HEALTH and SOCIAL CARE

ADVANCED GNVQ

Hilary Thomson

Caroline Holden

Dawn Collard

Gillian Hutt

Carolyn Meggitt

Jean Manuel

2ND EDITION

Hodder & Stoughton

A MEMBER OF THE HODDER HEADLINE GROUP

Orders: please contact Bookpoint Ltd, 39 Milton Park, Abingdon, Oxon OX14 4TD. Telephone: (44) 01235 400414, Fax: (44) 01235 400454. Lines are open from 9.00 - 6.00, Monday to Saturday, with a 24 hour message answering service. Email address: orders@bookpoint.co.uk

British Library Cataloguing in Publication Data
A catalogue record for this title is available from The British Library

ISBN 0 340 647809

First published 1995

Impression number	14	13	12	11	10	9	8	7	6	5
Year	2004	2003	2002	2001	2000	1999	1998			

Typeset by Wearset, Boldon, Tyne & Wear.
Printed in Great Britain for Hodder & Stoughton Educational, a division of Hodder Headline Plc, 338 Euston Road, London NW1 3BH by Scotprint Ltd, Musselburgh, Scotland.

CONTENTS

ACKNOWLEDGEMENTS

We would like to thank the following for their help and advice during the preparation of this book: Chrissie Rycroft for the correlation exercise; Silvia Aslangul (NESCOT) for career and work experience assignments; Sneh Kapoor for contributing some case studies in Chapter 4; Julie Rzezniczek for the contribution on M.E.; Margaret Evans for information from hospitals; Freda Dudfield for the exercise on listening skills; Nicola Crabbe and Tanya Grogan, students, for contributions to material on child abuse.

For their help with the second edition, we would also like to thank: Janet Miller for her additional material on Scotland; Milly Fink for her help with Chapter 4; John Rawlinson (University of Wales College of Medicine) for information on transactional analysis; and Jean Douglas.

Our special thanks go to our families for their support and encouragement.

For the reproduction of copyright material, the publishers would like to thank:

Ulrike Preuss/Format, fig. 2.2; Martin Mayer/Network, fig. 2.10; VCL/Telegraph Colour Library, fig. 2.11; Biophoto Associates, fig. 3.1; Bracegirdle and Freeman, figs. 3.5, 3.6, 3.9, 3.10, 3.11; P.M.G. Munro, Biopolymer Group, Imperial College, fig. 3.12; Accoson Ltd, fig. 3.49; Vitalograph, fig. 3.55a; Xavier Rovani/Network, fig. 3.57; Brenda Prince/Format, fig. 3.58; Jacques Grison/Network, fig. 3.59; J. Allan Cash Ltd, figs. 3.60, 4.2; Observer Magazine/Topham Picture Point, fig. 4.5; Health Education Authority, fig. 6.9.

INTRODUCTION

The recent development of General National Vocational Qualifications (GNVQs) has called for a new approach to study in the health and social care field.

Up until now, if you were on such a course (for example, BTEC or other courses aimed at preparing future caring professionals) you will have had to select relevant material from a variety of sociology, psychology, biology and statistics texts. This book, however, combines the relevant areas of these subjects and includes, in addition, a comprehensive guide to the structure of the health and social care systems, their operation, and experience in the workplace.

The book covers, chapter by chapter, the eight new mandatory units of the Advanced GNVQ 'Health and Social Care'. These mandatory units were set centrally and are the same irrespective of the awarding body offering the qualification (BTEC, RSA or City and Guilds). The mandatory units, and therefore this book, cover the fundamental skills, knowledge, understanding and principles common to a wide range of 'caring' occupations.

The GNVQ also requires four further units to be completed; these are to be chosen from a list of options. As these units are not centrally devised they vary from one awarding body to another, and therefore cannot be covered within this book.

Advanced GNVQ units are comparable in educational standard with A and AS Level, and it is possible as an A Level student to take one or more units which may be useful for your intended career. If you are such a student, this book is ideal for you as it will cover your chosen unit(s) as well as giving you essential background reading to cover each of the performance criteria.

The GNVQ programme sets outcomes but does not prescribe the course. You will find that the number of suggested activities within the book gives scope for you to follow your own learning pattern in the way that best fits your own resources and those of your school or college. In line with GNVQ practice, the use of project assignments, surveys, investigations of processes and services, and case studies is encouraged.

As well as completing eight mandatory units and four optional units, you must show the following 'Core Skills': 'Communication', 'Application of Number' and 'Information Technology', all of which are formally assessed, and 'Problem Solving' and 'Personal Skills', which are encouraged and may be recorded in your National Record of Achievement, but are not formally assessed and certified. The numerous activities suggested in this book provide ample opportunity for you to develop and practise all these skills; with reference to information technology skills, it is assumed that you will have the facilities to produce written reports on a word processor at least occasionally.

The Advanced GNVQ is assessed in two ways: through external tests, and from a 'Portfolio of Evidence' derived from projects carried out within the course. This book will help with both elements. An external written test, consisting of short-answers or multiple-choice questions and lasting for one hour, is taken for each mandatory unit (with the exception of Unit 2). Each chapter will help you to master the necessary underpinning knowledge, understanding and principles to reach the required high pass mark in the corresponding test. Because the tests can be sat at different times of the year, and you may repeat the tests until you pass, a text which allows you to study independently is obviously very useful.

The student-centred approach and the many activities allow you to take a leading role in the collection and presentation of evidence to be used for project-based assessment. On the basis of the Portfolio of Evidence, a Merit or a Distinction may be awarded if a level of performance above the basic requirement is demonstrated. Within the book activities are suggested which give you ample opportunity to develop and demonstrate the abilities on which the criteria for awarding grades focus. These are the ability to plan; to seek and handle information; to evaluate approaches, outcomes and alternatives; and to show quality of outcomes. The Portfolio of Evidence can also be used by people outside the scheme to examine the quality of your work, for example institutions of higher education.

Chapter 1 explores the rights and responsibilities of individuals and organisations in relation to equality of opportunity. Key legislation (or the lack of it) in this area is considered, alongside the ways in which people may attempt to seek redress for any discrimination they experience. The concept of discrimination is fully explored, giving advice for students about how they might carry out further research into its effects and consequences for service users, health and care workers and the general public. Finally, ethical issues and dilemmas for individuals and oragnisations in health and social care are described and illustrated with contemporary examples.

In Chapter 2 the role of interaction in influencing an individual's health and social well-being is examined. Forms of interpersonal interaction, i.e. communication and sensory contact, are described, as well as the varying customs regarding verbal and non-verbal communication that have evolved in different cultures, which if not properly understood can inhibit effective interaction. Particular reference is made, in investigating these issues, to care settings and caring relationships. Other constraints to effective interaction are also investigated: the effects of noise, the subtle inhibiting effects of stereotyping, as well as physical and emotional well-being, for example the degree of stress, being experienced by either participant in the interaction. The ways of minimising constraints in both one-to-one and group situations are examined: these include the use of practical avoidance measures, plus a range of counselling skills and an understanding of the basic values which underpin health and social care work.

Chapter 3 focuses on the physical aspects of health and social well-being. The organisation of structures within body systems, from cells to tissues and organs is described, as are the relationships between their main functions. The maintenance of a constant internal environment (homeostasis) is considered along with the effects of development and ageing on body systems. The final part of this chapter looks at methods of monitoring the healthy function of the human body, and provides students with secondary source data to analyse, such as ECG traces and blood cell counts, and the opportunity to undertake monitoring of the cardio-respiratory system themselves.

In Chapter 4 the focus is upon enabling students to appreciate the contributions of the disciplines of psychology and sociology to an understanding of health and social well-being. Human growth, development and change is approached from a psychological viewpoint, enabling students to explore a range of influences and unexpected pressures on patterns of human development. An evaluation of the support networks available to people is followed by an introduction to some of the key social factors which influence people from a range of different cultural backgrounds. There is also a critical assessment of socio-economic factors relating to the health of the population in the UK today. Questions are raised about how health and care services and policies for people could be improved.

In a rapidly changing area such as health and social care it is essential to have really up-to-date information on the organisation of its planning and provision. This is provided in Chapter 5, along with many suggestions for activities in both the classroom and workplace.

Chapter 6 contains an introduction to the development and implementation of care plans, which are an increasingly important aspect of care provision. It should be read in conjunction with Chapter 2, which covers some of the skills necessary for producing a care plan. Students are given guidance on the investigation of care plans within the workplace. The opportunity is also provided for readers to find out about their chosen careers. The services concerned with the promotion and protection of health and social well-being are described, and the legislation and ethical issues involved in these areas are considered. Students are given guidance to carry out an investigation into how service users both experience and influence health and social care provision.

Chapter 7 aims to raise health awareness by highlighting the areas in which people have genuine choices in following a healthier lifestyle: smoking, drug abuse in its widest sense, sexually transmitted diseases, HIV and AIDS, personal safety and security. The reasons for, sources of and methods used in health campaigns are investigated, and activities are structured to enable students to evaluate the effectiveness of a health education campaign.

Chapter 8 provides a comprehensive guide to research methods used in health and social care. Guidance is given on how to plan, produce and present a research project, and the reader will find this chapter useful for reference when carrying out many of the pieces of research suggested throughout this book.

The National Council for Vocational Qualifications states that 'Work placements can provide invaluable experience and a context for project work. Careful planning is required to exploit the full potential of learning opportunities provided by placements.' For these reasons an appendix has been included to give students and lecturers advice on how to go about setting up a work placement, and suggesting activities to be carried out before, during and after the placement. There are also activities throughout the book which can be carried out in the workplace. These have been indicated with the symbol **W**.

The GNVQ requires students to demonstrate an understanding of the 'value base' in health and social care work. The components of the value base are: freedom from any type of discrimination; maintaining confidentiality of information; promoting and supporting individual rights and choice; and supporting individuals through effective communication. All of these components are comprehensively covered within the book to give students the in-depth knowledge they will need.

Each chapter is followed by a short list of suggested further reading and useful resources, as well as details of works cited in the text.

1

EQUAL OPPORTUNITIES AND INDIVIDUALS' RIGHTS

This chapter describes why the principles fundamental to equality of opportunity legislation are important to health and social care practitioners. It goes on to explore the rights and responsibilities of individuals and organisations in relation to equality of opportunity. Key legislation (or the lack of it) in this area is considered, alongside the ways in which people may attempt to seek redress for any discrimination they experience. The concept of discrimination is fully explored giving advice for students about how they might carry out further research into its effects and consequences for clients, health and care workers and the general public. Finally, ethical issues and dilemmas for individuals and organisations in health and social care are described and illustrated with contemporary examples.

INTRODUCTION

All of us spend time wondering why people think and behave in the way they do. We puzzle over those nearest to us – our parents and our children; our neighbours; our teachers, fellow students or workers; our employers; our friends – as well as politicians and people we hear or read about.

Some people, particularly those working in occupations related to health and social care, generally have serious and pressing reasons for being concerned about people's behaviour and attitudes. A child is being abused; a school boy is truanting from school; a nursery-school toddler is crying and upset; a mother is severely depressed and suicidal; a young woman is losing weight rapidly as a result of drastically limiting her diet; a

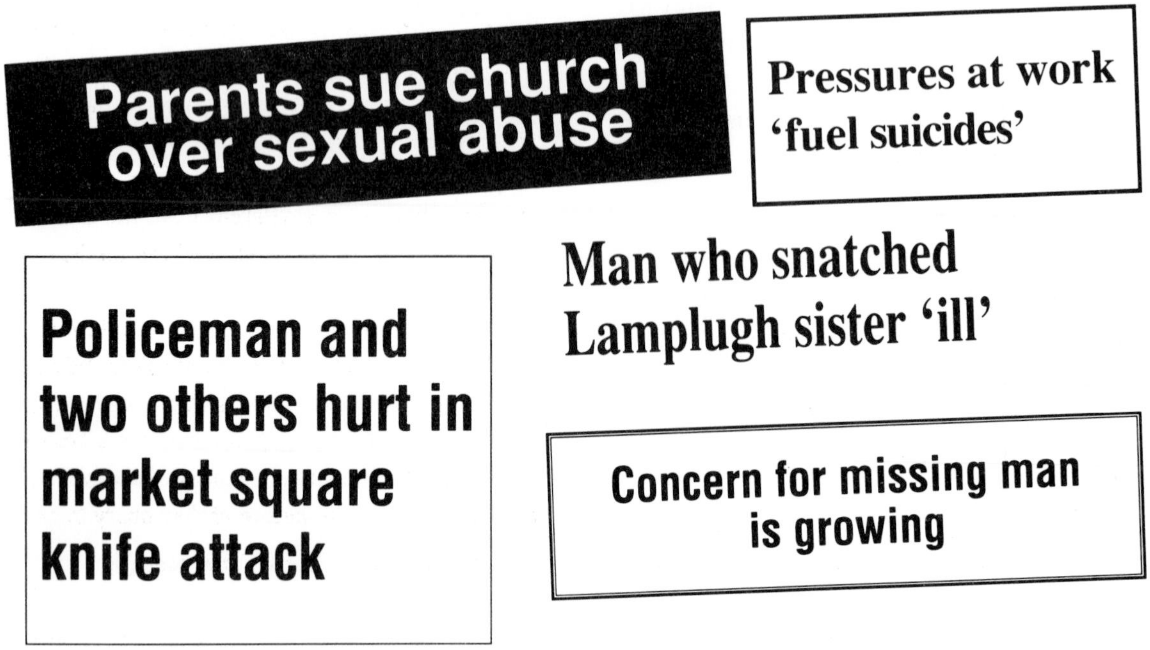
Parents sue church over sexual abuse

Pressures at work 'fuel suicides'

Policeman and two others hurt in market square knife attack

Man who snatched Lamplugh sister 'ill'

Concern for missing man is growing

teenager has run away from his foster-home; a man has just hit a nurse in Accident and Emergency . . . These and a thousand other such situations regularly confront workers in health and social care. Problems need to be tackled and the care, safety and welfare of patients and clients protected.

The search for possible explanations of why people think and behave in the ways they do draws on the theories, perspectives and research of social science. The work of sociologists and psychologists is studied, evaluated and, to a greater or lesser degree, applied to specific situations. Until we have a wider understanding of behaviour than that gained solely on the basis of our own personal experience, we may be unsure how to care for and help others with different experiences from our own. While the social sciences are unlikely to provide all the answers, they may enable us to ask more appropriate and critical questions, to understand the social context of people's lives and to have some appreciation of the perspectives through which others view their worlds. We can also use what we learn from social scientists to reflect upon our own experiences, so that we are more able to empathise with others seeking help and using services.

In this chapter the theories and research of social scientists will be used to explore some of the fundamental questions which health and social care workers will continually need to ask of themselves and of others:

- Where do our attitudes towards and ideas about other people come from?
- How do these attitudes, beliefs and ideas affect our behaviour towards others?
- How are people in societies affected by the attitudes and behaviour of other people around them?
- In what ways can the attitudes and behaviour of people in societies lead to prejudice, discrimination and the unfair treatment of others?
- How have people in this society sought to overcome the unfair treatment of others?
- How successful have key groups in this society been in influencing the development of legislation towards equal opportunities in Britain?
- What ethical, moral and social dilemmas are people working in health and social care occupations likely to face?

LEGAL RIGHTS AND RESPONSIBILITIES IN RELATION TO EQUALITY OF OPPORTUNITY

To those working in health and social care roles, the principles underpinning the legislation concerning equality of opportunity can prove important (see Table 1.1).

Combating prejudice and discrimination: equal opportunities legislation

The problems faced by the NHS in Britain are well publicised; as budgets are cut, hospital wards and clinics are forced to close, waiting lists for operations grow longer and services are run down. These events are given prominence on TV and in the press, especially when highlighted by charity campaigns to raise money for machinery and buildings previously funded by the NHS. In contrast, over the past ten years there has been considerable growth in the availability of and advertising for private medicine, promoted by images of luxury very different from the dingy wards and ramshackle facilities of the public sector.

It is therefore not surprising to have found that *inequality of access is a commonplace theme in accounting for health and illness, articulated out of both the political ideology of socialism and a broader-based expectation in Britain that the sick deserve the best of treatment, irrespective of their ability to pay.*

(Stainton Rogers, 1990, emphasis added)

Later in this chapter we consider the forms of

Table 1.1 The issue of equality of opportunity in health and social care

Principles underpinning equal opportunities legislation	Significance for health and care workers
The legislation establishes the RIGHTS of individuals to seek REDRESS for unfair discrimination.	This means that health and care workers can use the legislation, if necessary, to attempt to protect themselves against discrimination. They can also support and advise clients to do the same, should the need arise.
It establishes the RESPONSIBILITY of individuals and organisations to behave in a non-discriminatory way.	This supports all individuals and organisations in the field of health and social care who wish to develop active equal opportunities policies and practices.
The legislation emphasises the principle of providing EQUAL ACCESS to services and, wherever possible, EQUAL TREATMENT within those services.	This means that health and social care workers and the organisations they work for can take positive steps to improve the access to and uptake of health and care services amongst all user groups.
The principle of POSITIVE ACTION (see p. 17) is established.	This has allowed health and social care services to provide the backing necessary for particular groups who have suffered discrimination.

discrimination existing within a society. Just as there are different explanations for prejudice and discrimination, so there are different suggested 'solutions'. In highlighting the issue of 'inequality of access', the question of EQUAL OPPORTUNITIES becomes crucial, directing attention as it does to three fundamental questions:

1 In what areas of social and political life is it unjustified to treat men and women, members of different ethnic, cultural or religious groups, people of different ages, or people with special needs or learning difficulties differently?
2 Are there any areas of social and political life where it *may* be justified to treat anyone differently?
3 How could access to and treatment within education, housing, employment and the provision of goods and services be made equitable and fair?

HOW LAWS ARE MADE – THE ROLE OF INDIVIDUALS AND ORGANISATIONS IN FORMING LEGISLATION

When a new government comes into power after a General Election, it will normally have a number of policies it wishes to put into effect and these include social policies. During the course of a government's term of power, there may be particular circumstances that arise which also provide the motivation to formulate and implement policies. These may include changes in societal attitudes, economic changes, campaigning and pressure from certain groups in society or unexpected and traumatic events. Figure 1.1 gives a simplified description of the ways in which governments can turn ideas for social policies into law.

Key legislation in this country, such as the 1976 Race Relations Act, the 1975 and 1986 Sex Discrimination Acts and the 1981 Education Act (which laid down that local authorities must draw up statements assessing the needs of children with physical and mental disabilities or learning difficulties, with the implication that these needs should be met), paved the way for the issue of equal opportunities to be addressed by organisations and employers around the country. Figures 1.2–1.4 outline the major equal opportunities legislation now in place and the role of the Commission for Racial Equality (CRE) and the Equal Opportunities Commission (EOC) in implementing it.

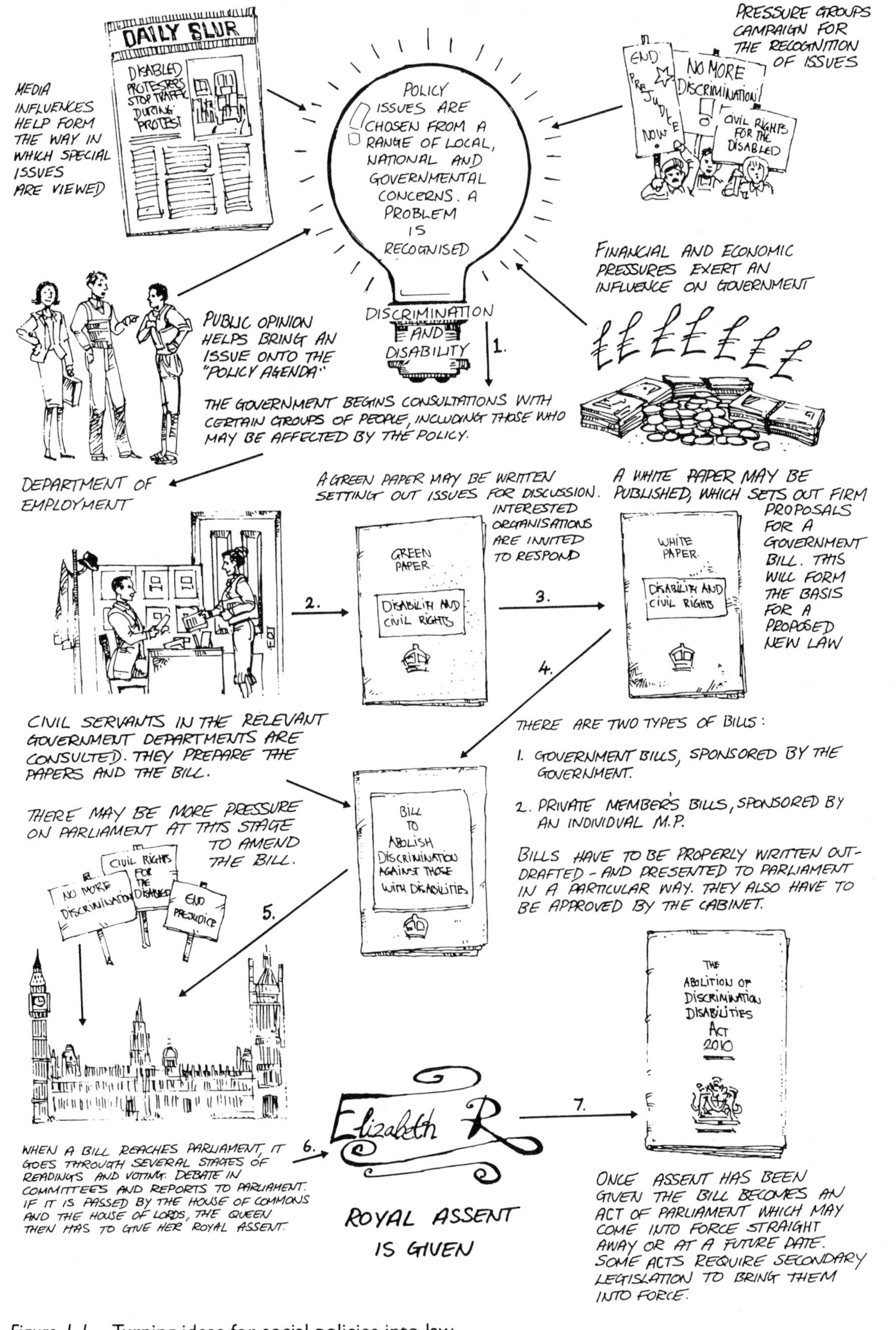

Figure 1.1 Turning ideas for social policies into law

THE SEX DISCRIMINATION ACTS 1975 AND 1986

With some exceptions in certain circumstances (and the Act does not apply to Northern Ireland), the 1975 and 1986 Sex Discrimination Acts make discrimination unlawful in:

- employment and training;
- education;
- the provision of goods, facilities and services;

These acts give people a right of access to the civil courts and industrial tribunals for legal remedies for unlawful discrimination.

Types of discrimination

Direct discrimination: definition and example

This occurs when one person is treated less favourably, on the grounds of their sex, than a person of the other sex is or would be treated in similar circumstances.

Example:

A child is refused a place in a nursery class and the only reason given is that there are 'already too many girls'.

Indirect discrimination: definition and example

This occurs when a requirement or condition, which cannot be justified on grounds other than sex, is applied to men and women equally but has the effect in practice of disadvantaging a considerably higher proportion of one sex than the other.

Example:

A girls' school insists that no pupils should be allowed to wear trousers as part of a school uniform. This indirectly discriminates against Asian girls in the school who follow a religious code of conduct requiring that they war garments which conceal all the lower part of the body (usually a fabric 'shift' dress).

The 1975 Act also set up

THE EQUAL OPPORTUNITIES COMMISSION

This has a statutory duty to enforce the Sex Discrimination Act (SDA) 1975 and the Equal Pay Act (EPA) 1970 (which came into force in 1975).

The EOC produces leaflets and guidelines on all types of issue related to equal pay and sex discrimination. It carries out research, awards grants to other groups for research, advises employers and trade unions on 'working towards equality' and assists individual or groups to fight cases of discrimination.

The Sex Discrimination Acts do not apply to work outside Great Britain; to cases where sex can be a 'genuine' occupational qualification; and to the armed forces. There is special provision for the police, prison officers, ministers of religion and competitive sport.

Victimisation

This occurs when an employer treats an employee (of either sex) less favourably than other employees are or would be treated on the grounds that the employee has or intends or is suspected of:

- bringing proceedings against the employer under the SDA or EPA;
- helped another to do so or took part in an EOC formal investigation or tribunal hearing;
- alleged that the employer or anyone else had contravened the SDA or EPA.

Example:

A social worker in a residential home gives evidence in proceedings under the SDA against a co-worker who has been accused of sexual discrimination against other employees. She is subsequently refused promotion.

Types of discrimination (only applicable in employment matters)

Direct marriage discrimination: definition and example

This occurs when a married person is treated less favourably, because he/she is married, than a single person of the same sex is or would be treated in similar circumstances.

Example:

An employer rejects all applications for posts from married people.

Indirect marriage discrimination: definition and example

This occurs when a requirement or condition which cannot be justified on grounds other than marital status is applied equally to married and single persons (of either sex) but has the effect in practice of disadvantaging a considerably higher proportion of married than single people (of the same sex).

Example:

A health authority issues application forms for student midwife posts on which applicants are required to state their sex and dates of birth of their children. Married female applicants for the posts with pre-school children subsequently receive letters stating they cannot be considered for 5 years because of their pre-school children. This arrangement is indirectly discriminatory because the requirement is indirectly discriminatory because the requirement or condition that an applicant must not have children of pre-school age is such that the proportion of married female applicants who can comply with it is considerably smaller than the proportion of female applicants who can do so.

(The EOC found southern Derbyshire health authority discriminating in this way in 1988. See EOC 1990.)

Figure 1.2 Sex discrimination acts 1975 and 1986

THE EQUAL PAY ACT 1970 (AMENDED 1983)

The most important provision of this legislation is that an employee is entitled to equal pay (and other contractual terms and conditions) with an employee of the opposite sex if:

(i) they are doing work which is the same or broadly similar;

(ii) they are doing work which has been rated as equivalent by an analytical job evaluation scheme; or

(iii) they are doing work of equal value in terms of the demands made on the worker (whether or not there has been a job evaluation scheme).

THE EMPLOYMENT PROTECTION ACT 1975

This gave women the right to paid maternity leave and the opportunity of returning to work afterwards.

Figure 1.3 Equal pay act 1970/Employment protection act 1975

THE RACE RELATIONS ACT 1976

With some exceptions in certain circumstances the Act protects every individual against racial discrimination:

- as a job applicant;
- as an employee or contract worker;
- as a home-buyer;
- as a tenant or prospective tenant;
- as a customer or client;
- as a school pupil, student or trainee;
- as a member or prospective member of a club;
- in many other situations.

It applies to:

All National Health Service (NHS) provision and personnel, including:

Health Authorities
NHS Trusts
Family Health Service Authorities (which provide GPs/Dental practitioners/Pharmacists/Opticians)
Community Health Councils
Community Health Services
Other voluntary organisations

It applies to:

All education and social services provision and personnel including:

Local authorities
Maintained and grant-maintained schools/colleges/higher education institutions
Education and Social Services Departments
Other voluntary organisations

The Race Relations Act was passed to strengthen the law against racial discrimination. It also set up

THE COMMISSION FOR RACIAL EQUALITY

which has the duties of:

- working towards the elimination of discrimination;
- promoting equality of opportunity and good relations between persons of different racial groups;
- keeping under review the working of the Act and, when required by the Secretary of State or when it otherwise thinks it is necessary, drawing up and submitting to the Secretary of State proposals for amending it;
- giving advice to people with complaints of discrimination and, in some cases, representing complainants in the courts.

. . . and most other areas of public life, although as yet it does not apply to immigration control or much of the prison service and police activity.

DIRECT DISCRIMINATION: DEFINITION AND EXAMPLE	INDIRECT DISCRIMINATION: DEFINITION AND EXAMPLE	DISCRIMINATION BY MEANS OF VICTIMIZATION: DEFINITION AND EXAMPLE
Direct discrimination is defined as treating a person less favourably than another on grounds of race and includes the segregation of people on racial grounds. **Example:** A receptionist at a dental practice tells black patients that there are no appointments available. She does so only on the basis of their colour.	Indirect discrimination takes place when someone, without necessarily intending to discriminate, effectively sets conditions for the use of services or for employment, for instance, which makes it harder for people from one racial group than another to make use of those services or get the job, and which cannot be justified. **Example:** A Community Health Clinic produces information leaflets in English about breast cancer and screening. The leaflets are distributed in an area where a substantial proportion of the population is not fluent in English. The Health Clinic refuses to translate the leaflets into the most commonly used languages in that area. In effect, this means that patients are required to read and understand English if they are to benefit from the advice contained in the leaflets	Discrimination by means of victimisation consists of treating a person less favourably than others are or would be treated in the same circumstances because that person has made a complaint or allegation of discrimination, has acted as a witness or informant in connection with proceedings under the Act, has been involved in any other way in its enforcement, or intends to do any of these things. **Example:** A nurse in a health clinic gives evidence in proceedings brought under the Race Relations Act against a doctor who has been accused of racial discrimination against black patients. The nurse is subsequently dismissed on unsubstantiated grounds.

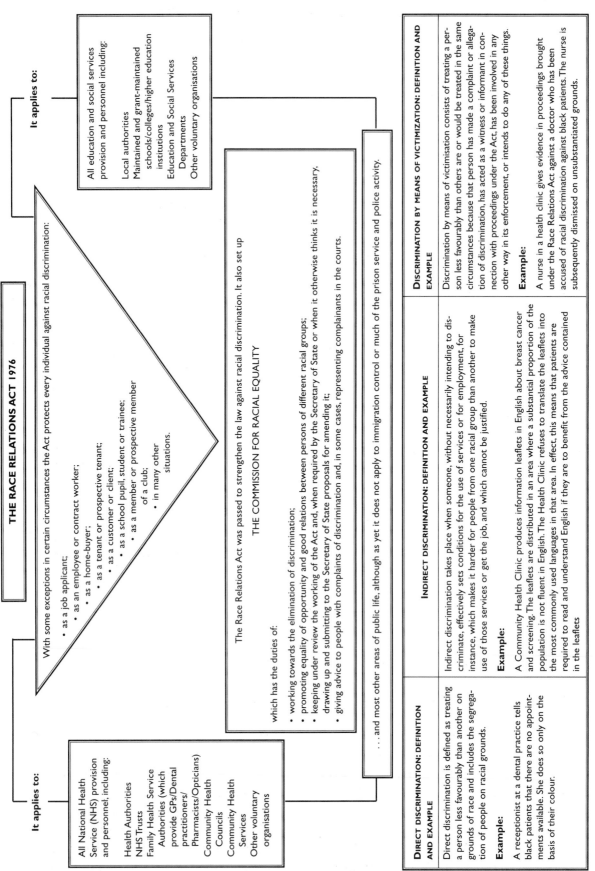

Figure 1.4 Race relations act 1976

LEGISLATION RELEVANT TO DISABILITY

Disabled Persons (Employment) Act 1944	Attempted to secure employment rights for disabled people. Under this Act, employers of 20 or more staff should employ at least 3% registered disabled people.
Education Act 1944	Specified that disabled children should be educated alongside their peers in primary and secondary education.
National Assistance Act 1948	Laid a duty on local authorities to 'arrange services for disabled people'. However, it forbade local authorities to make cash payments to disabled people.
Chronically Sick and Disabled Persons Representation Act 1970	Listed the services local authorities should provide and made it compulsory for local authorities to compile a register of people with disabilities and publicise services (which only need to be provided 'where practical and reasonable' to do so).
Education Act 1981	Sets out the requirements for the integration of children with special needs into the mainstream school system.
Disabled Persons (Services, Consultation and Representation) Act 1986	Provided professional and administrative approaches to the provision of services. Gives the person with disability the right to have an 'advocate', e.g. a social worker, to be present when needs are being assessed.

Figure 1.5 Legislation relevant to disability

Figure 1.5 summarises the legislative measures introduced since the Second World War relating to people with a disability.

Public support for equal opportunities at work for men and women has grown in recent years. A survey by the Family Policy Studies Centre in 1992 found that 85% of their respondents favoured laws against sex discrimination, but only 23% believed that opportunities are, in fact, equal. According to the 1992 Annual Report of the Equal Opportunities Commission, the number of women reporting sex discrimination at work rose by 40% in 1991–2. However, it is important to recognise that while equal opportunities legislation has generally been welcomed as a good thing, there are other perspectives on the issue of prejudice and discrimination which deserve serious consideration.

Some people have argued that the right-wing Conservative governments in power in this country since 1979 have not embraced and promoted the idea of equal opportunities quite so enthusiastically as they might. Organisations such as the CRE and EOC, which have focused upon legal initiatives as a way of making progress, suggest that these governments have failed to respond to proposals to strengthen and improve race relations and sex discrimination legislation. They point out that while discrimination continues to be a widespread phenomenon in Britain today, only a handful of discrimination cases succeed each year in industrial tribunals or courts. The CRE has said that when it first reviewed the 1976 Race Relations Act in 1985, it 'suggested many ways of making the law more effective. The government never responded formally, and little has changed.' In December 1994 Michael Portillo, the Employment Secretary, was reported to be considering a possible merger of the EOC and the CRE (*The Guardian* 8 December 1994).

There are fears, too, that as the European Community (EC) has not so far adopted a formal ban on racial discrimination, Britain's laws could be weakened if the single market comes fully into effect.

These arguments have led some to suggest not only that the powers of the CRE and the EOC are far too limited, but also that a focus on 'equal opportunities' alone is too weak and will not bring about the wider and more fundamental social changes in attitudes and in social and economic structure in society necessary to eliminate institutional prejudice and discrimination. For example, where people do not start out from an equal base, offering fair treatment may do little to redress more fundamental disadvantages faced by certain social groups, such as the experience of poverty and long-term unemployment. The following extract is from *The Independent*'s report on the first national survey of the blind:

MOST BLIND PEOPLE 'LIVING IN POVERTY'

Most blind people 'live at the extremes of poverty', are unemployed and do not go out on their own, according to the first national survey of people with visual handicaps, published yesterday by the Royal National Institute for the Blind.

Ian Bruce, the director-general of the RNIB, said the report showed that the blind 'are poorly served by hard-pressed social services departments, with fewer than one in five being visited even once at the time of their sight loss'.

The survey reveals that nearly 1 million people are eligible for registration as blind or partially-sighted – far higher than government estimates. There are 300,000 completely blind people in Britain, 119,000 more than previously thought.

The report, which was based on 600 interviews, says four out of five blind people of working age are unemployed. More than half have been out of work for five years. In both respects, the blind fare worse than the general disabled population, in which 31 per cent have found employment.

(The Independent, 16 October 1991)

RECENT ATTEMPTS TO PROVIDE NEW LEGISLATION RELEVANT TO DISABILITY

The Civil Rights (Disabled Persons) Bill 1994

This Private Member's Bill, proposed by Labour MP Roger Berry, was an attempt to provide an anti-discrimination law for the disabled on a model similar to the Sex Discrimination and Race Relations Acts. It did not succeed in becoming law. In May 1994 the Conservative Social Security Minister for the Disabled, Nicholas Scott, was called on to resign when he had to apologise for misleading the House of Commons over the Bill. His officials had been involved in the initial drafting of amendments put by backbenchers which resulted in the Bill running out of time.

The main provisions of this Bill would have been . . .

THE BILL'S SIX PROVISIONS

The Civil Rights (Disabled Persons) Bill is divided into six parts:

☐ Definitions determining who is covered by the bill, and the types of discrimination the bill prohibits.
☐ Provision to establish a Disablement Commission, which will monitor the effectiveness of the new laws and assist in their enforcement.
☐ Detailed provisions in the field of employment. Potential or actual employees with a disability are protected from discrimination, and employers are also required to make "reasonable accommodations" for disabled people in their workplace.
☐ Requirements on businesses, organisations and public bodies to make "reasonable accommodations" to the disability of a person who wants to use their services/facilities.
☐ Enforcement of the other parts of the bill. Civil rights for disabled people could be enforced by court injunctions and damages proceedings.
☐ Miscellaneous details, including the dates on which the regulations contained in the bill would come in to force.

(The Guardian, 21 May 1994)

Do we need anti-discrimination legislation on disability?

YES! – arguments in favour

1 Resource implications. Spread over, say, 20 years, the costs of such legislation would be affordable and would not be as great as some anticipate. People who otherwise cost a lot to support in benefits could be employed and paying tax and National Insurance – thus contributing to the economy.
2 Values and commitments. Without the protection of the law it is extremely difficult, if not impossible, for people with disabilities to challenge actions or decisions which are discriminatory. Other countries, such as the USA, Canada, Australia and New Zealand, have such legislation. Why not Britain?
3 Hidden agendas. Unless there is firm pressure from individuals and organisations in society to put forward a Civil Rights Anti-Discrimination Bill, the government may try to push forward less satisfactory legislation in the hope that people will believe that something at least is being done. However, if this legislation is 'weak', i.e. there are so many loopholes and 'get-out' clauses in it that it becomes worthless, the needs of people with disabilities will not be addressed.

NO! – arguments against

1 Resource implications. This legislation will cost too much. Some estimates have put the cost of such laws at £17 million. The money would have to be spent on adapting workplaces and services to make them accessible to and usable by people with disabilities. This would cut down the profits which employers could make, proving particularly expensive for small businesses.
2 Societal pressure. The legislation would be unworkable. There would be a large rise in court cases as people with disabilities pursued their claims. The general public might come to resent such legislation, causing even more harm and prejudice towards people with disabilities.
3 Values and commitments. Public education to change attitudes is needed more than anti-discrimination legislation.

In November 1994's Queen's Speech to Parliament, John Major included a Bill offering new rights for people with disabilities. These proposals are regarded by many organisations and groups representing people with disabilities as falling short of the full civil rights and anti-discrimination laws they sought from the Civil Rights (Disabled Persons) Bill. This new Bill will be handled by William Hague, the new Minister for Disabled People at the Department of Social Security. Students should be able to follow the passage of this legislation through Parliament in 1995–6.

The main provisions of this new Bill are . . .

NEW RIGHTS FOR DISABLED WELCOMED
Main points

- ☐ Employment quota system to be axed
- ☐ New right of non-discrimination at work
- ☐ Employers to make "reasonable adjustment" to premises
- ☐ New right of access to goods and services, including insurance and transport infrastructure
- ☐ Trading premises to be adapted where change "readily achievable" and subject to financial limit
- ☐ All new buses to be "low floor" design
- ☐ Drive to make schools more accessible for disabled
- ☐ National Disability Council to be created with advisory functions
- ☐ Cash grants to enable disabled people to buy own care services

In the Commons, however, the package seemed enough to satisfy most of the Conservatives who had backed the defeated private member's bill. No MP who won a high place in yesterday's ballot for such bills during the new parliamentary session gave a commitment to re-introduce a broader disability rights measure.

The Government's package was set out by William Hague, Minister for Disabled People, at the same time as Virginia Bottomley, the Health Secretary, confirmed a plan for disabled people to be given cash grants by local authorities to enable them to buy their own care services.

Mr Hague's proposals will be brought forward in a government disability bill during the new session. Mrs Bottomley's will not be put before MPs for another year and will initially be limited to "a relatively small group, probably those disabled people who are able and willing to manage their care".

Announcing his package in the Commons, Mr Hague said it went "substantially wider and deeper" than the July paper and reconciled the wishes of disabled people and what he called the legitimate interest of business.

Taken together with Mrs Bottomley's announcement, the measures represented the greatest single advance for disabled people. But it was "vital that the action we take has a realistic timetable, is practical and takes account of the impact on service providers", Mr Hague said.

Instead, disabled people would have a statutory right of non-discrimination at work. Employers of more than 20 people who treated a disabled person less favourably than others without "justifiable reason", or who failed to make "reasonable adjustment" to the workplace, could be taken to an industrial tribunal.

As well as adding the extra, qualified provision for traders to make similar adaptations to their premises – with redress available to disabled customers through legal channels not yet specified – the package includes new requirements in respect of insurance and other financial services, transport (exempting existing vehicles and trains) and education.

All schools will next year be checked for ease of accessibility for disabled children and adults. Funds will be made available by the Government for projects to improve ease of access.

Mr Hague said: "The more it is possible to educate disabled children with their able-bodied peers, the less we shall see adults avoiding, ignoring or feeling embarrassed by disabled people."

John Hannam, the most prominent Tory backer of the defeated private member's bill, congratulated the minister for going far wider with the package than had been expected.

Opposition MPs, however, were suspicious of the number of conditions and qualifications peppering Mr Hague's statement. Disability groups said they would be scrutinising the fine print.

David Brindle
and Patrick Wintour

(The Guardian, 25 November 1994)

ACTIVITY

1 The defeat of the Civil Rights (Disabled Persons) Bill in May/June 1994 generated a great deal of media publicity. Carry out further research into the proposals in the Bill, the reasons why it did not succeed and the views of organisations and groups representing

people with disabilities about this proposed legislation.

2 The Civil Rights (Disabled Persons) Bill was, in part, modelled upon the Americans with Disabilities Act 1990. From July 1995 US firms with 15 or more employees must not discriminate in applications procedures, qualification standards or any other terms and conditions of employment. Find out more about anti-discrimination legislation in other countries such as the USA and Scandinavia. Compare these with British legislation.

3 Study again the arguments above used for and against anti-discrimination legislation on disability in Britain. Arrange a debate to extend and develop these arguments, looking in particular at the interests and attitudes of key groups in the population such as the government, employers, people with disabilities, carers and pressure groups and charities campaigning on behalf of the disabled.

Social class and equality of opportunity

While some writers have been critical of the implementation and effectiveness of equal opportunities legislation, others have noted how the debate over social class, income and 'equality of access' to services and treatment is expressed in the public debate about private versus public health and social care services, an area where differential treatment has not been seen by governments as a form of discrimination comparable with sexism or racism. The treatment of the public as 'consumers' of health care is reflected in the following extract from the St Helier NHS Trust Publication, *Health Extra* +, May 1993.

The Maternity Wards at St Helier Hospital have seen the birth of over 3,500 new babies in the last year.

Over this year, the Maternity Wards have continued to improve their service, for example, new developments in the out patients service. 'Some mums find it difficult to get to the hospital during the day, so we have been setting up appointments for them, "out of working hours" ' said Shermane Peters, Clinical Midwife Manager on the Maternity Wards.

Tours of the Maternity Unit have also proved very popular with mothers and their partners. 'It gives an opportunity to meet the midwives, ask any questions and allows us to allay any anxieties or concerns' added Shermane.

Also available in St Helier Hospital, is the Private Ward, which has proved particularly attractive to women who would like a higher degree of privacy during their time on the ward. Maternity care is provided by an independent team of midwives, and doctors are always available. Peace of mind is added too, as the ward is at the centre of a large hospital, with all its high technology equipment.

Whichever option chosen by the mother and her partner, The Trust will care for the whole family in the considerate and compassionate manner, which women have come to expect, from this leader in the field of maternity care.

(Health Extra +, May 1993)

SHORTCOMINGS OF AND INCONSISTENCIES IN THE LEGISLATION

Laws, in theory, lay down what can or cannot be done in Britain. However, almost all laws passed in Parliament are debated before, during and after the process. Many are and remain highly controversial; others are complex and little understood or recognised; a few are all but completely ignored. Therefore the legislative process on its own is not enough to ensure that people exercise their rights and responsibilities as far as equal opportunities are concerned.

In itself, legislation to maintain equal opportunities has not proved sufficient to ensure:

- that the existence of the law is recognised or that it is understood;
- that there are adequate resources to put the law into effect;
- that 'loopholes' in the legislation have not been used to discriminate;
- that individuals can discover whether they are victims of unlawful discrimination in the first place. For instance, if an individual is turned down for a job or promotion, how can he or she be certain that this is because of his or her sex, race, cultural background, disability, etc.?;
- that organisations, employers and individuals change their long-term practices. even if they have been proved to have been discriminating in a particular area or against a particular individual. Many organisations may choose to respond to a situation such as this by paying costs or damages to the individual who has brought the case to a tribunal or to the courts, as in the following example:

PC Joginder Singh Prem, the Sikh constable who won £25,000 damages from Nottinghamshire Constabulary for racial discrimination and victimisation, was turned down for promotion to sergeant five times, despite passing the sergeant's and inspector's exams.

When he was rejected for the fourth time in 1991, he lodged a complaint with Nottingham industrial tribunal. After a fifth rejection in 1992, he filed a second complaint.

A month later, the force started disciplinary proceedings against him over his investigation of an assault.

PC Prem said: 'I was called a turban-headed git.

'I could tolerate that sort of slogan from junior officers, but life got difficult when they started saying it in front of senior officers who seemed to be supporting them.

'Nobody could ever touch my work effort. But instead of getting encouragement, all I had was discouragement and ridicule.'

Yesterday's settlement, which avoided a six-week tribunal hearing, included £10,000 for each of his two last rejections, which the force admitted were the result of racial discrimination.

The case, which comes more than two years after the force paid a total of £30,000 damages for race discrimination to another Sikh constable, Surinder Singh, and two sergeants, raises questions about the effectiveness of the equal opportunities policy set up in the wake of that case.

(The Guardian, 5 May 1993)

Nevertheless, in some organisations it does seem that the allegation of and investigation into discriminatory practices can provide the spur for long-term change. For example, a formal CRE investigation into admissions for medical training at St George's Hospital in London found direct racial discrimination. The computer program which was used for the initial selection of applicants for interview gave differential and less favourable weighting to women and ethnic minority candidates. The admissions policy has since been changed to eliminate discrimination;

- that the law is implemented. For example, the 1981 Education Act was accompanied by government guidelines that recommended that children with special needs should be assessed for 'statementing' within six months. A report in 1992 by the Audit Commission and Her Majesty's Inspectors found that some pupils were having to wait up to three years and that the average wait was 12 months.

Robert Clay should be starting school next term, but has yet to be assessed for his educational needs.

Robert is almost five and physically disabled. A year ago his mother, Catherine, wrote to her local county council's education department asking for a statement on his needs, and was refused.

Several attempts later the assessment has been agreed, but may be too late for him to start school

He should be going after Easter, but the

school is waiting to see how many hours' help he will get,' said Mrs Clay.

If a school thinks that a child who has not been assessed needs extra help, it has to apply to the Mainstream Support Group, set up by the education authority, to fund special needs sessions.

But there are many schools applying for a limited amount of money, so not all schools get what they say they need. Had Robert been assessed, he would automatically receive the help he needs.

'At the moment the school doesn't even know if it will be able to take him, because if it doesn't get funding for extra help, it can't afford to take him on.

The council could not comment on individual cases, said a spokeswoman.

(The Guardian, 29 March 1993)

- that the law is interpreted in the same way by everyone concerned. There is a legal requirement that disabled people should form 3% of all workforces of 20 or more people. This requirement is rarely regarded as an obligation. Employers can obtain exemptions, which approximately 60% of all employers have. Since 1947 there have only been 10 prosecutions under this requirement of the law which suggests to employers that they are not particularly at risk if they fail to comply with it.

ACTIVITY

1 Write to the EOC and the CRE (for addresses see list at end of chapter) for further information about sex discrimination and race relations legislation. These organisations publish many useful and free guides.

2 Test 'awareness' of the legislation by designing a small-scale survey and carrying it out in your school or college or on the general public (see Chapter 8 for guidance). There may also be opportunities to interview the people you meet during a work experience placement. How familiar are people with the laws? What are their attitudes towards the legislation?

IMPLEMENTING EQUAL OPPORTUNITIES

By the early 1980s it was clear that laws against unequal pay and sex discrimination would do nothing to tackle the entrenched patterns of inequality that had built up over centuries ... people have begun to insist that POSITIVE measures are needed in order to compensate for past discrimination.

(Coote and Campbell, 1982)

There has been a growing recognition that the legislation on racial equality, sex discrimination and special needs provided a starting point, but that there are other areas which organisations, employers and individuals need to address:

- Organisations (schools, local authorities, employers, hospitals, etc.) need to formulate equal opportunities policies of their own, specific to their own needs and concerns as well as complying with the law.
- Training and education in equal opportunities and race awareness need to be provided; there should be agreed procedures and policies which need to be monitored and evaluated.
- Recruitment and selection procedures need to be non-discriminatory.
- More flexible working arrangements and facilities (e.g. workplace nurseries) should be considered to encourage the recruitment and retention of women with children or carers looking after elderly or disabled relatives.
- Positive action policies to improve employment prospects for disadvantaged groups could be carried out where monitoring showed that particular groups have been under-represented in certain

types of work or grades of work (positive discrimination at the point of selection remains unlawful). Training for work in which one particular group had previously been under-represented may lawfully be provided and employers may encourage members of that group to take up work. One way of doing this is through job advertisements which encourage applications from a particular sex or ethnic group to apply for the post. Some examples are given on page 78. The advertisement for a manager for an Asian women's refuge is allowed specifically to request an 'Asian woman' because her ethnic background and sex constitute a 'genuine occupational qualification' for the job – i.e. she will provide services to particular groups in the community that may be done most effectively by an Asian woman. Similar criteria apply to the county council advertisement for temporary social workers for minority ethnic communities.

- Ethnic monitoring, which involves employers finding out how many people from ethnic minorities are employed, with the aim of giving everyone an equal chance, can be controversial unless some visible progress on these issues is subsequently made. At present, however, ethnic monitoring is carried out by only a small number of employers and public services.

ORGANISATIONAL RESPONSES TO THE LEGISLATION

The late 1970s and 1980s saw a wave of projects and programmes initiated in local authorities (particularly the Inner London Education Authority, ILEA), in individual schools and colleges, and in health and social services organisations in inner-city and urban areas. Some legislation of the 1980s, however, seemed contrary to the spirit of these initiatives. For example, Clause 28 of the Local Government Act 1988 stated that there would be a:

prohibition on promoting homosexuality by teaching or by publishing material.

(i) A local authority shall not:
  (a) intentionally promote homosexuality or publish material with the intention of promoting homosexuality;
  (b) promote the teaching in any maintained school of the acceptability of homosexuality as a pretended family relationship.

This section of the Act, although it has never been tested in the courts, has led to some confusion among staff employed by local authorities, such as teachers, social workers and youth workers. What exactly does 'promotion' mean? This confusion, in turn, may have led to a reluctance to discuss sexuality openly, leaving those in need of counselling and support rather vulnerable. In 1993 MPs voted to lower the age of consent for homosexual men from 21 to 18, but there is no anti-discriminatory legislation to protect gay men or lesbians.

A persistent theme in this political context has been the relationship between LOCAL GOVERNMENT and CENTRAL GOVERNMENT, including aspects such as the crisis in local government funding, local democratic initiatives and central government powers. Conservative governments have preferred the language of 'equal opportunities' to the more radical 'anti-racist' and 'anti-sexist' policies and programmes which have emerged in health, welfare and social work contexts.

ACTIVITY

Compare these two articles from *Community Care* (published within a month of each other in 1992). In the first extract, Tim Yeo is critical of 'anti-discriminatory' policies. In the second, Baroness Cumberlege calls on health authorities to promote 'equal opportunities'.

Devise a role-play in which these two junior health ministers are called on to explain and discuss their views.

BLACK STAFF WELCOME ANTIRACIST STANCE

Black social workers expressed concern this week at the government's criticisms of the social work training council's anti-discriminatory policies.

In a statement released shortly before its annual conference this weekend the Association of Black Social Workers and Allied Professions welcomed the growing prominence of race.

Supporting CCETSW's anti-racist guidelines, the association said it deplored the actions of those 'seeking to destabilise the process'. Junior health minister Tim Yeo has complained of CCETSW's emphasis on anti-discriminatory policies.

EQUALITY OPTION

Baroness Cumberlege, a junior health minister, has called on health authorities to promote equal opportunities and provide appropriate services for black and ethnic minority communities. Speaking at an open day of the London Chinese Health Resource Centre, she praised the work of Chinese social workers, doctors and nurses in care provision.

The 'torrent of new legislation' outlined in the extract below from *Community Care* (6 May 1993), together with the Education Acts passed in the 1980s and 1990s, in the political climate in which it has been implemented, has undoubtedly had an impact upon the financial and organisational commitment to positive action on equal opportunities in many health and social care contexts. A 'momentum for change' has, arguably, been slowed down.

A TORRENT OF NEW LEGISLATION

An extraordinary 145 pieces of legislation affecting local government have been passed by Conservative governments since 1979. What follows is just the tip of the legislative iceberg which has affected local government in the past few years. It includes some of the most controversial and most significant for social services.

- Housing Act 1988
- Local Government Act 1988 – included Clause 28
- Local Government Finance Act 1988 – introduced poll tax
- Local Government and Housing Act 1989 – restrictions on 'political activity' by local authorities
- Children Act 1989
- NHS and Community Care Act 1990
- Local Government Act 1992 – local government structures
- Local Government Finance Act 1992 – introduces council tax

ACTIVITY

Invite speakers/representatives from the main political parties to talk to your class about their views on how organisations should implement equal opportunities legislation.

Four interesting reports highlight the progress which has been made and the problems which remain.

1 The study *Racial Equality in Social Services Departments: A Survey of Equal Opportunities Policies*, carried out by the CRE in 1988 and published in 1989, focused particularly on equal opportunities and service delivery, i.e. whether all users of Social Services Departments could be said to be treated fairly. It provided the CRE with a 'snapshot of the state of development of equal opportunities practice in social services delivery in 1988, as reported by just over a third of the departments in England, Scotland and Wales'.

   The survey found that 66% of those departments had no written equal opportunities policy and most were not meeting their duties in law under section 71 of the Race Relations Act 1976, i.e. they were not ensuring that unlawful racial discrimination was not taking place and not promoting equality of opportunity and good relations between persons of different racial groups.

The CRE suggested that there was a need for departments to use a formal written policy rather than simply a general intention to treat all clients fairly.

In the survey, Social Services Departments were asked whether they had:

(a) adopted particular measures to meet the needs of ethnic minorities;
(b) adapted existing services to meet the needs of a multi-racial community.

In answer to (a), the particular measures most often cited were:

- the translation of social services information into relevant community languages;
- the use of an interpreting service;
- race relations training for staff;
- the appointment of specialist race advisers for services.

In reply to (b), the adaptations most frequently mentioned were:

- recruitment campaigns for ethnic minority foster and adoptive parents;
- guidelines for staff on the needs of ethnic minority children in care;
- training for staff involved in child care;
- involving members of the ethnic minority communities in planning for care, in the translation of leaflets and in outreach work;
- adapting the dietary requirements of meals-on-wheels services to ethnic minorities;
- changes to day centres to make them more attractive to ethnic minority users;
- the funding of ethnic minority groups who provided social services to the community.

ACTIVITY

The replies given by Social Services Departments to the CRE's survey questions provide a useful indication of the practical ways in which the needs of ethnic minorities might be taken into account when planning social services. Can you think of other ways in which services could become more responsive to needs in this way?

2 A report by the EOC entitled *Equality Management: Women's Employment in the NHS*, carried out in 1990 and published in 1992, concluded that discrimination against women in the NHS is 'deeply engrained'. The report suggested that 'High labour turnover and staff shortages are the inevitable consequence of the failure of the NHS to address issues of sex and marital discrimination, and to promote good-quality equal opportunities employment practices.'

3 *The Work of the Equal Opportunities Task Force 1986–1990: A Final Report*, published in March 1991 by the King Edward's Hospital Fund for London, pointed to 'glaring' racial inequalities in the NHS and called on the NHS to implement equal opportunities policies.

The task force found that while most health authorities had set up equal opportunities policies, relatively few had translated their policies into a timetabled programme for action, or had allocated responsibilities or sufficient resources. Most had failed to produce data about the ethnic composition of their workforce or monitor the outcome of selection decisions, especially in regard to promotion procedures and outcomes. Few health authorities complied with the recommendations of the CRE code of practice, while equal opportunities had not yet become part of the formal and routine duties of health service managers. The report concluded that action was needed immediately even to maintain the limited progress made during the 1980s, but that the new market-style NHS, effective from April 1991, could not alone be relied upon as the means of achieving racial equality in the NHS.

The King Edward's Hospital Fund for London Task Force was established in 1986 to help health authorities to implement equal opportunities policies for all racial groups in the health service, with the greatest emphasis upon employment. During its research, many authorities asked the Task Force for guidance on writing their equal opportunities policies. As a result, the Task Force produced a 'model policy' on race and discrimination.

4 *The Guardian* of 19 July 1993 reported on a study of equal opportunities in Southwark Council. This study appears to highlight some of the confusion and ambiguity surrounding equal opportunities issues in public services today.

RACE RANKLES COUNCIL STAFF

After interviewing more than 130 council staff, an outside consultant found that 'without any doubt' race was their main concern. 'Angry statements were recorded,' says the report. The council declared its opposition to all forms of racism and sexism nearly 10 years ago.

Disturbingly high numbers of staff said that colleagues made sexist or racist comments. A quarter of staff members had been made to feel uncomfortable or upset at work, and more than a fifth, disproportionately black and female, claimed that they had been discriminated against. But few felt able to make a formal complaint.

The report notes that more than 70 per cent of staff members felt that existing training and support under the equal opportunities provisions was inadequate, though most had little or no interest in receiving such training.

The consultants said that almost half the council staff had not received a copy of the council's equal opportunities policy statement. The statement and the council's recruitment procedures needed revision and overhaul.

ACTIVITY

1 What criticisms of the NHS and Social Services Departments are made in the four reports quoted above?

2 Does the institution in which you are studying have a formal, written policy on 'equal opportunities', 'anti-sexism', 'anti-racism', disability or special needs? If so, ask for copies of the policies and use these as a basis for discussion of the following questions (and if not, ask why not!):
- What general areas do these policies cover?
- Do you think that the policies should be rewritten in any way?
- Are these policies widely publicised in your institution?
- What practical changes/developments/initiatives are being taken in your institution as a result of these policies?
- Who in your institution is responsible for the implementation of these policies?
- Are there working parties, committees or informal or formal groups of people concerned with equal opportunities in your institution? If so, what are they doing?
- Are there particular equal opportunities or race equality issues which you think your institution should be addressing?

3 Working individually or in groups, make a list of the practical issues within social and health care contexts which you think equal opportunities and race equality policies should be trying to address.

4 What would you include in equal opportunities and race awareness training for staff working in a health or social care context?

5 A recent study of Asian women in North London found that only 3% of respondents said that they could turn to their GPs, social workers or health

visitors, and many were not aware of these services. What practical proposals and policies could be made to ensure better COMMUNICATION in health and social care contexts?

Systems of redress: enforcement of the legislation

ORGANISATIONAL

Where an organisation has a written EQUAL OPPORTUNITIES or similar POLICY, it may be possible for individuals who feel that they have suffered discrimination to use INTERNAL COMPLAINTS SYSTEMS to put forward their case. Sometimes such systems are intended for the use of employees only. Other organisations make them open to clients and/or the general public along the lines of the CUSTOMER COMPLAINTS procedures used in industry and retailing. For example, the Metropolitan Police use a grievance procedure, whereby an officer or a member of civilian staff can log a formal complaint and have the matter investigated. *The Guardian* newspaper reported that of the 339 grievances in the interim total for 1994, 47 involved gender and 18 were concerned with race. (*The Guardian*, 1 February 1995). Most Social Services Departments now have a written complaints procedure for clients (and may employ a Complaints Officer to deal with this work), as well as an internal grievance and disciplinary process for employees.

Cases of sexual harassment are sometimes dealt with internally and, where this is the case, usually involve an individual enlisting the support of a trade union or professional association. These organisations are likely to employ legal advisors who can assist the complainant.

However, where no such policy exists or where attempts to resolve the problem internally have failed, the individual may have to pursue their case through the legal system. This may be either at the level of the local community, such as through INDUSTRIAL TRIBUNALS, or in the country as a whole, through the courts. If all else fails, discrimination claims can be pursued beyond national boundaries, e.g. in the EU courts.

CONCILIATION AND TRIBUNALS

Cases of sex discrimination or racial discrimination not involving employment are dealt with in the courts. However, anybody who feels that he or she has been discriminated against unlawfully in employment or equal pay cases has a number of other courses of action open to them:

- The COMPLAINANT, as an individual, may bring a case before an INDUSTRIAL TRIBUNAL.
- Before doing so, the complainant can try two other courses of action. He or she may ask the employer concerned to:
  (a) complete a questionnaire giving reasons for the treatment which caused the complaint; or
  (b) answer a letter to the same effect.
  If there is no reply or the answers are unsatisfactory, this can be used as evidence during a hearing at an industrial tribunal.
- The complainant (or the employer) may ask a CONCILIATION OFFICER from the Advisory, Conciliation and Arbitration Service (ACAS) to attempt a settlement.
- If no settlement is reached and the complaint is still unresolved, an industrial tribunal will hear the case.

An industrial tribunal is an independent judicial body whose hearings are relatively informal. It consists of three people (see Figure 1.6). Tribunals sit in most areas and usually no costs or fees are charged. Complainants can present their own cases, employ a lawyer to act for them or ask another person to present the case.

There are time limits on presenting some cases to industrial tribunals: this must be done no later than three months from when the act complained of occurred for sex discrimination cases, but equal pay

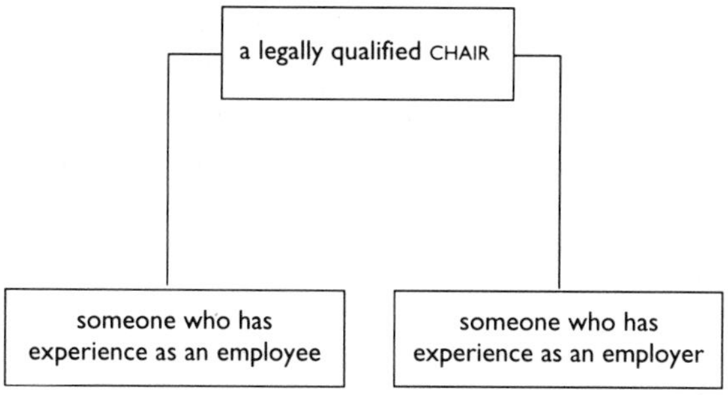

Figure 1.6 Composition of an industrial tribunal

complaints can be made at any time.

The burden of proof is on the complainant to show evidence that he or she has been discriminated against.

REMEDIES

If a tribunal upholds a complaint it may:

- declare the rights of both parties;
- award compensation, including special damages where there has been, for example, loss of earnings, and general damages for other situations such as injury to feelings. In very serious cases exemplary or aggravated damages can be awarded;
- recommend that the complained-against person should, within a specified time limit, take a particular course of action to reduce or stop the effect of any discrimination.

If an industrial tribunal hearing goes against a complainant, she or he may appeal to the Employment Appeal Tribunal if she or he feels that the law was misinterpreted. This appeal is heard by a high court judge and two lay members.

Further appeals can be made to the Court of Appeal (or Court of Sessions in Scotland) and finally to the House of Lords.

In certain cases the CRE and the EOC can take action to support individual complainants and/or conduct formal investigations into discriminatory practices.

Example of a case taken to a tribunal

In 1992 four male coroner's officers investigating sudden deaths in Birmingham's city coroner's office took a sex discrimination case under the Equal Pay Act to an industrial tribunal. They claimed that they were being paid about £1,000 a year less than a newly appointed female coroner's office for doing the same job. The new female employee was appointed to her post on a top scale, even though she was still training, and the four men involved had been doing the job for several years but were paid on a lower scale.

West Midlands Police Authority agreed to a substantial cash settlement with the men. One of the men involved said: 'It was sexual discrimination against men.'

PREPARING A CASE

Race through the 90s, a magazine produced jointly by the CRE and the BBC, produced some useful summary notes on preparing a complaint of discrimination:

Remember:

- No one will openly admit that they discriminated against you.
- It's not always easy to get the evidence you need.
- If your complaint is about promotion or unfair treatment at work, people you work with, managers and others may get resentful and label you a troublemaker.

It is important to:

- make detailed notes of conversations as soon as possible after the incident you are complaining about;
- keep copies of all letters and documents concerning your case;
- contact possible witnesses; keep in touch with them, in case they move;
- make sure you have a strong case. The law is very complicated. Your chances of winning are best if you have good legal advice and help throughout. Remember, the other side will usually have lawyers!

THE EUROPEAN COURT OF JUSTICE

The European Court of Justice sits in Luxembourg. It is composed of judges from each member state of the European Union who are assisted by Advocates General. The court considers any infringement of community law, or questions of interpretation. Rulings are final on European law, which takes precedence over national law.

Legal cases taken to the European Court of Justice have helped to clarify and interpret the laws on equal opportunities in EU countries such as Britain. The EU Treaty of Rome (Article 119), which states that men and women should receive equal pay for equal work together with the adoption of five Directives concerned with the general principle of equal treatment for men and women (see Table 1.2), means that there is a strong legal framework in the EU on equal opportunities.

A recent and controversial case taken to the European Court of Justice concerned equality of opportunity and pension rights. In May 1990 in the Barber case the European Court decided that men and women should receive the same pension entitlement for the same work at the same age. However, in October 1994 in the Coloroll case the Court decided that companies are free to insist that women must work to 65 to collect a full pension. (Previously women have only had to work to 60 to receive a full pension, while men, if they retired before the age of 60, received a reduced pension). Businesses argued to the EU that they could only afford to make men's and women's pensions equal by getting women to work an extra five years, rather than allowing men to receive a full pension at the lower age of 60.

Table 1.2 Women's rights and equal opportunities Directives of the European Union

1	The first Directive 75/117 created the obligation to apply the principle of 'equal pay for work of equal value'. It grants legal guarantees for the enforcement of this right and protects employees against dismissal on discriminatory grounds.
2	The second Directive 76/207, on equal treatment in employment, prohibits all sex-based discrimination at work. By implication it guarantees equal treatment with regard to recruitment, vocational training and promotion.
3	The third Directive 79/7, on equal treatment in social security matters, is aimed at achieving equal treatment in statutory social security schemes.
4	The fourth Directive 86/378, ensures equal treatment in occupational social security schemes.
5	The fifth Directive 86/613, on equal treatment in self-employment, applies the principle of equal treatment to men and women who are self-employed, including those in agriculture.

Source: Fact Sheet No. 1. *Women's Rights and Equal Opportunities Commission of the European Communities.*

OTHER AVENUES FOR REDRESS

The government has also published the 'Patient's Charter' which outlines patients' rights and avenues for complaints in general terms and also refers to special needs and 'respect for' religious and cultural beliefs. Copies are available from:
The Patient's Charter
FREEPOST
London SE99 7XU

Establishing and implementing equal opportunities policies: examples of local initiatives

Nirveen Kalsi and Pamela Constantinides, in their report *Working Towards Racial Equality in Health Care: The Haringey Experience* (1989), provide a clear demonstration of the difficulties and achievements involved in establishing and implementing equal opportunities policies. Nirveen Kalsi was appointed by the London Borough of Haringey to lead an ethnic minorities development worker project as part of a three-year development post. She describes the difficulties faced:

Establishing an equal opportunities policy, let alone getting it fully implemented, can take longer than anticipated, with unforeseen setbacks along the way. Similarly, changing patterns and methods of service delivery, and setting up structures through which the views of clients can be incorporated into the planning process, can be lengthy tasks.

Community organisations and health service managers can have quite different perspectives on the time-scales involved. Community groups, impatient for change, can become frustrated by the early lack of visible results, and this can lead to accusations of 'token' appointments, 'the appearance of activity', and 'marginalisation' of the issues. To community activists the health authority processes – set up a sub-committee, carry out a survey – can look like recipes for delayed action. Health service managers of the 1980s, on the other hand, sometimes feel almost swamped by the number and scale of changes and impending changes with which they have to contend. They feel beset by financial constraints. They want time – to become better informed, to be consulted, to assess budget implications. There can also of course be more trenchant resistance. Both management and staff may wish to avoid facing up to the uncomfortable issues surrounding health, race and inequality. They may prefer to cling to the notion that a 'colour-blind' service is by definition an equitable service and may wish to deny evidence which makes it clear that this is not so. There can be marked resistance to altering established practices in employment and promotion and a refusal to accept that these practices may be discriminatory.

(Kalsi and Constantinides, 1989)

Despite these problems Kalsi, working as a 'linkworker' with other health professionals, was able to develop specific priority areas for change in terms of race and health. These included:

- services for the growing numbers of elderly people of black/ethnic minority origin;
- mental health services;
- the setting up of a sickle-cell and thalassemia counselling centre;
- the writing of health promotion material in community languages other than English;
- the development of teams of 'linkworkers'.

The concept of a 'linkworker' has been adopted by other health authorities. In the following extract from its 1991 Annual Report, Wandsworth Health Authority sets out its linkworker scheme.

Most health promotion programmes and resources, especially those developed nationally, have been based on the needs of white individuals and groups.

Often these resources are not appropriate for use locally. The Linkworker Service largely works with non-English-speaking clients and has been proactive in terms of providing advice, consultancy and in-service education to NHS staff, as well as a service to clients using NHS services.

The aims of the Linkworker Service are listed below:

- To assist the Department of Public Health and the Health Promotion Service to identify health needs in the local ethnic and cultural minority community.
- To facilitate and improve communication between non-English-speaking clients and health professionals.
- To facilitate the understanding of cultural and other factors which need to be taken into account when care and advice are being given.
- To facilitate the provision of health care which is appropriate to the needs of the different cultural groups within Wandsworth Health Authority.
- To undertake proactive health promotion programmes in line with the Health Authority strategy and to contribute to the strategy.
- To identify opportunities and networks in support of local health promotion initiatives.
- To identify gaps in service provision.

Linkworkers are trained to participate in a three-way communication process involving the health professional, the client and themselves to enable everyone to get the best from the consultation.

Another of their roles is to identify the different views of health expressed by the various ethnic and cultural groups.

There is a continuing need for the Health Authority to listen to these views and to find ways of actively involving people from all races in assessing the service needs of the population.

ACTIVITY

1 Find out, by writing for information to the various organisations involved, what local initiatives on equal opportunities, race equality, disability and special needs exist in the areas where you live and/or study. You could write to:
- local hospitals;
- the Area Health Authority;
- the local county or borough council;
- the local Race Equality or Social Justice Council;
- community organisations, voluntary organisations and charities in your area.

2 If possible try to arrange for someone working on an initiative in this area to talk to your group or class.

ACTIVITY

Consider and discuss these situations:

Jane is admitted to hospital via casualty. She walked in declaring that she had just taken an overdose of paracetamol. She is 17. Two days later, while recovering from her treatment, Jane spits at one of the black nurses attending her and shouts racial abuse at her.

How should a situation like this be handled?

Jaswinder came to England to join her husband and his family. Her ordeal began when her husband threw her out with the four children.

'It was hard when I came here from Pakistan, what with young children and not knowing anybody or anything, and the neighbours always watching us and muttering to themselves when we passed.

'Then suddenly, one day, my husband just told me to leave this house and to take the children. I was stunned. I didn't know what to say, where to go, who to talk to. I have no relatives in England, and his relatives all took his side and didn't even want to see us. It was like it was my fault, even though I had done nothing wrong.

'I wasn't able to do anything, not even look after my children properly.... I thought I was going mad.... I saw the doctor and he gave me vitamin tablets and sleeping pills.... but I didn't tell him about my problems at home.... he couldn't change the way my husband and his family had behaved.... They finally sent me to hospital.'

(Race through the 90s, CRE and BBC Radio, 1992)

Could Jaswinder and her children have been helped in any other ways?

Working in groups, write 'case studies' like these, involving other instances where equal opportunities issues need to be considered. These might be based on your own experiences and observations or on situations you envisage might arise in health and social care contexts.

Swap these case studies with another group in your class and discuss the ones you have been given.

GENERAL SOURCES OF HELP AND ADVICE

Most trade unions have equal opportunity policies of their own and can provide advice and support for anyone wishing to pursue a complaint. A useful exercise would be to write to the national headquarters of trade unions in the health and social care field, asking them for information on the help that they can provide in this area. Relevant unions might include GMB, NUPE and UNISON.

Other organisations you could usefully contact might be:

- the Citizen's Advice Bureau;
- a local law centre;
- a local Racial Equality or Social Justice Council.

There is also a Health Information Service helpline run by the Department of Health, which can be reached on 0800 665544 (a Freefone number).

HOW INDIVIDUALS' RIGHTS CAN BE AFFECTED BY DISCRIMINATION

ACTIVITY

The following pages present some groupings of statistics, results of research studies and other information. Bearing in mind the limitations associated with data gathered from primary and secondary sources (see the section of Chapter 8 on 'Research Methods'), discuss the implications of each grouping of information.

What does this information indicate about life in Britain?

How can this information be explained?

RACE/ETHNICITY

ONE IN TEN NON-WHITE FAMILIES SUFFERS RACIAL HARASSMENT

One in ten ethnic minority households in London has suffered racial abuse, threats or physical attacks, according to recent research.

The study by the independent London Research Centre found that 48,000 households have experienced racial harassment: 64 per cent of those say family members have been verbally abused, 24 per cent report physical assault and 17 per cent have members who have been threatened because of the colour of their skin. The study also found that 10,000 white families had suffered harassment.

- Of London's 480,000 ethnic minority households 10 per cent say they have suffered racial harassment (sample: 6,500).
- 64 per cent of victims claim a member of the household was verbally abused; 24 per cent claim physical assault, and 17 per cent threats.
- Incidents were reported to the police in 51 per cent of all cases and 59 per cent of assaults.
- 32 per cent of households said they still felt threatened.
- 55 per cent of victims were owner-occupiers, 38 per cent council or association tenants, 7 per cent private tenants.

(The Independent, 11 March 1993)

The European Parliament is increasingly encouraging member states to act against racism. The Committee of Inquiry into Racism and Xenophobia made the following points in 1990:

- there were 7,000 racial attacks in the UK in 1989;
- institutional racism is prevalent in British society and ethnic minorities continue to be discriminated against in the justice system, job opportunities and recruitment;
- it is twice as difficult for black people to get jobs as whites;
- management can manipulate formal rules to their advantage to hinder, rather than help, blacks in their efforts to get jobs;
- without positive action, ethnic minorities may forever fail to join mainstream economic life;
- in 1988, more than half the ethnic minority population of Strathclyde had experienced racial attacks.

(European Parliament, 1990)

. . . racial discrimination has indeed continued to have a great impact on the employment opportunities of black people. . . . At least a third of the employers recruiting people to the jobs covered in this study discriminate against Asian applicants or West Indian applicants or both.

C. Brown and P. Gay, 1986, Policy Studies Institute)

We now have 4 black or Asian MPs out of 650, 1 senior Asian judge out of 500 at circuit level or above and 1 Asian Civil Servant out of 668 at under-secretary level or above, that is 0.15% compared to an economically active ethnic minority population of 4.7%.

(The Independent, 7 June 1991)

Thirteen of every 1,000 Asian babies die in their first year, compared with the national rate of five out of 1,000.

(Race Through the 90s, CRE and BBC 1992)

Compulsory detention under the Mental Health Act is twenty-five times more likely for 16–25-year-old blacks than for whites.

(Observer, 1 January 1987)

In 1985 DHSS figures showed that while overseas-born doctors in the NHS formed 28% of all hospital doctors, they were confined to the lower professional ranks.

(DHSS, 1986)

Although an estimated 8% of the NHS workforce is black or Asian, compared with 5.5% in the population as a whole, representation is concentrated among ancillary and lower-grade nursing jobs and among junior doctors.

(The Guardian, 9 December 1993)

In a survey entitled 'Equal Voice' carried out by Portsmouth University's social services research and information unit in 1992, it was revealed that most black and ethnic minority households interviewed in south-east Hampshire had not heard of the local council's Social Services Department; and more than one-third of those who had, did not know what services were on offer.

(Community Care, 28 March 1993)

SEX / GENDER

Women take overwhelming responsibility for domestic duties in Britain. Work mainly done by women in households includes washing and ironing (88%), preparing the evening meals (77%), looking after sick children (67%); the only work done mainly by men is repairing household equipment (82%).

(Social Trends, 1989)

Majorities of both sexes still regard certain occupations as being mainly suitable for men or women, but not suitable for both. For instance, majorities regard being a car mechanic as an exclusively male occupation, and substantial minorities of both sexes believe the same of the job of bus driver, police officer and bank manager. Similarly, substantial numbers of both sexes think women more suitable than men to be nurses and secretaries.

(Social Trends, 1990)

The average part-time working woman earns little over half as much per hour as a full-time working man while 4 out of 10 women are below the 16 hour threshold which legally denies them major employment rights. 82% of part-time workers are women.

(Options, November 1991)

Of those women who were in employment in 1990 (both employees and the self-employed), 81% were employed in three service sectors: 1. distribution, hotels, catering and repairs; 2. banking, finance, insurance, etc.; 3. other services which include nursing and education. (The corresponding figure for men was 53%.) A further 14% of women were employed in manufacturing, compared with 28% for men. Clerical and related occupations constituted the largest single category of women's employment (31%), followed by managerial and professional occupations (29%).

(Labour Market Quarterly Report, November 1991)

A FAIR COP?

Ethnic minority officers in police:

1990: 1.11%

1993: 1.45%

Table 1.3 Employment by occupation: Great Britain, 1991

Occupational group	Females 000s	% of group	Males 000s	% of group	Total 000s
1 Managers & administrators	1,118	30.7	2,527	69.3	3,645
Bank, building society & post-office managers	23	21.7	83	78.3	106
2 Professional occupations	915	38.4	1,470	61.6	2,385
Medical practitioners	32	32.3	67	67.7	99
Solicitors	17	23.0	57	77.0	74
3 Associate professional & technical occupations	1,112	49.2	1,146	50.8	2,258
Computer analysts/programmers	41	20.7	157	79.3	198
Nurses	**397**	**89.6**	**46**	**10.4**	**443**
4 Clerical & secretarial	3,047	75.2	1,007	24.8	4,054
Computer operators	146	70.2	62	29.8	208
5 Craft & related	414	10.7	3,462	89.3	3,876
Bakers, flour confectioners	16	35.6	29	64.4	45
6 Personal & protective services	1,530	65.4	809	34.6	2,339
Police officers (sergeant & below)	17	12.1	124	87.9	141
Hairdressers, barbers	**100**	**87.0**	**15**	**13.0**	**115**
7 Selling	1,242	62.0	760	38.0	2,002
Sales assistants	867	77.5	251	22.5	1,118
8 Plant & machine operatives	570	22.1	2,011	77.9	2,581
Assemblers/lineworkers	113	48.7	119	51.3	232
9 Other occupations	1,178	52.2	1,079	47.8	2,257
Postal workers, mail sorters	32	17.6	150	82.4	182
Cleaners, domestics	**709**	**87.3**	**103**	**12.7**	**812**
Inadequately described/not stated	19	35.2	35	64.8	54
All occupations	11,145	43.8	14,306	56.2	25,451

Source: Labour Force Survey (1991).

Table 1.4 School examination results, 1990/1991 (000s)

	England GCSE Grades A–C		Scotland SCE Ordinary and Standard Grades 1–3		Wales GCSE Grades A–C	
Subject	Females	Males	Females	Males	Females	Males
English	158.7	120.5	19.3	15.1	9.3	6.4
Mathematics	98.0	108.1	12.2	12.9	5.4	5.5
Biology	31.5	25.3	8.3	3.5	2.5	1.7
French	72.0	47.6	9.4	5.3	3.6	1.8
History	53.6	45.6	5.1	3.6	2.5	1.7
Chemistry	25.2	33.5	7.9	8.9	1.6	1.9
Physics	18.6	39.5	5.4	10.8	1.1	2.2
Computer Studies	12.4	15.9	2.0	3.7	1.2	1.6

Source: Department for Education; Scottish Examination Board Report 1991; Welsh Office.

Women officers in police:

1990: 11.6%

1993: 13.2%

Source: Her Majesty's Inspectorate of Constabulary.

Nine out of ten policewomen are verbally sexually harassed, according to research. One in ten has given serious thought to leaving the police because of harassment. Six in ten had offensive comments made about their appearance. Three in ten were subjected to unwanted touching.

Table 1.5 First destinations of school leavers, 1989/1990 (000s)

	England		Scotland*		Wales	
Leavers entering:	Females	Males	Females	Males	Females	Males
Degree courses and teacher training courses	35.2	37.9	3.9	4.1	2.5	2.1
Other full-time further and higher education courses	84.0	58.4	7.9	4.9	5.3	4.3
Labour market/destination unknown	162.7	199.9	24.9	29.1	9.4	12.1
All leavers	281.9	296.2	36.7	38.1	17.2	18.5

*1988/9 figures.
Source: Department for Education; Scottish Office; Welsh Office.

Source: Sex Discrimination in the Police Service in England and Wales, by Dr Jennifer Brown and Elizabeth Campbell.

(The Guardian, 28 September 1994)

OLD AGE

NEGATIVE ATTITUDES TOWARDS OLD AGE

Although old age is a status that all of us might expect to reach, negative attitudes about old age and 'the elderly' are common. To use Goffman's terminology, old age is a weakly stigmatised, discreditable status. Old age is not directly and inevitably discrediting for a number of reasons. Most importantly, it is often not immediately apparent how old someone is. In any case definitions of 'old' are indeterminate and so although negative attitudes and stereotypes are prevalent it is often difficult to know who is or is not 'old'. Hence old people who are fit, active and who look young are not stigmatised in the ways in which frail elderly disabled people may be. Indeed, the negative stereotypes of old age seem to be based upon the association between old age, sickness and dependency. Negative stereotyping highlights dependency, sickness and the inability to perform socially. A review by Lehr (1983) of studies of negative attitudes towards old age in industrial societies summarises the evidence as follows: 'Generally the image of the aged, aside from a few positive traits, is defined by negative characteristics such as decline and loss of functions and capacities. The aged are perceived as ill, retarded, tired, slow, and inefficient in their thinking; they are seen as asexual, or if even showing sexual interests, as ridiculous.'

Such negative, stereotypical attitudes are widespread in British society and are constantly reinforced in the media and everyday conversation. . . . Because an old person has difficulty with walking and eyesight, she or he is also presumed to have difficulty in understanding others, to be unable to make everyday decisions, and to have lost interest in world affairs and their own sexuality. As with other stereotypes the contradictory evidence of able and competent old people who manage their lives successfully is explained away by, for example, claiming they are 'exceptions'.

Most older people do not accept the stereotype of old age as applying to themselves, although there may be self-stigmatisation among some older people. Research shows that old people differentiate between how they look and their chronological age, and that their self-image is often that of being a younger person. . .

Not all old people are able to resist the negative label of 'being old', especially if they are dependent upon other people for a range of physical and social support. . . In such circumstances the attitudes of others can be said to create social handicaps for the old person and to create a 'self-fulfilling prophecy'.

Field, 1992)

Table 1.6 The over-65s in the UK population

	Numbers (millions)		% of total population	
	Aged 65–79	Aged 80+	Over 65	Over 80
1901	1.3 (65–74)	0.5 (75+)	4.7	1.3 (75+)
1921	1.9 (65–74)	0.7 (75+)	5.9	1.5 (75+)
1951	4.8	0.7	10.9	1.4
1971	6.1	1.3	13.4	2.3
1981	6.9	1.6	15.0	2.8
1989	6.9	2.0	15.6	3.5
Males	3.0	0.6	6.3	1.1
Females	3.9	1.4	9.3	2.4
Projected 2001	6.7	2.5	16.0	3.8

Source: Social Trends 1986 (Table 1.2) and 1991 (Table 1.3).

DISABILITY

Government statistics . . . independent research projects and personal experiences show that on nearly every indicator of participation in mainstream life disabled people come out extremely badly: for example on employment statistics, income levels, suitable housing and access to public transport, buildings, information (newspapers, radio and television) and leisure facilities.

(Vic Finkelstein, in Swain et al., 1993)

Poverty is also a restriction on the lives of people with learning difficulties. Those who live independently often rely on state benefits which are low: Flynn (1989) found that the average weekly income of 88 people in her study was £39 in 1985.

(Jan Walmsley, in Swain et al., 1993)

Table 1.7 Percentage of the population aged 65 and over in selected countries

	1980	2010	2030
Canada	9.51	14.61	22.39
France	13.96	16.26	21.76
Germany	15.51	20.35	25.82
Italy	13.45	17.28	21.92
Japan	9.10	18.62	19.97
UK	14.87	14.61	19.24
USA	11.29	12.79	19.49

Source: OECD 'Ageing populations: the social policy implications', Demographic Change and Public Policy, 1988.

After over a century of state-provided education, disabled children and young people are still not entitled to the same kind of schooling as their able-bodied peers, nor do they leave with equivalent qualifications. . . The majority of British schools, colleges and universities remain unprepared to accommodate disabled students within a mainstream setting.

(Mike Oliver and Colin Barnes, in Swain et al., 1993)

Disabled people are more likely to be out of work than non-disabled people, they are out of work longer than other unemployed workers, and when they do find work it is more often than not low-paid, low-status work with poor working conditions.

Mike Oliver and Colin Barnes, in Swain et al., 1993)

The NHS does not publish statistics about the employment of disabled women in the National Health Service. However, the statistics collected by the Employment Service from Health Authorities in 1990 showed that only 4 out of 215 District Health Authorities and Boards and one out of 17 Regional Health Authorities have more than 1% of staff in employment who are registered disabled. Eight Authorities and Boards employed no registered disabled staff at all. NUPE's survey of nurses showed that disabled nurses tend to be employed in the lower grades and that their disability has resulted from injury sustained in the course of their employment. NUPE points to a need for greater preventative measures and imaginative efforts to integrate nurses with disabilities into satisfying work.

(Equal Opportunities Commission, 1992, p. 40)

SEXUALITY

One in five young lesbian and gay men attempts suicide because of their sexuality, according to research by Trenchard and Warren for the London Gay Teenage Group.

(Kendra Sone, Community Care Magazine Supplement, 31 March 1994, p. 4)

Your discussions of these groupings of statistics and information should have produced some interesting ideas. They may well have involved some conflict or disagreement among members of your group in attitudes, ideas and beliefs expressed. There may have been considerable confusion in trying to find appropriate explanations for some of the trends illustrated. Social scientists involved in the production and evaluation of the kind of information illustrated above have been concerned to *make sense of it* – to relate it to the way people interact and to changes in the social, economic and political structures of the society in which we live. Just as yours may have done, their interpretations of the data differ in many respects; but certain common themes can be described.

Forms of discrimination

Social scientists have suggested that data such as those presented above can be explained by using the concept of DISCRIMINATION to refer to the unfair treatment or neglect of certain groups of people in society. They suggest that discrimination in societies such as Britain can arise in several ways:

1 At the level of *individual prejudice*, where people may have personal attitudes and beliefs which they use to prejudge other groups negatively (or, in some instances, positively). There are many forms of prejudice; the following are some of the major 'isms' we will consider in this chapter:

- *racism*: a belief in the inherent superiority of one race over all others and thereby its right to dominance;
- *sexism*: a belief in the inherent superiority of one sex over the other and thereby its right to dominance;
- *ageism*: a belief in the inherent superiority of one age-group over all others;
- *heterosexism*: a belief in the inherent superiority of opposite sex sexual relationships over same-sex sexual relationships.

And, of course, people may express a variety of prejudices towards people with disabilities. Common prejudices here often involve the idea that to be disabled is to lack intelligence or sensitivity. There is also a tendency to describe disabled people as either 'amazing' and 'courageous' because of the way they manage their disabilities, or to see them as dependent upon others for help and charity.

These categories are not mutually exclusive. They may interlink, as in prejudice towards 'old women' or 'black youth'.

Various forms of prejudice can also be held about people with a particular 'health status', i.e. with an illness, disability or condition which is either misunderstood (e.g. wrongly thought to be contagious) or seen as the direct result of some moral or behavioural inadequacy in the person concerned. It is well known that people with mental health problems or those with HIV or AIDS infections can find their illnesses severely stigmatising – to the point where they may suffer physical or verbal attacks from others, they may lose their job or their home, or they may be refused access to services or public places. Skin conditions such as psoriasis can be considered unsightly or (wrongly) 'catching' by others, making it difficult for people with these conditions to feel comfortable in places such as swimming pools or beaches.

People may also face prejudice from others because of their religious beliefs, customs and practices. These may range from beliefs that 'new religious movements', sects and cults may be 'brainwashing' new converts, to hostility towards plans to build a new mosque or Hindu temple in parts of Britain.

2 At the level of *individual behaviour* whereby people may discriminate towards others directly by, for example, using abusive language or refusing access to services, or indirectly by the tone of voice or body language used. It has been argued that these forms or types of discrimination (which may produce undesirable, painful or life-threatening experiences for people) are reinforced by the strategies which people use to deny, ignore and minimise the presence of discrimination in their own institutions, culture and personal behaviour. This COVERT discrimination contrasts with OVERT discrimination, which is openly practised, acknowledged and even justified. Covert discrimination may take the following forms (adapted from Dominelli, 1992):
   - *Denial strategies*, based on the idea that there is no such thing as cultural and institutional racism/sexism, etc., only personal prejudice in its crude manifestations.
   - *Colour- or gender-blind strategies*, which focus on the idea that all people are the same – members of one human race with similar problems, needs and objectives.
   - *Dumping strategies*, which rely on placing the responsibility for eliminating racism, sexism, etc., on the shoulders of the groups discriminated against.
   - *Omission strategies*, which rest on the view that racism, sexism, etc., are not important parts of social interaction and can be safely ignored in most situations.
   - *Devaluing strategies*, which acknowledge the presence of discrimination in general terms but fail to 'see' it in specific instances involving daily routines/interaction and in the testimonies and accounts of family, friends, colleagues, etc.
   - *Avoidance strategies*, where it is accepted that discrimination exists but there is a refusal or denial of the particular responsibility of the individual or institution to do something about it.

3 At the level of *institutional discrimination*, where there is public legitimation of prejudice. Within the structures and hierarchies of organisations, power can be used to exclude certain groups from access to resources, and to form (or to contribute to the formation of) general beliefs that such exclusion is justifiable.

4 At a *cultural* level, where people's 'common-sense' values, beliefs and ideas (i.e. those rarely questioned or challenged) can endorse and reinforce both individual prejudice and institutional discrimination. Here discrimination can be transmitted through history, through daily language and interaction and through media influences.

Stereotypes

Most social–psychological and (in sociology) interactionist theories of prejudice and discrimination have focused upon the following two ideas:

- that prejudice may arise from early socialisation and learning experiences, personality traits and the general psychological processes involved in attitude formation;
- that prejudiced attitudes and adverse 'labelling' may result in low self-esteem and a 'self-fulfilling prophecy' of low achievement.

STEREOTYPING PREJUDICE AND THE SELF-FULFILLING PROPHECY

The self-fulfilling prophecy and its influence on the caring professions is discussed on pages 84–85 in Chapter 2.

What is stereotyping?

Originally a term from printing, a 'stereotype' is now used to mean a simplified image of a whole group of people, for example a racial, national, religious, sexual or occupational group. Stereotyping is the attribution of characteristics that are presumed to belong to a whole group of people to just one individual.

It seems that we need stereotypes in order to categorise somehow all the different people we meet, watch and read about. They are cognitive shortcuts for dealing with all the information we receive: a convenient and lazy way of viewing other people. Our stereotypes influence our perception of events and our memory of them. They may also influence the way we behave towards others, and thus the way they feel and behave – the self-fulfilling prophecy.

Stereotypes make useful pigeon-holes. Unfortunately they usually have value judgements, often negative, attached to them.

Educated people are nowadays more aware of stereotyping and its dangers. Try asking friends what is the stereotype of, for example, Scots, the elderly, an immigrant group, nurses. They will probably be reluctant or embarrassed to say what they think the stereotypes are, especially if they are negative or derogatory, and will say that they do not agree with them. This is encouraging, but nevertheless, the people you ask will probably be in accord about what the stereotype for each group is held to be. That is because stereotypes are very common in our society and are reinforced by sections of the media.

Stereotypes are learnt by children from their parents and the majority culture – newspapers, TV, comics, books and films. Out-of-date stereotypes are often perpetrated in children's books, written years ago, which are still popular.

Sex-role stereotyping

In the 'Thomas the Tank Engine' stories the engines are all male, while the silly clattering carriages are all female.

In 1982 J. Penrose complained to *The Guardian* that the Ladybird Key Words Reading scheme was guilty of traditional sex stereotyping. Peter made all the important decisions, took charge more often and spoke more frequently than Jane. He was active and adventurous, Jane was totally passive.

It is not surprising, therefore, to find rigid sex-role stereotyping among adults.

> **ACTIVITY**
>
> Carry out a content analysis of a children's reading scheme book, using the following categories or others you can think of:
>
> - Who takes the initiative most often?
> - Who talks the most often?
> - How many times is the child featured with the same sex parent?
> - How many times is the child featured with the opposite sex parent?
> - Which child is the most active?

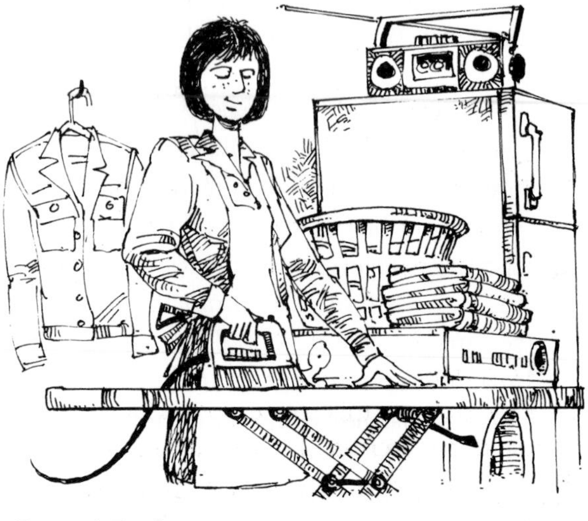

Figure 1.7 Stereotyping

ACTIVITY

Look at Figure 1.7.

- What type of stereotype does this picture show?
- Describe ways in which this stereotype is reinforced by society.
- Why do you think parents reinforce this stereotype with their children from an early age?

Racial stereotyping

Similarly, old children's books hold out-of-date racial stereotypes. The Captain W.E. Johns' Biggles stories, still in circulation, show a corrupt world being kept in order by clean-living white English men; the villains are usually big negroes, harsh Prussian officers or fat, suave Eurasians.

The fact that racism is still, despite the anti-discrimination laws, more prevalent in England than in many other mixed-race societies must be in part due to the stereotypes that have been absorbed into our culture. D. Milner (1983) wrote: 'When racism has taken root in the majority culture, has pervaded its institutions, language, its social intercourse and its cultural productions, has entered the very interstices of the culture, then the simple process by which a culture is transmitted from generation to generation in the socialisation process becomes the most important "determinant" of prejudice.'

ACTIVITY

Look out for examples of racial stereotyping in modern academic textbooks.

Prejudice

Prejudice starts with a stereotype. Allport suggested five increasingly violent stages of behaviour which may take place against any minority group:

- *Anti-locution* – hostile talk, racial jokes, verbal denigration and insult.
- *Avoidance* – keeping a distance but without inflicting any harm.
- *Discrimination* – exclusion from housing, employment, schools, clubs. The Race Relations Act covers three kinds of discrimination: direct discrimination, indirect discrimination and victimisation. Indirect discrimination is the most difficult to prove.
- *Physical attack* – violence against the person or property.
- *Extermination* – indiscriminate violence against a whole group.

ACTIVITY

Give a present day example of each of these stages of prejudice.

Social identity theory

Tajfel and Turner put forward social identity theory to explain the development of prejudice. The basis of this theory is that people, particularly those with low self-esteem and an intense need for acceptance by others, will identify with a group that has a positive social image. The more positive the image of the group, the more positive will be their social identity, and therefore their self-image. By emphasising how desirable the 'in group' is and how undesirable the 'out group', and by concentrating on those characteristics of the 'in group' which make it 'superior', people can make for themselves a satisfactory social identity, and it is this that lies at the heart of prejudice.

Scapegoating

This is suggested as another explanation for prejudice. When there are problems in society, like a shortage of housing and high unemployment, people find targets for their frustration and aggression. Minority racial groups are easy targets. The defence mechanisms of displacement and projection are involved in scapegoating.

The reduction of prejudice

To reduce everyday prejudice it is important:

- to meet people from discriminated groups on a personal level, and to see them performing in high-status occupations;
- to receive information from the media which breaks down the traditional stereotypes;
- to live in a society in which prejudice is actively discouraged.

ACTIVITY

A recent study by researchers at the London University Institute of Education shows ethnic minority groups outperforming 'whites' in GCSE examination results and entrance to university.

EXAM RESULTS

Ethnic minorities' exam performance compared with white pupils.

	Difference in points
Black African	+4.6
Black Caribbean	−0.6
Other black groups	+0.3
Indian	+8.2
Pakistani	+7.2
Bangladeshi	+6.3
Chinese	+10.7
Others	+5.7

Note: Differences of less than one point are not statistically significant and may have arisen by chance.

Source: The Times, Monday 27 June 1994.

- Investigate possible reasons for this.
- Discuss how, in the long term, popular stereotypes might change in response to information like this.

ACTIVITY

Whether or not we believe in stereotyped views of race, gender, age, disability, health status, religion and sexuality, their existence can be readily demonstrated.

Working in groups, for each of the areas above draw up lists of the most common negative stereotypes you have encountered. These stereotypes might take the form of popular jokes, beliefs or terms and labels used to describe the groups of people concerned. For example, 'women drivers are hopeless', or 'old people are grumpy'.

(You may find this a rather distressing experience because some of the terms used can be highly unpleasant . . . the intent to hurt is contained within them. If this happens, ensure that you discuss your feelings about this exercise with your group.)

How do you think these stereotypes have arisen?

- Why do people use them?
- What possible effects may these stereotypes have on the groups of people they describe?
- Is it possible to think of positive stereotypes for the groups mentioned above? If so, what would they be?
- Are positive stereotypes any more acceptable than negative stereotypes?

By growing up in this society, by incorporating its culture and history and by being exposed to the mass media, many people will become familiar with negative racial and sexual stereotypes, and with stereotypes relating to people with disabilities and older people.

Institutional and cultural discrimination – organisational and societal structures and processes

Negative ideas and assumptions are reinforced when dominant organisations in society (local and central government, the legal system, schools, the health and welfare services, private companies) conduct their affairs in ways resulting in distinctive patterns of social disadvantage. Discriminatory practices become part of general routines and rules.

The discrimination may not necessarily be recognised or intended (although it would be naïve not to believe that some forms of discrimination are deliberate). Limited access to buildings for people with disabilities, restricted access to promotion for some groups such as women or older workers, and transport policies which restrict movement to certain groups are all examples of the routine forms of discrimination which seem to continue in this society. This is partly because institutional discrimination can also persist through the omission of serious and active attempts within such organisations to overcome the unfair treatment of certain groups within the population. For example, racial discrimination has no central place in the EU Social Charter and there are no EU race equality directives.

ACTIVITY

1 Ask ten people from a variety of backgrounds to define and give examples of the terms 'prejudice' and 'discrimination'. Write down their responses and then analyse and compare them. What do people mean by these terms? What illustrations and examples of them do they give? Which definitions do you find most and least satisfactory, and why?

2 If you are doing a project on racism not exclusively based on Britain, you might consider looking at:
- the experience of migrant workers in EU countries;
- the conflict in the former Yugoslavia and the notion of 'ethnic cleansing'.

INSTITUTIONAL DISCRIMINATION?

RICHMOND COUNCIL IS IGNORING THE DISABLED

Richmond Council came under fire this week for failing to appoint any disabled staff this year.

Cllr Malcolm McDougall, chairman of the Personnel Sub-Committee which published the findings, claimed that few from either group had applied for the jobs.

'If they don't apply, they can't be appointed', he explained, and claimed that 'the council goes out of its way to show its equal opportunities policy'.

Asked about the legal requirement that disabled people should form three per cent of all workforces, Cllr McDougall revealed: 'this requirement is not generally regarded as being an obligation, but the council plays its part in encouraging equal opportunities'.

Cllr McDougall said the council is looking into adapting its premises for disabled workers, should it be necessary, and that 'the council is always willing to pursue any positive initiative'.

But local disabled leaders are not impressed. Alan Pinn, Chairman of Thames Valley's Disabled Drivers Association, told *The Times* 'it's an absolute disgrace'.

He went on: 'I believe that comments like those made by Cllr McDougall are out of touch with current thinking, and don't help the situation.'

(Richmond and Twickenham Times, 9 October 1992)

THE MEDIA'S ROLE IN CULTURAL DISCRIMINATION

PRESS 'GIVES SLANTED VIEW OF DISABLED PEOPLE'

National newspapers are presenting a partial and distorted view of people with disabilities and those who care for them, sometimes breaching the Press Complaints Commission's guidance on discrimination, according to a report published by the Spastics Society.

The choice of stories covered, and the language used, combine to portray disabled people – one in ten of the population – in a stereotyped and detrimental way, undermining their individuality, the Society said.

It was easier to find bad examples in the

tabloids, but the broadsheet press was also prone to sensationalising or marginalising the issues, it added. Both concentrated on fundraising, charity stories and personal interest medical stories, while disabled people are most affected by political and social issues. Community care, of profound interest to disabled people, was not covered by the tabloids in the periods studied, while stories about carers, sport, employment or local authority provisions for disabled people received little attention.

The report says that too often newspapers write about 'the disabled' or 'the handicapped', implying there is one homogeneous group, and that all disabled people are victims. It says newspapers often patronise, by referring to disabled people by their first name, as if they are small children in need of help. Conversely, anything a disabled person achieves, however minor, is heralded as worthy of congratulation.

Brian Lamb, head of campaigns at the Spastics Society, said that distorted reporting cut disabled people off from mainstream society. 'We hope this report will stimulate debate . . . and help point the way to good journalistic practice in the future,' he said.

The report, which analysed stories on disabilities over an eight-week period in late 1990, and two weeks last February, says the commission should ensure the Press 'avoids' prejudicial and pejorative reference to the person's race, colour, religion, sex or sexual orientation, or to any physical or mental illness or handicap.'

(The Independent, 3 December 1991)

ACTIVITY

Find (or record if from television) five examples of advertisements, pictures images or articles, each one of which, in your opinion, represents a different form or type of discrimination or prejudice, i.e. by race, sex, age, disability, etc. Indicate what you think is discriminatory about each of these images and articles.

Language and discrimination

One way in which discrimination enters culture is through the association between language and thought. The following is adapted from the publication of the National Association of Teachers in Further and Higher Education *Equal Opportunities Guide to Language* (NATFHE, 1993), which offers a useful discussion of the issues in this area.

Overtly discriminatory and offensive language is an obvious problem, and can be a disciplinary issue related to harassment and discrimination. Beyond this obvious area, however, there are problems in laying down guidelines, because language is a fluid and dynamic medium, and reflects the society in which it is used. It is constantly changing in response to changes in society, and to the perceptions of people within society.

However, language is not neutral; neither is it a simple transparent medium for conveying messages. Language can help to form, perpetuate and reinforce prejudice and discrimination. Because of prejudice, negative feelings and attitudes may come to be associated with a word or phrase which was originally coined with positive intention. No word is good or bad in itself. Its use can be judged on two criteria: the intention of the person using it, and the effect on the person about whom it is used. Few of us would have any hesitation about condemning words used with the intention to abuse or offend. But because of the frequent changes of terminology for describing groups which are the subject of prejudice, some people may use words which many now find offensive, although they have no intention of causing offence. The most positive line in these situations is to accept the wishes of the person/people offended, and use the terminology they would prefer.

GENDER

Sexist language is language that promotes and maintains attitudes that stereotype people according to gender. Non-sexist language treats all people equally, and either does not refer to a person's sex at all when it is irrelevant, or refers to men and women in symmetrical ways when their gender is relevant. It is accepted that stereotyping of the masculine can often affect men adversely. But the main problem with sexist language remains that generally it assumes that the male is the norm. The words 'man', 'he' and 'him' are often used in referring to human beings of either sex. This gives a distinct impression to the reader or listener that women are absent, silent or of no importance. This problem can be overcome by:

1 avoiding the use of he, his and him, by:

adding the female:	she or he, his or hers, s/he
using the first person:	I, me, mine, we, our, ours
using the second person:	you, your, yours
using the plural:	they, them, theirs.

2 avoiding composite words containing the word 'man', e.g.:

Instead of:	Try:
manpower	workforce, staff
manning	staffing, running
man-made	artificial, synthetic
to a man	everyone, without exception, unanimously
man hours	work hours.

In the workplace, biased language reinforces the stereotyping of men and women, and the fact that they are often typecast as being suitable for particular jobs. The gender description in such terms as 'male secretary', 'woman carpenter', 'male nurse', 'female director', reveals this typecasting. Linking jobs to gender can be avoided by using alternative expressions.

Instead of:	Try:
chairman	chair
headmaster	headteacher
businessman	business manager, executive
foreman	supervisor
policeman	police officer
salesman/girl	shop assistant/worker
stewardess/air hostess	airline staff/flight attendant.

RACE

Racist language is language that promotes and maintains attitudes that stereotype people according to their skin colour and racial origin. It often involves stereotyped attitudes to culture and religion. Non-racist language treats all people equally, and either does not refer to a person's race when it is not relevant, or refers to black and white people in symmetrical ways when their race is relevant. Although there may be examples of language which negatively stereotypes white people, the main problem with racist language in our society is that it is either deliberately offensive to or abusive of those who are not part of the Anglo-Saxon majority, or it assumes that majority is the norm and superior to all minorities. For examples, the term 'non-white' is directly exclusive, and implies deviation from the norm.

The controversies that surround the terminology in this area can be illustrated by the fact that even the term 'race' itself is loaded in the way it can be interpreted, and it does not carry the same meaning for all people. 'Ethnic minority', although widely used and accepted, is seen by many as containing both cultural and religious bias (the dictionary definition of ethnic is 'pertaining to nations not Christian or Jewish: gentile, heathen, pagan'). However, most institutions use 'ethnic monitoring', and until some alternative is found the term will remain in use. The term 'immigrants' is inappropriate to describe people who were born or have settled in Britain, although the word is frequently used inaccurately to refer to black people.

In the first part of this century, the terms 'Negro', 'coloured', etc., were widely used. The development of Black movements in the 1960s led to the use of the word 'Black' as a proud and assertive term, and for many people, from then until now, this has been the preferred term. However, its use is seen by some as restricted to those of African origin, and some people from Chinese or Asian backgrounds may prefer to describe themselves, and be described, as such. Although for many years the term 'coloured' has been regarded as offensive, the expression 'people of colour' to cover those who are not members of the white majority has recently become fashionable in America, and its usage is now appearing in Britain. The principle remains to follow the wishes of the person/people concerned before deciding what terminology to use.

A number of phrases and terms used in everyday speech can cause offence. Some, like 'nigger in the wood pile' and 'working like a black' have their roots in a more openly racist past, and should be avoided. There is also a problem with the use of the word 'black' as an adjective. It is parody to object to 'black' as a purely descriptive colour adjective, as in such terms as 'black coffee', 'blackboard', 'black car', etc. The problem arises because so many uses of 'black' involve negative and sometimes evil connotations, e.g. 'black magic', 'black mark', 'black sheep', etc.

DISABILITY

The term 'disability' is now widely used to cover people who may have a physical disability, a mental illness or emotional, behavioural or learning difficulties. The term 'disability', though contested by some, is more acceptable to many organisations controlled by disabled people than 'handicapped'. It takes into account that people may be disabled (i.e. prevented from being able to do something) not only by accidents (of birth, or otherwise), but by social organisation which takes little or no account of such people and thus excludes them from participating in the mainstream of society's activities.

Again we find that what is acceptable in one period causes offence in another, and there is a need to update our language on a regular basis. In education, for example, expressions such as 'ESN (Educationally Sub-Normal)', 'retarded', 'maladjusted' were once widely used. The expression 'special needs' was coined as an attempt to get away from those negative labels, and is still the coherent usage, although not acceptable to all disabled people. The term 'special educational needs' is not accurate, as in many cases the needs are not educational, but involve problems of access, etc. It can be dehumanising to use blanket expressions such as 'the deaf', and demoralising for disabled people to hear themselves constantly described as unfortunate victims.

Instead of:	Try:
mentally handicapped/ backward/dull	learning difficulty
spastic	cerebral palsy
mongol	Down's syndrome
cripple	person with disability/mobility impaired
idiot/imbecile/ feeble-minded	development disability
crazy/maniac/insane	emotional disability
The deaf	deaf person/person with impaired hearing
The blind	blind person/partially sighted person

AGE

It is now accepted that ageism is a form of prejudice and discrimination which must be taken seriously. In employment practices, although most managers now trumpet their equal opportunity policies and credentials, they are increasingly discriminating on the grounds of age. Language must be carefully constructed so as to combat this. The use of terms such as 'old fogey', 'dead wood', 'out of the Ark', 'geriatric', 'too old to change', 'over the hill', 'out of date', creates an environment in which it is possible to intimidate people into premature retirement. If we talked of 'more experienced', 'long-serving' instead of 'middle-aged' and 'the old guard', the intimidation could be avoided.

Effects of discrimination

Research into the effects of discrimination in the contexts of early education, health and welfare, and work is so wide-ranging that it would be impossible to summarise all the issues covered in the space available in this book. Instead, some of the main areas of concern raised by studies of the effects of racism, sexism, ageism and discrimination against people with disabilities are summarised below, along with the ideas for student assignments or projects and examples of key texts which students might find helpful. Work experience placements may provide opportunities for students to investigate some of these issues.

Students should bear in mind that the effects of discrimination can be both long term, resulting in patterns of disadvantage for whole groups in the population, and short term, resulting in immediate feelings of anger and/or the loss of feelings of worth and confidence. The exploration of these negative and damaging effects of discrimination should not, however, exclude three important further questions relating to the effects of discrimination:

1 What strategies do people use to overcome or challenge the discrimination and prejudice they may face?
2 What steps are being taken by groups and organisations to overcome the effects of prejudice and discrimination?
3 Are the effects of discrimination always experienced in the same way by members of a particular group in society? For instance, statistics about 'black unemployment', which group all ethnic minorities together, may mask different levels of disadvantage or success in the labour market experienced by some ethnic minority groups. In *Racial Equality: Colour, Culture and Justice*, Tariq Modood from the Policy Studies Institute suggests that 'cultural racism' is suffered most in the UK by those ethnic groups whose language, religion, customs and family structures are most different from the white majority norm.

SEXISM

Early education

Important issues to consider in the study of sex and gender in the context of early education at home/at playgroups or nurseries/within other childcare arrangements/in primary schools are:

- sex-role stereotyping and socialisation;
- the formation of gender identities and gender-linked labelling processes;
- the interaction between parents and children/carers and children/teachers and children, and between children themselves;
- the influence of cultural forms such as books, the mass media, songs, stories and play.

ACTIVITY

Ideas for projects and assignments

1 Carry out a content analysis of children's books, analysing the images of male and female characters which appear and the language used to describe them or which they are given to use. Interview children about their perceptions and understanding of sex roles and gender in the books they read.

2 Observe children's play in a setting such as a nursery, playgroup, infant school or playground. Are boys and girls playing different games in different ways? Is this reinforced by the organisation of the school/group/playground and the attitudes and behaviour of the adults caring for the children?

3 Interview parents or childcare workers about their perceptions of the differences between boys and girls and their approaches to caring for and working with each sex.

Key texts

Grabrucker, M. (1988), *There's a Good Girl: Gender Stereotyping in the First Three Years of Life*. London: Women's Press.

Best, L. (1993), 'Dragons, Dinner Ladies and Ferrets: Sex Roles in Children's Books', *Sociology Review*, vol. 2, no. 3, February 1993.

Health and social care

Studies of health, welfare and sex discrimination have looked at areas such as:

- why women form the largest proportion of 'carers' for elderly or disabled relatives and what implications this has for their lives;
- reproductive rights – access to abortion, contraception, fertility and IVF programmes; ante- and post-natal care; pregnancy and childbirth;
- access to adequate maternity and child benefits as well as other state benefits;
- the response of the authorities and organisations to women suffering sexual abuse, rape or other physical abuse;
- how social and health services might be provided in non-sexist and non-hierarchical ways so that divisions between the service providers and clients are minimised and prejudice and discrimination therefore lessened.

ACTIVITY

Ideas for projects and assignments

1 Contact any voluntary 'carers' organisation in your area (such as the 'Crossroads' scheme) to investigate their views about the pressures on women (and men) with regard to caring for elderly or disabled relatives.

2 Investigate the history of legislation relating to abortion, contraception and IVF in this and one other country, contrasting the development it has taken in the two examples chosen.

3 Carry out a survey among women with children, asking them about their views on maternity and child benefits, and investigating whether they feel that the current system leads to prejudice and/or discrimination against women when they return to work.

4 Find out what facilities and services exist in your area for women (or men) suffering from sexual or physical abuse. Are they adequate?

5 Write to your local health and social services organisations asking for details of any equal opportunities initiatives they are carrying out and ask to talk to some of the key workers involved.

Key texts

Abbot, P. and Wallace, C. (1990). *An Introduction to Sociology: Feminist Perspectives*. London and New York: Routledge (contains a useful chapter on 'Women, Health and Caring').

Faludi, S. (1991), *Backlash: The Undeclared War against Women*. London: Vintage (contains an excellent chapter on reproductive rights).

Roberts, H. (1993), 'Women, Health and Health Care', *Sociology Review*, vol. 2, no. 4, April 1993, pp. 18–21.

Work

Studies of gender and discrimination in the context of work have addressed:

- the reasons why women remain concentrated in the lower-status, less well-paid strata of occupations;
- whether there is a 'glass ceiling' for women at work which forms a barrier to promotion;

- how popular images of female employers in the 'caring professions' such as nursing contribute to prejudice and discrimination against them;
- problems and possibilities of part-time work and flexible working hours for women;
- the effects of attempts to combine paid work with domestic responsibilities and childcare.

ACTIVITY

Ideas for projects and assignments

1 There are many studies documenting the concentration of women in low-status, low-paid occupations, so there is the possibility here of carrying out an interesting overall survey of the issues using secondary sources.

2 Interview a particular category of women in one type of job to find out whether they think a 'glass ceiling' operates in their organisations.

3 Take one category of occupation in the health and welfare field and investigate the images and stereotypes that people hold about that form of work.

4 Carry out a survey of men and women working in the caring professions, asking what their ideal working arrangements would be and why.

Key text

Savage, J. (1985), *The Politics of Nursing*. London: Heinemann.

RACISM

Early education

As with sex and gender, important issues to consider in relation to the effects and implications of prejudice and discrimination in dealing with younger children are:

- the learning of racial stereotypes and images and the implications for 'labelling' and 'self-concept';
- the unintentional and sometimes intentional teaching of racist ideas, attitudes and cultural beliefs;
- structures of family life which reinforce an 'us and them' mentality and may contribute to hostility and lack of understanding between different groups in society.

ACTIVITY

Ideas for projects and assignments

1 Conduct an investigation into the way children see people from cultures and ethnic groups other than their own.

2 Visit a branch of a national chain of shops which sells books for children, such as The Early Learning Centre or W.H. Smith, and assess how many of the books on sale contain images of black or ethnic minority children or adults.

3 Hold discussions with a school or a playgroup which has a race equality policy to find out how that policy is implemented and what the attitudes and feelings of the staff and the children are towards it.

Key texts

Commission for Racial Equality (1989), *From Cradle to School: A Practical Guide to Race Equality and Childcare*. London: CRE (for address see list at end of chapter).

Milner, D. (1983), *Children and Race Ten Years On*. London: Ward Lock Educational.

Health and social care

Here studies have looked at:

- the extent to which Area Health Authorities and Social Services Departments have

COUNTY COUNCIL
WORKING TOWARDS EQUAL OPPORTUNITIES

SOCIAL SERVICES DEPARTMENT
INSPECTION UNIT

INSPECTORS

A number of opportunities arise for Inspector appointments during the period April to July 1995 owing to the cessation of fixed-term contract employees, retirement and career progression.

The duties of these posts include registering and inspecting private and voluntary residential care homes for adults and inspecting Local Authority homes. Applicants should have: experience of the practice and management of residential care; a recognised social services qualification; a commitment to promoting high standards of care and quality of life for residents.

Personal skills and abilities required include: a well organised approach to your work; good presentation, oral and written communication; negotiation; evaluation; confident manner in dealing with owners, managers and residents and working with colleagues in other agencies. Keyboard skills will be an advantage and training will be provided in the use of the Unit's computerised register, work processing and inspection management system.

You must be a car driver, an essential car user allowance is payable. Applicants must be prepared to work unsocial hours as necessary to meet the requirements of the work.

The Social Services Department particularly welcomes applications from Afro-Caribbean and Asian people and people with disabilities as they are under-represented in the department. (Race Relations Act 1976 Section 38(1)(b) applies.)

Job sharers welcome

CHILDREN AND FAMILIES SERVICE

TEAM LEADER - Hospital based

£22,008 – £24,275 p.a. inc.

A full-time (35 hours) fieldwork team leader is sought.

The Children and Families fieldwork service is divided into teams undertaking assessments or long-term work. There is a vacancy for a team leader in the assessment team, which has special links with all hospital paediatric services.

We are looking for social workers/managers with at least 3 years post qualification experience, most of which should be in children's fieldwork. Candidates should have experience of working in a hospital setting and preferably some managerial experience.

The ethnic minorities population in this borough is under-represented at this level and applications from black and other ethnic minorities would be particularly welcomed.

an equal opportunities employer

County Council

An Equal Opportunities Employer welcoming applications from all sections of the community.

TEMPORARY SOCIAL WORKERS FOR MINORITY ETHNIC COMMUNITIES
(2 POSTS – FULL-TIME OR PART-TIME)

Salary: **Social Work Grade (Qualified)**
£12,810 (Scp 23) – £16,194 (Scp 38) (Review)
£18,615 per annum (Scp 35)
(Pro rata if part-time)

Desirable qualifications: CQSW, CSS or equivalent qualifications in field related to Social Work.

We are seeking to recruit two temporary social workers who will assist in the County Council's aims to ensure that members of the ethnic communities from the New Commonwealth are provided with a social work service and that this service is developed in accordance with their needs.

Due to the specialised role it is essential that applicants are able to understand and communicate clearly in spoken and written English and spoken Gujerati and Urdu. It is also desirable to have a knowledge of Afro-Caribbean cultures and communities, and therefore members of this community would be welcome applicants.

Due to the funding arrangements of these posts, contracts will be offered on a fixed-term basis until 31st March, 1995. The County Council offers the following:

- a major commitment to training
- optional superannuation scheme
- car user allowance payable; facilities available for car loan or lease
- professional supervision
- re-location expenses up to £4,400
- a real commitment to Equal Opportunities
- attractive Local Conditions of Services complementing the National Scheme which can include additional annual leave, enhanced sickness provisions, etc.
- creche facilities
- It is essential that post-holders possess a full driving licence and have access to a vehicle during working hours.

For an informal discussion, please contact the Practice Manager.

MANAGER FOR ASIAN WOMENS REFUGE

in Birmingham. The successful applicant will be an Asian woman with a professional social work qualification, who is committed to developing services to Asian women and families in need. She will:

- speak Punjabi and at least one other South Asian language;
- be experienced in family and child care work;
- have some experience of management and/or supervising staff.

The post involves familiarity with the Benefits system; counselling of residents and their families; carrying overall control of the domestic budget; and understanding and implementing an Equal Opportunities policy.

The post is non-residential. Salary £16,500 – £18,500.

The post is exempt from the requirements of the Sex Discrimination Act under Section 52D and Section 7.

drawn up and/or implemented race equality policies;
- the issues of transracial adoption and fostering of ethnic minority children;
- the disproportionately large numbers of ethnic minority children taken into care in Britain;
- why most black elders in Britain today maintain themselves either on the level of income support rates or below the poverty level.

ACTIVITY

Ideas for projects and assignments

1 Write to your local Area Health Authority or Social Services Department asking if they have a race equality policy and, if so, whether you can have a copy. Your teachers or lecturers may be able to arrange for you to interview any key personnel in these organisations concerned with equal opportunities.

2 Investigate the issue of transracial adoption and fostering.

Key texts

Leicester City Council (1990), *Earnings and Ethnicity*. Leicester: LCC.

Community Care magazine (Reed Publishing Monthly Ltd, published monthly). Your local school or college library should stock this.

CRE publications generally; a list may be obtained from the address given at the end of this chapter.

Culley, L. and Dyson, S. (1993), 'Race, Inequality and Health', *Sociology Review*, vol. 3, no. 1, September 1993, pp. 24–27.

Work

There are a large number of concerns here, which include:

- why qualified black social workers remain relatively scarce – although there has been a small rise in successful applicants for professional social work courses;
- prejudice and discrimination against black and ethnic minority workers in the fields of health and social care.

ACTIVITY

Ideas for projects and assignments

1 Use secondary sources (the publications of the CRE and the Runnymede Trust are very helpful in this respect) to investigate the employment position of black and ethnic minority workers in this country.

2 Interview black or ethnic minority nurses, doctors and other health and social services professionals about their views on and experiences of racism. (You may find it helpful here to refer to the material on 'Interviews' in the section of Chapter 8 on 'Research Methods'.)

Key texts

Skellington, R. and Morris, P. (1992), *'Race' in Britain Today*. London: Sage.

Richardson, J. and Lambert, J. (1985), *The Sociology of Race*. Ormskirk: Causeway Press.

The publications of the Commission for Racial Equality will be useful; for address see list at end of chapter.

DISABILITY

Early education

Important issues here are:

- the integration of children with special needs into mainstream schools;
- the 'STATEMENTING' of children with special needs so their needs might be met;
- the stresses faced by families with under-fives with a disability and the services which would alleviate some of those stresses;

- the prejudice towards, labelling and self-image of children with disabilities;
- advocacy and EMPOWERMENT – i.e. that adults ensure that the wishes of the child are heard and considered and that the child is enabled (empowered) to make his or her wishes known to adults.

ACTIVITY

Ideas for projects and assignments

1. If a placement can be found in a school which has successfully integrated children with special needs, then it may be possible to investigate how this occurred.
2. Research into the stereotypes and images children hold of children with special needs or disabilities could be carried out.
3. If you know someone well who has a young child with a disability, it might be possible to use an unstructured interview to find out more about what the experience of having a child with a disability in the family can mean.

Key texts

HMSO (1991), *The Children Act Guidance and Regulations*, vol. 6: *Children with Disabilities*. London: HMSO.

Stow, L. and Selfe, L. (1989), *Understanding Children with Special Needs*. London: Unwin Hyman.

Health and social care

Many studies here look at:

- the experiences, including those of prejudice and discrimination, and the situations of people with disabilities, *from their own perspective*. There is much criticism and questioning of the very categories used in terms such as 'disabilities' and 'disabled person'. The essential focus of many studies is therefore on the social barriers to full participative citizenship which people with disabilities may face;
- images of disability and concepts of 'normal' and 'abnormal' and how they may have furthered the disadvantages faced by people with disabilities;
- the extent to which disabled people can participate in and/or control the provision of services and facilities intended for their use;
- the experiences of older people with disabilities who are noticing the effects of ageing.

ACTIVITY

Ideas for projects and assignments

1. Interview people with disabilities about how they view the terms and labels applied to them.
2. Get in touch with voluntary and self-help organisations for people with disabilities in your area and talk to the people who are involved in these about the issue of participation in the running of services and facilities.
3. Investigate the images and stereotypes of disability which appear in the mass media.

Key texts

Davies, T. (1994), 'Disabled by Society?', *Sociology Review*, vol. 3, no. 4, April 1994, pp. 15–19.

O'Hagan, M. and Smith, M. (1993), *Special Issues in Child-Care*. London: Ballière Tindall (contains a very good chapter on children and special needs).

Work

Important issues here are:

- the absence to date of anti-discriminatory legislation for people with disabilities along

the lines of that already provided in terms of race and sex;
- the discrimination faced by people with disabilities in applying for jobs;
- positive examples of where people with disabilities have been enabled (sometimes through the use of information technology) to obtain work.

ACTIVITY

Ideas for projects and assignments

1 Write to your local council, asking what proportion of registered disabled employees they have. Visit your local job centre to ask how many vacancies advertised by them have been filled by registered disabled people in the last year.

2 Find out more about the kinds of facility which would make it easier for people with disabilities to find employment.

Key text

Skett, A. (1993), *Caring for People with Disabilities.* London: Pitman Publishing.

AGE

Early education

Studies here have concentrated on:

- the lack of state-funded nursery and childcare provision in this country and the possible implications for children's emotional, social and intellectual development, as well as for equal working opportunities for working parents (especially women and single parents);
- the prejudice and discrimination faced by women who breast-feed their babies in public and the attitudes towards women and children implied by these reactions;
- the prejudice and discrimination faced by parents and carers towards children in general in public places, e.g. restaurants;
- the lack of inexpensive leisure facilities for young people.

ACTIVITY

Ideas for projects and assignments

1 Survey the provision of playgroup and nursery places in your area. (Your local council or community health clinic should be able to provide a list of playgroups/nurseries in the area.) What facilities are available? What do parents with under-fives in the area where you live think of these facilities?

2 Interview women who have breast-fed their babies in public places about their experiences.

3 Investigate the provision of leisure facilities for young people in your area. What do young people think of these facilities? Are they adequate?

Key texts

Contact the following organisations for useful reading material:

Association of Breast Feeding Mothers
Order Department
Sydenham Green Health Centre
Holshaw Close
London SE26 4TH

Pre-School Playgroups Association
61–63 Kings Cross Road
London WC1X 9LL

Health and social care

Studies here have covered issues such as:

- general prejudice and discrimination towards older people in society;
- child poverty.

ACTIVITY

Ideas for projects and assignments

1 Carry out a survey of young people's attitudes and perceptions of older

people. You may wish to refer to the material on questionnaires in Chapter 8 for advice on constructing an appropriate survey.

2 Contact the Child Poverty Action Group for information relating to this issue.

Key texts

All publications from the Child Poverty Action Group will be helpful. Write to:

Child Poverty Action Group
4th Floor
1–5 Bath Street
London EC1V 9PY

Field, D. (1992), 'Elderly People in British Society', *Sociology Review*, vol. 1, no. 4, April 1992.

Work

- A major concern is the barriers to employment and promotion faced by older people and the lack of any legislation to protect them from discrimination in this respect.

ACTIVITY

Ideas for projects and assignments

Find out if the local Job Club or employment training programmes in your area include groups for older people wishing to return to work. Find out if it would be possible to talk to some of the people who attend these sessions about their experiences.

Key texts

Family Policy Studies Centre (1991), Fact Sheet 2 'An Ageing Population'. London: Family Policy Studies Centre.

ETHICAL ISSUES IN HEALTH AND SOCIAL CARE PRACTICE

Reasons for ethical concern in health and social care

The relationship between health and social care workers and their patients and clients is a very special one for a number of reasons including the following:

- Health and social care workers may have considerable power over patients/clients.
- Such workers may be far more knowledgeable about ill-health, the benefit system or how to use the law courts, and this in itself may constitute a form of power.
- Many patients/clients are vulnerable; they may be sick, elderly, homeless or deprived in some way.
- Health and social care workers frequently have intimate and confidential knowledge of patient's/client's health and/or social circumstances.
- Decisions taken by health and social care professionals may have very significant consequences for patients/clients, e.g. they may determine whether someone is housed or whether a terminally ill patient continues to receive treatment.
- In the field of health care in particular, rapid scientific and technological advances have forced doctors and paramedical staff to make ethical decisions which neither they nor society at large have had to deal with before.

All of these factors indicate clearly that workers in health and social care are in a position to do harm as well as good, and therefore have a special responsibility at all times to be aware of and respect the ethical demands placed upon them by virtue of their professions.

ACTIVITY

Identify and explain how recent scientific and technological advances have created new moral questions for health and social care practitioners. One issue that might concern social workers and probation officers is the possibility of the electronic tagging of offenders. To find out more about this you could contact the Home Office.

Responsibilities of health and social care workers

All health and social care workers are of course bound by the general requirements of the law to respect the rights of patients and clients and to treat them equally, whether in the provision of health care, social services or in access to information.

The key pieces of equal opportunities legislation here are the Sex Discrimination Acts of 1975 and 1986 and the Race Relations Act of 1976, together with legislation relevant to the treatment of disabled people, the most recent being the Disabled Persons Act 1986. The government has announced its intention to proceed with a further Disability Rights Bill to cover employment opportunities, access to goods and services and building regulations, but it is unlikely that the final Act will grant people with disabilities the same rights guaranteed to those covered by the two main equal opportunities acts (although these Acts themselves are far from comprehensive).

The main provisions of the equal opportunities legislation are summarised in Table 1.1 on page 6.

ACTIVITY

Contact the Equal Opportunities Commission and the Commission for Racial Equality for more detailed information on the application of equal opportunities legislation to health and social care settings (for example access to housing).

In addition to general equal opportunities legislation there are other official government and local authority requirements relating to professional conduct such as the Patient's Charter and Community Care Charters. For example, the Patient's Charter states that:

- NHS workers have a duty to respect the privacy, dignity and religious and cultural beliefs of patients (Charter Standard No. 9).

In many cases ethical requirements are explicitly spelt out in professional codes of conduct. For example, nurses, midwives and health visitors are governed by the *United Kingdom Central Council Code of Professional Conduct*. Its main ethical provisions are:

- act always in such a manner as to promote and safeguard the interests and well-being of patients and clients (patient advocacy);
- work in an open and cooperative manner with patients, clients and their families, foster their independence and recognise and respect their involvement in the planning and delivery of care;
- recognise and respect the uniqueness and dignity of each patient and client, and respond to their need for care, irrespective of their ethnic origin, religious beliefs, personal attributes, the nature of their health problem or any other factor;
- report to an appropriate person or authority, at the earliest possible time, any conscientious objection which may be relevant to your professional practice;
- avoid any abuse of your privileged relationship with patients and clients and of the privileged access allowed to their person, property, residence or workplace;
- protect all confidential information concerning patients and clients obtained in the course of professional practice and make disclosures only with consent, where required by the order of a court or where

you can justify disclosure in the wider public interest.

Codes of conduct for other health and social care professionals are produced by their regulatory bodies such as the General Medical Council and the Central Council for Education and Training in Social Work. Professional associations and trades unions also provide guidance, such as the *British Association of Social Workers' Code of Ethics*.

There are 12 principles of social work practice:

1 Knowledge skills and experience used positively for the benefit of all sections of the community and individuals.
2 Respect for clients as individuals and safeguarding their dignity and rights.
3 No prejudice in self, nor tolerance of prejudice in others, on grounds of origin, race, status, sex, sexual orientation, age, disability, beliefs or contribution to society.
4 Empowerment of clients and their participation in decisions and defining services.
5 Sustained concern for clients even when unable to help them or where self-protection is necessary.
6 Professional responsibility takes precedence over personal interest.
7 Responsibility for standards of service and for continuing education and training.
8 Collaboration with others in the interests of clients.
9 Clarity in public as to whether acting in a personal or organisational capacity.
10 Promotion of appropriate ethnic and cultural diversity of services.
11 Confidentiality of information and divulgence only by consent or exceptionally in evidence of serious danger.
12 Pursuit of conditions of employment which enable these obligations to be respected.

Doctors are sometimes required to swear by the Hippocratic Oath, said to have been devised by the Greek physician Hippocrates 2,000 years ago. Part of it reads as follows:

'... I will prescribe regimen for the good of my patients according to my ability and my judgement and never do harm to anyone. To please no one will I prescribe a deadly drug, nor give advice which may cause his death... In every house where I come I will enter only for the good of my patients, keeping myself far from all intentional ill-doing and all seduction.... All that may come to my knowledge in the exercise of my profession ... which ought not to be spread abroad, I will keep secret and will never reveal.'

ACTIVITY

Identify the moral principles advocated by Hippocrates which remain central to the work of health care professionals today.

ACTIVITY

Write to the registration bodies and professional associations of various caring professions and request copies of their codes of ethical conduct. From these, identify the most important ethical principles shared by all of these groups and use this as a basis to draw up your own code of ethics for all health and social care workers.

ACTIVITY

Discuss the following.

- Can legislation force us to behave morally?

Assessment of risk

One of the major tasks of social workers, probation officers and clinical and community nurses is to assess the needs of patients and clients, particularly those deemed to be at risk from others or who may be a risk to themselves, their families or the wider community. These might include:

- psychiatric patients;
- dependent elderly people;
- young offenders;
- child abuse victims;
- people with learning difficulties.

Legislation which establishes the duty of health and social care workers in such situations includes the:

- Mental Health Act 1983;
- Police and Criminal Evidence Act 1984;
- Criminal Justice Acts 1988 and 1991;
- Children Act 1989;
- NHS and Community Care Act 1989.

This legislation is discussed in more detail in Chapter 6.

ETHICAL ISSUES

Important ethical issues arise from the exercise of such duties because they involve questions of the restriction of liberty and adjudication (having to make judgements) by health and social care workers, between the sometimes competing interests and wishes of individuals and their families and communities.

Child protection

Following the Children Act 1989, the assessment of children who might be at risk of neglect, or of physical or sexual abuse, was given priority. Social workers specialising in child protection are required to assess the (potential or actual) risk to children. Those who are felt to be vulnerable will be placed on the social services AT RISK REGISTER and their progress regularly monitored; in serious cases the child may be separated from their family. This is a very difficult decision to make and requires the social worker to weigh up the risk to the child of remaining in a potentially abusive situation against the risks to the child of having her/his family disrupted either by their removal to a PLACE OF SAFETY (such as a foster home) under an EMERGENCY PROTECTION ORDER or by the removal of the abuser (frequently a parent) according to criminal justice legislation.

Health and social care workers need to recognise that many children fiercely love and defend parents who have done them immense harm; these feelings must be acknowledged if further damage is not to be done to the child. Social workers must also of course respect the rights of the parent who remains innocent until proven guilty.

Case study: Protecting children

Three children, Louisa (aged six and a half), Sidney (aged four) and Ruth (aged six) live with their parents, Mr and Mrs Smith (aged 21 and 25 respectively) in a three-bedroomed first-floor flat rented from the council. Mr Smith is Louisa's father. Ruth and Sidney have a different father who is no longer in contact with the family. Mr Smith is unemployed and the family rely on Income Support.

Since Ruth was two years old there have been concerns about her not gaining weight for her age and height. These worries intensified last year when she was sexually abused by a neighbour.

Mrs Smith left home at 16, running away from her violent father. Mr Smith had an unhappy childhood after his mother left home when he was four.

Ruth was doing well at school but was always hungry and thirsty and often came inappropriately dressed and occasionally smelly. Health visitors who visited the home considered standards of hygiene and cleanliness there to be poor.

Social services were about to put Ruth's name on the Child Protection Register when Louisa was taken to hospital with a broken leg. X-rays revealed previous fracturing to ribs and one arm. All three children were immediately made the subjects of Emergency

Protection Orders and a social worker from the local authority Social Services Department was assigned to the family.

Within three days the local authority applied to the FAMILY PROCEEDINGS COURT to make the children the subject of an INTERIM CARE ORDER. An Order lasting eight weeks was granted by the Magistrate and was not disputed by the parents. A *Guardian ad Litem* (GAL) was appointed to represent the interests of all three children throughout the court proceedings and to instruct a solicitor on their behalf. A further Interim Care Order would need to be considered at the end of the eight week period and a final decision about what to do with the children would need to be made by the court in a further four weeks.

Background information: explanation of terms

- *Child Protection Register* – a list held by social services of all children at risk of harm.
- *Emergency Protection Order* – if a child is in danger he or she may have to be taken away from home quickly. Social Services (or the NSPCC) can go to a magistrate at any time and apply for an Emergency Protection Order which, if granted, means a child can be taken to a safe place or kept in a safe place for up to eight days. This order can be made to last for a further seven days if the court thinks it necessary.
- *Family Proceedings Court* – a local court where hearings are heard by Magistrates with special training in children's cases.
- *Interim Care Order* – an Order made by the Family Proceedings Court which means that social services will look after a child and decide where he or she will live as long as the Order lasts.
- *Guardian ad Litem* – a person appointed by the court to represent the interests of the child throughout the court proceedings. The GAL visits the children and takes their wishes and feelings into account when writing a report for the court. The GAL instructs a solicitor to stand up in court and speak on behalf of the child or children involved.

ACTIVITY

Imagine that you are the GAL and write a report advising the court on the best course of action to be taken for the children. Your report must consider the following issues:

- Should the children be returned home with their parents; returned home but with supervision from social services; live away from home with relatives or foster parents or be adopted?
- Is the level of risk to the children the same for all three of them? How could that 'level of risk' be assessed?
- How far can the wishes and feelings of the children be taken into account?

The Children Act 1989

The Children Act came into force in October 1991. The philosophy behind the Act is to encourage parents to continue to be responsible for their children, even where the family is disrupted, with support from social services where appropriate. The rights of children are also strengthened. The main points of the Act are as follows:

MAIN POINTS OF THE CHILDREN ACT

- A new concept of parental responsibility is introduced
- Parents will no longer lose parental rights when their child goes into care
- Parents and children will be consulted on care decisions
- Married parents will share parental responsibility, even if they later divorce
- Unmarried mothers will have parental responsibility, but the father will be able to acquire it by agreement or court order
- Care cases will start in the magistrates' court, more difficult cases will go to the county court or High Court. Specially trained judges and magistrates will hear cases
- Parents whose children are removed from home will be able to challenge the removal in court after 72 hours. Eight-day emergency

protection orders will replace 28-day place of safety orders
- Child assessment orders will allow a child to be examined at home, or elsewhere
- In most cases of divorce courts will make no order, otherwise custody and access will be replaced by residence orders and contact orders
- Children will be able to apply for their own residence and contact orders, as will grandparents and others with close links
- Local authorities must safeguard the welfare of children in need, including providing day care for under-fives and after-school care

(The Guardian, 14 October 1991)

Assessment of elderly dependent people

Access to assessment of care needs is a right for elderly dependent people under the NHS and Community Care Act (CCA). One of the aims of the Act is to draw a clear distinction between health care and social care and to enable elderly people to be cared for (or to care for themselves) within the 'community'. The health and social care worker will liaise with a variety of agencies including the health service, for example to arrange for district nursing support, and social services, perhaps to arrange for a home help to visit so as to assist the client to stay in their own home where this is possible and desirable.

Whilst the primary concern of those undertaking assessment will be to meet the needs of the elderly person, the practitioner will also have to take into account the needs and wishes of the client's family and/or close friends (as recommended in Royal College of Nursing guidelines for assessing health need in old age). This is because care in the community in practice often means unpaid care by close relatives (usually women) whose own needs and wishes may conflict with the needs of their elderly relative. The increased emphasis now placed on families providing care for their elderly relatives has led to some highly publicised cases of 'granny dumping', where families who feel that they can no longer cope 'dump' their elderly relatives in residential homes and hospital accident and emergency wards. Organisations representing carers (such as the Carers' National Association) have also highlighted often hidden incidents of abuse of the elderly by those caring for them. Clearly, in assessing and trying to meet the needs of elderly people, health and social care workers need to be alert to such risks.

ACTIVITY

Undertake research into the incidence of abuse of the elderly and 'granny dumping' by families. Consider what steps could be taken by health and social care workers to reduce the risk to elderly dependent people.

In Germany relatives of elderly people receiving institutional care are legally bound to make a financial contribution to such care. A government agency is charged with recovering money from relatives including grandchildren (deductions can be taken from salary). In Britain since the CCA, social care for the elderly has been means tested, which means that those who are deemed to have the resources must pay for their care, even if, as in the case of residential care, they must sell their home to do so.

ACTIVITY

Discuss the following.

- Do we have a moral duty to care for our parents and/or grandparents?
- Should the State translate any such moral duty into a legal duty?

Mental illness

In their assessment of risk to patients and clients who are suffering from mental illness, health and social care workers will have reference to the 1983 Mental Health Act. This

Act gives (some) doctors, nurses and social workers the right to detain individuals against their will in a mental hospital if the patient is deemed to be a risk to themselves or others. This is known as SECTIONING. (The Act is discussed in more detail in Chapter 6.)

Mental illness and community care

Following the NHS and Community Care Act, increasing numbers of people with mental health problems, as well as the elderly, are being treated in the community, either in their (family) homes or in small residential units. Here again health and social care workers must weigh up the benefits to the patient of being treated in the 'community' against possible potential risks to those living in that community. There is much evidence to support the view that care in the 'community' is a much better option for the vast majority of patients who are mentally ill, particularly where good community nursing and social work support are available. Unfortunately for some, care in the community will mean only the help of family or friends, or in some cases a life on the streets. Where adequate support is not available the costs to family and friends can be very high as the following letter illustrates.

For seven or eight years I was responsible for the care of my wife who suffered from progressive senile dementia. She was in the care of the community – I was the community. As the condition worsened it was necessary to keep a 24-hour watch. I could do no shopping unless a friend came in. She would get up in the middle of the night and attempt to wander off and turn on the gas without igniting it. She suffered complete loss of memory and was subject to occasional violent outbursts.

I sustained no serious injury but lots of small ones. We were both in our eighties but I was apparently considered capable. Towards the end, my wife was accepted into hospital for two week periods about every six weeks. In the end, the poor woman did not know who she was or where she was and I was on the verge of a nervous breakdown.

Despite my pleas she was refused hospital accommodation. In fact one of the two local mental hospitals was closed. I was obliged to find a private nursing home at £300 per week. My experience, which is typical of many, has shown me that the best and only satisfactory way to treat advanced cases of senile dementia is in a mental hospital with the necessary facilities, and a trained, qualified and caring staff.

Goodwin R. England.

Darley Abbey, Derby.

(The Guardian, 14 October 1991)

A number of recent well-publicised tragedies have highlighted problems with treatment in the community for people who are mentally ill and has thrown into relief the moral dilemmas facing health and social care professionals working in this field. A number of severely mentally ill patients receiving 'care in the community' have brought about their own deaths or the deaths of others. Recent examples include the case of Ben Silcock who climbed into a lions' den and was severely mauled, and the murder of an occupational therapist by a young man who was suffering from schizophrenia. The publicity in such cases has unfortunately not advanced rational debate on the care of those with mental illness, but has served to further entrench prejudice against those with mental health problems.

It certainly seems to be the case that while many people believe that there should be greater 'tolerance' and improved community provision for the mentally ill, this often evaporates when people are asked to accept people with such needs into their local community. A recent survey conducted by the Department of Health showed that a majority of people remain fearful of mental illness and would appear to have very stereotyped views of those who are mentally ill. Only 19% would trust a woman who had ever been a mental hospital patient to baby-sit for them, and nearly one-third believed that it was possible to spot the difference between a

'PSYCHIATRIC PATIENT FREED TO KILL'

'CALLS FOR STRICTER CONTROL OF MENTALLY ILL'

'SCHIZOPHRENIC MAULED BY LIONS'

'COMMUNITY CARE POLICY QUESTIONED'

'normal person' and one with mental illness. This may mean that even where care in the community is the best option for the patient, the fears of their families and the local community take precedence. This is not to say that some patients are not a danger to themselves and/or others, but that prejudice or fear should not be allowed to prevent reasoned debate about the best way of meeting the needs of those who are mentally ill.

Access to information

As we have seen above, a key requirement of many codes of ethics concerns the patient's/client's right of access to information. The ethical principles involved in providing access to information include respect for individuals and a recognition of their autonomy (literally, self-rule). This includes the right to decide, for example, what medical treatment is best for oneself or one's children. Access to information is central to such a decision-making process, and hence to the concept of INFORMED CONSENT, i.e. that true consent or agreement can be given only by someone who is in receipt of all the relevant information.

The Patient's Charter identifies rights of access to information for users of the NHS. Every citizen has a right:

- to be given a clear explanation of any treatment proposed, including any risks and any alternatives, before deciding whether to agree to treatment (right 5);
- to have access to his or her health records, and to know that those working for the NHS are under a legal duty to keep their contents confidential (right 6).

Similarly, in its Framework for Community Care Charters (August 1994), the Department of Health states that those who use community health care services must have the right of access to their own health records honoured. This right of access is enshrined in two pieces of legislation: the ACCESS TO MEDICAL REPORTS ACT (1988) and the ACCESS TO HEALTH RECORDS ACT (1990), which give patients a right of access to their health records after these dates. The main exemptions include cases where information has been provided by another identifiable individual (perhaps in a case of domestic violence) and where the disclosure of such information is likely to cause serious harm to the physical or mental health of the patient or someone else.

ACTIVITY

Ask to see your own medical records. (Check first of all that no application fee is charged.) How useful is the information to you?

EMPOWERMENT

Access to information is central to the idea of empowerment. This means, literally, to give people power and to treat them not as passive RECIPIENTS of health or social care (many patients are expected to be very patient!) but as active PARTICIPANTS whose needs and wishes must be respected. Some are very critical of the concept of empowerment because those who are powerless in society as a result of poverty or homelessness, say, cannot be given power simply by being handed certain information by health and social care workers.

Others, however, argue that providing patients and clients with access to relevant information is central to a recognition of them as individuals who are worthy of respect and who have rights to full consultation and participation in the decisions made by professionals concerning their health and social care. At the very least it should mean that patients and clients are provided with basic information about the help available to them so as to avoid the difficulties experienced by the following woman suffering from incontinence who eventually heard about a support group:

'Thank God I heard about you. I've been incontinent for years but I couldn't find out where to get help. The local chemist said all I had to do was go to the GP. The GP said no, the district nurse is for that. The district nurse said no, you need the social services, and the social worker said I should go and see my own GP.'

(Marianne Rigge, The Guardian, 23 November 1994)

The Department of Health believes that patients can be empowered through the publication of 'league tables' demonstrating the comparative performance of different hospitals (and possibly of individual surgeons) according to various 'performance indicators' (the first such league tables for Scottish hospitals were published in December 1994). It is argued that patients suffering from specific problems, and their GPs, will be able to find out where, and by what method, their condition has been most successfully treated and will be able to request a suitable referral. Others argue that such league tables do not provide unproblematic guidance as to the quality of treatment, and point out that few patients have any real choice as to where procedures are carried out.

The concept of empowerment is central to the NHS and Community Care Act. Social Services Departments are required to explain fully what care services are available and what they may cost. Certainly many individuals and their carers believe that the amount of information available has increased and that this has enabled many people to become more involved in decisions about their care (*Carers' World Magazine*, October 1994).

The Patient's Charter too is seen by the Department of Health as an exercise in empowerment, by setting out certain standards which the public can expect and which the health service must aim to achieve.

ACTIVITY

Write to the Department of Health for a copy of the Patient's Charter. Are the standards referred to the same thing as patients' 'rights'?

The trend towards greater equality in relationships between health and social care professionals and their patients and clients was highlighted by a recent conference held by the British Medical Association (BMA). With the help of a professor of moral philosophy, the BMA aims to draw up a new statement of 'core values', in part to 'enhance the doctor–patient relationship as the key attribute of medical professionalism' which will hopefully recognise that the doctor–patient relationship should be a partnership (BMA press release, 8 November 1994).

Confidentiality

Confidentiality refers to the privacy and restriction of information provided by the client (either voluntarily or involuntarily) in the course of treatment or the provision of services.

WHY IS CONFIDENTIALITY AN ETHICAL ISSUE?

From one ('utilitarian') point of view, without patients/clients being willing to disclose personal and sometimes very intimate and embarrassing information, health and social care professionals would not be able to do their job of advising and assisting clients and patients. Therefore it is a matter of prudence to maintain confidentiality. However, for others, to refuse to respect the confidentiality of information provided by patients and clients is to show disrespect for their feelings and wishes and to fail to acknowledge their full status as human beings. The requirement to respect confidentiality is enshrined both in law in the Data Protection Act and in the Patient's Charter and Community Care Charters.

LEGISLATION TO PROTECT CONFIDENTIALITY

Data Protection Act 1984

This Act protects information about living individuals held on computer and has been fully in force since 1987. The Act aims to ensure that all computerised personal data:

- is accurate and up to date;
- has been obtained fairly and lawfully;
- is used only for specified, lawful purposes;
- is kept confidential;
- is available for scrutiny (and possible correction or erasure) by those concerned.

Agencies must also take suitable precautions to prevent unauthorised access to, or disclosure of, computerised personal data.

SEXUALITY AND THE AGE OF CONSENT

The age of consent for heterosexual intercourse is 16. GPs or family planning clinics who provide contraceptive advice to people under 16 are therefore in a difficult position with regard to the law in that they may be seen to be aiding and abetting a criminal offence. Certainly many parents of under 16s believe they have a right to be consulted by GPs in such circumstances. However, in practice, the vast majority of doctors claim that their primary duty is to respect the confidentiality of their patient.

ACTIVITY

What issues are raised by this? Are GPs right to respect the confidence of their under-age patients even if it means that they tacitly condone the breaking of the law?

ACTIVITY

Obtain a copy of your own local Community Care Charter (all local authorities should provide these by April 1995) and familiarise yourself with the provisions for confidentiality and access to information in your area.

ACTIVITY

Case study

You are a psychiatric social worker and for the past year you have been supporting a client called Ann who is 30. She has a long history of mental illness and has been hospitalised (under 'section') on one occasion. However, during the past year she appears to have made considerable progress and, with your help, has managed to find a job as a minibus driver for a local children's charity. She enjoys her work very much and during the six months she has had the job her self-confidence has improved dramatically. Recently, however, she has appeared rather unkempt and has been late for several appointments with you. You discover that Ann has started drinking – 'just one or two to help me feel better and not when I am driving'. What do you do, knowing that if she does drink when she is working she will endanger the lives of the children using the minibus, but that if you report her you will forfeit her trust and her relationship with you that has been so important to her recovery?

Ethical dilemmas

An ethical dilemma can be defined as a situation in which an individual is faced with a moral choice in which he or she feels that both options are morally right (or wrong). A moral dilemma usually results in us feeling regret or remorse for the option that we rejected; even if we feel that in the circumstances we took the right decision, we still feel the moral 'pull' of the action that we decided not to undertake.

Moral dilemmas arise when we experience a conflict between the moral principles that we hold. For example, we may recognise that our duty as professionals is at all times to maintain the confidentiality of patients and clients. How do we reconcile this with the duty to act always in the best interest of the client, when doing so may require us to divulge confidential information about a client that we have promised not to reveal? Even though in many cases of ethical decision-making we will clearly feel that one option has a greater moral claim on us than another, we may still feel unhappy at the choices facing us.

IDENTIFYING THE BEST INTERESTS OF THE CLIENT

As we have seen, the primary concern of all those who work in the health and social care fields is (or should be) the well-being of clients or patients; all decisions taken should be in their best interests. However, in the face of political, financial and practical constraints the reality is often that the professional's duty is to do the best for the client in the circumstances prevailing.

Dilemmas may arise when the professional's view of the best interests of the client manifestly conflicts with the best interests of the client as perceived by the client's family or the wider community. Situations may also arise where the best interests of the individual must take second place to the best interests of society.

How do we define best interests? This is often incredibly difficult. For doctors and other health care professionals, recent advances in technology and medical techniques have meant that the best interests of the patient, perhaps of premature foetuses, may have been sacrificed to the demand that doctors save life at all costs as the following article from *The Independent* of 26 June 1993 explains:

WE SAVED THE BABY; UNFORTUNATELY, THE FAMILY IS CRACKING UP

Infants who five years ago might have died now survive, but with terrible handicaps. **Elaine Williams** looks at the price of success

Advances in medical science have many unforeseen consequences. The increasing ability of doctors to save new-born babies in intensive care, for instance, has results rarely discussed outside medical circles: what happens to those infants who survive but who are handicapped, sometimes severely?

Eleanor Barnes is director of the Family Fund, which issues grants to families with severely disabled children – and which increasingly finds itself picking up the pieces in the wake of medical success stories. Every day she sees the effects that looking after severely handicapped babies have on families on the breadline.

"A lot of our parents are cracking up, they cannot take any more. Some write to us in a suicidal state. The ethical issue – of whether a baby should be kept alive or not – is much broader than the life or death of that child. It is about a whole network of relationships involved in that child's life; the mother, father, siblings and the community. The question for doctors is not just 'Is this a viable baby?' but 'What is the community doing to support such babies?'."

Mrs Barnes believes many doctors have no idea of the circumstances into which they are sending the babies. She describes a typical application to the Fund: a nine-month-old spastic quadriplegic who has fits and is blind. "The family must have a telephone to make emergency calls, they must have a washing machine because of excessive laundry and the need to reduce infection, and they need grants towards transport costs in order to get the child out at all with all the equipment for naso-gastric feeding, oxygen and suction."

It is, says Mrs Barnes, a classic example of society failing to face the consequences of medical advance. "Does the DSS say to doctors: 'Unplug the baby – we're not prepared to pay for the parents to come to visit it'? If we are going to save life at all costs, then we must be prepared to provide the real costs of keeping that child alive."

Alice Russell, a social worker who assesses families for Family Fund grants, says that doctors underestimate the dedication that parents need in order to care for severely disabled babies and to cope with the pressures on them. Siblings suffer, and fathers often walk out.

"I visited a single parent with a tiny Down's syndrome child, premature and dreadfully handicapped. He was attached to three separate tubes; one administering oxygen, another liquid feeds, another taking waste products. That mother was coping with thousands of pounds' worth of equipment in a tiny council flat. She was totally alone. She had been sent home from hospital with the child and told he would probably not last the night. That child is now five months old."

Mrs Barnes identifies two pressing issues: one is the responsibility of the community in the support of this growing number of families; the other is the nature of the baby's own life. In her mind, the two are connected. Many of these babies, she believes, suffer enormous pain and face a poor future.

A practising Catholic who says her faith is crucial to her work, Mrs Barnes does not hesitate to consider death as an option for some of these babies. "I don't think doctors are nearly sensitive enough to the rights of the baby. A baby should have the right to die."

Some senior doctors are grappling with these issues. Dr. Geoff Durbin, director of the regional neonatalogy unit at the Birmingham Maternity Hospital, believes his unit has faced up to the dilemmas more than most. Few babies at the unit are kept on long-term respiratory support. He does not believe that death is always a poor option.

"I say: 'At this moment in time, would I wish this to be my baby?'. The purpose of offering care to immature babies is that the care provided produces a life of value to the individual, to siblings, to parents and to society. There is no purpose in doing it simply for the sake of survivors.

"If you make good decisions, clearly and simply, you carry the parents and staff through. We say to parents: 'We want your child to be able to play and communicate.' If that is not to be the case, then we don't believe it is right to carry on. Such explicit explanation is not usual. Doctors are frightened of getting it wrong; but if everything is up-front, the situation doesn't get out of control.

"If we make a decision to switch from intensive care, I don't believe that's a killing step, it's allowing a baby to die with dignity.

ACTIVITY

Read the article and identify moral arguments for and against such medical intervention in the lives of premature babies.

PASSIVE EUTHANASIA

The above illustrates the difficulty in identifying the best interests of the patient in the case of passive euthanasia. Passive euthanasia refers to the practice of not intervening to extend the life of a terminally ill patient, i.e. letting them die. This might be achieved by turning off a life-support machine or withdrawing a feeding tube.

There are some who argue that passive euthanasia can never be in the best interests of the patient because it is tantamount to killing. If you take this view, for a doctor or nurse to fail to save a life is as morally wrong as for them to deliberately take that life. There are certainly some doctors who believe that their moral duty is to save life at all costs. Others feel unhappy at 'playing God', i.e. making decisions as to who should be allowed to live and who should die. Some health professionals, however, are less concerned with this aspect than with the fact that frequently it is not possible to be sure that a person has no chance of recovery. Were such certainty always possible many doctors would feel convinced that the best interests of the patient would be served by allowing a patient incapable of independent life to die. From this point of view it is not life *per se* which is of moral consequence but the *quality* of that life, so that in many cases medical staff may experience no real conflict between the moral imperatives to save life and the desire to act in the best interest of the patient, where quality of life is so poor that the best interests of the patient are served by letting them die.

There have been many high-profile cases where the best interests of the patient (usually in a coma or a persistent vegetative state) have been violently contested. A famous example is the case of the Hillsborough disaster victim Tony Bland. Despite the agreement of Tony's parents, doctors caring for him had to approach to the House of Lords to win permission to disconnect his feeding tube and to allow him to die. The two following quotes illustrate how differently this decision was viewed:

'This is a great relief. The decision is in the best interests of everyone. Not just in the best interests of our family but for the nursing staff who have cared for Tony and, of course, for Tony himself.'

(Allan Bland, Tony's father)

'... there is no doubt that the Law Lords have ... undermined protection for people unable to speak for themselves – which ultimately must include the newborn handicapped, the aged, as well as patients in a persistent vegetative state.'

(Paul Tully, Society for the Protection of Unborn Children)

A more recent case involved a man in a persistent vegetative state whose wife was opposed to the doctors' decision to withdraw artificial feeding. In this case the health authority has obtained a ruling that the patient's best interests should be determined by the courts.

ACTIVITY

In pairs or small groups identify arguments to support the view that:

1 the patient's family should decide on the best interests of the patient;

2 only doctors should decide what is in the patient's best interests;

3 the courts should have the final say.

Rationing of health care

The issue of the rationing or 'prioritising' of health care raises significant moral questions. Some people argue that if adequate funding were provided there would be no need to ration or limit health care at all: that everyone in need of medical help would be able to receive it. Others argue that even if health care funding were increased, rapid advances in

medical technology and expertise, together with our apparently infinite demand for care, mean that it would still not be possible to provide everyone with all the health care that they demand.

There is little doubt that the rationing of health care already occurs; what concerns many practitioners is that such rationing does not take place according to any clear set of publicly agreed principles, but instead seems to happen in a rather arbitrary and unplanned way. The result may be that patients in certain parts of the country are offered a procedure which is denied to patients elsewhere, as the following articles suggest:

DOCTORS UNHAPPY OVER 'RATIONING'

Eight out of 10 GPs believe patients are suffering because of rationing in the National Health Service, as do nine out of 10 hospital doctors, says a survey published yesterday.

Ninety-seven per cent of 510 GPs who replied to questionnaires in Doctor magazine said they thought rationing was happening, with 75 per cent regarding it as an inevitable part of modern health care. But 84 per cent believed it was harming patients.

Many GPs said their treatment decisions were affected by factors other than clinical need. Only 4 per cent said their decisions were not affected by cost and 55 per cent said cost influenced their decisions either very much or quite a lot.

The doctors admit they are influenced by patients' life-styles as to what priority they attach to securing treatment for them. A GP's personal morality and the perceived usefulness of the patient to society also have a significant influence on treatment decisions.

Asked to list the most important treatments, reversal of sterilisation and in vitro fertilisation received a zero percentage support, and heart transplants just 1 per cent. Eighty per cent of doctors thought childhood immunisation was the most important treatment, with 38 per cent supporting anti-smoking education and 31 per cent hip replacement and care for the demented elderly.

(The Guardian, 30 September 1994)

DOCTORS SAY SOCIETY MUST DECIDE HOW HEALTH SERVICE RESOURCES SHOULD BE 'RATIONED'

'We don't use the word rationing – we call it priority setting,' said the official at the Department of Health.

This prize example of Orwellian double-speak is a sure sign that something significant is happening in the health service.

That something is the first public debate on rationing in health care – whether it is inevitable and, if so, who decides, and on what basis, between giving Mrs Jones a hip replacement or Mr Smith a heart transplant.

While there is nothing new about rationing, it has traditionally been done by means of waiting lists. It was covert. The system was controlled by GPs as the 'gatekeepers', who decided when to refer patients, and then by the consultants who controlled the outpatient and inpatient lists.

Now doctors are increasingly saying that they do not want this responsibility. They do not want the blame for not treating patients when money runs out or when their hospital does not offer a particular procedure.

According to the BMA under-secretary, Dr Andrew Vallance-Owen, that means doctors have to tell patients: 'I am sorry, you have this condition, but we don't treat it in this part of the country.' In effect, he says, 'it depends on your postcode as to whether you can have certain procedures'.

(The Independent, 2 March 1993)

A further concern has been that rationing of care may take place simply according to age so that certain procedures may be routinely denied to people over a certain age, regardless of whether or not they would benefit.

PHYSICIANS SLATE 'AGEIST' HEALTH BIAS

Elderly people are suffering discrimination at the hands of the health service, in breach of medical ethics, and possibly wasting resources, the Royal College of Physicians said yesterday.

Discrimination is sometimes explicit – some units have age limits for certain treatments – but in most cases it is unspoken, based on an assumption that the elderly should be at the back of the queue because they have less time to live.

At a press conference in London to launch the report, Professor John Grimley Evans, head of clinical geratology at Oxford University, said a study three years ago had found elderly people being denied access to coronary care units and to 'clot-busting' drugs after heart attacks.

'There has been an assumption that older people can't benefit from treatment, or have greater side effects, but there have been no scientific trials.'

Professor Leslie Turnberg, president of the College, said a public debate should be held if health care was to be rationed for the elderly.

'It is a worry to many of us that although it may not be overt and defined, there is a pattern of discrimination against elderly people on the basis of age, not need.

'When a scarcity of resources is driving the way we practice, people are making unconscious choices on the basis of life expectancy.'

The College's report states: 'The guiding principle upon which the provision of acute medical care to elderly people is based must be that there is to be no distinction or negative discrimination on grounds of age.'

(The Guardian, 11 May 1994)

In recognition of some of these concerns, a number of attempts have been made to find a 'fair' way of rationing health care according to an agreed set of principles. One famous example of the use of public consultation to determine health care priorities was in Oregon in the USA (of course public health care in America is very limited and, as in Britain, there is no rationing for those who can afford private treatment).

The ethical justifications of the Oregon experiment were that:

- it is more equitable (fairer) to guarantee everyone basic health care than to offer a

larger range of care to only some;
- explicit, publicly accountable decisions are better than the hidden rationing that happens now;
- health care priorities should be determined by the community as well as by doctors.

A range of medical and surgical procedures were categorised according to their perceived value to society, value to the individual and whether they were essential to basic health care. However, a further key criterion was a cost–benefit analysis, in other words a high cost, high benefit procedure may be ranked lower than a lower cost procedure of lower benefit. The following is a summary of the Oregon exercise:

DISEASES THAT ARE UNTREATED IN OREGON

In Oregon in the United States, 709 conditions and diseases were placed in order of priority in a scheme to provide the poor with a free health service. The state then decided how much it could afford. Conditions below 'line 587' are not funded.

This is a selection of the diseases that will not be treated in 120,000 poor Oregonians who cannot afford to pay for medical care.

- Benign skin tumours and moles
- Deformities of the spine
- Benign growths of vocal cords – which can affect the voice
- Acute viral hepatitis
- Cancers that have spread to other parts of the body, where treatment will not result in more than 5 per cent of the patients surviving for more than five years
- Male and female infertility, including treatment to improve ovulation
- Surgery on blocked fallopian tubes
- Removing raised scars
- Joint and muscle sprains
- Liver transplant for liver cancer
- Obesity
- Venereal warts
- Non-infectious gastroenteritis and colitis
- Coughs and colds

Treatment of alcohol and drug addiction does not even make it on to the list.

(The Independent, 2 March 1993)

QALYs

One such British attempt to develop a system of health care rationing has been the development of the concept of QUALYs, or Quality Adjusted Life Years. In this model treatments are ranked according to their costs, weighed against the projected increase in life expectancy and the quality of life that treatment will bring about. Using this approach some health authorities have withdrawn procedures such as varicose vein removal because, except in serious cases, such surgery does not increase life expectancy or sufficiently enhance quality of life.

There are of course many ethical questions raised by the QALY approach, not least that human beings are unique and as such it is very difficult to apply a purely technical formula which is likely to do justice to all cases. QALYs can also be seen as ageist in that the young are more likely to experience the most enhanced life expectancy from any given procedure. QALYs also seem to discriminate against people requiring continuing care and favour those needing immediate, one-off procedures; they also appear to fail to give sufficient priority to preventative medicine. Christine Hancock, general secretary of the Royal College of Nurses, believes that the money spent developing the QALY formula could be better used:

'If demand for health care were to be met in full we could avoid costly and unnecessary problems associated with waiting for treatment. Perhaps some of the money and effort at present spent on new ways of allocating resources ... could be used ... in providing essential services.'

(The Independent, 2 March 1993)

ACTIVITY

Draw up your own list of medical procedures and undertake research into people's health care priorities.

It might be useful to work in small groups to draw up a questionnaire to be targeted at different groups. Analyse any differences you find in terms of age, race, gender, those who have children and those who are childless, etc. What do your conclusions tell you about the practical possibility of rationing health care in an equitable way?

The right to know/who needs to know

PATERNALISM *VERSUS* FREEDOM OF INFORMATION: THE MEDICAL CONTEXT

We have established that access to information is the right of all patients and clients. Without possession of adequate knowledge, informed consent is impossible. This requires that individuals understand the treatment that is proposed for them and are able to make meaningful decisions about any choices they may have. However, there are many difficulties with the practice of informed consent in medical contexts, not least the question of how much information should be provided and the degree of patient understanding necessary.

There are two main views on this issue, both of which could be seen as compatible with the requirements made of health and social care workers in the legislation and guidelines governing their conduct.

One view, which might be called a paternalist view, holds that only the professional has sufficient knowledge and experience to reach a fully informed decision on treatment and/or service provision. It is thus up to the professional to determine what information, in her or his judgement, the client or patient needs to know. This notion of supplying information on a 'need to know basis' presupposes that patients and clients cannot generally cope with all the information that is potentially available and that such information may be confusing or distressing. With respect to this view, it is sometimes suggested that by simply seeking out the skills of a nurse or doctor, a patient is tacitly agreeing to any treatment deemed necessary. However, for all major invasive procedures the patient is required to give explicit consent by signing a consent form, and it is clear that without the patient having information as to the nature of their own medical condition and an understanding of what treatment will involve then their 'consent' means little. This is the view of those committed to freedom of information who believe that a surgeon has to reveal all the possible outcomes of a particular operation in order to obtain fully informed consent. Such a view holds that patients and clients should have full access to all information that may have a bearing on their case; it is not up to the health professional to decide on behalf of the patient or client what they can or cannot cope with or need or do not need to know. It may well be that not all clients have the capacity to fully assimilate the information with which they are provided, but this does not excuse the health care worker from making it available to them.

ACTIVITY

Consider the following situations:
A patient is about to receive an intramuscular injection. If the patient asks 'Will it hurt?' should he be told yes, it's likely to be very painful, or should the nurse say 'You may experience some discomfort?' Which is likely to be best for the patient?

A patient with metastasising cancer (spreading around the body) and only a few weeks to live has not been told his prognosis. Are medical and nursing staff justified in this because they believe that the patient's last days will be happier and more hopeful, or does the patient have a right to be told the truth?

Artificial resuscitation

To resuscitate someone is to revive them from an unconscious state or apparent death. In a hospital setting this may be undertaken using artificial respiration, cardiac massage and/or defibrillation. The heart muscle must be revived within three to five minutes, or irreversible brain damage occurs.

Many relatives of hospital patients are shocked to find out that the case notes of their loved one read 'not for resus' or DNR (do not resuscitate). In such cases medical staff have taken a decision, based on the age or condition of the patient, that if the patient's heart stops they will be allowed to die. What concerns us here is the question of who has the right to make such a decision and what rights patients should have to be consulted or informed about such decisions. In a recent study (reported in *The Guardian*, 5 November 1994, one-third of senior doctors questioned would not resuscitate otherwise healthy people over 70. In one hospital an 'opt-in' policy operates where nobody is resuscitated unless a specific decision is taken to do so. Less than 1% of consultants had ever consulted with the patients themselves over resuscitation decisions. In this study, 100 patients with an average age of 80 were asked whether they were upset by the question. In general people were positive and welcomed the opportunity to be consulted on such an important topic. However, of the 87 patients questioned who would have been resuscitated, 35 said they did not want it. There is certainly no doubt that the sight of a 'crash team' with all its hardware violently trying to resuscitate a tired and weak 80-year-old can be distressing and might lead anyone to question the wisdom of doing so.

It is argued by the authors of the report that just as doctors have a moral duty to disclose a patient's diagnosis, so too the question of resuscitation should be raised with patients and their wishes taken into account. However, the Patients' Association believes that such a practice could amount to cruelty and intrusion: 'When I'm 75 and slightly deaf and a bit blurry-eyed and weak and wobbly do you think that I'd want to be faced with that question?'

This raises a wider issue about access to information. Many patients who find being a patient a bewildering and rather threatening experience may feel less vulnerable and experience less enforced passivity if they are fully involved in decision making processes; they will feel like partners rather than patients. However, what of those patients, such as the one above, who do not feel that they can cope with such decisions and who would genuinely rather leave their care in the hands of those they perceive to be the 'experts'? Does this mean that the patient has forsaken the right to be treated as a person and their autonomy denied? No, legally the patient must still give their explicit consent to any invasive procedures and the patient reserves the right at any time to opt-in again to the decision-making process. One way of viewing this would be to say that the patient has the right to relinquish **responsibility**, but by doing so does not relinquish **autonomy**.

Ways of handling ethical issues

In some cases, as we have seen, there will be specific guidelines which aim to assist health and social care professionals in their decision-making about ethical issues, but even with comprehensive 'rulebooks' health and social care practitioners will not be able to avoid, at times, having to make very difficult moral decisions and acting upon them.

In social work ethical dilemmas or conflicts may be taken to a case conference. Advice may be sought from senior team members who are experienced in particular areas; at other times inter-agency conferences may throw light upon a particular issue and make decision-making easier.

Large hospitals will have their own ethics committees to which difficult cases may be referred. With regard to the ethics of medical research, the Department of Health now requires all health authorities to have Local Research Ethics Committees. These committees have eight to 12 members, including nursing staff whose professional code of conduct, as we saw, requires them to act as advocates for patients.

In some cases the advice of professional bodies will be sought, e.g. the BMA Ethics Committee or the Royal College of Nursing.

Similarly, trade unions such as Unison can provide advice and guidance, although of course their main aim is to safeguard the interests of their members.

Where technological and scientific advances threaten to open a whole new ethical can of worms a specific enquiry may be established to consider the ethical and hence legal ramifications of the issue and may propose new legislation. In January 1994 the Human Fertilisation and Embryology Authority undertook a public consultation exercise on the ethical implications of donated ovarian tissue in embryo research and assisted conception. Such consultations, particularly on obviously moral issues which would seem to cross partisan political lines, are likely to be very important in the formulation of legislation and social policy.

ACTIVITY

The Human Fertilisation and Embryology Authority reported in July 1994. Write for a copy of its final report and identify its main findings.

ASSESSMENT OPPORTUNITY ✔

SCENARIO

You are a sister/charge nurse on a medical ward with considerable experience of caring for seriously ill patients and their families and friends.

You have been asked to produce a training pack on ethical issues in nursing for use by student nurses. The aim of the pack is to provide practical help for new nurses to enable them to understand and deal with the ethical issues and dilemmas which they will face.

Your training pack will include the following:

1. A list of general ethical principles that you feel are central to the work of nurses;
2. A detailed discussion of each principle and an explanation of why it is important to the work of nursing staff;
3. A discussion and explanation of **ethical dilemmas** – to bring this alive for student nurses you will devise a number of case studies which illustrate the following:
   - dilemmas involved in identifying the best interests of patients;
   - dilemmas involved in the rationing /allocation of health care;
   - dilemmas involved in assessing risk to patients;
   - dilemmas involved in the issue of access to information and informed consent;
   - dilemmas involved in the issue of confidentiality.
4. A description of how such ethical dilemmas might be resolved, together with a discussion and evaluation of the possible effectiveness of these.

SOURCES FOR ASSIGNMENTS, INVESTIGATIONS AND PROJECTS

The best general reference/address/telephone number directory of all health and social services organisations, including those dealing specifically with equal opportunities, is the *Social Services Year Book* published annually by Longman Community Information and Reference. If your school or college library does not have a copy of this, your local public reference library will.

Child Poverty Action Group
4th Floor
1–5 Bath Street
London EC1V 9PY
Tel.: 0171 253 3406

Citizen's Advice Bureaux: see your local telephone directory.

Commission for Racial Equality (CRE)
10–12 Allington Street
London SW1E 5EH
Tel.: 0171 828 7022

Equal Opportunities Commission (EOC)
Overseas House
Quay Street
Manchester M3 3HN
Tel.: 0161 833 9244

General Medical Council
44 Hallam Street
London W1N 6AE

Human Fertilisation and Embryology Authority
Paxton House
30 Artillery Lane
London E1 7LS

The King's Fund (King Edward's Hospital Fund for London) publishes an extremely useful list of publications. Write for a booklist to:

Bournemouth English Book Centre
9 Albion Close
Parkstone
Dorset BH12 3LL

The Patients' Association
18 Victoria Park Square
Bethnal Green
London E2 9PF

Policy Studies Institute
100 Park Village East
London NW1 3SR
Tel.: 0171 387 2171

Runneymede Trust
11 Princelet Street
London E1 6QH
Tel.: 0171 375 1496

UKCC
23 Portland Place
London W1N 3AF

REFERENCES AND RESOURCES

Bowling, A. (1993), *What People say about Prioritising Health Services*. London: King's Fund Centre for Health.

Commission for Racial Equality, *Act for Equality: Strengthening the Race Relations Act*. London: CRE.

Commission for Racial Equality (1989), *Racial Equality in Social Services Departments: A Survey of Equal Opportunities Policies*. London: CRE.

Commission for Racial Equality (1992), *Race Relations: A Code of Practice in Primary Health Care Services*. London: CRE.

Coote, A. and Campbell, B. (1982), *Sweet Freedom: The Struggle for Women's Liberation*. London: Picador.

Cornwell, R. and Staunton, M. (1985), *Data Protection: Putting the Record Straight*. London: NCCL.

Dominelli, L. (1992) 'An uncaring profession? An examination of racism in social work', *Racism and Antiracism – Inequalities, Opportunities and Policies*. Eds: P. Braham, A. Ruttansi, R. Skellington. London: Sage.

Equal Opportunities Commission (1990) *Formal Investigation Report: Southern Derbyshire Health Authority* (March). Manchester: EOC.

Equal Opportunities Commission (1992a), *Equality Management: Women's Employment in the NHS. A Survey Report*. Manchester: EOC.

Equal Opportunities Commission (1992b), *A Guide for Employers to the Sex Discrimination Acts 1975 and 1986*. Manchester: EOC.

Field, D. (1992), 'Elderly People in British Society', *Sociology Review*, vol. 1, no. 4, April.

Gibson, P. (1993), 'Resuscitation – the Ethical Implications' *Nursing*, vol. 4, no. 26.

Giddens, A. (1989), *Sociology*. Cambridge: Polity Press.

Ginger, L. (1990), Practicals and Class Exercises for A, AS and GCSE Psychology.

Holmes, C. (1993), 'QALYs', *International Journal*

of Health Care Quality Assurance, vol. 6, no. 5.

Human Fertilisation and Embryology Authority (1994), *Report on Ovarian Tissue in Embryo Research and Assisted Conception*. London: HREA.

'Inside Anti-Discriminatory Practice', *Community Care Magazine Supplement*, 1–8, March 1994.

Kalsi, N. and Constantinides, P. (1989), *Working towards Racial Equality in Health Care: The Haringey Experience*. London: King's Fund Centre for Health.

King Edward's Hospital Fund for London (1991), *The Work of the Equal Opportunities Task Force 1986–1990: A Final Report*. London: King's Fund Centre for Health.

Modood, T. (1994), *Racial Equality: Colour, Culture and Justice*. London: IPPR.

National Association of Teachers in Further and Higher Education (1993), *Equal Opportunities Guide to Language*. London: NATFHE.

Race Through the 90s (magazine). London: CRE/BBC Radio.

Skellington, R. and Morris, P. (1992), *Race in Britain Today*. London: Sage.

Stainton Rogers, W. (1991), *Explaining Health and Illness: An Exploration of Diversity*. Hemel Hempstead: Harvester Wheatsheaf.

Swain, J., Finkelstein, V., French, S. and Oliver, M. (1993), *Disabling Barriers: Enabling Environments*. London: Sage.

TVEI (1992), *The Equal Opportunities Fact Pack*. London: Department of Employment Group.

Wandsworth Health Authority (1991), *Working Together for Health: Annual Report 1991*. London: Wandsworth Health Authority, Department of Public Health Medicine.

2

INTERPERSONAL INTERACTION

In this chapter the role of interaction in influencing an individual's health and social well-being is examined. Forms of interpersonal interaction, that is, communication and sensory contact, are described, as well as the varying customs regarding verbal and non-verbal communication that have evolved in different cultures, which if not properly understood can inhibit effective interaction. Particular reference is made, in investigating these issues, to care settings and caring relationships.

Other constraints to effective interaction are also investigated: the effects of noise, the subtle inhibiting effects of stereotyping as well as the physical and emotional well-being, for example the degree of stress, being experienced by either participant in the interaction.

The ways of minimising constraints in both one-to-one and group situations is examined: these include the use of practical avoidance measures, plus a range of counselling skills and an understanding of the basic values which underpin health and social care work.

INTRODUCTION

The health or social care worker must be able to communicate effectively with a wide range of other people: with patients or clients, who may be children, adolescents, young adults, middle-aged or elders; and with many different professionals (for example doctors, nurses, physiotherapists, teachers, the police), each of whom will have their own angle of perception and the jargon of their profession.

Lack of proper communication between the health or social care worker and the patient or client will mean that the patient/client will not receive the help he or she needs. Lack of proper communication between professionals can mean that a vulnerable client, for example a child 'at risk' or a frail old person, who is totally dependent for his or her safety and well-being on a carefully designed network of care and supervision, can be exposed to danger or accident, perhaps with tragic consequences.

There are two case studies in this chapter which illustrate many of the points we will discuss. Activities throughout the chapter apply to these cases, and you may want to refer to them on several occasions.

EXPLORING INTERPERSONAL INTERACTION

The positive and negative influences of interaction

Interaction with others plays an important part in the development of the self concept through the years of childhood and adolescence (see page 200), but it is also important for maintaining self-esteem in adulthood and old age.

The social support network of each individual encountered in care situations is likely to be a significant indicator of their feeling of personal well-being.

Isolated people are more at risk from mental, physical and social problems. A

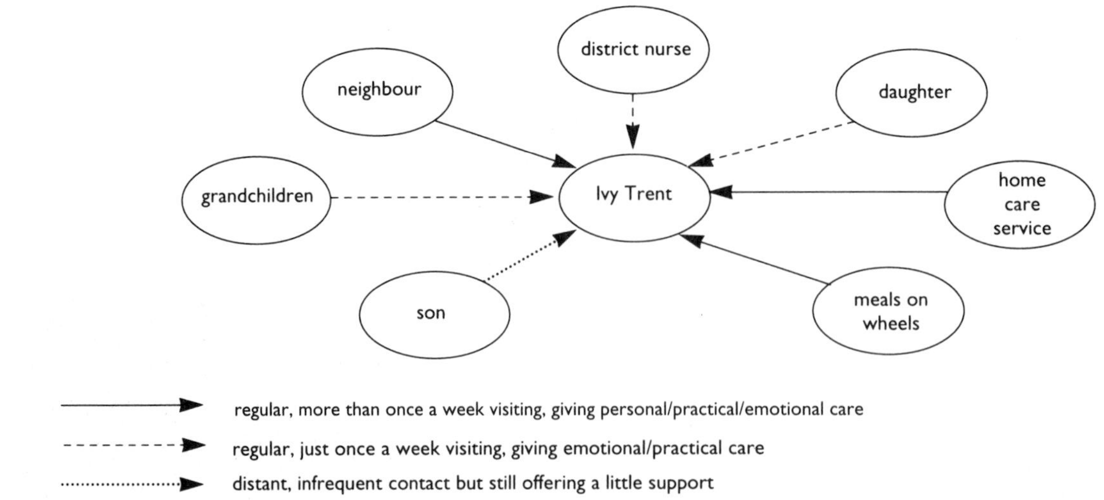

Figure 2.1 Eco map for Mrs Trent

strong social support network can prevent many problems and is greatly conducive to mental health and life satisfaction at all stages of the life cycle. Research has shown, predictably, that people who are more isolated tend to turn to formal agencies for help in times of trouble.

One way of clearly showing a person's social support system is by an 'eco map'. Figure 2.1 shows such a map for the case of Mrs Trent (see case study 1 on page 107).

Forms of interaction

Interaction may take place verbally, through language or sign language, by touch or by use of other high tech or low tech systems. It also takes place non verbally, through body language and environmental factors, and through activities which bring groups of people together in a common interest.

In the initial interview between health or social care worker and client, when the individual needs of the client are being tentatively assessed, the worker will be expressing a desire to help, both verbally and non-verbally.

The worker will, for example, greet the client using appropriately friendly and welcoming words, and matching the words with non-verbal signals – welcoming gestures and tone of voice. If a client has a communication difficulty, a great deal more non-verbal communication will be used.

Verbal communication

Interaction through language

Verbal communication concerns words or substitutes for words and refers to an individual's first language. This may be:

- a spoken language;
- a signed language (e.g. British sign language);
- another system of communication using technology.

The last type of communication may be through low-tech or high-tech means, depending on the specific needs of the individual and the resources available. For instance, a hearing aid is a simple low-tech means of improving communication, whilst in severe cases of disability, there are automatic computerised control systems available which can control a client's whole environment – heating, light, television, telephone – from a single control pad.

DEAFNESS AND HEARING IMPAIRMENT

Deaf or hearing impaired are terms used to describe a person with hearing problems but there are many different conditions that merit these labels. The British Association of Teachers

Figure 2.2 Communicating in sign language

of the Deaf (BATOD) makes the following distinctions:

- *Slightly hearing impaired* Children whose average hearing loss, regardless of age of onset, does not exceed 40 dB.
- *Moderately hearing impaired* Children whose average hearing loss, regardless of age of onset, is 41 dB to 70 dB.
- *Severely hearing impaired* Children whose average hearing loss is from 71 dB to 95 dB, and those with a greater loss who acquired their hearing impairment after the age of 18 months.
- *Profoundly hearing impaired* Children who were born with, or who acquired before the age of 18 months, an average hearing loss of 96 dB or greater.

A very important distinction for hearing impaired people and those who live with, work with or teach them is whether deafness occurred at a pre-lingual or post-lingual stage in their lives. In the UK it is estimated that over 2 000 000 people lie somewhere along a continuum of hearing impairment. The majority of these use hearing aids, but around 70 000–80 000 need to use forms of communication that do not depend on auditory input. Of these, 20 000–30 000 are pre-lingually deaf and this group needs to rely on visual-gestural systems of communication like British Sign Language (BSL).

From time to time a hearing impaired BSL user may need a BSL interpreter to turn their communications into spoken language and to convert spoken language into BSL. BSL is a highly complex language which uses the hands, body, facial expression and eyes. It has its own grammar and there is no one-to-one correspondence between words and BSL signs.

However, not all hearing impaired people need to use BSL, and others may have had limited exposure to it. Relatively few hearing

people are 'fluent' BSL users, so what does this mean for the hearing impaired learner? Although moves are being made to rectify the situation, some researchers believe that few deaf people achieve the potential that would be expected from their basic underlying intelligence. For this reason, both teachers of the deaf and educational interpreters for the deaf have a vital role to play in supporting the hearing impaired learner.

(Psychology Review, vol. 1, no. 2, November 1994)

Non-verbal communication

Non-verbal communication refers to all the body signals which we deliberately or inadvertently make when we are with other people.

It has been calculated that, on average, the total impact of a message owes 7% to the actual words, 38% to the 'paralanguage' (how we say the words) and 55% to our non-verbal signals. Argyle (1988) demonstrated that, where the non-verbal message contradicts the verbal message, the latter tends to be discounted. They found that the non-verbal style in which a message is communicated has five times more effect than the actual verbal message itself. Our non-verbal behaviour is the more reliable guide to our real feelings.

There are roughly eight kinds of non-verbal communication:

- paralanguage – the way we say things, tone of voice, timing;
- eye contact;
- facial expression;
- posture;
- gesture;
- touch;
- proxemics – how close we come to the other person/people;
- dress.

PARALANGUAGE

This includes the way things are said, the tone of voice, and the timing of speech.

Research into paralanguage has shown that:

- people are very accurate in assessing which emotion is being expressed by a speaker. The assessment is made from paralanguage cues such as loudness, pitch, rate of speaking, rhythm and inflection;
- these patterns of speech can be recorded and analysed on a machine called a speech spectograph. People who suffer from mental disorders tend to show unusually flattened speech patterns;
- when someone is in a highly emotional state, for example angry or anxious, they tend to stutter, repeat themselves and make more slips of the tongue than usual;
- when someone is not sure of what they are saying, or uncertain of how what they say will be received, they will say 'er' and 'um' more often than usual;
- the timbre of the voice, its softness or harshness, is also different in different emotional states;
- the timing of speech is important in communication. Very slow speech may indicate that a person is uncertain of what they are saying. Fast speech can indicate that a person is anxious or excited.

The listener will unconsciously register all these signals from the speaker, and from them guess his or her state of mind. In the active listening undertaken by those in the caring professions (see page 105), the signals from the speaker will be more consciously noted, and from them an appropriate assessment of the speaker's emotional state may be made.

ACTIVITY

Give a verbal message, for example 'You don't look very well today', to different subjects in:
- a friendly tone of voice;
- a hostile tone of voice.

What reaction do the subjects give?

Ask the subjects how the question made them feel, presented in the different styles.

Did they react more to the language, or the paralanguage?

What are the implications of this for carers?

EYE CONTACT

Eye contact can powerfully indicate emotion. The more eye contact someone has with another person, the closer they tend to feel to them. People who don't like each other tend to avoid eye contact.

Research has suggested that eye contact has four important functions in communication.

1. it regulates the flow of conversation;
2. it gives feedback to the speaker on what he or she has communicated;
3. it expresses emotion;
4. it informs both the speaker and the listener of the nature of the relationship they are in.

Other studies have shown that people who have strong emotional needs for approval make more eye contact than others; speakers also feel that if people are not looking at them, they are not attending to what they are saying.

A care worker who is listening to a client will therefore use eye contact to express sincerity and concern and to show that he or she is attending carefully.

FACIAL EXPRESSION

Research has shown that there are some facial expressions which have the same meaning all over the world. An example is the 'eyebrow flash' in which, when people greet each other, they rapidly raise and lower their eyebrows. This has been observed throughout human societies (and also among the great apes).

There are seven major groups of facial expression, which are recognised in virtually all human societies: happiness, surprise, fear, sadness, anger, interest and disgust/contempt. However, some cultures inhibit the expression of certain emotions, for example anger, which is perhaps allowed expression more in the West than in parts of the East.

ACTIVITY

Facial expressions

Write the names of different emotions on pieces of paper and put them in a hat. Take it in turns to take a piece of paper and mime the emotion written there. Which emotions are most easily recognised?

POSTURE

People may want to appear to others in a certain way. But how they really feel is often given away by body posture, or small unconscious gestures which demonstrate, for example, nervousness or anxiety. This is called emotional leakage.

GESTURE

People who are communicating together often show 'postural echo', i.e. they copy the gestures and posture of the person they are talking to. This demonstrates attentiveness and empathy.

ACTIVITY

Ask a group of people to divide into pairs and talk to each other. After several minutes ask them to 'freeze'.

Some pairs will be mimicking each other's posture and gestures.

Specify the gestures that are being copied.

Find out whether the couples who demonstrate postural echo know each other better than the couples who don't and demonstrate it.

Many gestures, for example head nodding, bowing or raising a thumb, are culture-specific, i.e. they mean something to people from one culture, but may mean nothing, or something entirely different, to those from another culture.

TOUCH

The amount of everyday touch which we will allow people to have with us is again culturally determined.

Those who work with distressed people, who are in fear, shock, pain or bereavement, know that there are times when touch, holding or hugging, is expressive and comforting when there are no suitable words.

PROXEMICS

This is another culturally determined method of communication. Each society has its own idea of personal space. For example, in Western Europe the normal conversational distance is 1–1.5 metres, but in some Arab countries it is very much closer than that.

ACTIVITY

How do you, in the library, on a crowded tube train, protect your own personal space? Do care arrangements, for example in hospitals or residential homes, take account of this need?

DRESS

The clothes of the care worker may be a uniform which will convey its own important/official/reassuring message. If a uniform is not worn, the clothes of the worker should not make an extreme statement expressing, for example, wealth, membership of a cult or sexual invitation. On the other hand, very drab and dowdy clothes reflect a lack of confidence and poor self-esteem, which might equally unconsciously deter clients, who will inevitably carry a set of stereotypes in their own minds (see also p. 123).

ACTIVITY

1 Draw an eco map to show Tracy's social support system (case study 2).

2 Draw an eco map to show Jean North's social support system (case study 2).

3 Find out from your local Social Services Department what facilities are available for the elderly in your area: Is there an occupational therapist attached to the Social Services Department? Are there specialist social workers who can supply equipment such as telephone and TV aids to help with communication for the deaf or hard of hearing, and to help with mobility and communication for the blind or partially sighted? Is day care available? Is respite care for short periods in a residential home available? Are personal alarms available? What kind of home help service is available and can hot or frozen meals be delivered?

AFFILIATION

There are some people who prefer being alone, but research has shown that many people find social isolation very disturbing. Solitary confinement is seen as highly unpleasant. The desire to affiliate is seen as a fundamental human characteristic. Theories of affiliation include the following:

- The need to affiliate has been passed on, as an innate human characteristic, from our human ancestors who lived in groups.
- Affiliation is learned during infancy and childhood.
- It is a human instinct to seek out others.

Research has shown that:

- isolation leads to fear, and fear increases the desire to be with other people;
- fear, from whatever cause, increases the desire to be with other people;
- we seek other people when we need reassurance;
- we seek other people when we need approval.

The body of a mentally ill man was found in his council flat weeks after he died and nearly six months after he was last seen by his community psychiatric nurse, an inquest heard yesterday.

Malcolm McDuff, who lived in Walthamstow, north London, had not had his monthly injection to control his schizophrenia since last December.

Police found his body lying in an armchair last week, after being called in by neighbours who had not seen Mr McDuff for over a month.

(The Guardian, 2 June 1994)

ACTIVITY

Read the extract on this page about the man not found for weeks after he died.

Loneliness and isolation from others, if not a chosen way of life, lie at the heart of a range of mental disturbances.

Consider (a) personality and (b) social factors that could lead to loneliness and isolation from others in childhood, adolescence, early adulthood, middle age and old age. (Refer to Erickson's 'life stages' in Chapter 4.)

ACTIVITY W

In any acute hospital ward two determinants of affiliation, fear and the need for reassurance, may be strongly in evidence.

In the course of communicating with patients you may find an opportunity to ask them:

- When they first came to hospital, did they just want to be alone or did they appreciate having other people around?
- Did they feel worried or afraid at any time?
- If so, did they seek reassurance from the hospital staff or other patients in adjoining beds, or did they wait for visiting time?

The negative influences of being in a group

Isolation from others may lead to mental disturbances, but it is also possible in many contexts to feel lonely in a group, i.e. unable to be oneself and communicate in a satisfying way with others. This experience can lower self-esteem and lead to feelings of oppression and depression.

If a client or patient is not given adequate mental stimulation (i.e. their intellectual needs are not met), this can result in the poor performance of certain tasks or a slower recovery or even a decline.

As with communication needs, before a client's intellectual needs can be met, their intelligence and level of education will have to be assessed. How they have previously spent their time (e.g. their type of employment, hobbies and interests) will also be relevant. Short-term goals are generally seen as more readily achievable than long-term ones, especially by the older person.

ACTIVITY

1 You work in a large residential home for elders. What programme of activities would you suggest to help towards your clients' intellectual needs? (See the examples given in the newspaper article below.)
How would you evaluate the effectiveness of this programme?

2 If you have had the opportunity to carry out any work experience, can you give examples of good and bad practice in meeting intellectual needs? (Don't forget confidentiality.)

STUDENT ENROLS AT 106

Mrs Tabitha Barker, 106, has enrolled at Farnborough College of Technology, Hants, to study a course in Reminiscence.

The former caretaker, who retired at the age of 86, believes that hard work is the secret of her great age.

Ms Jennie Espiner, senior lecturer, at the college, said: 'We couldn't have asked for a more appropriate student for this course. Mrs Barker's recollections are crisp and clear and span many generations.'

The course aims to encourage students to think of themselves as living history.

(The Daily Telegraph, 30 December 1994)

An unsatisfactory nursing home for the elderly would provide an example of some of the negative effects of being in an uncongenial group situation:

The set-up will be familiar to anybody who has had to contend with residential nursing homes: a pokey bedsitting room, with luck; a communal 'living room' where dowdy armchairs are arranged deadpan along the walls, populated by unstimulated, infinitely sad people *not* looking at the permanently blaring television. Mid-morning trolleys with instant-coffee-already-with-milk-and-sugar, disgusting food aimed at the lowest common denominator (people whose teeth don't function), a complete absence of intellectual stimulus and negligible privacy. Clothes vaguely and too infrequently washed, never properly pressed. A pronounced tendency to 'calm' patients with tranquillisers, which only make them confused and (quietly) miserable. And nurses who call you by your Christian name when they don't just call you 'Granny' or 'Dearie', and who address you as though, just because you're there, you must have an IQ of two.

(The Times, 11 June 1994)

Compare this with the positive environment, in which infirm individuals are treated with respect, as described here:

My mother's nine lives suddenly began to run out just before Christmas 1990. For some time, she had been able to stay at home only thanks to a cobbled-together succession of resident home-helps with nursing training.

This form of care had worked well, but suddenly (there had been another tiny stroke) we needed to add a night nurse. There wasn't really room in the house and, decisively, my stepfather couldn't take the strain. Overnight, my mother was in a nursing home. It was private and expensive: £380 a week is the figure that sticks. It was considered better-than-average. And it was a prison for body and mind. And then my mother's former doctor told us about Amesbury Abbey. It was hopeless, the waiting list was miles long: but he would take us there. You never knew.

We arrived at the tail-end of lunch, but we went to the restaurant – a proper restaurant, not a canteen: flowers again, table napkins and pretty table mats at small tables, reproduction Georgian chairs. Uniformed waitresses, not nurses, and good smells coming from the kitchen when the service doors opened. We went walkabout, met people, asked if we might glance at where they lived; proudly, they welcomed us into large rooms or suites, full of their own furniture, pictures and books. There was a physio unit, its staff obviously in the business of getting people on their feet.

And slightly away from the house, clusters of mews houses: sheltered housing, as I was later to discover, which meant what the name implies rather than a mere emergency bell to summon a warden.

We would have to find £15,000 for a fully returnable deposit for a room; otherwise, it cost much the same as the place of abandoned hope my mother was in. Within a week, my mother was regaining both spirits and mobility. I think, with a little more time, she might even have recovered sufficiently to return home. The nine lives really were up: she collapsed a fortnight later, with fatal pneumonia; but with despair giving way to hope, some fragment of that old promise was redeemed.

(The Times, 11 June 1994)

ACTIVITY

Read the accounts of two different nursing homes for the elderly.

List the key physical and psychological factors which led to the pleasant environment in the second example.

What effects, psychological, intellectual and physical, was their environment having on the residents?

What effects, psychological, intellectual and physical, was the environment in the first example having on the residents?

The writer of these articles suggests the following checklist when looking round potential homes:

NURSING HOME CHECKPOINTS

1 The smell as you walk through the door.
2 Ask for the menu. Look at the crockery.
3 Ask about visiting hours. 'No restrictions' is the right answer.
4 Does it look like a nursing home?
5 Are the people there happy, well groomed, sure of themselves?
6 Watch matron's face when asked if there is a bar.

Assuming that the home is acceptable, people will have different views on entering it. The move will involve some:

- loss of independence;
- change in status;
- change in environment.

Their views and feelings on these points and many others can usefully be elicited through interviews and/or questionnaires.

ASSESSMENT OPPORTUNITY ✓

1 Devise a questionnaire for elderly people (perhaps in a hospital ward or in the community) to ascertain attitudes towards residential care.

2 Choose one response that shows a positive attitude towards residential care and one that shows a negative attitude. If the respondents are agreeable, conduct an in-depth interview with them to try to identify the factors which might account for the differing attitudes.

3 Identify the factors in:
- self-concept
- attitudes
- personality

that would lead to:
- positive and
- negative

reactions on the part of an elderly person to the prospect of going into residential care.

4 Write an imaginary case study of:
- an old person who welcomes residential care;
- an old person who hates the idea of 'going into a home'.

ACTIVITY W

The following are ideas for projects you could carry out while working in a care organisation.

- Set up a questionnaire for people at a day centre for the disabled, or for the elderly.

  Complete task 2 or task 3 from the Assessment opportunity above for this questionnaire. Select one or two positive and one or two negative replies, and investigate these further using in-depth interview techniques.

  Relate your findings to aspects of self concept and personality.

- Observe small children in a day nursery, and their attachment and separation behaviour.

  Research attachment behaviour (see next section on 'Attachments').

  Relate the observed behaviour to your research on attachment.

NB Always check with your work placement supervisor before carrying out research.

The effects of gender, age and culture on social interaction

THE EFFECT OF GENDER ON SOCIAL INTERACTION

In 1974, a major review of books and articles on sex differences in motivation, social behaviour and intellectual ability was undertaken by Maccoby and Jacklin (*The Psychology of Sex Differences*).

They found that many popular stereotypes are not borne out by the evidence. Myths include:

- Girls are more sociable than boys.
- Boys are more 'analytic' than girls.
- Girls are 'auditory' while boys are 'visual'.
- Girls have lower self-esteem than boys.

Some differences were supported by evidence:

- Boys are more aggressive than girls.

In fact, verbal aggression, fantasy play and physical aggression are more noticeable in boys than girls from about two and a half years of age.

- Girls are superior to boys in verbal ability.

Girls' verbal abilities appear to mature more rapidly in the early years (though not all studies support this theory). From pre-school age to puberty, verbal abilities between the sexes are similar. But from about 11 years, research shows that girls tend to develop superior verbal ability up until and possibly beyond adolescence.

- Boys are superior to girls in visual-spatial ability.

This involves the visual perception of figures or objects in space and how they relate to each other. Male superiority in this seems to emerge in adolescence and to continue through adulthood.

- Boys are superior to girls in mathematical ability.

There is not such a marked sex difference in this ability as in visual-spatial ability, but research shows that from about 13 years, boys' mathematical skills increase faster than girls'.

However, although these differences appear in the research, there is a tendency to exaggerate them. Maccoby later argued that:

- **In behaviour, boys and girls are more alike than they are different.**

ACTIVITY

Discuss Maccoby and Jacklin's findings in relation to the nature/nurture debate: how far do you think these sex differences are inborn, and how far do you think they are nurtured?

With regard to the sex differences, which have emerged from the research, how could you enhance interaction with males and females of different age groups?

THE EFFECT OF AGE ON SOCIAL INTERACTION

The type of social interaction individuals prefer varies through the life cycle. What are the particular requirements of the different age groups?

Social disengagement theory (Cumming and Henry, 1961), based on a five year study of 50–90 year olds in the USA, suggests that society withdraws from the ageing individual (through retirement, grown children, death of spouse), while at the same time the individual withdraws from society (through reduced social activity). The theory suggests that those with a sense of psychological well-being may be happy with this state of affairs.

However, other research has shown that many elderly people remain socially active and 'engaged', and reports relatively high levels of contentment.

Changes in society, including improved health care, earlier retirement age and higher educational levels, have meant that many elderly people in the 1990s have a choice of lifestyle available to them. They may be as socially active or inactive as they wish, as long as they enjoy adequate health and sufficient income.

Activity

Find out what facilities and activities are available for the different age groups in the area in which you live.

Is more support required for one age group? What would you suggest?

THE EFFECTS OF CULTURE ON SOCIAL INTERACTION

Different cultures can have very particular effects on interaction. See the earlier section in this chapter on touch and proxemics for specific examples.

Activity

1 Choose one of the minority racial groups living in England.

2 Are religious beliefs important to this group? If so, what are they? How do these beliefs affect the behaviour of the men, the women, the male children and the female children? How might these beliefs and behaviours affect communication with those of a different religion, the agnostic or the atheist?

3 Research their traditions and customs. What behaviour is expected of the women? What behaviour is expected of the children? How do they express joy and anger? What are their customs regarding touch, of family members and friends? What are the common gestures of their culture? Do they have special customs regarding eye contact and proxemics? What are their accepted forms of address and respect.

4 Religious beliefs and customs will affect interaction between individuals.
With the minority group you have chosen to study, specify how customs influence the following interactions:
How do -

- men and women who are non family members interact?
- men and women within the family interact?
- women of different ages interact?
- the women behave in mixed gatherings?
- the women interact with the children?
- the men interact with the children?
- the women interact with the elders?
- the men interact with the elders?

5 Analyse how these customs differ from British customs.

6 Discuss how the cultural differences could inhibit communication between a British care worker and a client from this minority racial group.

Factors which affect interpersonal interaction

ACTIVITY BASED INTERACTION

Interaction will be enhanced by activities in areas of common interest, such as sport, music, card playing, arts and crafts. In these activities, enthusiasm and slight ability are more important than the subtle skills involved in purely social contact. They might, therefore, be particularly recommended for those who feel isolated, lack confidence, or have other special needs. Successful participation in a group activity enhances self-esteem and self-confidence, which will spill over onto other aspects of living.

ACTIVITY

Make a list of activities and possible common interests which could enhance interaction between individuals at each of the life stages (using Erickson's stages of psychosocial development as a basis).

Referring to the case studies on pages 107 and 109, would you consider that the lives of Ivy Trent, Tracy Congdon, or Frank and Jean North would be enhanced by activity based interaction? If so, what would you suggest?

ENVIRONMENTAL

Arrangement of chairs in the interview room

The interview room should, if possible, be at a comfortable temperature and free from distracting noises.

The arrangement of the furniture is significant. One chair higher than the other, or a large desk as a barrier, are non-verbal symbols of power and dominance, which are unhelpful in the caring context as the client probably already has low self-esteem and may feel fear. Therefore the worker and the client should sit on chairs of equal height. If a desk is used it should be made clear that this is so that the worker can take essential notes. It is best if interviewer and interviewee sit on two sides of the desk (an arrangement used by many GPs).

Sackeim *et al.* (1978: in Hayes and Orrell, 1993) found that the left side of the face is far more expressive of emotion than the right side. They suggest that the reason for this is that the left half of the face is controlled by the right side of the brain, which is thought to deal with artistic, emotional and intuitive skills, while the left side of the brain is thought to deal with logical reasoning and language. So perhaps the interviewer should have a good view of the left side of the client's face.

Arrangement of chairs for groups

There should be sufficient space for all the members of the group to sit comfortably with an acceptable amount of 'personal space' between them – the interaction will be affected if group members have to sit too close, or too far apart from each other.

Lighting

Lighting should be adequate in both individual and group situations, so that reading and writing can be performed if necessary. Very bright light can seem harsh and unwelcoming, not conducive to the possible discussion of personal details. Dim light promotes an unhelpfully intimate atmosphere.

Heating

The room should be a comfortable temperature. A room that is too hot or too cold will provoke physical discomfort; in the group situation it will promote time-wasting complaints and attempts to improve the situation.

Noise

Continuous or intermittent noise is distracting and can interfere with important thought processes.

Optimising the environment

ACTIVITY

1 Work out ways of optimising the physical environment in one to one and group situations.

2 Design suitable activities to enhance the interaction of the following groups:
- exuberant toddlers;
- newly retired people;
- ex-psychiatric patients recently discharged into the community;
- adolescents with low self-esteem;
- women principally at home with small children.

Further factors which inhibit interpersonal interaction with individuals

DISTRACTIONS

A continuous noise outside an interview room is a distraction, but interaction between two people will be inhibited far more by interruptions. Suppose a client is telling his or her personal story to a care worker when the phone rings or there is a knock at the door. The worker takes his or her attention from the client and talks for some minutes to the person on the telephone, or the person at the door, about another matter entirely. The client will feel devalued, that his or her crucial communication is unimportant, and therefore that he or she is unimportant. The client will feel angry, and when the worker at last turns back, may have decided not to reveal any more about him or herself – worker/client communication will have broken down. Any interruptions should therefore be dealt with briefly, with the worker making it clear that the client and his or her problems are the current priority.

DOMINATING THE CONVERSATION

Care workers are there to listen and should put their own concerns to one side. However, they may perhaps unintentionally dominate the conversation in any of three ways:

1 Making the client's story their own story: 'Oh, I'm sorry to hear that happened to you. My own sister/niece/uncle had a similar experience . . .'
2 By assuming responsibility for working out the problem and giving the client only a minor role. An extreme example would be to set out a treatment/care plan, then impose it on the client.
3 By trying to scrutinise every area of the client's life, regardless of the actual service he or she requests.

MANIPULATION

The care worker or client can be manipulative if either one of them has a hidden agenda in the interaction. There are also specific ways in which each side may manipulate the other.

The care worker

This may be direct or indirect. Care workers may manipulate clients by manoeuvring them to choose modes of action in accordance with the care workers' judgement, in such a way that the clients are not aware of the process. If they are aware of it, they feel 'moved about' against their will.

Or care workers might use persuasion in a controlling way to urge clients to accept their decisions. This demotes the clients to playing a minor role in the play of their own lives, and denies them rights to personal choice and independence.

The client

This can happen when a client goes to several agencies for help and complains at each new agency about the lack of help received at the last agency. Such clients are often plausible and much time may be wasted.

BLOCKING THE OTHER'S CONTRIBUTION

In one-to-one, face-to-face interaction, communication can be blocked by one participant in a number of ways, verbal and non-verbal, some of which are subtle and minimal.

The care worker may block the communication of the client in many non-verbal ways, for example:

- a look of boredom;
- a yawn;
- the slightest expression of disgust;
- a smile at the wrong time;
- withdrawal of eye contact, turning away;
- drumming the fingers;
- fidgeting.

The care worker may block the communication of the client verbally by, for example:

- changing the subject;

- being critical;
- misunderstanding;
- joking at the client's expense.

ACTIVITY W

Practise interview skills by interviewing a friend about one of their interests. Try to get some in-depth information by preparing some questions in advance, and using open rather than closed questions.

Interview skills can be practised in role-plays with the case studies of Ivy Trent and Tracy Congdon (described at the end of this chapter).

On work experience, the supervisor at the day centre or hospital might suggest individuals who would enjoy being interviewed. Patients/clients would be assured that:

- they would not have to answer any questions they did not like;
- their names would not be used;
- they would be helping the students complete a project.

The content of the interview could be agreed in advance with the volunteer, for example to cover:

- the client's childhood; or
- the client's employment history.

Students would:

- prepare questions in advance;
- study interview skills;
- tape-record the interview, with the knowledge of the volunteer.

Two willing volunteers should be found, with contrasting needs, and one with a communication disability.

Social and cultural constraints to effective interaction

CULTURE AND GENDER MATCHING

Ideally 'culture and gender matching' should be achieved between the helper and the person in need, i.e. the helper should be of a similar class background and racial type and of the same gender as the person in need.

As this is often not possible, the worker must use empathy and attempt to communicate with the client on the client's level.

It is obvious that communication between two individuals will be hampered if one of the parties has a poor grasp of English, for example if they come from an ethnic minority group.

However, it is also possible for people who speak the same language not to understand each other.

LANGUAGE AND SOCIAL CLASS

In 1961 Bernstein, an English sociologist, put forward his theory of *restricted* and *elaborated* codes of language.

Bernstein claimed that working-class and middle-class children in England speak two different kinds of language. The working-class style of speech tends towards a *restricted* code, which:

- is syntactically crude;
- is repetitive;
- is rigid;
- is limited in its use of adjectives and adverbs;
- uses more pronouns than nouns;
- involves short, grammatically complete and incomplete sentences;
- is context-bound;
- makes frequent use of uninformative but emotionally reinforcing phrases such as 'you see', 'you know', 'wouldn't it' and 'don't I';
- tends to emphasise the present, the here and now;
- is poor at tracing causal relationships;
- does not permit the expression of abstract and hypothetical thought;
- rarely uses 'I' and conveys much meaning non-verbally.

The *elaborated* code, as used by the middle class:

- is syntactically more complex and flexible,

with longer and more complicated sentences;
- makes use of a range of subordinate clauses, as well as conjunctions, prepositions, adjectives and adverbs;
- allows the expression of abstract thoughts;
- makes frequent use of 'I';
- uses more nouns than pronouns;
- is context-independent;
- makes the meaning explicit;
- emphasises the precise description of experiences or feelings;
- tends to stress the past and future rather than the present.

Stones (1971) gave examples of imaginary conversations on a bus between a mother and child:

Mother: hold on tight
Child: why?
Mother: hold on tight
Child: why?
Mother: you'll fall
Child: why?
Mother: I told you to hold on tight, didn't I?

This is a fairly typical restricted code type of conversation, with very little attempt by the mother to explain or reason. Contrast this with an elaborated code mother and her child:

Mother hold on tight, darling
Child: why?
Mother: if you don't you'll be thrown forward and you'll fall
Child: why?
Mother: because if the bus suddenly stops, you'll jerk forward onto the seat in front.

Bernstein's theory has been criticised as making a value judgement, implying that middle-class speech is 'superior' or closer to the 'Queen's English' than working-class speech. But, this debate aside, those working in the health or social care professions should be aware of the difference between restricted and elaborated codes of speech. It is very possible that a worker speaking the elaborated code and a client speaking the restricted code may misunderstand each other and fail to communicate properly at all (see page 84).

BLACK ENGLISH

Similarly, but more obviously, English black children and adults speak in dialogues which show a restricted code. It has been found that they do not speak fully and comfortably in their own language when with whites.

Labov (1970: in Gross, 1992) demonstrated this:

A young black boy, Leon, was asked by a friendly white interviewer to tell him everything he could about a toy.

The eight-year-old boy said very little and remained silent for most of the time.

In a second situation Leon was interviewed by a black interviewer. This time he answered the questions with single words or sounds.

On these first two episodes, Leon would have been labelled 'non-verbal' or 'linguistically retarded'.

However, in a third situation he sat on the floor, shared a bag of crisps with his best friend, and with the same black interviewer asking questions in the local dialect, conversed in a lively way.

In 1972 Williams (Gross, 1992) devised the BITCH test (black intelligence test of cultural homogeneity), which was specially designed to measure the true abilities of black children, written in the dialogue in which they are skilled, instead of the usual Standard English. When white children were tested using only black dialect sentences they did very badly indeed.

LANGUAGE AND CULTURAL DIFFERENCES

During middle childhood, children may begin to fall behind seriously at school if they have not mastered the middle-class 'elaborated' code of English used in school, perhaps because they come from immigrant communities or if their parents only use a 'restricted' code.

It is at this age that children become aware of the implications of belonging to a particular cultural or religious group. They realise that this affects their family rules, family activities and diet, which may be different from those of the majority. If they belong to a sect or racial minority group which is subject to prejudice in the area, they will become aware at this age of stereotypes and may absorb the stereotype of their own particular group into their own self-concept (see the section on stereotypes and self-fulfilling prophecy on page 34).

A good school, which believes in the value of each individual, can help substantially in overcoming these difficulties.

LANGUAGE DIFFERENCES AND COMMUNICATIONS IN THE CARING PROFESSIONS

In the 1970s, J. E. Mayer and Noel Timms studied the views of 61 clients who had requested help from the Family Welfare Association. The clients were predominantly working class. Social workers at the Family Welfare Association (FWA) had access to limited funds to help clients with pressing debts, but mainly their aim was to help people with relationship problems, particularly marital difficulties.

Some clients approached the FWA for help with paying, for example, an electricity bill.

Typically, the social worker, who was trained to look behind a 'presenting' problem for an 'underlying' problem, would sort out some financial help and then try to find out if there was an underlying problem, by asking about the past or about present relationships.

In the case of dissatisfied clients it seems that the workers were using the elaborated code – they were trying to take the problem out of context and relate it to past difficulties, trying to get the client to look for causes behind getting into debt so that the situation would not recur.

But the client using the restricted code could not see any point in looking to the past, trying to make causal relationships, or talking hypothetically.

The result of this failure in communication meant that the worker felt frustrated, while the client felt that the worker's questions were irrelevant, time-wasting and 'nosey'.

For health workers, similar communication problems can arise if, for example, a doctor talks to a patient as if the patient had also received a medical education, and describes symptoms and treatments in technical terms. This will often leave the patient bewildered and anxious.

Interpersonal constraints to effective interaction

If a helper is unaware of the stereotypes and prejudices he or she holds in his or her own mind, these will unconsciously raise a barrier against effective communication between helper and client. It is essential that the helper has sufficient self-knowledge not to let his or her own prejudices interfere in the helping process. (See Chapter 1 for further information on stereotypes.)

Sex role stereotyping, racial stereotyping and the relationship of stereotyping with prejudice are discussed on pages 33–36 in Chapter 1.

SELF-FULFILLING PROPHECY AND LABELLING

Stereotypes are not easily discarded. They influence our perceptions and our social interactions, and can lead us to interact with those we stereotype in ways that cause them to fulfil our expectations. Children are particularly vulnerable to this, but so too are adults who hold a low status in our society.

Many psychological studies have demonstrated this. The following are two examples.

1 In 1966 Rosenthal (Hayes and Orrell, 1993) showed that expectations affect how much a child achieves. In one study, teachers in an American school were told

that certain children (of average ability and randomly picked) would show dramatic improvements over the next year. After a year these children had shown dramatic improvements, presumably because the teachers, without realising it, had started to treat these children differently, unconsciously giving them extra help and encouragement.

This self-fulfilling prophecy can work negatively as well, and most unconscious racism in British schools works in this way. If children are perceived to be less able, for example because of their accents, they may gradually come to believe, because of the way they are treated, that they are less able, and will underachieve dramatically.

2 Aronson and Osherow (1980: in Gross, 1992) reported an experiment with third graders (nine year-olds) in the USA, conducted by their teacher Elliott.

She told her class one day that brown-eyed people are more intelligent and 'better' people than those with blue eyes. Brown-eyed students, though in the minority, would be the 'ruling class' over the inferior blue-eyed children, given extra privileges and the blue-eyed students were 'kept in their place' by such restrictions as being last in line, seated at the back of the class and given less break time.

Within a short time, the blue-eyed children began to do more poorly in their schoolwork and became depressed and angry and described themselves more negatively. The brown-eyed group grew mean, oppressing the others and making derogatory statements about them.
The next day, Elliott announced that she had lied and that it was really blue-eyed people who are superior. The pattern of discrimination, derogation and prejudice quickly reversed itself; she then de-briefed the children.

Several similar studies have replicated this scenario with other populations.

Labelling a person can be self-fulfilling in this way, especially if a person is a child, and the people doing the labelling are 'significant others' such as parents or regular teachers. Up to adolescence, children believe what they are told by their carers. Therefore, if they are often described as, for example, lazy, difficult, clumsy, they may well absorb these labels into their developing self-concept and become these things. Fortunately, positive labels such as good, helpful, enthusiastic can also be self-fulfilling by the same means. At adolescence, children might reassess what they have been told they are in the light of what they feel they are, but this process might involve considerable acting out and argument.

Labels and the caring professions

Labels have often been used by people who work in the caring professions. Before patients and clients were allowed by right to see their own medical or social work records, words such as 'nice' or 'difficult' tended to be put into reports. Such words would influence the perception of those reading the reports, and the patient or client would be treated accordingly. Open access to records has put an end to this overt practice, but care workers must constantly be on their guard against the easy tendency to label and stereotype. It is important that people in the caring professions are aware of any stereotypes they hold in their own minds, so that they can overcome them. Such self-awareness is necessary so that all patients/clients are approached equally and with an open mind.

ACTIVITY

1 Look through children's books, old and new, tabloid newspapers, comics and current TV programmes.
List examples you have found where gender, racial class or age stereotypes are being reinforced or deliberately reversed.

2 Another kind of individual stereotype involves inferring what somebody is like

psychologically from certain aspects of their physical appearance. Attractive-looking people are attributed with all kinds of positive characteristics (the 'halo effect').
Using pictures cut from magazines, carry out an experiment to test the following hypothesis: 'that on first impression attractive-looking people are attributed with positive characteristics and high-status jobs, and unattractive people with negative characteristics and low-status jobs'.
What is the danger of this kind of stereotype to workers in the caring professions?

ACTIVITY

1 Make notes on different attitudes patients/clients have to themselves and their health, focusing on one case study.

2 Make notes on cases you observe where professionals influence the way in which patients/clients view their own health, again focusing on one case study (NB respect confidentiality – do not use actual names).

Psychological well-being

STRESS AND DISTRESS AND THE CARE WORKER

Care workers not only have to contend with the ordinary and sometimes extraordinary stresses of life, which affect all people, but also the special stresses caused by interaction with their client.

Self-knowledge should help the carer compartmentalise his or her own problems, so that they do not interfere in the interaction with the client. However, stress caused by the interaction itself can promote confusion and frustration in the care worker.

It is important for the care worker to remember that a client who has always had difficulty with relationships is likely to elicit the same emotions in the worker as they have elicited in all their former relationships.

An example of this is the passive/aggressive personality.

This personality disorder is a lifelong process which does not make the person suffering from it anxious. Typically, the person does not understand why they have difficulties in their relationships or at work. The style involves communicating hostility in an indirect and apparently non-assaultive manner. Passive aggressives hurt others, not by doing things, but by failing to do them.

Examples

- The person who fails to turn up to an important meeting commits an aggressive action to everybody who does.
- The individual who agrees to support a certain motion and then remains neutral when the votes are cast causes considerable mischief.

Experienced counsellors will realise that the building up of frustration and irritation within themselves is being subtly caused by the behaviour pattern of the client, and realising this makes it easier to deal with their own anger.

External stressors that might affect the client or care worker are shown in Table 2.1. Table 2.1 was devised in 1967, but is still a quick method of assessing one's own stress level. More recent research has emphasised just how important social networks are in easing levels of stress, and how different household structures affect people differently. For instance, single women are found to live longer and healthier lives than their married counterparts. Older married men, on the other hand, are less prone to heart attack and other illnesses symptomatic of stress than older single men.

Table 2.1 Social Readjustment Rating Scale (SRRS)

Rank	Life event	Mean value
1	Death of spouse	100
2	Divorce	73
3	Marital separation	65
4	Jail term	63
5	Death of close family member	63
6	Personal injury or illness	53
7	Marriage	50
8	Fired at work	47
9	Marital reconciliation	45
10	Retirement	45
11	Change in health of family member	44
12	Pregnancy	40
13	Sex difficulties	39
14	Gain of new family member	39
15	Business readjustment	39
16	Change in financial state	38
17	Death of close friend	37
18	Change to different line of work	36
19	Change in number of arguments with spouse	35
20	Mortgage over $10,000	31
21	Foreclosure of mortgage or loan	30
22	Change in responsibilities at work	29
23	Son or daughter leaving home	29
24	Trouble with in-laws	29
25	Outstanding personal achievement	28
26	Wife begins or stops work	26
27	Begin or end school	26
28	Change in living conditions	25
29	Revision of personal habits	24
30	Trouble with boss	23
31	Change in work hours or conditions	20
32	Change in residence	20
33	Change in schools	20
34	Change in recreation	19
35	Change in church activities	19
36	Change in social activities	18
37	Mortgage or loan less than $10,000	17
38	Change in sleeping habits	16
39	Change in number of family get-togethers	15
40	Change in eating habits	15
41	Vacation	13
42	Christmas	12
43	Minor violations of the law	11

The amount of life stress a person has experienced in a given period of time, say one year, is measured by the total number of life change units (LCUs). These units result from the addition of the values (shown in the right column) associated with events that the person has experienced during the target time period. The SRSS was intended to predict the onset of illness. Several studies have indicated that individuals who experience many significant life changes (and score 300 life change units or over) in a given period—for example one year—have a greater susceptibility to both physical and mental illness than those with a lower score.
Source: Holmes, T. H. and Rahe, R. H. (1967), 'The Social Readjustment Rating Scale', *Journal of Psychosomatic Research*, Vol. II, pp. 213–218.

Physical and emotional well-being

PHYSICAL WELL-BEING

Before communication can be established, any handicaps in hearing and sight must be ascertained. This is especially important with the elderly, who may have difficulties seeing or hearing that are not immediately obvious.

In the case of elderly people about to be discharged home from hospital (like Mrs Trent – see Case Study 1 on page 107), multidisciplinary health assessments are often made, with the social worker acting as coordinator. Assessments might be made by a physiotherapist, an occupational therapist, a district nurse and a social worker, each of whom will have different areas of concern.

In 1989 a study of Runciman described the factors that different professional groups perceived as important to check in an assessment. The areas to be checked, and their practical applications, were:

- mobility — inside, outside, steps, balance, etc.
- exercise — on exertion, e.g. chest pain, leg pain
- lower limbs — feet, circulation, ankles, ulcers
- skin — pressure areas, itching
- vision — reading, glasses
- hearing — door-bell, conversation, aids
- self-care — washing, bathing, toileting, dressing
- continence — bladder, bowels, day, night, frequency
- house and
- household tasks — garden, heating, hazards, security

• nutrition	diet, appetite, cooking, weight, teeth/dentures
• finance	benefits, pensions
• medication	drugs prescribed/taken, side-effects
• medical history	
• services	voluntary/private, health visitor, GP, home help, meals on wheels
• mental status	memory, orientation, mood, sleep, grief
• attitudes	to health, housing, help, carers
• social support	relatives, friends, neighbours, amount, stress
• aids	walking, toileting, bathroom, kitchen
• communication	telephone, emergency help

ACTIVITY

1 Read Case Study 1 on Ivy Trent (see page 107).

2 Divide into groups and take one role each of:
- physiotherapist;
- occupational therapist;
- district nurse;
- home care worker.

3 Find out what are the responsibilities and special concerns of your profession with regard to the elderly.

4 Refer to the checklist in the text. What questions would you ask Mrs Trent on the home visit? Write a list.

5 Go through each room of her flat – kitchen, toilet and bathroom, bedroom, living room. Think of each part of the day. What help would she need? What aids or equipment could you help her with?

EMOTIONAL WELL-BEING

Those who work in the caring professions notice in the course of their work that there are some people who cope courageously with incredible hardships and difficulties in their lives, while at the other end of the spectrum there are those who 'break down' in the face of a relatively minor crisis. It is though that everyone has their breaking point, but what is it that gives such inner strength to some individuals?

Some psychologists, who believe in nature rather than nurture, would propose that personality types are inherited and inborn. Eysenck and Wilson (1991) wrote:

> It is nothing short of tragic that so many mothers (and perhaps fathers too) worry about the bringing up of their children and blame themselves for anything that seems to have gone wrong, as if their actions in looking after their children were primarily responsible for their character and their abilities and achievements. The truth, of course, is simply that the influence of parents is strictly limited; their major contribution to the future of their child is made when they join their chromosomes and shuffle their genes into the unique pattern that will forever after determine the looks, the behaviour, the personality and the intellect of the child. How much more relaxed the parents could be if only they realized the limitations which nature has put on their later contributions!

But many psychologists and psychiatrists would disagree with this, believing that mental health and strength are due to nurture, particularly in the first years of life (see page 205 in Chapter 4).

THE EFFECTS OF STRESS AND DISTRESS ON THE CLIENT

'Difficult' clients

A client approaching a social care worker may feel one or more of the following: low self-esteem, a feeling of failure, high anxiety, shame, guilt, fear or grief.

By using defence mechanisms, these negative emotions may come across as belligerence or aggression, or perhaps flippancy. Professional workers will be able to interpret this behaviour, at first to themselves, and later, when the time is right, to the client. They will use calming and listening skills (see page 105) to reduce the client's anxiety and lower his or her defences.

The effects of strong emotion

A sudden shock can produce physical and psychological symptoms. Trembling, shaking, temporary loss of memory, sleeplessness and lack of concentration are common symptoms of shock or stress that may be quite long-lasting. See Chapter 4 for a discussion of grief and stress.

Care workers will be aware of the symptoms of stress and realise that the client is not acting in his or her 'normal' manner. They will also know that a time of crisis, when a person is thrown into a state of disorganisation and remembers other times of crisis in his or her life, may also be a significant opportunity for personal growth and change.

Behavioural/emotional needs and life stages

At each life stage an individual has certain emotional and behavioural needs. If these are not met, behavioural disturbances may result. Table 2.2 sets out these stages in schematic form.

ACTIVITY

Refer to the two case studies on pages 107–111 in this chapter.

1 *Ivy Trent*
What are the emotional needs of Mrs Trent?
What behaviour might she show if these are not met?

2 *Tracy Congdon*
What are Tracy's emotional needs?
What behaviour does she show that indicates emotional problems?

3 *Frank North*
What are Frank North's emotional needs?
What behaviour does he show that indicates emotional problems?

Ways of optimising effective interaction

CLIENT RIGHTS AWARENESS AND THE VALUES UNDERPINNING SOCIAL CARE WORK.

The charter of rights for someone receiving a service at home from social services

Most local authorities will draw up their own charter of rights for clients receiving social services, based on the general guidelines outlined in the Citizen's Charter. There are specific government recommendations for certain matters – for example, the document 'Working Together' deals with child abuse, and its guidelines will be adapted to the special circumstances of different localities. The following charter of rights is specific to Surrey Social Services, but may be considered as representative.

1 The right to remain living in your own home if that is what you want.
2 The right to maintain your chosen lifestyle.
3 The right to have your personal dignity respected irrespective of physical or mental disability.
4 The right to be treated as an individual, whatever your physical or mental disability.
5 The right to personal independence, personal choice, personal responsibilities and actions, including acceptance of risk.

Table 2.2 Life stages and emotional/behavioural needs

Life stage	Life event threats	Behavioural needs	Examples of behavioural disturbances if needs are not met
Infant	Frequent changes of carer; indifferent carer, abuse	Security; attachments; physical comfort	Withdrawn; passive
Young child	Neglect; deprivation; abuse (emotional, physical, sexual)	As for infant; also space and permission for play and self-expression in a safe environment. Stimulation, encouragement and friendships	Failure to thrive, clinging, dependent behaviour, indiscriminate friendliness, aggression, enuresis, recurrent nightmares
Adolescent	Peer group pressure into substance abuse, petty crime Family discord or breakdown may lead to delinquency or eating disorders Feeling of failure at school may lead to truancy	Enough freedom for expression of own developing identity but also caring control Friendships, good relationships with adults, encouragement, achievement	Confusion, aggression, moodiness, substance abuse, eating disorders (anorexia nervosa and bulimia), truancy, delinquent behaviour
Adult	Infertility (for those who feel the need for children) Separation and divorce Ill-health Unemployment Mental illness, especially depression Homelessness	Intimate, long-lasting relationships Reproduction and nurturing Employment, which provides identity, security, social contacts and the ability to provide for dependants	Depression Regression Loss of self-esteem Alcoholism Shoplifting Gambling Wife- or husband-battering
Elder	Bereavement and loss Ill-health and loss of mobility Reduced income Isolation	Maintained contacts with family members, social contacts, interests, good health and mobility, sufficient income	Depression Withdrawal Self-neglect

6 The right to personal privacy for yourself, your belongings and your affairs.
7 The right to have cultural, religious, sexual and emotional needs accepted and respected.
8 The right to receive care appropriate to your needs from suitably trained and experienced workers.
9 The right to have, and participate in, regular reviews of your individual circumstances, and to have a friend and adviser present if you so wish.
10 The right to participate as fully as possible in the drawing up of your own care plan.
11 The right to be fully informed about the services provided by the Department, and of any decisions made by the Authority's staff that may affect your personal well-being.
12 The right of access to personal files.
13 The right of access to a formal complaints procedure and to be represented by a friend or adviser if you so wish.
14 The right to be represented by an advocate if you so wish, or are unable to make personal representation through mental incapacity.

Boundaries on these rights

1 **Rights:** In all situations it is social services' policy to respect people's dignity, individuality and confidentiality along with their rights to independence, choice and control over their own lifestyle. Therefore Surrey County Council has produced this Charter of Rights.

2 **Responsibilities:** Your personal choices and actions have consequences which may affect other people. Therefore, as a user of services at home, you are obliged to ensure that others are not disturbed or put at risk by your actions. For example, you have a responsibility to provide a safe working environment for those who enter your home to provide services.

3 **Risks:** It is important to realise that living at home independently brings an element of risk. Some degree of risk is a normal part of life for everyone. Avoidance of risk leads to an unhealthy way of life.

4 **Restrictions:** Some people with severe physical disabilities, learning disabilities, or mental health problems cannot exercise their rights in full. It is essential, though, not to take away their rights unnecessarily – and any restriction will be strictly limited and reviewed regularly.

INDIVIDUALISATION

Individualization is the recognition and understanding of each client's unique qualities and the differential use of principles and methods in assisting each toward a better adjustment. Individualization is based upon the right of human beings to be individuals and to be treated not just as a human being but as *this* human being with his personal differences.

(Felix P. Biestek, 1990)

This value incorporates the principle of freedom from any kind of discrimination.

The role of the social worker

The skill of individualisation requires the following attributes in the care worker:

- freedom from bias and prejudice;
- knowledge of human behaviour, from psychology and medicine – not just from personal experience;
- ability to move at the client's pace;
- empathy – the ability to enter into the feelings of other people;
- ability to keep perspective: the emotional involvement of the care worker should be controlled.

Practical ways of individualising

The care worker may intend to individualise and not do so effectively; following these principles will demonstrate that he or she is doing so in a way the client cannot miss:

- thoughtfulness in details, such as timing appointments to help a mother with schoolchildren;
- privacy in interviews, ensuring that the care worker can give full and undivided attention and reassurance about confidentiality;
- care in keeping appointments;
- preparation for interviews – review the client's record before the interview starts;
- engaging the client – let clients make their own decisions, select their own goals and fill out their own forms, thus stimulating their self-confidence.

PURPOSEFUL EXPRESSION OF FEELINGS

Purposeful expression of feelings is the recognition of the client's need to express his feelings freely, especially his negative feelings. The care worker listens purposefully, neither discouraging nor condemning the expression of those feelings, sometimes even actively stimulating and encouraging them when they are therapeutically useful.

(Felix P. Biestek, 1990)

Benefits to client of purposeful expression

- It relieves tensions and anxiety in the client

who after 'letting off steam' will be able to see his or her problem more clearly.
- The care worker will understand more about the client.
- The client/worker relationship will be strengthened.

Boundaries

Expression of feelings must be limited to those the agency can cope with. For example, deeply disturbed emotions need handling by a psychiatrist.

CONTROLLED EMOTIONAL INVOLVEMENT

The controlled emotional involvement is the care worker's sensitivity to the client's feelings, an understanding of their meaning, and a purposeful, appropriate response to those feelings.

ACCEPTANCE

Acceptance is a principle of action wherein the care worker perceives and deals with the client as he or she really is, including his or her strengths and weaknesses, congenial and uncongenial qualities, positive and negative feelings, constructive and destructive attitudes and behaviour, maintaining all the while a sense of the client's innate dignity and personal worth.

The purpose of acceptance is therapeutic: to aid care workers in understanding each client as they really are, thus making casework more effective; and to help each client free themselves from undesirable defence, so that they feel safe to look at and reveal themselves as they really are, and thus to deal with their problems in a more realistic way.

CLIENT SELF-DETERMINATION

The principle of client self-determination is the practical recognition that clients need, and have a right to, freedom in making their own choices and decisions. Care workers have a corresponding duty to respect that right, recognise that need, and stimulate and help activate that potential for self-direction by helping the client to see and use the available and appropriate resources of the community and of his or her own personality.

The client's right to self-determination, however, is limited by the client's capacity for positive and constructive decision-making, by the framework of civil and moral law, and by the function of the agency.

It is this value which emphasises the need for each individual to maintain his or her own identity, through exercising choice and independence.

The main reasons for enabling client self-determination are:

- to allow the client to regain self-confidence, which may have been lost in the present crisis;
- to allow the client to draw from that self-confidence a renewed ability to solve his or her own problems;
- to enable the client, through making his or her own choices and plans, with the support of the care worker, to experience personal growth and increased maturity.

Four practical ways in which the care worker might enable client self-determination

- Help the client to see his or her problem or need clearly and with perspective. This is done using listening and interview skills.
- Acquaint the client with the relevant sources of help available in the community. The client should know precisely what help is available in the community. But it is up to him or her how far to use it.
- Introduce stimuli that will activate the client's own dormant resources. Through the care worker/client relationship, abilities in the client that had been crushed by the current crisis will be released.
- Create a client/care worker relationship in which the client can grow and work out his or her own problems.

It is unacceptable for care workers to impose plans on a client. A client will make progress in social responsibility, emotion adjustment and personality development only if he or she is allowed to exercise freedom of choice and decision.

The limitations on client self-determination

- Not all clients are equally capable of making their own decisions.
- A client cannot intrude on the rights of others without their consent.
- A client has the right to take some risks with his or her own safety but not with the safety of others.
- A client's plans and decisions should keep within the law.

THE NON-JUDGEMENTAL ATTITUDE

The non-judgemental attitude is based on a conviction that the function of the care worker excludes assigning guilt or innocence, or degree of client responsibility for causing the problems or needs, but does include making evaluative judgements about the attitudes, standards or actions of the client. The attitude, which involves elements of both thought and feeling, is transmitted to the client.

In helping clients it is important to understand their failures and weaknesses, but it is not the function of the care worker to judge.

The care worker provides the non-judgemental atmosphere and within this the client develops the strength to see him or herself objectively, and to do what is necessary for constructive change.

Boundaries

The non-judgemental attitude does not mean indifference to value systems, or to social, legal or moral standards.

CONFIDENTIALITY

Confidentiality is the preservation of secret information concerning the client which is disclosed in the professional relationship. Confidentiality is based upon a basic right of the client; it is an ethical obligation of the care worker and is necessary for an effective service. The client's right, however, is not absolute. Moreover, the client's secret is often shared with other professional persons within the agency and also in other agencies; the obligation then binds all equally.

One way in which 'confidentiality' could be described would be as having to do with people's rights over the property of their secrets. It is useful to make an analogy with material belongings, because this can help to highlight how much worth people attach to information concerning themselves and their lives, and the seriousness of the damage which can occur when their ownership rights in this area are infringed.

It therefore follows that 'to extract a person's secrets from him under false pretences, or to pass them on to others when they have been entrusted in confidence, might constitute a more serious violation of personal rights than the stealing of a material object' (Felix P. Biestek, 1990).

Breach of confidentiality has been likened to theft, but it is more serious. The invasion of privacy resulting from a failure in confidentiality often leads to a greater and more fundamental loss than does theft.

Confidentiality relates directly to the principle of respect for other people.

A client wants to be reassured about confidentiality. But as the case will be recorded, his or her secrets will be known to the typist and the supervisor. The counsellor or care worker is not a freelance worker, but part of a social agency. The client should understand this.

How far this information should be communicated outside the agency is a different matter.

The client should be assured of the following rights:

- Other agencies and individuals should only be consulted with the client's consent (this may be overridden in extreme cases such as that of a child at risk).
- Records should only show information that is essential to provide the service, and in

many instances should be available to the scrutiny of the client.

Boundaries of confidentiality

The client's right to confidentiality is limited by:

- the rights of other individuals;
- the rights of the care worker;
- the rights of the hospital/social agency;
- the rights of society as a whole.

> **ACTIVITY**
>
> The Code of Professional Conduct is issued by the United Kingdom Central Council for Nursing, Midwifery and Health Visiting. It states:
>
> Each registered nurse, midwife and health visitor shall act, at all times, in such a manner as to justify public trust and confidence, to uphold and enhance the good standing and reputation of the profession, to serve the interests of society, and above all to safeguard the interests of individual patients and clients.
>
> Write to the UKCC (for address see list at end of chapter) and ask for a copy of the Code. Read the section on confidentiality.

Anyone working in the health and social care fields is expected to understand and honour scrupulously the requirements of confidentiality. The following extract is an example of the formal commitment to do so that workers in a care institution may be expected to sign.

The following statement has been taken from the DHSS Steering Group on Health Service Information and should be adhered to by all hospital staff:

> 'In the course of your duties you may have access to confidential material about patients, members of staff or other health service business. On no account must information relating to identifiable patients be divulged to anyone other than authorised persons, for example medical, nursing or other professional staff, as appropriate, who are concerned directly with the care, diagnosis and/or treatment of the patient. If you are in any doubt whatsoever as to the authority of a person or body asking for information of this nature you must seek advice from your superior officer. Similarly, no information of a personal or confidential nature concerning individual members of staff should be divulged to anyone without the proper authority having first been given.'

The focal word in the definition of 'confidential' is TRUST. A patient must be able to have complete trust in the hospital and its staff with regards to private and personal information which they have given about themselves. A patient has a right to expect that information given in confidence will be used only for the purpose for which it was given and will not be released to others without their consent.

As a representative of the hospital, on a work placement programme, you are expected to ensure that you:

- Never discuss patients or hospital business with other persons either inside or outside the hospital.
- Never give out information regarding a patient to anyone.
- Always refer persons who are requesting information to your supervisor.

> **ACTIVITY**
>
> Read the following clinical profile and try to answer the questions at the end.
>
> 1 Mrs Irene McGregor is a 55-year-old married woman who lives on a housing estate in the suburbs of a large city. She has been admitted for a hysterectomy related to fibroids.
>
> 2 A routine chest radiograph shows evidence of previous tuberculosis. Other investigations are normal. In the past she has had no serious illness, but 10 years

ago she was investigated for possible epilepsy.

3 She has three children, all of whom are well, but one has recently been suspected of drug-taking. She has told this only to the social worker. Her husband is a postman and she works part-time in a shop. There is an elderly mother-in-law who lives nearby and is visited daily by the family.

4 She is naturally anxious about the operation, and the fact that her eldest son may be involved with drugs has made her particularly anxious about her admission. She is otherwise well adjusted.

- This information, except for that associated with her son, has been obtained from the case-sheet. Who should have access to it?
- How much of each of the four points of information listed above should be shared with members of the professional staff?
- How much should be shared with other members of the team: e.g. porters, receptionists, etc.?
- Do all members of staff need to know all the information?
- During the weekly ward meeting, a member of the nursing staff feels that the patient is more anxious than she should be. How much information about the son should be divulged and openly discussed?

It is sometimes useful, when deciding on who should be given confidential information, to separate people into the following groups:

1 Those who must know.
2 Those who should know.
3 Those who could know.
4 Those who shouldn't know.

A typical team on a medical or surgical ward would include doctors, nurses, social workers, physiotherapists, dieticians, pharmacists and others. Related to this team are secretaries, receptionists, porters and ward maids. These individuals are vital to the working of the team. Look again at Mrs McGregor and the issues and questions which have been raised. Divide the professional groups, the supporting staff, and others into the categories listed above.

Confidentiality, outside the health care team: So far it has been assumed that information about an individual *might* be shared between members of the team. There are circumstances, however, when information about a particular patient is requested by other groups. Consider Mrs McGregor again. Information is requested by the following. Would you divulge it?

- The husband: He asks for information about the medical problems.
- A close friend: A neighbour (female) asks to see the ward sister and requests information about treatment.
- The social services: They are concerned about possible problems at home while the patient is recovering. They want details of the family background.
- The police: Questions are being asked about possible drug problems in the area and they suspect her son.
- The press: They have found out from the police that her son is a possible addict. They telephone you for information.
- Your colleagues: You meet a colleague at a social event. He (or she) is very interested in family problems associated with drug-taking. He asks if you know anyone who might be able to help in this important research project.

These points raise important issues in confidentiality, and you should now be clearer about when, and to whom, you would divulge information.

Computers and records: The introduction of computers and databases has provided a new element in the maintenance of confidentiality.

It has also introduced a new problem, that of access to records by patients. While it has always been possible (but rather difficult) to obtain access to case-sheets, the Data Protection Act makes the provision for this clear. While final decisions about access to computer-based medical information still remain to be made, there are fundamental moral questions which need to be answered.

- Should patients have a right of access to their own medical information?
- Will this prevent the writing down of sensitive information?
- Who else should have access to the information? Should all relatives be allowed to see it?
- What safeguards would you include to make the records confidential?

ACTIVITY

Consider the following dilemmas involving the values underpinning health and social care work. In each case, decide:

- Whose rights are being violated?
- Whose rights should take priority?
- What course of action should be taken?

1 A newly married man comes to see a social worker. He confesses that he recently on one occasion sexually abused his young step-daughter. He is desperate to get help so that this does not happen again. He was himself abused as a child; he has not told his new wife this, nor the fact that he has approached her daughter. He pleads that his wife should not know, fearing that she would have no more to do with him.

2 A teenager is benefiting from a series of counselling sessions in which she is discussing family problems. She reveals that a short while ago she stole something quite substantial from a shop, but swears that she will never steal again.

3 An elderly man is desperate to return from hospital to his own flat which is in a filthy state because of the numerous cats he keeps which have no access to outdoors. His health is frail following a heart attack and his movement limited. Hospital staff are pressing him to go to a residential home for his own well-being and safety, but he has lived in his flat for 50 years and feels that it is his home.

4 A mentally handicapped couple are considered fit to live in the community, and following discharge from hospital are housed in a ground-floor council flat. The woman is more severely handicapped than her husband. There have been complaints from neighbours about dirt and smells. The social worker visits and finds that the flat is very dirty and that the couple's standard of personal hygiene is very low (both have head lice and wear unwashed clothes). There is, however, a little food in the fridge and both husband and wife insist that they are managing. They do not want to move, or be parted.

Conveying the core conditions of counselling

In the process of interaction with the client, conveying the core conditions of counselling, i.e. warmth, understanding, sincerity and the positive value of others, is essential.

Manner is extremely important and includes paralanguage, eye contact, facial expression, gestures and proxemics.

A warm smile and open, welcoming gestures with a friendly tone of voice, will convey warmth and sincerity to an anxious client.

A care worker's manner is one of his or her professional tools and must always be used, even if he or she is rushed and under pressure.

CONVEYING WARMTH

Conveying warmth in the initial stages of the interview is very important. The client may have personal and painful data to reveal and will decide not to do so if the worker is in any way cold and rejecting.

Warmth may be conveyed non-verbally by:

- a warm smile (facial expression);
- open welcoming gestures;
- a friendly tone of voice (paralanguage);
- a confident manner – this reassures the client that something can be done;
- offering physical help – for example a guiding arm to an elderly or distraught person;
- the general appearance of the care worker;
- the physical arrangement of chairs in the interview room;
- calm movements.

And verbally by:

- the use of friendly words that nevertheless show appropriate respect;
- the expression of a desire to be of help;
- a clear explanation of how long the interview will last;
- reassurance about confidentiality;
- a clear assessment at the end of the interview about what has been achieved and the arrangement of a follow-up, if necessary.

CONVEYING UNDERSTANDING

A care worker conveys understanding through empathy, acceptance and a non-judgemental attitude. These are values which underpin social care work and are described in full in the third part of this chapter.

A client often experiences great relief at being able to tell his or her truth without getting an emotional reaction from the other person. This process, sometimes called 'ventilation', lowers anxiety and can, if the worker provides warmth and acceptance, be sufficient in itself to let the client see his or her own solution to the problem without further help. (This is the therapeutic value of the confessional.)

Understanding is also conveyed where the care worker shows knowledge and acceptance of the particular physical, cognitive and social needs of the client. Understanding is also shown when the worker can paraphrase what the client has just said (see pages 98).

CONVEYING SINCERITY

Warmth, understanding and sincerity are all communicated by the use of eye contact, which shows interest and attention.

Sincerity is also conveyed by:

- the worker clearly stating at the outset how long the interview will last;
- reassurance about confidentiality, while explaining its boundaries;
- clear assessment at the end of the interview about what has been achieved.

CONVEYING THE POSITIVE VALUE OF OTHERS

Conveying the positive value of others may be done using the following non-verbal signals:

- smiling;
- eye contact;
- listening skills;
- calm movements;
- open gestures.

Both verbally and non-verbally the following values may be shown through:

- empathy;
- acceptance and a non-judgemental attitude;
- respect for the individual;
- freedom from any type of stereotyping or discrimination;
- assurance of confidentiality, with its boundaries explained;
- encouragement of the client's self-determination, self-respect and dignity;
- conveying warmth, understanding and sincerity and beginning and ending the interview positively.

Positive avoidance measures

Examples of positive avoidance measures are:

- reducing noise;
- minimising distractions;
- sensible arrangement of chairs;
- avoiding stereotyping;
- confirming others' perceptions;
- seeking feedback;
- reflective listening.

SEEKING FEEDBACK, PARAPHRASING AND REFLECTION

The attempt by the carer to try and imagine and understand the world as it appears to the client is an aspect of empathy. This understanding is demonstrated to the client by means of feedback, showing that the carer has understood what it is like to be in the client's position. Techniques used here include paraphrasing and reflection.

Example of paraphrasing

Student: The problem is getting from my technology class, which doesn't end till 3 p.m., in time to catch the bus to get me to the sports centre with the other students.

Counsellor: So there's a real timetabling problem for you here.

Example of reflection

Client: I've been to six interviews and still haven't got a job. I always prepare myself. I don't know what's happening.

Counsellor: You have obviously tried very hard and are upset and frustrated by what has happened.

In paraphrasing, the carer summarises the content of what the client has said, demonstrating that it has been fully understood. In this way, the carer can check that he or she has indeed got the essential gist of what the client said; and the client will be helped by having a perhaps rambling story presented concisely and clearly back to them.

In reflection, the carer reflects back feelings to the client, in this way clarifying the emotional content of what has been communicated, thereby helping the client in self-knowledge by perceiving the effect the problem is having on the client. In this way the carer also reflects empathy.

In practice, paraphrasing the content and reflecting the emotional message are not easily distinguishable.

ACTIVITY

Rank each reply below according to whether you think the response is highly empathetic, moderately empathetic or non-empathetic.

1 Paraphrasing

Statement from client:

I'm frightened about the prospect of leaving home to go to college. I realise that it's necessary and I'm even a little excited by the thought, but deep down it feels very scary.

Reply from counsellor:

(a) You're trying to weigh up the pros and cons of leaving home.

(b) You are both attracted and repelled by the prospect in store.

(c) Right now, you're on the horns of a dilemma.

(d) There appears to be an uncomfortable decision facing you.

(e) Leaving home is never easy.

Statement from client:

I'm worried about my father. He's not been well for a long time and now he seems to be getting depressed about his health.

Reply from counsellor:

(a) Parents can become a real trial as they get older.

(b) There's nothing you can do; best to get on with your own life.

(c) Your father's health and emotional state appear to be causing you a lot of concern.

(d) You're concerned about your father's long-term health and well-being.

(e) It's been a long time since your father was in good health and this is worrying you.

2 Reflection

Statement from client:

I can't make up my mind about whether I really want this job. I don't feel confident, but my spouse is pushing me hard to accept.

Reply from counsellor:

(a) It seems like you are under a lot of pressure at the present time and feeling very uncertain. It feels like a very uncomfortable position to be in.

(b) I know just what it's like. I was in exactly the same situation as you last year. Men/women are all the same.

(c) Don't worry. Leave matters to settle for a day or two and I'm sure that you will arrive at the correct decision.

(d) Your spouse seems to be making life very difficult for you. I wonder why?

(e) It sounds as though you don't really know what to do for the best.

DEMONSTRATING SKILLS OF INTERPERSONAL INTERACTION

Support needed for effective interaction

PROMOTING COMMUNICATION WITHIN GROUPS

A group comes into being when a number of people share a common goal which they know cannot be achieved by any one of them alone.

Individuals in a small group are still communicating face-to-face, but everybody's behaviour is influenced by the larger number of participants. Many psychological experiments have been performed in the area of group pressure, and collective responsibility, and readers are referred to the studies of obedience conformity and bystander apathy which may be found in any psychology textbook and which provide useful insights into group interaction.

Types of groups

In the health and social care settings there are many group formations. Two major types are:

- *multidisciplinary groups*, e.g. doctor, police officer, teacher, social worker and perhaps a parent at a conference on a child 'at risk'; or a doctor, physiotherapist, ward sister, occupational therapist, dietician and social worker at a ward meeting (see Case Study 1 on Mrs Ivy Trent at the end of the chapter);
- *groups of people in similar situations*, e.g. groups of people with similar diseases or disabilities, or people who have applied to be foster-parents awaiting their first child.

Each professional group has its own perception of a patient's problems and, if rigidly held, this can act as a barrier to communication with members of the other professions, to the detriment of the patient. It is important that the social worker, who often coordinates multidisciplinary assessments, is able to communicate clearly in speech and writing without the use of jargon, and is able to understand the jargon of each profession in order, if necessary, to interpret it for other members of the team. Small details can have important consequences in these cases and should not be misunderstood.

ACTIVITY

M. Preston-Shoot in 1987 identified the following types of group:
- social or recreational groups;
- group psychotherapy;
- group counselling;
- educational groups;
- social treatment groups;
- discussion groups;
- self-help groups;
- social action groups;
- self-directed groups.

Think of a group that would come under each of these headings.

The development of a group

A group which is assembled for a certain purpose and with regular meetings proposed develops through certain stages. Theorists have named these stages differently, but all are agreed on what happens at each stage. Tuckman and Jenson (1977) called these stages of group development:

- forming;
- storming;
- norming;
- performing;
- adjourning.

The group leader

The role of the group leader will vary slightly according to the type of group, but always involves the difficult task of being sometimes central, sometimes motivating others, sometimes in the background, and then back in the centre again.

The forming stage

In this stage members of the group move from finding out information about the group (orientation and exploration) in parallel communication directed at the leader, to increased communication with each other. The group and the leader are tested by each member to see if trust can be established.

Anyone joining a group will be aware that they will have to sacrifice individuality, and they will want to know whether the benefits of joining a group will compensate for this. The leader will take this and any similar opportunity to point out that the members of the group, by sharing their interests and problems, are in a position to understand and thereby help one another.

In the early meetings, a group leader will need to be able to perform the following tasks:

- give a short presentation of himself or herself;
- ask each member to give a similar presentation;
- go over the information that was given to members before they joined the group;
- amend any aims and agreements;
- acknowledge initial uncertainties;
- get each person to say what they hope to gain from the group;
- summarise issues as they are presented;
- establish norms for listening and accepting;
- help the group interaction: 'Does anyone else feel like this?';
- play the part of the absent member by putting into words what people may want to say but are not yet ready to risk;
- show concern for each individual;
- when asked questions, sometimes say: 'Does anyone else know the answer to that?'.

The storming stage

'Storming' is the period when people argue about how they see the group's function and structure. People reveal their differences and their personalities; some may be overbearing and disruptive. At this stage the question each group member is asking internally is no longer 'Do I belong?' but 'Do I have any influence here?'. Pairings and subgroups might have formed among members of the group. Underlying the overt communications, a struggle for power and control is taking place, and there is a tendency to polarise around certain issues.

The leader and the group are tested further. The group may break down at this stage if the leader does not provide enough security, while individual members query if they are going to get what they came for.

At this stage the group leader must:

- keep calm in the face of conflict between members of the group or towards the leader;
- not retaliate when his/her authority is challenged; the challenge may be due to ambivalence about membership or a transference reaction;
- model acceptance and openly recognise that people are different;
- not give particular attention to difficult or isolated members;
- try to choose the right time to intervene to

encourage progress and the right time to keep quiet;
- start handing over responsibilities to the membership.

The norming stage

When this stage is reached it means that group cohesion has been established. Intimate and personal opinions may be expressed by members to each other. People start to look for 'affection', i.e. signs that they are accepted by the wider circle. Sharing information, cooperation and decision-making by consensus leads to action.

Members identify with the group and its future; there is a growing *esprit de corps* and 'we' talk develops.

At this stage rules for meetings are established. Norms are set up, specifying for example the kind of behaviour group members may expect from each other. Some groups opt for a business-like atmosphere, others find a more relaxed atmosphere appropriate. There will be some ritual ownership of seats, regular high attendance and a feeling of some exclusivity. Such norms are likely to make it difficult for new members to join the group. A lack of conformity to the group's norms can lead to scapegoating or group pressure to conform. New leadership may come from within the group and this may result in altering basic group norms.

The tasks for the group leader at this stage are to:

- retreat from a directing role into a listening, following one, therefore letting people help each other;
- facilitate the group by observing the group and commenting on what seems to be happening, offering ideas of his or her own and asking the group what their perceptions are;
- ask him or herself, and perhaps the group, what is going on here? What is this issue really all about? An apparently superficial and irrelevant topic, discussed heatedly, might hide a deeper issue.

The performing stage

When performing occurs the group is working together to solve problems. It is no longer dependent on the leader, who moves into the background. The leader's tasks now are to:

- observe how the members of the group communicate with each other and deal with the tasks before them;
- show interest and express praise and appreciation of efforts (positive reinforcement);
- continue to model confidence, attitudes and problem-solving.

The adjourning stage

This is the ending stage that follows the achievement of a task. All groups have to end at some time, or they may cease to be productive. Members will feel a sense of loss but also a sense of achievement. At this stage the leader becomes more active again. His or her tasks now are to:

- set goals for the time left in partnership with the group;
- review experiences, emphasising gains as well as feelings of loss;
- mention and encourage interests outside the group;
- help the group return to the planning stage if they want to continue, but with some other purpose;
- evaluate the sessions and ask for feedback.

Different levels of participation in groups

Robert Bales in 1955 studied the performance of small, initially leaderless, discussion groups. He made the following observations:

- People do not participate to equal degrees. One or two members contribute much more than the others.
- The active members give information and offer opinions.
- The less active members confine themselves to agreeing or disagreeing, or asking for information.

- Group participants distinguish between the person they think the most influential and the person they like best.

Leadership styles

There has been much research into the leadership role in group performance, and four distinct styles have been described.

The autocratic style

One member, usually the chairperson, holds the floor most of the time. He or she imposes his or her will on the others in the group, who may resent being 'steamrollered' and may lose interest in issues where their suggestions are not welcomed. A fair amount of work can, however, be achieved.

Example of this style in a health or social care setting: A ward meeting where time is limited and several patients' needs must be discussed. The meeting would be led by the consultant, senior doctor or ward sister.

The laissez-faire style

Here a group does not have a leader, but may have a care worker who acts as a facilitator. Decisions are taken, but no one is chosen to carry them out. The meeting may be fun but little is achieved.

Example: A group meeting primarily for comparing notes and mutual social support – perhaps a group of first-time mothers with their babies.

The democratic style

This recognises that everyone has a contribution to make. Leaders are elected for a term, or the leadership role rotates among all the members. A democratic group is one that takes the decision-making processes very seriously. Where unanimity is impossible, a vote is taken.

Example: Ongoing case conferences about children 'at risk', deciding whether they should be taken into care.

The collective style

A collective will avoid leadership roles altogether and work as a team of equals arriving at unanimity. In the health and social care context, a care worker might be present to act as a facilitator. This style entails long group discussions, but once decisions are taken, everyone feels committed to carry them out.

Example: A collective style might be chosen by a group of people with a certain disease or disability who feel the general public should be more aware of their needs.

Factors which inhibit interpersonal interaction in groups

Distractions

Distractions which would interrupt the development of the group might include:

- outside intermittent noise (aircraft, pneumatic drill, chairs being pushed around on the floor above);
- constant knocking at the door – someone wanting to speak to a group member;
- telephone ringing – as above;
- group members coming and going all at different times;
- one group member leaning out of the window to talk to people outside;
- one group member distracting the others by silly behaviour.

Some of these potential pitfalls can be avoided by careful choice of venue. The leader can ask the group to solve the other problems itself.

Irrelevant topics

Sometimes a group may heatedly and at length discuss a topic that seems irrelevant to the task in hand. Advanced group-work skills enable the leader to see the real meaning of the apparently irrelevant topic and explain to the group how this topic links to the main task.

Dominating member

One person may be aggressive and outspoken, with the rest hiding their feelings so as not to be different or unpopular.

The leader can point out that what the outspoken member is saying is felt by a lot of people, even though they may not admit it. The leader can explain that though some

Figure 2.3 Distracting behaviour

people may fear conflict, it does occur, and it is important to have the courage to confront it. If the leader does not handle the dominator in the group, members will start to be absent, or lose their tempers.

Blocking other people's contributions
The problem with allowing someone to dominate a group is that this stops others with useful things to say from contributing. Intervention has to take place early on to prevent group structure hardening.

Stimulating silent members counteracts the dominance of the voluble member as well as making the group structure a more functional one. The leader should thank the monopoliser for all his or her contributions and state clearly that he or she would like to hear everyone's point of view.

Manipulation
At the other extreme from the dominator, a person may manipulate a group by remaining silent. Some groups resent this, believing that the person is quietly judging them or not sharing. The leader should ask pleasantly for a contribution from a silent member, thus modelling respect for each member. Conveying an interest in hearing from people can also be done non-verbally with a touch, gesture or eye contact.

The group may be manipulated by any of its members, including the leader, if they have a hidden agenda for the group.

Facilitating group work

Assertiveness
Assertive behaviour facilitates communications in groups and therefore it is useful if the leader explains the principles of assertion to certain groups at the outset.

Assertiveness in an individual or group situation may be defined as standing up for your basic rights and beliefs, without isolating those of others, and making your behaviour 'match' your feelings. It is distinct from both passive and aggressive behaviour.

Those who behave passively:

- allow others to make decisions for them;
- feel helpless, powerless, inhibited, nervous and anxious;

- rarely express feelings;
- have little self-confidence;
- do best when following others;
- are fearful of taking the initiative;
- feel sorry for themselves to the point of martyrdom.

Those who behave aggressively are:

- very expressive, to the point of humiliating and deprecating others;
- obnoxious, vicious, egocentric;
- able to make others feel devastated by an encounter with them;
- giving out the message that they are OK but the other person definitely is not.

If you are assertive in your behaviour, you:

- are expressive with your feelings, without being obnoxious;
- are able to state views and desires directly, spontaneously and honestly;
- feel good about yourself and others too;
- respect the feelings and rights of other people;
- can evaluate a situation, decide how to act, then act without reservation;
- are true to yourself;
- value winning or losing little compared with the value of expressing yourself and choosing for yourself;
- may not always achieve your goals, but the resolution isn't always as important as the actual process of asserting yourself;
- are able to say what you have to say, whether it is positive or negative, leaving the other person's dignity intact.

Most people are assertive at some times with some people, but it is possible to learn to be assertive in situations which cause stress.

ACTIVITY

Make an assertiveness self-assessment table. Each group member can make a hierarchy of the least and most anxiety-provoking situations for them.

Then make a daily log of successful assertive interactions.

Non-verbal techniques of assertion in the group situation include:

- a good eye contact;
- confident posture, standing or sitting comfortably;
- talking in a strong, steady voice;
- not clenching one's fist and not pointing one's finger.

Assertive verbal behaviour includes:

- avoiding qualifying words (such as 'maybe', 'only', 'just');
- avoiding disqualifying phrases (such as 'I'm sure this isn't important but');
- avoiding attacking phrases (such as those that begin with 'you'; substitute assertive phrases that use 'I' language, e.g. 'I feel . . .'.

Other assertive behaviours to practise in the group situation are:

- the 'broken record' – calm repetition of the assertive message;
- 'fogging' – accept criticism comfortably without being defensive;
- 'negative enquiry': purposely invite criticism (this prevents manipulation);
- silence, and listening reflectively.

Adapting communication to other physical and cognitive abilities and individuality

As in the one-to-one situation (see the first part of this chapter), the care worker or leader assesses the abilities and needs of the group members and communicates appropriately.

For example, with a group of elderly people, some of whom are partially deaf and some of whom are visually impaired, communications might have to be both written and spoken, with non-verbal gesturing increased.

Children, those with a poor grasp of English and the mentally handicapped are other examples of groups where the leader would specially adapt his or her methods of communication.

Supportive skills

Warmth, understanding and sincerity are supportive skills. These are conveyed by the leader in the group situation by: modelling respect for each member of the group; assertiveness (verbal and non-verbal); confidence; attitudes; and problem-solving.

Humour can be used to relieve tension but must not involve teasing.

ACTIVITY **W**

Practise group work in the classroom by using the case studies of Ivy Trent and Tracy Congdon (in this chapter) for role-play.

In the course of study, you may do a project in groups, for example a video project. Each participant can analyse the development of this group.

On work experience, any meeting of professionals which the student attends could be used to analyse group communication.

Students should prepare in advance of their analysis:

- a record sheet
- a sociogram
- an analysis grid

to record who communicates with whom and what contribution each member makes.

Discuss ways in which you could improve your own interaction skills.

PROMOTING INTERACTION BETWEEN INDIVIDUALS

Environmental factors which encourage effective communication are described earlier in this chapter (see page 80).

The initial interview between health/social care worker and patient/client

The first interview with a client is of crucial importance. The client may well be in a state of acute anxiety and distress, and may, depending on the problem, feel shame about asking for help at all. The way in which the worker handles the initial interview will therefore determine whether the client will receive help and whether he or she will return. From the point of view of the health or social care worker, the purpose of the first interview is threefold:

- *screening*, to find out whether the person is eligible for the service offered;
- *information gathering*, involving the amassing of concrete facts about the situation and what led to it;
- *assessment or 'diagnosis'* of the problem and assessment of the client/patient – general physical health, personality strengths and weaknesses, and the strength of his or her social support network in the community.

Care workers will naturally take in first impressions from the posture, dress, manner and speech of a client. But their professional training will have taught them the importance of self-knowledge, so that they will be aware of any stereotypes and prejudices they might hold, and so be able to keep an open mind (see Chapter 1). People are far too complex to be summed up rapidly, and though workers might make a tentative assessment of a client's personality, they will be prepared to change and adapt it as the interview, and subsequent interviews, progress.

Workers should be well acquainted with the physical, social and psychological needs of the various age-groups (Chapters 3 and 4), and will have specialised knowledge of some of these, depending on the worker's profession. They should be aware that at a time of acute anxiety people will look, dress and act differently from normal, that they must use listening skills (see below) and that clients who have painful material to reveal may talk about something else entirely, only to reveal the true nature of the trouble just as they are leaving.

Active listening and responding

On the whole we are poor listeners. Research shows that we tend to listen in short 30-second spurts before losing attention. We tend to hear items we are interested in and not attend to others. If we are bored and if we dislike the speaker's personality, mannerisms, accent or appearance, we may 'switch off', and follow more interesting thoughts of our own.

Active listening, the listening required in a caring context, calls for concentration; it is hard work and tiring.

Eye contact

Typically the interviewee, the person talking, looks away at times, then looks back now and then to check that the interviewer is still attending.

The listener's eye contact tends to be stronger.

Posture

The listener should keep the body and hands neat and relaxed.

An occasional nod acts as positive reinforcement, i.e. it can encourage the client when he or she is saying something useful or helpful.

Interview skills

The '5WH Test' is a useful standby formula to obtain information in a fact-finding interview. This stands for sentences that start with why (use this sparingly), who, what, when and where? A sixth useful question word is how? Sensitive use of these key words can elicit a lot of fundamental information.

For example: what is the problem, when did it start, who could help, where should we begin to sort it out, how have you managed so far?

Effective counsellors should demonstrate the following seven qualities.

1 *Empathy or understanding*: the effort to see the world through the other person's eyes.
2 *Respect*: responding in a way which conveys a belief in the other's ability to tackle the problem.
3 *Concreteness or being specific*, so that the interviewee can reduce confusion about what he/she means.
4 *Self-knowledge and self-acceptance*. The interview should have these qualities and should be ready to help others to gain them.
5 *Genuineness*: being real in a relationship.
6 *Congruence*: so that the words we use match our body language.
7 *Immediacy*: dealing with what is going on in the present moment of the counselling session, as a sample of what is going on in someone's everyday life.

The skills of interviewing may be broken down into 20 points or 'micro-skills'. Skills 1–13 are the more basic skills of interviewing:

1 Let a person finish talking without reacting.
2 Be able to reflect back accurately to the interviewee the content of what they have said and their feelings.
3 Be able to paraphrase what the interviewee has just said.
4 Be able to summarise what has been said in order to move the interview forward.
5 Be able to define your own role clearly to the interviewee.
6 Be able to use open questions, rather than closed questions which lead to a yes or no answer and tend to close the topic.
7 Be able to use prompts to encourage the person to continue, especially if an important area has been reached and the interviewee suddenly goes quiet.
8 Be able to tolerate silences of about five seconds. Silences are often the client's best thinking times, in which she/he is deciding what is the best thing to do.
9 Be able to control your own anxiety at what the client is revealing, which may strike some personal chord with you, and be able to relax.
10 Be able to provide direction and keep the interview in focus.
11 Be able to set mutual goals.
12 Be able to discuss and generate alternative plans of action.
13 Be able to begin, sustain and end the interview well.

Skills 14–20 are more advanced skills, and time and practice are needed to develop them.

14 Be able to draw out feelings from the interviewee.
15 Be able to offer tentative understanding and interpretation of what has been happening.
16 Be able to see how the interviewee affects your own emotions.
17 Be able to focus on the 'here and now' as well as 'there and then'.
18 Be able to recognise and confront ambivalence and inconsistencies.
19 Be able to tolerate painful topics.
20 Be able to evaluate the costs and gains of what was achieved.

ACTIVITY

A In this task you will learn what it feels like *not* to be listened to.

1 Divide into groups of three.

2 One of the group talks to the other two on a subject, for example 'one good thing that has happened to me this week'.

3 The other two listen intently for one minute. They then switch off and stop listening until given a sign to stop the exercise.

4 Repeat the exercise twice with each member of the group taking the role of the speaker.

After this exercise, you should each answer the following questions:

- For the listeners – was it easy or difficult to stop listening?
- For the speaker – how did the two students show with their body language that they had stopped listening?
- What did it feel like to be listened to intently?
- What did it feel like not to be listened to?
- What do you think makes a good listener?

B In this task, you will attempt to tap into the emotion behind a person's words.

1 In groups of three, each talk in turn on a topic, for example 'if I could change one thing about myself'.

2 The two listeners listen intently and observe the body language of the speaker, trying to recognise the emotion behind the words.

Case Study 1: Ivy Trent

Mrs Ivy Trent is 76 years old and a widow. She has had a stroke and is now in a wheelchair. She is remaining in hospital while her future is considered. She is rather deaf. Her progress is slow, but medical staff think she will be able to walk with aids in time. She is rather afraid of going home and managing alone. She lives alone in a low-rise block of council flats, on the first floor. There are working lifts. She has one good neighbour/friend. Her daughter lives quite near and visits once a week. Her son lives a long way away but could offer some financial help. Mrs Trent feels that her children should help more. They haven't even suggested that she should live with them.

HOSPITAL STAFF

The *consultant* has done what can be done medically for Mrs Trent. Now it is time for her to leave hospital and continue physiotherapy as an out-patient. He urgently needs the bed for new cases.

The *ward sister* agrees with the doctor that Mrs Trent ought to leave hospital. She has become quite 'institutionalised' – she depends on ward routine. The ward sister thinks that Mrs Trent likes the security of being in hospital. She finds her rather demanding.

The *occupational therapist* has noticed that Mrs

Trent's progress is slow physically but that she has the strength to start walking again once the will is there. Mrs Trent has enjoyed occupational therapy sessions, chatting with the other patients, and her right hand has improved sufficiently for her to try various crafts. She has also practised household tasks from her wheelchair – boiling a kettle, making tea and toast, boiling an egg. The occupational therapist feels that perhaps Mrs Trent would enjoy a day care centre if there is one locally.

The *physiotherapist* finds that Mrs Trent's progress has been rather slow. She doesn't seem all that motivated. But the physiotherapist is convinced that in time, with continued physiotherapy, Mrs Trent will be able to walk with a tripod or a zimmer frame. Out-patient physiotherapy is available.

FRIENDS AND RELATIVES

Mrs Trent's *daughter*, Mrs Baker, lives nearby and will visit once a week, but she is married with children, and has a job, and is very busy. Her relationship with her mother has not always been that good. She says very strongly that she cannot have her mother to live with her, it would not work (though she does not say this directly to her mother). However, she will continue to visit once a week. Her children like to see their grandmother.

Mrs Trent's *son*, Mr Trent, lives a long way away. He cannot have his mother to stay with him (he makes various excuses). But he can give a little financial help – enough for some aids around the flat, perhaps an electric wheelchair. He can only stay around for a few more days while his mother's future is decided, because of the pressure and demands of work.

Mrs Smith, an *elderly neighbour and friend*, can go round for a chat every day and make a cup of tea. She and Mrs Trent have been friends for years. But she would be too frail to lift Mrs Trent if she fell.

SERVICES

The *home care service* provides help with personal care, such as help with getting up, washing and dressing. Care at home is available seven days a week, as well as evenings and weekends. The personal care worker will sometimes give practical help with shopping or cooking.

The *meals on wheels organiser* can have frozen or hot meals delivered to the home five days a week. What about the weekends?

The *day care centre* provides company and activities and helps clients cope with day-to-day problems that might arise at home. Transport can be arranged. Chiropody and hairdressing are available. Day care can be provided one or two days a week including weekends.

The *district nurse* will call once a week at first to help the patient with any incontinence and the prevention of pressure sores.

STAGES IN PLANNING MRS TRENT'S DISCHARGE FROM HOSPITAL AND FUTURE CARE

1 At a multidisciplinary ward meeting, the consultant, ward sister, physiotherapist, occupational therapist and social worker give their assessment of the patient.
2 The social worker talks to Mrs Trent. She cannot stay in hospital; what does she really want to do?
3 The social worker talks to relatives – Mrs Trent's son and daughter – to hear their views.
4 Home visit with patient. Present at this multidisciplinary meeting will be the social worker (acting as coordinator), the physiotherapist, the occupational therapist, Mrs Trent and her elderly neighbour. Calling in briefly will be the home care organiser, meals on wheels organiser and the district nurse. A thorough physical assessment of the patient in her own home will be made and suggestions for aids and gadgets to help her will be put forward by the physiotherapist and occupational therapist. A careful plan, going through every hour of the patient's day, will be made and special plans will be made for

Sundays and bank holidays when services may not be available. A decision will be taken whether Mrs Trent could cope alone while still in her wheelchair, or whether discharge should be postponed until she can take several steps unaided.

Case Study 2: Tracy Congdon (*suitable for role-play*)

Characters involved in the inquiry into the future of Tracy Congdon, aged 8:

Jean North	Tracy's mother
Frank North	Jean's husband and Tracy's stepfather
William Beatty	Tracy's uncle and previous foster-father
Susan Beatty	Jean's sister and Tracy's aunt and previous foster-mother
Alison Greene	Tracy's teacher at Harville Junior School
Terry Hill	social services

THE SITUATION

Frank and Jean North have been married for one year. They have taken their six children (three each) from previous marriages out of care, with the council's approval of course, and are living in a council house in Harville. Tracy, who is the subject of this inquiry, used to live with the Beattys, who took her when she was nine months old, when Jean left her first husband, Alan Congdon, Tracy's father. Mrs Beatty is Jean's sister. Tracy is now 8 years old and has been at home with Frank and Jean for a year.

The family appear to live quite happily together, but neighbours have gossiped about Tracy's appearance. They say she frequently has bruises and a black eye; she has been seen carrying heavy sacks of shopping up the steep hill to her home; and one neighbour is reported as seeing all the North children except Tracy being bought ice-cream. One of the children ate his ice and gave Tracy the dry cornet. Frank North has been heard shouting and swearing in the house. He used to drink regularly and rather heavily. Jean North is quiet and withdrawn, but has no time for the 'authorities'.

Nevertheless, the North family is now complete again, and with Tracy they might hope to resume normal life.

THE BRIEF

You are all attending a Social Services Department meeting held to consider the case.

It is the brief of the reporting groups to interview each character and to decide whether Tracy should be returned to care, or whether she should remain at home. In the latter case you may make recommendations as to future action (regular social worker visits, etc.). Each member of the group should take notes on the progress of the interviews, and one members should be elected to report on these and to communicate to the rest of the class the decision of the group. Remember that whatever you decide will have a lasting impact on the life of this child.

Your only concern is for the health and well-being of Tracy.

SOME THOUGHTS TO HELP YOU

It may be detrimental to move Tracy again; she has been in this environment for one year and will only just be settling in.

The natural bond of blood between mother and child has always been regarded by the courts as important, and it has been their practice to encourage families to live together wherever possible, provided that the child's life does not appear to be in danger.

There is no positive evidence of ill-treatment; but hearsay suggests that Tracy might be punished harshly, and that she is more familiar with the Beattys.

Terry Hill is a qualified and experienced social worker.

There are two main alternatives: (a) leave her at home under the eye of the social services, or (b) return her to the Beattys. You may, though, recommend she be placed in council care under a care order.

Remember: You must be able to justify your decision, with reference to the characters you have interviewed. Do not try to trip them up with questions about intricate details of family life; you should judge them by their feelings about Tracy, their past record and your assessment of their reliability in the future.

THE CHARACTERS

Jean North

You are 38 years old and have been married once before. You and Frank, the three children from your first marriage and the three from Frank's first marriage, aged between 1 and 11, live quite happily together. You are not over-houseproud, but the home is kept reasonably clean and the children are all well fed. You do not go out to work. The only problem is that Frank drinks rather heavily at times and then picks on your daughter Tracy. He does not mean to do this, but appears not to be able to control himself. Tracy is rather an annoying child. She does not eat properly, wets her bed, is moody and quiet. She day-dreams a lot and does not immediately do what she is told. You insist, however, that she should not return to your sister's home, as a family should stick together and a girl's place is with her mother. You must persuade the committee of this. The neighbours are nasty-minded and have spread rumours of the ill-treatment of Tracy deliberately to cause trouble. Tracy's teacher, Miss Greene, is just as bad – school is a waste of time anyway, the children just play with sand all day. The social services have no business to interfere with your private life. Tracy must stay with you.

Frank North

You are 42 years old and have been married once before, your first wife having divorced you. You are now quite happy with Jean, and you and she, the three children from your first marriage and Jean's three, live on your wages as a factory-hand. In the past you have shown a weakness for drink and, when drunk, tend towards violence. However, you mean to turn over a new leaf, to work harder and to look after your family better. You try very hard to treat all the children alike, but somehow Tracy gets on your nerves. You tend to smack her more often that the others but you have never really hurt her. You hope very much that the family can be kept together so that a stable home can be built up. It would break Jean's heart to lose Tracy now, and you must convince the committee that you and she are good parents.

You also strongly resent the interference of busybodies like the social services people, your sister-in-law and her husband, and so on. 'Live and let live' is your motto.

William and Susan Beatty

Susan is Jean North's sister, and the two of you cared for Tracy from when she was nine months old, when Jean divorced her first husband, Alan Congdon. Tracy's return to her mother one year ago caused you and the child great distress. Until then she had been a normal, happy girl. Now, on the very few occasions Jean has let you see her (the three of you are hardly on speaking terms), she has been quiet and looked depressed. She always seems to be crying. You have heard from neighbours that she is ill-treated; you know that Tracy's stepfather, Frank, drinks heavily and is a 'bad lot'. You cannot understand what Jean sees in him. You are very anxious that Tracy should come back to you and to what you regard as her real home, and you will go to any lengths to achieve this.

Alison Greene

You have been Tracy's teacher at Harville Junior for two years. When she first came to you she seemed a normal, happy child. Her foster-parents, Mr and Mrs Beatty, though not very 'bright', were interested in her education and clearly looked after her well. However, when Tracy returned to her real mother, all that changed. She lost weight, became quieter and sadder, and was often absent without excuse. Mrs North takes no interest in the school and is not concerned for Tracy's education, although this is not unusual in the best of families.

You are convinced that Tracy is ill-treated at home and have mentioned this often to the Education Welfare Officer. He has told you that this information has been passed on to Terry Hill who is in charge of Tracy's case, but nothing else has happened about it. You are very worried about Tracy, but have no evidence to support your beliefs.

Terry Hill

You work for the Harville Social Services Department and you are responsible for Tracy Congdon, aged 8. One year ago you were responsible for returning her, against her will, to her mother and stepfather, under a court decision. However, she seems to have settled down reasonably well. On your fairly infrequent visits to the house, you have thought she looked pale and perhaps rather thin, but otherwise well cared for. You have heard rumours from neighbours about Tracy being ill-treated, but have no evidence that these are true; the area is well known for its gossips and scandal-mongers. You know nothing against the stepfather, Frank North, except that he has been 'short' with you on your visits. He does not like social workers interfering in his private life – but then, few people do.

You have over 60 other cases to deal with, and among these Tracy's is far from the most urgent. The time taken to investigate her case in detail might be better spent saving old people's lives (from the cold) and dealing with urgent child abuse cases where lives are in danger. In your experience, this sort of minor family problem sorts itself out as the child settles down. It always takes some time to get used to the change, but it is worth it in the end to see a child with her real mother.

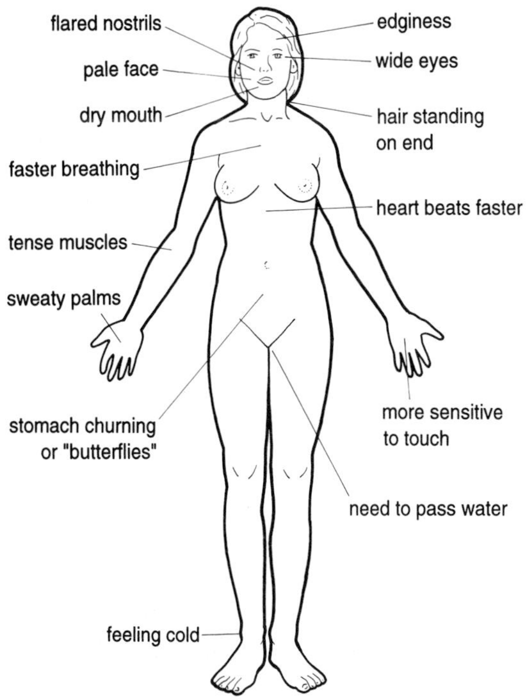

Figure 2.4 Short-term effects of stress

ANALYSING METHODS OF INTERACTING WITH CLIENTS IN HEALTH AND SOCIAL CARE

Effects of care settings on clients

Research has shown that any significant changes in our lives can be a source of STRESS; this is because we have to adjust and adapt to change. The body responds to a stressor in a number of ways (see Figures 2.4 and 2.5). Most of us have experienced the short-term effects of stress:

- feeling 'butterflies' or a churning sensation in the stomach before an examination or an interview;
- sweaty palms or the feeling of the hairs on the back of the neck standing up when in a frightening situation.

These responses to a stressor prepare our body for quick action – the 'fight' or 'flight' reaction. After responding to a threat, the person often says 'I don't know where I found the strength to run – my legs turned to jelly at first and my throat went dry'. The release of adrenaline and other hormones into the blood enables us to act rapidly to deal with the event.

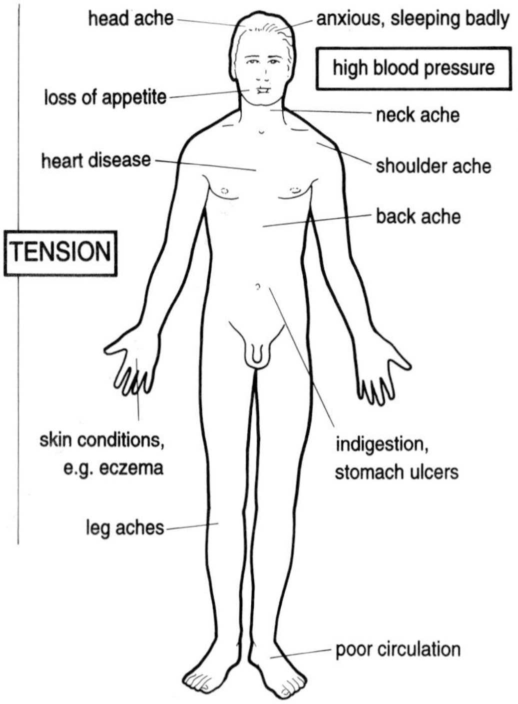

Figure 2.5 Long-term effects of stress

ADMISSION TO HOSPITAL

For many people admission to hospital, even when it is planned, is a stressful event. However welcoming the staff, the patient will probably experience any or all of the following stressors:

- loss of identity;
- unexpected events, if admission is as a result of an accident or sudden illness;
- unpleasant symptoms, e.g. pain or vomiting;
- loss of function, e.g. loss of mobility or sensation;
- loneliness;
- unfamiliar surroundings and relationships;
- altered status and role.

ACTIVITY **W**

See how many stressors you can identify in a patient or client. Record your observations, remembering to preserve confidentiality.

There are many ways in which a carer can reduce the harmful effects of these stressors:

- Give patients information about their environment and what will happen to them. However busy a ward is, time must be allowed to welcome patients; to show them where their 'home' will be and where they can find facilities, e.g. toilet, telephone, assistance.
- Promote understanding of the patient's physical and psychological symptoms. Medical jargon should be translated into simple-to-understand language.
- Offer treatment to alleviate symptoms. Many carers now appreciate the benefit of a more holistic approach and can offer massage, aromatherapy and other relaxation techniques.
- Offer support and companionship with others. Most patients gain valuable support from those with similar problems. 'A problem shared is a problem halved.'
- Suggest different and more positive ways of perceiving what is happening to the patient.
- Provide aids to increase physical strength and functioning. Physiotherapists and occupational therapists are trained in methods of enabling patients to regain function following a stroke or visiting the patient's home prior to discharge to install physical aids such as grip rails in the bathroom.

It is essential that *all* advice given to patients is closely monitored by trained personnel.

RELATIVES UNDER STRESS

Most of the stressors described above are felt equally by relatives, who may be unable to visit their loved one as often as they would wish and who perceive hospital as a strange and threatening environment.

Carers can minimise their stress:

- simply by showing relatives that the patient is being cared for as well as possible;
- by explaining everything that is being done for the patient;
- by asking the relatives how they are feeling.

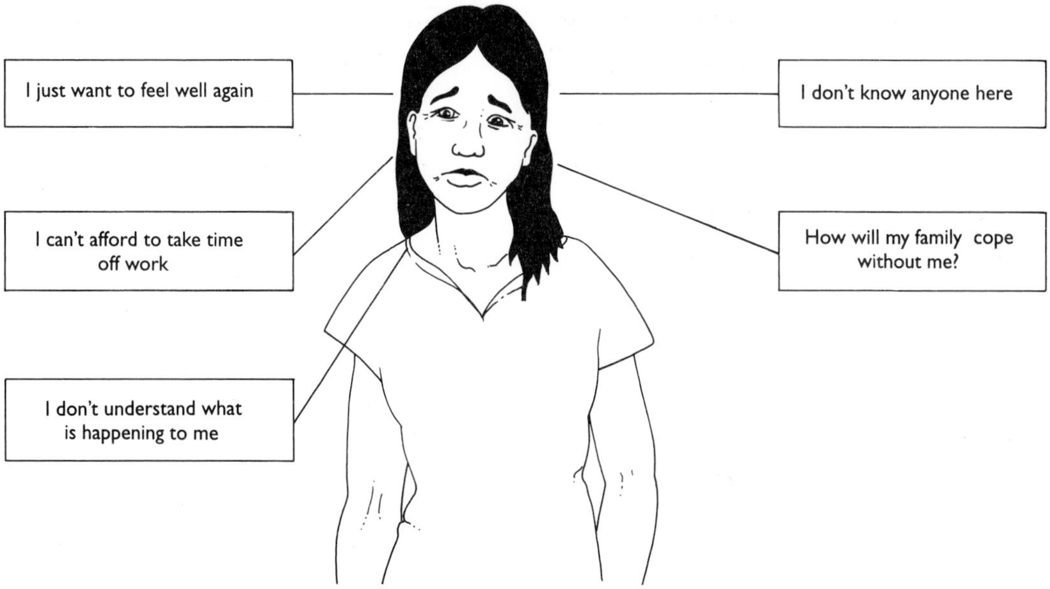

I just want to feel well again
I can't afford to take time off work
I don't understand what is happening to me
I don't know anyone here
How will my family cope without me?

Relatives undertaking individual care at home may be under more stress. There are many reasons for this:

- *feeling inadequate*, i.e. lacking the expertise to interpret symptoms or to relieve pain when oral medication fails;
- *fatigue* – sleep may be interrupted by the patient's poor sleep patterns or hallucinations;
- *guilt* – if the carer can no longer cope, then the relative may have to be admitted into hospital.

The community nursing staff can help by regular visits to give both practical help and advice and by being on call to sort out problems, e.g. with medication.

COMMUNICATION BETWEEN PEOPLE OF DIFFERENT CULTURES

Some ethnic and religious minority groups in the UK form their own subgroup within the larger society. The beliefs, customs and values related to ill-health and social well-being are very important aspects of the culture of the subgroup.

The most obvious difficulty in communication that might arise is that of language difference. It is not uncommon for a sick person in this context to seek help in the first instance from a healer from their own culture who shares and understands their cultural background and who practises medicine which is familiar to the sick individual. Other problems related to health and social well-being may be:

- *interpretation*. Knowing a culture's language does not automatically guarantee fluent communication; an interpreter may be asked to translate the language, but may have difficulty in getting across the *concepts* and *actions* that are new to the client. For example, if a woman from a totally different culture who was about to give birth was taken and placed in a delivery suite in a hospital in the UK, there would be severe communication difficulties; even if an interpreter was present, the situation would be completely alien to the woman and all the concepts surrounding the event would be incomprehensible.
- *obtaining information*. The accessibility of both health and social care services depends on people knowing how to obtain the relevant information; often leaflets are printed in several languages but they must still be available in the right places.

Stress or anxiety can also affect the nature of the caring relationship.

Barriers to effective functioning in a care work group

Stress has many definitions and is not necessarily a 'bad' thing. Stress provides the adrenalin necessary to sustain intense effort and to handle several problems at the same time; however, it also has the effect of draining the individual's physical and emotional resources. At the personal level, stress can cause real pain and suffering; at the organisational level it causes disruption and loss of 'production'. Obviously we are not dealing with PRODUCTS within care organisations, but we are striving towards common goals. The success of the whole organisation depends on cooperation between its members. In this context, stress arises from:

- the way we think about ourselves and our circumstances;
- the meaning we give to the demands we judge are being made on us;
- the value we put on the importance of caring for others.

Research has shown that there are severe stress problems among the professions with the responsibility of providing client care and treatment. Groups and individuals affected are:

- nurses;
- doctors;
- remedial therapists;
- social workers;
- radiographers;
- medical social workers;
- teachers.

Causes of stress within the care organisation include:

- low morale;
- confusion over individual roles in the hierarchy of the organisation;
- the responsibility for providing care for patients and clients who are ill or disadvantaged;
- poor or absent communication with superiors and colleagues;
- ambiguity over which tasks should take priority during the working day;
- excessive workload (both quantitative, i.e. having too much work to do, and qualitative, i.e. finding the work too difficult);
- feelings of personal inadequacy and insecurity.

Stress is discussed in Chapter 4.

- Unmanaged stress lowers our resistance to illness.
- Several diseases have long been linked with stress.
- Recent research has shown that the common cold is also linked to stress.

METHODS FOR DEALING WITH STRESS

Systematic desensitisation

This involves learning to make a new response, for example relaxation, to stimuli that invoke anxiety.

Changing attitudes

This can be achieved by reducing cognitive dissonance which is the discomfort a person feels when they hold two conflicting attitudes. For example, they may enjoy smoking but know that it damages their health.

Relaxation

Relaxation simply means doing nothing with the muscles. It may be practised in small intervals during the day, when:

- holding on the telephone;
- stopping at a red light;
- sitting in an office.

ACTIVITY

The muscle groups around the head, face, neck and shoulders are particularly important areas in tackling stress: a great deal of tension may accumulate in these muscles.

1 Work down through the head and shoulders; check that tension has left the top of the head, forehead, jaws, cheeks, tongue, neck.

2 Tense each area of the body in turn, concentrating on the tensed area, then breathe out, telling yourself to relax and let go.

ACTIVITY

Count down from ten to zero, and as the numbers go down be aware that the tension is going down correspondingly.

Visual imagery is helpful:

- Imagine a pile of work at ten and visualise it shrinking as the numbers decrease, and disappearing at zero.
- Imagine a slowly descending elevator which opens at ground level on to a tropical, scented garden or a wide, sunny beach.

Biofeedback

Modern technology enables an individual's internal responses to, for example, relaxation exercises to be measured, so they can watch the internal effects of their efforts.

Exercise

Exercise provides a way of releasing a great deal of the muscle tension and general physical arousal which accumulates in our response to stress. A regular exercise programme yields physical and psychological benefits. Physical gains include:

- improved stamina;
- reduced total peripheral resistance in blood circulation;
- lower systolic and diastolic blood pressure;
- increased inner size of arteries;
- increased number of capillaries;
- lower blood lipids;
- improved lung capacity;
- improved muscular strength.

The psychological benefits of exercise include:

- a greater ability to concentrate;
- more energy;
- a firmer appearance;
- reduced anxiety and hostility;
- an elevated mood;
- improved immune response;
- better sleep;
- better control of body weight.

Case study: Rachel

Rachel, a student nurse, wrote about her feelings on first starting work on a medical ward:

I had heard a lot of rumours about the ward from other nurses – that Sister was a real tyrant and that you never got a proper lunch break because there was always an errand to run on the way – but I was looking forward to the challenge of something different. I found it easy to get on with the patients but was very nervous when confronted by the cardiac monitors; everyone else seemed to be so confident and competent. There was such a lot of routine work to do that I never felt able to ask how to do a certain procedure; the only times when it was possible to glean information from senior staff was when visitors came, and then all the senior staff seemed to disappear into Sister's office for tea – I busied myself with the patients who never had any visitors.

The first time I saw a patient die was dreadful – she was only 33 years old and had a loving husband and two small children. At least I had enough nursing knowledge to know that the death was imminent, but I still found it very emotionally draining and often found myself thinking about it and how unfair life was to some people. There are times when I felt like giving up nursing but then I would be chatting to a patient and realise how rewarding a profession it was – it's people that really count, isn't it?

ACTIVITY

1 Identify and write down the stressors (the factors producing stress) which Rachel mentions.

2 How could colleagues help reduce the effect of these stressors for Rachel, and for themselves?

3 How can Rachel alleviate the stress she is feeling?

4 Find out about 'Type A' and 'Type B' personalities from psychology textbooks. Are some personalities more suitable than others for nursing education?

Anxiety

Unresolved anxiety will lead to stress. The physical effects of anxiety developed originally as aids to survival, triggered off by dangerous situations (the 'fight or flight' response). There are two types of anxiety:

- *objective anxiety*, caused by external stressful events;
- *neurotic anxiety*, caused by subjective, often unconscious feelings which arise within the individual.

Although they have different sources, both types of anxiety is experienced as the same painful emotional state.

Objective anxiety can be coped with by changing the circumstances of the environment in which a person functions. For example, a social worker who is worried about their ability to cope with a difficult client can enlist help from colleagues or even transfer responsibilities, if necessary.

Neurotic anxiety cannot be removed by external events. Consequently, the ego develops additional ways to protect itself from these internal threats, called the EGO DEFENCES:

- *Repression*: Unpleasant memories and thoughts are banished from consciousness and forced into the unconscious mind. This process of repression requires much mental energy and can quickly lead to abnormal behaviour.
- *Regression*: The individual behaves as they did in an earlier phase. Immature behaviour is characteristic of those experiencing this phenomenon.
- *Sublimation*: Sublimation occurs when an individual diverts their energies away from the area of work which they are finding difficult and instead devotes himself or herself completely to other things. For example, a hospital ward manager whose record-keeping skills are inadequate might channel all their energies into staff development issues, thereby replacing the need to deal with essential administration with the unnecessary concern for trivial matters.
- *Projection*: Simple projection occurs when a person unconsciously attributes to another person a characteristic that is in fact his own. Personal feelings of dislike, hatred or envy that one person feels towards another and which give rise to internal feelings of neurotic anxiety are projected on to that person. What was originally an *internal* threat is now experienced as an *external* threat. Instead of feeling 'I hate you', projection changes this to 'you hate me'. The extreme case is that of the PARANOID who feels continually threatened by everyone with whom they come into contact.

Poor communication

In most small groups, there are few restrictions on who communicates with whom. However, in larger groups and organisations, unrestricted communication becomes unwieldy and inefficient, if not impossible. In these circumstances communications networks are established. These networks:

- reinforce the status and role characteristics of the group;
- protect group leaders from being overloaded with requests and information;
- allow for rapid and efficient transmission of news, goals, information and commands throughout the group.

When lines of communication are unclear, individual job satisfaction is found to be lower and overall efficiency is adversely affected.

Lack of motivation

Employees in care organisations are motivated by:

- the need to earn a living;
- the need for job satisfaction;
- the need for security of tenure;
- the need for the respect of colleagues.

Motivation is a general term referring to the regulation of NEED-SATISFYING and GOAL-SEEKING behaviour. If we remember Maslow's hierarchy of human needs (see page 205), when DEFICIENCY NEEDS are not met, motivation increases to find ways of satisfying them and is likely to decrease when they are met.

All human beings need to feel important and appreciated and this particular need is especially significant from adolescence onwards. Clients who have mental health problems may have a negative self-image linked to low self-esteem. It is the carer's role to help clients develop a more positive self-image as part of therapy.

When needs are being met, a person's motivation may well increase to seek further fulfilment of the same needs. SELF-ACTUALISATION may be summed up as: 'What a person *can* be, he or she *ought* to be', i.e. it refers to the fulfilment of one's *potential*.

Neither sanctions (e.g. punishments or threats) nor motivation to perform can be successful if the individual does not understand clearly what is expected of him or her (their role).

Discrimination

Discrimination occurs when a person is treated differently from others, in an unfair way, simply because of his or her membership of a particular group. Discrimination does not only occur on the basis of race – people may be discriminated against because of their class, age, sex or physical disability. A male nurse may experience discrimination within a care organisation because his female colleagues see his progress up the career pyramid as being helped by his gender.

Any employee working in a care organisation will function less effectively as a team member if he or she feels discriminated against.

Conflict of interest

This occurs when a person does not behave in accordance with expectations attached to a role because to do so would place too great a strain on that person. The individual who cannot resolve this conflict of interest may suffer feelings of inadequacy, embarrassment and guilt.

COPING WITH STRESS IN CARING

Self-awareness is vital to identifying the necessary steps in the coping strategy. The 'stress and coping model' designed by Roy D. Bailey (Bailey, 1985) is a very useful tool for anyone working in the caring professions (see Figure 2.6).

The model begins with the *appraisal of an external demand*, e.g. a hospital nurse is confronted by an emergency admission from a road traffic accident. The nurse either unconsciously or consciously initiates *coping by dynamic self-regulation*, e.g. the nurse tries to alleviate their own and the patient's anxiety. If successful, the demands are no longer threatening to the nurse and the particular form of coping is terminated. If the coping

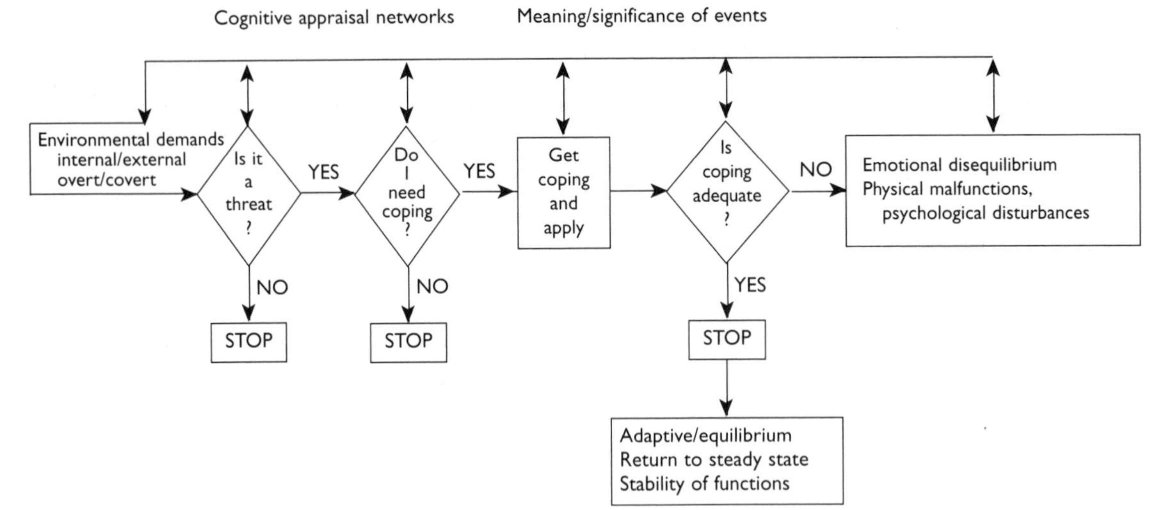

Figure 2.6 Dynamic self-regulation flow-systems model for stress and coping. *Source*: Bailey, 1985

mechanism is not successful, EMOTIONAL DISEQUILIBRIUM results. This may lead to other problems, e.g. long-term stress symptoms or drug dependency.

The flow-diagram of the model in Figure 2.6 shows that:

- not every demand need to be stressful to the health care professional;
- it is possible to evaluate highly individual appraisals of professional demands;
- coping need not always be successful, i.e. a reduction in anticipated or experienced stress is not guaranteed merely because the worker has tried to cope with the source of the stress (the stressor).

The two main tools used in coping with stress are:

- problem-solving (these skills are acquired during the professional training of the care worker);
- emotional processing (this form of coping may take the form of anxiety-reduction training or stress-management skills).

All health care professionals must have access to services which prevent or reduce undesirable forms and levels of stress:

- *Prevention:* counselling services and stress-management facilities should be available to all health professionals so that stress and its effects may be prevented.
- *Restoration:* counselling and stress-reduction facilities should also be made available for those in advanced stages of stress to restore equilibrium and stable functioning.
- *Staff support services:* counselling, stress management and stress reduction should be presented early on in the professional training as part of the staff support services available to all those beginning work in the caring professions.

ACTIVITY

1 Think of a stressful event, e.g. an exam, a driving test or an interview.

2 Arrange it into the 'stress and coping model' format.

3 In groups, choose one of the following strategies for coping with stress, research its usefulness and present your findings to the rest of the class:
   - progressive relaxation;
   - systematic desensitisation;
   - transcendental meditation;
   - autogenic regulation training;
   - stress inoculation training.

4 As a class, evaluate the different methods and decide in which situations each would be most effective.

Communication between individuals: transactional analysis

Transactional analysis (TA) is a neo-Freudian theory developed by Eric Berne (1964) and is a means for understanding personality and interpersonal communication and for changing behaviour. TA helps in the interpretation of the interactions that occur within a relationship; it does not focus at all on the circumstances surrounding the relationship. Important concepts in this model are:

- ego states;
- games;
- scripts;
- strokes.

EGO STATES

Each individual is viewed as possessing three EGO STATES which become integrated into personality in the early years of life and which give rise to patterns of feelings and behaviour in adult life.

These elements, co-existing in all of us, are as follows:

- *The parent*: Those aspects which lead us to behave with responsibility for, or authority over, others. The basic model for this is likely to be our own parents, or parental figures, in early life. The parent may be a 'critical' or 'controlling' parent, emphasising what we 'should' or 'ought' to do and the use of power in relationships.
- *The adult*: Those aspects which lead us to think rationally, to use reasoning and logic in our dealings with others, to respond to the world through developing knowledge, understanding and consciously invoked skills.
- *The child:* Those aspects which are impulsive, creative, spontaneous, irrational, intuitive and emotional. (All of these are normal elements of a balanced, healthy adult life.) The 'natural' or 'free' child manifests this through uninhibited play, fun and curiosity. The 'adapted' child, however, is shown when we are inhibited by having learnt that our freedom is curtailed by others; it is characterised by feeling small and saying 'I can't' or, rebelliously, 'I won't'.

At any one time we may be aware of the dominance of one of these ego states. In interactions between two people, therefore, there is a transaction between one of these aspects of each individual. Consider the following situation in which James Jones, who has a stomach-ache, is talking to Elsie Griffiths, a nurse:

JJ: 'My tummy is really sore.'
EG: 'Now come on, pull yourself together, we can't have you crying like this now, can we? Just take this medicine.'

James is predominantly interacting with the nurse from his *child ego state*, and she is responding from her *parent ego state*. At other times, when James is in his office as a police inspector and when Elsie is a student in her further education classes, each would interact very differently. The same situation might have given rise to the following interchange:

JJ: 'The pain seems to be here – on the right side of my lower stomach. What do you think is causing it?'
EG: 'You'll need a more thorough examination, but a possible cause is an inflamed appendix.'

In each of these examples, a COMPLEMENTARY TRANSACTION occurs. In the first, child speaks to parent and the response is from parent to child. In the second example, adult speaks to adult and adult responds to adult.

Now consider the following:

JJ: 'Could you tell me exactly what is going on in my stomach?'
EG: 'Now then, it's nothing for you to worry about, Jimmy; just you snuggle down in bed and I'll bring you a nice hot-water bottle.'

Here the transaction is *crossed*: an adult-to-

		References
PARENT	Life as taught My theories, laws, rules, rituals, customs	Conservative part of you clings onto tradition and rejects the new. Uses words like 'should' and 'must'. Role model for you when you parent others or play an authoritative role. Part of you which copies your own parents and their values
ADULT	Life as found My checking things out, risk-taking, testing	Questions and explores, non-emotional and objective. Uses words like 'now', 'where' and 'why'. Parts of you made by you
CHILD	Life as felt My emotional responses, intuitions, impulses	Playful, sexy, rich in fantasy and creativity. Uses words like 'now', 'can't' and 'won't'. Fantasises and day dreams carried over from childhood: memories of being dependent and free as a child.

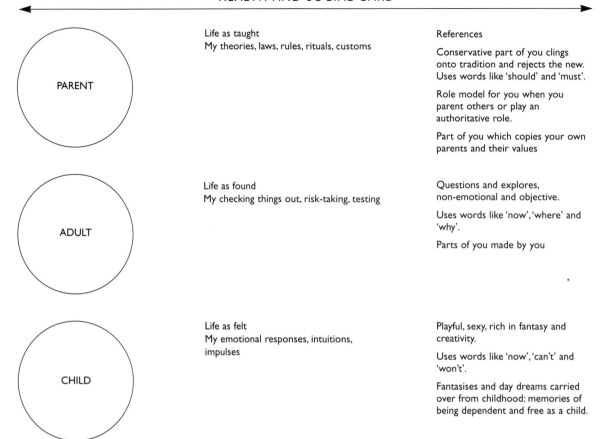

Figure 2.7 A transaction model of ego function

adult question is met by a parent-to-child response. Such an exchange will feel unsatisfactory and may lead to frustration. Rapport is unlikely to develop.

GAMES

Berne (1964) also described repetitive patterns of behaviour, or 'games', which are manipulative strategies used by people to avoid more direct, honest or assertive ways of communicating or achieving outcomes. In such a game, those involved tend to behave according to their roles in the game, rather than engage in a genuine interpersonal encounter. A common game in the caring professions is the RESCUE GAME. This game, which involves three interchanging roles, could become stuck in a 'drama triangle' (see Figure 2.9). There are three roles:

- the *attacker*;
- the *victim*;
- the *rescuer*.

Typically, a person presenting in the role of a patient may perceive himself or herself as passive, helpless, a *victim* of some outside circumstance, seeking help. Health care workers, such as nurses, perceive themselves as having enough power, ability or skills to help other people and to achieve satisfaction by so doing, thus taking on the role of *rescuer*. So far, the roles are *complementary* – the angelic nurse and the poor patient need and fulfil each other. However, if the patient doesn't get better, respond or show appropriate gratitude, the nurse (who has done all she can) feels helpless and thwarted, seeing the patient now not as poor and helpless, but as bad and deviant. The nurse is now in the *victim* role and sees the patient as a *persecutor* or *attacker*. The roles change again as the nurse feels frustrated and becomes firmer, now adopting a *persecutor* role with the patient, who is then reconfirmed in the *victim* role – and as a result is further *disempowered*.

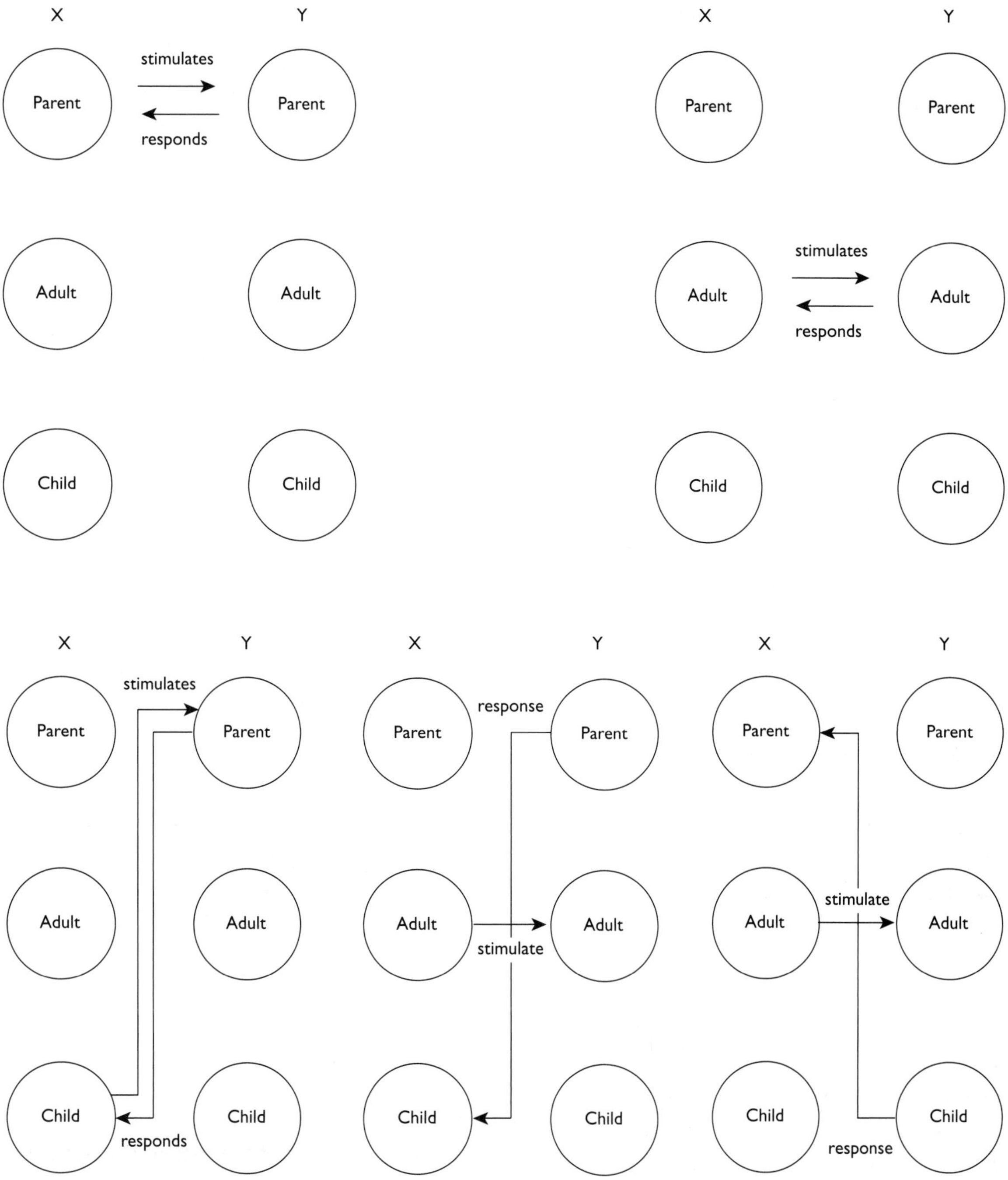

Figure 2.8 Transactional analysis: (a-c) complementary transactions; (d-e) crossed transactions
Source: Oliver, 1993

Methods used to improve the caring relationship

ORGANISATIONAL INFORMATION

Hospitals and social care settings are now much less forbidding to the newcomer than in the past; most units or wards have a board which displays information about the staff, usually with photos. Patients and clients are given a card which informs them about their NAMED NURSE or KEY WORKER. All information has to be presented in an easy-to-digest form because too much information given in

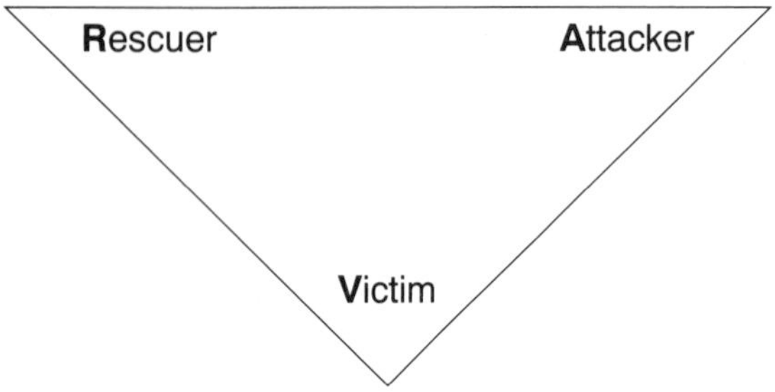

Figure 2.9 The drama triangle

cramped text will put the recipient off reading it.

ENVIRONMENTAL CHANGES

Most hospitals and residential care institutions in the UK were built during the reign of Queen Victoria; over the subsequent years many adaptations have been made to provide the sort of patient and client care that is appropriate for the twentieth century. The trend has been away from the old, dark buildings with their long corridors and 'Nightingale'-style wards, towards airy, light edifices with a central nursing station and fewer patients to a room. A patient's environment has a very important role in their rate of recovery. Richard Ulrich, an American architect, studied the recovery rate of two groups of patients who had had their gall bladders removed. One group he placed in a part of the ward which had a view of trees; the other group faced a blank wall. The benefits to the 'tree view' group were:

- shorter post-operative stay;
- fewer negative evaluative comments from nurses;
- fewer analgesics (pain-killers) used.

The use of environment as part of helping communication is relevant to every care setting; small changes – such as pictures on the walls, fresh colours, refreshment facilities for clients and visitors to enjoy together, and furniture arranged to encourage communication – can all enhance the caring environment (see Figure 2.10).

Figure 2.10 Admission of a patient

THE NAMED NURSE

The introduction of the named nurse and of a more well-defined admissions procedure in hospitals and other care institutions has led to a better relationship between carers and their clients. Some wards or units have introduced the practice of TEAM NURSING which enables a greater use of SKILL MIX.

SKILL MIX

The introduction of skill mix in community nursing and health visiting is a response to the need to rationalise costs by employing cheaper staff with specific skills. The Patient's Charter (Department of Health, 1992) emphasises a 'service provision' approach and a move away from the generic health care worker who views patients and clients as 'my patients' or 'my families'.

Advantages of skill mix

- Can create new opportunities for practitioners, e.g. learning management skills.
- Can lead to more opportunity for the practitioner or team leader to focus on wider issues, e.g. health promotion.
- May lead to greater job satisfaction for team members.
- Patients and clients may benefit from the collective experience shared by the team.

Disadvantages of skill mix

- Nurses may be viewed as too expensive a resource.
- Support workers are replacing trained nurses, de-skilling nurses and eroding the professional role.
- Supervision of untrained staff is more difficult to carry out effectively in the community than on a hospital ward.
- Can lead to job dissatisfaction if the practitioner feels 'de-skilled'.
- May make the concept of the 'named nurse' (enshrined in the Patient's Charter) more difficult to implement.

ACTIVITY

Obtain a copy of the Patient's Charter. Before work experience in a hospital, discuss in groups whether you believe the aims of the Charter can be fulfilled. Prepare a schedule for a structured interview to be carried out in the work placement; your brief is to find out facts and ideas on the issue of *skill mix* and the *named nurse*. Follow the guidelines in Chapter 8 (Research Methods).

PERSONAL APPEARANCE OF HEALTH WORKERS

The debate about nurses wearing uniforms has raged for decades. Historically, the primary purpose of the uniform was to maintain standards of hygiene and efficiency; now that a plastic apron can cope with the dirtier aspects of any nursing task, many feel that the traditional uniform should go.

Paediatric nurses usually wear practical tabard aprons decorated with nursery rhyme or cartoon characters, and doctors rarely wear the traditional white coat.

Nursery nurses and social care workers often wear a customised sweatshirt and trousers; most large Accident and Emergency Departments now have a cubicle decorated to provide a non-threatening environment for traumatised children (see Figure 2.11).

EMPOWERMENT

Patient advocacy is a growing movement, in which users of health and social services provide each other with mutual support. An advocate is someone independent of these services who befriends an individual user of services on a one-to-one basis and represents his or her interests to the professionals.

Empowerment incorporates the principle of advocacy and aims to enable clients to exercise some power over the care they receive; at the individual level, some people are better able than others to represent their

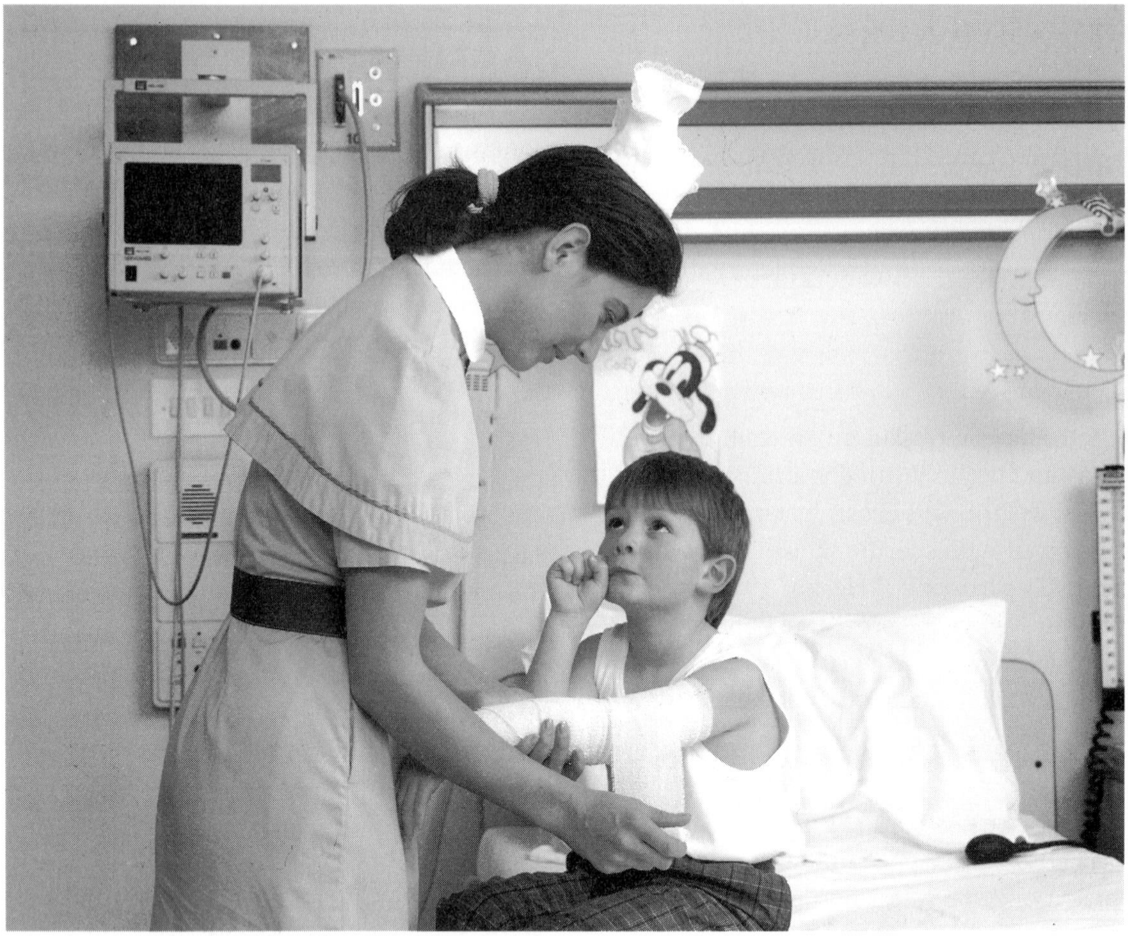

Figure 2.11 Accident and Emergency department cubicle for children

own interests to health care professionals, and those who pay for private health care feel that they can influence the doctor for whose services they pay directly; those who rely on the NHS have no such direct leverage.

Methods used to improve interpersonal interaction

IMPROVING OWN PERFORMANCE

A professional carer can demonstrate listening and attending by using verbal and non-verbal communication (see page 105). Egan's SOLER technique is a firm basis for showing non-verbal attending. It should be used flexibly, so that it feels natural. The carer should:

- sit **S**quare, i.e. opposite the client or patient; **S**
- maintain an **O**pen posture; **O**
- **L**ean forward slightly; **L**
- maintain **E**ye contact; **E**
- be **R**elaxed. **R**

THE IMPORTANCE OF FEEDBACK

Communication becomes true communication only when there is feedback; it should be a two-way process, with one responding to the stimulus of another. *Empathic responding* (see page 106) shows patients and clients that you can see things from their point of view and that you understand their needs and concerns.

ASSESSMENT OPPORTUNITY ✓

Task One

Read the following case study.

Daniel had just celebrated his first birthday when he was badly scalded on both arms; he was rushed to the local Accident and Emergency Department and admitted to the paediatric ward. His parents, June and Peter, were encouraged to be with him, and June was able to spend all day playing with and comforting her son. Daniel was discharged from hospital after five days and referred to the Burns Unit of a hospital an hour's drive away from his home. The consultant decided that skin grafts were necessary and Daniel was admitted for treatment. Although it was not an emergency admission, Daniel was whisked out of his father's arms by a nurse who hurried down the corridor to the dressing rooms to await examination of the injuries by a doctor. For the next one and a half hours, Peter and June listened helplessly to Daniel's screams; when they asked if they could be with their son, they were told that parents were not allowed in the dressing rooms and the reason for the delay was that the doctor had been held up in the operating theatre.

During the next few weeks, June was able to live in at the hospital, but this was regarded as a privilege rather than as an automatic right. June acquired knowledge of the rules and routines of ward life through observation, experience and discussion with other mothers after they had returned to their living quarters. Learning by making mistakes was often a painful and humiliating process; June had seen another young patient being helped to walk around his cubicle by holding his mother's hands, but when she was doing the same with Daniel, a nurse passing the room said 'You shouldn't let him walk around on his donor area, you know'. The staff seemed too busy to answer questions; the routine was difficult to understand as so many decisions seemed to be taken on an *ad hoc* basis.

June repeatedly asked if she could stay with Daniel during the distressing ordeal of the dressing room, but was always told 'I'm afraid parents aren't allowed in the dressing room'. One day, two weeks after admission, the consultant and junior doctor were passing the entrance to Daniel's cubicle and June overheard them saying that they wanted 'to take a look at this one'. June asked them if she could accompany them and the consultant replied 'Of course, if you think it will help the child.' The staff in the dressing room were very pleasant and allowed June to hold and reassure Daniel. The staff always allowed June to assist after the first time.

Visitors, parents and staff all wore gowns and masks and siblings were not allowed on the ward because of the risk of infection. Most parents feel a tremendous sense of guilt if their child suffers a burn or scald, and this feeling was compounded by the trauma of the admissions procedure.

Task Two

1 Look back to the section on Transactional Analysis (page 119). Identify the transactions that took place between June and the professionals at the Burns Unit.

2 Outline four aspects of the caring relationship which you believe could be improved, and describe the constraints to interaction.

3 Describe the methods which a professional carer could use to improve the problems mentioned above.

On work experience

In a child care setting:

- Try to find out about how the 'settling in' period is managed in the nursery or school.

- If possible, observe a child who is new to the placement; what emotions does the child show?
- What information is given to parents/carers of the child about the settling in period?

In a hospital:

How is a planned admission to hospital managed?

- Are there a lot of forms to fill in?
- Does the hospital or unit operate a 'named nurse' policy?
- How much written information is given to patients and their relatives?
- Is the environment welcoming – could anything be done to improve the caring relationship?

In a residential home for the elderly:

Arrange to interview one of the residents, to find out the following:

- How he or she felt when entering the home for the first time.
- What changes he or she would like to see in the general running of the home.

NB Always ask permission from your work placement supervisor before undertaking any research, and offer to show the questions you will be asking.

REFERENCES AND RESOURCES

Aggleton, P. (1990), *Health*. London: Routledge.

Allen, I., ed. (1990), *Care Managers and Care Management*. London: Policy Studies Institute.

Argyle, M. (1988), *Bodily Communication*, London: Routledge.

Atkinson, R.L. (1993), *Introduction to Psychology*, 11th ed. US: Harcourt Brace Jovanovich College Publishers.

Bailey, R.D. (1985), *Coping with Stress in Caring*. Oxford: Blackwell Scientific.

Berne, E. (1964), *Games People Play*. London: Penguin.

Biestek, F.P. (1992), *The Casework Relationship*. London: Routledge.

Blaxter, M. (1990), *Health and Lifestyles*. London: Routledge.

Bond, J. and Bond, S. (1986), *Sociology and Health Care*. Edinburgh: Churchill Livingstone.

Burton, G. and Dimbleby, R. (1988), *Between Ourselves: An Introduction to Interpersonal Communication*, ch. 5. London: Edward Arnold.

Butrym, Z.T. (1986), *The Nature of Social Work*. London: Macmillan.

Coulshed, V. (1990), *Social Work Practice: An Introduction*. London: Macmillan Education.

Davey, B. and Popay, J. (1993), *Dilemmas in Health Care*. Milton Keynes: Open University Press.

Egan, G. (1986), *The Skilled Helper*. California: Brooks/Cole.

Eysenck, H. and Wilson, G. (1991), *Know Your Own Personality*. London: Penguin.

Frankl, V. (1983), *Man's Search for Meaning*. New York: Pocket Books.

Gill, D. and Adams, B. (1988), *The ABC of Communication Studies*. Walton-on-Thames: Nelson.

Gross, R. (1992), *Psychology: The Science of Mind and Behaviour*, 2nd ed. Sevenoaks: Hodder and Stoughton.

Handy, C. (1985), *Understanding Organizations*. Harmondsworth: Penguin.

Harris, T. (1970), *I'm OK, You're OK*. London: Jonathan Cape.

Hayes, N. and Orrell, S. (1993), *Psychology: An Introduction*, 2nd ed. London: Longman.

Heywood-Jones, I. (1988), 'The Buck Stops Here', *Nursing Times*, vol. 84, no. 17, pp. 50–2.

Hinchliff, S., Noma, S.E. and Schober, J.E. (1989), *Nursing Practice and Health Care*. London: Edward Arnold.

Maccoby and Jacklin (1974), The Psychology of Sex Differences. Stanford, California: Stanford University Press.

Mackay, L. (1989), *Nursing a Problem*. Milton Keynes: Open University Press.

Mares, P., Hailey, A. and Baxter, C. (1985), *Health Care in Multiracial Britain*. London: HEC/NEC.

Maslow, A.H. (1954), Motivation and Personality. New York: Harper.

Mayer, J.E. and Timms, N. (1970), *The Client Speaks: Working Class Impressions of Casework*. London: Routledge and Kegan Paul.

Milgram, S. (1963), *Obedience to Authority*. New York: Harper & Row.

Moreno, J.L. (1953), *Who Shall Survive? Foundations of Sociometry, Group Psychotherapy and Sociodrama*. New York: Basic Books.

Murgatroyd, S. (1985), *Counselling and Helping*. London: International Thomson Publishing Ltd.

Oliver, R.W. (1993), *Psychology and Health Care*. London: Bailliere Tindall.

Pedler, M., Burgogyne, J. and Boydell, T. (1986), *A Manager's Guide to Self-Development*. London: McGraw-Hill.

Phelps, S. and Austin, N. (1989), *The Assertive Woman*. London: Arlington Books.

Preston-Shoot, M. (1987), *Effective Groupwork*. London: Macmillan Education.

Runciman, P. (1989), 'Health Assessment of the Elderly: A Multidisciplinary Perspective' in *Social Work and Health Care*, Taylor, R. and Ford, J. (eds). London: Jessica Kingsley.

Steiner, C. (1974, 1990), *Scripts People Live*. New York: Grove.

Stewart, I. (1989), *Transactional Analysis Counselling in Action*. London: Sage Publications.

USEFUL ADDRESS

United Kingdom Central Council for Nursing,
Midwifery and Health Visiting
(PC Division)
23 Portland Place
London W1N 3AF

3

HEALTH AND SOCIAL WELL-BEING: PHYSICAL ASPECTS

This chapter focuses on the physical aspects of health and social well-being. The organisation of structures within body systems, from cells to tissues and organs, is described, as are the relationships between their main functions. The maintenance of a constant internal environment (homeostasis) is considered along with the effects of development and ageing on body systems. The final part of this chapter looks at methods of monitoring the healthy function of the human body, and provides students with secondary source data to analyse, such as ECG traces and blood cell counts, and the opportunity to undertake monitoring of the cardio-respiratory system themselves.

BODY SYSTEMS: LEVELS OF ORGANISATION

What is the human body made up of?

When you ask yourself this question, what springs immediately to mind? Do you think first of organs such as the lungs or heart, or do you think of tissues such as muscle and blood? Perhaps you think of cells, or even of the molecules making up those cells, such as carbohydrates or lipids. You may even think of atoms such as carbon, hydrogen and oxygen. Any of these answers would be valid, as the structure of the body can be considered at a molecular level, at a cellular level, or as a collection of tissues, organs and systems.

The following information and exercises will guide you through the main aspects of each of these levels of organisation which are summarised below.

cells → tissues → organs → organ systems

Cellular organisation

ACTIVITY

Using a light microscope, either prepare your own slide of wrist cells using the instructions below or observe prepared slides of cheek cells. Calculate the magnification. (You do this by multiplying the magnification of the eyepiece by the magnification of the objective lens.)

To prepare a slide of wrist cells: wash your wrist thoroughly; apply transparent sticky tape firmly; remove and place sticky side up on a slide; add a drop of methylene blue and apply a coverslip.

ELECTRON MICROSCOPES can magnify an object up to 500,000 times. This enables us to examine in detail the many organelles found in a cell.

ACTIVITY

- Find out about and identify the organelles labelled A–E in Figure 3.1. Choose from: plasma membrane, nucleus, ribosome, endoplasmic reticulum, mitochondrion.
- Calculate the actual width of the nucleus.

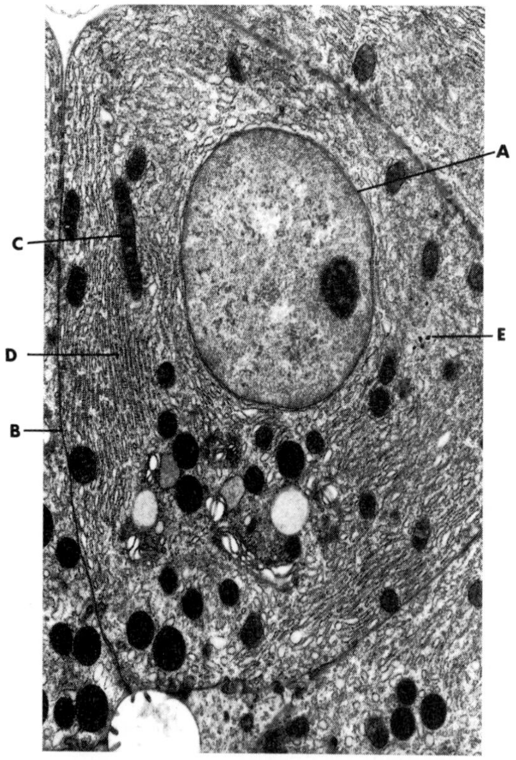

Figure 3.1 Electron micrograph of a cell from the pancreas

- Write a paragraph on the functions of the nucleus, ribosomes, endoplasmic reticulum, mitochondria and plasma membrane.
  (You will find further information about the plasma membrane and mitochondria in the next sections of this chapter.)

TRANSPORT IN AND OUT OF CELLS

Cells can be thought of as individual 'packets' of living matter. They are surrounded by a flexible envelope, the plasma membrane, which retains the contents of the cell and separates it from the outside world. However, cells are not isolated from their environment – food materials, oxygen and waste materials, for example, must be moved constantly in opposite directions across the plasma membranes. The movement of materials across the plasma membrane may be by diffusion, osmosis, active transport, phagocytosis or pinocytosis.

Diffusion

Definition: Diffusion is the process by which a substance moves from a region of high concentration of that substance to a region of low concentration of the same substance.

ACTIVITY

- Drop a crystal of potassium permanganate (potassium manganate VII) into a beaker of water. Observe the spread of the purple colour by diffusion.
- What everyday examples of diffusion can you think of?

Osmosis

Definition: The passage of water from a region where it is highly concentrated to a region where its concentration is lower, through a partially permeable membrane.

ACTIVITY

- Copy Figure 3.2. Indicate on which side water is highly concentrated, on which side its concentration is lower, and in which direction water will move by osmosis.
- Use potato chips of identical size placed in different concentrations of salt or sugar solution to investigate osmosis. Plot a graph to show how length changes with increasing concentration.
- Plant cells have cell walls which are rigid enough to prevent excessive uptake of water. Animal cells do not have cell walls. What do you predict would happen to a red blood cell placed in pure water?

Active transport

Diffusion and osmosis are passive processes, i.e. they do not require energy. Active transport, however, does require the expenditure of energy as it involves moving molecules against a CONCENTRATION GRADIENT

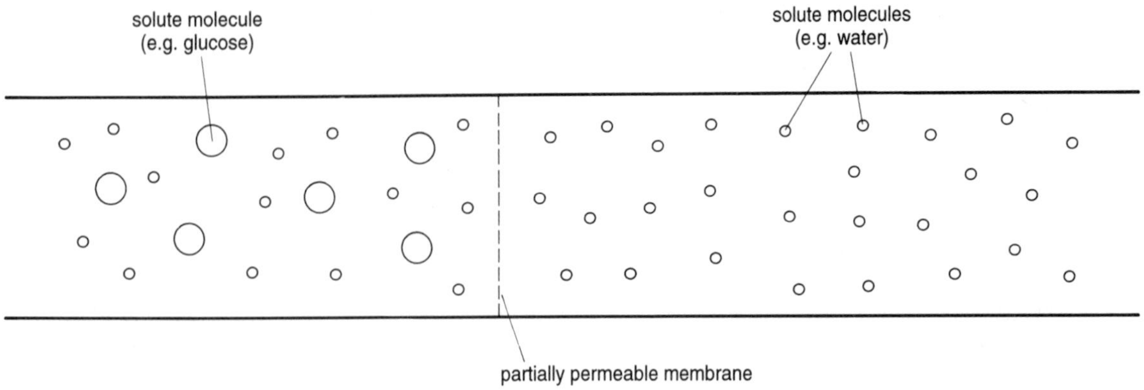

Figure 3.2 Osmosis

(i.e. from a region of low concentration to one of higher concentration).

The plasma membrane is spanned by proteins (Figure 3.3a) and it is thought that these convey molecules from one side to the other.

Phagocytosis

Particles which are too small to be taken in by diffusion or active transport can be taken up by phagocytosis. The plasma membrane forms a cup-shaped depression around a particle, which is then pinched off to form a vacuole (Figure 3.3b).

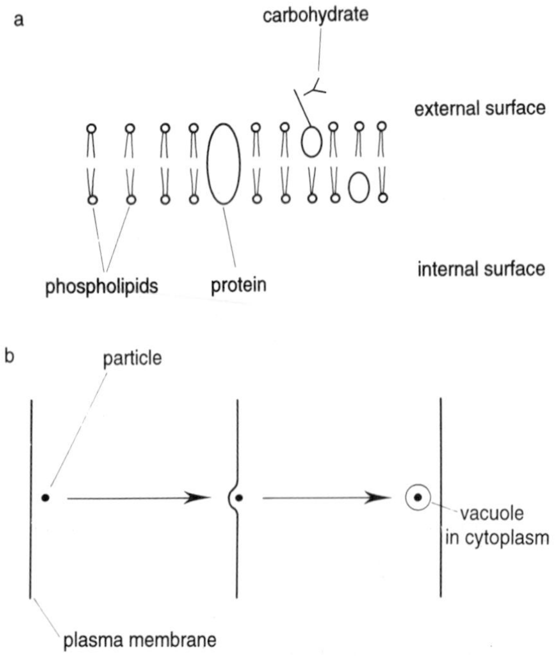

Figure 3.3 a) Diagram of plasma membrane, b) phagocytosis

ACTIVITY

- In cells which take in a lot of material by active transport and phagocytosis, which organelle is likely to be present in particularly high numbers to supply the necessary energy?
- Phagocytosis only occurs in a few specialised cells. Can you find examples of such cells?

Pinocytosis

This is very similar to phagocytosis but involves much smaller vacuoles. Pinocytosis is used for the uptake of liquids, not solids.

CELLULAR RESPIRATION

All living systems require a constant supply of energy in order to maintain the processes of life, including the synthesis of large molecules, cell division, reproduction and movement. The energy initially comes from the sun, and is captured in chemical form by plants during photosynthesis. Proteins, carbohydrates and fats are produced as a result of photosynthesis. All these molecules contain energy and enter the human body in the food consumed.

Cellular respiration is the metabolic process by which cells release energy from food in order to sustain their activities. Cells use carbohydrate in the form of glucose to release energy. In aerobic respiration the glucose is oxidised to carbon dioxide and water.

$C_6H_{12}O_6 + 6O_2 \rightarrow 6CO_2 + 6H_2O + \text{ENERGY}$

The metabolic reactions that occur in aerobic cellular respiration can be divided into three stages:

- Glycolysis (in the cytoplasm)
- Krebs (tricarboxylic acid) cycle (in mitochondria)
- Electron (hydrogen) transport system (in mitochondria)

The glucose is gradually broken down during glycolysis and Krebs cycle. The energy that is released is not used directly, but is transferred into ADENOSINE TRI-PHOSPHATE (ATP) which is the short term energy store for all cells. It is this molecule that is used to supply energy for the life-sustaining cellular processes.

Glycolysis and anaerobic respiration

Glycolysis is the breakdown of glucose, a six carbon molecule, into two molecules of the three carbon compound pyruvic acid. Two molecules of ATP are produced. This occurs in all cells and is an anaerobic stage. This means that it does not require oxygen. In aerobic respiration, the pyruvic acid then enters the next stage of respiration: Krebs Cycle.

In anaerobic organisms such as yeast, the pyruvic acid is converted into ethanol and carbon dioxide. The next two stages of respiration, Krebs Cycle and the Electron Transfer System, do not take place.

In human beings, anaerobic respiration takes a different form. Aerobic respiration normally occurs and anaerobic respiration only takes place when anoxia (a shortage of oxygen) is temporarily present. This can happen in muscle cells during periods of strenuous exercise when the circulatory system is not able to maintain the supply of oxygen in enough quantity.

The product of glycolysis, pyruvic acid, is then converted to lactic acid, with the release of only a little energy. This occurs in the cytoplasm. The amount of energy released in this type of anaerobic respiration is only 5% of that released in aerobic respiration when glucose is completely oxidised. Lactic acid is toxic and can cause cramp which will make the person stop the muscular activity. When enough oxygen has accumulated again in the muscle the lactic acid is changed back into pyruvic acid. This then enters the next stage of respiration, and all the lactic acid is removed from the muscle tissue and completely broken down to carbon dioxide and water. In the process of lactic acid production, an 'oxygen debt' occurs. This is 'repaid' after exercise by continued deep and rapid breathing.

Krebs cycle (tricarboxylic acid cycle)

Although some of the energy in the glucose has been released in glycolysis, most of it remains 'locked up' in the pyruvic acid molecules. These enter the mitochondrion and, in the presence of oxygen, are broken down into carbon dioxide and hydrogen atoms in a cycle of reactions called the Krebs Cycle. The carbon dioxide is removed as a waste product and the hydrogen atoms are passed on to hydrogen carriers.

The Krebs Cycle is an interconversion centre for many molecules. Fatty acids from fats, and amino acids from proteins, can enter the respiratory pathway here, or fats and some amino acids can be built up from the intermediate compounds in the cycle.

The electron transfer system

This also takes place within the mitochondrion. It is where the energy, which is now in the hydrogen atoms combined with their carriers, is finally converted to ATP. The majority of the ATP produced during respiration is produced at this stage. Oxygen is needed for this process and the hydrogen atoms combine with the oxygen to form water.

ACTIVITY

Look at Figure 3.4a. Explain the level of oxygen consumption before, during and after exercise. Discuss the four phases

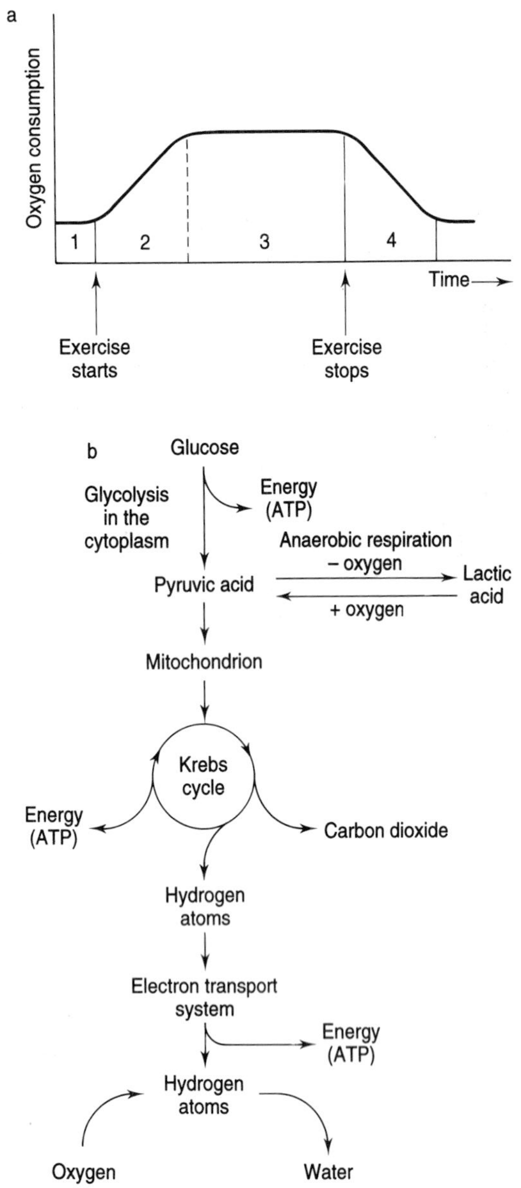

Figure 3.4 a) Oxygen consumption before, during and after exercise, b) Stages in cellular respiration

indicated on the graph, relating your answer to the three stages in cellular respiration described above and summarised in Figure 3.4b. Mention why the oxygen consumption does not return to the resting level straight away after exercise.

Tissue organisation

Cells are grouped together to form tissues. A tissue may consist of one type of cell, for example squamous epithelium, or of many types of cell, for example blood. There are four main groups of tissues: epithelial tissue, connective tissue, muscle tissue and nervous tissue.

EPITHELIAL TISSUE

EPITHELIAL TISSUE lines the internal and external surfaces of the body. Its general function is protection, for example against injury or infection. It may also be adapted for a more specialised function such as absorption, secretion or excretion. Epithelial tissues are classified according to the shape of the cells and the number of layers. When there is only one layer of cells the epithelium is called simple. One surface of the cell is free and the opposite surface rests on a basement membrane derived from the underlying connective tissue.

An example of this is simple squamous epithelium (see Figure 3.5). This is found where molecules pass through the cell walls by diffusion. The cells are thin to allow this to happen easily.

When there are many layers of cells the epithelium is called stratified squamous epithelium. The lowest layer is attached to the basement membrane. Protection is the main function of stratified epithelia; examples are the epidermis of the skin, where the outer layers are cornified, and the lining of the vagina (see Figure 3.6).

ACTIVITY

Find information to complete Table 3.1. Where possible the drawings of cell shape should be made from an examination of microscope slides.

CONNECTIVE TISSUE

CONNECTIVE TISSUE is a term which covers a very wide variety of tissues whose general common function is support. The cells of connective tissue are surrounded by a large amount of intercellular substance called the

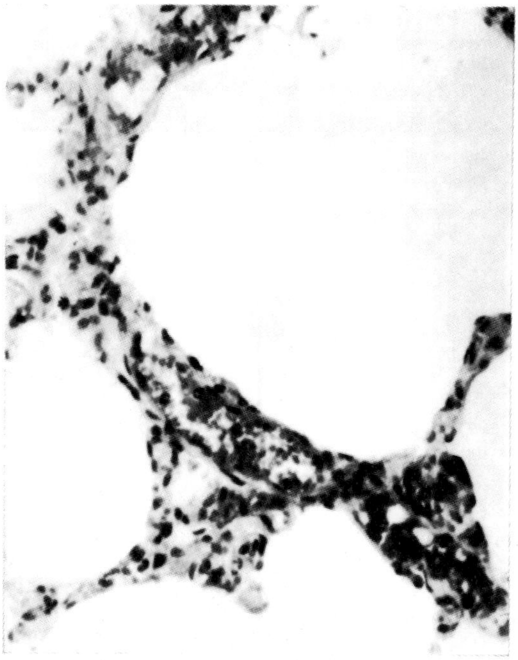

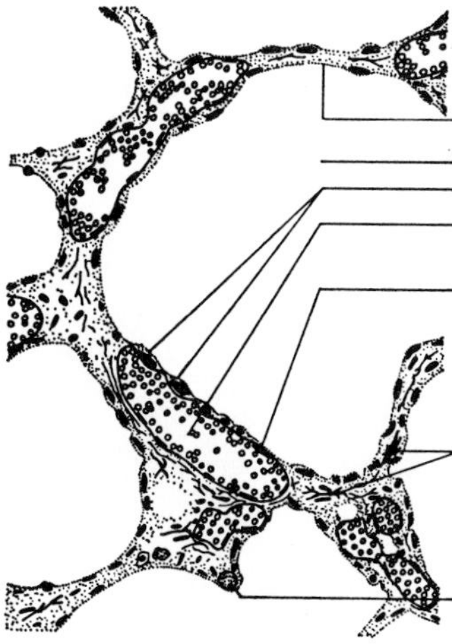

Figure 3.5 Simple squamous epithelium
Source: An Atlas of Histology, by W.H. Freeman and B. Bracegirdle, Heinemann, 1966.

matrix. Connective tissue may be classified in several ways. Figure 3.7 gives one example of classification.

Vascular tissue

Blood

Blood is found circulating within the cardiovascular system, i.e. within the heart and blood vessels.

> **ACTIVITY**
>
> Figure 3.8 shows the components of blood. Which of these can you identify in Figure 3.9? If possible, examine a prepared slide of blood under the microscope and identify as many of the components as possible.
>
> List three ways in which the structure of the red blood cells makes blood efficient at carrying out its main function.

> Red blood cells have a lifespan of about three months. How are the waste products from their breakdown excreted?

Lymph

Lymph is a milky liquid which is rich in fats and contains lymphocytes. It is carried in LYMPH CAPILLARIES which merge to form LYMPH VESSELS. These have a structure similar to veins, including valves which ensure that the lymph moves in one direction only.

Lymph is derived from TISSUE FLUID which bathes all the cells of the body. Tissue fluid is derived from blood, and is the means by which materials are exchanged between cells and blood. The lymph system drains into the circulatory system, so this means there is a constant flow of liquid from the blood to the tissue fluid, to the lymph and back into the blood.

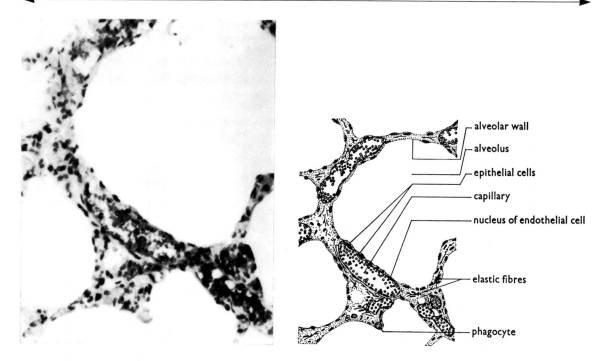

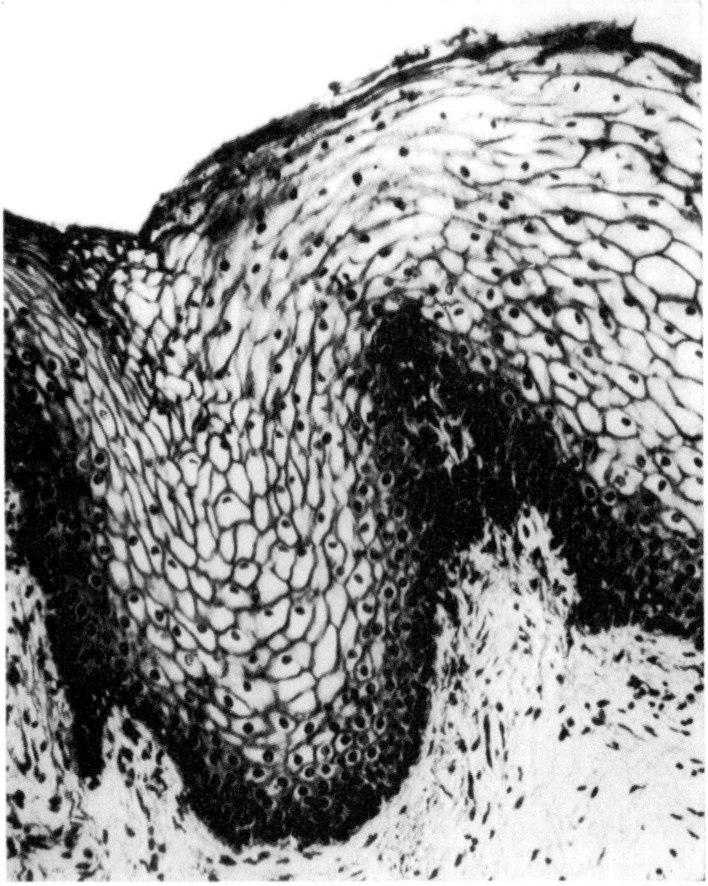

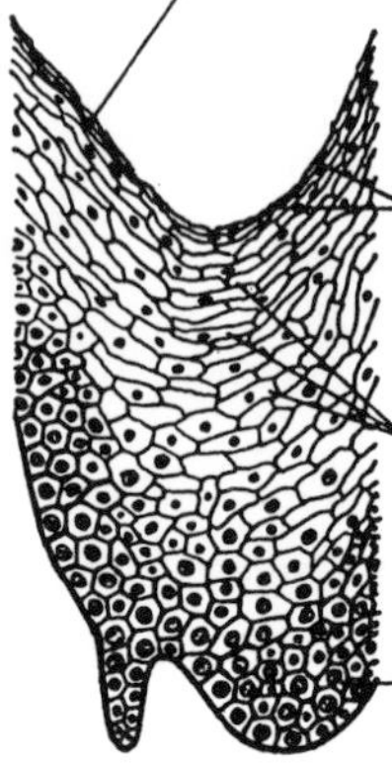

Figure 3.6 Stratified squamous epithelium
Source: An Atlas of Histology, by W.H. Freeman and B. Bracegirdle, Heinemann, 1966.

Skeletal tissue

Cartilage

Cartilage gives support and helps maintain shape. It contains fibres of the protein collagen which give it strength, and a jelly-like matrix (background substance) which allows it to return to its original shape after deformation. Unlike other connective tissues, it has no blood vessels or nerves of its own.

ACTIVITY

List the places in the body where cartilage may be found.

Bone

The matrix of compact bone is made up of collagen together with inorganic substances such as calcium, magnesium and phosphorus. These components are arranged in concentric circles, called LAMELLAE, around a HAVERSIAN CANAL containing an artery, a vein, lymph vessels and nerve fibres. OSTEOCYTES or bone cells are found in the spaces in the lamellae known as LACUNAE, and fine channels called CANALICULI link lacunae (Figure 3.10).

ACTIVITY

- If possible, look at bone tissue under the microscope. Try to identify the features described. To gain a three-dimensional picture of bone, examine longitudinal as well as transverse sections.
- The combination of the protein (collagen) and the inorganic substances makes bone very strong. To show that both components are important, try the following (take care).

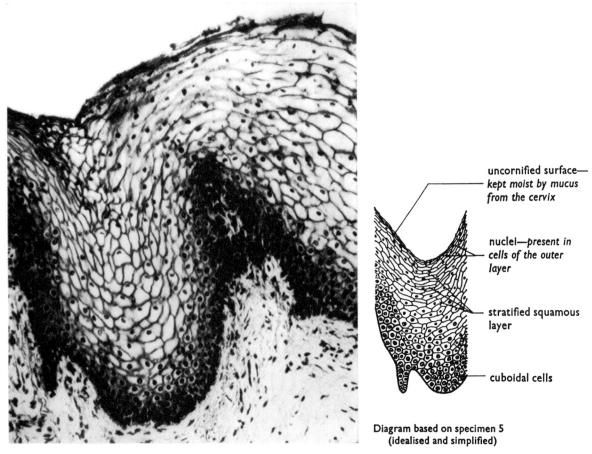

Table 3.1 Epithelial tissues

	Type	Shape of cells	Location in body	Functions
Simple One layer of cells	Squamous			
	Cuboidal			
	Columnar			
	Ciliated			
	Pseudo-stratified		Lining urinary tract Trachea	Protection
Compound More than one layer of cells	Stratified squamous			
	Transitional			

(a) Put a chicken bone in 2 M acid (care!) until it becomes flexible. This removes many of the inorganic substances.

(b) Burn a chicken bone over a Bunsen burner. This will remove much of the protein.

From your observations, which component of bone makes it:

(i) hard but brittle;

(ii) strong but flexible.

- Obtain a long bone from a butcher. Carefully saw it in half lengthwise (your butcher may do this for you). Make a drawing to show the positions of spongy bone, compact bone, marrow and cartilage.
- Bone is obviously important in providing a framework for supporting the body, and providing a means of attachment for muscles which then operate the bones as a system of levers for locomotion. Can you find three other functions of bone?

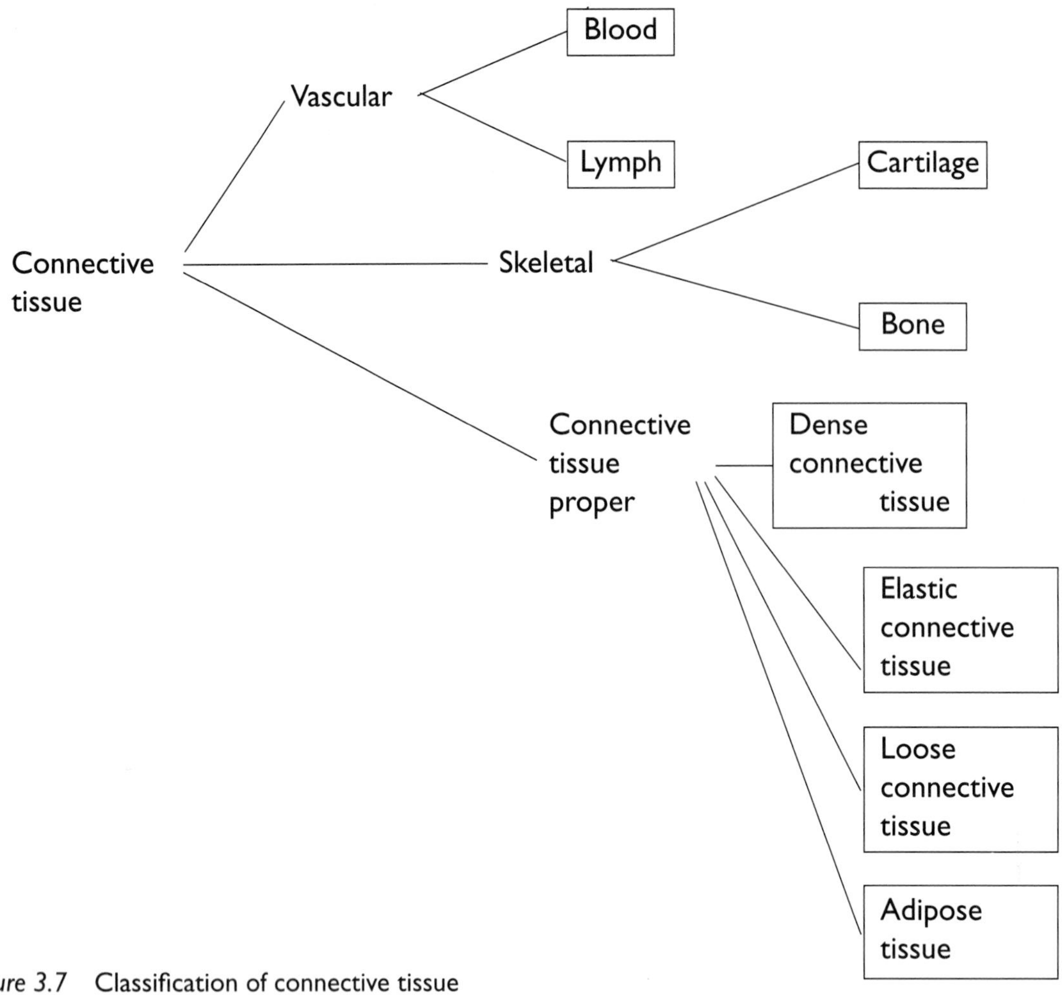

Figure 3.7 Classification of connective tissue

Connective tissue proper

Table 3.2 Locations and function of connective tissue proper

	Location	Function
Dense connective tissue	Tendons, ligaments	Strong attachment between structures; tendons link muscle to bone; ligaments link bone to bone
Elastic connective tissue	Lung tissue; walls of arteries	Allows stretching
Loose connective tissue	Dermis of skin, mucous membranes, blood vessels, nerves, body organs	Strength, elasticity, support
Adipose tissue	Subcutaneous layer of skin; around heart and kidneys; marrow of long bones; padding around joints	Insulation, support, protection, energy reserve

Component	Appearance	Function	*Nos. of cells* mm^{-3}
Plasma	Straw-coloured liquid	Matrix in which a variety of substances are carried e.g. vitamins, products of digestion, execretory products, hormones	
Red blood cells or *erythrocytes*	Biconcave discs full of the red pigment haemoglobin. No nucleus 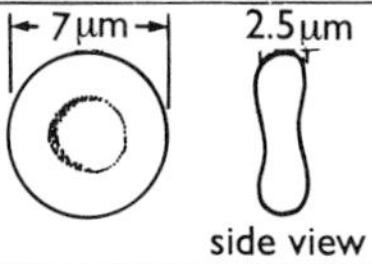 7µm 2.5µm side view	Carriage of O_2 and some CO_2	500,000
White blood cells or leucocytes			
(a) *Granulocytes*	Granular cytoplasm. Lobed nuclei		
Neutrophils	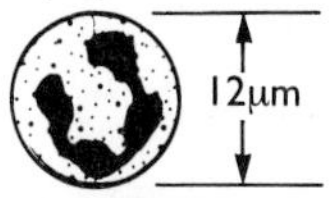 12µm	Engulf bacteria	4,900
Eosinophils	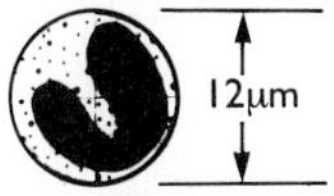 12µm	Anti-histamine properties	105
Basophils	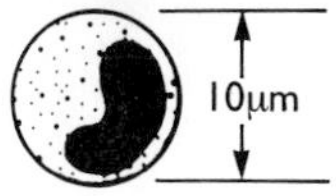 10µm	Produces histamine	35
(b) *Agranulocytes*	No granules seen under light microscope		
Monocytes	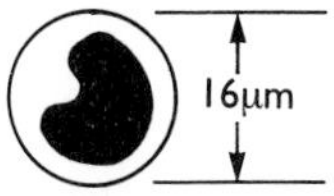 16µm	Engulf bacteria	280
Lymphocytes	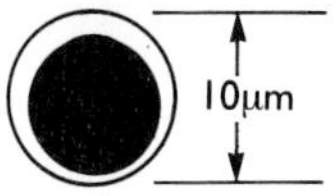 10µm	Antibody production	1,680
Platelets	 3µm	Clotting	250,000

Figure 3.8 The components of blood

MUSCLE TISSUE

MUSCLE TISSUE makes up about 40–50% of body weight. Three types of muscle are present in the body: cardiac muscle, involuntary muscle and voluntary muscle.

Cardiac muscle

CARDIAC MUSCLE is found only in the heart. It is capable of rapid, rhythmic contraction and relaxation. To allow the waves of contraction to spread over the heart, the muscle cells, or fibres, are branched and connected to one another.

Involuntary muscle

INVOLUNTARY MUSCLE, also known as **smooth, unstriped** or **unstructured muscle**, is found in the walls of the intestinal, genital, urinary and respiratory tracts and the walls of blood vessels. It can contract rhythmically and does not tire easily. The muscle cells are spindle-shaped and organised into bundles of sheets.

ACTIVITY

Explain why muscle contraction is necessary in each of the locations listed above (intestinal, genital, urinary and respiratory tracts, and the walls of blood vessels).

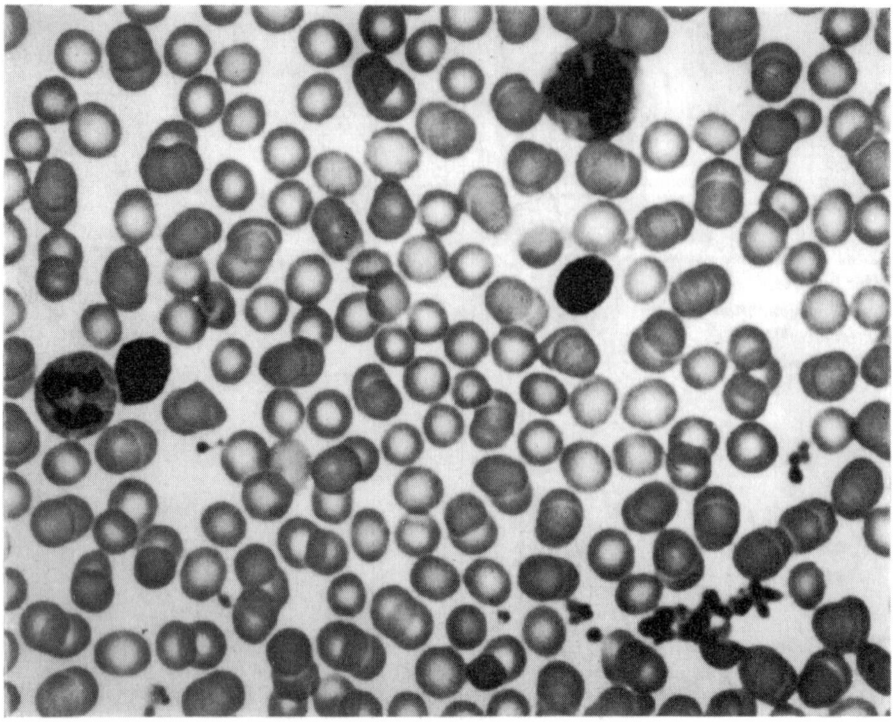

Figure 3.9 Photomicrograph of blood cells and platelets (×1,600)
Source: An Atlas of Histology, by W.H. Freeman and B. Bracegirdle, Heinemann, 1966.

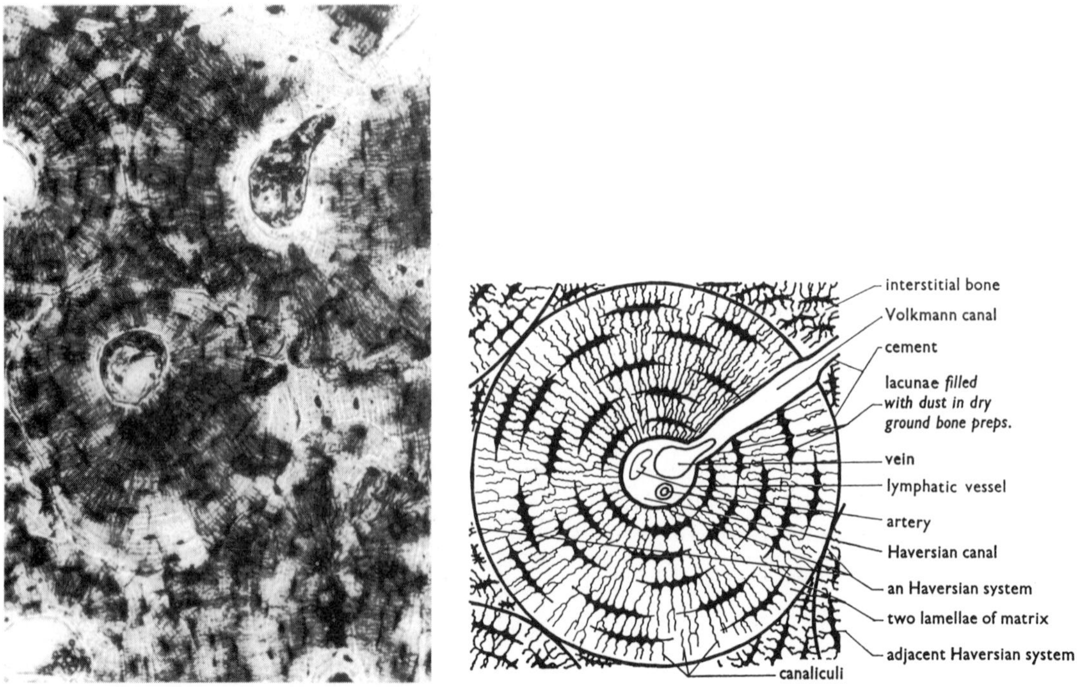

Figure 3.10 Transverse section of compact bone (×100)
Source: An Atlas of Histology, by W.H. Freeman and B. Bracegirdle, Heinemann, 1966.

Voluntary muscle

VOLUNTARY MUSCLE, also known as **skeletal**, or **striated muscle**, is attached to bone and moves parts of the skeleton. It is capable of powerful, rapid contractions, but tires quickly. The structure of skeletal muscle fibres is shown in Figure 3.11a.

ACTIVITY

Take a small piece of muscle (e.g. beef steak) and using a mounted needle tease out one of the numerous fibres it is made of. Mount this on a slide in a drop of saline, and examine it under the microscope. Draw what you see.

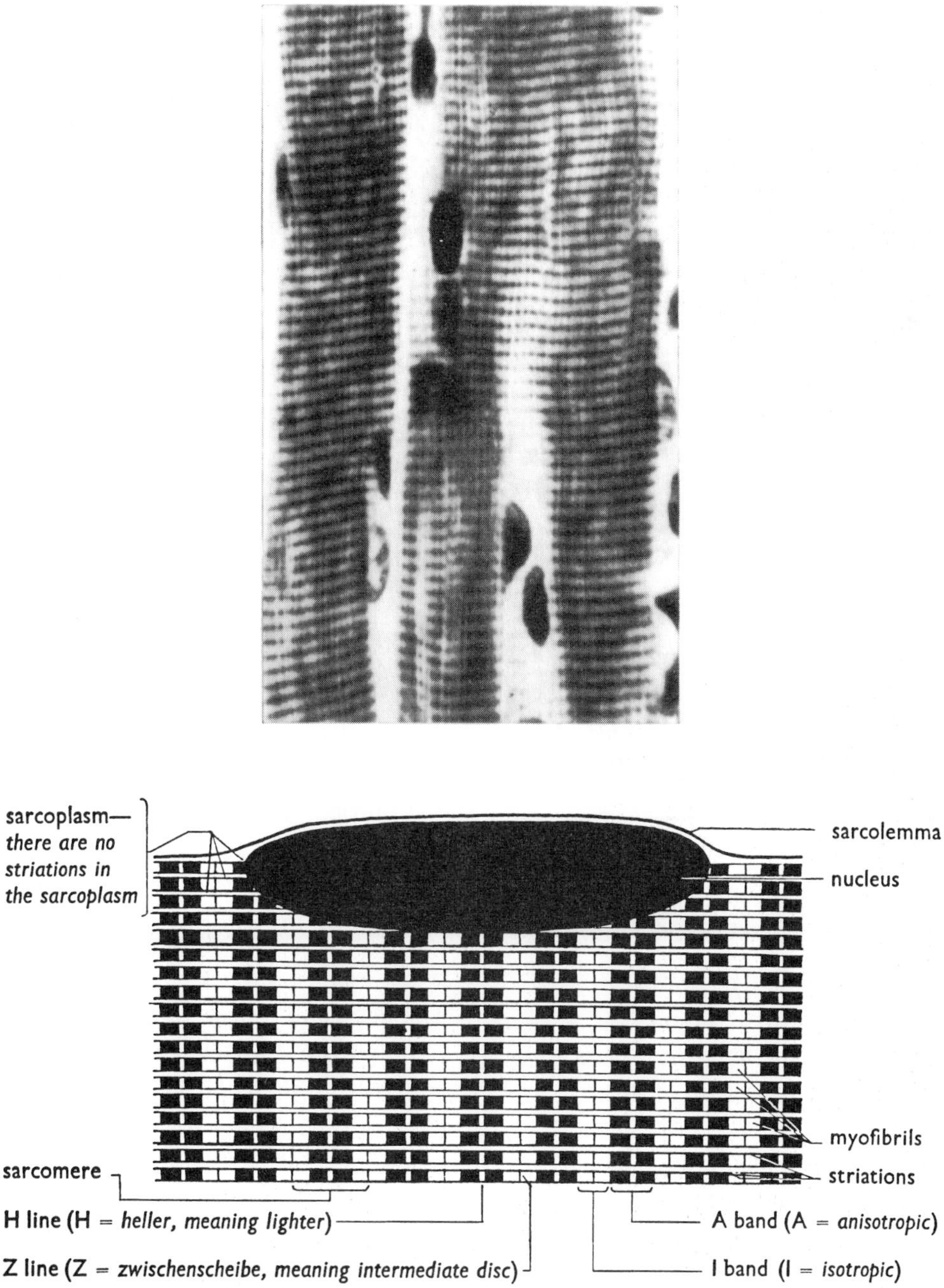

Figure 3.11 a) Structure of a skeletal muscle fibre, b) diagram based on electron micrographs
Source: An Atlas of Histology, by W.H. Freeman and B. Bracegirdle, Heinemann, 1966.

Each muscle fibre contains from several hundred to several thousand MYOFIBRILS (Figure 3.11b). These run longitudinally and are made up of thick and thin filaments. The thick filaments comprise the protein MYOSIN, and the thin filaments consist of the protein ACTIN. It is the arrangement of these filaments which gives this muscle its striped appearance. When the muscle contracts, the thick and thin filaments slide over each other so that the myofibrils shorten.

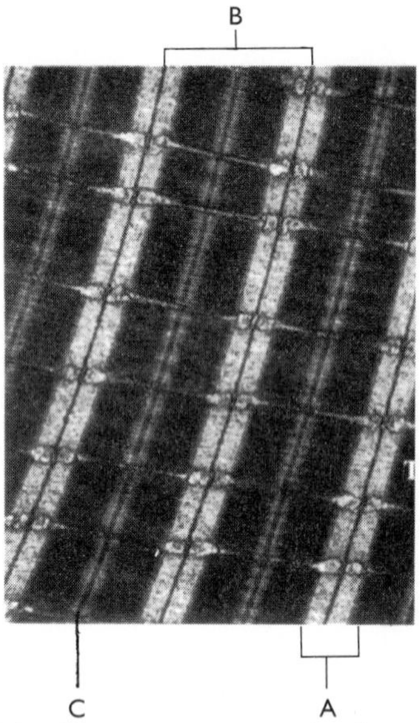

Figure 3.12 Electronmicrograph of part of a striated muscle (×7,650). *Source:* P.M.G. Munro, Biopolymer Group, Imperial College, in *Biological Science*, N.P.O. Green, G.W. Stout and D.J. Taylor, Cambridge University Press, 1985.

ACTIVITY

Use Figure 3.12 to help you answer the following questions:

- Identify the parts A–C indicated in Figure 3.12.
- What happens to the lengths of parts A, B and C during contraction of this tissue?
- What happens to the length of the dark band during contraction?

NERVOUS TISSUE

NERVOUS TISSUE is composed of nerve cells, or NEURONES, which are capable of transmitting an electrical impulse. A neurone contains a nucleus which is found within a CELL BODY (Figure 3.13). Parts of the neurone known as DENDRONS transmit the impulse to the cell body, and parts known as AXONS transmit the impulse away from the cell body. Some neurones are covered with a fatty sheath and are known as MYELINATED; the remainder are unmyelinated.

Neurones are found throughout the body where they form the nervous system. This consists of the CENTRAL NERVOUS SYSTEM (CNS) and the NERVES. The central nervous system comprises the brain and the spinal cord.

- Neurones which conduct impulses from the internal and external environments towards the CNS are called *sensory neurones*.
- Neurones which conduct impulses away from the CNS to effector organs like muscles and glands are called *motor neurones* (Figure 3.14).
- Neurones which conduct impulses from sensory to motor neurones are called *intermediate neurones*.

The ability to respond to stimuli is a feature of all living organisms. Neurones are especially adapted to enable the nervous system to carry out its functions, which are:

- to collect information about the internal and external environments;
- to process and integrate the information, usually taking into account previous experience;
- to act on the information, by coordinating the activities of the body.

The neurones transfer information very rapidly from sense cells to the central nervous system, and then convey messages back to effector organs to enable fast responses to be made.

ASSESSMENT OPPORTUNITY ✓

1 Provide a report which explains the role of each organelle in a human body cell.

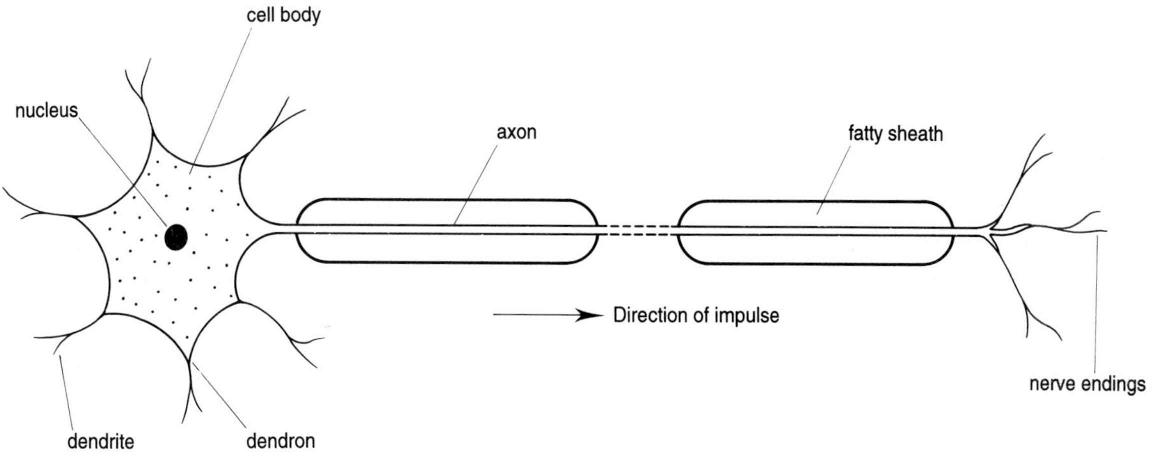

Figure 3.13 Motor neurone

2 List the key features of each of the following tissue types:
Epithelia
Connective
Muscle
Nervous
Note how each type of tissue is adapted to perform its function.

3 Look at photomicrographs of each of the following tissues:
Squamous epithelium
Compound epithelium
Compact bone
Blood
Skeletal muscle
Neurones
First identify each photomicrograph, and then identify the structures shown.

4 Provide a report which summarises the processes involved in cellular respiration. Clearly identify the anaerobic and aerobic phases.

Organ organisation

As we have seen, tissues are groups of similar specialist cells. They have a common origin and function.

Tissues are grouped together to form organs. Several different types of tissue combine to make one organ which has one or more physiological functions.

BODY SYSTEM ORGANISATION

Most organs do not function independently but in groups called organ systems. These can also be called body systems.

The following are the human body systems:

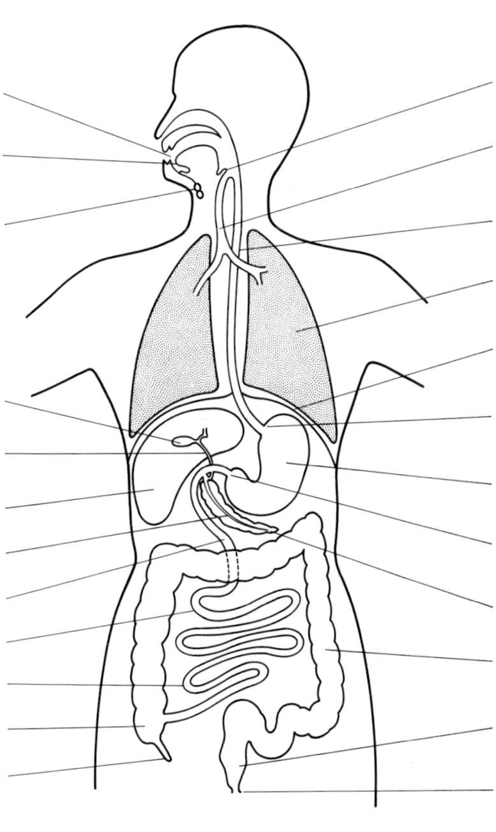

Figure 3.14 The Alimentary Canal

- Digestive system.
- Cardiovascular system.
- Immune system.
- Respiratory system.
- Renal system.
- Reproductive system.
- Endocrine system.
- Musculo-skeletal system.
- Nervous and sensory system.

INTER-RELATIONSHIPS OF BODY SYSTEMS TO PERFORM FUNCTIONS

Body systems work together to perform the different functions of the body.

For energy supply	→	digestive, liver, cardiovascular, respiratory.
For communication	→	cardiovascular, endocrine, nervous, sensory.
For support and locomotion	→	musculo-skeletal, nervous.
For reproduction	→	reproductive organs, endocrine, cardiovascular.
For excretion	→	renal, respiratory, skin, liver.
For defence	→	skin, immune system, cardiovascular lymphatic.

The liver and skin are included in this list as they are very important in many functions, although they are not body systems in the strictest sense.

THE DIGESTIVE SYSTEM

Nutrients

The nutrients in food provide the body with energy and with the raw materials for synthesis of new molecules and growth.

The following are important in the diet:

- Carbohydrates
- Proteins
- Fats
- Water
- Minerals
- Vitamins
- Roughage

Water, minerals and vitamins can enter the blood stream in the form in which they are taken in, but carbohydrates, proteins and fats must be digested first.

The digestion, absorption and metabolism of food

To be of value to the body, the food that is ingested through the mouth must be broken down mechanically and chemically. It can then enter the blood stream and be distributed to all living tissues in the body.

Digestion and absorption take place in the ALIMENTARY CANAL (see Figure 3.14), which runs from the mouth to the anus. It is muscular, with layers of circular and longitudinal muscle. The circular muscles, by contracting and relaxing alternately, push the food through the various regions of the alimentary canal, where it is first digested and then absorbed. The wave-like motion causing food to move along is called PERISTALSIS.

Digestion is the process by which insoluble food consisting of large molecules is broken down into soluble smaller molecules. These smaller molecules, in solution, pass through the walls of the intestine and eventually enter the blood stream. Digestion is brought about by hydrolytic enzymes. These are special proteins which are able to speed up the reactions causing the breakdown of proteins, carbohydrates and fats taken into the body in the diet. The elements of water, –H and –OH, are added to certain bonds in the large insoluble molecules. The bonds then break down, releasing the soluble small molecules.

- Proteins are broken down into amino acids.
- Fats are broken down into fatty acids and glycerol.
- Carbohydrates are broken down into glucose and other monosaccharides.

In the alimentary canal, the mechanical

breakdown of food into smaller pieces takes place first, followed by digestion and absorption. Each part of the alimentary canal is adapted to its own particular role in this sequence of events.

ACTIVITY

Copy the diagram in Figure 3.14 and label the parts of the alimentary canal and the associated organs. Choose from the following: anus, rectum, appendix, epiglottis, gall bladder, liver, bile duct, lung, diaphragm, stomach, colon, pancreas, pyloric sphincter, cardiac sphincter, salivary gland, tongue, mouth, pancreatic duct, duodenum, ileum, colon, oesophagus, caecum, jejunum.

Briefly note the role of each of the parts that you label and write one paragraph to summarise the function of each organ.

ABSORPTION

Some absorption takes place in the duodenum and jejunum, but most takes place in the ileum.

Figure 3.15 details the structure of one villus. There are 20–49 villi to each square millimetre of the ileum wall.

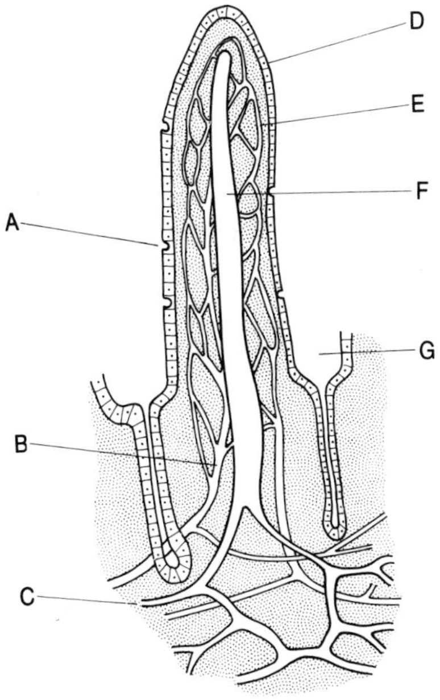

Figure 3.15 Longitudinal section of a villus

ACTIVITY

1 Look at a prepared slide of the ileum, either a transverse section or a longitudinal section. Try to identify the tissue types and structures.
List five structural adaptations which make the ileum suitable for its functions, particularly absorption.

2 Label the parts A–G of the villus in Figure 3.15.
Choose from: network of blood capillaries, lacteal vessel, Crypt of Lieberkuhn, blood vessels supplying villus, branch of lymphatic system, mucus-secreting goblet cell, epithelium.

3 Explain how each of the following are absorbed and explain how each reaches the blood system:
- fatty acids,
- glycerol,
- amino acids,
- monosaccharides,
- vitamins,
- minerals.

So that body cells can make use of the food that is eaten, the nutrients must pass out of the alimentary canal into the bloodstream to be transported to where they are needed. The gut wall presents a barrier for the nutrients to cross.

THE LIVER

The liver is a large lobed structure which lies just beneath the diaphragm and partly overlapping the stomach. It receives oxygenated blood from the hepatic artery and deoxygenated blood is removed in the hepatic vein. In addition it receives all the blood leaving the alimentary canal in the hepatic portal vein. This is unlike other blood vessels in the body in that it both originates and terminates in organs. This special arrangement exists because the liver is responsible for regulating the level of many solutes in the blood. The composition of the blood leaving the alimentary canal will be determined by the diet, and therefore it will not be suitable to be released directly into the general circulation. This internal regulation function of the liver is one of the many homeostatic mechanisms in the body. Homeostasis is the process by which the body regulates internal conditions so that metabolic processes proceed at a constant rate.

ACTIVITY

1 Find out about the structure of the liver and look at a microscope slide of a transverse section of liver. Identify as many of the features as you can.

2 Find out how the liver is involved in carbohydrate metabolism.

3 How is the liver involved in heat production and therefore temperature regulation?

4 The liver is important in excretion. Find out how it excretes:
(a) excess proteins and amino acids,
(b) worn-out red blood cells.

THE CARDIOVASCULAR SYSTEM

The cardiovascular system consists of the following tissues and organs:

- the heart (see Figure 3.17, page 147);
- the circulatory system: arteries, veins, capillaries;
- the blood;
- the lymph.

The heart and circulatory system

The role of the heart and circulatory system is to carry blood between various parts of the body. Each organ has a major artery supplying it with blood from the heart and a major vein which returns it.

ACTIVITY

Copy Figure 3.16 and add the names of the vessels numbered 1–19. Use arrows to show the direction of blood flow. Shade the vessels containing oxygenated blood red, and those containing deoxygenated blood blue.

The flow of blood is maintained in three ways:

1 *The pumping action of the heart.*
2 *The contraction of skeletal muscle.* The contraction of muscles during movement squeezes the veins and increases the pressure of blood within them. Pocket valves in the veins prevent backflow of blood and ensure that it flows to the heart.
3 *Inspiratory movements.* The pressure in the thorax is reduced when breathing in, and this helps to draw blood back to the heart.

HEART STRUCTURE AND ACTION

ACTIVITY

1 Copy Figure 3.17 and label the parts A–Q. Indicate with arrows the direction of blood flow.

2 Note the function of each of the parts labelled A–Q.

3 Using a guide, dissect a heart (e.g. the heart of a sheep). Relate the diagram to the actual structure.

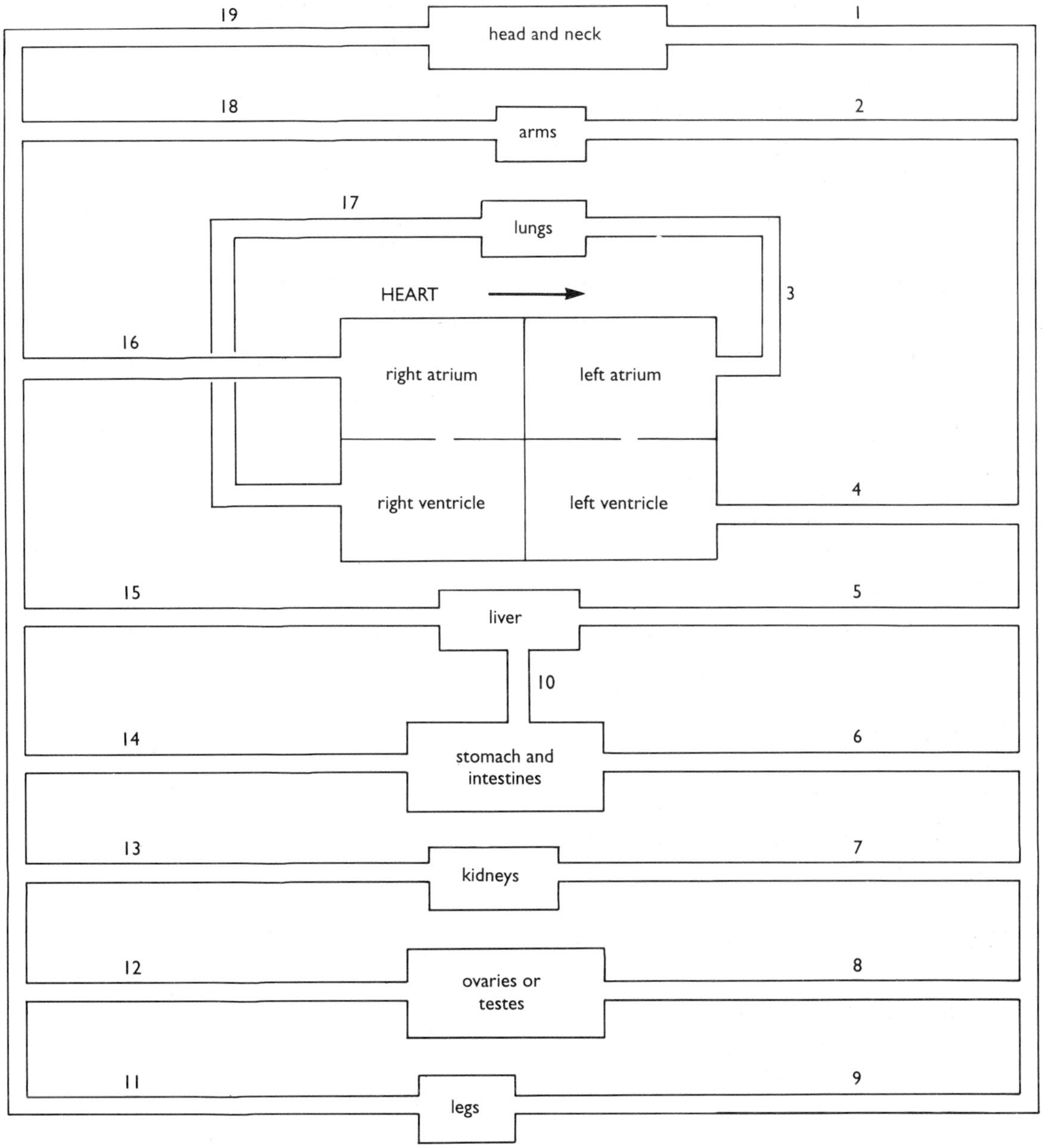

Figure 3.16 General plan of the human circulatory system

ARTERIES, VEINS AND CAPILLARIES

ARTERIES carry blood away from the heart. VEINS carry blood to the heart. CAPILLARIES connect arteries and veins and form a network in the tissues.

FUNCTIONS OF THE BLOOD

The functions of each type of cell in the blood are shown in Figure 3.8.

A major role of the blood is TRANSPORT.

THE RESPIRATORY SYSTEM

The respiratory system consists of the following:

- *Air passages* connecting the respiratory surfaces with the outside air. These passages are found in the nose and nasal cavities, the mouth and throat, the trachea and the two bronchi. The passages are covered by mucus secreted by goblet cells in the ciliated epithelium which lines them. The

ACTIVITY

Copy out the table and complete it.

Materials transported	Examples	Transported to:	Transported from:	Transported in:
Respiratory gases	Oxygen			Haemoglobin in red cells
	Carbon dioxide			
Organic nutrients	Glucose Amino acids Vitamins			
Mineral salts	Calcium Iodine Iron			
Excretory products	Urea			
Hormones	Insulin Anti-diuretic hormone			
Heat	Metabolic heat			

How is the blood involved in:

- communication,
- energy supply,
- reproduction?

mucus traps particles from the incoming air and also moistens it. The bronchi lead into further passages, the many bronchioles.

- *The respiratory surface*, which is formed by 300 million air sacs, the alveoli, in each lung. The total respiratory surface area is approximately 90 m^2. The surfaces of the alveoli are moist and form the site of gaseous exchange of oxygen and carbon dioxide. Each alveolus is surrounded by a capillary network, which conveys deoxygenated blood to the alveoli and oxygenated blood away from the alveoli.
- *The structures which cause the breathing mechanism and ventilation of the lungs.* Air is moved in and out of the air passages and the alveoli. The structures involved are the diaphragm, ribs, intercostal muscles and pleural membranes. The latter secrete pleural fluid into the pleural cavity; the function of the fluid is lubrication. Pressure in this cavity is always lower than that in the lungs, so that the lungs expand to fill the thorax.

ACTIVITY

1 Copy the diagram of the respiratory system (Figure 3.18).

2 Label the structures A–H.

3 Briefly note the function of each structure.

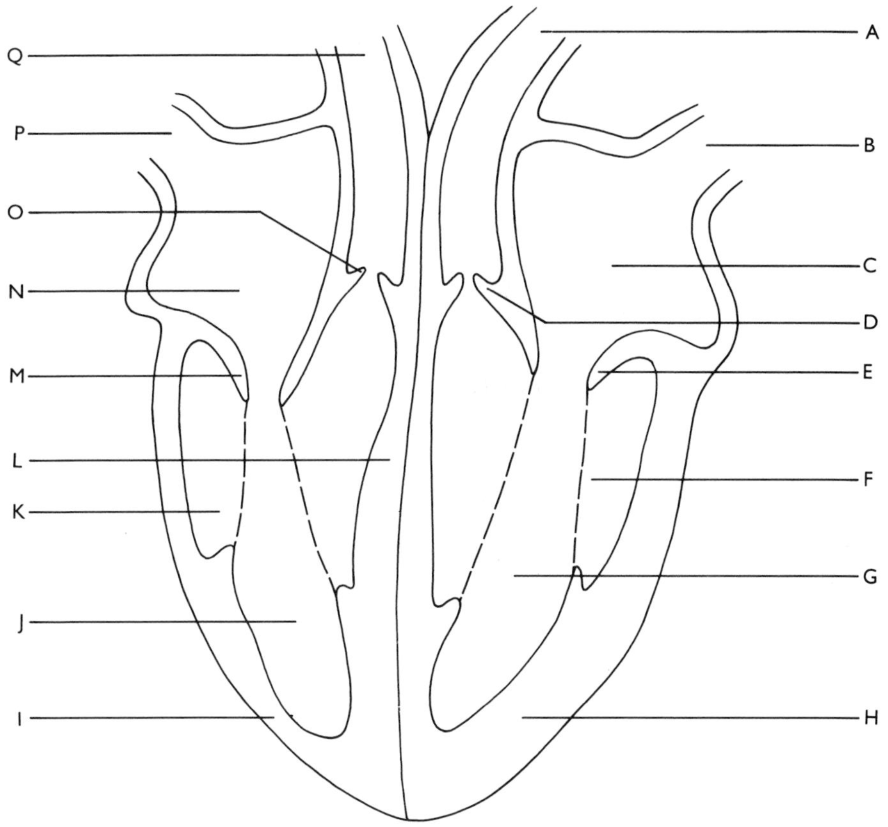

Figure 3.17 Structure of the heart

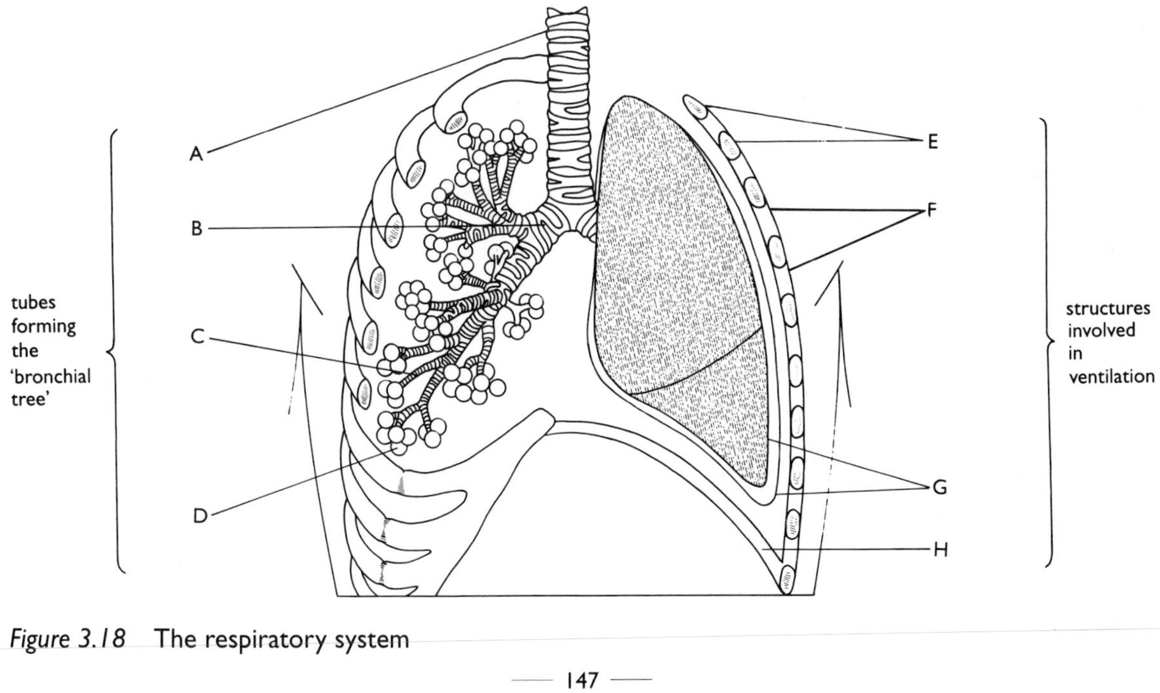

Figure 3.18 The respiratory system

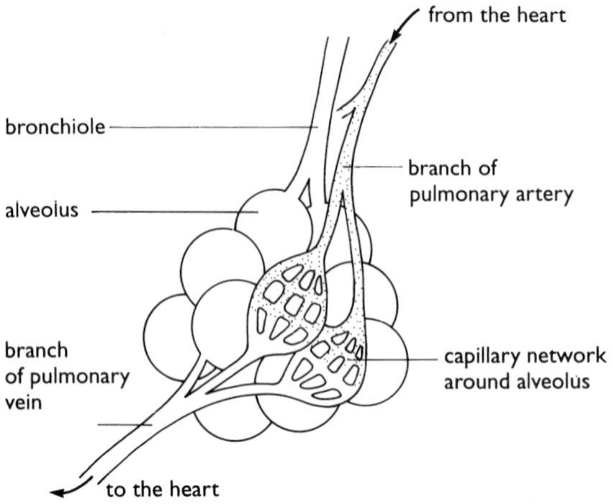

Figure 3.19 A group of alveoli

ACTIVITY

1 Look at Figure 3.19. Why is it advantageous for the terminal chambers of the respiratory system to be divided into numerous small compartments rather than one larger spherical chamber?

2 What is the function of the capillary network covering the terminal group of alveoli?

Gaseous exchange at the alveoli

Each alveolus is made up of thin cells (squamous epithelium) and some elastic and collagen fibres (see Figure 3.5). The network of capillaries that surrounds the group of alveoli brings blood from the pulmonary artery. The capillaries unite to form the pulmonary vein. The capillaries are also lined with squamous epithelium, and are very narrow so that the red cells within them are squeezed as they pass through. This slows down the flow of blood, allowing more time for diffusion, and increases the surface area for the diffusion of oxygen into the cells. The oxygen from the inspired air dissolves in the moisture lining the alveoli and then diffuses across the alveolar and capillary walls into the plasma. From here it diffuses into the red blood cells and combines with the respiratory pigment, haemoglobin. Carbon dioxide diffuses from the blood into the alveolus to leave the lungs in the expired air.

ACTIVITY

1 Inspect Figure 3.20. Why is the surface of the alveolus covered by a layer of water?

2 What properties are possessed by the squamous epithelial cells, which line both the alveolar and the capillary walls that make them particularly suitable for their function here?

3 By which physical process do the oxygen and carbon dioxide molecules pass across the alveolar and capillary walls?

4 What role does the respiratory system play in energy supply and excretion?

Ventilation of the lungs

Ventilation of the lungs is brought about by changes in the volume of the thorax.

The rhythmical breathing movements occur 12 to 20 times a minute.

INSPIRATION (BREATHING IN)

The volume of the thorax is increased by two movements:

1 The muscles around the edge of the diaphragm contract and pull it downwards so that it flattens.
2 The lower ribs are raised upwards and outwards by contraction of the external intercostal muscles which run obliquely from one rib to the next. The internal intercostal muscles are relaxed at this time.

The volume of the lungs increases as the volume of the thorax increases because the lungs are thin and elastic. Thus air is drawn in (see Figure 3.21a).

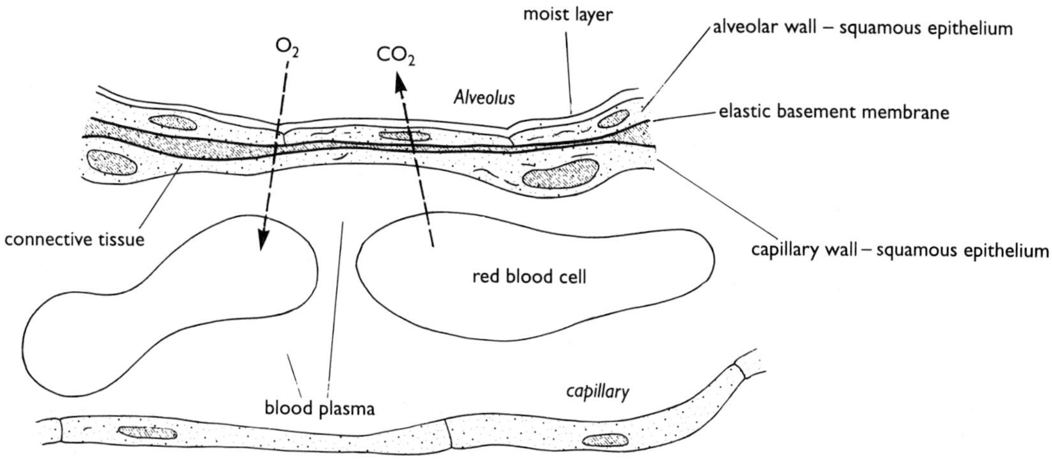

Figure 3.20 Gaseous exchange in an alveolus

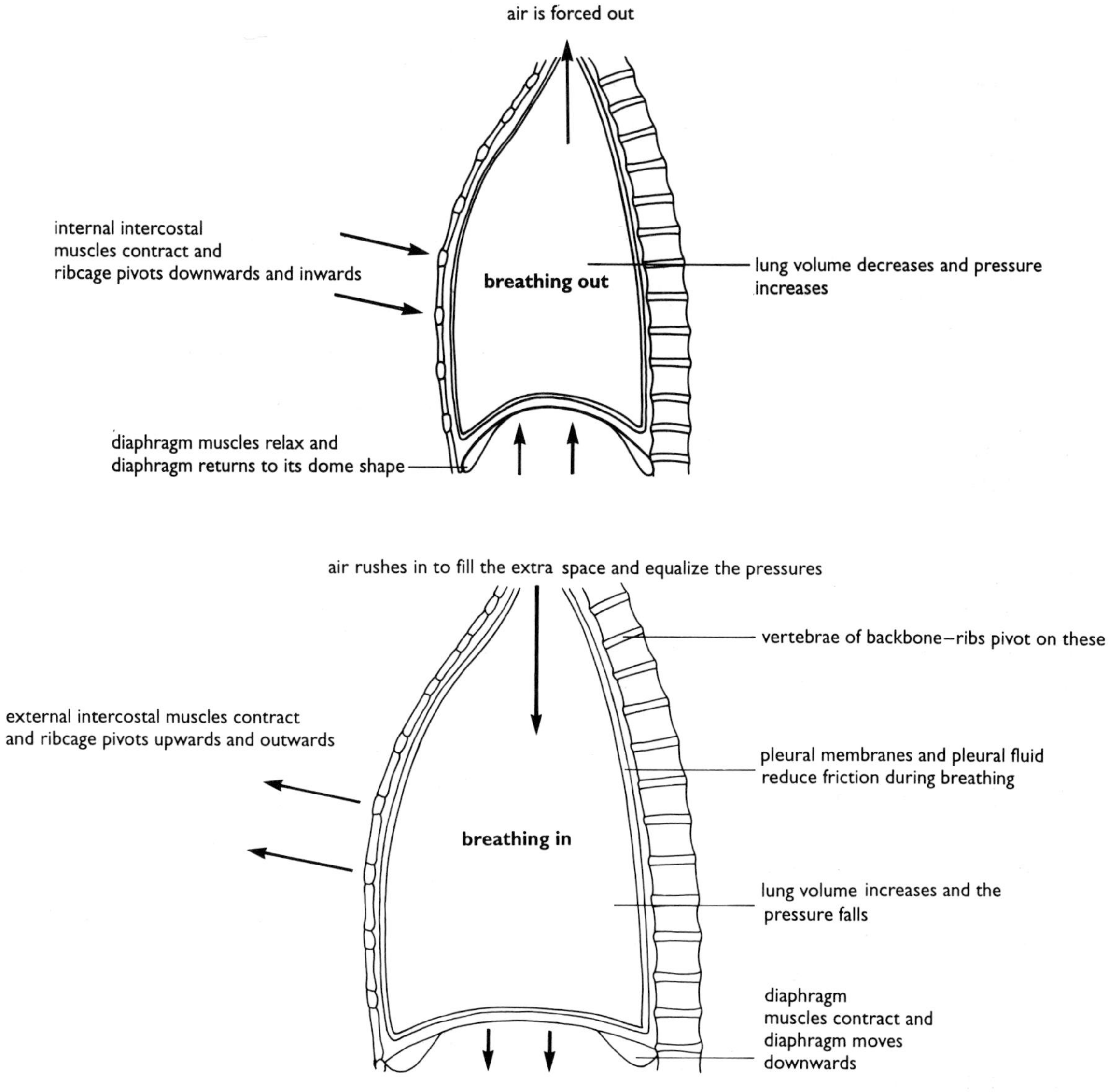

Figure 3.21 Breathing (a) in, (b) out

EXPIRATION (BREATHING OUT)

The muscles of the diaphragm relax so that it resumes its dome shape. The external intercostal muscles relax and the internal intercostal muscles contract. The volume of the thorax decreases and therefore the lungs contract and air is expelled (see Figure 3.21b). This is largely a passive process.

THE NERVOUS SYSTEM

The nervous system responds very rapidly to stimuli. The messages, in the form of impulses, are carried by nerve cells or NEURONES. These are described earlier in the chapter (page 141). The shape of the neurone varies, depending on its function. A motor neurone is illustrated in Figure 3.13. Some neurones are covered with a fatty sheath and are known as myelinated. The remainder are unmyelinated.

Both the central and peripheral parts of the nervous system are made up of neurones. Neurones may be bundled together and wrapped in connective tissue to form NERVES. The nervous system consists of the CENTRAL NERVOUS SYSTEM (CNS) and the nerves (or PERIPHERAL NERVOUS SYSTEM). The central nervous system consists of the brain (Figure 3.22) and the spinal cord (Figure 3.23).

ACTIVITY

1 Find out the functions of each of the parts labelled in Figure 3.22.

2 Look at a prepared slide of spinal cord (transverse section) under the microscope. How many of the features labelled in Figure 3.23 can you find? Under high power, look for the cell bodies in the grey matter.

- Neurones which conduct impulses from the internal and external environments towards the CNS are called SENSORY NEURONES.

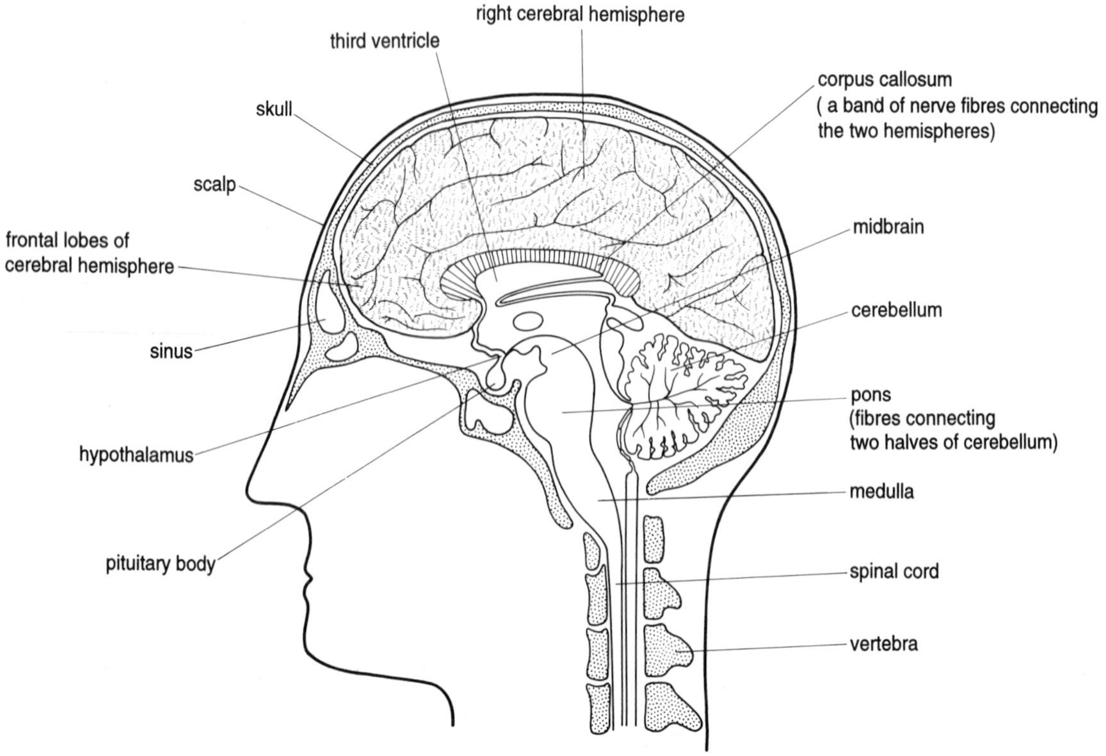

Figure 3.22 Section through the head to show the brain

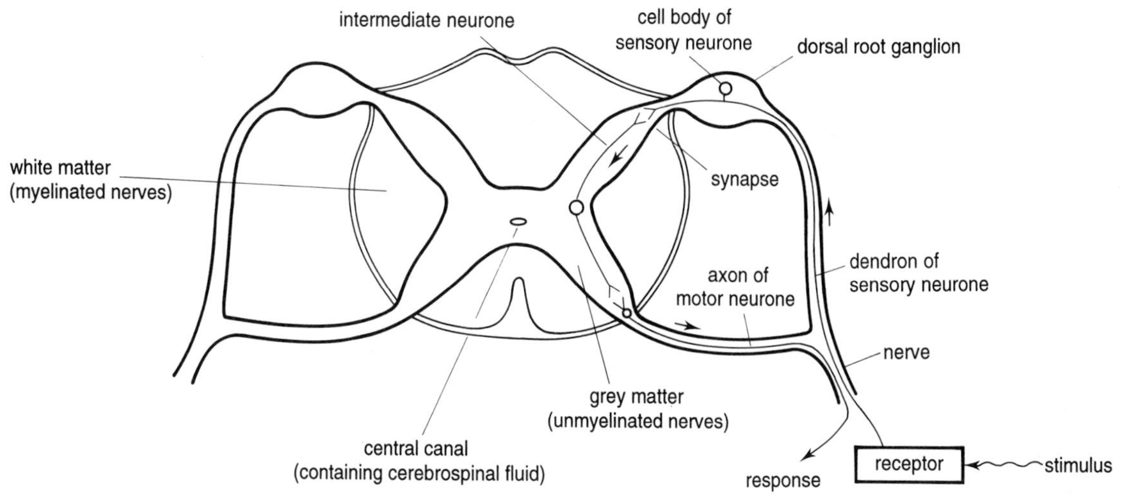

Figure 3.23 Transverse section through the spinal cord showing the reflex arc

- Neurones which conduct impulses away from the CNS to effector organs like muscles and glands are called MOTOR NEURONES (see Figure 3.13).
- Neurones which conduct impulses from sensory to motor neurones are called INTERMEDIATE NEURONES.

These three types of neurone can connect to form a REFLEX ARC (see Figure 3.23) which is involved in an automatic response.

ACTIVITY

- In Figure 3.23 identify the three types of neurone described. Compare the relative lengths of their axons and dendrons.
- Describe the pathway of the impulse involved in the withdrawal of a finger from a pinprick.
- Try one of the simplest reflexes, the knee jerk. Sit with the right thigh crossed loosely over the left knee in such a way as slightly to stretch the extensor muscle of the leg. If someone now taps the right knee tendon (just below the knee cap) a sharp extension of the leg should result.

Autonomic nervous system

The peripheral nervous system consists not only of the *somatic nervous system*, which activates voluntary responses, but also the *autonomic nervous system*, which controls activities of the internal environment which are normally involuntary. Obviously this latter system plays a vital role in aspects of homeostasis.

Sense organs

Changes in both external and internal environments occur all the time and responses to these are vital to ensure survival. Some cells are specialised to enable us to be sensitive to stimuli; these sensory cells are grouped together to form sense organs. They link to the central nervous system so that a rapid response can be made to the stimuli.

ACTIVITY

The skin

The skin has touch, pressure and pain receptors. Look at Figure 3.38. The Meissner's Corpuscles are sensitive to touch and the Pacinian Corpuscles are sensitive to pressure. The more of these per unit area, the more impulses are sent to the brain in response to stimuli and the more sensitive the skin. Devise, carry out and produce a report on a series of experiments to determine the sensitivity of pressure receptors on different areas of skin on the human body.

The eye

The eye contains photoreceptor cells and produces an ever changing image of the visual field at which it is directed. Investigate the structure of the eye by looking at a diagram of a vertical section through the eye and describing the function of the parts labelled. You may be able to obtain an eye of a sheep or cow for dissection. Explain why we need sight.

The ear

The ear has two functions: hearing, and maintaining balance. Find out how the structure of the ear is adapted to these functions.

THE MUSCULO-SKELETAL SYSTEM

The coordinated contraction and relaxation of muscles attached to the bones of the skeleton allows us to move our bodies. Bones articulate with each other at movable joints, which allow manoeuvrability. The skeleton is strong enough to support the weight of the body during movement. It is especially adapted to allow bipedal movement (walking upright on our hind limbs). The skeleton also has a major role in the protection of delicate organs.

The skeleton is made of bone and cartilage. The detailed structure of these tissues is described earlier in this chapter.

The skeleton can be considered in two parts:

- *the axial skeleton* consisting of the skull, vertebral column and the ribcage;
- *the appendicular skeleton* consisting of the girdles and limbs.

ACTIVITY

1 Look at Figure 3.24 and briefly outline the function of each of the labelled parts. (In addition, some bones have very specialised functions. For example, red blood cells are produced in bone marrow, and the middle ear ossicles are made of bone).

2 The functions of the skeleton can be described under four headings:
   - support;
   - protection;
   - movement;
   - muscle attachment.

   Write a paragraph explaining how the skeleton carries out these functions and note which particular bones are involved.

3 Find out about the structure of the vertebral column and note the function of each of the types of vertebra. How are they adapted to their function?

   The first two neck vertebrae are called the atlas and axis respectively. How do they articulate with and support the skull?

Joints

The bones of the skeleton articulate at joints. The actions of the muscles bring about the movement of bones at synovial joints. The articulating surface of the bones is covered with pads of articular cartilage. The joint is enclosed by fibrous capsule, and ligaments stretch from bone to bone. Lining the capsule is a synovial membrane which secretes synovial fluid into the capsule.

ACTIVITY

Look at Figure 3.25 of a synovial joint. What are the functions of the following parts: fibrous capsule, ligament, synovial fluid and synovial membrane?

Find out about the four main types of synovial joint. Explain how the structures

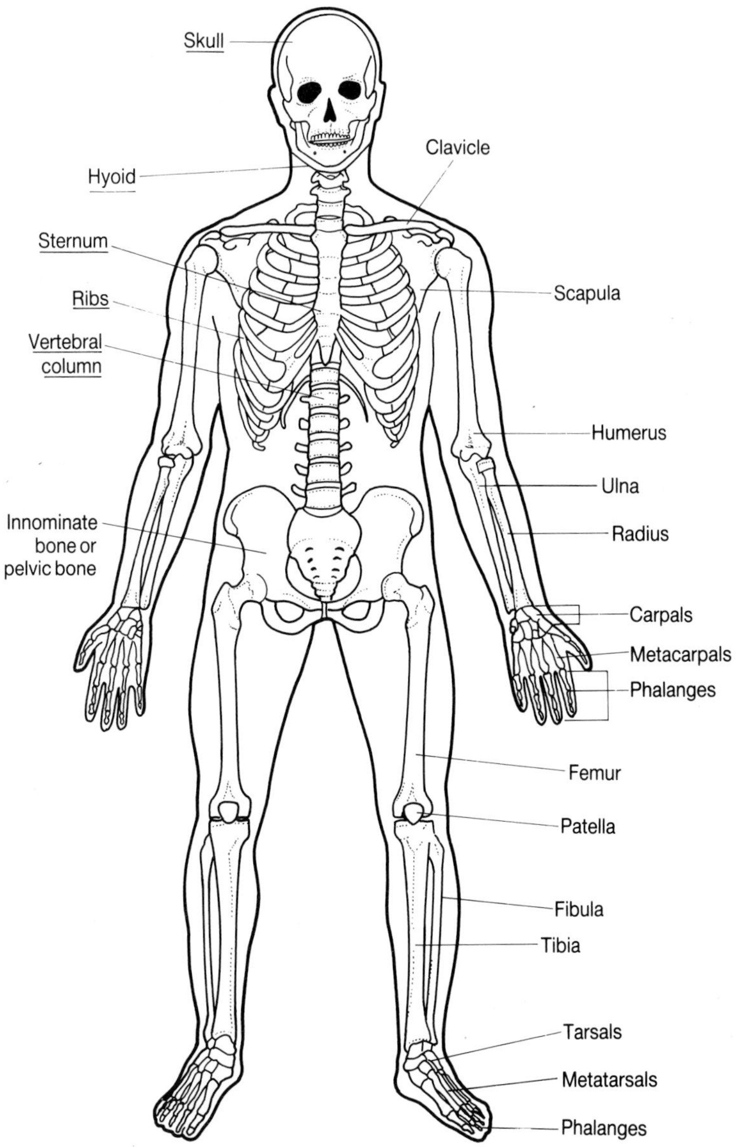

Figure 3.24 The human skeleton

of the different joints allow four different types of movement in the skeleton:

- gliding;
- hinge;
- ball and socket;
- pivot.

Muscular movement

Voluntary muscles cause movement of the skeleton as they contract and relax. They can contract to about one-third or one-half of their resting length. The structure and mechanism of contraction of voluntary muscle are described earlier in this chapter (page 139). Contractions of voluntary muscle are brought about as a result of nerve impulses reaching the muscle. The nerve fibre terminates at the muscle with a special structure, the motor end plate. This enables the nerve impulse to pass into the muscle fibre.

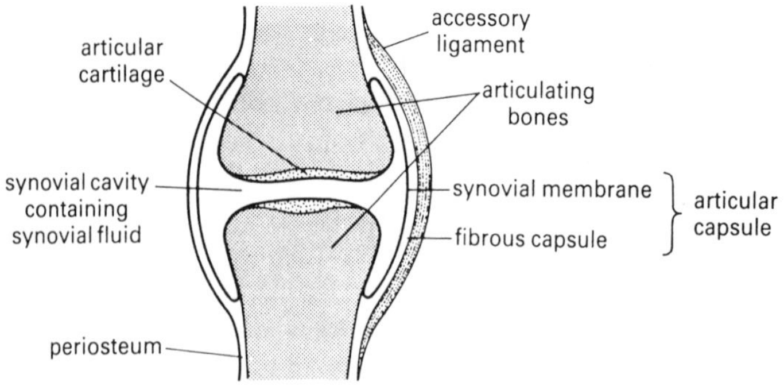

Figure 3.25 A synovial joint

ACTIVITY

Find a photomicrograph of motor end plates on muscle fibres.

Identify the nerve fibres, the motor end plates and the muscle fibres. Explain how the nerve impulse triggers contraction of the muscle cell.

The muscles are attached to the bones by tendons and act across joints. The limbs are worked as lever systems. The muscles can only contract a short distance, but because they are attached near a joint, the movement at the end of the limb is greatly magnified. The biceps muscle of the arm may contract only 80 or 90 mm, but the hand will move 60 cm.

ANTAGONISTIC PAIRS OF MUSCLES

Muscles work in antagonistic pairs across a joint. In the case of the limbs they are called flexor and extensor muscles, according to whether they bend or straighten the limb.

ACTIVITY

Look at Figure 3.26 which shows the antagonistic pair of muscles in the arm. Explain how they work.

Find out about antagonistic pairs of muscles in the leg and explain how walking is achieved. How do we keep upright?

What role does the nervous system play in support and locomotion?

THE REPRODUCTIVE SYSTEM

Sexual reproduction involves the fusing of two sex cells called gametes, one the male spermatazoon and one the female ovum. This process is called fertilisation or conception. The reproductive system is responsible for producing the gametes and enabling internal fertilisation to occur within the body of the woman. The resulting cell is called a zygote, and this develops into an embryo and then a foetus. The female reproductive system is adapted to enable the foetus to develop to a certain stage before birth occurs.

ACTIVITY

- Look at Figure 3.27. Note the function of the following structures:
  ovary, funnel of oviduct, oviduct, uterus, cervix and vagina.
- What size can the uterus reach in pregnancy? What is the role of the smooth muscle of the uterus wall?
- Look at Figure 3.28. Compare this with a microscope slide of the ovary. You can see various stages in the development of the ovum in a follicle. Find out more about these stages of development, and how the ovum is released. Make a series

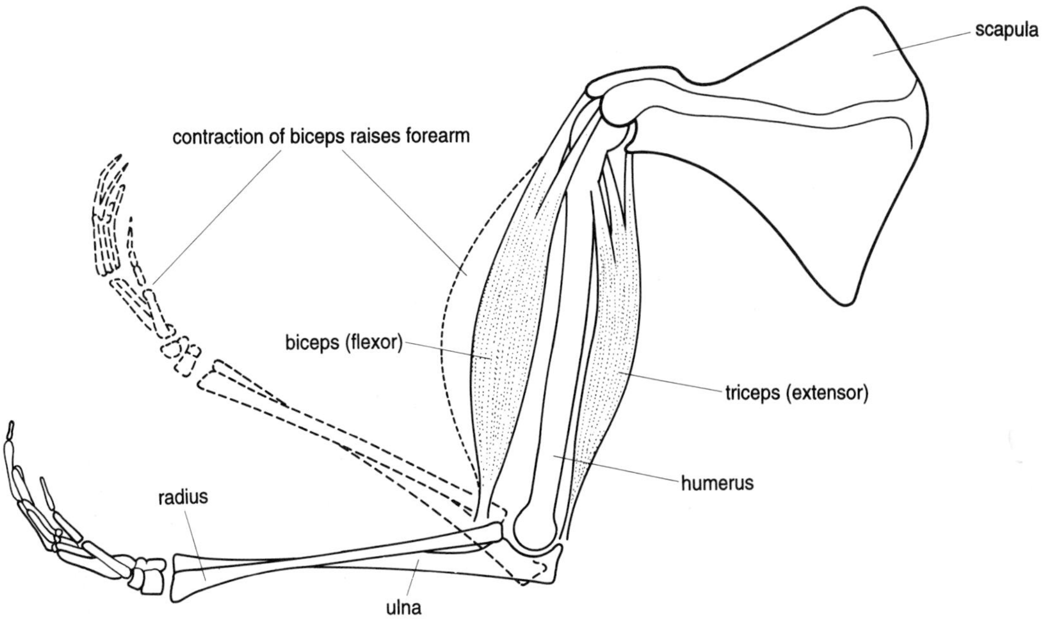

Figure 3.26 Antagonistic pairs of muscles

of annotated diagrams to illustrate the process.

- Look at Figure 3.29. Identify the hormones A, B, C and D. Explain the variation in their levels during the menstrual cycle and their roles. Include the events occurring in the ovary and the uterus wall in your account. Exactly what triggers ovulation?

ACTIVITY

- What are the advantages and disadvantages of the testes being outside the abdominal cavity?
- What is the role of the testosterone produced in the testes? Mention the role in the testes themselves as well as the link to the secondary sexual characteristics.

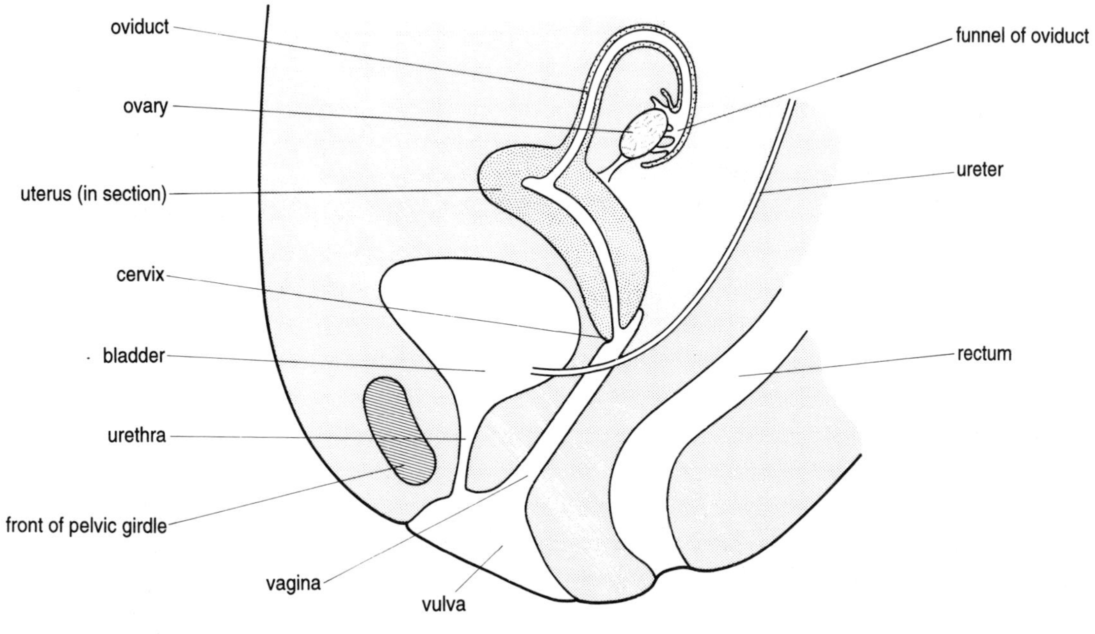

Figure 3.27 Female reproductive system

- Look at Figure 3.30. Describe the role of the following structures: penis, testis, sperm-producing tubules, epididymis, sperm duct, prostate gland, Cowper's gland and urethra.
- Describe how copulation and how ejaculation of spermatozoa into the vagina occur.
- Look at a microscope slide of spermatazoa. How are the spermatozoa adapted to their function?
- Examine a microscope slide of a section of the testis. Identify what you see.
- Explain the role of the circulatory system in reproduction.

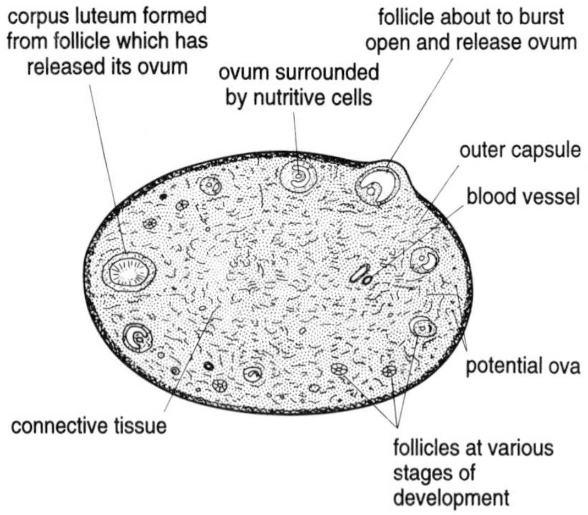

Figure 3.28 Longitudinal section of an ovary

THE RENAL SYSTEM

The kidneys produce urine and are the main organs of the urinary system. This system is often called the EXCRETORY SYSTEM because an important function of the kidneys is the excretion of nitrogenous waste, mostly in the form of urea, dissolved in the urine. The body cannot store excess proteins, so amino acids that are not immediately required are broken down in the liver to make urea. This is carried in the bloodstream to the kidneys for elimination. All the blood in the body passes through the kidneys in five minutes.

In addition, the kidneys carry out the following regulatory mechanisms:

- Regulation of the water content of the body fluids (and hence the volume of the body fluids).
- Regulation of the chemical composition of the body fluid (e.g. sodium chloride).
- Regulation of the pH of body fluid.

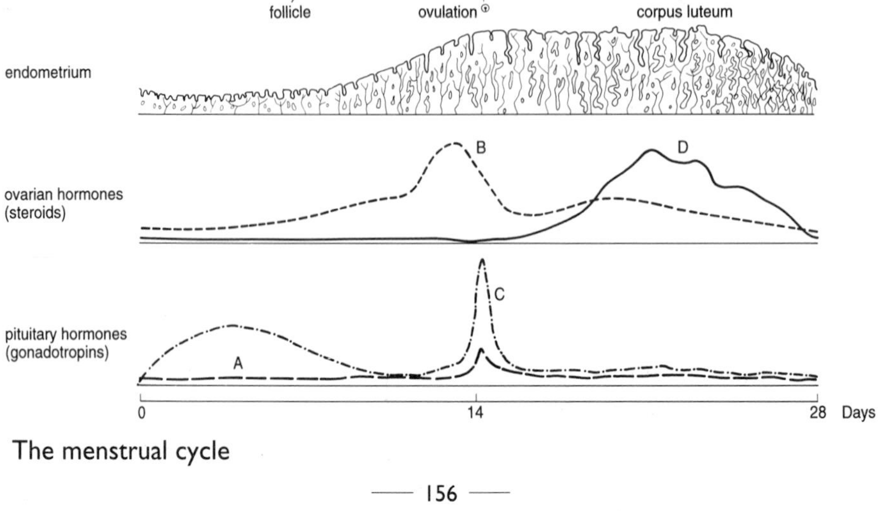

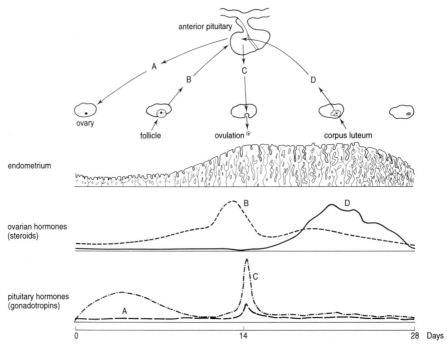

Figure 3.29 The menstrual cycle

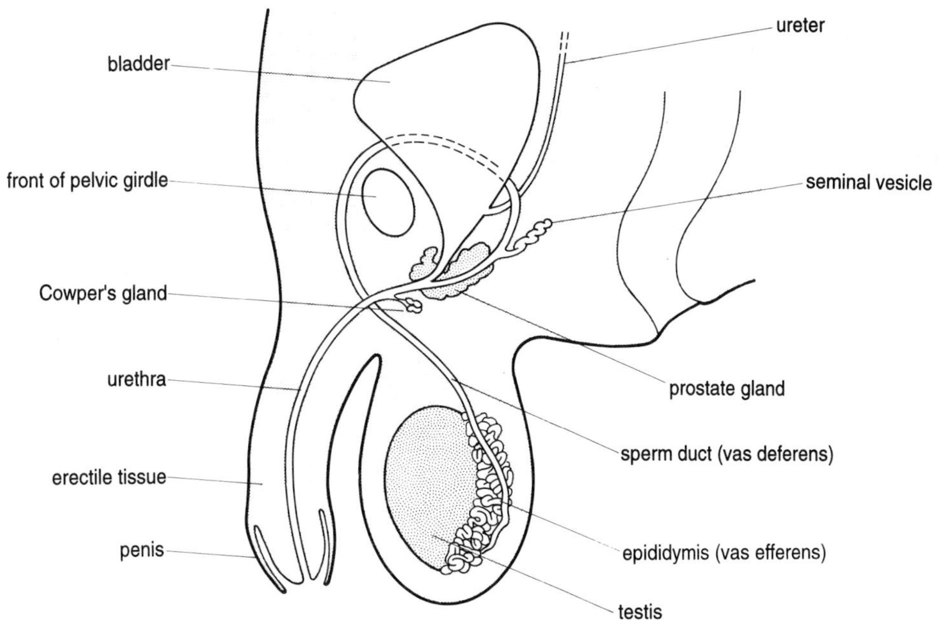

Figure 3.30 Male reproductive system

ACTIVITY

Figure 3.31 shows the urinary system.

- Distinguish between the ureter and the urethra. What is the function of the bladder? What is the role of the renal vein?
- The urea arrives at the kidney in the renal artery. Look back at Figure 3.16 (page 145). How does the urea get to the kidneys from the liver? List the blood vessels it travels through. What other important chemical arrives in the renal artery?
- Cut a kidney (e.g. from a lamb or pig) in half longitudinally with a sharp knife. Draw what you see, labelling as many structures shown in Figure 3.32 that you can see. (A nephron is too small to see.)

Detailed structure of the kidney

Each kidney has many blood vessels and approximately one million nephrons or kidney tubules. It is these tubules that carry out all the regulatory functions listed above.

The renal artery divides into many smaller arterioles, which eventually lead to the glomeruli, a small knot of capillaries, in the Bowman's capsules.

ACTIVITY

Look at Figure 3.33. Then examine a prepared slide of kidney cortex under a microscope. Can you find the Bowman's

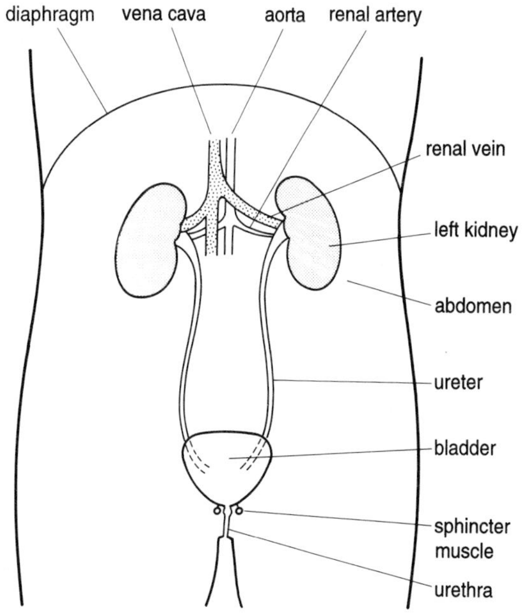

Figure 3.31 The urinary system

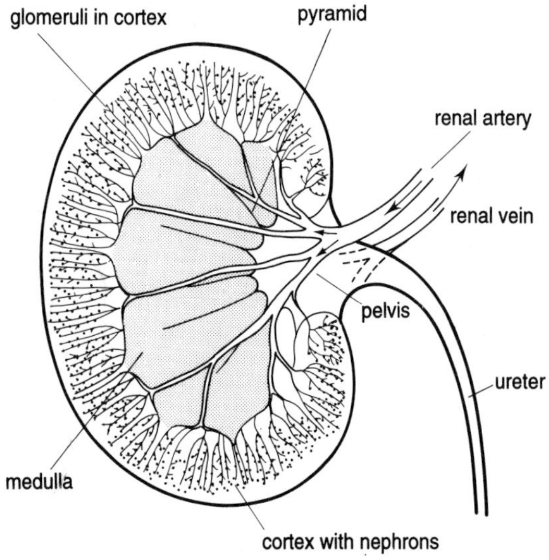

Figure 3.32 The structure of the kidney

capsules, each containing a glomerulus, and transverse sections of the tubules of the nephron? There will also be blood vessels; you may be able to see some red blood cells.

How the kidney functions

The blood pressure in the glomerulus is very high. This high pressure forces about one-fifth of the water from the plasma, taking with it small molecules, through the walls of the capillaries of the glomerulus and the walls of the Bowman's capsule into the capsule space. Both these walls are composed of squamous epithelial cells.

The liquid formed in the capsule space is called the glomerular filtrate or fluid, and the process by which it is formed is ultrafiltration.

ACTIVITY

- Can you think of two reasons why the pressure of the blood in the glomeruli is so high?
- How are the squamous cells found in the capillaries and Bowman's capsule adapted to their function?
- Look at Table 3.4 and note the differences between the blood leaving the glomerulus and the glomerular filtrate. How do you account for these differences? (Think about the sizes.)
- About 50% of the urea and much of the mineral content of filtrate are reabsorbed back into the blood. How do you account for the higher concentration of these in the urine?

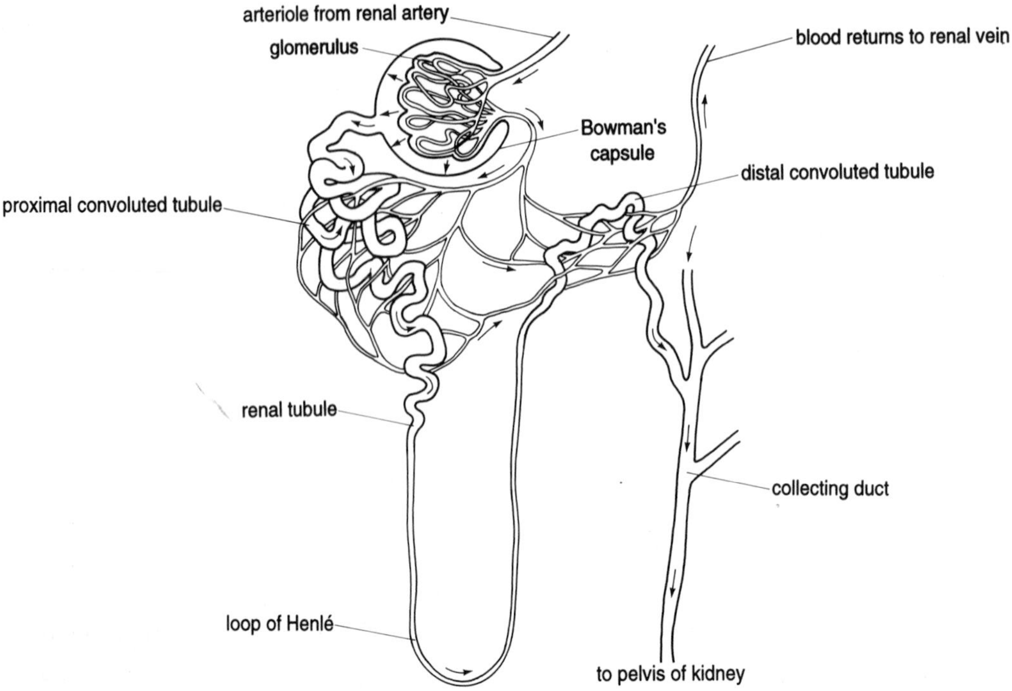

Figure 3.33 The nephron

Table 3.4 The differences between the blood leaving the glomerulus and the glomerular filtrate

Blood leaving the glomerulus	Glomerular filtrate
Water	Water
Plasma proteins	–
Platelets	–
Red blood cells	–
White blood cells	–
–	Glucose
–	Amino acids
–	Urea
–	Minerals

As the glomerular filtrate flows along the nephron its composition changes. This is because there are many substances in it which are needed by the body and must therefore be reabsorbed back into the bloodstream. Much of the water and glucose, and most of the mineral salts and amino acids, are among the substances which must not be excreted. If there was not any reabsorption of the water the body would be totally dehydrated in three minutes. Urea, other molecules and the water which is to be excreted are left in the nephron and eventually form urine. Most of the reabsorption occurs in the proximal convoluted tubule.

The loop of Henle causes a build up of salt in the medulla. As the collecting ducts pass through this area, water moves out of the filtrate by osmosis. The amount of water reabsorbed in this way is under the control of anti-diuretic hormone. How this works will be discussed in the 'Homeostasis' section later in this chapter.

The collecting ducts convey the urine to the pelvic region of the kidneys. From here it passes down the ureter to the bladder.

THE IMMUNE SYSTEM

Natural defences against disease

Resistance to pathogenic microbes entering the bloodstream is brought about by several mechanisms. These include the following:

- A hydrolytic enzyme in *tears*.
- The *skin* has a dead, horny layer which is difficult for micro-organisms to penetrate.
- The cell layers which line the mouth, respiratory surfaces, alimentary canal and vagina contain *antimicrobial enzymes* and produce *mucus* to trap particles. In the respiratory tract, *cilia* can sweep these particles away.
- The *acid* in the stomach will kill many micro-organisms.
- If a wound occurs, *clotting* of the blood will help prevent the entry of micro-organisms.

If the mechanisms above fail and micro-organisms enter the bloodstream there are processes which may be able to eliminate the pathogens:

- phagocytosis;
- immune response.

The immune response

Immunity is the ability of an organism to resist disease by the recognition of foreign material and the production of chemicals which help to destroy this material. The foreign material carries antigens. These are proteins or polysaccharides on the outer surface of the foreign material, which may be bacteria, fungi or viruses, or even a transplanted organ. Sometimes the antigen may be actually released from the pathogenic microbe. The chemicals which combat the antigens are called antibodies, which are proteins and are produced by lymphocytes. Each antibody is specific to a particular antigen; it combines with it and prevents it from doing harm.

There are two types of lymphocyte involved in the immune response:

1 *T-lymphocytes*. These are formed in the bone marrow but mature in the thymus gland. They then enter the lymphatic system and the lymph nodes, where they stay before multiplying and circulating around the body upon invasion by foreign antigens. These lymphocytes combat fungi and

initial invasion by viruses. They are involved in the rejection of foreign tissues, such as those of an unmatched transplanted organ. The lymphocytes carry the antibodies, and the whole cell must contact the antigen in order to attack it.

2 *B-lymphocytes.* These are formed and mature in the bone marrow and then travel to the lymph nodes. When an antigen reaches the lymph node the B-lymphocytes divide rapidly and produce antibodies which travel around the blood system as immunoglobulins. Immunoglobulins provide protection against bacteria and reinfection by viruses.

Types of immunity

PASSIVE IMMUNITY

PASSIVE IMMUNITY is the result of antibodies being passed into the body in some way other than being produced by the individual.

A foetus or newborn infant may obtain antibodies from its mother either across the placenta or in breast milk. This is a type of natural passive immunity. It does not last long because the antibodies are soon destroyed in the liver.

Alternatively, passive immunity may be acquired artificially by the injection of antibodies from another mammal. Horse serum containing antibodies can be used in the treatment of diphtheria and tetanus in humans. Again, immunity is only temporary.

ACTIVE IMMUNITY

ACTIVE IMMUNITY occurs when the individual manufactures his or her own antibodies. Active immunity may be the result of a natural infection. Once the body has been invaded by the antigen, antibodies start to be made. The reaction is slow, and the antibody level reached is not very high, so the individual will suffer from the disease. However, next time the same antigen affects the body there is a rapid response, and a high level of antibody is rapidly reached. The symptoms of the disease will not occur; this is why most people suffer from diseases like mumps and measles only once.

It is possible to induce the body to produce antibodies without suffering from the disease. This is the basis of vaccination when the antigen is injected in some form. There are different types of vaccination, depending on the form of the antigen.

- *Living attenuated micro-organisms.* These are living pathogens which multiply, but they have been weakened, e.g. by heating or by culturing them outside the human body, so that they are unable to cause the symptoms of the disease. Examples include the vaccines against measles, tuberculosis, poliomyelitis and rubella (German measles).
- *Dead micro-organisms.* Although harmless, they still induce antibody production. Examples include vaccines against typhoid, influenza and whooping cough.
- *Toxoids.* In some cases (e.g. diphtheria and tetanus) the toxin alone will cause antibody production. The toxin can be made harmless (e.g. with formaldehyde) and used as a vaccine.
- *Extracted antigens.* The antigens can be taken from the pathogens and used as a vaccine. For example, influenza vaccine can be prepared in this way.
- *Artificial antigens.* The genes responsible for antigen production in a pathogen can be transferred to a non-pathogen. This harmless organism can be grown in a fermenter where it will produce the antigen which can be harvested and used in a vaccine.

All the above methods produce what is known as *active* immunity because they cause the individual to synthesise his or her own antibodies.

ACTIVITY

- Which type of immunity acts most immediately, active or passive? Which type of immunity is longer lasting, active or passive? Suggest a situation in which passive immunisation would be more useful than active.

- Look at Figure 3.34. Explain the meaning of the four types of immunity and give examples of each.
- Newborn babies are resistant to a variety of diseases. Explain why this resistance does not last long and why a vaccination programme is begun at three months.
- Find out about the vaccination programme that is provided in the UK. Discuss any problems that have occurred in the operation of this programme.
- Look at the graph in Figure 3.35. How does the information shown here help to explain why most people get mumps and measles only once?

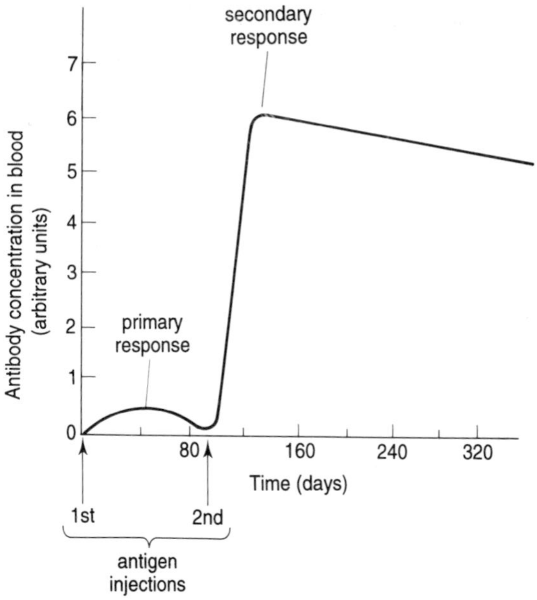

Figure 3.35 Changes in the level of antibody in the blood following two injections of antigen
Source: Advanced Human Biology, Simpkins and Williams, Unwin Hyman Ltd, 1987

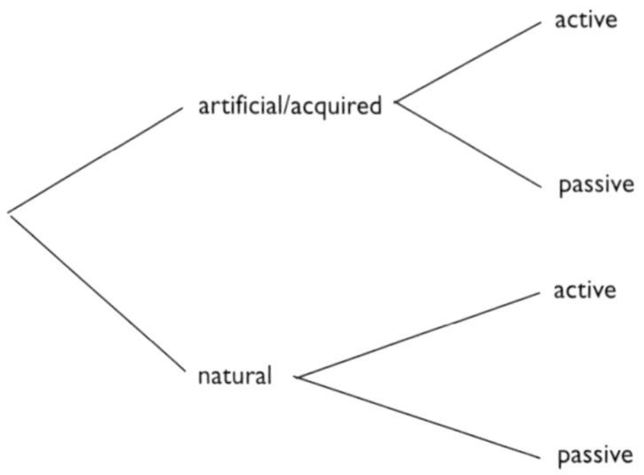

Figure 3.34 Summary of types of immunity

THE ENDOCRINE SYSTEM

We possess two coordinating systems: the nervous system (described earlier in the chapter) and the endocrine system. The nervous system gives us rapid control, whilst the endocrine system regulates more long-term changes. The two systems interact so that the internal environment is kept constant and responses are made to changes in the external environment.

The endocrine system is made up of glands which are ductless and secrete hormones directly into the blood stream. They travel to particular organs, the target organs. Hormones are effective in small quantities. Most endocrine glands are influenced by the pituitary gland, which is linked to the hypothalamus. This can be considered as an important link between the endocrine and nervous systems.

ACTIVITY

1 In an outline diagram of the human body, indicate the positions of the major endocrine glands: pituitary, thyroid, parathyroid, pancreas, adrenal, ovary, testis.

2 Summarise the action of the anterior and posterior pituitary bodies in regulating the other glands. Explain the links with the hypothalamus.

3 Draw up a table with four columns:
(a) Endocrine organ (b) Hormone produced
(c) Target organ (d) Action
Complete the table for all the glands listed above.
(Refer to the section on reproduction for some of your answers.)

HOMEOSTASIS AND EQUILIBRIUM SYSTEMS

Very little change can be tolerated within the human body. The external environment is almost constantly changing. This means efficient mechanisms are needed to prevent corresponding changes within the body. The maintenance of a constant internal environment is known as HOMEOSTASIS.

> **ACTIVITY**
>
> Make a short list of changes which you think could occur within the body. Items on your list might include changes in temperature; levels of waste such as urea and carbon dioxide; oxygen level; amount of water and salts present in the body; blood sugar level; blood pressure; and pH.

In this section we will limit ourselves to looking at body temperature, blood sugar level, water balance and respiratory rate, and the systems concerned with their equilibria.

Homeostasis and feedback mechanisms

NEGATIVE FEEDBACK

Although there is a huge variety of homeostatic functions within the body, they all work through the same basic mechanism.

- To control a factor, a RECEPTOR must detect any changes in level of that factor.
- The receptor must then communicate with an EFFECTOR which will bring about the necessary corrections.
- The changes back to the 'norm' or 'reference point' will then be detected by the receptor and the system will be turned off.

This mechanism is known as NEGATIVE FEEDBACK (see Figure 3.36). (NB A *feedback system* is any circular situation in which information about

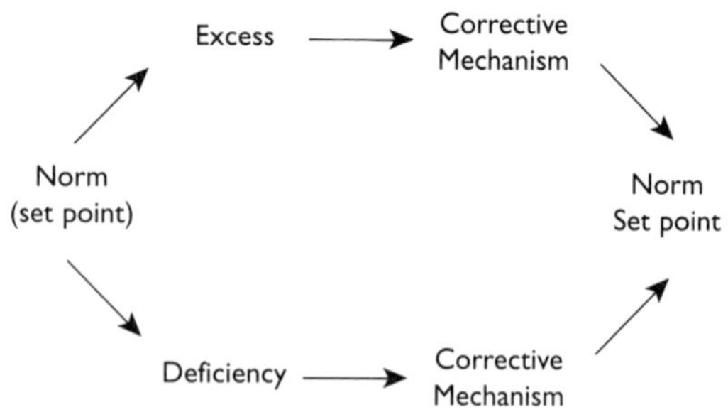

Figure 3.36 Negative feedback

the status of something is continually reported (fed back) to a central control region. The type of feedback system that *reverses* the direction of the initial condition is a *negative* feedback system.)

Control systems

Within the body there is division of labour, with different systems carrying out different functions. To perform effectively, these different systems must be controlled to ensure that they work in a coordinated fashion.

Communication between systems is vitally important. There are two forms of communication:

- *Nerves*
  The nervous system has been considered earlier in this chapter. Temperature regulation and respiratory rate are examples of homeostatic mechanisms under nervous control.
- *Hormones*
  Water balance and blood sugar level regulation are examples of homeostatic mechanisms which are under hormonal control.

BODY TEMPERATURE REGULATION

The normal core temperature in humans is 37.5°C. (Core temperature refers to the tissues below a level of 2.5 cm beneath the surface of the skin. Temperatures in other regions can fluctuate considerably (see Figure 3.37).

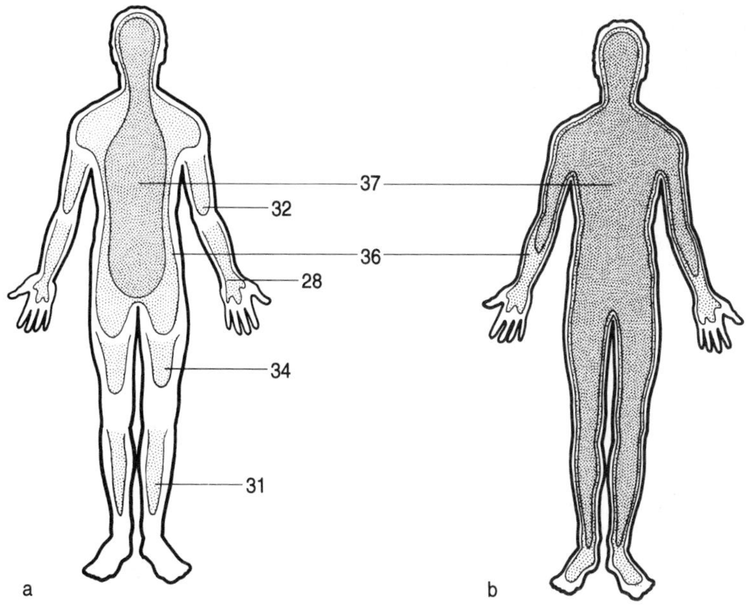

Figure 3.37 Temperature (°C) on the surface of the body (a) in a cold environment and (b) in a hot environment
Source: Advanced Human Biology, Simpkins and Williams, Unwin Hyman Ltd, 1987.

ACTIVITY

- Measure your oral temperature. Drink a cup of hot tea or a glass of cold water and note how long it takes for the temperature to return to the original level. Why do you think that it is more accurate to take the rectal temperature than the oral temperature?
- Although 37.5°C is given as the 'normal' temperature, there will be a range of values around this norm.

Using a very sensitive thermometer, for example one supplied for checking ovulation, investigate the range of temperature values
(a) between people;
(b) in the same person at different times.

Deviations from the normal temperature of 37.5°C cause changes in METABOLIC RATE. Metabolism, the sum total of reactions in the cell or body, is controlled by ENZYMES, which are biological catalysts. Enzymes in the body work most efficiently at about 37.5°C.

ACTIVITY

1 Find an account of the 'lock and key' mechanism by which enzymes function and use this to write an account of why enzymes are less efficient at temperatures:
(a) lower and
(b) higher
than 37°C.

2 Using the following apparatus and materials, design, carry out and evaluate an experiment to investigate the effect of temperature on enzyme action. (Your evaluation should include any sources of error, and suggestions for improvements and further work.)
Apparatus and materials:
- test tubes and rack;
- wax pencil for labelling;
- pipette (5 cm^3);
- white tile;
- glass rods;
- water baths and thermometers;
- diastase solution (25 cm^3 of 0.2%): enzyme which breaks down starch;

- starch solution n(25 cm^3 of 0.2%);
- dilute iodine (turns blue-black in the presence of starch).

Body temperature abnormalities

Low body temperature: When the core temperature falls below 35°C the person is said to be suffering from HYPOTHERMIA. A state of hypothermia is sometimes induced in heart surgery because it allows the surgeon to carry out repairs to the heart without the risk of brain damage to the patient. The body temperature is lowered to 15°C, which reduces the metabolic demand of the brain cells without damage, for up to one hour. At this lower metabolic rate, the brain cells can exist on a reduced blood supply.

ACTIVITY

If you suspected an elderly relative was suffering from mild hypothermia what actions would you take?

High body temperature: A fever, or abnormally high body temperature, may be caused by infection from bacteria and viruses or, less commonly, by heart attacks, tumours or reactions to vaccines. What happens is that the body's 'thermostat' is set too high. This means that at a normal temperature of 37.5°C the person will feel cold and shiver, i.e. they have a *chill*. When the person feels warm and starts sweating, this indicates that body temperature is falling.

It is thought that, in some ways, fever is beneficial:

- the high temperature may inhibit the growth of some bacteria and viruses;
- the heart rate increases so that white blood cells are delivered to sites of infection more rapidly;
- the increase in the rate of chemical reactions with increased temperature may help body cells to repair themselves more quickly.

The harmful effects of a fever can be dehydration or even permanent brain damage. Death results if the body temperature rises to 44.4–45.5°C.

The role of the skin in temperature regulation

Temperature control is the chief homeostatic function of the skin. If changes in body temperature from 37.5°C are to be prevented, the amount of heat produced in the body must be equalled exactly by the amount of heat lost from the body.

The blood vessels close to the surface of the epidermis (see Figure 3.38) can dilate and contract. In warm weather, when the need is to lose heat, surface blood vessels in the skin dilate or swell (VASODILATION). Blood is thus brought nearer to the surface of the body and heat loss occurs via conduction, convection and radiation. In cold weather, when the need is to conserve heat, the vessels contract or shrink (VASOCONSTRICTION), blood travels lower down in the skin and heat energy is retained (see Figure 3.39).

SWEATING is an efficient way of losing excess heat. The body is covered with sweat glands, and in very hot conditions humans may produce up to 1,000 cm^3/h of sweat. As mentioned above, the evaporation of water uses energy (2.5 kJ/g). When sweat evaporates from the skin surface, energy as latent heat of evaporation is lost from the body and this reduces body temperature.

ACTIVITY

Explain why sweating is an inefficient method of heat loss in a humid environment?

The insulating effect of clothes has been mentioned above. The body also has its own methods of insulation.

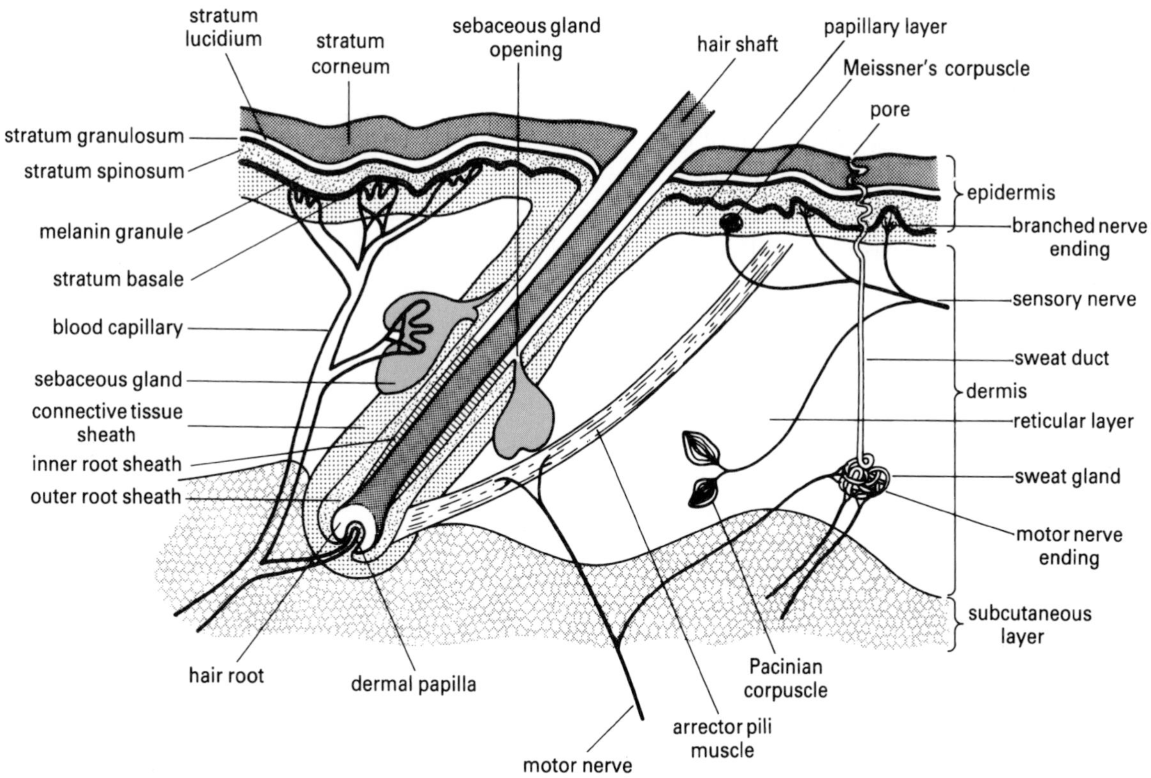

Figure 3.38 Vertical section through the human skin

- In response to decreasing temperatures the ERECTOR PILI MUSCLES contract, raising the hairs on the skin. This allows a layer of warm air to become trapped which acts as an efficient insulator (i.e. poor conductor of heat).
- SUBCUTANEOUS FAT is an effective insulator.

ACTIVITY

- Females tend to have more subcutaneous fat than males. What can you predict about their ability to maintain a constant body temperature as the environmental temperature drops?

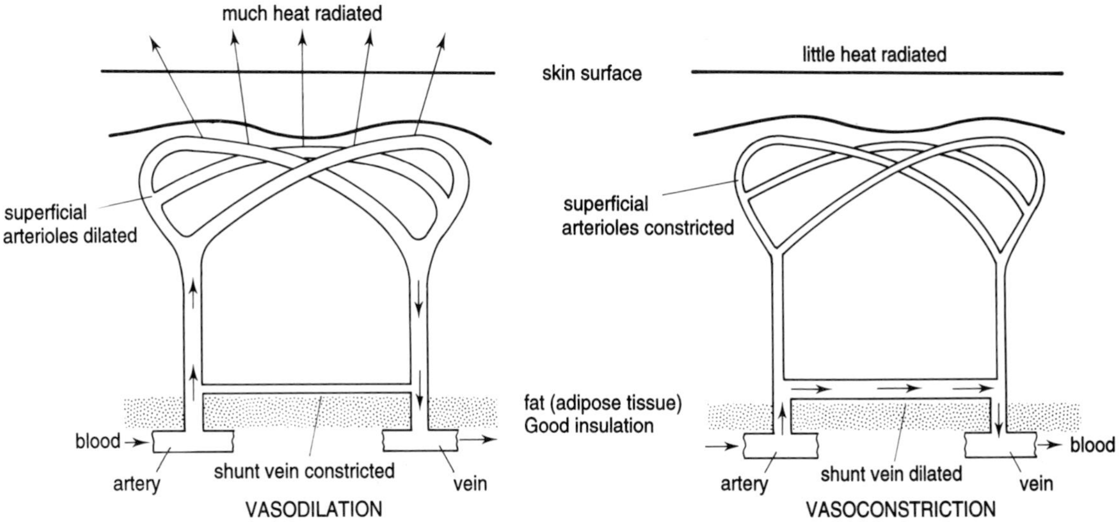

Figure 3.39 Vasodilation and vasoconstriction

THE ROLE OF THE HYPOTHALAMUS IN TEMPERATURE REGULATION

The hypothalamus is a small section of the base of the brain, weighing only 4 g (see Figure 3.22). It is attached to the rest of the brain by numerous nerves. As well as having a nervous function, the hypothalamus is involved in endocrine functions. However, temperature regulation is entirely under nervous control.

The hypothalamus has a thermoregulatory centre which monitors the temperature of blood passing through it. In addition it receives nervous information from receptors in the skin about external temperature changes. Any reduction in blood temperature will bring about changes in the body which conserve heat. Any rise in blood temperature will bring about changes in the body to lose heat.

The role of the hypothalamus in temperature regulation is summarised in Figure 3.40.

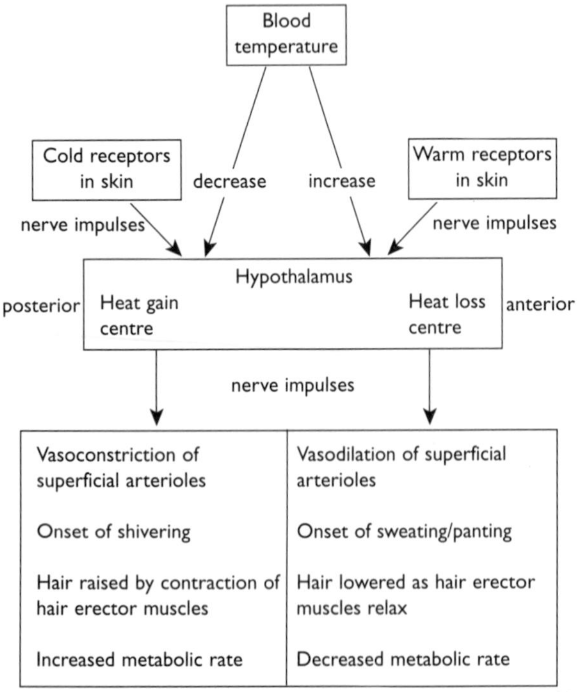

Figure 3.40 The role of the hypothalamus in temperature regulation

CONTROL OF RESPIRATORY RATE

This is under nervous control. In the medulla oblongata of the brain (see Figure 3.22) is a breathing centre. In the aortic arch and the carotid arteries there are chemoreceptors which are sensitive to minute changes in the concentration of carbon dioxide in the blood. When the level rises, nerve impulses go from the chemoreceptors to the breathing centre and then to the diaphragm and intercostal muscles. The breathing rate then increases in order to remove the excess carbon-dioxide.

We can also consciously control our breathing rate.

ACTIVITY

Draw a flow diagram to illustrate the control process described above.

CONTROL OF WATER IN THE BODY

Antidiuretic hormone (ADH): the role of the kidneys

The role of the kidneys in excretion is discussed earlier in the chapter.

The body controls changes in the amount of water in the body by regulating the permeability of the collecting ducts. The osmotic potential of the blood is detected by OSMORECEPTORS in the hypothalamus of the brain (Figure 3.22). If the osmotic potential drops (i.e. less water, more salt), a message (in the form of a nervous impulse) is passed to the posterior pituitary gland, resulting in the release of ANTIDIURETIC HORMONE or ADH. This is carried in the blood to the kidneys where it causes the collecting ducts to become more permeable to water. More water can then leave the filtrate, resulting in more concentrated urine and an increase in the osmotic potential of the blood.

ACTIVITY

- Find out the positions of the hypothalamus and posterior pituitary gland.
- Draw a flow chart to illustrate the correction of a drop in the osmotic potential of the blood as described above.
- Explain what would happen if the osmotic potential of the blood were to rise. Draw a flow chart to illustrate this.
- A person who suffers from the uncommon disease of DIABETES INSIPIDUS is unable to produce sufficient ADH. What can you predict about the volume and concentration of the urine they produce?

CONTROL OF BLOOD SUGAR LEVEL

The normal blood glucose level is 90 mg in 100 cm^2 of blood. The nervous system is especially sensitive to changes in this level. Carbohydrate taken in the diet is spasmodic, so there is a system which relies on the build up and breakdown of glycogen in the liver to remove or add glucose to the blood (see Figure 3.41). This system is under hormonal control.

ACTIVITY

Look at the negative feedback diagram (Figure 3.41) which shows the control of blood sugar level by insulin. Summarise the information shown in the diagram.

Find out more about the role of the pancreas and the two hormones that are produced by the two different types of cells. What is the name of the second hormone secreted by the pancreas? How does it work with insulin to help regulate the blood sugar level?

Look at a microscope slide of a vertical section of the pancreas and see if you can identify the two types of hormone-secreting cell. Can you see any blood vessels or capillaries? Why is it important for endocrine glands to have a blood supply?

THE KEY EFFECTS OF AGEING ON BODY SYSTEMS

Many changes occur in the body as it develops and ages.

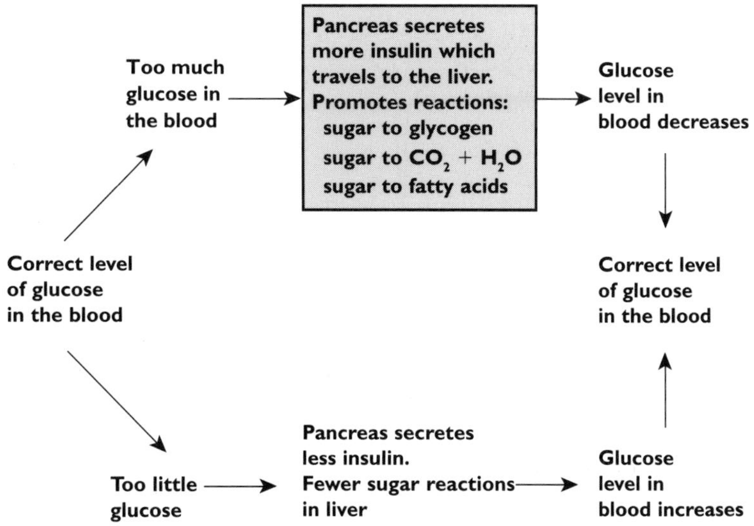

Figure 3.41 The control of blood glucose level by insulin

Growth after birth

At birth, all the organs are complete. All the organs continue to grow, but at different rates. Nervous tissue has grown most rapidly during gestation, and subsequent growth is slow. The skull and brain normally reach adult size by the fifth year. The long bones of the axial skeleton grow fastest after birth and they have special areas of growth which are called EPIPHYSICAL AREAS. This differential growth in different parts of the body results in changes of proportion during development.

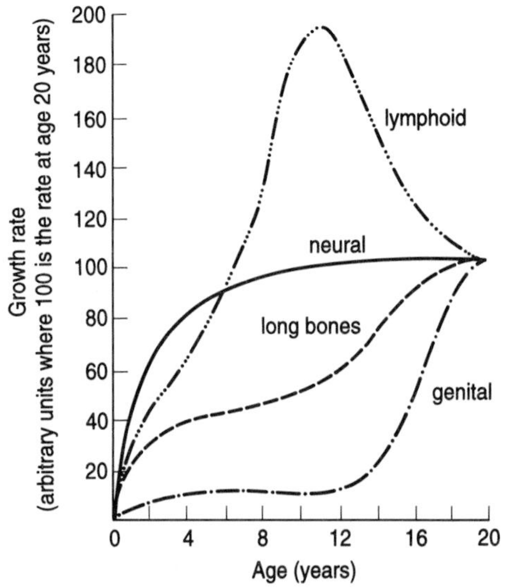

Figure 3.42 Differential growth rates in some tissues

ACTIVITY

Look at Figures 3.42–3.44. Differential growth rates of various tissues and organs are shown, together with the resulting change in proportions in different parts of the body, with the increase in age up to 25 years. The rate of growth, measured by height, is also shown.

Summarise the information shown in the illustrated data, and explain why the proportions of the different parts of the body change with increasing age.

Changes in the support and locomotion system

The musculo-skeletal system shows signs of ageing during the 40s, when people start to feel a loss of strength. Muscles become weaker and less flexible.

By the 50s, hips, knees, feet, and spine start to stiffen up, as the cartilage in the joints wears thin and becomes harder. Connective tissue, for example in tendons and ligaments, starts to lose its elasticity. Joints start to lose their mobility.

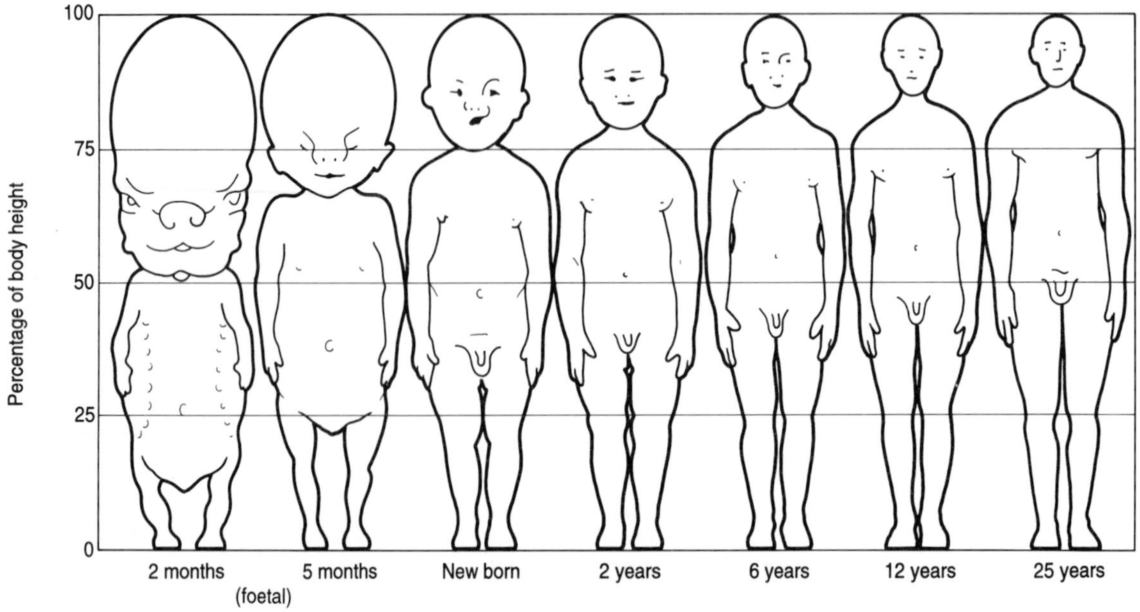

Figure 3.43 Disproportionate growth of different parts of the body throughout life

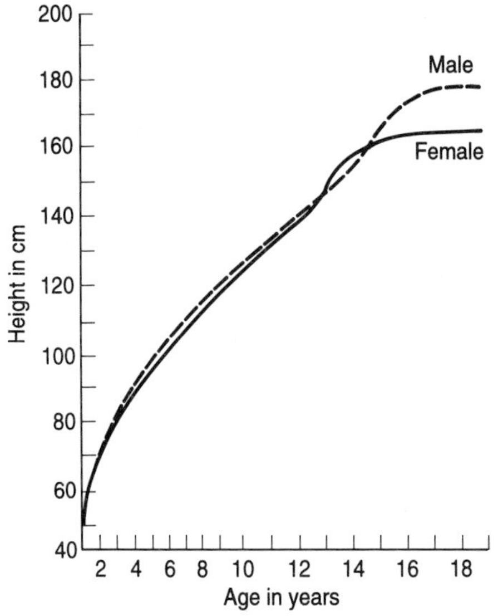

Figure 3.44 Growth curve for males and females (height)

Bone density becomes reduced as the calcium content is lowered, and osteoporosis and brittle bones can result. An older person breaks bones more easily.

By the 60s, almost thirty percent of muscle is lost and what remains begins to degenerate. The contraction of the discs between the vertebrae is responsible for the hunching of the back and the shrinkage seen in the elderly, which can be called 'negative growth'.

Changes in the reproductive system

THE CHANGES THAT OCCUR DURING PUBERTY

In young women between the ages of 10 and 14, the ovarian tissues begin to respond to the anterior pituitary gonadotrophic hormones, follicle stimulating hormone (FSH) and luteinising hormone (LH). FSH causes maturation of the follicles in the ovary and they start to produce OESTROGEN. LH causes the formation of the corpus luteum in the ovary which then releases PROGESTERONE.

Oestrogen and progesterone have several effects on the body. Bones grow, height increases rapidly, the pelvis becomes broader, and fat is deposited on the shoulders, hips and thighs.

Secondary sexual characteristics develop: fat is deposited in the breasts and hair grows on the pubis and under the arms.

The secondary sex organs also begin to develop. Fallopian tubes lengthen, uterus muscles enlarge and the lining proliferates. The onset of menstruation occurs and the vaginal epithelium thickens.

In young men between the ages of 13 and 16, testicular tissues become responsive to the anterior pituitary gonadotrophic hormones, follicle stimulating hormone (FSH) and interstitial cell stimulating hormone (ICSH). FSH stimulates spermatogenesis and ICSH causes secretion of testosterone by the interstitial cells of the testis.

Testosterone has several effects. Secondary sexual characteristics develop. Hair grows on face and pubis, and the larynx enlarges and the voice deepens. Bones grow and muscles develop and the proportions of the body alter.

The secondary sex organs develop. The penis, scrotum and prostate all enlarge.

ACTIVITY

1 In the female, what is the distinction between the primary sex organs and secondary sex organs? What are the secondary sexual characteristics?

2 What are the two hormones that are produced in the female at the onset of puberty and where are they produced?

3 What effects do these two hormones have on the female
(a) general body features?
(b) secondary sexual characteristics?
(c) secondary sex organs?

4 How are these changes significant to the reproductive role?

5 What are the male primary sex organs? What are the secondary sex organs and what are the secondary sexual characteristics?

6 What are the two hormones that are produced in the male at the onset of puberty? Where are they produced?

7 What are the effects of these hormones on the male
(a) general body features?
(b) secondary sexual characteristics?
(c) secondary sex organs?

LATER CHANGES IN THE REPRODUCTIVE SYSTEM

The MENOPAUSE occurs in women, usually between the ages of 45 and 55. The woman no longer ovulates and therefore can no longer reproduce. As a result of the drop in hormone levels of PROGESTERONE and OESTROGEN:

- the ovaries, uterus and cervix shrink;
- the Fallopian tubes shorten;
- the walls of the vagina lose elasticity;
- mucus production decreases and becomes alkaline.

From their 40s onwards, men can still play a reproductive role, but certain changes occur in their reproductive system:

- *sperm production* decreases;
- *sexual arousal* takes longer;
- *erections* are less frequent and do not last as long;
- *ejaculations* are less powerful and less frequent.

The onset of all the changes in the male and female reproductive system is gradual and can be accommodated as long as psychological factors do not interfere.

ACTIVITY

Research the causes, signs and possible symptoms of the menopause. Use the following list as a guide:

- define the climacteric;
- possible emotional effects on the woman and her family;
- hormone replacement therapy (HRT);
- other available treatments.

The effects of age on homeostasis

MAINTENANCE OF BODY TEMPERATURE

Various factors affect the control of body temperature throughout life.

Surface area:volume ratio
The larger a person's surface area:volume ratio, the faster their heat loss.

ACTIVITY

1 Who has the largest surface area:volume ratio, a new born baby or an adult?

2 Put 50 cm^3 of boiling water into a 50 cm^3 beaker and 1,000 cm^3 into a 1,000 cm^3 beaker.

- Work out the approximate surface area:volume ratio for each.
- Take the temperature of each immediately and than at regular intervals (e.g. every minute).
- Plot a cooling curve, i.e. temperature (°C) against time (minutes).
- What conclusions can you draw?

Level of activity:
Most of the heat produced by the body comes from RESPIRATION (the breakdown of food in the cells to release energy). The rate at which this heat is produced is known as the METABOLIC RATE. During strenuous exercise, more likely to be undertaken by younger people, the metabolic rate may increase to as much as 15 to 20 times the normal rate. Shivering, or automatic repetitive contraction of muscles, can cause body heat production to rise to about four times the normal rate.

Newborn infants do not have the ability to shiver. However, they do have deposits of specialised adipose tissue, known as 'brown fat', between their shoulder blades. This tissue is metabolically more active than ordinary fat, and can produce large quantities of heat. These fat deposits atrophy with increasing age.

State of development of the body:
The basal metabolic rate (BMR) is a measure of the rate at which the body breaks down foods (and therefore releases heat) when a person is at rest. The BMR varies according to age and sex.

At the age of five the BMR is around 220 kJ m^{-2} h^{-1}. After this age males have a slightly higher BMR than females. There is a fairly steep decrease in the rate over the years until 20 is reached. At 20 the BMR of females is 150 kJ m^{-2} h^{-1} on average, and 160 kJ m^{-2} h^{-1} for males. Then there is a steady decrease and by the age of 80 the BMR has reduced to about 130 kJ m^{-2} h^{-1}. This means that elderly people produce less heat.

The BMR decreases with age because:

- The proportion of energy used to build and maintain tissue declines with age.
- The amount of heat lost decreases as surface area:volume ratio decreases from birth to adulthood (see above).
- The amount of brown fat decreases with age (see above).

The difference in BMR between males and females is because females generally have a higher fat:muscle ratio than males, and the level of respiration is lower in fat than in muscle.

Diet:
The temperature of food and drinks consumed obviously influences the body temperature. It is important that anyone vulnerable to hypothermia, because of decreased heat production, is encouraged to consume hot food and drink. Equally, cold drinks can be very useful in helping to keep body temperature down in very hot conditions.

ASSESSMENT OPPORTUNITY ✓

1 Write a report describing how body systems carry out the functions of communication, support and locomotion, reproduction, energy supply excretion and defence.
Take each of the functions listed above and note which body systems contribute to the function and its control. Describe the role that each body system has in each function. You need not include details of the structure of the body systems, but diagrams summarising how each function is carried out would be helpful.

2 Write summary notes on the homeostatic mechanisms involved in controlling body temperature, blood sugar level, water, and respiratory rate. Identify the normal ranges for temperature, blood sugar and respiratory rate.

3 Write a short report describing changes in the support and locomotor systems, and also the female and male reproductive systems, throughout life.

MONITORING AND MAINTAINING A HEALTHY BODY

Electrocardiographic measurement

(Refer back to pages 144–147 to remind yourself about heart structure and the cardiac cycle.)

The heart is MYOGENIC, i.e. it has an 'in-built' mechanism for initiating the contraction of the cardiac muscle fibres. This allows it to continue beating for quite some time when removed from the body and placed in an appropriate solution at 37°C.

The stimulus for contraction originates at the SINO-ATRIAL NODE (S-A node), which is also known as the PACEMAKER (Figure 13.45). A wave of excitation passes from the S-A node across the muscle fibres of the atria, which causes them to contract. This wave spreads at approximately 1 m/s. The fibres of the atria are completely separated from those of the ventricles, except for the region in the right atrium called the ATRIO-VENTRICULAR NODE (A-V node). The A-V node is connected to the BUNDLE OF HIS, a strand of modified cardiac fibres which gives rise to finer branches known as PURKINJE TISSUE. Impulses are conducted rapidly along the bundle (5 m/s) and spread to all parts of the ventricles. Both ventricles contract simultaneously and this starts approximately 0.15 s after the atria have completed their contraction.

ACTIVITY

Redraw a simple diagram of the heart from Figure 3.45, showing the position of the S-A and A-V nodes and bundle of HIS. Put arrows on to show the direction of the spread of the wave of excitation described above.

The spread of the wave of excitation during each heartbeat can be detected at the surfaces of the body by electrodes which must be placed in particular positions (Figure 3.46). The signals need amplifying before they can be recorded and the patient must be relaxed. The display of these signals over a period of time is an ELECTROCARDIOGRAM (ECG). A typical ECG trace is shown in Figure 3.47.

- P wave shows contraction of atria;
- Q, R and S waves show contraction of ventricles;
- T wave shows relaxation of ventricles.

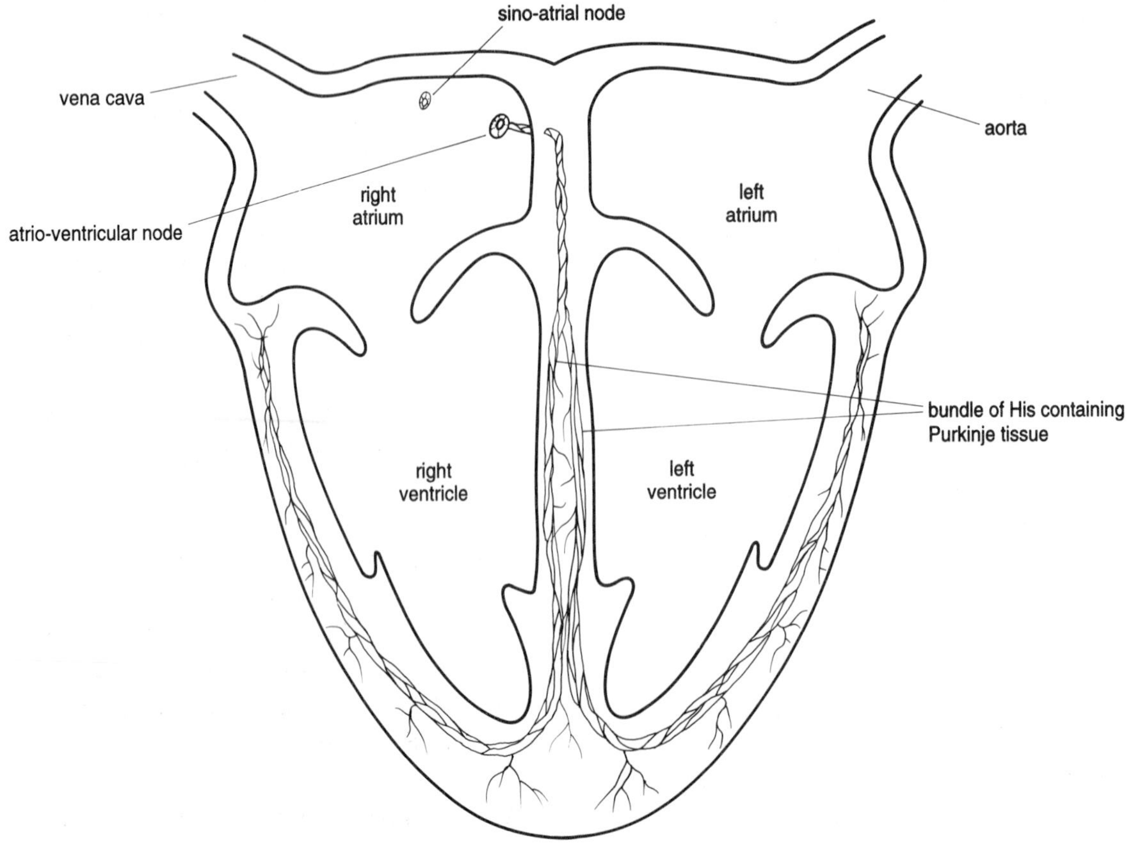

Figure 3.45 Structure of the heart

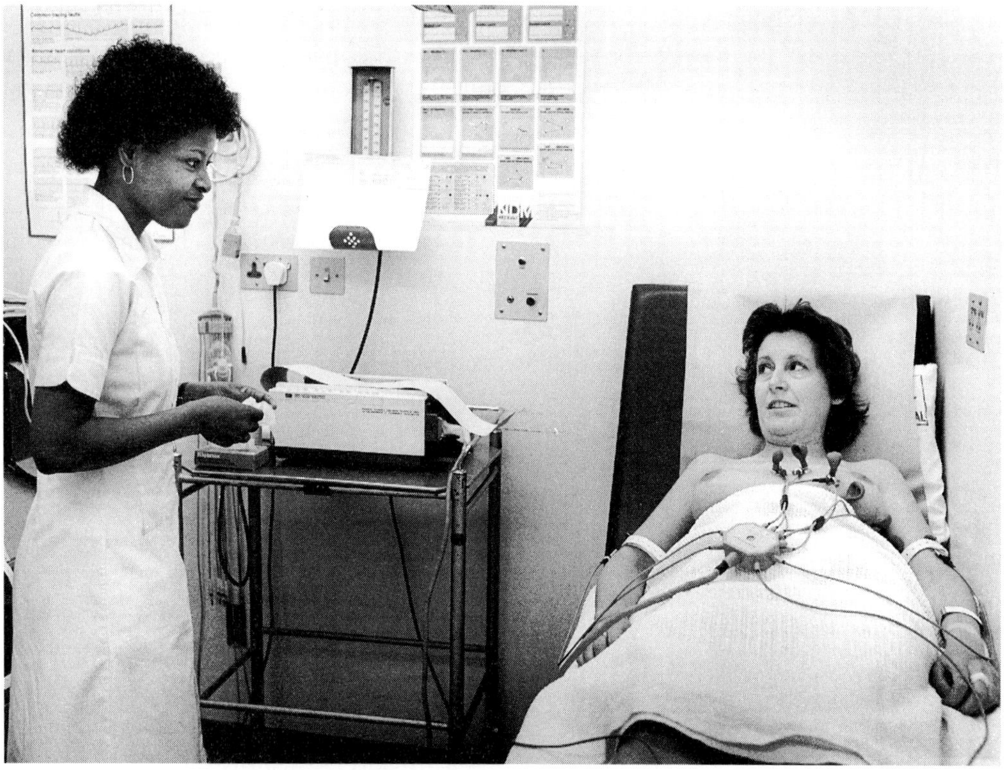

Figure 3.46 The production of an electrocardiogram (ECG)

ACTIVITY

1 • Look at Figure 3.47. How many heartbeats are shown? Work out the heart rate in beats per minute.

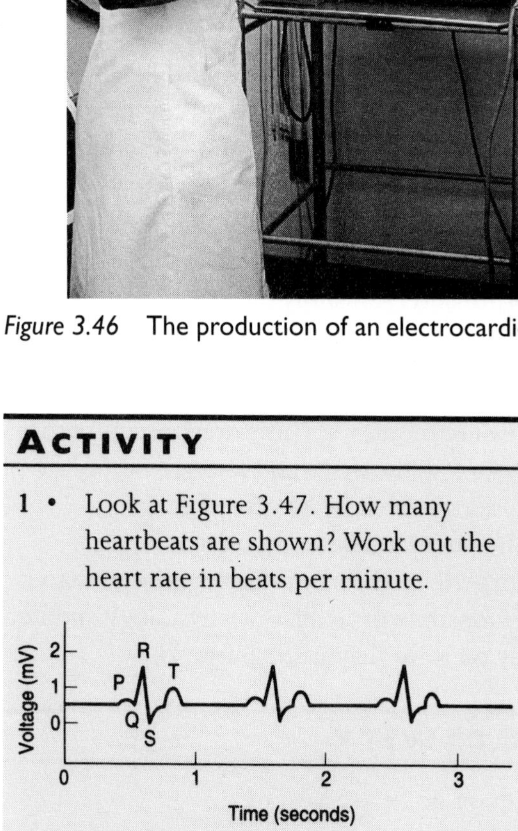

Figure 3.47 A typical ECG trace

• Figure 3.48 is the ECG trace from a patient with a heart defect. What differences can you see compared with Figure 3.47?

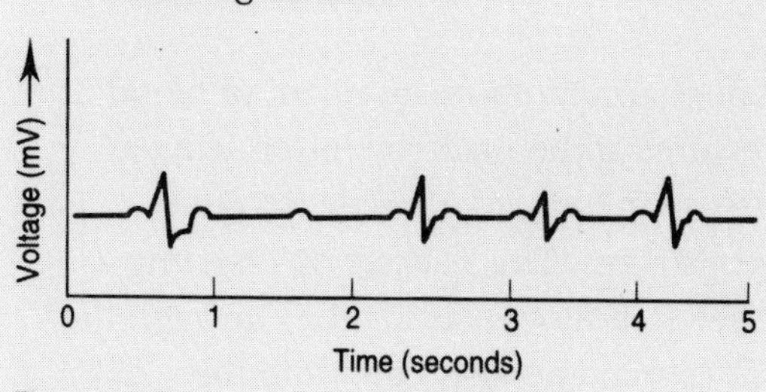

Figure 3.48 An abnormal ECG trace

2 If possible use an ECG computer program which describes the physiological basis of the ECG and the way in which it is recorded, and presents simulations of traces.

3 You may have the necessary equipment for producing an ECG trace within the biology or physics department of your school or college. If you have access to this equipment you could design and carry out an experiment to test the effect of a factor such as smoking or caffeine consumption on the heart.

4 The ECG trace can be either displayed on a screen while the electrodes are attached to the patient, or a permanent trace can be drawn. What do you think are the relative merits and drawbacks of each recording method?

5 What other 'bioelectric' events can be recorded and measured?

Monitoring the blood

(Refer back to pages 144–146 to remind yourself about the structure and functions of blood.)

BLOOD PRESSURE

A MERCURY COLUMN SPHYGMOMANOMETER is used for measuring blood pressure. Because it involves no direct contact with the bloodstream, it is straightforward, quick and easy to use. However, it is not as accurate as methods which do involve contact with the bloodstream, and may not be suitable if patients have a very low blood pressure.

The sphygmomanometer (Figure 3.49) consists of an inflatable cuff which is placed around the patient's arm; a small hand pump for inflating the cuff; a valve which is used to control the pressure in the cuff; a mercury pressure meter (manometer) which records the pressure inside the cuff and a rubber tube which connects the cuff to the manometer. It is used as follows:

1 The cuff is placed around the arm just above the elbow at heart height. Air is pumped in until the high pressure stops blood flowing through the brachial artery (on the inside of the arm). At this point no pulse will be felt and if a stethoscope is placed on the artery no sound is heard.
2 The pressure in the cuff is slowly released by opening the valve. This allows blood to begin to spurt through a small opening in the artery. This can be heard with a stethoscope as a tapping sound. The pressure in the cuff at this point is the same as the maximum blood pressure during each heartbeat (SYSTOLIC PRESSURE).
3 The tapping sounds continue as the pressure falls until the blood vessel remains open through the pulse period and the sounds disappear. The pressure in the cuff is now equal to the lowest blood pressure during each heartbeat (DIASTOLIC PRESSURE).
4 Blood pressure is therefore recorded as two numbers – the systolic over diastolic pressure. A healthy heart will give a reading of approximately 120/80 mmHg.

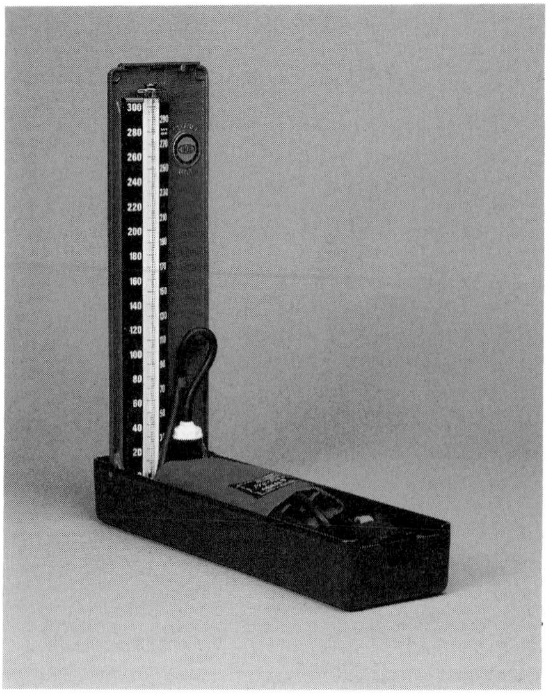

Figure 3.49 A sphygmomanometer

Many schools and colleges have digital blood pressure monitors. These do not require the use of a stethoscope and also give a readout of pulse rate. Because the use of a sphygmomanometer requires skill, an inexperienced person should use it only to demonstrate principles of physiology and not rely on it for diagnostic purposes.

ACTIVITY

If you do have access to a sphygmomanometer, carry out an investigation to find out if there is a correlation between blood pressure and age (see page 406 in Chapter 8 for details on how to carry out a correlation study).

A more accurate measurement of blood pressure can be made by introducing a PRESSURE TRANSDUCER directly into the bloodstream. This is done by inserting a catheter (hollow plastic tube) through the skin (percutaneously) and into the appropriate blood vessel. The transducer can be already mounted at the end of the catheter, or introduced once the catheter is in place. Alternatively, if monitoring is to take place over a long period, the transducer can be surgically implanted at the appropriate site.

A transducer is any device which changes a physiological variable into an electrical signal. In this case the transducer is attached to a thin, flexible diaphragm. Movements of the diaphragm produced by the flow of blood are converted into electrical signals by the transducer, which can then be recorded.

ACTIVITY

The use of the sphygmomanometer is a *non-invasive* technique and the use of electronic pressure transducers is an *invasive* technique.

- What is meant by 'non-invasive' and 'invasive'?
- What do you think may be the possible advantages and drawbacks of non-invasive and invasive techniques in general?

BLOOD FLOW

Non-invasive techniques

Pulse: The pumping action of the heart causes a regular pulsation in the blood flow. Because the arteries have muscular walls (see page 137) they alternately expand and recoil as the blood flow varies, and this can be felt in arteries near the surface and lying over a bone or other firm tissue. Pulse is strongest in arteries closest to the heart. Figure 3.50 shows the places at which pulse may be determined. A trace can be made (Figure 3.51), which shows not only the pulse rate but rhythm and volume.

Taking the pulse by hand: The pulse is usually checked during the course of a physical examination because it can give clues to the patient's state of health. Two fingertips are pressed against the wrist just below the base of the thumb to feel the pulse in the radial artery. The features that should be noted are:

- *the rate* – between 60 and 80 beats per minute in fit individuals. The pulse rate usually corresponds with the heart rate, which varies according to the person's state of relaxation or physical activity.
- *the rhythm* – an abnormal rhythm may indicate a heart disorder; when the heart is beating very fast, some of its beats may be too weak to be detectable at the pulse.
- *the character* – if the pulse feels 'thready' or weak, it may be a sign of shock; if the pulse feels very full or 'bounding', it may be a sign of respiratory disease.
- *the vessel wall* – this should feel soft when the pulse is felt; a wall that feels hard may be a sign of *arteriosclerosis*.

ACTIVITY

Usually, the pulse is counted for 15 seconds and then converted into beats per minute. What is the formula for making this conversion?

Compare the following in a person who takes regular exercise (e.g. competes at a high level in a sport) and a person who does not take exercise.

- Resting pulse rate.
- Pulse rate after a set exercise (e.g. one minute of 'step ups').
- Time taken for pulse rate to return to the resting rate.

(Plot pulse rate against time on a graph.)

NB For safety reasons, make sure that the exercise you suggest is easily within the capabilities of your subjects.

Doppler ultrasound: This technique depends on the fact that sound waves reflected from moving objects change frequency (and therefore there is a change of tone). You may have noticed this when a siren on a vehicle moves past you and you hear a sudden fall in pitch, i.e. the frequency of the siren note was higher when it approached you than when it receded from you (see Figure 3.52). To measure the speed and direction of movement

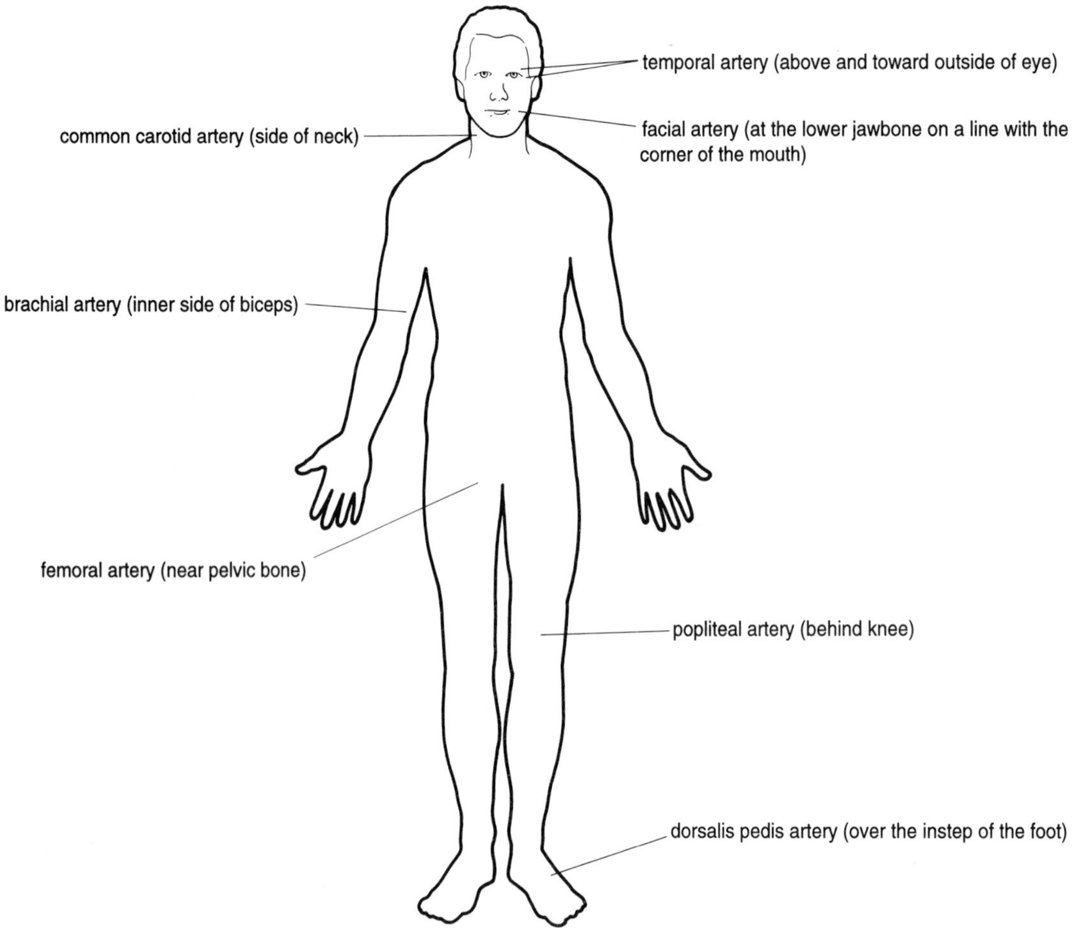

Figure 3.50 Location of pulse measurement

of the blood, ultrasound waves (high frequency sound waves) are directed from a transmitter on to blood vessels (Figure 3.53). These waves are reflected from the moving red blood cells and detected by a receiver. The faster the blood is moving, the greater the change in frequency of the waves. Abnormal changes in frequency can indicate a blockage due to a clot (thrombosis) or narrowing of the blood vessels.

Invasive techniques

A catheter can be inserted into the blood vessels to measure blood flow (see 'pressure

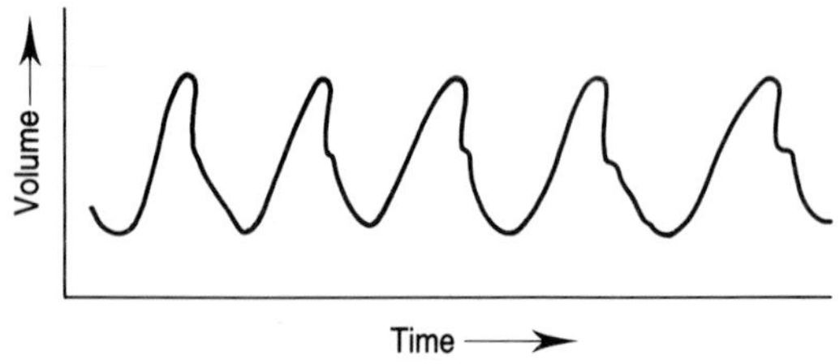

Figure 3.51 Trace of carotid pulse

transducers' above). The catheter can be manipulated through the chambers of the heart. Sometimes a small balloon is inflated at the end of the catheter so that it will be moved along by the bloodstream. Dye can be injected along the catheter and X-rays taken to investigate blood flow (see below).

CHEMICALS IN THE BLOOD

The level of some of the chemicals transported within the blood can be tested relatively easily. Two such examples are given below.

Glucose

After starch or sugar is eaten and digested it is absorbed into the bloodstream as glucose. The hormone insulin is produced when the blood sugar level is high; it brings the level back down again mainly by transporting glucose into the cells. However, in diabetes insulin is

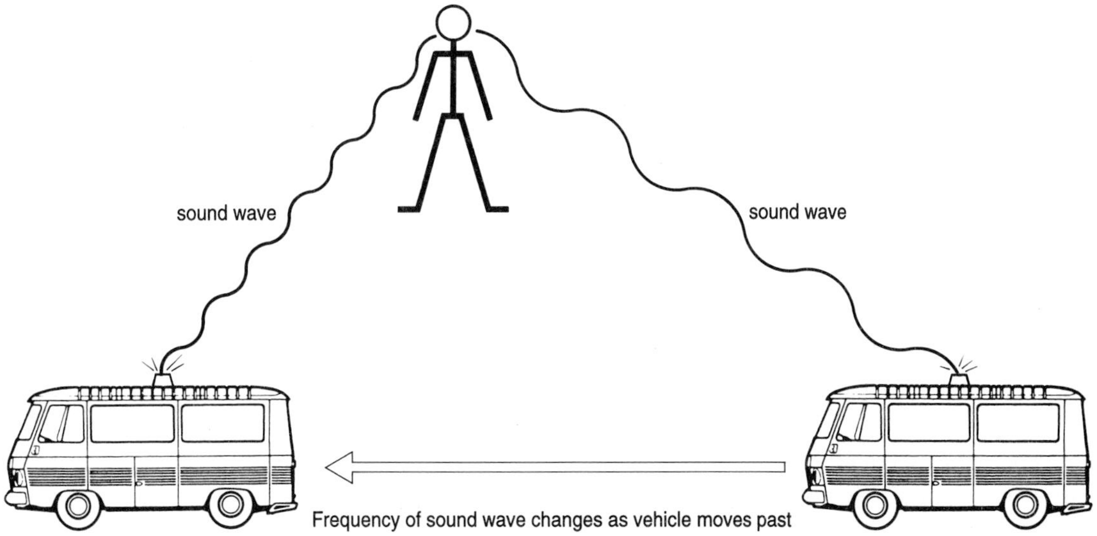

Figure 3.52 Example of the Doppler effect

either lacking or ineffective, and so glucose is in such a high concentration in the blood that it 'spills over' into the urine.

If the blood sugar level is too high the diabetic can inject himself or herself with insulin. In the past, diabetics assessed their insulin needs every so often by testing their urine for glucose. However, by the time glucose is in the urine, blood glucose levels will be unacceptably high and it is realised now that even slightly high blood sugars can cause long-term damage to various organs. For this reason, diabetics are now recommended to test their blood sugar level twice a day by a finger-prick technique.

ACTIVITY

Find out:

- Why does insulin have to be injected rather than taken orally?
- To what long-term complications are diabetics susceptible?

Cholesterol

Cholesterol is a steroid from which all other steroids in the body are formed. It can be produced in the liver, but the major source of cholesterol in the body is the diet.

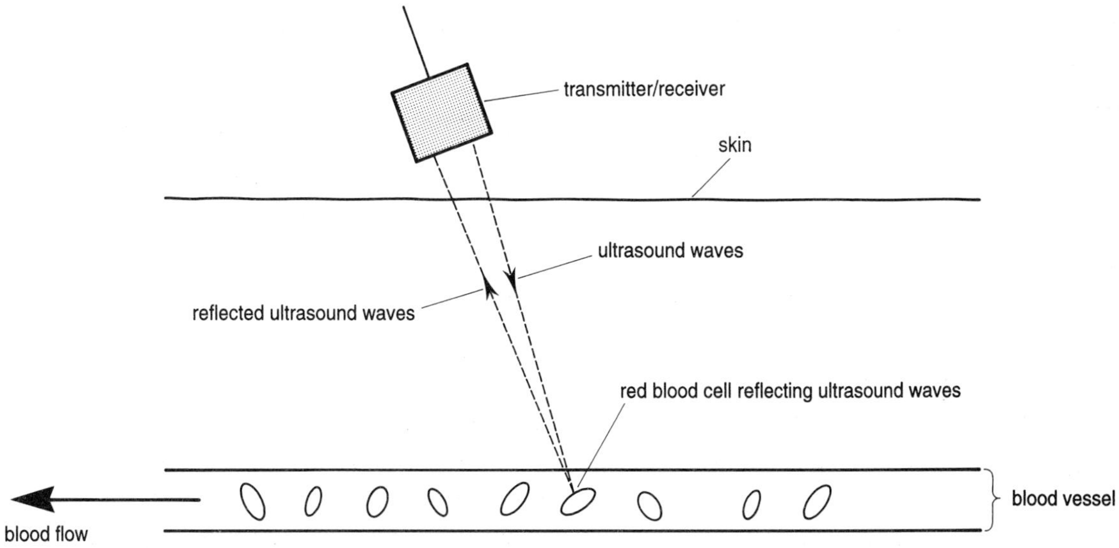

Figure 3.53 Doppler ultrasound measuring blood flow

ACTIVITY

Find out:

- What is a steroid?
- Which foods are particularly rich in cholesterol?

Cholesterol is excreted in the bile and when present in large amounts can form cholesterol gallstones which block the bile duct and cause severe discomfort. Excessive amounts in the blood can lead to its deposition in the walls of the arteries, leading to ATHEROSCLEROSIS (narrowing of the arteries). This increases the risk of blood clot formation which may block blood vessels (ARTERIAL THROMBOSIS). If this occurs in the heart or brain it is often fatal.

Home cholesterol testing kits to measure cholesterol level in the blood can be bought from most chemists; these are *not* suitable for use in schools or colleges as they involve obtaining a blood sample. This is done by pricking a finger with a sterile lancet. The test works by first filtering the blood and then using a two step process involving a colour change to measure the level of cholesterol. Table 3.5 shows the risk indicated by the results obtained.

BLOOD CELL COUNTS

The most commonly ordered haematology test is the COMPLETE BLOOD COUNT (CBC). This generally includes the determination of the amount of haemoglobin; the determination of the percentage of blood volume made up of red blood cells (haematocrit); a red blood cell count; a white blood cell count; a differential count in which the percentage of each type of white blood cell is calculated; and observations on the appearance (morphology) of red blood cells, white blood cells and platelets.

Machines are usually used in laboratories to give a very accurate and rapid count of red blood cells. However, these cells may be counted manually with the aid of a counting chamber called a HAEMOCYTOMETER (Figure 3.54). Because the depth of the blood sample in the chamber is known (0.1 mm), and the distances between the grid lines are known (e.g. 0.0025 mm for the smallest square), the number of blood cells in a known volume can be counted. The blood is diluted to prevent it from clotting, and the cells in at least 80 of the smallest squares are then counted. To make sure cells are not missed or counted twice, the right-hand rule is applied. This means that cells which are partially in the square are counted at the top and right-hand margins, but not counted at the bottom or left-hand margins.

ACTIVITY

Look at Figure 3.54b and estimate the number of red blood cells in a given volume of the diluted blood. Do this by counting the number of cells in 80 squares and calculating the volume of diluted blood in that area (see measurements above). Express your answer in cells per dm^3.

A normal red blood cell count for men is approximately $5.5 \times 10^{12}/dm^3$, and for

Table 3.5 Risk related to amount of cholesterol in the blood

Cholesterol in blood (mmol/l)	Up to one additional risk factor	Multiple risk factors
Up to 5.2	Within desirable limits	Low risk
5.3—6.5	Low risk	Medium risk
6.6—7.8	Medium risk	High risk
Over 7.8	High risk	Very high risk

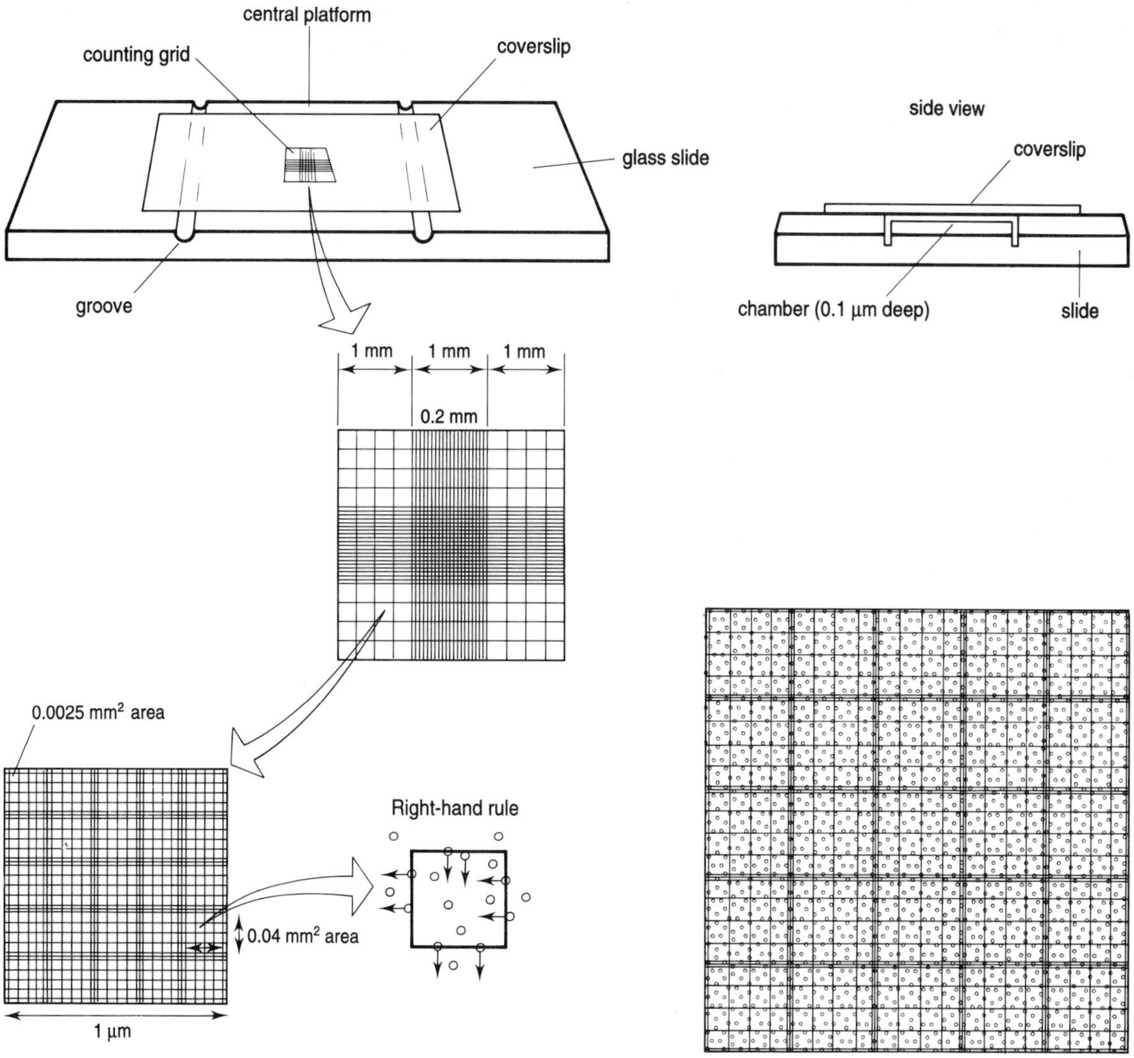

Figure 3.54 Haemocytometer

women approximately $4.8 \times 10^{12}/dm^3$. A low number of red blood cells indicates that a person may be suffering from ANAEMIA, which might have been caused by a nutritional deficiency, bone marrow failure or blood loss.

An increase in the number of white blood cells indicates a state of inflammation or infection. Because each type of white cell plays a different role, determining which types have increased (differential count) aids in the diagnosis of the condition (see Table 3.6).

Table 3.6 Differential counts

Type of white blood cell	Normal %	Revised level indicates
Neutrophils	60–70	Damaged by invading bacteria
Eosinophils	2–4	Allergic reaction
Basophils	0.5–1	
Lymphocytes	20–25	Antigen–antibody reactions
Monocytes	3–8	Chronic infection
Total w.b.c.	100	

ACTIVITY

Look at the blood counts for the three patients shown below. Can you find any abnormal readings and suggest possible reasons for these?

Patient	A	B	C
Sex	female	male	male
Red blood cells (1012/dm3)	3.0	5.2	6.1
White blood cells (% of total white blood cell count)			
Neutrophils	65	60	3
Eosinophils	3	8	1.5
Basophils	0.5	5.0	0.5
Lymphocytes	23	20	23
Monocytes	8.5	7	2

Respiratory measurements

RESPIRATORY FLOW RATE

Peak flow estimation is the commonest test of lung function. This can be carried out with a simple piece of equipment known as a peak flow meter. The person is asked to blow into it as quickly as they can. The rate at which air is expelled (peak expiratory flow) is recorded on a dial and is normally between 400 and 500 dm^3 of air per minute. The value varies according to the time of the day, so several readings should be taken over a period and averaged.

ACTIVITY

Peak flow meters are inexpensive and widely available in schools and colleges. If you can obtain one, carry out an investigation to compare peak flow rate in two groups of people, for example:

- males versus females;
- smokers versus non-smokers;
- people who exercise a lot versus people who do not exercise;
- asthma sufferers versus non-sufferers.

If possible, find out how to average your results using Student's t-test for unmatched samples.
NB Do not forget to follow the manufacturer's instructions, particularly with regard to safety.

Forced expiratory time can be measured with just a watch. This is the time taken to empty the chest from full inspiration (i.e. from breathing in as far as possible) to breathing out as far as possible. Normally this should be done in less than four seconds. If it takes more than six seconds this indicates a significant airflow obstruction.

Lung volumes

A SPIROMETER (see Figure 3.55) can be used to measure lung volumes.

- TIDAL VOLUME is the volume of air breathed in and out in one normal breath and is usually about 400 cm^3.
- VITAL CAPACITY is the maximum amount of air a person can breathe in and out; it is usually between 3 and 5 cm^3.

ACTIVITY

Find out what is meant by the terms below:

- expiratory reserve volume;
- inspiratory reserve volume;
- respiratory rate;
- pulmonary ventilation.

If you have access to a spirometer, measure your tidal volume and vital capacity. Measure yourself for the terms above.

NB You should not use a spirometer unsupervised. Ensure that you are aware of all the safety precautions.

PERFUSION

PERFUSION is the passage of fluid through a tissue, but generally the term is used to mean the passage of blood through the lung tissue to pick up oxygen and release carbon dioxide. The levels of these gases in the blood can be

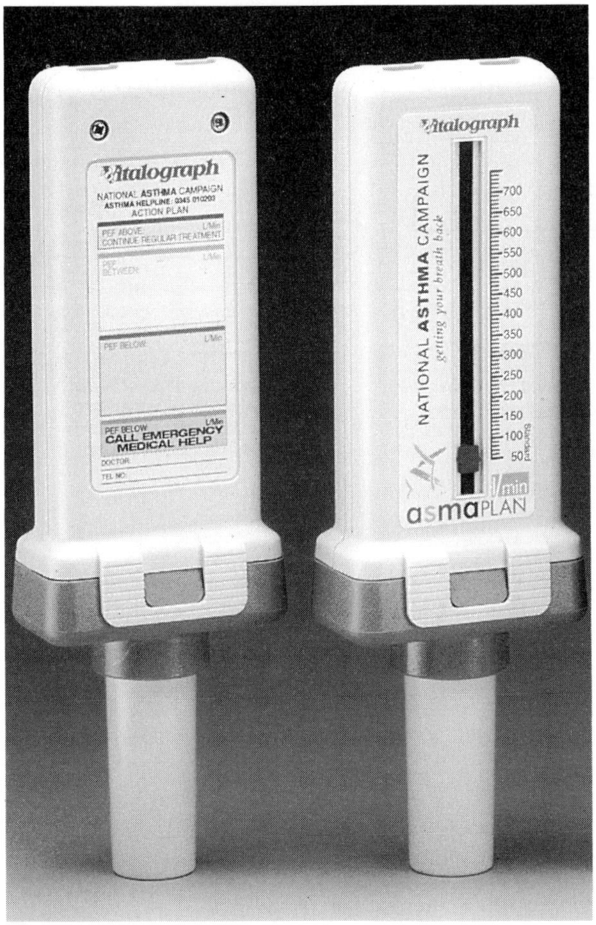

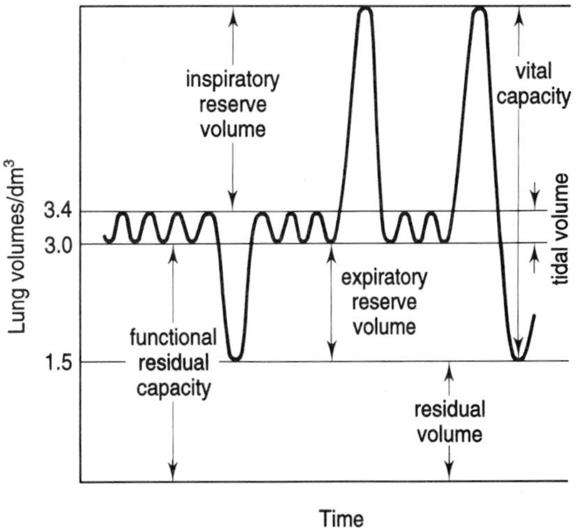

Figure 3.55 (a) Spirometer and (b) Spirometer trace from a normal male

measured to indicate how well a person is perfused. This BLOOD GAS ANALYSIS is performed on the arterial blood as this contains the oxygen absorbed from the air in the lungs. The blood sample may be taken from the wrist or groin; a local anaesthetic may be given because the procedure is more painful than taking the normal venous blood sample.

Imaging techniques

Imaging techniques are used to examine the tissues of the body. There are many different techniques employed and some of the most commonly used are explained below.

ACTIVITY

Before you read the following sections, note down all the examples of imaging techniques you can think of.

RADIOLOGY

This branch of medicine is concerned with the use of radiation and radioactive substances.

X-RADIOGRAPHY is probably the best-known imaging technique. It is likely that you have had at least one X-ray examination. Figure 3.56 shows how X-rays are produced. A high voltage accelerates a beam of electrons (negative particles that are found in atoms) towards a target, in a tube from which all the air has been removed. (Because electrons are so small it is important that there are no comparatively large air molecules around which could deflect them from their pathway.) The electrons collide with a tungsten target and cause the production of X-rays. The greater the current, the greater the number of electrons hitting the target and the more intense the X-rays. The higher the voltage, the greater the energy and

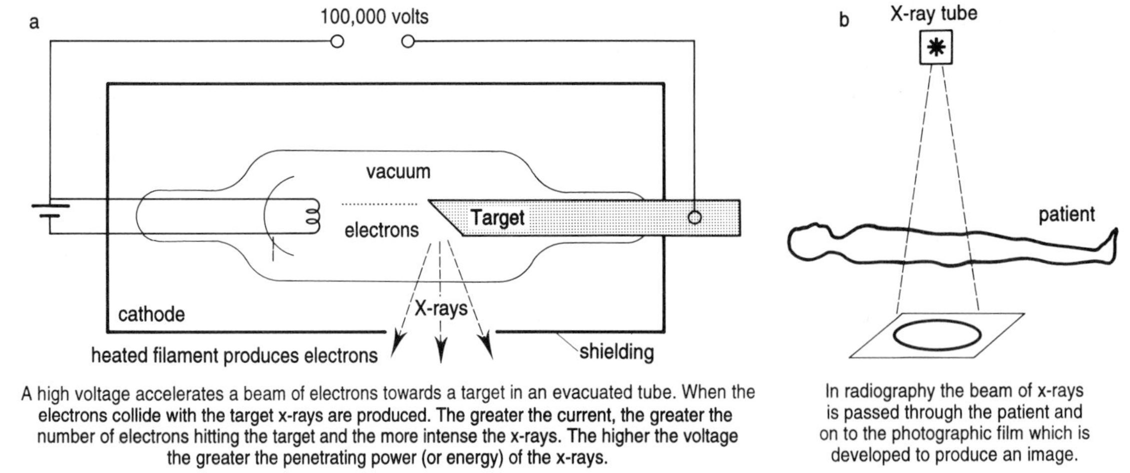
a
100,000 volts
vacuum
electrons
Target
cathode
X-rays
heated filament produces electrons
shielding
A high voltage accelerates a beam of electrons towards a target in an evacuated tube. When the electrons collide with the target x-rays are produced. The greater the current, the greater the number of electrons hitting the target and the more intense the x-rays. The higher the voltage the greater the penetrating power (or energy) of the x-rays.
b
X-ray tube
patient
In radiography the beam of x-rays is passed through the patient and on to the photographic film which is developed to produce an image.

Figure 3.56 The production of X-rays

penetrating power of the X-rays. X-rays are directed on to the area of the body under investigation, and pass through it to record an image on photographic film. The more dense tissues, such as bone, absorb more X-rays than less dense body tissues. This means the strength of X-rays reaching the photographic film varies, which produces images of varying densities known as RADIOGRAPHS (Figure 3.57). RADIOGRAPHERS are responsible for producing the radiographs, and specialist doctors known as RADIOLOGISTS interpret the radiographs. X-rays are used in determining the nature of a disorder (diagnosis). Chest X-rays are commonly taken because the sizes of the heart and lungs can be seen, as can areas of inflammation or fluid.

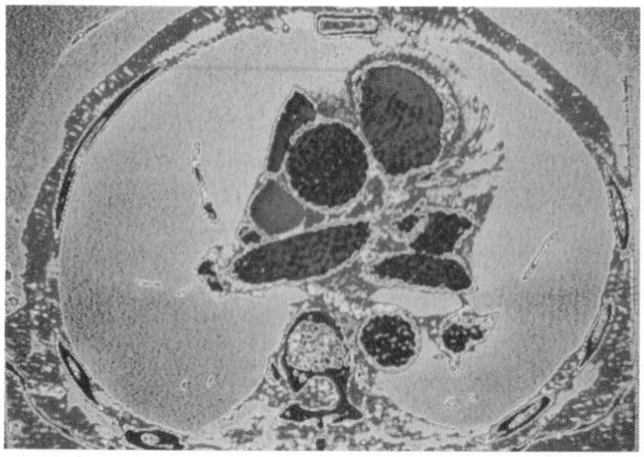

Figure 3.57 Radiograph of the heart

ACTIVITY

- What diseases do you think could be diagnosed and investigated with a chest X-ray?

RADIOOPAQUE DYES (contrast media) can be used to show more detailed information than a simple X-ray. These dyes, which absorb X-rays, are injected into the tissue under investigation to highlight empty spaces and outline soft tissues. They are, therefore, particularly valuable for examining hollow organs such as the bowel. The exact techniques depend on the area of the body to be examined (see Table 3.7).

BODY SCANNING: A detailed picture of the soft tissues of the body can be obtained by producing a CAT scan (Figure 3.58). CAT stands for COMPUTER AXIAL TOMOGRAPHY. A series of X-rays, taken at fractionally different depths of tissue, is analysed by computer. This method produces images of a slice of the body. The most common use of the CAT scan is in examining the brain. Unlike conventional X-rays, the CAT scan can differentiate between normal tissues, abscesses and blood clots. The procedure is safe and quick, but unfortunately, the expensive equipment necessary is not widely available.

ACTIVITY

Find out what possible harm may be caused by the use of X-rays. What safety measures are used to protect:

- patients?
- radiographers?

Why are X-rays unsuitable for monitoring foetal development?

MAGNETIC RESOURCE IMAGING (MRI)

MRI is the latest imaging technique used in hospitals (see Figure 3.59). This technique can produce images which are similar to and, in certain parts of the body (including the brain, spinal cord and heart), superior to those of the CAT scanner, but without the radiation hazard. It offers an early diagnosis of many conditions including cancer.

ULTRASOUND

Tissues in the body can be examined by the use of ULTRASOUND (high-frequency sound waves). The ultrasound is transmitted into the body, where it is reflected at the boundaries between different types of tissue. The time lapse and intensity loss of the reflected ultrasound (returning signal) allows the nature and position of the tissues to be deduced. The sound waves are generated by a hand-held device which is placed over the area to be scanned (Figure 3.60). The echo of the returning waves is recorded and analysed by a computer which forms a screen image. Ultrasound scans cause no damage to the tissues and for this reason are routinely given to pregnant women to monitor foetal development. The scans reveal the size and position, and, therefore, the age of the foetus; they can also detect foetal or placental defects. The procedure is also used to guide the needle into the uterus during amniocentesis.

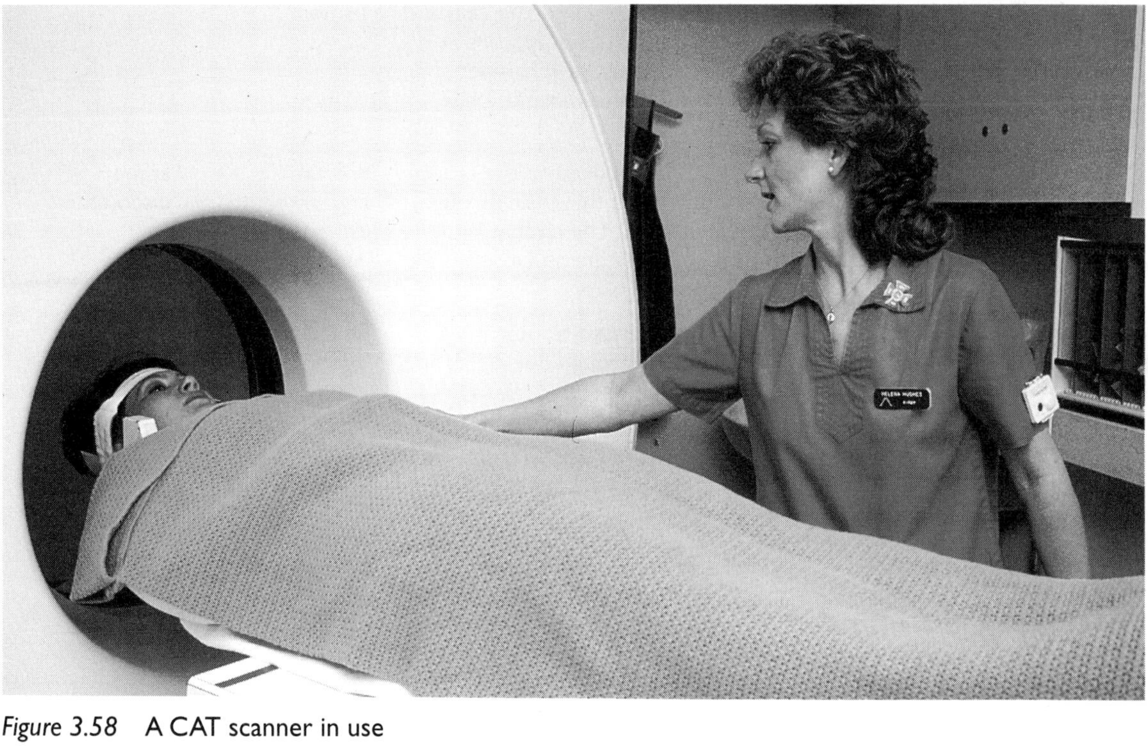

Figure 3.58 A CAT scanner in use

Table 3.7 Examples of techniques using contrast media

Technique	Body part examined	Method of administration	Examples of diseases diagnosed	Side effects
Angio-graphy/ Arterio-graphy	Blood vessels	Thin tube placed in the blood vessel (local anaesthetic and light sedation used). Dye injected. X-ray taken.	Blood clots, Artheriosclerosis, Arteriosclerosis, tumours	
Barium studies	Digestive tract	For the oesophagus, stomach and duodenum a barium meal is given. The patient fasts overnight then swallows a porridge-like drink containing barium. S/he lies on a table which can be tilted to coat the entire area under investigation and the stomach may be distended with air. Several X-rays are then taken over a period of about an hour. For small and large intestine a barium enema may be given.	Hernias, ulcers, colitis, tumours	Barium meal may cause constipation Barium enema may cause uncomfortable muscle spasms
Cholecystogram	Gall bladder and common bile duct	Tablets containing dye are swallowed after the evening meal. The dye enters the blood and circulates until it is absorbed by the liver. By the morning the dye has accumulated in the gall bladder. The patient is then given a fatty meal to stimulate the release of bile, so that the common bile duct can also be seen.		
Cholangio-gram	Bile ducts in the liver	Dye is injected into the vein and within 20 minutes appears in the bile ducts, or it can be injected directly into the bile duct.	Tumour	
Cysto-gram	Bladder and urethra	Dye is introduced to the bladder via a thin tube through the urethra. The patient is asked to urinate and a series of X-rays are taken.	Prostatic enlargment, urinary tract infection	Some discomfort
Hystero-salpingogram	Uterus and fallopian tubes	Dye introduced to uterus via a thin tube through the vagina and cervix.	Blocked fallopian tubes	
Lymph-angiogram	Lymph system	Dye injected into a lymph vessel (usually at the top of the foot). This spreads throughout the lymph system.	Hodgkin's disease, Lymphoma	
Myelogram	Space surrounding spinal cord with vertebral column	Dye injected into the space (lumbar puncture). Table tipped to allow the dye to travel the length of spinal chord.	Spinal tumours	

Pyelogram	Kidneys	Patient fasts overnight before dye is injected into a vein. This then travels through the blood to the kidney.	Kidney stone. Tumour
Venogram	Vein	Dye is injected into vein in hand or foot.	Blood clot (eg deep vein thrombosis)

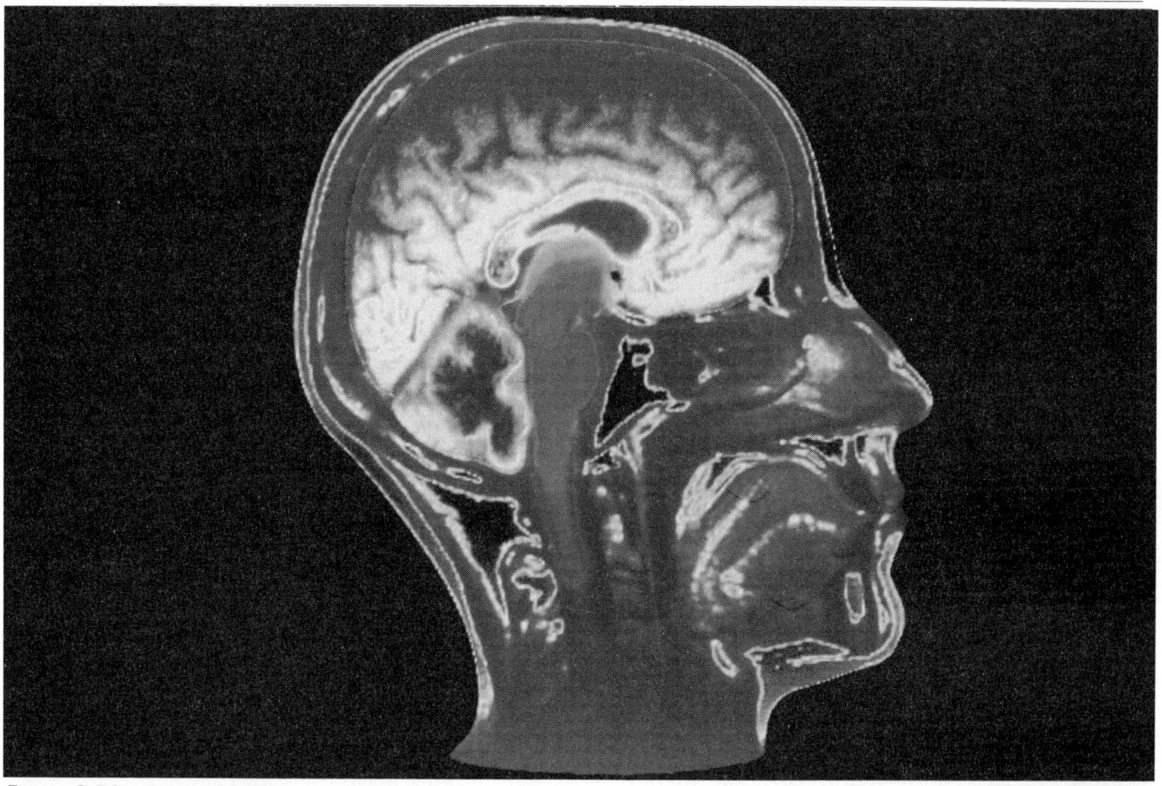

Figure 3.59 Lateral MRI scan of the head

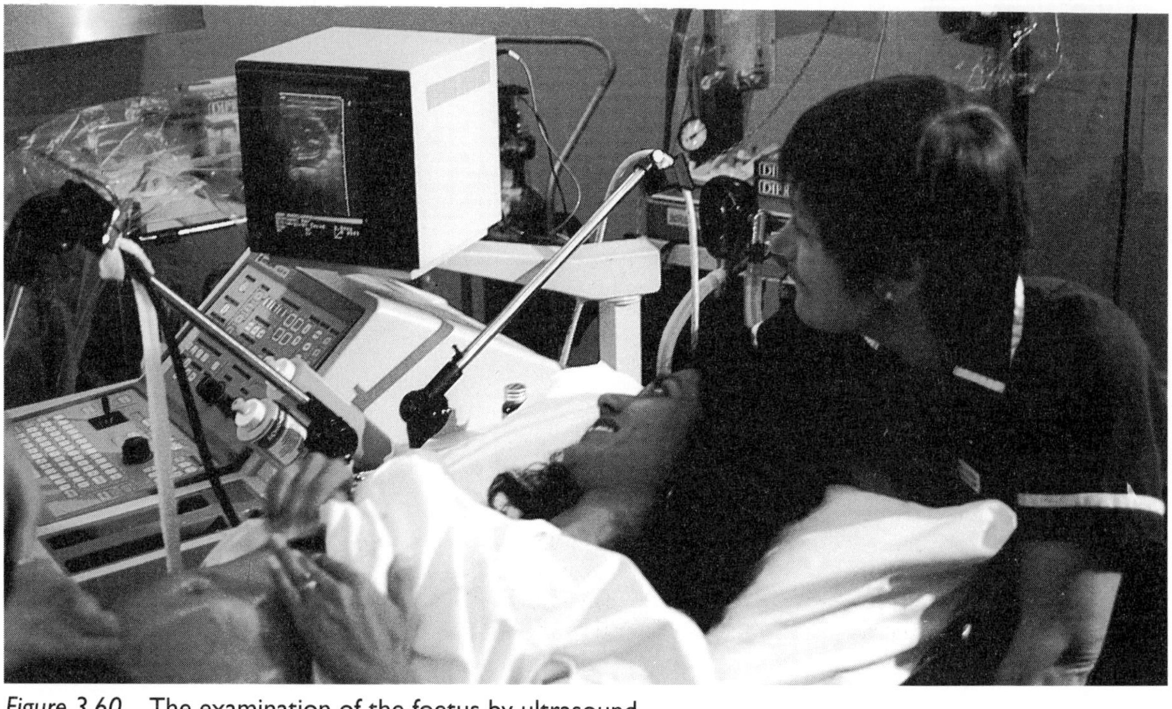

Figure 3.60 The examination of the foetus by ultrasound

Increasingly, ultrasound is also being used in other areas of diagnosis such as tumour location. For example, the pattern of blood vessels in an ovarian cyst can be studied. This can give a vital clue in spotting the very early development of cancer.

ASSESSMENT OPPORTUNITY ✓

- Produce an analytical report based on the monitoring of one individual's cardio-respiratory system (you could monitor yourself or a volunteer). Draw valid conclusions about the physiological status of the person monitored.
- If you had the equipment and resources mentioned in this chapter, what additional data would be useful to help you monitor the cardio-respiratory system?
- Explain the role of imaging techniques in displaying anatomical features.

RESOURCES

Physiological measurement technicians at local hospitals may be able to provide further secondary source data. If possible, visits to local physiological measurement and radiography units should be arranged.

An ECG computer program which describes the physiological basis of the ECG and the way in which it is recorded, and presents simulations of traces, and a unit with electrodes which attach to thumbs and ankles, and which can be attached to a BBC microcomputer to give an ECG trace, are available from the suppliers, Philip Harris.

USEFUL ADDRESSES

Association of Respiratory Technicians and Physiologists
Pulmonary Function Department
General Hospital
Steelhouse Lane
Birmingham B4 6NH

College of Radiographers
Wimpole Street
London W1
Tel.: 0171 935 5726/8

Electrophysiology Technologists' Association
Neurophysiology Department
Selly Oak Hospital
Raddlebury Road
Birmingham B29 6JD

4

HEALTH AND SOCIAL WELL-BEING: PSYCHO-SOCIAL ASPECTS

In this chapter the focus is upon enabling students to appreciate the contributions of the disciplines of psychology and sociology to an understanding of health and social well-being. Human growth, development and change is approached from a psychological viewpoint, enabling students to explore a range of influences and unexpected pressures on patterns of human development. An evaluation of the support networks available to people is followed by an introduction to some of the key social factors which influence people from a range of different cultural backgrounds. There is also a critical assessment of socio-economic factors relating to the health of the population in the UK today. Questions are raised about how health and care services and policies for people could be improved.

HUMAN GROWTH AND DEVELOPMENT

Aspects of human development

THE DEVELOPMENT OF LANGUAGE AND COMMUNICATION

Language is an organised system of symbols which humans use to communicate. These symbols may be spoken, written down (as in handwriting or braille) or signed (as in sign language used by those who are deaf or without speech). Spoken language is made up of basic sounds, called PHONEMES, which are combined to form more complex sounds with meaning, called MORPHEMES. For example, 'st' and 'op' are phonemes; 'stop' is a morpheme.

The acquisition and sequence of language development appear to occur in the same stages universally, regardless of culture, training or cognitive ability. Maturation and experience both play an important part in language acquisition.

Four stages of language development have been identified. Some of the main landmarks in these stages of acquiring speech are described below.

Pre-linguistic

The ability to use the voice draws on a number of skills, e.g. controlling breathing, face muscles and tongue muscles. Studies have shown that by the time babies are just a few hours old, they seem to be able to distinguish speech from other sounds, and may have a genetically acquired preference for listening to human speech.

Babbling

At two to six months babies start babbling, i.e. making sounds similar to human speech, but they are not just imitating what they have heard. Some of the sounds that babies make do not occur in the language their parents use, e.g. British-born babies make sounds that only occur in the Japanese and Chinese languages.

Babbling is probably a genetically acquired response, but it can have some communication value and can be modified by social learning. The baby enjoys making these noises when alone in its cot. Babbling has intonation patterns, like speech, with rising inflections and speech-like rhythms. The repetition of syllables over and over again is called ECHOLALIA, e.g. da da da da da.

Babbling occurs at roughly the same age in babies worldwide. Even deaf babies born to deaf-mute parents babble – and on average at the same time as hearing babies. However, deaf babies tend to stop babbling at around nine or ten months, presumably because of a lack of feedback from their own voice.

Language – nature and nurture

Although language appears to be genetically acquired and to develop universally through a maturational process, there is much evidence to show that babies benefit from social interaction, which enhances the development of speech. Infants enjoy and respond to human companionship. Research has shown that babies of just a few months old move their bodies in INTERACTIONAL SYNCHRONY, i.e. in rhythm with the human speech they are exposed to. Other research has shown that from about six weeks old, the babies' behaviour changes in the presence of the mother: they move their hands in a different way, change the expression on their faces, move their lips as if trying to speak, and take 'turns' at 'speaking' with their mothers.

Thus early, innate responses, like babbling and hand movements, may be modified and encouraged by interaction with the baby's carers. On the other hand, it is known that children brought up in deprived circumstances, such as the poorly run orphanages studied by Skeels and Dye, and described by Gross, suffer from poor language development.

Therefore it appears that sensitive social interaction, reinforcement, as provided in the pleased response a carer makes to a baby's vocalisation, and the opportunity to hear and imitate other human voices without continual background noise, are all required for optimal speech development.

The first words – from one to two years

From about 12 months two important changes occur:

1 The infants are now mature enough to be able to control their vocal chords, tongue and breathing.
2 The infant's brain is now mature enough to know that the sounds made or heard can stand for something that they know, e.g. dada, milk, doggie.

The following landmarks occur at this age:

- *Jargon* – this is the overlap of babbling and patterned speech (words);
- *First words* – these are often invented. A baby's first word is when they consistently use the same sound to label the same thing;
- First words are often ordinary words reduced to their simplest sounds, e.g. as 's' is a difficult sound to make, spoon becomes poon;
- Mistakes with pronouncing words;
- *Holophrases* – these are words which convey complex messages, e.g. 'milk' may mean I want more milk or, on another occasion, I spilt my milk.

Active and passive vocabulary can be defined as follows:

- *Active vocabulary* – the number of words a child can use. Typically, a child can use 10 words by 15 months, 50 words by 19 months and 200 words by 2 years.
- *Passive vocabulary* – the number of words a child can understand. A child of one to two years always understands more than he or she is able to speak.

ACTIVITY

Referring to a textbook, summarise the main errors that children make in their early speech.

Table 4.1 Telegraphic speech development

	Child's age (in months)		
Sentence	25.5	30	35.5
I showed you the book	I show book	Show you the book	CORRECT
I will read the book	Read book	I read the book	CORRECT
Do I like to read books?	To read book?	I read books	CORRECT

Source: An introduction to Child Development, by G.C. Davenport (Collins, 1994).

Early sentences

Stage 1 grammar

Typical two-word utterances, in which children leave out the least important words, is called *telegraphic speech* (Brown, 1973). The following example (Table 4.1) from Brown's 10 year longitudinal study shows the rapid progress children make between two and three years of age. By three years even the last difficult sentence can be imitated correctly.

By three years of age a child may have a vocabulary of about 1,000 words.

Stage 2 grammar

- *Overgeneralising* – children are beginning to acquire the rules of grammar, but tend to use the same rule in every case, as is demonstrated in their grammatical mistakes, e.g. sheeps, goed, wented. A demonstration of children's rule learning ability was conducted by Berko in 1958. He showed the children a picture of an imaginary creature called a wug (Figure 4.1). He told them this is a wug. He then showed a second picture showing two of the creatures, and asked to complete the sentence 'There are two _______'.
- *Overextension* – for example 'doggie' may be used to refer to all animals.

Later speech

- *Pronunciation* – up until the age of five years, most children have trouble with at least one phoneme;
- *Overmarking and redundancy*, e.g. the girl pushed the door and then the boy he repushed the door once more.

At five years a child can join quite complicated sentences together and is ready for school, which relies heavily on a child's ability to understand and use language.

Theories of how language is acquired include Skinner's (1957) theory which explains the acquisition of language in learning theory terms, i.e. language is learned through the same processes as all other behaviour – selective reinforcement, shaping and imitation.

Against this and other nurturist views, is Chomsky's naturist theory which states that we are born with an ability to formulate and understand language.

ACTIVITY

Research the evidence for and against each of these theories.

Most psychologists would take the view that the acquisition of language is partly due to

This is a wug
Now there is another one.
There are two of them.
There are two _______.

Figure 4.1 Berko's (1958) diagram for testing children's use of the rule for forming plurals (*Taken from*: Gross, 1992)

maturation, partly due to learning and partly due to social interaction.

Genie

Genie was a child brought up in conditions of severe deprivation in one room, and beaten if she made a noise. When found at the age of 13 years she had no speech. Curtiss (1977) taught her to speak to a certain extent, and it is probable that Genie's progress would have continued if her care circumstances had allowed this. However, it is unlikely that she would ever have acquired perfect speech.

ACTIVITY

Watch the video of Genie, or read Curtiss's report. Does this case show evidence for a critical period for learning speech or not? What progress in vocabulary and grammar did Genie make? It was not possible to ascertain whether Genie had been mentally retarded at birth or not.

ACTIVITY **W**

Observe children during work experience. Make notes of the ages of various children and record their speech utterances. Give examples you have heard of echolalia, holophrases, telegraphic speech and the other speech landmarks described above.

INTELLECTUAL DEVELOPMENT

Some aspects of Piaget's theory of cognitive development

By continuously interacting with the outside world, a child constructs a set of structures. This is the process of intellectual growth, which develops over time and is dependent on two major principles: organisation and adaptation.

Organisation

Schemas are a way of organising experience which makes the environment simpler and more predictable. A schema may be thought

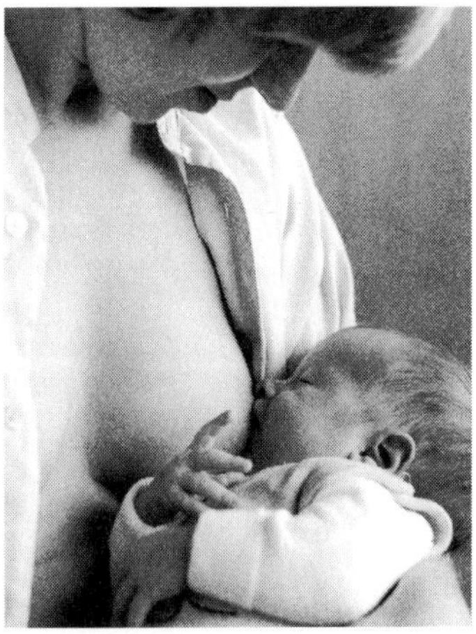

Figure 4.2 A suckling baby

of as the basic building block of intelligent behaviour. A baby's schemas are inborn reflexes, such as sucking, each of which operates separately from other schemas. Later, larger structures which are more inclusive will develop, constituting the typical abilities and understanding of each developmental stage.

Adaptation

Underlying the changes involved in the process of intellectual development are FUNCTIONAL VARIANTS. These are fundamental aspects of the developmental process which remain the same, and work in the same way, throughout the various stages. Piaget identifies three:

1 assimilation;
2 accommodation;
3 equilibration.

The baby sucks at anything that touches the lips or is put into the mouth. The baby applies this schema to all objects he or she sucks, *assimilating* them. The baby has to change the way he or she sucks differently shaped objects, in this way demonstrating *accommodation*. The child will be in a state of balance or *equilibrium* brought about by equilibration. If already existing schemas are inadequate to cope with new situations, for example a new object calls for a different

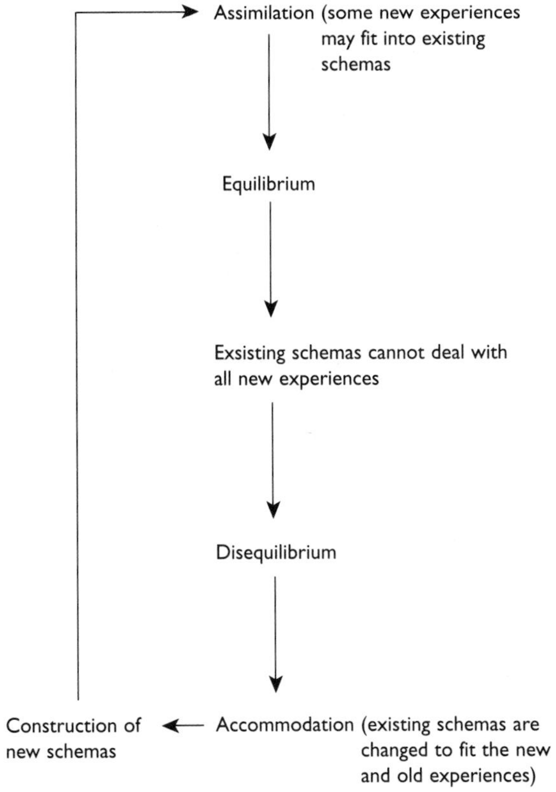

Figure 4.3 Functional variants in the process of intellectual development

method of sucking, then the child is pushed into a less comfortable state, of disequilibrium; to restore the balance, he or she must change one or more of the schemas, i.e. the baby must accommodate.

Development proceeds through the process shown in Figure 4.3. The most significant developments take place in the first 15 years of life.

Stages of cognitive development

Piaget describes four stages:

1 the sensorimotor (0–2 years);
2 the pre-operational (2–7 years);
3 the concrete operational (7–11 years);
4 the formal operational (11–15 years).

The ages corresponding to each stage are only approximations: children move through the stages at different speeds, the difference often being due to environmental factors. However, the sequence of stages is always the same because it depends partly on biological maturation. Later stages build on earlier ones and involve reconstructing at a new level what was achieved at an earlier stage.

In the sensorimotor stage (birth to two years) the baby's intelligence is practical, and its interactions with the environment are overt, either sensory (seeing, hearing) or motor (grasping, pulling). The baby shows a lack of OBJECT PERMANENCE, i.e. when a toy is seen, heard or felt it exists, but when it is not seen, heard or felt it is as if it no longer exists. At six to seven months a baby will reach for a familiar object if part of it is showing. If the object is totally covered up, even if the baby sees you covering it up, he or she will not search for it. From eight months the baby will search for a completely hidden object. At 12 months a baby will search for an object hidden under several layers of cloth.

The sensorimotor stage is also important mainly for the development of the GENERAL SYMBOLIC FUNCTION. Three manifestations of this are:

- *language:* action leads to thought which is reflected in language;
- *deferred imitation:* the ability to copy something seen or heard when the model (the person doing the action) is no longer present, as when a child 'feeds' its doll in the way it has been fed by its own mother;
- *representational or make-believe play* (about 18–24 months): one object is used as if it were another.

The *pre-operational stage* (two to seven years) is divided into two parts:

(a) the pre-conceptual (two to four years);
(b) the intuitive (four to seven years).

The whole pre-operational stage is influenced by:

- egocentrism;
- conservation.

The pre-conceptual child has difficulty with relative terms. Piaget noticed that children at this stage will tend to classify objects and events in a way that lacks adult logic. For example, present bricks of two sizes and two colours, red and blue, and ask a child between two and four years old to divide the bricks into big red bricks and small blue bricks. The child can only classify things on the basis of a single attribute at a time – either colour or size, but not both at once.

The pre-conceptual child also has difficulty with arranging objects on the basis of a particular dimension, for example increasing height.

At this age a child typically perceives the world from their own point of view only. A child at this stage conversing with one of his or her peers will express their own thoughts out loud and not take the other's point of view into consideration. When telling the mother something, the child does not set the scene, assuming that the listener knows it already, and does not consider any other point of view. This EGOCENTRICITY can lead to difficulties in play, especially in the two to three years age group where discord may arise. Only later, when the child begins to integrate the wishes and demands of others, will cooperative play take place.

The concept of cause and effect is developed at this stage but is still very limited. An example of this is the concept of IMMANENT JUSTICE, whereby an accident may be perceived by a child as a punishment for some misbehaviour by the victim, whereas to an adult the accident would seem spontaneous. Care workers who deal with children of this age should be particularly aware of this concept and sensitive to the fact that young children involved in accidents, or admitted to hospital, may see these events as punishments.

ANIMISTIC THINKING is prevalent at the pre-conceptual stage. This is the belief that inanimate objects are alive. The child attributes human emotions and needs to inanimate objects. Piaget believed that the child reasons in the following way: if our shadow moves and follows us when we walk, it must be alive. The family car, being filled with petrol, is having a 'drink'. Many popular children's books promote this concept (e.g. Thomas the Tank Engine). It is through animism that a cuddly toy or doll may come to be a child's constant and trusted companion at bedtime or at times of stress.

The 'intuitive' child, at four to seven years old, may have developed the kinds of thinking described above, but they are still very limited in their ability to think logically. In the latter part of the pre-operational period, children become more capable of classifying rather than quantifying events and objects, and integrate them into their developing mental skills. Therefore problem-solving becomes more prevalent at the age of four to seven years, but the child still does not appear capable of explaining how he or she has solved the problems. It is for this reason that Piaget termed this the intuitive stage of the pre-operational period.

CONSERVATION, the concept that certain properties do not alter while undergoing certain transformations, comes in stages:

conservation of numbers	5–7 years
conservation of length	7–8 years
conservation of matter	8–10 years
conservation of area	8–9 years
conservation of weight	10–12 years
conservation of volume	12–14 years

ACTIVITY W

Conservation of numbers

- Make a row of objects, for example buttons.
- Have a pile of buttons nearby and ask the child to reproduce the original row.

A child at the first stage of conservation of numbers will make a rough approximation of the original row (different number but same length). A child at the second stage will reproduce the row exactly.

Conservation of length

- Place two sticks of exactly the same length next to each other, with each end in line. A child of the appropriate age, if asked, should state that the sticks are of equal length.

- Keeping the sticks parallel, move one stick upwards so that its top is higher than the other. Ask the child which stick is the longer. A child who has not yet attained conservation of length will state that the stick which has been moved is the longer.

Conservation of matter

- Take a piece of play dough and form it into two equal-sized balls.
- Ask the child if the balls are equal in size.
- If the child agrees that they are equal, roll out one ball into a sausage shape, allowing the child to observe what you are doing.
- Ask the child which shape contains the most play dough.

Conservation of area

- Make two large squares of card, to represent two meadows.
- Make two smaller squares to represent two 'potato plots'.
- Cut up one of the potato plots and distribute it around one of the meadows.
- Ask the child:
  (a) Is there still as much room for potatoes?
  (b) Is there still as much room for cows to graze?

  Conservation of area appears to be attained in stages: a child will typically say yes to (a) before being ready to say yes to (b).

Conservation of weight

- Using two balls of clay, use a pair of weighing scales to show the child that each ball of clay is equal in weight to the other.
- Change one of the balls of clay into a sausage shape.
- Ask the child to predict the relative weight of the two shapes.

Conservation of volume

- Pour some water into a tumbler.
- With the child watching, pour the water from the tumbler into a long thin glass.
- Ask the child whether the tumbler or the thin container contains more water.
- What did the child say? How did Piaget account for this?

In the *concrete operational period* (seven to 11 years) the child has a more integrated cognitive system to consult than in the preceding intuitive stage. Logic and reasoning play key roles. There is greater equilibrium, greater cognitive stability and less egocentricity, enabling conservation and classification skills to become established.

The *formal operational period* (12 years onwards) signals the onset of mature thought – the final equilibrium state towards which the intellect has been moving through childhood. The adolescent continues to classify objects and events as they did in the concrete operational period, but now they consider the results of such operations as propositions; they will now go further by attempting to make logical connections between them.

Implications of Piaget's theory for the caring professions

There have been criticisms of Piaget's theory, but it has contributed to our understanding of the intellectual development of the individual and the possible implications for the carer. The consideration of ideas of immanent justice, animism, accommodation and assimilation may provide an insight into a child's understanding of his or her predicament, e.g. illness, hospitalisation or abuse.

A sick child may endure considerable fear in trying to deal with new information in relation to his or her existing knowledge. Many misconceptions may arise, and from them childhood beliefs which seem at the time entirely real, whether benign or frightening. The key to overcoming fears lies in the intellect's ability continually to integrate new information and modify ideas accordingly. The sick child therefore needs not only appropriate explanations, but more importantly a patient exploration and understanding of his or her beliefs, fears and misconceptions.

EMOTIONAL DEVELOPMENT

Attachments

Deprivation and privation

Psychologists since Bowlby have been divided about how important the mother is to the child's emotional development. There is agreement, however, that the formation of strong attachment bonds (not necessarily with the biological mother) before the age of three years is vital to the emotional health of the growing child.

If these bonds have been made, and are then for some reason disrupted, perhaps by divorce, death, moving house or hospitalisation, the child will be distressed, the distress typically showing three phases: protest, despair and detachment. This distress can with time and care be overcome, more quickly if an infant can be with someone else to whom he or she is attached.

What is far more serious for the long term is if an infant fails to make any bonds at all (privation). This may happen if a baby has multiple changes of carer, or if he or she is in the kind of institution where staff change regularly and 'favouritism' is discouraged, or if the child has emotionally neglecting parents (see section on emotional abuse on page 224). A child may then suffer from 'affectionless psychopathy' (Bowlby) which is characterised by:

- a phase of very clingy, dependent behaviour, followed by
- attention-seeking behaviour and indiscriminate friendliness, and finally
- a personality which shows no feelings of guilt, is unable to keep rules and is unable to form lasting relationships.

A life on the fringes of society, or involvement in crime, is a strong possibility for such people. Psychopathy is rare, but behaviour that tends towards it is observed quite commonly.

For an infant it is certainly better to have loved and lost (deprivation) than never to have loved at all (privation).

Bowlby's theory was based on two main principles:

1. *Monotropy.* This concept, based on the studies of imprinting behaviour in animals suggests that a special attachment developed between a mother or mother substitute that was different in quality from all other attachments.
2. *Maternal deprivation.* Bowlby argued that separation from the mother or mother substitute in infancy may lead to serious problems later, including juvenile delinquency and affectionless psychopathy.

Therefore, a mother should stay at home and look after her small children, rather than go out to work.

Considerable evidence has been gathered which refutes both of these principles.

- *Monotropy.* Studies have shown that infants typically make several strong attachments in infancy, and may even make a stronger attachment to someone they see only briefly every day, e.g. the father, than to the person who takes care of them all day, especially if the daytime caretaker is depressed and unresponsive.
- *Maternal deprivation.* The studies Bowlby used to support his theory were frequently studies of children in institutions whose development was retarded. This developmental retardation could be explained by other kinds of deprivation besides maternal deprivation, e.g. stimulus deprivation. Cross-cultural studies also appear to contradict this theory – in many societies infants are not brought up by their mothers and do not suffer harm as a result. Deprivation studies, such as the Freud and

Dann study of orphans who grew up in a Nazi concentration camp, show that it is bond formation that is important, not the person with whom the bond is formed.

Research by M. Rutter showed:

1 that it is stress in the family home rather than maternal deprivation which leads to juvenile delinquency;
2 it is privation rather than maternal deprivation which leads to affectionless psychopathy.

However, important changes have resulted from Bowlby's work:

- Children in hospital are now often accompanied by a parent, for the well-being of both.
- Institutions now place equal emphasis on emotional as well as physical care.
- In problem family situations, social workers must weight up the physical danger to the child against the emotional trauma of removing a child from home.
- Increased, but still not sufficient, childcare provision for working mothers.

ACTIVITY

1 What two physiological effects does a new baby's crying have on its mother?

2 Give reasons why the consequences of divorce on a small child may be more damaging than the consequences of the death of one parent.

Attachments: summary

- There is no foundation for the belief that the biological mother is uniquely capable of caring for her child.
- The 'mother' does not even have to be female.
- Multiple attachments rather than a distinct preference for a mother-figure is the rule rather than the exception for even young infants.
- Attachment is unrelated to the amount of physical care-taking the baby receives from the attachment figure.

Attachments are determined by:

- *Intensity of interaction*: quality of time is more important than quantity of time.
- *Sensitive responsiveness* to the baby's needs by the carer.
- *Consistency*: people must be a predictable part of the child's environment.

ASSESSMENT OPPORTUNITY – PART I ✔

1 Find out the visiting arrangements at the children's ward in your local hospital. What are the effects of these arrangements on the conditions of the sick child?

2 Observe for 15 minutes a mother and baby. (If a live mother and baby cannot be arranged, you might be able to watch a video.)

3 Note:
- age of baby;
- relationship of carer to baby.

4 Note what the carer does with body, voice, eye contact.

5 Note how the baby responds.

6 Write down a case study of this mother and baby from your notes.

7 How much do you think your presence affected the behaviour of the mother?

8 Discuss which factors favour attachments and which inhibit them, using books from the library for your research.

Case study: Anthony

The following description of Anthony's case is

taken from 'The Lost Boys', *Sunday Times*, 22 September 1991.

The police started calling for Anthony when he was 4. He got into trouble from the moment he was allowed to play outside his home on a big pre-war housing estate in west London. First he abused bigger boys with racial taunts until they beat up his eldest sister. (Anthony, they felt, was too small to hit.)

Then he smashed a neighbour's windows and discovered vandalism. At the age of 5 he learnt about theft, breaking into a BT van and stealing the equipment.

'He always denies everything. It's never him,' his mother says. 'He's done so many things I can't remember half of them. I've done everything they've told me to, like keep him in and stop his treats and put him in his room and leave him. But he just climbs out of the window.'

Home is a clean but sparsely furnished ground-floor flat. There are no books; the only wall-fitting is an electric clock. There used to be a telephone, but it melted when one of Anthony's younger sisters burnt the flat down.

Trying to alter Anthony means tackling emotional damage that goes back to birth. He was sick with lung trouble from the age of three months, passed much of his infancy in hospital, and from the age of 18 months spent his days in a nursery because another baby, Frances, had come along. His mother adored the new child, regarding Anthony, by contrast, as spoilt.

At the nursery, Anthony hit other children as soon as he could walk. 'I thought it was normal because he was only two. All kids are spiteful at that age. He was just very active,' Bridget says. But his violence continued. Bridget stopped his medication, believing it was the cause, but it made no difference.

Anthony's teachers arranged child guidance and mother-and-son counselling with a psychologist. Nothing changed.

At infants' school the teachers kept a book in the playground for the names of misbehaving children. If a child featured twice in one week, a letter was sent to parents. Anthony was named twice a day; the school wrote only if he did *not* appear. That happened once, and his mother rewarded him with a budgie, christened Gazza. Within days Gazza was forgotten and Anthony was back in the book.

In some ways, he is a bright and endearing child, who climbs trees and loves pigeons, often bringing them home. When he grows up, he says, he wants to be a policeman.

But wherever he goes, his behaviour is the same. When he and his sister were given summer holidays with host families outside London this year, Frances returned with a present and a promise that she would be welcomed again. Anthony's hosts said the family was glad to see the back of him.

Asked about the holiday last week, Anthony said: 'I don't know. I forget now. I forget everything.'

His mother, living a cycle of boredom during the day, and 'murderous' weekends with all the children home, sees her only hope in a move from their estate. Unless this happens, she believes, Anthony is doomed.

'If he carries on the way he's going now, he will end up in prison. I know it's horrible to say. But I don't see any future for him.'

ASSESSMENT OPPORTUNITY – PART 2 ✔

Read Anthony's story. Then use the following questions as the basis for discussion or a written essay.
Is Anthony an 'affectionless' child?

- What stresses did he experience in infancy which might have contributed to his present behaviour?
- Identify the ways in which his home is deprived?
- What positive signs are there? Does Anthony demonstrate any attachments at all?
- What help would you suggest for Anthony and children like him?

Psychological and social causes of the increasing crime rate among juveniles

There has been recent national concern at and a heated debate about possible causes of juvenile crime. Proposed causes of this, based on research over the years, have included separation from the mother at an early age, a failure to form any strong attachment bonds in infancy (affectionless psychopathy), and long-standing marital discord, as well as social factors such as high unemployment, poverty, alienation from school and truancy. Now, controversially, the lack of a socially responsible father in many families is also seen as a contributory cause.

The importance of the father

In the past the father has been seen as having mainly indirect value as an emotional and economic support for the mother. The notion of 'paternal deprivation' has hardly been considered until the present day. While the importance of a father's secondary role as provider of emotional and economic support for the mother has changed but not diminished, research is now showing that children raised without fathers are more likely to be poor, do badly at school, have a drink or drug problem and end up in jail.

The role of the father does not supplant that of the mother, and should be viewed as providing increased involvement with his children and concern for their social and emotional welfare, both directly in partnership with the mother and through support for the mother.

The father is now considered to be of direct emotional and social significance to the developing child in the following ways:

- A father is an important attachment figure for small children, who form a different quality of attachment with their mother and father and choose one or other according to the circumstances. For example, the mother might be preferred as a source of comfort, the father as a playmate.
- A father provides an adult male role model which is important for girls, but seems to be particularly necessary for boys.
- Research indicates that affection and discipline from two parents protects against acquiring a criminal record. One of the factors must be that where there are several children, two parents can provide more affection, supervision and discipline than one parent trying to do everything alone.

There is now a large body of American and British data to demonstrate the disastrous effects of raising children without fathers. In the USA, more than 70 per cent of all juveniles in state reform institutions are from fatherless homes. Studies suggest that the most damaging lack in lone-parent families is the example of two adults engaging in negotiation and concession, a model of behaviour that may be sometimes irreplaceable in a child's development. Easier divorce, while improving the happiness of adults, can thus reduce children's experience of give-and-take.

(The Times, 6 July 1993)

Single-parent families

There has been recent extensive media coverage, and some would say victimisation, of single-parent families.

The concern raised about the growth of single-parent families is not focused so much on the more mature single parent who has become homeless as a result of marital breakdown but wishes to be independent and work. A greater worry, from the psychological point of view, is the growth of 'illegitimate' births among teenagers and women between 20 and 24 years, the traditional child-bearing age. Many young single women today may talk of having a baby without a husband or long-term partner as utterly normal. The mother receives from the baby the unquestioning love she finds nowhere else.

Other reasons have been suggested for this growing trend:

- Young men leaving school unqualified and

jobless are considered 'not worth marrying'.

- Young women are responding to this 'by having children outside marriage and relying on state benefits'. They may also find that having a baby gives them priority on the council housing list.

(*phrases in quotation marks from* The Times, *June* 1994)

ACTIVITY

Find out who gets priority on the council housing list in the area in which you live. How are priorities of need determined?

ACTIVITY

Discuss the psychological difficulties or benefits that children face in:

- family change due to divorce:
- a family that has always been fatherless.

On some housing estates today there is a lack of men.

Something is missing on the Meadow Well estate on North Tyneside. There are women and children aplenty, and scores of youths. But where have all the fathers gone? Most of them seem to have vanished: to the pub, the betting shop, prison, or points unknown.

That men should get and hold a job, live with their children, plant the garden, keep an eye out for the local villains or organise a Scout troop is an idea so detached from the reality of life at Meadow Well as to be farcical.

Meadow Well has become a classic sink estate of impoverished women, deprived children, loutish adolescents and a prevailing nihilism.

(Sunday Times, 11 July 1993)

The problems on this estate are not its design (the houses are well spaced) or a lack of community initiatives (many programmes have been started here); they reflect deeper problems – of 'growing illegitimacy and family breakdown, the reduction in the work ethic and rising crime' (*Sunday Times*, 11 July 1993).

What problems or benefits might occur for a child raised in a single-parent family, on an estate surrounded by similar families, without the back-up of relatives?

A report carried out by Family Policy Studies Centre and Crime Concern 1993 states that more emphasis needs to be placed on the roles played by men in bringing up children and their influence on the raising of socially responsible adults. The report states: 'This is not merely because men so heavily outnumber women as known offenders, but because the role of fathers in raising pro-socially responsible children has been unjustly neglected.'

There is now a national campaign to prevent youngsters turning to crime, and courses on parental skills will be offered in areas across the country. The following extract from *The Times*, July 1993, describes examples.

A block of flats and the lives of its residents have been transformed by the provision of a neighbourhood centre offering a range of support facilities for young mothers and fathers.

The flats on the ground floor of one of three tower blocks at Hockwell Ring, Luton, Bedfordshire, have been converted to provide a community room, nursery, toilets and reception areas. A nursery school and 'mums and tots' club operates five days a week and, once a week, there is a drop-in club for mothers and children and a lunch club. A six-week basic child-care course has been held and a ten-week course for those who want a certificate is planned.

Inside Lancaster Farms young offenders' institution, Lancashire, staff are also running a parentcraft course for young men aged 17 to 21. The course includes talks on sexual behaviour, contraception and how to feed, bath and look after a baby.

ACTIVITY

Discuss the following questions in your class, or in smaller groups.

- The growth of the idea, starting in the 1960s, that people should not have limits on their happiness or rights – including the rights both to have children and to get divorced – has been blamed for the breakdown of the traditional family. Do you agree with this? What other reasons might there be for changes in family structure?
- In some cultures the extended family (grandparents, uncles, aunts, etc.) all help each other in raising children, so that there is less pressure on the 'nuclear' family. Could anything be done in this country to encourage the extended family? Or do you think this would be a backward step?
- Should more effort be made to give good parenting models on popular television programmes such as daily 'soaps'? Or do you think this is already being done?
- If the father's role in the family is important, what qualities should he possess? What behaviour should he show? What behaviour should he not show?
- Find out what parenting courses and other types of support are offered to young mothers and fathers in the area where you live.

Showing emotion

An intense emotion comprises the following components:

- perception of stimulus (person, object or event);
- physiological arousal, involving the autonomic nervous system (see Chapter 3);
- cognitive appraisal of the state of affairs;
- facial expression;
- reactions to the emotion.

Physiological changes associated with emotion

During emotional arousal the sympathetic division of the autonomic nervous system is activated as it prepares the body for emergency action and energy output. As the emotion recedes, the parasympathetic system – the energy-conserving system – takes over and returns the body to its normal state.

ACTIVITY W

- List other bodily changes that take place during emotional arousal.
- Research how polygraphs are used in lie detection. What are the problems in using arousal to detect lies?

Identifying emotion

The James–Lange theory

The James–Lange theory of emotion argues that the emotion we feel arises from our perception of the physiological state of the body, which is activated in response to a person or event. 'We do not weep because we feel sorrow; we feel sorrow because we weep' (James). Similarly we are afraid because we run; we are angry because we shout.

ACTIVITY

- Study the James–Lange theory using a textbook.
- Put one letter in each box so that the diagram below describes the James–Lange theory of emotion.

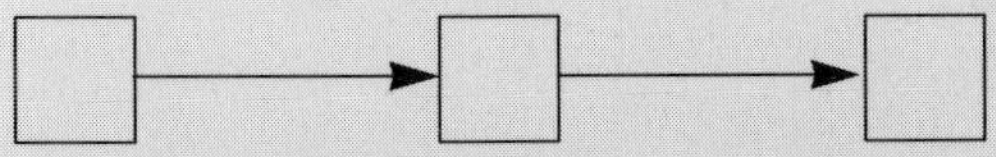

A – physiological response
B – perception of emotional stimulus
C – perception of emotion

The James–Lange theory argues that because different emotions feel different, each different emotion must have its own distinct pattern of autonomic activity, and therefore autonomic arousal differentiates the emotions. Others have criticised this, saying that the heart beats harder in both anger and fear, therefore the pattern of autonomic arousal does not seem to differ much from one emotional state to another.

Research seems to show that there are some physiological differences between the emotions, but not sufficient differences to prevent 'errors' in interpretation. One study showed that subjects in a high fear condition, walking over a swaying bridge 230 ft over the Capilano Canyon, were more likely to 'fall in love' with an attractive female experimenter than those in a low fear condition crossing a stable low bridge.

ACTIVITY

Look up Schacter and Singer's (1962) theory of emotion in a textbook. How does this theory differ from the James–Lange theory?

Personality development

This section discusses the self-concept and how it develops, outlines the nature–nurture debate on personality, and investigates the differing psychological perspectives on personality. These alternative viewpoints have led to various methods of measuring personality, which are also discussed.

THE SELF

Development of personality is best understood in terms of the development of an individual's self-concept. We cannot fully understand a person's behaviour unless we also understand what that behaviour means for that person. When we say we know someone well, part of what we mean is that we know what they think of themselves. Behaviour that appears the same may have two different meanings if performed by two people with different self-concepts: for example, of two elderly people accepting that they need residential care, one might be genuinely seeking company, safety and dependency, while the other might feel depressed at the prospect of loss of valued independence, but realise that circumstances have left no option.

Development of the self-concept occurs mainly in childhood and adolescence, although our self-concept continues to be revised to a certain extent throughout life.

Traditionally self-concept is seen as a term covering three main components:

- the self image;
- the self-esteem;
- the ideal self.

The self-image

The self-image refers to the kind of person we think we are.

ACTIVITY

- Ask yourself the question 'Who am I?' 20 times. Then count up the number of your answers that refer to:
  (a) social roles (the social self);
  (b) personality traits (the personality);
  (c) physical characteristics (the bodily self).
- For the whole of your group of students, work out the highest-scoring and lowest-scoring of these three categories. This test, first used by Kuhn in 1960, has since been used on seven-year-olds and undergraduates. Seven-year-olds typically describe themselves mainly in terms of physical characteristics ('I've got blue eyes'), with an average of five answers relating to social roles, while undergraduates describe themselves much more in terms of social roles (average 10 answers).
- If 16–18-year-olds describe themselves mostly in terms of personality traits, what does this say about the change in the self-image as individuals grow up?
- Use the test on:
  (a) a child at puberty
  (b) a middle-aged person.

  What categories would you expect to predominate in the list of each? Why?

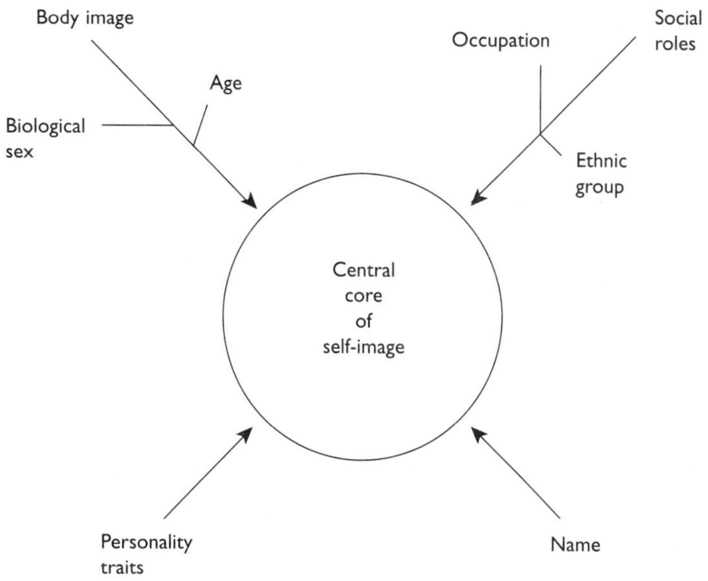

Figure 4.4 The central core of self-image

The bodily self: the body image

When our body changes, so our body image and thus our self-concept changes. Body changes occur to all individuals:

- at adolescence, a time of rapid growth and change;
- in the ageing process, a more gradual change that will also affect the body image (e.g. loss of looks, strength);

and to some individuals:

- with major surgery, e.g. amputation or mastectomy;
- with dramatic weight gain or loss (the disorder anorexia nervosa involves a disturbance of the body image: sufferers claim to feel they are fat when emaciated (see Figure 4.5).

Self-recognition

Self-recognition is usually confined to the fact; even adults have difficulty recognising their own bodies in photographs.

ACTIVITY

Without mirrors, or reflective surfaces, how would we obtain our body image?

Social roles

Change in social roles also affects the self-image, positively or negatively. For example, a man who loses his job, or is forced to take an inferior job, will feel his loss of status and decision-making powers reflected in the way other employees treat him, as well as the loss of earnings; these feelings may then be reflected in his dress, manner and posture.

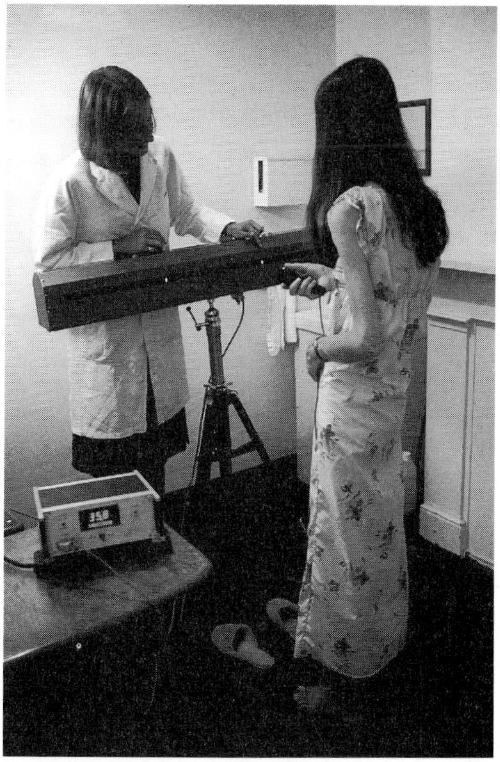

Figure 4.5 Anorexia nervosa

Examples of major social role changes through the life cycle which may affect the self-image include:

- leaving school;
- starting work;
- redundancy;
- parenthood;
- disability.

Self-esteem

Self-esteem has been defined as 'a personal judgement of worthiness, that is expressed in the attitudes the individual holds towards himself' (Coopersmith, 1967). Coopersmith's important study of self-esteem, using as subjects hundreds of nine to ten-year-old boys, none of whom had any obvious emotional disturbance, found that those who scored high on self-esteem:

- were doing better at school;
- were more often chosen as friends;
- were not unduly worried by criticism;
- enjoyed participating in things;

while those who scored low in self-esteem:

- were isolated;
- were fearful;
- were reluctant to join in;
- were self-conscious;
- were over-sensitive to criticism;
- under-rated themselves;
- under-achieved in class.

Coopersmith studied the highest and the lowest scorers in depth, and found a correlation with methods of parenting.

Parents of boys with high self-esteem:

- had high expectations of their children but also provided sound models;
- regarded their children as important and interesting people;
- knew about their friends and interests;
- were neither permissive nor punitive;
- gave rewards for good behaviour;
- used occasional withdrawal of love for bad behaviour.

Parents of boys with low self-esteem:

- were unclear about their expectations for their children;
- considered their sons as not very important;
- stressed their rights and powers as parents;
- treated their sons as thought they were a burden;
- gave unpredictable discipline, veering between over-strictness and over-permissiveness.

Coopersmith followed the boys into adulthood and found that the high self-esteem boys continued through life to outperform the low self-esteem boys.

Styles of parenting differ, and psychologists have tried to categorise these many differences. Figure 4.6 shows one method of characterising the various styles.

Authoritative parents combine control with acceptance and child-centred involvement. Their control and demands are combined

	accepting responsive child-centred	rejecting unresponsive parent-centred
demanding controlling	authoritative	authoritarian
undemanding not controlling	indulgent	neglecting

Figure 4.6 Child-rearing practices
Source: after Maccoby and Martin 1983, in *Introduction to Psychology*, Atkinson, R. (Harcourt Brace, 1993).

with warmth, nurturance and two-way communication. Children's opinions and feelings are consulted when family decisions are made, and explanations and reasons are given for any punitive measures if these are imposed.

Research shows that the children of such parents tend to be independent, self-assertive, friendly with peers, and cooperative with parents. They seem to enjoy life and have a strong motivation to succeed.

Authoritarian parents also attempt to control and assert their power over their children, but without warmth and nurturance. They attempt to set an absolute set of standards, and they value obedience, respect for authority, work, tradition and the presentation of order.

The children of such parents tend to be moderately competent and responsible but they also tend to be socially withdrawn and to lack spontaneity. The girls seem to be particularly dependent on their parents and to lack achievement motivation. The boys tend to be more aggressive than other boys. Some studies have found a link between authoritarian parenting and low self-esteem in boys (Coopersmith, 1967).

Indulgent parents are accepting, responsive, child-centred parents who place few demands on their children and exercise little control.

The children of such parents tend to show more happiness and vitality than children of authoritarian parents, but their behaviour tends to be immature in that they lack self-reliance, social responsibility and impulse control over, for example, aggression.

Even though authoritarian and indulgent parents have completely opposed child-rearing styles, both have children who tend to show little self-reliance, and may have problems with aggression.

Most *neglecting* parents do not neglect in the extreme sense that would be termed child abuse. But they are very parent-centred, concerned with their own interests and activities, and uninvolved with those of their children. Typically, if their children are not at home they do not know what they are doing. They are uninterested in events at their children's schools, have few conversations with their children and do not consider their opinions.

The children of such parents tend to be moody, impulsive and aggressive. They tend to truant from school and may start drinking, smoking and dating at earlier ages than their peers.

Extreme neglect by parents constitutes emotional abuse. These parents are emotionally unavailable to their children. They are detached, emotionally uninvolved, often depressed and uninterested in their children.

Emotionally abused children show clear disturbance in their relationship and increasing deficits in all aspects of psychological functioning by the age of 2. Their deficits are actually greater than those of children whose parents physically abuse them (Egeland and Sroufe, 1981).

Apart from cases of extreme behaviour in parents, as in severe neglect and child abuse, it should be noted that links between parenting style and children's personality, though evident, are not as strong as researchers might expect:

- The two parents in a family might have different styles of parenting.
- The high divorce rate might mean that a woman has to change 'styles' when she has to work full time.
- Parents use different approaches at different times, so different children in the family have different experiences.
- Following an unexpected family crisis, such as unemployment, accident or illness, child-centred parents might become more parent-centred.
- Grandparents or other relatives who see the child regularly might provide aspects of parenting not provided by the mother or father.

It is not always immediately apparent if a person has high self-esteem:

- Hooligans and members of delinquent groups may have low self-esteem that they cover with aggression.
- Individuals with high self-esteem may cover it with modesty and self-deprecation for social reasons ('I'm never going to pass this exam').
- Females may artificially depress their own performance so as not to outshine their male partners.

The ideal self (idealised self-image)

Our ideal self is the kind of person we should like to be. This can vary in degree – we may see room for improvement in certain areas or we may want to be totally different from the way we are. In general, the greater the gap between our self-image and our ideal self, the lower our self-esteem (see section on Carl Rogers, page 205).

ACTIVITY

- Make up sets of cards with positive and negative character traits written on them.
- Pick out the traits which describe how you would ideally like to be (ideal self).
- Arrange them in a list.
- Now pick out cards which describe you as you really are (self-image).
- Arrange them in a list.
- How close is your self-image to your ideal self?

The development of the self-concept

Four factors influence the development of the self-concept:

- the reaction of others;
- comparison with others;
- social roles;
- identification.

The reaction of others: Up until adolescence children believe what they are told by their carers, and are likely to perform to the labels they have been given by the process of the self-fulfilling prophecy (on labelling and the self-fulfilling prophecy see Thomson *et al.*, 1994).

ACTIVITY

How do your self-ratings compare with ratings of you by others? Work with someone you know well.

- Write a short paragraph describing yourself.
- Write a short paragraph describing your friend.
- Ask your friend to do the same thing.
- Compare your results.

Which is more favourable, your self-rating or your friend's rating of you? Why?

Comparison with others: Some children find themselves on the receiving end of situations like that shown in Figure 4.7. Such comparisons, repeatedly made, will be incorporated into the child's developing self-concept, encouraging low self-esteem. Adults also compare themselves with others. In the absence of objective standards of what is right, other people are used for evaluation purposes.
Social roles: When we take on a new social role, we start to see ourselves differently. By this means the self-concept is continually revised throughout the life cycle.

ACTIVITY

List social roles, positive or negative, that might be chosen, or imposed upon:

- the primary-school child;
- the middle-school child;
- the adolescent;
- the young adult;
- the middle-aged person;
- the old person.

What effect would these have on the individual's self concept in each case?

Figure 4.7 Comparison with others may cause low self-esteem

Identification: A child will learn a style of behaviour by imitating a role model. Through the process of imitation the learning becomes internalised, so that the child comes to identify with that person. This is the social learning approach outlined at the beginning of this chapter, which argues that much of our learning of social roles, e.g. our sex role learning, occurs through the process of identification.

PERSONALITY

The nature–nurture debate applies to personality development and is described on page 88 in Chapter 2 (emotional needs).

Eysenck (1991) puts the naturist viewpoint (page 88). Carl Rogers and the phenomenologists put the nurturist viewpoint (below).

Maslow's hierarchy of needs

The psychologist Maslow proposed in 1954 that there is a hierarchy of needs, ascending from the basic biological needs to more complex psychological needs that become important only after the basic needs have been satisfied. This hierarchy can be represented in a pyramid diagram (see Figure 4.8).

The needs at one level must be at least partially satisfied before those at the next level start to motivate behaviour. When food and safety are difficult to obtain, the relief of those needs will dominate a person's actions and higher motives are of little importance. Artistic and scientific efforts do not flourish in societies in which people have to struggle for food, shelter and safety. The highest motive, self-actualisation, can be fulfilled only after all other needs are satisfied.

Carl Rogers: self-concept and positive regard

Carl Rogers (1902–87) developed his theory from his work with emotionally troubled people. He was impressed with what he saw as the individual's innate tendency to move towards growth, maturity and positive change. He argued that human beings have a need to develop their potential as fully as

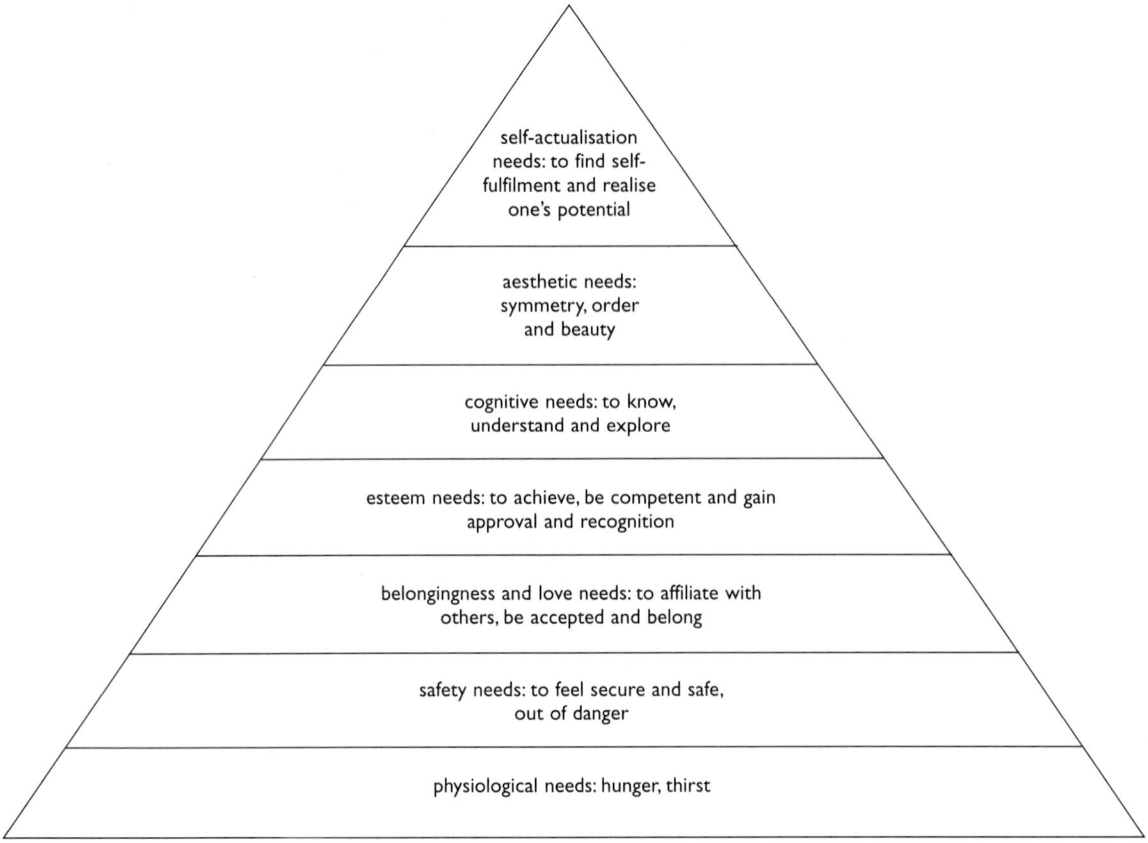

Figure 4.8 Maslow's hierarchy of needs
Source: Maslow in *Psychology: an introduction*, Hayes, N. and Orrel, S. (Longman Group UK Ltd, 1993).

possible. From his clinical work, he saw neurotic or psychotic problems developing when this aspect of a person's personality is consistently denied.

Everyone has an ideal self-concept, a way they would like to be, and people are troubled if their self-concept does not measure up to their ideal. In mentally healthy people, their self-concept is close to their ideal self-concept.

All individuals have a need for positive regard from other people. Rogers believed that people are likely to show greater mental health, and live more fully, if they are brought up with unconditional positive regard. This means that they feel themselves specially valued by one or two people even when their feelings, attitude and behaviour are less than ideal.

Rogers insisted that most, if not all, of his neurotic clients had parents who did not give their children a strong sense of being loved and approved of unconditionally. The child got the message that he or she wasn't really loved at all – the parents would have liked some other, ideal child, who never misbehaved. Therefore, these children grow up striving for approval from others and ignoring their own self-actualisation in the process. People like this tend to have very unrealistically high standards for their own behaviour, i.e. their ideal self-concept doesn't correlate strongly with their own self-concept.

Rogers developed the idea of ENCOUNTER GROUPS. Personal growth is achieved by unconditional positive regard from other members of the group. Once defences are broken down, people can help each other. People are able to sort out their own problems, he felt, if put in a situation in which they had unconditional positive regard from someone else. A therapist could provide that relationship, so long as the therapist was warm, accepting, genuine and non-directive. This relationship is central to the healing process.

Personality may be defined as an individual's characteristic patterns of thought, emotion and behaviour which influence his or her reactions to the environment. Personality psychology aims to describe and define these individual differences. There are many diverse approaches to this subject, and many psychologists are eclectic, choosing among the approaches to arrive at their own integrated view of personality. The following sections outline the main approaches.

Personality type and physical type

'Yond Cassius has a lean and hungry look; he thinks too much: such men are dangerous . . . Would he were fatter' (Shakespeare: *Julius Caesar*, Act 1, scene 2). The idea that body build and personality type are interrelated has long been prevalent, and is reflected in popular stereotypes such as the 'gentle giant'. The soft round body type (endomorphic) has been related to a relaxed, sociable temperament; the muscular and athletic body type (mesomorphic) has been related to a courageous, energetic and assertive temperament; and the tall and thin body type (ectomorphic) has been related to a fearful introverted, artistic temperament. Such theories of personality are not currently much used, as they are considered by some to oversimplify complex factors.

Trait theories

In a sense we are all trait theorists. We describe ourselves or others as patient, outgoing, hardworking, etc. Psychologists have attempted to go beyond the layperson's trait conceptions to formalise this approach.

Allport argued that personality traits are organised in a kind of hierarchy, some having a stronger influence on an individual's behaviour than others:

- *Cardinal disposition:* one dominant disposition that people have which influences almost all aspects of their behaviour.
- *Central dispositions:* most people have five to ten central dispositions that direct many aspects of their lives.
- *Secondary dispositions:* less important interests which still affect behaviour.

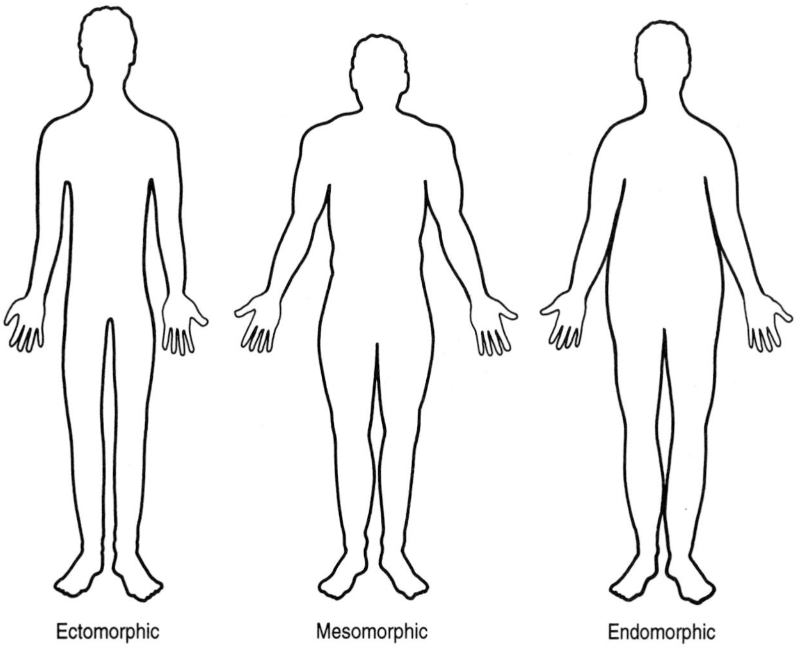

Figure 4.9 Differing builds of human beings

Factor–analytic theories

There are approximately 18,000 words in the English language that refer to characteristics of behaviour. Cattell (1986) condensed this to under 200 terms by eliminating rare words and near-synonyms. By rating a number of people on these traits and factor-analysing the results, he established a list of 16 basic traits:

- warm;
- intelligent;
- emotionally stable;
- dominant;
- cheerful;
- conscientious;
- bold;
- sensitive;
- suspicious;
- imaginative;
- shrewd;
- guilt-prone;
- experimenting;
- self-sufficient;
- self-disciplined;
- tense.

Cattell devised a questionnaire comprising more than 100 questions to measure an individual on each of these traits; a yes or no answer to each question gives a score for one of the factors.

H. Eysenck also uses factor analysis, but of a more restricted kind. His major factors are introversion/extroversion and emotional instability/stability.

If Cattell identified 16 basic traits and Eysenck works mainly with two, how many basic personality traits actually are there? Many trait researchers are finding a compromise, with a growing consensus around some version of the 'Big Five' personality dimensions (see Table 4.2).

Personality testing on this model is much used in occupational psychology – in choosing the right people for certain jobs. However, it has been much criticised: most people prefer to be seen as extrovert and, seeing what each key question is aimed at, answer according to how they wish to be seen rather than according to how they actually are.

Table 4.2 The 'Big Five' personality dimensions

Big Five Dimensions	Facet scales
Neuroticism	Anxiety Hostility Depression Self-consciousness Impulsiveness Vulnerability
Extroversion	Warmth Gregariousness Assertiveness Activity Excitement seeking Positive emotions
Openness	Fantasy Aesthetics Feelings Actions Ideas Values
Agreeableness	Trust Straightforwardness Altruism Compliance Modesty Tender-mindedness
Conscientiousness	Competence Order Dutifulness Achievement striving Self-discipline Deliberation

Source: Deary and Matthews (1993).

ACTIVITY

- Carry out an example of a trait test (e.g. from Eysenck, *Know Your Own Personality*).
- Analyse your results.
- Did almost everybody turn out to be extrovert?
- Do you think they saw the key questions coming?

Another major criticism of this approach is that it assumes people are consistent over various social situations, which many think is not the case. In the face of life crises, many people show the very opposite to their normal character traits.

ACTIVITY

- Choose a person who frequently appears in the media.
- How would you describe their personality?
- Would you expect them to behave consistently according to that outline over most social situations?
- Do you think that the popular outrage that is expressed in the tabloid press when a well-known figure acts out of character with their public image is due to the fact that people expect and need consistency from others?

The psychoanalytic approach

Sigmund Freud was the creator of psychoanalytic theory. Freud compared the human mind with an iceberg (see Figure 4.10), and gave primary importance to unconscious mental influences.

According to Freud's theory, the personality is composed of three main parts:

- the id;
- the ego;
- the superego.

Psychosexual development occurs in five stages (see Table 4.3)

Freudian theory is currently academically unpopular yet many psychotherapists still depend at least in part (some heavily) on the psychoanalytic approach. Such psychotherapists are particularly interested in assessing unconscious wishes, motivations and conflicts. Tests that have been developed to assess these are known as PROJECTIVE TESTS. Projective tests present the client with an ambiguous stimulus, and it is proposed that because of the ambiguity, the client projects his or her personality on to the stimulus. The client is encouraged to use their imagination and say whatever they think they can see within the stimulus. This is known as FREE ASSOCIATION.

Two widely used projective tests, the results of which can be quantified and which have been shown to have a degree of reliability and validity, are:

- the Rorschach test, a series of ten cards, each displaying a complex inkblot (see Figure 4.11);
- the Thematic Apperception Test (TAT), a series of 20 ambiguous pictures (see Figure 4.12).

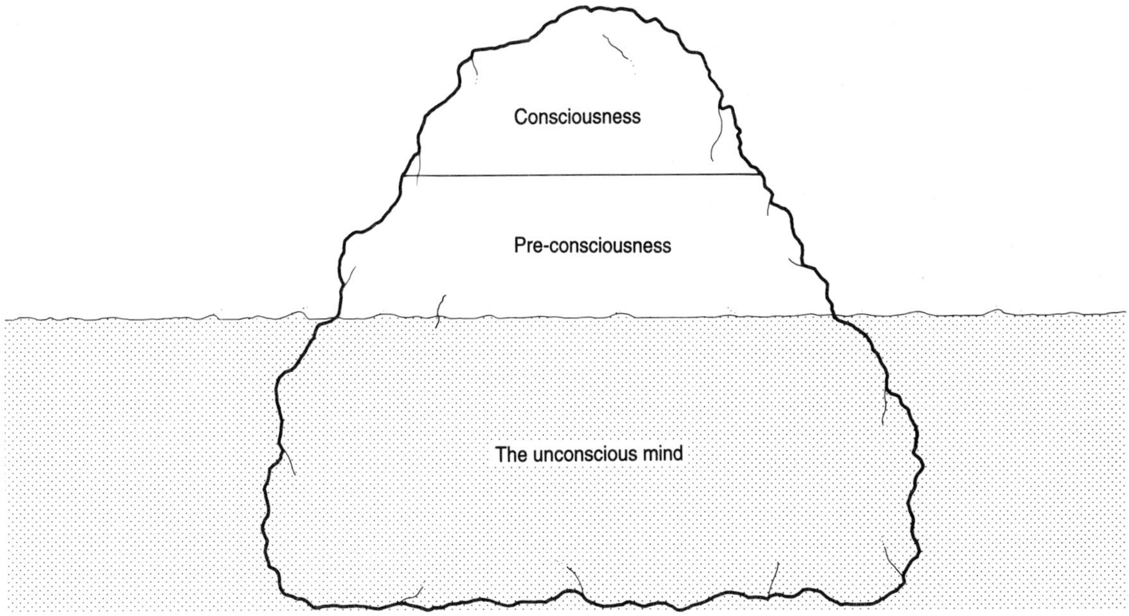

Figure 4.10 Freud's three territories of the mind

Table 4.3 Freud's stages of psychosexual development and implications for carers

Stage	Age (yrs)	Erotogenic zone	Associated personality characteristics	Implications for carers
Oral	0–1½	Mouth	Relaxed and generous feeding is thought to lead to optimistic, friendly and cooperative traits. Difficulties or deprivation may lead to a constant search later on for oral gratification, through smoking, drinking, eating	A carer will observe that babies derive great pleasure from sucking things and putting things in their mouths. A sick child, who may be fed naso-gastrically, will not have this pleasure. The nurse may therefore encourage thumb sucking or dummy sucking.
Anal	1½–4	Anus	Conflict at this stage can lead, according to this theory, to obstinate, fastidious, miserly and excessively orderly character traits (the anal personality). The theory also links this stage to performing for others, sculpting, potting and gardening.	Badly organized 'toilet training' can lead to a nervous child, and in some cases encopresis. This theory would imply that it is unwise to insert any foreign objects (e.g. thermometer) into the anus of a child over 1 year old.
Phallic	4–6	Genitals	A child of this age is developing a masculine or feminine identity. According to this theory, the Oedipus complex occurs at this stage and must be resolved.	A child of this age explores his or her own body and a carer should not be disturbed to find a child holding his or her genitals.
Latent	6–12		This is a stage of intellectual development. Children are now less concerned with their bodies; sexual activity remains dormant; they are learning about their environment.	A child of this age needs games, sports and stimulation and prefers to mix with others of the same sex. The carer can provide intellectually and competitively suitable games – computer games and ward management (bed positions etc.) can be used to improve the environment for this age group.
Genital	≥12		An awakening of sexual feelings occurs at this age involving emotional upheavals, romantic infatuations and confusions.	A carer should devote time to listening and talking to adolescents, and also offer them privacy to think and listen to music.

ACTIVITY

The pictures used in the TAT tests, and the inkblots used for the Rorschach tests, are similar to those used by practicing clinicians.

- Select five subjects from different age groups.
- Ask them for their reactions:
  (a) to the inkblot (Figure 4.11) – what do they see?
  (b) to the picture (Figure 4.12) – what story comes to mind?
- Carefully record their reactions.
- Analyse your results

In psychotherapy such tests are helpful in suggesting possible areas of conflict to be explored. They are not used alone to assess personality, but in conjunction with other sources of data (for example, the client's history, observations of behaviour).

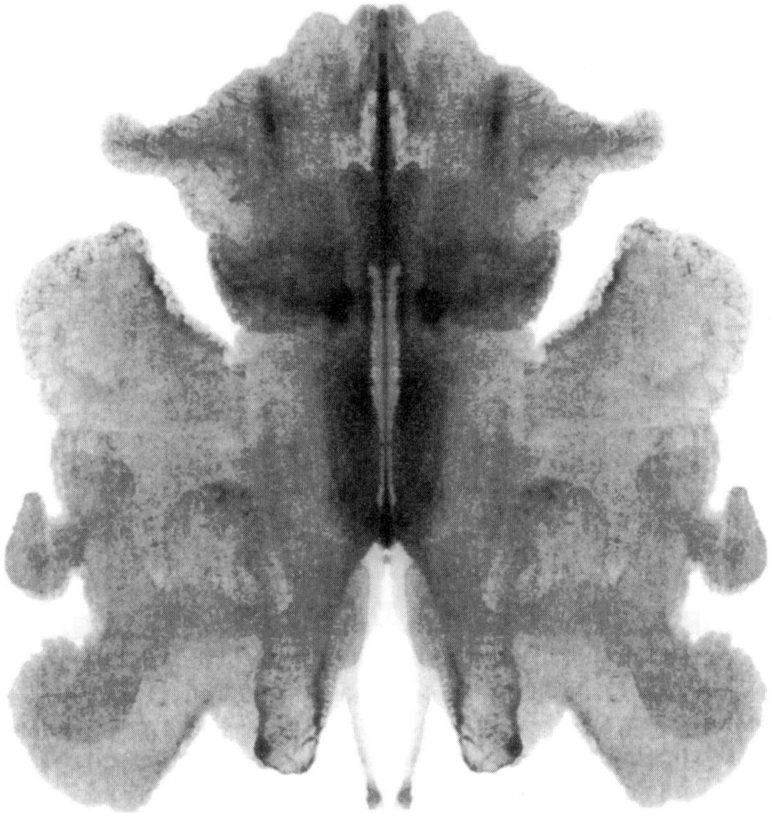

Figure 4.11 An 'inkblot' similar to those used in the Rorschach test
Source: Atkinson (1993), *An Introduction to Psychology*

The social learning approach to personality

Give me a dozen healthy infants, well-formed, and my own specified world to bring them up in and I'll guarantee to take any one at random and to train him to become any type of specialist I might select – doctor, lawyer, artist, merchant-chief and, yes, even beggar-man and thief,

Figure 4.12 A figure similar to those used in the thematic apperception test (TAT)

regardless of his talents, penchants, tendencies, abilities, vocations, and race of his ancestors.

(Watson, 1930)

The social learning approach proposes that the processes of learning, particularly OPERANT CONDITIONING, shape the individual's behaviour repertoire to be adaptive to their environment. Individuals are, by this view, extremely modifiable. Behaviour therapy, widely used in many different forms, has developed from the social learning approach.

The phenomenological approach

Adherents of this approach believe that people, given the correct circumstances, are basically good and motivated towards self-actualisation (see Maslow's hierarchy of needs on page 206).

Humanistic psychologist George Kelly believed that the psychologist's goal should be to find the dimensions that each individual uses to interpret himself or herself and his or her social environment. These dimensions are the individual's own PERSONAL CONSTRUCTS. Kelly's Role Construct Repertory Test ('rep test') is used to measure an individual's personal constructs.

ACTIVITY

Look up Kelly's 'rep test' in a psychology textbook. Work through the test.
NB It is usual to include yourself as one of the eight important people.

The nature–nurture debate

The nature–nurture debate is central to many issues in psychology, to the study of:

- perception;
- intelligence;
- language development;
- personality development;
- altruistic behaviour;
- schizophrenia.

The nativists believed that we are born with certain capacities: these may be incomplete or immature at birth, but develop gradually after birth. This development proceeds through the genetically determined process of maturation, with learning and environment playing a minimal role or none at all.

The empiricists believed that all our knowledge and abilities are acquired through learning and experience.

Today, most psychologists would not see development as a genetic versus environmental process, but would see themselves as interactionists, believing that we are each born with certain genetic tendencies, but stimulation and environmental influences are crucial in determining how, or indeed whether, these tendencies and capacities develop.

Biologists distinguish between the GENOTYPE, i.e. the set of genetic characteristics we inherit, which is fixed from conception, and the PHENOTYPE, the overall physiological and behavioural characteristics that the person develops which develops and changes all the time. Therefore, throughout life there is an interaction between our genes and our environment, so that both are of equal importance, and work together.

ALTRUISTIC BEHAVIOUR – IS THIS NATURE, THE SELFISH GENE OR NURTURE?

The selfish gene

Sociobiology represents an extension of Darwin's evolutionary theory, and attempts to understand all types of social behaviour among animals and humans, including altruism and aggression, in evolutionary terms.

Among animals, various examples of altruism have been observed. For example, dolphins will often group around an injured individual to push it up to the surface where it can breathe, rather than abandon it; a rabbit will drum its feet on the ground, therefore increasing the chances of other rabbits escaping and therefore eventually reproducing, while at the same time reducing its own chances of escaping and also drawing the attention of the predator to itself.

This seems at first to go against Darwin's theory of natural selection, that the strongest and fittest of a species will survive to reproduce. However, if an animal is conceptualised as a set of genes, and genes distributed across kin, then biological altruism is shown to be 'selfish'. A mother animal allowing herself to be killed in the process of saving her three offspring from a predator will have saved one and a half times her own genes (each offspring inherits half of its mother's genes), thereby making a profit in terms of the survival of her own genes in her relatives.

This was Hamilton's theory of kin selection (1964), which suggests that individuals are selected to act not to maximise their own fitness, but to maximise their inclusive fitness, for the survival and reproduction of their kin. Thus the apparent paradox of biological altruism may be resolved. Dawkins (1991) defines the selfish gene as 'all replicas of a particular bit of DNA distributed across the world. A gene might be able to assist replicas of itself sitting in other bodies. If so, though this might appear as individual altruism, it would be brought about by gene selfishness.'

What about cases of 'altruism' among animals where they are not related? Trivers (1971) proposed the principle of '*delayed reciprocal altruism*', by which animals will return favours to other animals who have done them a good turn. For example, male baboons who do not have a partner sometimes form a temporary alliance with another solitary male baboon. They find a male and female who are courting. One of them attacks the male so that the other can mate with the female. The males who give this kind of help are more likely to later receive help in return, so that reciprocation occurs.

Biological altruism in humans

Parental care and human kidney donation may be seen as examples of kin selection in humans, whereas blood donation may be seen as an example of delayed reciprocal altruism in humans.

ACTIVITY

Whole professions and occupations are concerned with helping others who are not related. Analyse the biological motivations of those who wish for example to work in the medical profession.

- Could their motives be partly explained by the selfish gene?
- List the psychological motives that might also be involved (e.g. intrinsic and extrinsic satisfaction, social learning (imitation), guilt, the wish to be good (moral and religious learning) and attachment).

Dawkins believes that, despite the selfish gene, it may be possible for a man to show true disinterested altruism: 'We are built as gene machines . . . but we have the power to turn against our creators. We, alone on earth, can rebel against the tyranny of the selfish replicator.'

SCHIZOPHRENIA

This mental illness is illustrative of the nature–nurture debate. This disease takes several forms and there is not always agreement about the diagnosis. Symptoms may include:

- thought disturbances;
- auditory hallucinations – hearing voices;
- delusions, e.g. delusions of grandeur, delusions of persecution;
- thought process disorder – an inability to keep to the point, and an apparent inability to screen out irrelevant stimuli, so that a mass of associations, many of them unrelated to the main point, appear in the speech. This juxtaposition of unrelated words and phrases has been called a 'word salad';
- flattening of affect – indifference to other

people's feelings, blunting and/or loss of appropriate emotional responses;
- psychomotor disorders, e.g. catatonic stupor – assuming a fixed position for a long period of time;
- loss of will power or drive.

Much research has attempted to demonstrate a genetic component in schizophrenia. Adoption studies have shown that babies born to schizophrenic mothers who are then adopted into families with no history of the disease are five times more likely to be diagnosed schizophrenic than adopted children whose natural mothers were not schizophrenic. Such evidence would seem to support the notion of a genetic susceptibility.

The nurture case was presented in an extreme form by R.D. Laing, who along with other researchers led the anti-psychiatry movement of the early 1960s which rejected the medical model of mental disorder. He believed that schizophrenia arises within families which use pathological forms of communication, especially double binds – contradictory messages in which, for example, a mother encourages her son to give her a hug and then tells him not to be such a baby, or where a mother states she wants her daughter to come home from hospital, and then proceeds to discourage her from leaving.

In his work he argued that their personal lives were intolerable and unliveable. The case studies documented in his book *Sanity, Madness and the Family*, do indeed portray family life at its confused and hypocritical worst, and support his hypothesis that the schizophrenic symptoms displayed by one member of each of these families may be no more than the tortured ruses of people trying to deal with the conflicting demands put upon them. A reader in the 1990s can see many advantages in the present social climate, in which families where relationships are not working can break down and reform without provoking social notice or disapproval.

However, later studies have indicated that the confused communications and disturbed emotions in families which include a schizophrenic member may occur, not necessarily as a *cause* of that behaviour but as a *result* of parents trying to cope with a child's maladaptive behaviour and unclear communications both prior to and following the diagnosis of schizophrenia.

Laing, maintaining his hypothesis, now sees schizophrenia as itself a natural way of healing our own appalling state of alienation called normality, and believes that the schizophrenic is an exceptionally eloquent critic of society.

The interactionist view is taken by Zubin and Spring 1977 who conclude that some people have a greater genetic predisposition towards schizophrenia then others, and whether or not this will develop depends on environmental stresses. Traumatic events (e.g. the early death of one or both parents) are found with greater than average frequency in the backgrounds of people who develop schizophrenia.

ACTIVITY

Down's syndrome

Read about Down's syndrome. Research the nature and nurture elements in this condition. How have views on this condition changed with increasing knowledge?

INTELLIGENCE

Fierce debate has taken place in the past as to whether intelligence is due to nature or nurture. Present thinking takes an interactionist approach.

It has been proposed that intelligence comprises the following components:

- the ability to learn and profit from experience;
- the ability to think or reason abstractedly;
- the ability to adapt to the uncertainties of a changing world;
- the ability to motivate oneself to

accomplish effectively the tasks one needs to accomplish.

Influences on intellectual ability

Interaction

Is intelligence nature, nurture or interaction? A first principle of developmental genetics is that each organism is a unique product of the interaction between genes and environment at every stage of life. Gould (1981) makes the point: 'Genes do not make specific bits and pieces of a body, they code for a range of forms under an array of environmental conditions. Moreover, even when a trait has been built and set, environmental intervention may still modify inherited defects.'

ACTIVITY

Research the Skeels and Dye (1939) study on children at a state orphanage.

- What factors enabled the children who were moved to the institution for the mentally retarded to progress so much better?
- What were the long-term benefits for these children?
- Does this study support nature, nurture or interaction as the primary determinant of intelligence?

Genetics

Genetic determinants of intelligence are strong. The average correlations between IQs of relations are as follows:

between the parents and their natural children	0.40
between identical twins	0.86
between fraternal twins	0.60
between siblings reared together	0.47
between siblings reared apart	0.24
between parents and their adopted children	0.31

Environment

Though partly inherited, intelligence is susceptible to the environmental influences, as the above figures show: the correlation between the intelligence of siblings reared together is higher than when they are reared apart. Also, various studies have shown that the intelligence of adopted children is higher than would be predicted on the basis of their natural parents' ability.

Given two children with the same genes, the child with:

- better prenatal and post-natal nutrition;
- the more intellectually stimulating home;
- the more emotionally secure home;
- the more appropriate rewards for academic accomplishments;

will attain the higher IQ score when tested at first grade (six years old). Children from impoverished homes typically show a decline in intellectual performance after the age of two years, and this effect is long-lasting. Preschool experience such as nursery school tends to promote similarly long-lasting benefits.

Project Headstart was set up in the 1960s in the USA to try to improve the preschool experiences of disadvantaged children and to compensate for unstimulating home environments. The project included extra classes, tuition, playgroups and visits. All the children showed some increase in IQ immediately after the programme, but from then on, for several years, their improvement was not maintained. However, when the Headstart children grew into teenagers and were retested at age 15, and compared with a control group who had received no preschool programme, they showed the following advantages:

- higher scores on tests of reading, arithmetic and language use;
- less likely to need remedial classes;
- showed less antisocial behaviour;
- more likely to hold after-school jobs.

Thus the beneficial influence of nursery education may lie dormant until puberty.

The type of stimulation provided in the

programmes was typical nursery-school play and activity. Encouraging the involvement and interest of the parents to provide increased stimulation at home was found to be the most important factor.

PART-TIME SCHOOLING FROM AGE THREE URGED

Only a quarter of British three- and four-year-olds receive a good quality nursery education, according to a report published yesterday. The report, by the Royal Society of Arts, says that part-time schooling should be compulsory from the age of three, but full-time school should not start until children are six ...

The Start Right report, which includes a detailed study of the benefits of nursery education, contrasts sharply with government claims that while there is room for improvement, most children are already receiving a good pre-school education ...

Professor Kathy Sylva, a member of the advisory group on the report, said a good nursery class must offer a balanced curriculum, properly trained teachers, small groups and a partnership with parents. Anything less would not have the lasting desirable effects which could be seen in pupils who had received the best in nursery education. 'We are arguing not just for any old pre-school education, because research studies show that isn't going to have a lasting impact. We are arguing for high-quality provision,' she said. The report says that the government should aim to have a new system of centres where children and their parents could learn together. The cost would be about £1bn a year, most of which would be recovered by making education for five-year-olds part-time only.

The main findings:

- Full-time school should not start until six.
- Part-time nursery education should be compulsory from three.
- Child Benefit could be linked to parents' attendance at parenting classes.
- Nursery schooling should be provided at 'family centres' where parents could learn alongside their children.
- All nursery-school teachers should receive a full professional training.
- A new code of conduct should govern all pre-school education.
- The new system should be in place by 1999.

(The Independent, 1994)

ACTIVITY

1 • Describe an environment for a young child which would offer social, sensory and intellectual stimulation.
  • Describe an environment for a young child that would offer none of these things.

2 Many mothers work. They have a choice of where to place their children (although this is often severely limited by availability and cost):
  • with relatives;
  • with childminders;
  • in a playgroup;
  • in a workplace creche;
  • with a nanny.

  What are the advantages and disadvantages to (a) the child, and (b) the mother, of each of these different settings:
  • for age group 0–2 years?
  • for age group 2–5 years?

MOTHER JAILED FOR LEAVING GIRL ON HER OWN

A young single parent was jailed for six months yesterday, after a court was told she left her two-year-old daughter at home alone during the day, five days a week, for almost a year while she went to work ...

For the first 10 months the mother returned home at lunchtime to feed her daughter, but the girl became upset when she had to go back to work. 'She could not cope with that, but rather than getting help she then left the child alone all day from 8.45 until 5.45 from August until October.

(The Independent, 3 August 1993)

MOTHER TO APPEAL OVER PRISON TERM

The mother said she left the child unattended during the day because 'it was a choice between food and clothes and a childminder'.

Ms Evans [of the Daycare Trust] said the case was not an isolated one. 'It is fairly common for women to leave children at home if arrangements for their care fall down. Not all employers are sympathetic to the presence of sick or wandering children in the workplace.'

(The Independent, 4 August 1993)

Expected life changes

EIGHT PSYCHOSOCIAL STAGES IN THE LIFE CYCLE

Erik Erikson (b. 1902), accepting some parts of Freud's theory of the personality and the psychosexual stages, believed that development continues throughout the life cycle. He identified eight psychosocial stages. Each one centres on a developmental crisis where a choice must be made between two conflicting personality characteristics.

These eight stages, summarised in Table 4.4, may be used as a basis for exploring the changing needs of the person and the way in which personal identity is established.

Stage 1: basic trust versus basic mistrust (0–1 years)

The quality of care that a small baby receives is important if the baby is to develop a sense of the world as a safe and comfortable place to be, as opposed to a place full of hazards.

If the baby is cuddled, played with and talked to, and his or her needs met as they arise, the baby will sense that people are dependable and helpful and that the world is safe. This sense of trust allows the baby to accept new experiences and to learn gradually to tolerate fear of the unknown.

Stage 2: autonomy versus shame and doubt (1–3 years)

The child's cognitive and muscle systems are developing and he or she is becoming more

Table 4.4 Erikson's eight psychosocial stages

Number of stage	Name of stage (psychosocial crisis)	Radius of significant relationships	Human virtues ('qualities of strength')	Approximate ages
1	Basic trust versus basic mistrust	Mother or mother-figure	Hope	0–1
2	Autonomy versus shame and doubt	Parents	Willpower	1–3
3	Initiative versus guilt	Basic family	Purpose	3–6
4	Industry versus inferiority	Neighbourhood and school	Competence	7–12
5	Identity versus role confusion	Peer groups and outgroups, models of leadership	Fidelity	12–18
6	Intimacy versus isolation	Partners in friendship, sex, competition, cooperation	Love	20s
7	Generativity versus stagnation	Divided labour and shared household	Care	Late 20s–50s
8	Ego integrity versus despair	'Humankind', 'my kind'	Wisdom	50s and beyond

mobile. The child's range of experiences and choices is also expanding. The child is just beginning to see himself or herself as a person in its own right and is beginning to sense independence.

This stage has sometimes been called the 'adolescence of childhood', as the child, though in many ways still a baby with a baby's needs, also wants to do everything for himself or herself. This can be a demanding time for parents who are often caring for a small baby as well. In this age group there are wide cultural/family/class differences on matters such as weaning and toilet training.

Stage 3: initiative versus guilt (3–5/6 years)

Rapid development takes place at this stage, physically, intellectually and socially, and the child is eager to try out growing skills and abilities to achieve all sorts of new goals.

The child wants to ask questions, indulge in fantasy play, play alone and be with other children, run and jump, climb and ride a bike.

At this age a child's physical and intellectual development will be affected by DEPRIVATION (see Table 4.5), especially sensory and intellectual deprivation. A home without space to play, toys to play with, books to look at, things to see, hear or touch will have detrimental effects on the child's development. Many children do not have access to a safe place outdoors where they can play with others.

Many people believe that free nursery education, where children have space to run around in a safe environment and freedom to express themselves with paint, sand and fantasy play, should be available to all preschool children. For those from deprived homes it is a necessity, while those from the most stimulating homes benefit from the social contact of nursery school.

The policy of Social Services Departments today is to promote the welfare of children in need by providing services to help them to be brought up within their own families as far as possible. If a child has to be taken into care, foster family homes are used in preference to institutions. When choosing a foster home the child's race, religion, culture and language

Table 4.5 The various forms of deprivation that can affect small children

Age group particularly affected	Type of deprivation	Effects
0–3 years (also 3–5 years)	Lack of basic care: warmth, food and clothing	Lack of food can lead to 'deprivation dwarfism'
	Lack of mother or other sensitive, caring adult to become attached to	Failure to make attachment bonds can lead through retarded development to maladjustment
2–5 years	Lack of sensory stimulation – colour, taste, sound, things to feel, e.g. in a flat with no access to outdoors	Will hamper intellectual development
2–5 years	Lack of intellectual stimulation – books, toys, conversation	Will retard speech and otherwise hamper intellectual development, as above. Boredom has also been related to behaviour disturbance
3 years–adolescence	Stressed relationships between adults	May lead to neglect of child Also, family discord has been related to behaviour problems and acquiring a criminal record
	(controversially) Lack of father or father-figure	Increased likelihood of: poor attainment at school Substance abuse Acquiring a criminal record

will be taken into account, as well as their particular personality and needs. Foster-parents have to be visited and approved by social services before they are registered and allowed to take a child.

Foster-parents receive support and counselling from social workers and they receive a professional wage. The support is particularly necessary in the early weeks of a fostering when a child, who may have had many previous disappointments, will be testing them to the limit.

Regular support and advice is especially important to families who foster children who have previously been abused, for the foster-parents will find that here, the best of intentions are not enough. Such children may show very odd and disturbing behaviour, and foster-parents need to be told what to expect and how to handle the behaviour over a long period.

ACTIVITY

Find out about the care of children in need in the area you live in.

- Are there many community homes?
- Are children placed with foster-parents where possible?
- Are family aides available to help during a temporary crisis (if, for example, a mother has to go into hospital and the father cannot take time off work to look after young children)?
- Are free day care places available?

Stage 4: industry versus inferiority (7–12 years)

Industry refers to the child's concern with how things work, how they are made and their own efforts to make things.

This is reinforced when the child is encouraged by adults, who now are no longer confined to the parents. Teachers begin to be very significant in the child's life, and the child, helped by teachers and parents, begins to develop all sorts of new skills valued by society.

The peer group becomes increasingly important, relative to adults, and plays an important part in the development of self-esteem. Children begin to compare themselves with other children as a way of assessing their own achievement.

Self-esteem and the esteem of others stem largely from completing tasks successfully, being allowed to make things and being given guidance and encouragement by adults.

A child may have potential abilities which if not nurtured during this period may develop 'late or never'. A lack of encouragement, and cold, uninterested or critical parents, may lead to a failure to achieve new skills and a sense of failure and low self-esteem.

Language and cultural differences

At this age children may begin to fall behind seriously at school if they have not mastered the middle-class 'elaborated' code of English used in school, perhaps because they come from immigrant communities or if their parents only use a 'restricted' code. See the sections on 'Bernstein's theory' and Labov's work on 'black English' in Chapter 2.

It is at this age that children become aware of the implications of belonging to a particular cultural or religious group. They realise that this affects their family rules, family activities and diet, which may be different from those of the majority. If they belong to a sect or racial minority group which is subject to prejudice in the area, they will become aware at this age of stereotypes and may absorb the stereotype of their own particular group into their own self-concept (see the section on stereotypes and self-fulfilling prophecy on page 204).

A good school, which believes in the value of each individual, can help substantially in overcoming these difficulties.

Stage 5: identity versus role confusion (12–18 years)

The growth spurt that proceeds from

ADOLESCENCE is rapid. Erikson has said that the previous trust in the body's mastery of its functions, enjoyed in childhood, is thereby disturbed. The adolescent has to learn to 'grow into' the new body. For a long time it will not feel comfortable or 'fit' properly.

At the social level, Western culture, with its emphasis on extended education, has invented adolescence as a slow transition from childhood to adulthood.

The stereotype of storm and stress, conflict and rebellion which the western world has of adolescence is reinforced to a considerable degree by the media. Many magazines and sections of the clothing and music industry both serve it and profit from it. But research has shown that for many teenagers the adjustments and the negotiations of various freedoms are achieved relatively peacefully.

At the psychological level, adolescents re-experience the conflicts of early childhood as they seek to establish their own identity separate from that of their parents. The adolescent needs support and security at home. Unfortunately, many marriages break up as children reach adolescence, perhaps partly because of the shifts in family relationships at this stage.

An adolescent experiencing discord at home may turn to substance abuse or delinquent behaviour. An adolescent with a different personality type, from a different background, might develop an eating disorder.

A child who has been brought up in a minority culture might at adolescence reject the customs they were brought up with in favour of the mainstream culture. Adolescents can be extreme in testing out various identities, so they might reject everything about their upbringing, only remembering the good things about it at a later stage.

The major developmental task of adolescence is for the individual to develop a sense of identity, by integrating all the images they have of themselves as son/daughter, pupil, friend, brother/sister, and reflecting on past experiences, thoughts and feelings. If adolescents are successful in this task, they will emerge from this stage with a clear sense of where they have been, who they are, and where they are going.

Those who came positively through the earlier stages of development are more likely to achieve an INTEGRATED PSYCHOSOCIAL IDENTITY at adolescence.

Whatever the final outcome of this stage, Erikson believes that some form of turmoil or upset of identity is inevitable: 'at no other phase of the life-cycle are the pressures of finding oneself and the threat of losing oneself so closely allied'. To have a sense of self-identity is to have a 'feeling of being at home in one's body, a sense of knowing where one is going and an inner assurance of anticipated recognition from those who count'.

Stage 6: intimacy versus isolation (20s)

For Erikson, the attainment of identity by the end of adolescence is a prerequisite of the ability to become intimate with another person. By this he means much more than just making love, and includes the ability to share with and care about another person. The essential need is to relate our deepest hopes and fears to another person and to accept another's need for intimacy in turn. The intimate relationship may indeed not involve sexuality at all and describes the relationship between friends as much as that between husband and wife.

Our personal identity only becomes fully realised and consolidated through sharing ourselves with another and, if a sense of intimacy is not established with friends or a marriage partner, the result in Erikson's view is a sense of isolation, of being alone without anyone to share with or care for.

Intimacy is normally achieved, according to Erikson, in the twenties (in young adulthood).

Stage 7: generativity versus stagnation (late 20s–50s)

According to Erikson, middle age – the

thirties, forties and fifties – brings with it either generativity or stagnation (self-absorption).

GENERATIVITY means that the person begins to be concerned with others beyond the immediate family, with future generations and the nature of the society and world in which those generations will live.

Generativity is not confined to parents but is displayed by anyone who is actively concerned with the welfare of young people and with making the world a better place in which to live and work.

Failure to establish a sense of generativity results in a sense of STAGNATION in which the individual becomes preoccupied with his or her personal needs and comforts. Such people indulge themselves as if they were their own or another's only child.

Many writers believe that most adults never attain generativity: that men get 'stuck' in the industry stage and women in the adolescent stage.

However, too much can be made of the so-called 'mid-life crisis' – 'crises' can occur at every age. Later in middle age there is the 'empty nest syndrome' when all dependants go.

Thus the adult has to cope with a series of changing roles: starting work, marriage, parenthood, coping with dependants, the empty nest.

Stage 8: ego integrity versus despair (50s and beyond)

Anderson (1978) claims that old people face a painful wall of discrimination that they are often too polite or too timid to attack:

- they are not hired for new jobs despite long experience (age discrimination);
- they are edged out of family life.

The elderly have a very low status compared with both children and adults.

However, many 60-year-olds would not see themselves as elderly; 70-year-olds regard those over 80 as old, not themselves.

In Erikson's view, the major task of ageing is to reflect on one's life, and to assess how worth while and fulfilling it has been. If on the whole the positive has outweighed the negative, then the individual will end his or her life with greater ego integrity than despair. Individuals will achieve ego integrity:

- if they are convinced that life does have a meaning and does make sense;
- if they conclude that what happened in their life was inevitable and could not have happened in any other way;
- if they believe that all life's experiences had their value and that good and bad experiences were times of learning and psychological growth;
- if they come to see and understand their own parents better because they have now experienced adulthood and maybe raised children of their own;
- if they see that the cycle of birth and death is something they have in common with all other human beings, whatever the difference in culture, status, lifestyle. Understanding this makes it easier to face the prospect of death.

ACTIVITY

Take two children from different backgrounds and imagine their experiences through the life cycle. For example:

1 A Bangladeshi boy whose parents speak very little English and who live in a high-rise flat in a large, run-down council estate in an inner city. The father is unemployed, the boy has several siblings and other relatives living nearby. There is considerable unemployment in the area, and much racial abuse, especially against the Bangladeshi community. The boy is close to his parents, and is intelligent.

2 Read again the case study of Tracy Congdon in Chapter 2. Try to predict her experience through the life cycle.

LOSS AND BEREAVEMENT

He who pretends to look on death without fear lies. All men are afraid of dying, this is the great law of sentient beings, without which the entire human species would soon be destroyed.

(Jean-Jacques Rousseau)

Loss is experienced in many ways, not necessarily involving the death of a loved one:

- growing up involves loss of infancy support networks;
- going to school involves temporary separation from parents;
- changing school involves loss of familiar surroundings.

Obviously, there are corresponding 'gains' here as well, e.g. the child gains new friends and experiences with each change in circumstance. Other life events that involve loss are:

- new siblings (loss of parental attention);
- death of a sibling;
- bereavement, as grandparents grow older and die;
- loss of parent through separation, divorce or death;
- ending or changing relationships;
- unemployment (either parent's, sibling's or one's own);
- miscarriage or stillbirth;
- disability (loss of a sense of the future and of security);
- birth of a handicapped baby (parents may grieve for the 'normal' child they have lost);
- caring for people with dementia or Alzheimer's disease.

Each loss may be seen as a preparation for greater losses. How the individual reacts to the death of a loved one will depend on how they have experienced other losses, their personal characteristics, their religious and cultural background and the support available.

Grief

Grief is a normal and necessary response to the death of a loved one. It can be short-lived or last a long time. Grief at the death of a husband, wife or child is likely to be the most difficult to get over. Grief can take the form of several clearly defined stages:

1. *Shock and disbelief.* Numbness and withdrawal from others enables the bereaved person to get through the funeral arrangements and family gatherings. This stage may last from three days to three months.
2. *Denial.* This generally occurs within the first 14 days and can last minutes, hours or weeks. No loss is acknowledged; the bereaved person behaves as if the dead person was still there. Hallucinations are a common experience; they may consist of a sense of having seen or heard the dead person or of having been aware of his or her presence.
3. *Growing awareness.* Some or all of the following emotions may be felt and each conspires to make many people feel that they are abnormal to experience such harsh emotions:

    - *Longing:* the urge to search, to try to find a reason for the death.
    - *Anger*, directed against any or all of the following: the medical services; the person who caused the death, in case of accident; God for allowing it to happen; the deceased for abandoning them.
    - *Depression:* the pain of the loss is felt, often with feelings of lack of self-worth. Crying, or letting go, usually helps to relieve the stress.
    - *Guilt:* this may be guilt for the real or imagined negligence inflicted on the person who has just died; or the bereaved can feel guilty about his or her own feelings and inability to enjoy life.
    - *Anxiety*, often bordering on panic, as the full impact of the loss is realised. There is worry about the changes and new responsibilities and future loneliness. There may even be thoughts of suicide.

4. *Acceptance.* This usually occurs in the second

year, after the death has been re-lived at the first anniversary. The bereaved person is then able to re-learn the world and new situations with its changes without the deceased person.

The most meaningful help that we can give any relative – child or adult – is to share his feelings before the event of death and allow him to work through his feelings, whether they are rational or irrational.

(Elizabeth Kubler-Ross)

Research has shown that counselling can help to reduce the damage to physical and mental health which sometimes follows the loss of a loved one. Most people come through the healing process of grief with the help of relatives and friends. Those who may be in particular need of help are often those:

- with little or no family support;
- with young children;
- who have shown particular distress or suicidal tendencies.

Bereavement counsellors try to establish a warm, trusting relationship with the bereaved person. This is done initially by listening with patience and sympathy; accepting tears as natural and even desirable. Bereavement counselling should not be undertaken by individuals working alone. The support of a group under professional guidance is crucial, as close contact with intense grief can be very stressful and emotionally demanding.

How to help someone who is suffering from loss

- DO be available.
- DO let your concern show.
- DO allow them to cry if they want.
- DO allow them to talk about their loss as much as they want.
- DO reassure them that they did everything that they could.

- DON'T avoid them because you feel awkward.
- DON'T say you know how they feel.
- DON'T change the subject when they mention their loss.

The following poem was written by 'Kate', who was unable to speak, but was occasionally seen to write. After her death, her locker was emptied and this poem was found. It was first printed in the *Sunday Post* in 1973 and has since appeared in newspapers and magazines all over the world.

KATE

What do you see nurses
What do you see?
Are you thinking
When you are looking at me,
A crabbit old woman
not very wise,
Uncertain of habit
with far-away eyes,
Who dribbles her food
and makes no reply,
When you say in a loud voice
'I do wish you'd try'
Who seems not to notice
the things that you do,
And forever is losing
a stocking or shoe,
Who unresisting or not
lets you do as you will
with bathing and feeding
the long day to fill,
Is that what you're thinking,
is that what you see?
Then open your eyes nurse,
You're not looking at me.
I'll tell you who I am
as I sit here so still,
I'm a small child of ten
with a father and mother,
Brothers and sisters who
love one another,
A young girl of sixteen
with wings on her feet,
Dreaming that soon now
a lover she'll meet;
A bride soon at twenty,
my heart gives a leap,

Remembering the vows
that I promised to keep;
At twenty-five now
I have young of my own
Who need me to build
a secure and happy home.
A young woman of thirty
my young now grow fast,
Bound to each other
with ties that should last;
At forty my young ones
now grown will soon be gone,
But my man stays beside me
to see I don't mourn;
At fifty once more
babies play round my knee,
Again we know children
my loved one and me.
Dark days are upon me,
my husband is dead,
I look at the future
I shudder with dread,
For my young are all busy
rearing young of their own,
I'm an old woman now
and nature is cruel,
'Tis her jest to make
old age look like a fool.
The body it crumbles,
Grace and vigour depart,
There now is a stone
where once I had a heart:
But inside this old carcase
a young girl still dwells,
And now and again
my battered heart swells,
I remember the joys
I remember the pain,
And I'm loving and living
life over again,
I think of the years
all too few – gone too fast,
And accept the stark fact
that nothing can last.
So open your eyes nurses
Open and see,
Not a crabbit old woman
look closer – see ME.

ACTIVITY

1 Explain the idea of loss in its widest sense, giving examples of loss experienced at all life stages.

2 How would you explain the death of a loved grandparent to a child of six years?

3 Outline the stages of grief that are normally experienced following a bereavement.

4 Find out about support services for the bereaved in your area.

5 Interview anyone who has suffered a bereavement and make brief notes.

Unexpected life changes

Unexpected life changes may include being a victim of crime (see page 230) or suffering disability or serious illness. Other examples could include child abuse and eating disorders.

CHILD ABUSE

The experience of the abused child has been compared with that of hostage victims and concentration camp inmates. A few days as a hostage can change the whole psyche of an adult; this should indicate how much damage intermittent violence, emotional battery (criticism, shouting) and then occasional kindness will inflict on an unknowing, inadequately verbal child. The abused child is asked to love and obey his or her warders and protectors, but at the same time is psychologically and physically degraded, and often receives violence for no consistent reason. As a result, the child internalises feelings of self-blame, guilt, low-esteem and a need to fail.

Emotional abuse and neglect

Parents who neglect their children, who are

cold, are too busy with their own lives, and who continuously fail to show their children love or affection, are abusing them emotionally. They may simply be uninterested, or they may continuously threaten, taunt, criticise or shout at a child.

The child feels unloved and unlovable, loses confidence and self-esteem, and becomes nervous and withdrawn. Children who are emotionally neglected usually show signs of being unhappy in some way. They may appear withdrawn or unusually aggressive, or they may have lingering health problems or difficulties at school. Emotional abuse hurts children very deeply. The effects on the child's personality can be very serious and make it hard for him or her to form successful relationships as he or she grows up.

The following extract is a description by a nine year-old boy, Jamie, of his experience:

I used to get into bad tempers all the time because I wanted my mum and dad to love me and be interested in me, but they kept telling me I was a bad boy.

One day I made my mum so angry, she hit me. Later she told me she was sorry and that she had telephoned some people called the NSPCC who could help make us happy. I thought they would take me away. But they didn't. They said that I wasn't bad and that what had happened to me wasn't my fault.

We went to the NSPCC every week. My mum and dad talked about how they felt and I told them how angry I was. I know now that my mum loves me, and she shows it.

My mum and dad pay me lots more attention, and I'm so much happier now.

Physical abuse

Physical abuse occurs when parents or adults deliberately inflict injuries on a child, or knowingly do not prevent them. Abusing actions include hitting, shaking, squeezing, burning or biting. They also include using excessive force when feeding, changing or handling a child. Giving a child poisonous substances, inappropriate drugs or alcohol, and attempting to suffocate or drown a child, are also examples of physical abuse.

Physical abuse is on a scale which has a smack on one end and violent battering at the other. Punishments on the child, once started, tend to escalate. Sometimes just one child in a family is physically abused. Often a step-parent, who has not bonded down the years with a child, is involved. Sometimes highly aggressive and psychotic personalities are involved, who have little hope of becoming reasonable parents, and these cases are the ones reported in the press. In the majority of cases the children who have been battered can eventually be returned successfully to their homes. Frequently their parents desperately want to make a happy home for their family. Their motivation is high, but most are emotionally immature people who expect too much from their children and punish them too severely for 'faults' that are really just part of normal development. They may also fuss over them, sometimes with over-protective fanaticism.

In cases of child abuse, a detailed longitudinal family history should be obtained. When decisions have to be made about whether abuse has occurred, and what should be the future of the child and family, the parents' own family background will be taken very seriously into account. Worrying events in the parents' background would include:

- violent childhood (observed or experienced);
- inadequate or inconsistent parenting;
- significant periods in hospital/care;
- persistent truancy/under-achievement in school;
- lack of close adolescent friendships;
- left home when very young;
- poor employment record;
- no close friendships;
- brief cohabitations/marital relationships;
- record of criminal violence;
- obsessional personality traits;
- alcohol or drug abuse.

The opposite of these factors, or the absence of them, would be seen as hopeful signs.

Physical abuse can cause injuries including bruising, burns, fractures, internal injuries and brain damage, and, in extreme cases, death. Shaking is more dangerous than people are aware and may cause brain damage or blindness. Beaten children often feel they are to blame and have low self-esteem. When they are older they tend to be aggressive and bully younger children. Some forms of physical punishment are inbuilt in our culture, though this is not the case in other cultures. There is a link with criminality: John and Elizabeth Newson wrote in 1989: 'The measures which stand out as most predictive of criminal record before the age of 20 are having been smacked or beaten once a week or more at 11, and having a mother with a high commitment to corporal punishment at that age'.

Medical presentation

Some injuries presented at the surgery or casualty department could only have been caused by assault, but the majority of injuries are more difficult to assess – they could have been caused by abuse or by accident. The following characteristics would tend to imply abuse rather than accident:

- A long unexplained delay between the incident and presentation for treatment (in serious injuries).
- The injuries could not have happened in the way described.
- There may be injuries of different ages.
- There were no witnesses.
- The parents are touchy and hostile and have unrealistic expectations of the child.
- The parents might hint at other problems.

Sexual abuse

This takes place when an adult forces a child to take part in a sexual activity, using the child to satisfy his or her own sexual desires. This can involve actual sexual contact or exposing children to pornographic videos or magazines. Sexual abusers may be single men who are sexually attracted to children, and the theory is that they feel inadequate in relationships with adults of their own age. They are capable of abusing very many children over the course of their adult life. Imprisonment removes such offenders from society, but does not act as a deterrent to their behaviour. Some wish to stop offending but need professional help to do so.

Sexual abuse also occurs within the home. Theories about the origin of the problem relate in some way to the abuse of power, especially by men over their daughters. The pattern of family relationships varies significantly: isolated families in rural areas; promiscuous families with a wide variety of sexual relationships between the different family members; or apparently highly moralistic and protective families, where the father turns to his daughter for sexual gratification because of marital problems no one wishes to acknowledge.

Sexual abuse can have very damaging and long-lasting effects. Children are confused because of their normal desire for physical affection and they feel that they are to blame for what has happened. They have to be told that they are never to blame. They may grow up feeling worthless and may, as young adults, become abusers themselves.

Finkelhor (1980) identified factors that might place a child at greater risk of sexual abuse. Many abusers are skilful in assessing and exploiting the emotional needs of vulnerable children. Finkelhor's factors include:

- living in a family with a stepfather;
- having lived at some time without the mother;
- not being close to the mother;
- having a mother who had a poor education;
- having no affection from the father;
- having two friends or fewer.

Note the importance of a close relationship with the mother as a protective factor.

Table 4.6 Coping with life event threats using ego defence mechanisms

Age group	Life event threat	Possible defence mechanism which might be used
Baby	Disruption of attachment bonds	Regression Denial
Child	Child abuse	Repression Denial Displacement Reaction formation
Adolescent	Delinquent behaviour Substance abuse Eating disorders	Displacement Regression Displacement Regression
Adult	Separation and divorce	Rationalisation Projection
	Unemployment	Regression Displacement
Elders	Bereavement	Denial

The ways in which abuse can threaten identity

The following are the ways in which abuse can threaten the identity of children, but adults suffering abuse (e.g. wife battering) will suffer in similar ways.

- Lack of trust in other people.
- Feelings of worthlessness.
- Loss of self-esteem and self-confidence.
- The child may feel he or she is to blame for what happened but is too ashamed to tell anyone for years. The child's behaviour will still be affected.
- The child becoming an adult will have difficulty forming relationships and may always expect or even seek out relationships which have an abusing content.
- If there has been no intervention, counselling help or personal reflection on the child's experience, he or she may also become an abuser.
- The child is more likely to turn to alcohol or drugs than others.
- The child is more likely than others to turn to crime.

Coping with child abuse

To cope with the stress of abuse, a child may adopt the following defence mechanisms (see Table 4.6):

- *Repression:* A child may push the memory of the abuse out of consciousness and forget what happened. But the repressed memory will still affect the child's behaviour; the child may, for example, suffer recurrent nightmares.
- *Denial:* If a parent or older sibling was involved, a child may deny that anything happened, out of confused loyalty and a need for security.
- *Displacement:* A child might act out what has happened to him or her with toys or smaller children.
- *Reaction formation:* A child might grow up fearing (in the case of physical or sexual abuse) any kind of physical contact from others.

Methods of protection from and prevention of child abuse

B. Gillham (1991) suggests three levels of prevention, particularly relating to child sexual abuse.

Primary prevention

- Increasing awareness of parents, teachers and other carers that child abusers are to be found at all levels of society, are often young or youngish men (and sometimes women), and may be in positions of responsibility towards children or may seek other involvement with children.

- Recognising that boys are almost as much at risk as girls, *particularly after the age of 10*.
- Teaching children simple rules about dealing with approaches from strangers.
- Teaching children *specific* information about access to private/sexual parts of their body – rules can be made relatively simple.
- Establishing a more conspicuous social vigilance about child sexual abuse so that potential abusers might be deterred.
- Establishing a penal policy which removes from circulation serious and persistent child abusers because they represent a disproportionate and long-term risk to the child population.
- Providing children with education in personal and social relationships so as to sensitise them to interpersonal abuse in all forms.

Secondary prevention

- Creating an atmosphere in schools and families (by formal and informal means) whereby children feel able to report abuse; and providing them with a vocabulary – at least for body parts – which will enable and permit them to disclose abuse they are experiencing.
- Parents, teachers and others *acting* on their suspicions (which may result in *primary* prevention, if a persistent abuser is stopped).
- Teachers, in particular, being alert to signs of sexual abuse in children (principally oblique forms of disclosure) but *not* relying on supposed behavioural or psychological indicators, most of which are non-specific to any aetiology, let alone sexual abuse.
- A clear recognition of the fact that children rarely lie about sexual abuse.
- Vigilance in the case of 'at risk' children, especially girls who are not with their natural fathers (an increasingly large category because of current rates of divorce and separation).
- When the offender is in the child's home, *removing him or her*, or, if that is impossible, removing the child.

Tertiary prevention

- Providing a sympathetic, undramatic, supportive response to the disclosure.
- Keeping formal interviewing and 'treatment' to a minimally intrusive level.
- Communicating to children that blame and responsibility are not theirs even if they 'cooperated' or 'consented'.
- Providing counselling services for adults who have current adjustment problems attributable to sexual abuse in childhood.

In a typical Social Services Department today there will be several specially selected and trained social workers working in conjunction with the police. The following outline of the course an investigation into child abuse might follow is taken from Surrey Social Services:

- police and social work team share their information and agree a course of action;
- team interview the informant;
- visit the family;
- seek parental consent to interview the child;
- joint social work/police interview;
- if consent is refused, consider whether a Place-of-Safety Order should be sought and take legal advice about a medical examination;
- interview and take statements from witnesses;
- arrange a medical examination, if necessary;
- interview the suspect, usually at a police station.

For resources in the community for helping with child abuse and other life event threats – refugees, family units, etc. – see the References and Resources section at the end of this chapter.

ACTIVITY

Choose one of the life stages described earlier in this chapter, then:

1 Collect as much information as you can about this life stage from newspapers, magazines and textbooks.

2 Prepare a poster illustrating individuals coping successfully/unsuccessfully with this life stage.

3 Find out the names of charities and helping agencies for this age group.

4 Answer the following questions as they apply to your chosen age group.

- What are the problems they most commonly have to deal with?
- Why do these problems arise?
- What help are the agencies able to offer?
- What social changes would the agencies like to see?

EATING DISORDERS

Anorexia nervosa

Anorexia nervosa is a recognised eating disorder among women today. Between one in 100 and one in 250 women are likely to be affected; sufferers are most frequently found among the higher social classes in the developed world. The disorder is occasionally, but rarely, seen in men (only 10% of sufferers are men).

Anorexia nervosa is characterised by severe weight loss (see Figure 4.5), wilful avoidance of food, and intense fear of being fat. It is popularly, but wrongly, called the 'slimmer's disease'. Features of the disorder are:

- weight loss;
- overactivity and obsessive exercising;
- tiredness and weakness;
- lanugo (baby-like hair on body; thinning of hair on head);
- extreme choosiness over food.

The criteria for diagnosis established by the American Psychiatric Association can be described as follows:

- intense fear of becoming obese which does not diminish as weight loss progresses;
- disturbance of body image, e.g. claiming to feel fat when emaciated;
- weight loss: at least 25% of original pre-illness body weight; or, if under 18 years of age, weight loss from the original pre-illness body weight plus projected weight gain expected from growth charts, which may be combined to make at least 25%;
- refusal to maintain body weight over a minimal normal weight for age and height;
- no physical illness that would account for the weight loss.

The causes of anorexia nervosa are much debated. The following are some theories:

- Dieting is seen by sufferers as a way of controlling their lives.
- Sufferers do not wish to grow up and are trying to keep their childhood shapes. In part, this may be influenced by the media obsession with achieving the 'perfect' (i.e. slim) body and also by the desire to defer the turbulence of adolescence.
- Some specialists see it as a true phobia about putting on weight.
- Feminist writers have suggested that the condition may be related to a new role for women within society.
- The development of eating disorders may be seen as the avoidance of adult sexual feelings and behaviours.
- The individual is over-involved in their own family so that when she or he enters adolescence there is a confrontation between the peer group and the family.
- Some specialists believe that the real cause is depression, personality disorder or, rarely, schizophrenia.
- Some doctors point to the hormonal

changes related to weight loss and absence of menstruation, and regard anorexia nervosa as a physical illness that is caused by a disorder of the hypothalamus (part of the brain concerned with hunger, thirst and sexual development).

Hospital treatment is often necessary to help the sufferer return to a normal weight. Treatment is usually a combination of:

- a controlled re-feeding programme, sometimes via a naso-gastric tube in severe cases;
- individual psychotherapy;
- family therapy.

Occasionally drug abuse and alcohol abuse also occur and these require specific treatment. Drug treatment may be needed if there is a depressive or other illness.

Psychotherapy may be needed for months or even years after the sufferer has achieved a more normal weight. Relapses are common whenever there is the slightest stress.

About 50% of all patients treated for anorexia nervosa in a hospital continue to have symptoms for many years; 5–10% later die from starvation or suicide.

Bulimia nervosa

Bulimia is often, but not always, a variant of anorexia nervosa. There has been a rise in the number of males suffering from this disorder, although most sufferers are girls or women between the ages of 15 and 30. Bulimia nervosa is characterised by episodes of compulsive overeating usually followed by self-induced vomiting.

As with anorexia, there is no single cause to account for the condition. Many of the theories advanced are linked closely to those put forward to explain anorexia nervosa, and include:

- a morbid fear of fatness;
- a constant craving for food developed after months or years of fasting.

Features of the illness include the following:

- The sufferer may be of normal weight or only slightly underweight.
- Bingeing and vomiting may occur once or several times a day.
- The sufferer may often become clinically depressed and even suicidal.
- In severe cases, repeated vomiting leads to dehydration and loss of the body's vital salts, especially potassium; this may result in weakness and cramps.
- The acid present in gastric juices may damage tooth enamel.

Often the bulimic carries out the bingeing and vomiting in secret, so the main difficulty in treating the illness lies in persuading the sufferer to accept treatment.

- Psychotherapy and/or anti-depressant drugs may be used.
- As with anorexia sufferers, supervision and regulation of eating habits are essential, and there is often the need for hospital admission.
- Relapses are common and closely linked to stress.

ACTIVITY

1. Collect as many magazines aimed at women between the ages of 16 and 60, particularly issues for the months January to August, and list and analyse the different 'reducing' diets offered to their readers.

2. Find out how many magazines cater *specifically* for the person trying to slim.

3. Discuss the prevalence of slim role models on film and in television. Would it be 'healthier' if such media reflected society more honestly? NB 40% of adult women in the UK wear size 16 clothes.

VICTIMS OF CRIME

Twenty years ago the victims of crime had few rights, and little attention was paid to their needs. Now the pain and suffering caused by crime is more widely recognised. The charity Victim Support has played an important role in bringing the needs of victims to public and political notice.

The Victim Support movement has a central role to play in our criminal justice system and our society. A society which neglects the victims of crime condones the crime itself. It is vital that the needs of victims are made a top priority in the criminal justice system, and that Victim Support groups have the capacity to give assistance to the victims of crime whenever it is needed.

(The Rt Hon Paddy Ashdown, MP)

Quick facts

- Every year in the UK one person in five is a victim of crime.
- Many people who suffer a crime become victims again within a few days.
- Last year, Victim Support offered help to over one million victims of crime, 50% more than five years before.

Case study

My son Daniel was 17 and studying for A Levels. He went out one Friday with friends and came back very distressed and covered in blood.

Two lads had jumped on Daniel as he walked home. He was knocked to the ground, and kicked in the face and ribs. Two women who recognised the attackers ran up shouting and the lads ran off. The incident had a terrible effect on me. I would sit and sob, and could not concentrate on anything. Victim Support were very kind and reassured me that my reactions were not unusual. They arranged for someone to come and see me that afternoon. The police had left us to decide whether we wanted charges brought. The volunteer helped me to think this through, and to talk about it with my husband and Daniel. To our relief, Daniel and his friend decided they wanted the lads arrested. They pleaded guilty and some months later Daniel got compensation.

We would like to thank Victim Support for their invaluable help, and for giving us the confidence to go through with this. We know we made the right decision, and that as victims of crime we are not alone.

(Courtesy of Victim Support)

ACTIVITY

Write to Victim Support for further information on their work. Consider ways in which people you know have been affected by crime, and discuss how Victim Support might have helped.

Support methods

The importance of informal support networks provided by friends and family is described in Chapter 2.

For those who are isolated in society, or who for various reasons do not wish to reveal their difficulties to those they know, perhaps feeling that their special needs would not be understood, there is a wide range of organisations available to help with general problems.

These include:

- Citizens Advice Bureau;
- personal safety;
- relationships;
- alcohol and drugs;
- help for the elderly;
- racial harassment;
- help for the disabled;
- keeping children safe;
- problems with children;
- eating disorders.

Examples of such organisations, many of which offer immediate help in the form of telephone lines, are given here. Details of these and other services are shown in public places such as public libraries and colleges, and some are listed in *Yellow Pages*. A general agency such as your local Citizens Advice

Bureau should have a full list of these organisations.

The following extracts have been taken from advertisements and organisation brochures.

CITIZENS ADVICE BUREAU

Citizens Advice Bureaux provide the largest advice service in the country. They give free information, support and assistance to people on a wide range of subjects, from employment rights to problems with consumer goods and services. This advice is delivered professionally by fully trained voluntary and paid staff. Over 700 bureaux make up the CAB Service, with a total of nearly 1,400 outlets.

Citizens Advice Bureaux pride themselves on providing a service for everyone as well as giving information on any subject, and actively welcome volunteers from all walks of life. The CAB Service is committed to equal opportunities for clients and staff. Bureaux are increasingly ensuring that they are accessible to people with mobility difficulties and hearing impairments. Telephone services are expanding for elderly and disabled people, and more services are being provided to meet the needs of ethnic communities.

Top six categories of enquiry

1. Debt advice is now the largest category of enquiry in bureaux. In many areas, specialist money advice units have been set up to cope with the increasing number of multiple debt enquiries.
2. The CAB Service has seen enquiries about social security multiply in the last decade. These include questions relating both to the benefits and to the system for administering them.
3. Employment enquiries doubled throughout the 1980s and continue to rise. They can include anything from help with finding a job to advice on terms and conditions of employment and on dismissal and redundancy.
4. Housing enquiries range from house purchase and tenancies to mortgage arrears and homelessness.
5. A wide spectrum of family and personal problems are brought to Citizens Advice Bureaux, from the care of old and young people to marital difficulties and bereavement.
6. Faced with the complexity of the legal system, more and more people are seeking help from their local bureau. Advice is sought on legal aid, procedures in the County Court, and complaints against the police and the legal profession.

PERSONAL SAFETY

BT offer an advice service and leaflet on how to deal with malicious callers: Tel.: 0800 666700, where a recorded message will advise you. If you need further advice, dial 150 (free), between 8am to 6pm, Monday to Saturday.

Citizens Advice Bureaux: They can help you get legal advice. Get the number of your nearest CAB in the local phone book.

London rape crisis centre offers a confidential telephone counselling service run by women. The helpline is for women and girls who have been raped or sexually assaulted and who require advice and support. PO Box 69, London WC1X 9NJ. Tel.: 0171-837-1600. Open: Mon–Fri, 10am–11pm Weekends 10am–10pm.

National AIDS Helpline is a freephone facility offering confidential information, advice and support to anyone concerned or worried about HIV/AIDS. National Aids Helpline: 0800 567123. Open: 24 hours a day, 7 days a week.

Rape Crisis Centres: If you have been raped, they will give you help and support. Find the nearest centre by calling 0171 837 1600. In Scotland 0131 556 9437.

SOCIAL SERVICES: If you or your children need to get away from a violent man, social workers at your local council can put you in touch with a nearby refuge for women. Their 24-hour emergency number will be in the phone book.

The Suzy Lamplugh Trust: 14 East Sheen Avenue, London SW14 8AS. A national charity for personal safety. Tel.: 0181 392 1839.

Victim Support Schemes: If you have been attacked, they can help you cope. Ask the police to put you in touch.

Women's Aid Federation provide an advice service, and set up refuges for victims of domestic violence. Their national helpline is 0117 963 3542.

RELATIONSHIPS AND CONTRACEPTION

Lesbian and Gay Switchboard is a confidential telephone helpline offering support, information and advice for lesbians and gay men. The helpline also provides an opportunity to talk through any concerns or anxieties you may have about your own sexuality.

Message Home is an answerphone service for anyone who has left home, so they can pass on a message to let relatives or friends know they are safe. Message Home: Tel.: 01705-733899. Open: 24 hours a day, 7 days a week.

Pregnancy Advisory Service Limited offer a confidential service to females including:

- pregnancy testing
- emergency contraception
- cervical smears
- abortion advice and help
- sterilisation, etc.

Pregnancy Advisory Service Limited is for use by any woman of any age. Some charge may be made – so ask first. Pregnancy Advisory Service Limited, 11–13 Charlotte Street, London W1P 1HD. Tel.: 0171 637 8962. Open: Mon–Fri, 9am–5pm, Sat Mornings.

RELATE used to be called the Marriage Guidance Council. It is a registered charity, with about 400 counselling centres throughout the country. RELATE has over 50 years' experience of helping people with their relationship problems, and understands how hard it can be to keep a marriage going nowadays.

RELATE helps people through difficult and unhappy stages in their relationships. This is mainly done through marital or relationship counselling, which takes place in a comfortable and relaxing room and usually takes several sessions (each session lasts about an hour). Some RELATE centres also offer a variety of other ways of helping:

- *Sex therapy*, where specialists offer help for a wide variety of sexual problems. This work has an outstanding measure of success: not only does the sexual relationship improve, but so does the marriage itself.
- *Family counselling*, which helps children caught in the breakdown of their parents' marriage, at a time when their parents are least able to help them.
- *Education and training*, which covers a wide area ranging from relationship education in schools to retirement preparation and counselling for the elderly. RELATE also helps the helpers: specialist training courses are run for people such as doctors, teachers, social workers, police officers, priests and managers in industry.

RELATE also runs a nationwide book service, Books With Care, which sells books by mail-order on every kind of problem. A series of free booklists can be obtained by contacting your local RELATE centre, or from the Bookshop at Rugby headquarters (National HQ, Herbert Gray College, Little Church Street, Rugby CV21 3AP. Tel.: 01788 773241.

ALCOHOL AND DRUGS

Leaflets on drugs are available from the Health Publications Unit, No 2 Site, Heywood Stores, Manchester Road, Heywood, Lancashire OL10 2PZ – including 'Drugs & Solvents – you and your child'; 'Drugs – a parents' guide'; 'Solvents – a parents' guide'.

25 Hour Drug Advice Line can be used by anyone concerned about their own or someone else's alcohol and/or drug use. Tel.: 0181 767

8711. Open: 24 hours a day, 7 days a week. This confidential telephone helpline provides information on:

- drugs
- alcohol
- HIV/AIDS
- other organisations/services/agencies who can help.

ADFAM National, 5th Floor, Epworth House, 25 City Road, London EC1Y 1AA. Tel.: 0171 638 3700. A charity for the families and friends of drug users. It provides a National Helpline offering information and confidential support.

DICE (Drop in Counselling/Education) offer a free and confidential service providing information, advice and support on:

- drugs/HIV/hepatitis
- drug use and safer sex
- HIV counselling and testing.

DICE can be used by anyone:

- drug users, their families and friends;
- anyone concerned/requiring information about drug use.

Tel.: 01737 779789, 50 Station Road, Redhill, Surrey RH1 1PH.

FAMILIES ANONYMOUS: The Doddington & Rollo Community Association, Charlotte Despard Avenue, Battersea, London SW11 5JE, Tel.: 0171 498 4680.

NARCOTICS ANONYMOUS is a worldwide organisation offering free and confidential advice and information on drugs and drug use. Their helpline can be used by all those concerned about their own or other people's use of drugs. NARCOTICS ANONYMOUS: 0171 272 9040 (information; 0171 498 9005 (helpline).

Quitline is a telephone helpline offering confidential, sympathetic and non-judgmental advice and support to those wanting to stop smoking. Quitline send out free information packs and can refer you to local stop smoking groups.

Quitline can be used by anyone wanting to stop smoking or by those helping others to give up. QUITLINE: 0171 487 3000. Open: Mon–Fri, 9.30am–5.30pm.

Release offer free and confidential information and advice on all drugs (illegal and prescribed), to anyone concerned about themselves or others. Also provide help and information on the legal aspects of drugs.

Appointments can be made if you need to see someone. RELEASE, 388 Old Street, London EC1V 9LT. Tel.: 0171 729 9904. Open: Mon–Fri, 10am–6pm, 0171 603 8654. Open: 24 hrs a day, 7 days a week.

RE-SOLV (The Society for the Prevention of Solvent and Volatile Substance Abuse). 30A High Street, Stone, Staffordshire ST15 8AW. Tel.: 0178 581 7885. Deals solely with solvent misuse. They publish leaflets, booklets and videos and know about local agencies who can help.

SADAS (Surrey Alcohol and Drug Advisory Service), 50 Station Road, Redhill, Surrey RH1 1PH. Tel.: 01737 780253.

SCODA (Standing Conference on Drug Abuse), Waterbridge House, 32–36 Loman Street, London SE1 0EE. Tel.: 0171 928 9500. They have a full list of local services throughout the country.

YOUTH ACCESS: Magazine Business Centre, 11 Newark Street, Leicester LE1 5SS. Tel.: 0116 255 8763. Mainly for the under-25s. Will put a caller in touch with a local agency.

HELP FOR ELDERLY PEOPLE

You can get advice on security when answering the door in the leaflet 'In doubt? Keep them out', available from your police station, or write to Home Office, Public Relations Branch, Room 151, 50 Queen Anne's Gate, London SW1H 9AT.

AGE CONCERN: You can call this group for

pensioners at their head office on 0181 679 8000. In Scotland 0131 228 5656.

CRUSE – BEREAVEMENT CARE offer free and confidential support, counselling and help to anyone who is bereaved. CRUSE Bereavement care, 8 Romany Court, Mill Street, Redhill, Surrey RH1 6PA. Tel.: 01737 762008. Open: Mon–Fri, 9.30am–5pm.

HELP THE AGED: For help on a lot of problems, call the advice line on 0800 289 404.

The *Help Shop* is a service for anyone requiring free, up-to-date information on anything related to local services. They can help with housing matters, adult education, trading standards queries, leisure and recreation, environmental health issues, etc. So, either ring them or call in for a visit. Help Shop, 35 Station Road, Redhill, Surrey RH1 1QH. Tel.: 01737 770333.

NATIONAL DEBTLINE is a telephone helpline providing confidential, expert advice and information on all kinds of debt. Includes practical help on:

- dealing with creditors;
- working out a personal budget;
- filling in court papers;
- housing and benefits advice.

They also supply callers with a free self-help pack on dealing with debts. NATIONAL DEBTLINE: 0121 359 8501. Open: Mon and Thurs, 10am–4pm; Tues and Wed, 2pm–7pm (24 hour answerphone service).

SAMARITANS are there for anyone in need of someone to talk to – whether suicidal, despairing or lonely. They offer a free and confidential service. SAMARITANS: 01737 248444. Open: Telephone helpline – 24 hours a day, 7 days a week. Office – 8.30am–10pm.

Saneline provide a telephone service offering guidance and support to both the sufferers of mental illness and those who care for them. They can also put you in touch with a local self-help group. SANELINE: 0171 724 8000. Open: 2pm–12 midnight; 7 days a week. Answerphone outside these hours.

VICTIM SUPPORT SCHEMES: If you have been assaulted or robbed they can help you get over it. Your local police will put you in touch with the nearest group.

RACIAL HARASSMENT

In an emergency, dial 999 and ask for the police. For general advice contact your local police station to speak to your local crime prevention officer or community relations officer.

CITIZENS ADVICE BUREAUX: Your local Citizens Advice Bureau can also give advice and put you in touch with a victim support scheme.

THE COMMISSION FOR RACIAL EQUALITY was set up by the Race Relations Act 1976 and works towards the elimination of racial discrimination and the promotion of equal opportunity between people of different racial groups. Their address is: 10–12 Allington Street, London SW1E 5EH. Tel.: 0171 828 7022. They will also have the number of your local Racial Equality Council.

HELP FOR THE DISABLED

BENEFIT ENQUIRY LINE for people with disabilities. We are members of a Department of Social Security team that has been specially set up to give you advice over the phone. During a single FREE call we can tell you about the benefits available to you and how to claim them. If you are a friend or adviser to someone with a disability, we can advise you too.

We know about some of the problems that people with disabilities face when trying to find out what money is available in benefits from Social Security. And we are specially trained to help you if you don't know what questions to ask. Just phone this number FREE: 0800 181794 10am–4pm Monday to Friday.

KEEPING YOUR CHILDREN SAFE

Many police forces and schools organise

Junior Citizen or Crucial Crew schemes for junior school children. They teach them how to cope with everyday dangers both in the home and outside. They also encourage good citizenship. Ask your children's school or your local community police officer about these programmes. You can also contact Crime Concern for information about Crucial Crew.

The police and social services will investigate any suspected case of child abuse, ill treatment or neglect. If you believe a child has been abused in any way or put in fear of an assault, contact them or the NSPCC immediately. There are a lot of groups who can help. Your doctor may be able to tell you which one is best.

ANTI-BULLYING CAMPAIGN offer confidential advice, support and understanding to young people and parents who are affected by bullying at school. ANTI-BULLYING CAMPAIGN: 0171 318 1446. Open: Mon–Fri, 9.30am–5pm.

CHILDLINE: 0800 1111. This is a free telephone line offering confidential counselling for children in trouble or danger, or for worried parents. You can write to Childline at Freepost 1111 London N1 4BR.

CRIME CONCERN, Signal Point, Station Road, Swindon, Wiltshire, SN1 1FE. Tel.: 0179 351 4596.

EXPLORING PARENTHOOD: A national charity who offer factsheets and a counselling service. You can contact them at Latimer Education Centre, 194 Freston Road, London W10 6TT. Tel.: 0181 960 1678.

KIDSCAPE: They are at 152 Buckingham Palace Road, London SW1W 9TR. Tel.: 0171 730 3300.

MOTHERS OF ABUSED CHILDREN: 0169 733 1432 after 6.30pm. Based in Cumbria, provides telephone counselling for victims, parents and people who have been abused in the past.

NATIONAL CHILDREN'S HOME CARELINE: 0181 514 1177.

NATIONAL SOCIETY FOR THE PREVENTION OF CRUELTY TO CHILDREN (NSPCC): The London head office is on 0171 825 2500, or look for local branches in your phone directory.

NSPCC CHILD PROTECTION HELPLINE: 0800 800 500. 24 Hrs a day, 7 days a week. A free and confidential national helpline offering counselling to anyone concerned about children being at risk. Calls may be made by parents, relatives, friends and children themselves.

PARENTLINE: Westbury House, 57 Hart Road, Thundersley, Essex SS7 3PD. Tel.: 0126 875 7077. Offers help and advice to parents who are under stress, or experiencing difficulties with a child.

ROYAL SCOTTISH SOCIETY FOR THE PREVENTION OF CRUELTY TO CHILDREN (RSSPCC): They are at: 41 Polwarth Terrace, Edinburgh EH11 1NU. Tel.: 0131 337 8539.

THE SAMARITANS: a charity that helps the lonely or suicidal. Numbers are in the local phone book or the operator will put you through. You can get help on the phone or face to face.

EATING DISORDERS

EATING DISORDERS ASSOCIATION offer help and understanding for families, friends and sufferers of anorexia and bulimia. You can either write to them or phone their helpline. If you need advice and help they can put you in touch with someone locally. EATING DISORDERS ASSOCIATION, Sackville Place, 44 Magdalen Street, Norwich, Norfolk NR3 1JU. Tel.: 01603 621414 – general helpline. Open: Mon–Fri, 9am–6.30pm. Tel.: 01603 765050 – youth helpline (up to age 18). Open: Mon, Tues and Wed, 4pm–6pm.

STATE SUPPORT

The Welfare State helps those in need with a range of financial benefits, and with practical and psychological care provided by Social Services Departments, organised to offer services to every part of the UK.

Social Services Departments are government funded and therefore have to ration their resources. Targeting of resources, once a matter of secret negotiation, is increasingly being made available for public scrutiny. Decision-making is therefore done within a policy framework which is published openly and is subject to consultation and appeal. The following information is published by Surrey Social Services. The activity at the end of this section suggests investigation of social services priorities and targeting of resources in different areas of the country.

WHAT DOES SOCIAL SERVICES DO?

Social Services helps children and families with difficulties, people who are elderly and frail, and people with physical disabilities, learning disabilities and mental health problems.

Some people may go to Social Services for advice and help during a sudden crisis. Others may need Social Services' long term help, maybe with a member of their family who has a physical disability or maybe with an elderly relative. Sometimes Social Services has to act to protect individuals, especially children.

HOW DO I GET A SERVICE?

Step 1

Contact your local Social Service Centre. You can discuss your situation confidentially with the case manager at the centre and, together, you will be able to work out what you need in the way of help, support and services.

During these discussions you can always have a friend or relative represent you if you want.

Step 2

Once it is clear what you need, the case manager will be able to tell you whether or not it will be provided by Social Services or whether you should be referred to a more appropriate organization.

Step 3

If the help that you need is to be arranged by Social Services, then the case manager might ask a specialist to discuss your needs with you in further detail and consider various options.

Step 4

These different options will be discussed between you, the case manager, and whoever will be providing the services whether from the statutory, voluntary or private sector. The cost will be worked out, including any contribution expected from you. At this stage (not before), Social Services has to establish whether it can afford to pay for the service you need.

Step 5

If the money is available, the case manager will make sure you get the service you need and that its quality is satisfactory. Regular reviews of your situation will take place and you will be invited to take part in them.

Step 6

If you are not happy with the service you are receiving or want to alter it, discuss this with your case manager.

These steps are in line with NHS and Community Care Act 1990 and are intended to give you greater choice and involvement.

As an example, the targeting of resources for people with sensory and physical disabilities is shown below.

SERVICES FOR PEOPLE WITH SENSORY AND PHYSICAL DISABILITIES

Who is included in this care group?

People aged 18–64 who need help because of a physical disability or illness or because of sensory disabilities.

What we are aiming for

Surrey Social Services aims to promote the social functioning and health of people with physical or sensory disabilities to enable them to follow their chosen lifestyle with maximum independence.

We want to help people with a physical and/or sensory disability to:

- Live and receive the support they need in local and ordinary settings

- Have choice and control over their own lives and live as independent and normal lives as possible
- Have access to a range of social services; health promotion services; general and specialist health care; social, leisure, educational and employment opportunities in their local community
- Know about the full range of services and opportunities, and how to access them

Definitions of need

The levels of needs of people with physical disabilities are defined in terms of the frequency with which they need help from others and in terms of their ability to live safely and independently.

HIGH NEED

People who need daily or continuous help, for example people who are unable to do one or more of the following personal care tasks safely or independently, ie without help or aids/equipment:

- get in and out of bed
- eat and drink
- prepare light snacks
- get to and use the WC/commode
- get dressed
- wash hands and face
- strip wash

and/or people with a visual disability who are unable to function safely and independently.

MODERATE NEED

People who need help several times a week, but less often than every day, for example people who are unable to do one or more of the following independently, ie without help and/or aids/equipment:

- bath themselves
- do the shopping
- do light or heavy house work
- cook meals

LOW NEED

People who need help intermittently or not more than once a week, for example people who have some disability which minimally affects independence.

What are our priorities?

In view of the current gap between needs and resources, Surrey social services have adopted the following policy on priorities and targeting of resources for disabled people.

Purchase of individual care packages

Services will be provided to those disabled people who are in high need as defined previously. This will include:

- People who have no other support with caring
- People who receive help from carers who need support with caring
- People with sensory disabilities who are unable to live safely and independently (from Surrey social services).

Preventive services

Social Services will work in partnership with other agencies to support and stimulate preventive services which are available to people at all levels of need. Our resources will be directed to funding services, projects and schemes rather than individuals so that people in low, moderate and high need may all benefit.

Assessment

All people approaching or being referred to social services will receive an assessment. Where the assessment shows that a person is not eligible for service under the priorities and targeting policy, people will receive advice on and/or be redirected to other appropriate agencies or services.

Packages of care

Services provided for individuals will vary according to the particular needs of each person, and the extent to which other support is available. For example, a person assessed as being in high need would require high levels of support if they are living on their own and have little other support. Another person with equally high levels of need may require very different levels and types of care if they are supported by a carer. Of course that carer may well need help to share the care.

ACTIVITY

1 Investigate the priorities and the criteria for eligibility for social services in the area in which you live.

- How are resources targeted?
- Do the social services work with other agencies, and/or the independent sector, to develop a range of support for people in high need?
- What preventative services for each client group – the elderly, those with sensory and physical disabilities, those with learning disabilities, those with mental health problems; children and families – are provided?

2 Find out the welfare benefits available for each of the above client groups.

THE INDIVIDUAL IN SOCIETY

Beliefs, ideas and values: the influence of socialisation

However helpless and dependent they may seem, within a few weeks of being born, babies will show signs of their need for emotional contact and INTERACTION with others. They smile, they cry, they babble, they reach out and they are particularly fascinated with the human face. As they grow and develop, they learn more about interacting with others, they acquire language and they begin to understand how others behave and how they, in turn, are expected to behave in particular situations. Learning the meaning of social behaviour and the values and beliefs of others is the way CULTURE is learned, re-learned and shared by each new generation. Culture is a 'set of guidelines – both implicit and explicit – which the individual inherits as a member of a particular group, and which tells him how to view the world, and how to behave in it in relation to other people, to the natural environment and to supernatural forces and gods' (McAvoy and Donaldson, 1990).

The process of learning the culture of a society (and/or of a subgroup or subculture within that society) is called SOCIALISATION. It is a continual process, lasting throughout our lives and involving the use of language, symbols and ritual. As we join different groups in society we learn new things; the initially strange becomes more familiar as we become accustomed to the new situation. At the same time as we adapt to or absorb values from the people around us, we also contribute as individuals, however minutely, to the culture of our group and/or the wider society. We may challenge ideas, question attitudes or join with others in diverging from usual patterns of behaviour. As a result, changes in society inevitably occur.

There is a debate about whether our experience of socialisation during childhood and the attitudes, values and ideas we encounter in our families, friends and neighbours (PRIMARY SOCIALISATION) is a much more powerful and influential one than any subsequent experience and socialisation gained from a wider variety of contexts – the family, friends, peers, schools, the media, religious organisations, colleagues at work, etc. (SECONDARY SOCIALISATION). Are ideas and values learned in the early years of life more difficult to alter or change later? Why should this be the case?

ACTIVITY

1 The process of socialisation can be grasped by thinking back to a time and a situation which was new to you, such as your first days at a new school, in a new job, in a new country, staying with a family other than your own for the first time . . .

What were your initial impressions and feelings? Did initially strange and difficult situations gradually become more familiar? How did this happen? What were you learning that made you gradually change the way in which you viewed this situation?

2 Do you think that early childhood experiences are particularly important? Why or why not? Interview several people older than yourself, asking them this question. Have their attitudes, values and beliefs altered significantly during their lives?

How do our attitudes, beliefs and ideas affect our behaviour towards others?

In many Western, industrialised societies, the beliefs, ideas and values people absorb from others and test out through their own experiences as they grow up from childhood to adulthood are unlikely to be completely coherent – a neat package which never varies. The term MORES refers to customs that have become part of a society's morality. For example, 'saving', rather than spending all our money at once, is generally seen as good for us as individuals and good for society as a whole. Nevertheless, even if a child learns a consistent set of moral and religious ideas from his or her family, sooner or later that child will hear contrary, different ideas and will understand that other people may have other perspectives. Hence the basis on which we adopt or reject certain values and ideas and make them our own is an interesting process for study.

ACTIVITY

Make a list of ten values, ideas or beliefs about life in this society which you hold, for example:
'I don't believe in stealing'
'I believe that it is important to care for others'
When your list is complete, think about where those ideas, values and attitudes came from. Have you always held those attitudes? Has a particular experience led you to hold a certain belief?

Discuss your list with other people.

Look again at your list. If you were asked 'How do your attitudes, values and beliefs influence your behaviour', what would be your response?

You may well find that several problems arise in trying to answer the last question in the Activity on this page. For example:

- Not all our ideas and values are always fixed and 'set'. We may be unsure about what we think on many issues. For example, we may be 'toying' with the idea of joining a church or a religious organisation.
- We may hold ideas and attitudes but not act on them. For example, we may 'believe' that working hard is a virtue but may often avoid doing it ourselves.
- Our attitudes may be reinforced and strengthened if people we are close to or people we associate with share them. For example, we may decide to protest at something we regard as unjust if others are also doing so.
- We may hold certain ideas but feel prevented from acting upon them by the behaviour of others around us or others we perceive to be more powerful than ourselves, and perhaps threatening. For example, we may wish to declare our teachers boring and incompetent but feel worried about how such a protest might affect our grades!
- We may simply be unaware or only half-aware of the reasons for our behaviour and the ideas which shape it. Many cultural factors influence us without any conscious knowledge, and we may not know what hidden ideas and prejudices we carry

around with us and how they play a role in our lives. For example, a student nursery teacher may suddenly realise that they have been telling off the children in their class in the same way that they were reprimanded as a child.

- The material circumstances of our lives and certain experiences can be positive or negative, or a mixture of both. Negative, traumatic episodes in our lives may leave us with views and beliefs we might rather not have but which we find difficult to abandon. For example, a woman who has been raped may feel uneasy in the presence of all men and see all men as a possible threat to her safety.
- We may express certain ideas overtly (openly to others) while simultaneously holding different and often contradictory attitudes. For example, a patient may say to the doctor, 'I've come to ask you for advice about these bouts of colds and 'flu I seem to keep getting', while thinking, 'I know what's wrong with me really: I'm over-worked and need a holiday but I bet he won't give me a prescription for that!'

Even if there were universal agreement upon what 'acceptable' behaviour was, and children grew up into societies learning and adopting accepted and socially approved ways of behaving, it is highly unlikely that every individual would always conform to the written or unwritten rules of social life. We often follow these social rules or NORMS out of habit or without particular reflection or thought. For example, we learn to wait patiently in supermarket checkout queues or, when entering a doctor's surgery, we wait for the doctor to ask us what is wrong before starting to explain. However, social relationships are problematic. Many experiences – a disability, a traumatic accident, the move to a new country or area of a country, the break-up of a family through divorce or bereavement – may lead people to behave towards and relate to others in unconventional, unexpected and therefore sometimes socially disapproved-of ways. In addition, we all bring to every social situation our unique personalities.

However, it is sometimes the case that the values, attitudes and ideas which we question the least are the ones which appear to us to embody 'common sense', ones which appear 'given' and 'natural'. Problems regarding the impact of these commonsense ideas on others may arise when:

- different groups of people from different cultural, religious, economic or social backgrounds evolve different ideas of what constitutes common sense;
- certain groups in society have the power to, and do, attempt to persuade others that their versions of common sense are the only correct ones;
- different views of common sense come into conflict.

ACTIVITY

1 Romantic love is a natural part of human experience and is therefore found in all societies, in close connection with marriage.

2 How long people live is dependent upon their biological make-up and cannot be strongly influenced by social differences.

3 In previous times the family was a stable unit, but today there is a great increase in the proportion of 'broken homes'.

4 In all societies some people will be unhappy or distressed; therefore rates of suicide will tend to be the same throughout the world.

In small groups or pairs, discuss each of the four statements above. With which (if any) does your group tend to agree most strongly? What reasons do people in your group give for agreeing with these statements? Are there any statements with which your group tends to disagree? What reasons do people in your group give for disagreeing with these statements?

Now read the following comments on these statements:

Each of these assertions is wrong or questionable, and seeing why will help us to understand the questions sociologists ask – and try to answer – in their work.

1 As we have seen, the idea that marriage ties should be based on romantic love is a recent one, not found either in the earlier history of Western societies, or in other cultures. Romantic love is actually unknown in most societies.

2 How long people live is very definitely affected by social influences. This is because modes of social life act as 'filters' for biological factors that cause illness, infirmity or death. The poor are less healthy on average than the rich, for example, because they usually have worse diets, live a more physically demanding existence, and have access to inferior medical facilities.

3 If we look back to the early 1800s, the proportion of children living in homes with only one natural parent was probably as high as at present, because many more people died young, particularly women in childbirth. Separation and divorce are today the main causes of 'broken homes', but the overall level is not very different.

4 Suicide rates are certainly not the same in all societies. Even if we only look at Western countries, we find that suicide rates vary considerably. The suicide rate of the United Kingdom, for example, is four times as high as that of Spain, but only a third of the rate in Hungary. Suicide rates increased quite sharply during the main period of industrialization of the Western societies, in the nineteenth and early twentieth centuries.
(Giddens, 1989, p. 14)

The Activity on this page suggests that a useful skill for anyone working in health and social care is to be prepared to ask of any of our beliefs: 'Is this really so? What evidence is there for this idea or belief?'

This leads us into asking perhaps the most controversial question so far. If it is useful to question and examine our beliefs and ideas (particularly in the light of the possible impact they may have on others), how do we EVALUATE them? How can we tell if we are 'right' or 'wrong'? The study of the social sciences is often an unsettling experience in itself because of this focus on questioning and because of the variety of possible ways of seeing things and of theories and explanations which it provides. This will be illustrated in the next section of this chapter. What happens when people's beliefs and ideas are different from those they live, work and socialise with or provide health and care services to? What tensions might arise? What strategies could be used to minimise potential areas of conflict and disagreement and maximise mutual understanding and acceptance?

Ethnic and cultural diversity in Britain

Britain is now an ethnically and culturally diverse society which nevertheless retains a dominant 'white' culture and population. What implications does this have for the ways in which we learn about other cultures and cultural traditions? How does our knowledge or lack of it about other ethnic, cultural or religious groups affect our behaviour towards people from those groups? To what extent is behaviour we regard as different from 'our own' seen as deviant or wrong?

THE CONCEPT OF DEVIANCE

SOCIAL DEVIANCE occurs in most societies, but what is regarded as 'deviant behaviour' by one society or group of people may be different from what is seen as deviant in another. What is seen by some as unacceptable, immoral or even criminal behaviour at one time in history may also change, becoming acceptable or even gaining approval.

In nineteenth century Britain, religious and moral beliefs strongly influenced peoples' views on marriage, sex and birth control. The subject of sex was not openly discussed, and nakedness was avoided in the home and in public. The only contraceptives that could be bought until the 1880s were quite expensive, extremely difficult to find out about or obtain, and generally unreliable. There were pessaries or the Dutch Cap for women, and leather or rubber sheaths for men.

The general climate of 'respectable' opinion was one of disapproval when it came to sex. The very idea of being able to enjoy it without the 'natural' result of producing children was quite shocking and unacceptable to most people.

(Adams, 1982)

Today there is still strict disapproval from the Catholic Church for the use of artificial contraceptives such as the Pill, the coil (or IUD), the sheath or sterilisation for men and women. Nevertheless, public, medical and governmental attitudes in the UK towards the use of contraception have changed considerably, especially over the last 25–30 years. The subject is taught in schools, discussed by couples, and help and advice is available from doctors, clinics and charities.

ACTIVITY

- Which groups in today's society may still regard the use of artificial contraception as socially deviant? What reasons do they have for their beliefs?
- Why do you think that attitudes towards the use of contraceptives have changed?
- It could be suggested that the use of artificial contraceptives by unmarried people and those in their teens is still regarded as more socially deviant than its use among married people and adults. Do you agree with this? Why might this be the case?

DEFINING ETHNICITY AND RACE

There have been minority ethnic groups and small settlements of black people in Britain for several hundred years. In this sense Britain has been a multi-ethnic society for a long period of time. However, since the 1950s there have been particular changes in the composition and size of Britain's black and Asian populations. There are some problems in obtaining a clear picture of these changes and even more difficulties in assessing their possible significance for health and welfare provision.

One problem is that ethnicity is not easily defined. Skellington and Morris, (1992) suggest that:

'Race', racial groups and categories . . . are not things that are given . . . objective facts waiting to be used – but concepts that have to be constructed. This construction involves a number of stages: differences of a certain kind between people have to be discerned; these differences have to be considered consequential; and these perceived shared attributes, such as skin colour, nationality, or regional or ethnic origin, have to become the basis for defining groups or categories of people.

(Skellington and Morris, 1992, p. 18)

Different sources of official or research-derived statistics use different bases for classifying people. Some may use legal nationality, others skin colour, others ethnic origin by country of birth or parents' country of birth. You may have come across some of these systems for classifying people if you have ever been asked to complete an 'ethnic monitoring form' or asked for your own 'self-assessment' of ethnicity.

ACTIVITY

1 Try to collect together examples of 'ethnic monitoring forms'. For example, your school or college may include

questions on ethnicity on the application forms it uses for potential new students or staff.

2 Discuss the use of these sorts of questions. Why are they used? What problems might arise in their use?

3 How would or do you describe yourself if asked to do so on forms such as these?

Ethnicity is therefore not an easily measurable thing. A 'white' person who was in fact born in eastern Europe but immigrated into this country in their twenties may, despite years of living here, still 'feel' Polish or Czech or Rumanian. A 'black' person born in Britain may feel British and have little cultural association with the country where their parents were born. People of mixed ethnic origin are sometimes consigned to an 'other' category on ethnic monitoring forms, thus conveying a certain confusion about the whole process of trying to categorise ethnicity.

A second difficulty is that:

there is no racialised data collection on the number of people claiming welfare benefits, using some form of personal social services, seeking health care (other than as inpatients), coming into contact with the police or appearing in courts.... It is impossible therefore ... to make any meaningful comparisons between the experiences of people of different ethnic origins and point to any desirable policy changes.

(Skellington and Morris, 1992, p. 21)

However, the 1991 Census was the first in Great Britain to include a question on ethnic group. *Social Trends* 24 shows that slightly over 3 million people (5.5% of the population) described themselves on their Census returns as belonging to an ethnic minority group. The proportion of the people who are in ethnic minority groups varies from area to area.

Minority ethnic groups are most concentrated and isolated in the former mill towns of Lancashire and Yorkshire, according to a new study which challenges the idea that Britain is truly multi-cultural.

Although numbers of black and Asian people are highest in inner London, the study shows that the areas most densely populated by ethnic minority groups are in the North and Midlands.

A Bangladeshi family in Oldham, Greater Manchester, is almost 50 per cent likely to have a

Table 4.7 Population by ethnic group and age, Great Britain, 1991

Ethnic group	% aged: 0–15	16–29	30–44	45–59	60 and over	All ages (= 100%) (000)
Ethnic minority group						
Black Caribbean	21.9	27.6	20.0	19.6	10.9	500
Black African	29.3	32.1	26.7	9.2	2.7	212
Black other	50.6	30.8	12.4	4.2	2.1	178
Indian	29.5	23.9	25.9	13.8	6.8	840
Pakistani	42.6	24.0	19.2	10.4	3.7	477
Bangladeshi	47.2	23.3	14.8	11.4	3.3	163
Chinese	23.3	29.7	29.4	12.0	5.7	157
Other Asian	24.4	25.2	33.0	13.3	4.1	198
Other	41.7	24.9	19.9	8.5	5.0	290
All ethnic minority groups	33.0	26.0	22.6	12.6	5.8	3,015
White	19.3	20.4	21.2	17.0	22.1	51,874
All ethnic groups	20.1	20.7	21.2	16.8	21.2	54,889

Source: Social Trends 24, data from Office of Population Censuses and Surveys; General Register Office (Scotland).

Table 4.8 Population by ethnic group and region, Great Britain, 1991, (000)

Region	Black[a]	Indian, Pakistani or Bangladeshi	Other ethnic minority groups	All ethnic minority groups	White	All ethnic groups	Ethnic minority groups as a percentage of total population
	891	1,480	645	3,015	51,874	54,889	5.5
North	5	21	13	39	2,988	3,027	1.3
Yorkshire & Humberside	37	144	33	214	4,623	4,837	4.4
East Midlands	39	120	29	188	3,765	3,953	4.8
East Anglia	14	14	15	43	1,984	2,027	2.1
South East	610	691	395	1,695	15,513	17,208	9.9
Greater london	535	521	290	1,346	5,334	6,680	20.2
Rest of South East	74	170	104	349	10,179	10,529	3.3
South West	22	17	24	63	4,547	4,609	1.4
West Midlands	102	277	45	424	4,726	5,150	8.2
North West	47	147	50	245	5,999	6,244	3.9
England	875	1,431	605	2,911	44,144	47,055	6.2
Wales	9	16	16	42	2,794	2,835	1.5
Scotland	6	32	24	63	4,936	4,999	1.3

[a]Black Caribbean, Black African and Black other.
Source: Social Trends 24, data from Office of Population Censuses and Surveys; General Register Office (Scotland).

Bangladeshi neighbour. In Tower Hamlets, east London, which has the biggest Bangladeshi community, the equivalent chance is 22 per cent.

David Owen, author of the study, says the findings show that, contrary to casual assumptions of a multi-cultural society, the reality is of marked geographical separation among ethnic groups.

"In much of Britain, people from the white group may only occasionally come into contact with people from minority ethnic groups. But where minority ethnic groups tend to concentrate, the white ethnic group may only just form the majority of the population," Mr Owen writes in Population Trends, the quarterly journal of the Office of Population Censuses and Surveys.

(The Guardian, *14 December 1994)*

In 1991 the proportion of the population from ethnic minorities in rural areas was below 1%, whereas the proportions for most

Table 4.9 Population of working age economic activity rates (%) by age, sex and ethnic group, Great Britain, Spring 1993

Ethnic group	Age group 16–19	20–29	30–39	40–49	50–59/64	Males aged 16–64	Females aged 16–59
White	62.0	82.1	84.5	86.7	69.0	86.1	71.9
Black[a]	41.7	75.2	75.2	87.3	70.3	80.4	66.0
Indian	25.1	72.5	77.6	86.3	61.3	80.8	61.4
Pakistani/Bangladeshi	35.4	52.8	52.1	50.2	41.1	72.3	24.8
Other[b]	47.0	60.0	68.7	84.3	75.5	76.0	58.6
All ethnic groups[c]	60.1	81.0	83.5	86.4	68.7	85.6	70.8

[a]Includes Caribbean, African and other black people of non-mixed origin.
[b]Includes Chinese, other ethnic minority groups of non-mixed origin and people of mixed origin.
[c]Includes ethnic group not stated.
Source: Social Trends 24, data from Employment Department, © *Crown copyright 1994.*

London boroughs and metropolitan districts were over 5%. Three in every five people from ethnic groups were under the age of 30, compared with two in every five in the population as a whole.

THE CONCEPT OF SUB-CULTURE

Despite the problems in defining ethnicity and race discussed above, black and ethnic minorities in Britain are often viewed as subcultures – groups of people whose 'view of the world, while developed from the larger culture in which they live, and sharing many of its values and concepts, also has certain unique, distinctive features of its own.' (McAvoy and Donaldson, 1990, p. 19).

There may also be subcultures within subcultures, so that, for example, the Asian population in Britain may be made up of social, religious and regional subcultures.

These cultural differences may generate tensions:

> At the interface between different cultures – or between members of different subcultures – a culture clash can occur. In this situation, one set of (often hidden) assumptions and concepts encounters a different set of assumptions and concepts. This may not only result in poor communication between the two parties, but also in feelings of bafflement, irritation, or even hostility in one or both parties.
>
> *(McAvoy and Donaldson, 1990, p. 19)*

There may also be expectations among the dominant white culture that black people in Britain should gradually adapt to or assimilate white cultural traditions (including dress, religion, family and sexual norms and mores), abandoning their own practices and beliefs. Refusal to do so may be seen as SOCIAL DEVIANCE, i.e. as non-conformity to given norms accepted by a significant number of people in a community or society.

As far as health and social care is concerned it can unfortunately sometimes be only one step from viewing other cultures as 'deviant' to blaming them for their problems and failure to be 'more like us'. Ethnic minorities come to be seen as deficient or lacking in something possessed by the white majority.

These views can, however, be questioned:

- What exactly is the dominant white culture in Britain? Does such a thing exist? For an interesting perspective on this question see the extract from *The Guardian* below.
- Are there distinct ethnic, cultural and/or religious 'subcultures' in the UK?
- To what extent should or could those from ethnic, cultural or religious minorities adapt to a dominant culture? What does it mean to be black and British?
- How do certain sets of ideas and beliefs come to be more widely held, more popular and more taken for granted than others at particular times and/or among particular groups of people? (Refer back to the activity on page 241.)

AMERICAN DREAMS AND NIGHTMARES

"Hi dad!" said eight-year-old Zoe. I was home from the City. They were plugged into TV, as usual. "Hello kids – what are you watching?"

"Oh, it's 'Fresh Prince of Bel Air' " says Tom, 10. "It's really cool – Will just pulled the chair from under Carlton . . ."

"Yeah – and he landed right on his butt!" says James, 12. "He he hee . . ."

I'm in England but they're in America. OK, so they're physically situated, like me, in England. But in their imaginations, in their hearts, in their dreams and deep in their souls, America is where they think they are, where they want to be, where they belong. They dress like Americans, talk like Americans, behave like Americans. If they were a dish, they'd be apple pie and ice cream.

Funny that – because all three are as English as roast beef. Since they were born upon this sceptered isle, they've breathed nothing but England's cool soft air.

These guys dress like Harlem blacks, with baseball caps worn backward, baggy jeans and hooded tops. They ghetto-blast rap music, break-dance, moonwalk. They watch American TV shows end-to-end – a non-stop diet of cartoons and boy-meets-girl schmaltz with plastic people, cute expressions, Kermit voices, corny gags – and gales of canned laughter that make the word "hysteria" sound subdued. Almost unEnglish. But my kids and all their mates think it's great. Their TV heroes are Screech, Chuckle, Fred Flintstone, Rugrats, the Avenger Penguins and Mighty Morphin Power Rangers.

"James – what would you like to do for your birthday?"

"Oh – could I go to the movies? The guys at school say Mrs Doubtfire/Mask/Forrest Gump is really ace."

So we go to the virtual reality world of the local American multi-screen. The foyer decor you could describe as Functional Ronald MacDonald. And though we're actually in High Wycombe it seems everybody comes from Brooklyn or Little Rock – all wearing US gear and queuing for popcorn, Coke, hamburgers and 26-flavours of ice cream. Consume, consume – "Daddy can I have . . . ?"

My kids are already fluent in American. If they were publishers of Hello magazine they'd rename it Hi. When Zoe plays with her dolls – "Bay Watch"-type chicks called Barbie and Sindy – she talks to them in the tones of Malibu. She learned the English alphabet on the sidewalk of Sesame Street.

"Zoe," I asked her the other day "What's the first letter of your name?"

'Zee," she said without hesitation.

"Tell me – why do you speak American to your dolls?"

"I like the way they talk there," she said. "If you say something like they say it in America, it sounds better."

Tom likes the schools on American TV. "They're more *realistic*," he says "than the school I go to . . .t." When he grows up, he'd like to settle-down stateside.

Does it matter? Yup, I think it does. Don't get me wrong – I've been to the place where my children "live", and I like it. But America is another place, a foreign country. I prefer England, goddammit! But my kids – and millions like them – have their own "special relationship" with the US of A – a one-way street of cultural colonisation.

And we – I'm sorry to whinge – are too demoralised, as people and as a country, to care. Anyway, we're all busy apeing America ourselves. So why not "live" there? – it is, after all, the Real Thing . . .

(The Guardian, 15 February 1995)

RESPONDING TO CULTURAL DIVERSITY

Chapter 1 of this book considered some of the ways in which health and care organisations had attempted to respond to equal opportunities and race relations legislation. These responses have included many recommendations for trying to understand more about the personal beliefs and preferences of different ethnic/cultural and religious groups. There have been attempts to understand more about differences in:

- the use of body language;
- touch (e.g. feelings about physical examinations);
- the distance between individuals (e.g. attitudes towards privacy);
- accepted forms of address and respect (e.g. attitudes towards professionals);
- diet;
- religious practices;
- preferences for types of medical treatment;
- birth and death customs (reactions to pain, loss and injury);
- sexual attitudes and roles;
- the language spoken and understood;
- washing and toiletting routines.

ACTIVITY

Study the comparisons made below between some of the religious and cultural beliefs of Jews and Hindus. What implications might these beliefs and practices have for people working with Jewish or Hindu clients?

Judaism

Social customs

- Modest dress for women – Jewish patients not to be treated in mixed wards.
- Medical treatment – Religious guidelines exist governing abortion, organ transplantation and donation, fertility treatment and contraception. No post-mortems permitted except in emergencies or when civil law requires.

Birth customs

- Pregnancy may be terminated during childbirth up to the point when the head has been delivered, if this is necessary to save the mother's life. After this point the life of the foetus may not be sacrificed even to save the mother's life.
- Circumcision of boys is usually carried out on the eighth day after birth.

Hinduism

Social customs

- Hindus prefer to wash themselves with running water, e.g. showers.
- Medical treatment – Hindu women generally much prefer to be treated by female staff.

Birth customs

- If possible, the mother and child should rest at home for 40 days after the birth, during which time the mother should not prepare food.

(Adapted from the *Concise Guide to Customs of Minority Ethnic Religions*, by D. Collins, M. Tank and A. Basith.)

Building on this tradition have been studies which have looked at the health beliefs of black and ethnic minority British people, because these may influence the types of conditions that people bring to doctors, how they present them to the doctor and, ultimately, the type and quality of the treatment or advice they may be given.

ACTIVITY

An interesting class exercise or opportunity for research would be to investigate different cultural perceptions of health and illness among fellow students or within your community. Some questions you might ask could be:

- What value do different ethnic/minority groups attach to 'health'?
- What approaches do people have towards 'becoming healthy' or being in 'perfect health'?
- How is illness/disease viewed?
- What is ill-health attributed to?
- What contact have people had with health (and care) services in Britain? Have these been positive or negative in any respects?

Other questions may be asked about different perceptions of specific illnesses, diseases, medical conditions or childbirth/death practices and beliefs.

Did any clear differences in health beliefs occur between members of various ethnic minority, cultural or religious groups? Were there more similarities than differences? How might you explain your findings?

These positive responses to cultural diversity, which try to take into account social influences on behaviour, recognise and respect different cultural practices. They also question stereotypical views and avoid over-broad generalisations.

> There is no such thing as the typical Asian patient, no more than there is a 'typical European patient' or a 'typical British patient'.
>
> *(McAvoy and Donaldson, 1990, p. 22)*

One of the factors which makes it difficult for health and social care professionals to respond to the needs of black and ethnic minority clients in the UK is that there is little published research about race and poverty or race and health.

WELFARE PROVISION

There is currently little published social policy research about race and poverty, and official statistics on welfare issues rarely contain a breakdown by ethnic origin. For a useful summary of what does exist, see Chapter 6 of Carey Oppenheim's book *Poverty: The Facts* (Oppenheim, 1993). Her analysis raises several issues which you may wish to explore in greater depth:

- Unemployment, low pay and poor working conditions are more likely to affect people from ethnic minorities in Britain than they are 'white' people.
- There is some evidence to show that while people from ethnic minorities (especially Asian people) are less likely overall to claim benefits, black people and other ethnic minority groups are more likely to claim Unemployment Benefit and Family Income Supplement.
- How far have racism and racial discrimination affected the delivery of welfare services and excluded ethnic minority groups from employment opportunities?
- To what extent have immigration policies disadvantaged people from ethnic minorities? The 1971 Immigration Act ruled that the wives and children of Commonwealth citizens could enter the UK only if a sponsor could support and accommodate them without recourse to 'public funds' such as Income Support, Housing Benefit and Family Credit.

HEALTH PROVISION

There is a similar 'invisibility' of black and ethnic minority groups in official studies of the health of the population. For an excellent discussion of race, ethnicity and health see Chapter 8 in *The Social Context of Health and Health Work* by Linda J. Jones (1994). Jones suggests the following:

- Most studies which have looked at the health of black and ethnic minority groups have tended to focus on patterns of morbidity (illness) and mortality (death) for adults born abroad (such as the Immigrant Mortality Study England and Wales 1970–1980). These studies have found that immigrant groups had higher mortality rates than average. However, Jones argues that this is more likely to be a reflection of the concentration of immigrant groups in lower social classes and semi-skilled and unskilled occupations, rather than their ethnic origin. This makes them more vulnerable to the health disadvantages associated with low income, poor housing and poor health care facilities and access to these (Jones, 1994, p. 306). Racial and class disadvantages reinforce each other.
- The more recent studies of black and ethnic minority groups indicate that their health concerns are similar to those of the rest of the population.
- Attempts to change the patterns of behaviour among ethnic minorities seem to be contributing to medical problems (e.g. exhorting Asian mothers to attend antenatal clinics more often in an effort to lower the risk of infant mortality) are racist because they ignore other issues such as social class or poverty which might also be linked to the problems experienced. For example, although babies born to Asian mothers have been found to be more at risk of infant mortality, the high rates of anaemia and low maternal weight of Asian women might better explain this than their reluctance to attend antenatal clinics. In other words, MATERIAL as well as CULTURAL factors might be at work.

ACTIVITY

Read the following extract from a newspaper and answer the questions below.

MINORITIES SUFFER POOR HEALTH CARE

BY CELIA HALL

Medical Editor

Two new studies of the health and lifestyles of black and ethnic minorities have revealed disquieting differences between these groups and the population as a whole.

The first national survey of behaviour and attitudes published today by the Health Education Authority (HEA) has found that health messages are not getting through.

The second survey, *Health, Race and Ethnicity*, from the King's Fund, the independent research organisation, echoes the theme. Chris Smaje, the report's author, said: 'Minority ethnic groups generally experience poorer quality contact with the health service than the white population. Caribbean people are more likely than whites to be committed compulsorily to psychiatric care and this occurs more often through the police."

The HEA survey, *Black and Minority Ethnic Groups in England*, a £330,000 investigation of Afro-Caribbean, Indian, Pakistani and Bangladeshi communities in England, found the health of these groups is being significantly damaged by cultural barriers and illiteracy.

At the same time, ethnic groups tended to suffer economic disadvantage, which increased their risks of ill health.

The report found high levels of illiteracy, and less understanding than in the general population of the significance of smoking, diet and weight on health.

Dr Michael Chan, director of the NHS Ethnic Health Unit, said: "The survey provides the most complete and up-to-date comparative data on the health of black and south-asian groups in England." He said it should help in targeting information about primary health care and cancer screening.

The survey found that health information had not been received or was not accepted.

A quarter of Indians and two in five Bangladeshis said they had not come across any health education at all. There was little interest in information about alcohol, drugs or contraception.

While only 15 per cent of women generally have never had a cervical smear, 30 per cent of Indian women, 46 per cent of Pakistani women and 60 per cent of Bangladeshi women have never been screened for signs of cervical cancer.

A third of Indian men who smoked said they did not know what effect it might have on their future health.

Both surveys are set against a background of greater incidence of diseases in the groups. The death rate among South Asians is 40 per cent higher and the risk of stroke in Afro-Caribbeans is double that of the general population.

(The Independent, 23 January 1995)

1 Briefly summarise the results of the two surveys discussed in the article.

2 The HEA survey claims that the health of Afro-Caribbeans, Indians, Pakistanis and Bangladeshis in Britain is being damaged significantly by *cultural barriers* and *illiteracy*. Why do you think that minority ethnic groups appear to experience poorer quality contact with the health services? What exactly are the 'cultural barriers' which may prevent better communication? Give possible examples.

3 What recommendations could you make to improve this situation?

4 Investigate in more depth the specific health and social care problems which may be faced by particular cultural groups in Britain. For example, Vietnamese refugees in Britain are often still an isolated group. Contact Deptford

Vietnamese Health Project in London for a useful report *Vietnamese Refugees: Towards a Healthy Future*.

5 People of West Indian origin in Britain apparently suffer from a higher rate of schizophrenia than the population as a whole. Why should this be? (The government has recently commissioned a three-year research project, in the north London borough of Haringey, to identify factors that may account for the high schizophrenia rate among black people.)

6 Certain ethnic minority groups in Britain are more likely than the population as a whole to be affected by the genetic conditions of sickle cell anaemia and thalassaemia. Is there sufficient research into the causes and treatment of these conditions? What services exist to help people affected by them?

The next section of this chapter takes a closer look at the ways in which health and well-being may be affected by socio-economic factors such as class and poverty. When studying this it will be worth returning to the issues raised here. Jones argues that:

> . . . a health policy which only tackles cultural barriers will not redress the structural inequalities that undermine attempts to provide an equal, comprehensive and needs-based health service. The problems that black and ethnic minority groups face – racial harassment, lower incomes, higher levels of unemployment and poor housing – continue to exist over time and continue to influence their health chances, both as patients and as health service workers.
>
> *(Jones, 1994, p. 328)*

THE EFFECT OF SOCIO-ECONOMIC FACTORS ON HEALTH AND SOCIAL WELL-BEING

Introduction – the political context

With politicians arguing that the amount of money which can be spent on health and social care services for people is limited, pressing questions on the relationship between health, social and economic circumstances become a prominent element in public and political debates. For example:

- What are the choices, or lack of them, which arise for individuals and families in relation to their health as a result of the income and other ECONOMIC RESOURCES (savings, winnings, inheritance, etc.) available to them?
- Can people be said to be contributing to their own ill-health by choosing to spend their money on an unhealthy lifestyle, by making the wrong choices in their diet and by showing a defeatist and passive response to difficult life situations?
- Alternatively, how might people's health be affected by social and economic factors outside their control?
- Even if there were total agreement upon what a healthy lifestyle was, would everyone be equally able to choose to follow it?
- What impact could differing levels of income and economic resources have on people's lifestyles, their resulting health and their ability to cope with life-event threats?

Government health education campaigns have generally targeted the individual and his or her lifestyle, exhorting us to exercise more frequently, eat less fat, avoid dangerous drugs and so on: in other words, implying that good health is to a very great extent within the grasp of anyone.

In Britain the right of everyone to health

care is increasingly being questioned, raising ethical dilemmas for medical and social workers about who should be treated or helped. Two articles reproduced here illustrate some of the current debates:

BEING ECONOMICAL WITH HEALTH

I am a first year undergraduate at the London School of Economics. I receive a London weighted grant of £2,845. In January I was diagnosed as having a kidney disease and a leaking heart valve and I have to take prescribed medication indefinitely. Also, my heart complaint means that I have to take prescribed antibiotics prior to dental treatment.

In the summer I have to make two visits to London to see consultants which will cost over £30 in rail fares. I did apply for help with NHS costs but as one who is not the 'most vulnerable' I have to pay £4.25 per prescription, dental charges up to £60 per course of treatment and travel costs up to £21 per week. Your leader writer is obviously not in my shoes. When s/he writes (May 21) that they have 'no quarrel' with prescription charges of £4.25.

(letter to the Guardian, 25 May 1993)

HEART SURGERY COULD BE LIMITED TO NON-SMOKERS

More hospitals are likely to adopt a formal policy of limiting vital heart surgery to non-smokers because of financial pressures and increasing waiting lists, a leading specialist on medical ethics said yesterday.

Commenting on reports that heart surgeons in Manchester and Leicester are turning away smokers who refuse to give up, Dr Richard Nicholson said: 'This is not surprising. In the long term it is the kind of decision that will be made much more frequently as the pressure on society not to waste health-care resources increases'. Similar policies are already in operation informally in hospitals around the country.

Dr Nicholson, editor of the *Bulletin of Medical Ethics*, said such policies were similar to those adopted in the early days of liver transplants, when alcoholics were excluded. 'It is an interesting ethical question for much wider debate', he said.

In a letter to the *British Medical Journal*, the Manchester surgeons said treating smokers was 'pointless'. They spend longer in hospital, were less likely than smokers to make a full recovery and more likely to need another operation.

(The Independent, 24 May 1993)

ACTIVITY

1 The letter to *The Guardian* reproduced in the text was written in response to government proposals in May 1993 to increase prescription charges to £4.25 per item. In what way does this writer believe that his or her ability to maintain his/her health is affected by his/her income?

2 What other groups (besides students) in the population of this country may face difficulties in paying for health and welfare services if they are not provided free of charge?

3 Investigate and make a list of charges including current prescription charges which are now made for health services and treatments within the NHS – for example, many dentists now refuse to take on new NHS patients and most dental treatments other than routine check-ups for adults now involve charges for most patients.

4 The article about heart surgery from *The Independent* quotes some Manchester surgeons as saying that 'treating smokers was "pointless" '. Do you agree that treatment should be withheld from those who could be argued to have contributed to their own ill-health?

5 Arrange a debate along the lines of question 4, both immediately before and

after embarking upon a study of this unit of work. In discussing the issues raised above, sociological evidence relating to income, class, poverty and unemployment will be discussed.

Using demographic characteristics to assess the health and social well-being of the population

Enquiry into the formation of health chances and social well-being has been influenced by the political context outlined above. Some of this research has focused upon structural health and welfare inequalities, while other investigations have stressed the influence of personal behaviour. In general, however, research producing definitions and assessments of the overall health and well-being of the population has been produced by:

- the medical profession;
- other health and welfare agencies;
- government enquiries resulting in reports;
- the analysis of these and other official statistics such as the *Census*, the *General Household Survey* and *Population Trends*.

A HEALTHY NATION

- Average lifespan is increasing by two years every decade: a boy born in 1996 can expect to live until he is 74, a girl until nearly 80
- Marked changes in the type of food we eat since the 1970s has led to an increase in the consumption of breakfast cereals, pre-cooked dishes and white meat, and a fall in the amount of eggs, sugar and red meat we buy
- Around a quarter of both men and women interviewed reported having at least one cardiovascular disease disorder
- More than two-thirds of adults had cholesterol levels above the desired level
- Around a fifth of all adults in England had not taken 20 minutes of moderate or vigorous exercise in the four weeks prior to being interviewed
- Male unskilled or manual workers are three times more likely to smoke than professionals
- Just over half of men and just under half of women aged 16 to 64 in England were overweight or obese in 1991–92
- Male unskilled or manual workers are three times more likely to smoke than professionals
- Nearly two in five men aged 18–24 drank more than the recommended maximum weekly amount
- During the six-month period ending 31 March 1993, over 20 000 people with drug problems sought help from drug services in the UK for the first time or after an absence of six months or more
- Death rates from lung cancer among males fell by almost half between 1971 and 1992 – but the rate for women rose by a sixth
- There were almost 26 million new out-patient attendances at NHS hospitals in 1993–94 – more than a fifth more than in 1981
- Suicide is three times more common among men than women
- On 31 March 1994 one in 16 hospital patients had waited over a year for admission, on 31 March 1991 it was one in six
- Government expenditure on the NHS in 1993/4 was more than three fifths more in real terms than 1976–77
- In 1993 there were 36 000 children on child protection registers in England, Wales and Northern Ireland – more than a third were considered at risk of physical injury
- The number of deaths in the UK is projected to rise from 658 000 deaths in 1993 to peak at 830 000 in 2051, when those born in the 1960s baby boom will be in their 80s
- The number of births each year in the UK is projected to exceed the number of deaths until the year 2027
- The proportion of lone mothers increased gradually until 1987, but since then has increased rapidly, so that almost one in five mothers with dependent children was a lone mother in 1992
- In 1993 there were 6.3 deaths per thousand

live births, which is nearly a third less than the rate five years ago
- The average stay as a hospital in-patient in 1993 was nine days for a male and seven days for a female
- The older we get the longer we stay in hospital – the average stay for a five to 15-year-old was four days compared with 14 days for someone aged 75 or over
- In 1993 it is estimated that 2 100 new AIDS cases will have been diagnosed in England and Wales. Sex between men and women accounted for nearly one in five of these cases in 1993, compared with one in nine in 1990

(Nursing Times, 8 February 1995)

As can be seen from the summary of the latest social trends above, these assessments of health and well-being can be based on an extremely wide range of factors, including:

- the incidence of disease or illness – morbidity;
- death or mortality rates;
- the incidence of disability and dysfunction;
- the incidence of suicide;
- life expectancy;
- infant mortality rates;
- crime rates;
- divorce rates;
- rates of abuse (racial, sexual, etc.).

The latest trends in some of these areas are given briefly below. Students are strongly advised to consult relevant publications (such as *Social Trends*, *Population Trends* or the *General Household Surveys* to extend and update their knowledge).

GENERAL POPULATION TRENDS – A SUMMARY

- The United Kingdom had a population of 58.0 million at mid-1992. The mid-1992 population estimate for England was 48.4 million, for Wales 2.9 million, for Scotland 5.1 million, and for Northern Ireland 1.6 million.
- The UK population is estimated to have increased by 197 thousand (0.34 per cent) between mid-1991 and mid-1992. This change is made up of increases of 170 thousand in England, 7 thousand in Wales, 4 thousand in Scotland, and 16 thousand in Northern Ireland. Northern Ireland had the largest increase in proportionate terms, 1.0 per cent, compared with 0.35 per cent in England, 0.24 per cent in Wales, and 0.08 per cent in Scotland.
- The total period fertility rate in England and Wales in 1992 was 1.80, as compared with 1.82 in 1991 and the long-term replacement level of 2.1.
- There were 690 thousand live births in 1992 in England and Wales, 9 thousand fewer than in 1991. Thirty-one per cent (215 thousand) were born outside marriage. Of these, 55 per cent were jointly registered by both parents who lived at the same address.
- The average age of mothers at childbirth, 27.9 years, was the highest since 1957.
- There were 854 thousand conceptions leading to a birth or a legal abortion in England and Wales in 1991, 2 per cent fewer than in 1990. The number of teenage conceptions fell by 10 per cent.
- The number of abortions of residents in England and Wales, having risen over a number of years to a peak in 1990, fell in 1992 for the second year running, to 160 thousand.
- The provisional number of marriages in England and Wales in 1992 was 311 thousand, up 1 per cent in 1991.
- Nearly a fifth of unmarried people in Great Britain aged 16–59 cohabit.
- The number of deaths in England and Wales in 1992 was 558 thousand, the lowest figure since 1967.
- Net civilian migration into the UK in 1992 was estimated at 34 thousand.
- There has recently been net migration from England to the other three countries of the UK. Within England in 1992 net migration out of the mainly urban regions towards the more rural ones continued.

(Daniel Capron, in Population Trends, *no. 75, Spring 1994)*

Table 4.10 Change in size of selected age-groups, England and Wales, 1981–1992

	Mid-year population (000)			Rate of change per thousand	
	1981	1991	1992	1981–91	1991–2
All ages	49,634	51,100	51,277	3	3
Children					
0–15	10,910	10,303	10,407	−6	10
0–4	3,006	3,431	3,455	13	7
5–9	3,196	3,223	3,259	1	11
10–15	4,708	3,650	3,694	−25	12
Working ages					
16–64/59[a]	29,796	31,351	31,402		2
16–29	10,425	10,892	10,674	5	−20
30–44	9,711	10,818	10,806	4	−1
45–64/59[a]	9,660	9,641	9,923	11	29
Pensionable ages				0	
65/60 and over[a]	8,928	9,446	9,467		2
65/60–74[a]	5,999	5,826	5,843		3
75–84	2,389	2,811	2,777	5	−12
85 and over	541	810	847	−3	47
				16	
				41	

[a]Pensionable age is 65 for men and 60 for women.
Source: Population Trends, no. 75, Spring 1994, data from Office of Population Censuses and Surveys.

AGE STRUCTURE

The age distribution of the population has changed in the last 30 years:

- the proportion of young people under 16 has fallen;
- the proportion of over-75s has increased.

Both these trends are expected to continue.

At present there are 33 children under 16 to every 100 people of working age. There are now also 30 people of pensionable age to every 100 of working age – a ratio which is projected to rise until 2031, when it is estimated that there will be nearly one person of pensionable age to every two of working age (using the pre-1995 pensionable ages of 65 for men and 60 for women) (*Population Trends*, Spring 1994).

MORTALITY

There were 634,000 deaths in the UK in 1992, a decrease of 2% on 1991. The *expectation of life at birth* is about 73 years for males and 79 years for females in England and Wales, a little lower for both in Scotland and Northern Ireland. The proportion of deaths due to respiratory diseases has fallen for all age groups, while the proportion caused by cancer has grown among females of all ages and men over 40 years. The proportion of *suicides* by young people, especially males, has increased sharply.

Every year, almost 5,000 people take their own lives in Britain, with young men, Asian women and country dwellers being particularly vulnerable. In the last 10 years, suicides of young men under 25 have gone up by 71% outnumbering women by 4 to 1. Suicides and attempted suicides among Asian women aged 15–24 have quadrupled since 1976, and they are three times as likely as white women of the same age to attempt to kill themselves – and 21.2 times more likely to succeed.

Infant mortality (in the first year of life) continues to decrease. Infant mortality rates (deaths under one year of age per 1,000 live births) decreased from 7.4 in 1991 to 6.6 in 1992 – the lowest recorded level. Perinatal mortality rates (stillbirths and deaths in the first week of life) were also, in 1992, the lowest ever recorded.

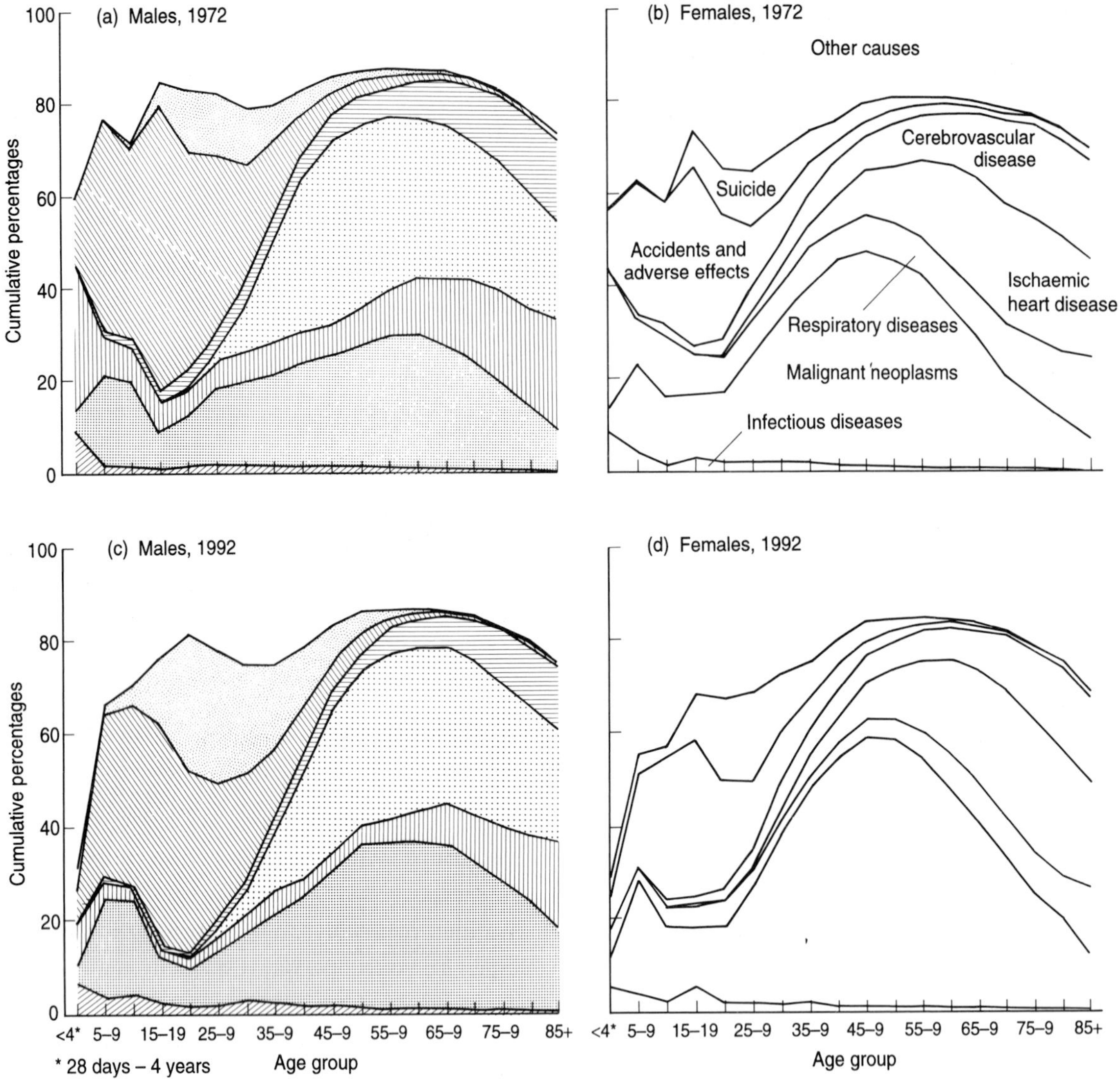

Figure 4.13 Causes of death in men and women of England and Wales, 1972 and 1992

DIVORCE

There has been an increase in divorce rates affecting all age groups. The 25–29 years age group shows the highest rate of divorce, among both men and women. Britain's divorce rate is the second highest in the European Union. It is estimated that one in four children born in 1994 will experience the divorce of their parents before they are 16 years old, if present trends continue.

Major influences on health and social well-being

DIFFERENCES IN INCOME, ECONOMIC RESOURCES AND WEALTH

A wide range of official reports covering the distribution of income, of personal wealth, of work and earnings and of the regional distribution of income, all confirm that the gap between the rich and the poor in Britain is growing wider.

In their book, *Income, Poverty and Wealth*, Thomas Stark and Giles Wright use official

Table 4.11 Divorce by duration of marriage, United Kingdom, 1961–1991

	Year of divorce			
Duration of marriage (%)	1961	1971	1981	1991
0–2 years	1.2	1.2	1.5	9.3
3–4 years	10.1	12.2	19.0	14.0
5–9 years	30.6	30.5	29.1	27.0
10–14 years	22.9	19.4	19.6	18.3
15–19 years	13.9	12.6	12.8	12.8
20–24 years		9.5	8.6	9.5
25–29 years	21.2	5.8	4.9	5.0
30 years and over		8.9	4.5	4.1
All durations (= 100%) (000)	27.0	79.2	155.6	171.1

Source: Social Trends 24, data from Office of Population Censuses and Surveys; General Register Office (Scotland). © *Crown copyright 1994.*

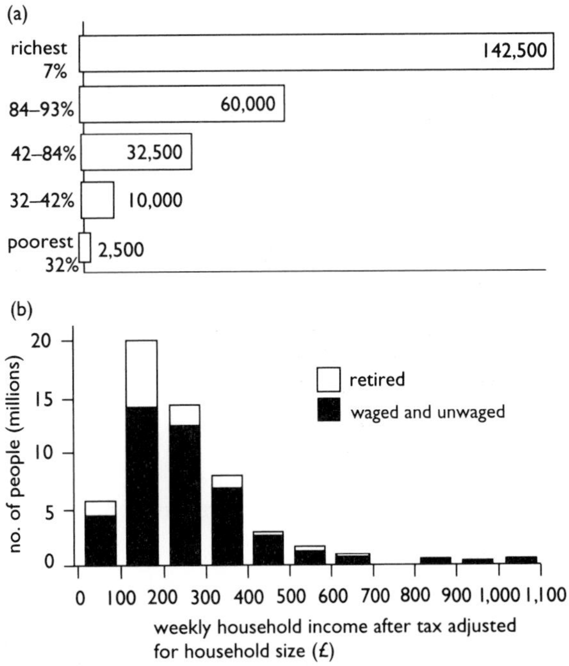

Figure 4.14 Wealth and income distribution
Source: The Guradian, 20 July 1993; wealth statistics from Inland Revenue, income distribution statistics from Institute for Public Policy Research

statistics and the result of government surveys to show how, throughout the 1980s, the share of disposable income taken by the top 10% of the population has steadily risen, while the poorest fifth of all households suffered a fall in their average income between 1987 and 1989. This trend was confirmed by a Labour Commission on Social Justice report in July 1993 which suggests that nearly two-thirds of the population has an income below the family average of £250 a week and that extremes of income are wider than at any time since 1886.

In February 1994 the Institute for Fiscal Studies published a study of tax trends in the past ten years. This showed that, over this period, the richest 10% of households in the UK have become £30 a week better off and the poorest 10% of households £3 a week worse off (reported in *The Guardian*, 9 February 1994).

There are also marked and widening regional differences in average household income. Greater London in the late 1980s was the most prosperous region, with average incomes 26% above the national average. At the other end of the scale, the least well-off regions – namely Northern Ireland and Wales – had average incomes only 73% and 82% respectively of the national average.

The *Regional Trends Survey* of 1993, published by the Central Statistical Office, indicates that weekly incomes are substantially higher in the south-east than in other parts of the country

Table 4.12 Divorce: by sex and age, England and Wales, 1961–1991 (per 1,000 married population)

	1961	1971	1981	1991
Males				
16–24	1.4	5.0	17.7	25.9
25–29	3.9	12.5	27.6	32.9
30–34	4.1	11.8	22.8	28.5
35–44	3.1	7.9	17.0	20.1
45 and over	1.1	3.1	4.8	5.6
All aged 16 and over	2.1	5.9	11.9	13.6
Females				
16–24	2.4	7.5	22.3	27.7
25–29	4.5	13.0	26.7	31.3
30–34	3.8	10.5	20.2	25.1
35–44	2.7	6.7	14.9	17.2
45 and over	0.9	2.8	3.9	4.5
All aged 16 and over	2.1	5.9	11.9	13.4

Source: Social Trends 24, data from Office of Population Censuses and Surveys. © *Crown copyright 1994.*

(it should be borne in mind that the cost of living is also higher in the south-east). One in five households in the south-east has a weekly income greater than £650. This rate is four times higher than in Northern Ireland.

Personal wealth remains concentrated among the richest 10% of the population – a trend confirmed by the latest in a line of similar reports. The Joseph Rowntree Foundation Inquiry into Income and Wealth reports that:

ROWNTREE REPORT:

- Gap between rich and poor greatest since second world war
- Since 1977, number with income less than half the average trebled
- Twice as many children in poorest 10th of society as in top 10th
- Richest 10th of population owns half of country's wealth

(The Guardian, 10 February 1995)

Table 4.13 Registrar-General's classification of social class

Social class		Examples of occupations
I	Professional	Lawyer, doctor
II	Intermediate	Teacher, nurse, manager
III(NM)	Skilled non-manual	Typist, shop assistant
III(M)	Skilled manual	Miner, cook, electrician
IV	Semi-skilled manual	Farm worker, packer
V	Unskilled manual	Cleaner, labourer

POVERTY

There is no official definition of poverty. Two poverty lines drawn from official and quasi-official data are commonly used:

- Income Support level;
- 50% of average income after housing costs.

In her book, *Poverty: The Facts*, Carey Oppenheim (1993) suggests that:

- Using either poverty line, between 11 million and 12 million people in the UK were living in poverty in 1988/89.
- In 1988/89, 4.4 million people were living below the level of the government's 'safety net' of Income Support. A principal reason for this is the low take-up of benefits. According to government figures, one in four of those eligible for Income Support do not claim it, and around one in two do not claim Family Credit to which they are entitled.
- Certain groups face especially high risks of poverty: 50% of lone-parent families, 42% of single pensioners, 69% of families where the breadwinner(s) are unemployed and 26% of families with an adult in part-time work lived in poverty (defined as below 50% of average income after housing costs) in 1988/89. There are no poverty figures broken down by ethnic origin, but Afro-Caribbeans and Asians have much higher rates of unemployment and are more likely to have low wages or to rely on inadequate benefits.
- Between 1979 and 1988/89 the composition of the poorest 10% of the population changed: pensioners fell from 31% to 14% of the poorest 10%; families with children grew from 50% to 54%; and single people without children more than doubled from 10% to 22%.

ACTIVITY

Examine the points made about those in poverty.

1. Work out what proportion of the total population of the UK is below the 'poverty line'.
2. Suggest reasons why the take-up of benefits is low.
3. Why do certain groups face a higher risk of poverty than others?
4. What factors could account for the changing composition of the poorest 10%?

Children are more at risk of poverty than the rest of society

Children growing up in lone-parent families have a much higher risk of poverty. In 1989, over three-quarters (76%) of children in lone-parent families – 1.4 million – were living in poverty (defined as on or below Income Support level), compared with 13% of children in two-parent families – 1.35 million.

A survey undertaken by the Department of Health and published at the beginning of 1995, showed a record number of children being placed on protection registers. The figure for 1993/4 was 28,500; 15% more than the previous year. A spokesman for the Association of Directors of Social Services commented that likely factors included:

- stresses caused by the rising number of marriage break-ups,
- the growing number of lone parents,
- the increase in families living on social security.

In 1985, there were one million children living on income support; in 1995 there were 3 million. The Association believed that there was a direct correlation between these figures and the increased number of referrals.

Women are more at risk of poverty than men

The Child Poverty Action Group estimates that in 1989 around 5.1 million women were living in poverty (defined as on or below Income Support level), compared with 3.4 million men. Low wages, lone parenthood and inadequate social security benefits and childcare provision all contribute to women's poverty.

ACTIVITY

The statistics quoted here give only the briefest introduction to the debate about levels of income, wealth and inequality in Britain. Use secondary sources to investigate these issues in more depth.

How have these factors been studied in relation to health?

The broad conclusion of most studies investigating the relationship between levels of income, economic resources and health is that deprivation and inequality in income, housing and employment status contribute to inequalities in health. Key pieces of research include the Black Report on *Inequalities in Health* (1980), *The Health Divide* by the Health Education Council (1987) and *The Nation's Health* (1988). (For details see the References list at the end of the chapter; see also Chapter 5.)

Drawing mainly on data published in the 1970s, the Black Report concluded that despite the existence for more than thirty years of a health service expressly committed to offering equal care for all, there remained a marked class gradient in standards of health, with substantial increases in the rates of both mortality and morbidity (illness) as one moves down the social class scale from class I (professional workers) to class V (unskilled manual workers). Moreover, not only did the report draw attention to the large inequalities in health between the social classes, it also argued that these differences were not declining. Indeed, the report pointed out that social class differentials in mortality, as measured by standardised mortality ratios (SMRs), had *increased* since the 1930s.

The extent of the class inequalities in health was perhaps most dramatically illustrated by the calculation of what the Black Report called 'excess deaths'. Using data for England and Wales, it calculated that if classes IV and V had had the same mortality rate as class I, then during the three-year period from 1970–72, the lives of 74,000 people under the age of seventy-five would not have been lost. This estimate included the 'excess' deaths of almost 10,000 children.

(Waddington, 1989)

SOCIAL CLASS is the most widely used indicator of the social and economic circumstances of individuals. In the study of health inequalities, social class is used to show how social and economic circumstances are related to the health experiences and expectations of individuals. It may be argued by some that since the end of the Second World War overall living standards in the UK have risen. People have more opportunity to purchase consumer goods, take holidays abroad and live in clean and sanitary housing, for example. Nevertheless, most social scientists believe that social class is still an important factor in the distribution of life-chances, although there is fierce debate about the extent to which people perceive themselves to 'belong' to a particular social class and whether or not their behaviour is affected by their class position. It may be misleading, for example, to see 'the poor' as one class: different groups of people may be poor for very different reasons. Gender and race may be factors as important as class in explaining people's position in society.

There are different ways of defining social class, but for the purposes of research, social scientists carrying out large-scale research have tended to measure social class in terms of one single factor: OCCUPATION.

The Black Report and many other pieces of research have used occupational class scales such as the Registrar-General's Scale. According to this classification:

- men are allocated a social class according to their own occupation;
- married women are ascribed the social class of their husband;
- children in two-parent families are ascribed the social class of their father;
- single women living alone, or with their children, are allocated a social class according to their own occupation.

As Clare Blackburn writes, many criticisms have been directed at the use of this measurement of class:

Some groups are poorly described by measures of social class based on occupations, for example, those who have never had a job, those who do not have a job now and married women who are classified according to their husband's social class.

The Registrar-General's classification is based on a hierarchy that reflects the traditional status of male occupations. It does not always accurately reflect the status or experiences associated with women's occupations.

It ascribes to all members of the same family the same social class. Thus it fails to recognize that some members of a family may experience poorer social and economic circumstances than others.

Social-class measures do not reflect that social class experiences are different for Black people and white people, just as they are for men and women.

(Blackburn, 1991)

Other researchers have also suggested that there is a need to find better measures of inequality in populations. Illsley has suggested that the top 20% of the population should be compared with the bottom 20%. Others have argued that large-scale research should at least be supplemented with smaller-scale studies which look in more depth at how inequalities are generated and sustained in everyday life.

Recently there has been some controversial debate about the concept of 'underclass'. Originally a term used by some sociologists to describe groups of the population so disadvantaged in relation to the majority that they could not even be considered part of a 'working class' (they might experience extremely high levels of unemployment, homelessness, social problems), in 1989 it became a more familiar term in use by the media. This was largely because an American, Charles Murray, began to publish, in the UK, his view of the underclass. Murray is a right-wing writer who argues that state benefits should largely be withdrawn, forcing people to bear the consequences of their behaviour. He argues that the underclass in Britain is made up of single parents and unmarried mothers whose lack of control over their children is a direct cause of high crime rates, high structural unemployment and the decline of the family. These views appeared to fit in well with the Conservative government's 'Back to Basics' campaign – itself subject to much debate.

ACTIVITY

1 Do you consider yourself as belonging to a particular social class? If so, which one? Use this question to start a discussion about people's definitions of class. How could or should it be defined?

2 There is no official definition of poverty. Would you agree with the definitions of poverty adopted in Oppenheim's study (those relying on Income Support or those who receive only 50% of the average national income after housing costs)?

3 The following is one attempt by social scientists to draw up a list of conditions which could be held to represent 'underprivilege' (the Jarman 8 underprivileged area index). The more factors which apply to a household from the list, the more likely they are to be underprivileged. Do you agree that this list could be a useful way to measure underprivilege? Could you write a better one?

- elderly living alone;
- under five years old;
- one-parent household;
- unskilled head of household;
- unemployed;
- lacking exclusive use of a basic amenity;
- a household with more than one person per room;
- has moved house within 12 months;
- was born in the New Commonwealth or Pakistan.

Trends in income, class and health

- At almost every age, people in the poorer social classes (IV and V) have higher rates of illness and death than people in wealthier social classes (I and II).
- A study by Smith *et al.* (1990), reported in the *British Medical Journal*, argued that the disparity in death rates between the social classes is widening and that as changes in income distribution continue to occur, such disparities can be expected to increase. Good health and longevity are most directly related to levels of affluence.
- Blaxter (1990), analysing data from the Health and Lifestyles Survey, has found that the apparent strong association between social class and health was primarily one of income and health. Other studies have shown how changes in income levels can correlate with changes in health. This may explain how social class differences in health can widen, despite rises in absolute income and living standards. Around the year 1950, the proportion of the population living in relative poverty was at its lowest level since 1921, with only 8% of the population living in relative poverty. By 1987 the number of people living in poverty had risen to 28% of the population. With overall rises in living standards over the century, death rates for the poor have not fallen as fast as death rates for the rich. Being healthy seems, then, to require a level of income which allows families to enjoy similar living standards and participate in a similar way as families with higher incomes (adapted from Blackburn, 1991).

The following trends are taken from Blackburn (1991):

- In 1986, babies born to social class IV and V families were 148% more likely to die in the perinatal period than babies born to social class I and II families.
- In 1986, babies born to parents in social

classes IV and V had a 178% greater chance of dying in the post-neonatal period than babies of social class I and II parents.

- Two-thirds of all low birth-weight babies are born to working-class mothers.
- The mortality rate for all causes of death tells us that children aged one to five, from social classes IV and V, are twice as likely to die as their counterparts from social classes I and II.
- Large-scale longitudinal studies show that children from manual classes suffer more respiratory infections and diseases, ear infections and squints, and are likely to be of shorter stature than their counterparts in non-manual classes.
- Children from manual social classes are also more likely to have less healthy teeth. In 1983, children from manual social classes had twice as many decayed teeth as their counterparts in non-manual classes.
- Surveys indicate that class inequalities in health experiences between classes are greatest for limiting long-standing illnesses, with unskilled manual classes reporting rates that are double those of professional classes, less steep for long-standing illness and only evident for acute illness reporting at age 45 and over.

ACTIVITY

1 Carry out research, using secondary sources, into the differences in levels of MORBIDITY and MORTALITY by social class for illnesses not mentioned here, such as cancers, heart disease, high blood pressure, obesity, arthritis, haemorrhoids, alcohol-related disease and mental illness.

2 What possible explanations can there be for the trends illustrated above?

Unemployment and health

Most research shows beyond doubt that there is an association between unemployment and ill-health. Mortality rates, rates of long-standing illness, rates of disability and rates of psychological disturbance have all been shown to be higher among the unemployed than among those with jobs. A higher risk of suicide and diseases such as stomach ulcers has also been traced in part to the effect of unemployment.

Ill-health may occur as a result of:

- the threat of job loss;
- the actual event;
- the state of being out of work.

ACTIVITY

An important question, of course, is whether poor health leads to or results in unemployment or whether the reverse effect occurs. Read the extract below and discuss the issue in relation to this case.

When news filtered through last May of possible mine closures – Westoe among them, Mr Frelford, whose job was looking after the skip-loading plant, started to worry. Work was hard to come by in a borough where unemployment is 26.7 per cent. There was a time when he might have got a job in the shipyards as an electrician, but Swan Hunter's failure to win a £170 million contract for a Royal Navy helicopter carrier ruled that out. Younger men might retrain, but he was 39. Colleagues took jobs as security guards, or cleaners for £1.60 an hour – but they worked 80-hour weeks, and he had a family.

Black October came and went. The 800 miners at Westoe were told that the colliery might shut in six weeks or six months. Some were ecstatic: they were the older ones, looking forward to a handsome redundancy payoff and an early retirement. Mr Frelford did not take the news well. For the next six months of uncertainty he suffered from not being able to plan, of thinking 'this week is the last week'.

There were reports that he had taken time off work for 'anxiety', that he had had a breakdown and been taken into hospital.

He came back to work looking normal. He

worked as conscientiously as ever. 'But it played on his mind,' said Michael Meughen, 44, a colleague. 'It must have done. But I didn't know anything about it.'

He was the kind of man who drank three pints at most, exchanged a few words about football and then went off home to the wife.

Last Wednesday, David Frelford took his children to school, as he did every day, and went in to see John Pattison, Mowbray Junior School's headteacher. 'He was showing genuine concern about Jack', said Mr Pattinson. 'There were no problems mentioned. I knew he had been made redundant . . . but he seemed perfectly happy.'

On Thursday morning, David Frelford dropped his children off, went home, put the chain on the front door and bolted the back door at the top and bottom. Then he wrote a note, climbed the stairs, went into the bathroom, poured petrol over his clothes and with a match, set himself alight.

(The Independent, 24 May 1993)

Housing and health

People who live in unhealthy homes usually suffer from other forms of social and economic disadvantage, so it becomes difficult to disentangle the effect of housing conditions on health from other factors. Moreover, there may be links between housing conditions and health not necessarily linked to poverty. For example, it has been suggested that the trend towards centrally heated homes with fitted carpets has increased the likelihood of allergies resulting from 'dust mites'.

Nevertheless, the strong relationship between health and housing can be related to four aspects of that housing:

- geographical location – where people live;
- patterns of tenure;
- the poor layout and design of homes;
- costs of fuel and other essential services.

GEOGRAPHICAL LOCATION

Low-income families, especially one-parent families and black families, are much more likely to be housed in neighbourhoods that are unattractive, densely populated, with poorly maintained houses and few communal areas and amenities.

The concept of ENVIRONMENTAL POVERTY can be used to refer to housing areas where there is a lack of, or lack of access to, gardens, parks, play space, shopping facilities, health centres, etc. Pollution from noise, litter, dirt and airborne pollutants such as metal particles (e.g. lead) can also be a factor in environmental pollution in inner cities and areas near industrial plants. Psychological and stress-related illnesses may be higher in environmentally poor areas, along with respiratory illnesses, chesty coughs, etc. Infections caused by poor hygiene facilities may also be increased.

Child accident rates are higher among poorer social groups and can be linked to the difficulties of supervising children in environmentally poor areas. The Child Accident Prevention Trust estimates that 250,000 childhood accidents a year can be attributed to bad housing design.

Homelessness may be considered under this heading. Surveys of the living conditions of families in hotel accommodation and their health status show that this accommodation is often overcrowded and insanitary, with poor access to cooking facilities.

The number of empty homes in England has risen by 30 per cent in 10 years to reach an all-time high of 864,000, according to local authority returns reaching the Department of the Environment.

Over the same period, the recorded figure for the number of homeless has more than doubled from roughly 170,000 people in 1983 to more than 400,000 today.

In both cases, the figures (see Figure 4.15) are thought to represent only a fraction of actual totals.

(The Guardian, 1994)

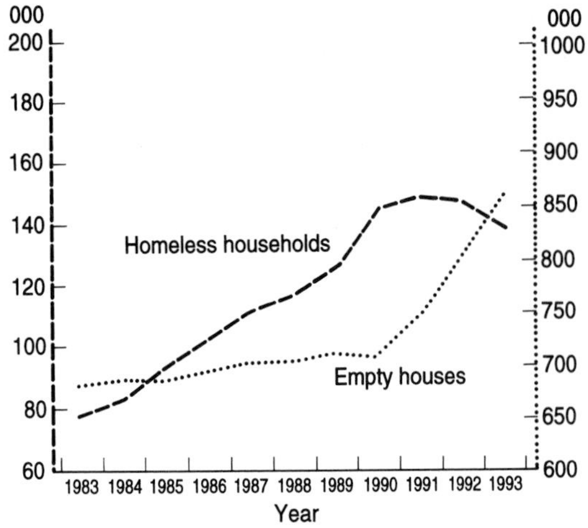

Figure 4.15 Homes: supply and demand, 1983–1993 *Source*: Shelter

PATTERNS OF TENURE

Research shows that owner-occupiers are likely to have the lowest death rates and council tenants the highest. A study by Kogevina (1990) showed that male council-house tenants were more likely to die from cancer of the face, oesophagus, stomach, larynx, bladder and lungs, and women tenants were especially more likely to die from cancer of the cervix, than owner-occupiers.

Damp is a major health hazard in certain types of rented accommodation, especially when families cannot afford to heat their homes. Spores from fungi in damp or dilapidated housing appear to lead to a greater frequency of respiratory symptoms, e.g. wheezing, runny noses, sore throats, headaches, fever and irritability. If children are adversely affected, their progress and development at school may also be impeded by frequent absence. Certain viruses also appear to thrive in damp conditions.

POOR LAYOUT AND DESIGN OF HOMES

Children who live in flats have higher incidences of respiratory infections than children who live in houses.

People who live in flats have higher incidences of emotional disturbances and mental health problems. Parents worry about the safety of their children. Vandalism, graffiti and racial and sexual attacks are increased where flat or block design is poor and there is no clear responsibility for communal areas or walkways.

People with disabilities often have great difficulty adapting small houses to their needs: for example, rooms are often too small to accommodate wheelchairs.

Lack of privacy and storage space in overcrowded homes can lead to considerable domestic tensions and physical and psychological problems.

COST OF FUEL AND OTHER ESSENTIAL SERVICES

Where low income affects housing choice, it also affects the 'choice' of fuel for many families. Owner-occupiers may more often be able to choose the form of heating they prefer. Tenants usually cannot. Fuel bills are often high because of damp conditions, condensation and poor insulation. They usually account for a greater proportion of the expenditure of low-income families than of higher-income families. They are often a major source of debt; gas disconnection rates have risen since 1981.

The imposition of high VAT rates on fuel bills (8% in 1994–5 and due eventually to reach 17.5%) has also caused controversy. Consumer groups and charities, such as Age Concern, have argued that high VAT rates on fuel bills hit the elderly on low incomes particularly hard despite, in 1994, an increase in weekly pensions of 50p for single people and 70p for couples. Elderly people may restrict their use of heating, thus putting them at risk of illness and hypothermia. The government claims that cold weather payments to vulnerable people on income support (£8.50 in 1994–5) and home insulation grants could alleviate many problems.

A newer source of debt and disconnection for lower-income families is failure to pay water rates. Research published in March 1995 by the Policy Studies Institute, suggests that rapidly rising levels of water bills have forced almost two million households into debt and danger of disconnection (Herbert and Kempson, 1995). With rising rates of water disconnections in the news, some people are asking whether this may soon become an additional and serious source of health risk to low-income families.

Physiological, psychological and behavioural effects of poverty

The following outlines a few of the main effects on health of low income, poverty and lack of economic resources. It should be used as a basis only for further discussion and research.

PHYSIOLOGICAL EFFECTS: POVERTY AND DIET

In June 1991 the National Children's Home charity commissioned a survey on the eating habits of low-income families in Britain. The results suggested that one in five parents regularly denied themselves food through lack of money, and one in ten children under the age of five went without enough to eat at least once a month. The report claimed to have found a direct relationship between those on the lowest income and those with the poorest diet.

The National Children's Bureau study of child poverty in 1993 argued that there is unmistakable evidence of a sharp rise in child poverty since 1979. This means that there are more children living in temporary accommodation such as bed and breakfast, with the adverse effects that this is likely to have on their health and education. There are also more children exposed to health problems because of poor housing. There is a link between prolonged unemployment and family breakdown, exposing more children to the stresses that this involves; and more children eat a poor diet, thereby becoming exposed to possible adverse effects on their physical growth and development.

Studies such as these have often provoked politicians into claiming that, with careful planning and shopping, one could eat a very healthy diet on Income Support levels.

TORY TELLS POOR TO GROW OWN VEG. TURN OFF TV AND STOP MOANING, HE SAYS.

Tory Toby Jessel made a turnip of himself last night by saying the poor should grow their own vegetables to save cash.

The wealthy MP told them to stop moaning about having no money, stop watching so much telly and get allotments.

He said: "If more people could be encouraged to have allotments and grow vegetables, then if they are in poverty that would help alleviate their situation."

His advice came as Tory MPs and ministers hit out at an independent report which said the nation's poor are getting poorer.

Cabinet Minister John Redwood added to the uproar by saying hard-up mums should quit smoking and breast-feed babies to save money.

Maverick MP Mr Jessel told a Commons debate that in his constituency of Twickenham, West London, a third of allotments were disused. Mr Jessel, 60, who lives in a mansion next door to Hampton Court Palace, said: "No one wants to be bothered.

"They sit in front of the television for hours on end, complaining about their poverty and not growing vegetables when they could do so easily and cheaply."

Shadow social security minister Donald Dewar said: "Allotments are fine.

But I am much more worried by evidence that life expectancy in poor areas is ten years less than in leafy suburbs."

Garden

Last night Mr Jessel defended his remarks, saying: 'I have a garden and growing vegetables is enjoyable. My speech was very close to the real world."

Welsh Secretary Mr Redwood, 43, rapped Labour and the BBC for backing claims in the Rowntree Report that poverty has worsened.

Labour's Nigel Griffiths said: 'Anyone who thinks powdered milk and smoking are prime causes of poverty needs their head examined."

(The Sun, 16 February 1995)

PSYCHOLOGICAL EFFECTS

Poverty appears to increase the number of stressful life events for families and makes it more difficult to overcome the stresses.

Poverty can mean relative powerlessness and lack of control over events which can increase a sense of helplessness and depressive illness.

The coping mechanisms to which people may resort to overcome stress may lead to worse problems, e.g. drug abuse, heavy consumption of alcohol, smoking.

BEHAVIOURAL EFFECTS

Here we return to the questions posed at the beginning of this section. The poor are often chastised and urged to act more responsibly by choosing healthier lifestyles and behaviours.

Is this a realistic and fair criticism?

ACTIVITY

Politicians often claim that it is possible to eat healthily on Income Support levels.

1 How far do you agree with this claim?

2 In a group in your school or college, design a diet to feed yourselves for three or four weeks on the amount of money you would have if you were on Income Support.

Social policy, health and well-being

Demographic, social and economic trends affecting populations, households and families are only some of the influences on the ways in which social policies are constructed and health and welfare services provided. There are many other influences, political, economic and social.

Part of the problem in analysing and accounting for policy changes is that we encounter a 'chicken and egg' situation. To what extent have governments incorporated their awareness of current social changes into the construction of social policies, and to what extent have some social policies and forms of welfare provision actually driven or caused social change, e.g. further or increased incidence of ill-health, poverty and need for support? This leads to problems for researchers, politicians and members of the public in trying to measure or determine the 'effect' of social changes on a particular social policy or element of health or welfare provision. Some writers, such as Malcolm Wicks, have suggested that governments should, when proposing new policies or legislation, always try to work out in advance what the likely or intended effect of these policies and proposals would be on families. These, he suggests, could be written out as a 'family impact statement' (see Wicks, 1991).

ACTIVITY

Working in small groups, try to produce a 'family impact statement' for each of the following (as yet imaginary) welfare policy proposals. What do you think the likely effects of these proposals on the health and well-being of families would be? What other information would you ideally need to be able to produce one of these statements 'for real'?

Policy proposals

1 To abolish, from the beginning of the next financial year, universal child benefit. Child benefit would be payable only to those mothers on low incomes and would become a means-tested benefit.

2 To provide nursery school places for all three year-olds whose parents wanted them for their children.

3 To provide a new and expanded national network of Well Woman and Well Man clinics in every local area of the country.

4 To make statutory provision for three months' paid paternity leave for men and to extend and improve maternity pay.

5 To raise benefits for lone-parent families.

6 To pass a law forbidding both parents to be in full-time paid employment if they have children of pre-school age.

ACTIVITY

Debate and discuss the following.

1 What evidence is there that structural inequalities in health exist in Britain?

2 Who is responsible for 'the nation's health'?

REFERENCES AND RESOURCES

Adams, C. (1982), *Ordinary Lives a Hundred Years Ago*. London: Virago.

Anderson, A. (1978), *Old is not a four letter word*, Across the Board Journal (May issue).

Atkinson, R.L. (1993), *Introduction to Psychology*, 11th ed. US: Harcourt Brace Jovanovich College Publishers.

Black Report (1980), *Inequalities in Health*. London: Penguin.

Blackburn, C. (1991), *Poverty and Health: Working with Families*. Oxford: OUP.

Brown (1973), *A First Language – the early stages*, London: Allen and Unwin.

Capron, D. (1994), 'A Review of 1992', *Population Trends*, vol. 75.

Collins, D., Tank, M. and Basith, A. (1993), *Concise Guide to Customs of Minority Ethnic Religion*. Hampshire: Arena.

Coopersmith (1967), *The antecedents of self esteem*, San Fransisco: Freeman.

Davenport, G.C. (1994), *An Introduction to Child Development*, London: HarperCollins.

Dawkins, R. (1991) *The Selfish Gene*, Oxford University Press.

Dobraszczyc, U. (1989), *Sickness, Health and Medicine*, Sociology in Focus series. London: Longman.

Eysenck, H. (1991), *Know Your Own Personality*. London: Penguin.

Finkelhor (1980), *Risk factors in the sexual vicitimisation of children*, Child Abuse and Neglect (volume 4).

Giddens, A. (1989), *Sociology*, Cambridge: Polity Press.

Gillham, B. (1991), *The Facts about Child Sexual Abuse*. London: Cassell Educational.

Gross, R. (1992), *Psychology: The Science of Mind and Behaviour*, 2nd ed. Sevenoaks: Hodder and Stoughton.

Hayes, N. (1984), *A First Course in Psychology*. Walton-on-Thames: Nelson.

Hayes, N. and Orrell, S. (1993), *Psychology: An Introduction*, 2nd ed. London: Longman.

Health Education Council (1987), *The Health Divide*. London: HEC.

Herbert, A. and Kempson, E. (1995), *Water, Debt and Disconnection*. Policy Studies Institute and the National Consumer Council.

Jones, D.N. and Pickett, J. (1993), *Understanding Child Abuse*, 2nd ed. London: Macmillan Educational.

Jones, L. (1994), *The Social Context of Health and Health Work*. London: Macmillan Press Ltd.

Kumar, V. (1993), *Poverty and Inequality in the UK: The Effects on Children*. London: National Children's Bureau.

Leach, P. (1993), 'Should Parents Hit Their Children?' in *The Psychologist*, vol. 6, no. 5, May 1993.

McAvoy and Donaldson (1990), *Health Care for Asians*. Oxford: Oxford Medical Publications.

Oppenheim, C. (1993), *Poverty: The Facts*. London: Child Poverty Action Group.

Robertson, J. and J. (1989), *Separation and the Very Young*. London: Free Association Books.

Rutter, M. (1988), *Maternal Deprivation Re-assessed*. London: Penguin.

Schacter and Singer (1962), *Cognitive, social and physiological determinants of emotional state*, Psychological Review Journal.

Skellington, R. and Morris, P. (1992), *'Race' in Britain Today*. London: Sage.

Skinner, B.F. (1957), *Verbal Behaviour*, New York: Appleton Century Crofts.

Social Services Yearbook 1993. London: Longman Community Information and Reference.

Social Trends 24 (1994), London: HMSO.

Tucker, N. (1990), *Adolescence*. London: Wayland.

Waddington, I. (1989), 'Inequalities in Health', *Social Studies Review*, January 1989.

Wicks, M. (1991), 'Family Matters and Public Policy', in M. Loney *et al. The State or the Market: Politics and Welfare in Contemporary Britain*, 2nd ed. London: Sage.

5

THE STRUCTURE AND DEVELOPMENT OF HEALTH AND SOCIAL CARE SERVICES

In a rapidly changing area such as health and social care it is essential to have really up-to-date information on the organisation of its planning and provision. This is provided in Chapter 5, along with many suggestions for activities in both the classroom and workplace.

THE PROVISION OF HEALTH AND SOCIAL CARE SERVICES AND FACILITIES

Provision of health and social care is through a combination of STATUTORY, VOLUNTARY and PRIVATE ORGANISATIONS with INFORMAL CARE playing an important part.

ACTIVITY

What do you understand by the terms:

- statutory;
- voluntary;
- private;
- informal?

Give examples of each.

Health care

STATUTORY PROVISION

The central government department responsible for health and personal social (welfare) services is the DEPARTMENT OF HEALTH (DoH). Each government department is headed by a Minister, who may be designated Secretary of State.

The Secretary of State for Health is responsible for the broad policy and central administration of health and welfare services.

ACTIVITY

1 Who is the current Secretary of State for Health?

2 What do you know of their actions in this role?

On a local level the provision of health services is the responsibility of the regional and district health authorities of the National Health Service (NHS), and the welfare services are provided through Personal Social Services (or social work) Departments of local authorities.

The NHS was introduced in 1948 as one area of welfare expansion pioneered by the Beveridge report and fought for by the then Labour minister Aneurin Bevan. It is now a central part of the country's 'health care system' but is not the only agent or organisation which provides health care. (The debate over what actually constitutes health care is too wide to be considered here. Individuals, families, communities, the personal social services, the private sector (e.g. the pharmaceutical companies and private hospitals), the media (in health promotion campaigns), the trade unions, local government and international organisations (such as the Red Cross) can all be said to be providing resources for improving people's health.)

The NHS has undergone several changes and reorganisations since 1948; these have been the outcome of discussions between 'government ministers and civil servants on the one hand, and a range of pressure groups on the other' (Ham, 1992, p. 7), with the medical profession, represented by the British Medical Association (BMA), being perhaps the most influential of these groups.

The key features of the NHS were that:

- the services should be provided *universally* to everyone;
- it would be funded mainly from general taxation, with National Insurance contributions making up only a small part of the total finance.

By 1987, however, a widening gap had emerged between the money provided by the government for the NHS and the funding needed to meet increasing demand (Ham, 1992, p. 44). In response to this, an extra £101 million was to be spent in the UK on health services and a new ministerial review of the future of the NHS initiated. This review did not directly tackle the funding shortfall which had emerged in the 1980s, but focused on how resources could be used more effectively through changes to the delivery of health services. It proposed:

- that hospitals should compete for resources in an internal market;
- that doctors should be made more accountable for their performance;
- that doctors should be more involved in management;
- that general management must be promoted.

Two White Papers, *Working for Patients* and *Caring for People*, paved the way for the NHS and Community Care Act 1990. This Act triggered another wave of reforms of the NHS. The Act retained the principle (in theory) of a health service available to all, free at the point of delivery and financed mainly by taxation. The most significant change was an attempt by the government to improve efficiency and quality in services by separating the *purchase* of health care from its *provision*.

Providers in the NHS were divided into three groups:

1. *Primary care:*
   - the general practice system;
   - indicative prescribing budgets (the amount of money GPs are allowed to spend on drugs for their patients);
   - the dental service.
2. *Secondary care:*
   - hospitals;
   - NHS Trusts;
   - directly managed units;
   - waiting lists;
   - the independent sector.
3. *Tertiary care:*
   - specialised treatment in a highly developed unit.

Purchasers and their organisations were divided into four groups:

1. *Purchasers of primary care:* family health service authorities.
2. *Purchasers of secondary care:*
   - district health authorities;
   - GP fundholders.
3. *Regional health authorities.*
4. *Special health authorities.*

This division of functions was promoted by:

- offering GPs new contracts with the NHS whereby they could become fundholders, controlling their own budgets;
- allowing hospitals to become self-governing Trusts, run by boards of directors accountable to the Department of Health;
- a move, in general, towards 'care in the community', with the future intention that hospitals will eventually care almost entirely for the acutely ill rather than

provide long-term care for the elderly or mentally ill, as some do at present.

In 1991, health authorities lost responsibility for providing health care and instead became purchasers of services from competing hospitals and Trusts.

In 1992, the government introduced the Patient's Charter which claimed to set out three important new rights for the public in relation to health services. These were:

- to be given detailed information on local health services, including quality standards and maximum waiting times;
- to be guaranteed admission for treatment by a specific date no later than two years from the day when your consultant places you on a waiting list;
- to have any complaint about NHS services – whoever provides them – investigated and to receive a full and prompt written reply from the chief executive or general manager.

The structure of the NHS is constantly changing. Eight English regional health authorities were set up in April 1994, replacing the previously existing 14 (see Figure 5.1). More changes are to follow and it is currently proposed that district health authorities will be merged with family health service authorities from April 1996.

The most recent signs of change in the health service (in May 1994) are of some local authorities wanting to take over the purchasing role and to run health services once again, coordinating these with their community care policies. Conservative-controlled Wandsworth in south London and Labour-run Birmingham are both interested in the idea. They are arguing that people do not understand the new purchase–provider NHS and feel unable to influence changes within it because so many of its institutions are unaccountable and unelected.

This section explains the structure of the NHS as it exists at the time of publication (see

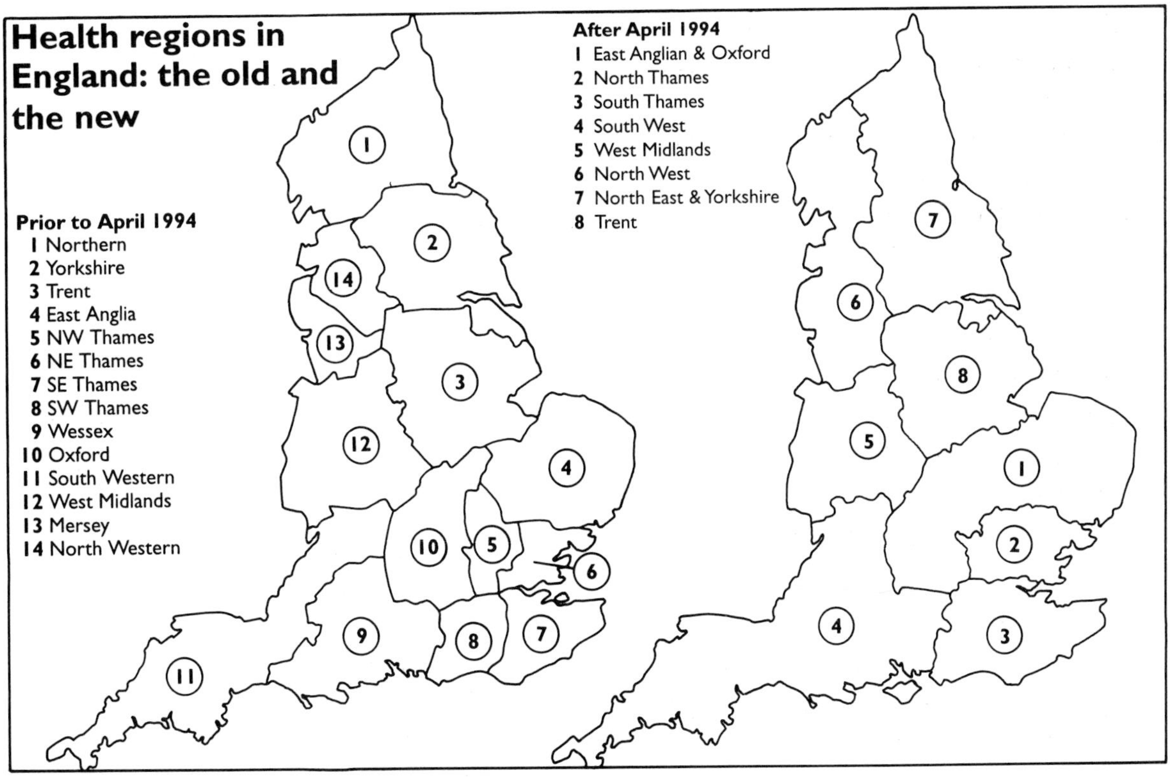

Figure 5.1 Changes to the English Regional Health Authorities in April 1994
Source: *The Guardian*, 22 October 1993

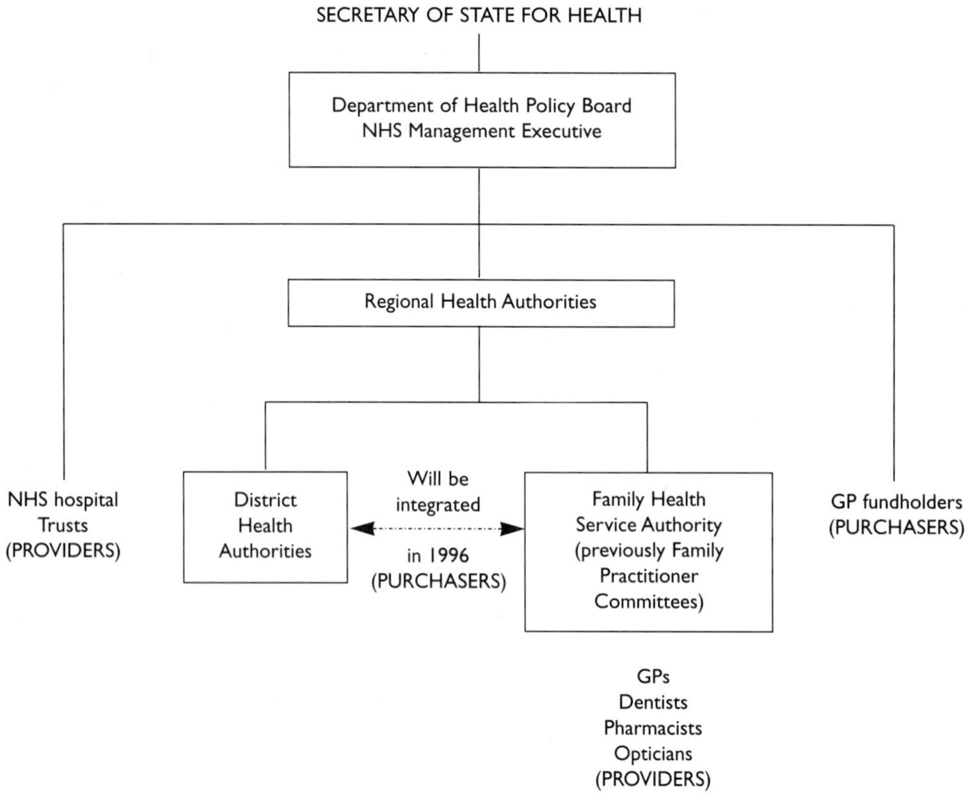

Figure 5.2 The current structure of the NHS in England

Figure 5.2), but the reader should always be aware of any actual or proposed changes.

ACTIVITY

1 Find out what health provision was available before the foundation of the NHS in 1948.

2 Find out what changes to health provision are now being made.

The Welsh Office, Scottish Office and Northern Ireland Office, each of which is headed by its own Secretary of State, are responsible for health services in their respective areas. There are no Regional Health Authorities.

- Wales has nine District Health Authorities and eight Family Health Service Authorities (FHSAs).
- Scotland has 15 Health Boards. (These combine the role of District Health Authorities and FHSAs.)
- Northern Ireland has four Health and Social Services Boards, which look after personal social services as well as health.

Regional Health Authorities

England is divided into eight Regional Health Authorities. The functions of the Regional Health Authority are:

- determination of regional priorities (e.g. how much kidney transplant surgery should be done);
- regional planning (e.g. location of specialities such as neurosurgery);
- allocation of resources to District Health Authorities, Family Health Service Authorities and fund-holding general practitioners;
- monitoring District Health Authorities' activities and relative costs;
- provision of major building projects;
- securing coordination among District Health Authorities;
- employment of medical and dental consultants and senior registrars (except in

health teaching areas where there is a university medical school).

District Health Authorities

Each region contains a number of District Health Authorities, 210 in all. The functions of the District Health Authorities are:

- assessing local health needs;
- employment of medical and other staff;
- planning and administering the appropriate health services (under guidance from the Regional Health Authority): for example, they have to make annual contracts with hospitals agreeing in advance the services the hospitals will provide and the price to be paid for them.

Each District Health Authority is responsible for the hospitals and Community Health Services in the district.

ACTIVITY W

Use your local activity and workplace visits to answer the following questions.

1 What is the name of your Regional Health Authority?

- Draw a map to show the area it covers.

2 What is the name of your District Health Authority?

- Draw a map to show the area it covers.
- Can you find any information on the age structure of this population?

Hospitals

In England and Wales there are approximately 2,500 hospitals, in Scotland 355 and in Northern Ireland 59.

In April 1991, major changes were made to the organisation of the NHS. The emphasis was put on health authorities becoming purchasers of the health services their residents need, and local hospitals and other units becoming providers of those services. Hospitals could choose to remain directly managed by health authorities, or to become NHS Trusts. These Trust hospitals became responsible for managing their own affairs without intervention from district or regional management. In the NHS and Community Care Act 1990, Trusts were given freedom to exercise the following powers:

- to employ staff on terms they consider appropriate;
- to buy and sell property;
- to enter into NHS and other contracts;
- to undertake, commission or make facilities available for research;
- to provide, or make facilities and staff available for, staff training;
- to carry out functions jointly with other bodies;
- to treat private patients and generate income subject to this not interfering with other obligations;
- to accept money, land and other property on trust.

For further information on NHS Trusts, contact the NHS Trust Unit at the Department of Health (for address see list at end of chapter).

ACTIVITY

1 How many NHS hospitals are there in the area covered by your District Health Authority?

- Are any of these Trust hospitals?

2 If you have access to a Trust hospital:

- Interview a member of staff to find out what they consider to be the advantages and disadvantages of trust status (a) to staff and (b) to clients.
- Design and use a questionnaire to find out whether members of the public are aware of the Trust status of their local hospital and, if they are, their perceptions of the advantages and disadvantages of this.

3 Are any of the hospitals in your area (NHS or Trust) specialised, for example, for maternity, mentally disordered or long-stay patients?

4 If possible, visit one of the hospitals in your area (see appendix) and prepare a report on its organisation. To help you with this, first prepare a description of its physical layout and structure and then find out about the following (use formal interviews, informal chats, printed leaflets and notice-boards as sources of information):
- catchment areas;
- size – number of patients;
- staffing levels;
- management structure:
- departments (make a chart): pathology, accident/emergency, out-patients, pharmacy, speech and language therapy, etc.

Write down what you *think* each department does, and then find out what they *really* do.

Include in your report a brief description of the hospital's history and development, and its plans for the future.

Community Health Services

The purpose of the Community Health Service is to deliver local health care. Its aims are to provide the following:

- a personalised service;
- a client-centred approach to care;
- accessible services available to all;
- a quality service to agreed standards;
- a highly trained workforce to deliver such a service;
- a widely available written statement of service provision;
- an integrated service with other agencies.

ACTIVITY

Find out how your local Community Health Service is organised. (Your local library or Health Clinic will probably have the relevant information.)

- Is it divided into neighbourhoods?
- How many clinics are there?
- What types of nurse make up the nursing team?
- What liaison is there between the Community Health Service and GPs?
- Which of the services below does your Community Health Service provide?

Alcohol counselling	Diabetic service
Ophthalmic services	
Dietician	Ante-natal
Orthoptic clinic	
Enuresis (bedwetting)	
Parentcraft	AIDS
Audiometry	Family Planning
Physiotherapy	
Baby clinics	Footcare
Psychosexual counselling	
Bio-mechanics	General advice
Psychologist	
Health visiting	Child health
Post-natal	
Hearing aid batteries	Chiropody
Speech and language therapy	
Child protection	Health promotion
School nursing	
Dentistry	HIV/AIDS
Toddler's clinic	
Immunisation	Terminal care
District nursing	
Incontinence services	Welfare foods
Drug abuse	
Older persons' clinic	Well woman clinic

Family Health Service Authorities

The Family Health Services Authority is responsible for purchasing the front-line or PRIMARY CARE services.

These services have important preventative as well as diagnostic and curative roles to play in medical care.

The providers of these services are;

- general practitioners (there are about 32,000 GPs in Britain);
- dentists (there are about 17,000 dentists);
- opticians (there are about 9,000 ophthalmic opticians);
- pharmacists (there are about 12,000 retail pharmacies under contract for prescriptions with the NHS).

ACTIVITY

In the area covered by your Family Health Services Authority, find out:

1 About GPs:

- How many of the residents are registered with a GP?
- How many GPs are there in the area? (How many males/females)
- Calculate the average number of patients per GP.
- How many practices are there in the area?
- How many of the practices have wheelchair access?
- How many of the practices have practice nurses; health visitors; district nurses; a psychiatric nurse; a chiropodist; a speech and language therapist; other health professionals?
- How many of the GPs carry out minor surgery?
- What percentage of women are screened for cervical cancer?
- What other screening services do the GPs in the area provide?
- What percentage of children are immunised?
- How many of the GPs offer a family planning service?

2 About dentists:

- How many dentists are there in the area? (How many males/females?)
- How many of these dentists give NHS treatment?
- How many of these dentists will take on new NHS patients? (NB Some will take new children on for NHS treatment, but not new adults.)
- Find out how much dentists are paid for various treatments (a) under the NHS, and (b) privately.

3 About pharmacists:

- How many pharmacies are there?
- What is the role of the pharmacist?

4 About opticians:

- How many opticians are there? (NB The FHSA has no control over the location of opticians.)
- Distinguish between ophthalmic opticians, ophthalmic medical practitioners and dispensing opticians.

GP fundholders

Since 1990 GPs working in large practices of 7,000 or more patients have been offered the opportunity to become 'fundholders'.

The fund is given to GPs by the Regional Health Authority. It can be used to purchase services (e.g. hospital treatments, out-patient services and diagnostic tests) which would usually be paid for by the District Health Authority. It is also supposed to cover most of the drugs that GPs prescribe. The amount each GP receives depends on factors such as their past drugs budget and which providers of services they use.

This money is used to purchase most drugs prescribed, diagnostic tests, and hospital care for their patients. Like District Health Authorities, fundholding GPs can make their own contracts with hospitals and decide themselves where to have their patients treated.

GP SURGERY FIRST TO BE STRIPPED OF FUNDHOLDING

A family doctor practice in Sheffield has been stripped of its fundholding status after running up a reported £100,000 deficit and placing a block on the referral of non-urgent patients.

The medical centre was among the surgeries that set the pace for the Government's NHS changes, opting for fundholding status and the power to control its own budget in April 1991. It is the first practice to have fallen foul of Department of Health rules and guidance governing fundholding.

The move is bound to embarrass Virginia Bottomley, Secretary of State for Health, who has consistently proclaimed fundholding as one of the success stories of the NHS changes and the split of service functions into purchasers and providers of health care.

Helen Jackson, Labour MP for Sheffield Hillsborough, is pressing the all-party Commons public accounts committee to investigate the finances of the practice. Last year, the centre, which serves 12,000 patients, set up a company which provided medical treatment to the practice. Critics argued that such companies made a nonsense of the purchaser–provider split. Ms Jackson said: 'I understand the practice ran out of money at the end of last year, but nobody wrote to inform the patients as far as I know.'

(The Independent, 10 March 1993)

ACTIVITY

1 Read the extract from *The Independent* on this page, which gives an example of problems which may be encountered with fundholding.

2 If possible, speak to a fundholding GP to find out what advantages and disadvantages of the system he or she has identified.

3 What do you consider to be the possible advantages and disadvantages?

PRIVATE PROVISION

It is estimated that expenditure on private health treatment in Britain is the equivalent of about 5% of NHS expenditure. The private sector falls into three categories.

1 'Off-the-shelf' products

Commercial 'off-the-shelf' sales of medicines, drugs and appliances in chemists' shops and supermarkets (informal or self-care) has an estimated annual value of £1,036 million. NHS prescription charges have risen to a level that makes many commonly prescribed medicines cheaper to buy directly over the counter from a pharmacist (see Figure 5.3).

2 Private treatment by doctors

Private treatment is provided by some family practitioners and specialists who are mainly hospital based.

Frequently, private treatment is financed by insurance (70% of private hospital admissions are covered by insurance).

There are about 200 private hospitals and nursing homes in Britain, and private treatment is also given in some NHS hospitals. 'Pay beds' may be reserved by hospital doctors for their private, fee-paying patients. Patients using 'pay beds' are generally in single rooms, and may be offered more attractive food than standard NHS food, but the treatment they receive will be the same as that given to an NHS patient.

ACTIVITY

1 Carry out a survey of the amount spent per month on 'off-the-shelf' health products. How does this vary with age?

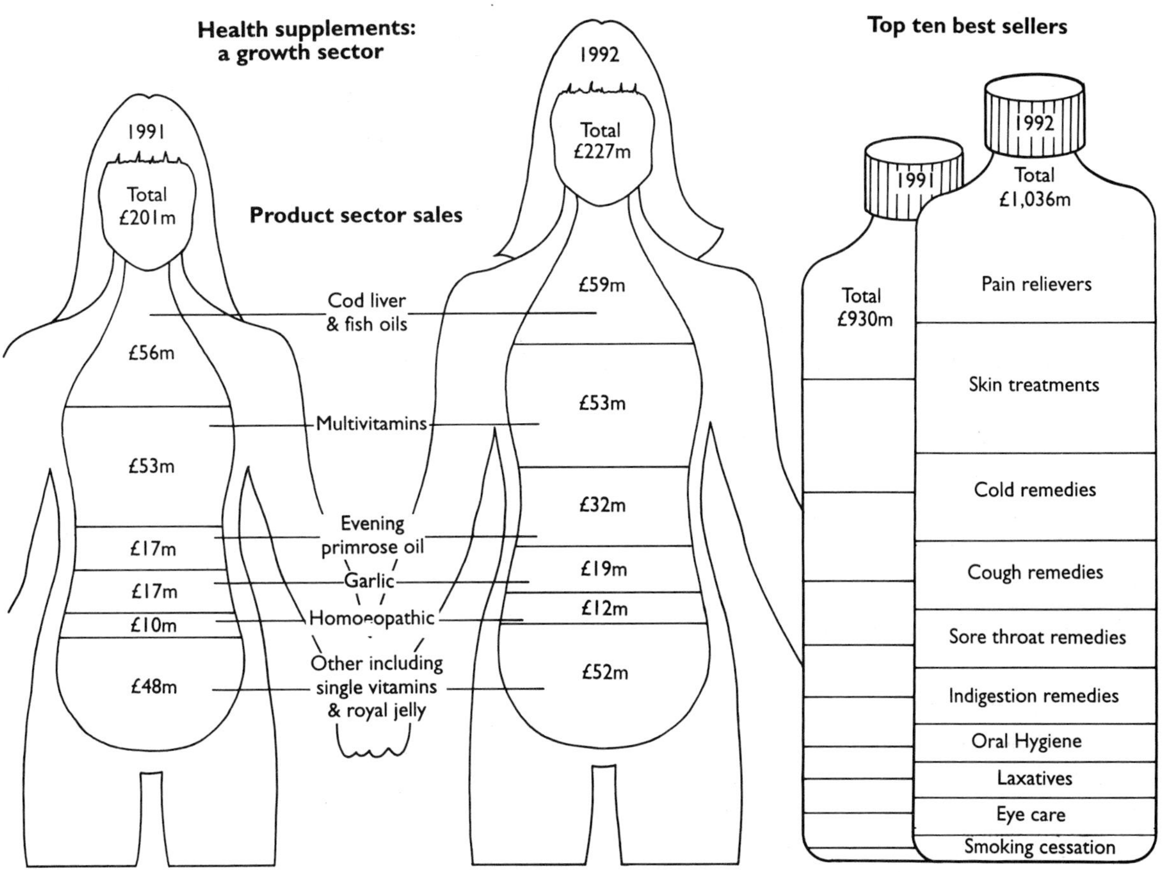

Figure 5.3 Over-the-counter pharmacy sales, 1991 and 1992
Source: *The Independent*, 2 June 1993

NB Think carefully about confidentiality before carrying out your research.

2 Find advertisements for private health insurance schemes and compare the services offered.

- How do the costs vary with the age of the insured?
- Can you find examples of large organisations that provide health insurance for their employees?

3 If possible, interview a person who has had hospital treatment privately. Compare his or her experiences with a patient having similar treatment in an NHS hospital.

- Why did the first person choose private treatment?
- Did it meet his or her expectations?

4 Organise a debate, or role-play a debate, on the motion: 'The private sector should be phased out of health care in this country.' Each side should be given time to prepare a list of the main advantages/disadvantages of a private health sector.

Complementary medicine

Some areas of complementary medicine practised by well-trained professionals, such as osteopathy and chiropractic, which provide treatment where orthodox medicine has often been weak, are quite well established. Other areas of complementary medicine are less widely accepted and less scientific.

There is no law controlling the qualifications of practising complementary therapists. This means it can be difficult to choose a reputable therapist, although some organisations can give some guidance (for example, the Institute for Complementary Medicine and the Council for Complementary and Alternative Medicine: for addresses see list at end of this chapter and Chapter 6). An increasing number of GPs are now practising alternative therapies, such as acupuncture and homeopathy (see Chapter 6).

ACTIVITY

1 Have a 'brainstorming' session to list all the areas of complementary medicine you can think of.

2 Question people who have used complementary medicine to find out:

- why they chose complementary medicine;
- how they chose their therapist;
- if they were happy with their treatment.

VOLUNTARY PROVISION

A VOLUNTARY ORGANISATION is an association or society which has come into existence of its own accord; it has been created by its members rather than being created by the state. Within voluntary organisations some workers are salaried (i.e. voluntary organisations are not staffed solely by volunteers). The volunteer organisations play a relatively minor role in health care provision compared with the NHS. However, with the introduction of the 1992 Community Care (Residential Accommodation) Act, they are increasingly important providers of certain services.

ACTIVITY

1 In a group 'brainstorming' session, generate a list of voluntary organisations concerned with health care provision (e.g. British Red Cross, Multiple Sclerosis Society, League of Friends of local hospitals . . .).

2 Complete your list by checking with your local library, hospital and health care centre.

3 What do you think are the characteristics of a good volunteer? What do you think a person gains from doing voluntary work?

ACTIVITY **W**

Select one (or a few) organisations each, and find out about:

- the services provided (for example: Are they a pressure group?; Do they lobby for improvements/recognition of need?; Are they a provider of services not available through other routes?);
- if these services are available from other agencies, is there evidence that this organisation better meets the needs of its clients?;
- the roles of salaried and volunteer staff;
- staff training;
- how the organisation is financed;
- the history of the organisation.

Social care

STATUTORY PROVISION

At the start of this chapter it was explained that the Department of Health is responsible for the broad policy and central administration of welfare services, which are provided on a local level through the Personal

Social Services (social work) Departments of local authorities.

These local Social Services Departments provide caring services to improve the quality of life of:

- elderly people;
- people with disabilities;
- people with learning disabilities;
- people with mental health problems;
- children and young people;

and their families and carers, so they can live as independently and as safely as possible.

The services provided include:

- assessing needs;
- providing personal help;
- social work;
- day care facilities;
- residential and respite care facilities;
- occupational therapy (OT);
- rehabilitation;
- supplying specialist equipment;
- an emergency service, 24 hours a day, 365 days a year.

Social workers in the second half of this century have had to address twin aspects of their role. They have been increasingly expected to provide *care* and *control*: to give personal help to people and to exercise the power to make decisions about the direction of other people's lives.

In 1968 the Seebohm Report on the social work profession suggested:

- that the many and varied existing local authority welfare services be brought together in new Social Services Departments and become a new important force in local government;
- that social workers should be trained to be able to cope with a wide variety of problems, rather than for narrower areas of expertise, such as children's welfare.

The 1970 Local Authority Social Services Act implemented some of Seebohm's recommendations and, with the first universally recognised professional qualification in social work (the CQSW, awarded in 1971), by the mid-1970s social workers as a profession had gained increased professional status and wider statutory and legal powers.

However, this was accompanied by an increasing separation between *field* social workers, based in Social Services Department area offices, and *residential* social workers, based in residential homes. The latter were paid on lower rates, and had less professional status and training.

The 1970s also saw a greater dissatisfaction among some social workers with the individual casework approach. Partly under the influence of the growing popularity of sociology as a discipline, problems of poverty and inequality were attributed to wider structures in society. It was therefore seen as inappropriate to expect people to be able to solve their own social problems, even with social work 'help'. Some social workers advocated 'radical social work', or community work, along with social and political action to change society. The 1980s and 1990s have also seen challenges to the traditional social work methods from feminists, black people, people with disabilities and gay and lesbian people.

In ever more stark contrast to these views, from 1979 the policies of the Thatcher and Major Conservative governments promoted three ideas:

- the need to reduce spending on welfare;
- the need to reduce people's dependence on a 'nanny state';
- the desire to encourage private and voluntary provision of services and self-help.

These ideas set up further challenges to the social work profession. It was implied:

- that much of what the social worker did was unnecessary or could be done by others;
- that social workers were concerned above all to raise their own professional status;

- that social workers were misguided 'do-gooders' or interfering busybodies.

The Barclay Report of 1982 tried to promote the concept of 'community social work'. It suggested that more social work time should be spent supporting informal carers and self-help groups in the community. The Griffiths report of 1988, on the other hand (implemented by the NHS and Community Care Act 1990), attempted to redefine the role of social workers as 'care managers' and promoted 'care in the community'. Social workers were now to act as coordinators in putting together 'packages of care' for individuals on the basis of assessment of need, and then to identify others to meet those needs –making a distinction between 'purchaser' and 'provider'.

Public inquiries and a series of child abuse scandals prompted the 1989 Children Act. This, together with other legislation such as the 1983 Mental Health Act, has increased and made more complex the legislative framework of which social workers must be aware. Social Services Departments are beginning to reorganise to provide more specialist social work teams to cope with these demands.

At the same time, social workers are being encouraged to form into inter-agency, multi-disciplinary teams and to work much more closely with teams of other health and care professionals such as health visitors, doctors, teachers, probation officers and the police, in managing their cases and the need of 'clients'. Some people are arguing that these changes have led to a situation where managerial, bureaucratic and organisational skills and knowledge have come to be those most valued in social workers.

(For an excellent review of this whole area, students are referred to Clarke (1993), on which much of the above summary draws.)

ACTIVITY

Write a paragraph to demonstrate that you understand what is meant by each of the services listed in the text. For example, what are respite care, occupational therapy and rehabilitation?

ACTIVITY W

1 Look at Figure 5.4, which outlines different client groups and the services generally available to them through the Social Services Department.

2 Choose one client group, and investigate the social services available to them in your locality. (Within the class of students it may be possible to cover each of the client groups, and for the information gathered to be shown on a series of posters.)

The Department of Health is not the only government department concerned with social care provision. The Department of Social Security (DSS) also plays a major role.

This department is responsible for the national administration of social security, which includes:

- National Insurance;
- war pensions;
- Child Benefit;
- Child Support Maintenance;
- Attendance Allowance;
- industrial injuries;
- Mobility Allowance;
- Care Allowance;
- Family Credit;
- Housing Benefit;
- Income Support.

The DSS has regional and local offices.

The social security system originally developed in the earlier part of the twentieth century as an attempt to provide a 'safety-net'

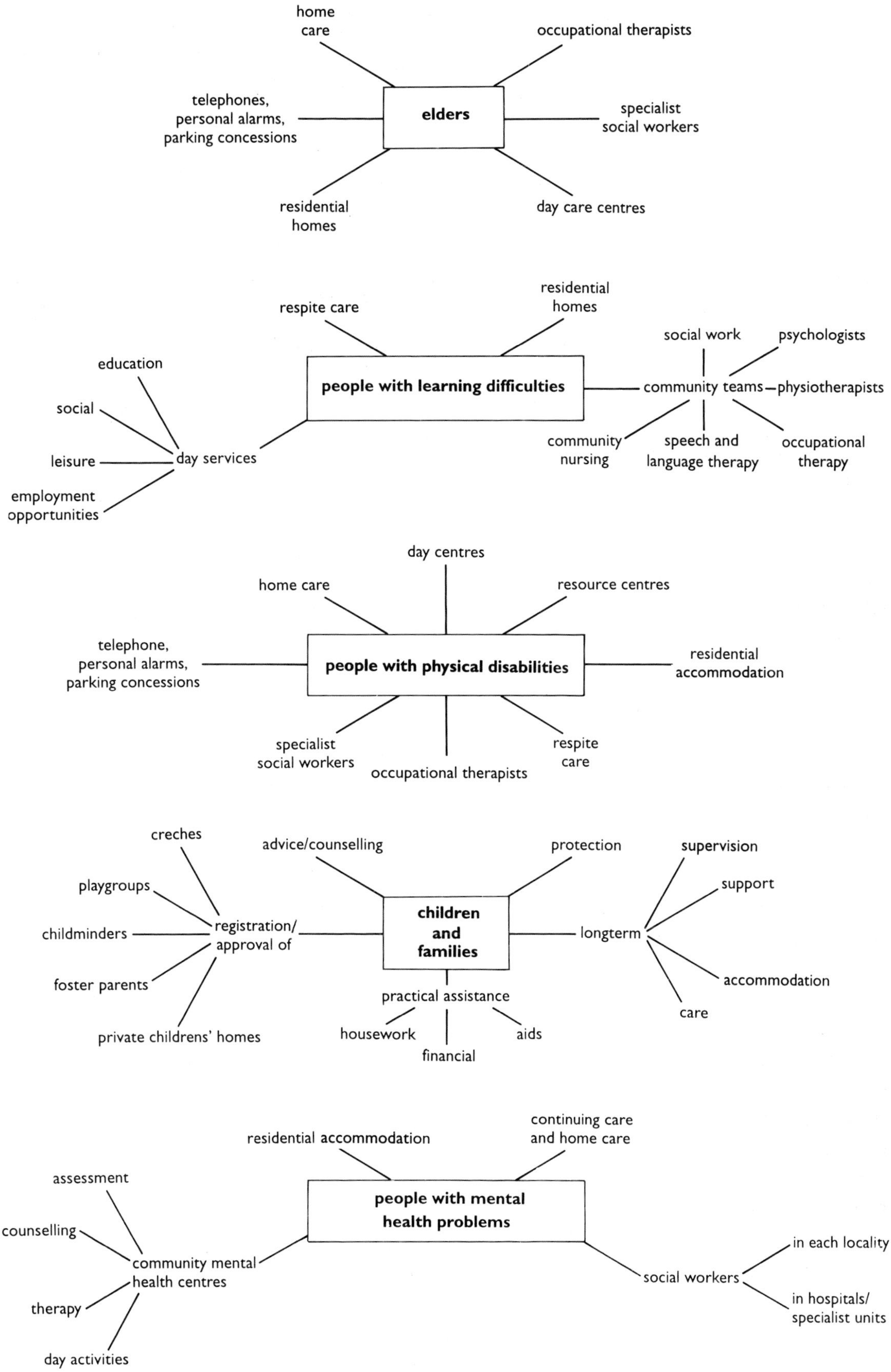

Figure 5.4 Different client groups and the services generally available to them through social services
Source: Surrey County Council Social Services Department

of assistance to those who, through unemployment, ill-health, old age or other factors, could not earn an adequate wage to keep out of poverty.

One of the main aims of the 1944 Beveridge Report and of the post-war Labour government was to provide 'a guarantee by government to all its citizens of an income sufficient to ensure an agreed minimum standard of living' (Lowe, 1993, p. 122). Social security was to provide a means whereby no one should be at risk from absolute poverty.

Social security provision took three main forms:

- National Insurance benefits, paid for by NI contributions;
- means-tested benefits, paid for through general taxation;
- universal benefits, paid for through general taxation.

By the 1960s and 1970s the huge costs of social security and the little impact the benefits seemed to be having on poverty levels generated a growing demand for benefits to be 'targeted' more 'cost-effectively' on those considered to be the most in need. This demand intensified the debate over what an agreed 'minimum standard of living' should be. What were (and are) adequate levels of social security? A further debate centred on the apparent existence of a poverty/unemployment trap – the disincentive to an increasing number of claimants to take low-paid work because, with the loss of benefits, an increase in tax liability and travel costs, their real income could actually fall. These debates remain important and have led, under the Conservative governments of Margaret Thatcher and John Major, to further trends:

- The move towards the privatisation of the provision of some benefits. For example, the government has encouraged a huge increase in the number of people with 'personal' pensions. It has made little real increase in the value of the basic state pension – perhaps intending to encourage greater numbers of people into taking up private pension plans.
- Further means-testing, for example, to limit the receipt of non-contributory benefits to the better-off. There have been suggestions that Child Benefit should be targeted at those on low incomes rather than remain a benefit payable to all mothers.
- A tightening up of the eligibility criteria for certain benefits, or even cash-limiting certain benefits, i.e. when the allocated fund of money for a certain benefit runs out, no more can be paid in that financial year.
- Tougher conditions on the receipt of benefits, imposing additional tests on claimants before they can qualify.
- Modernising the social security system, i.e. responding to changes in family life so that, for instance, part-timers should not be excluded from the National Insurance system.

In 1986 Parliament passed the Social Security Act. This:

- brought in Income Support to replace Supplementary Benefit. Benefits were targeted more at lone parents and the disabled;
- brought in Family Credit, which replaced Family Income Supplement. This new benefit provided extra income for those in low-paid jobs;
- brought in the Social Fund, which provides grants and loans payable to those with exceptional needs.

The Social Security (Incapacity for Work) Bill of January 1994 proposed the introduction of a new social security benefit – Incapacity Benefit – to replace Sickness Benefit and Invalidity Benefit. It also proposed two new tests of incapacity for work which would apply generally in the social security system.

The current pattern of benefit provision is

complex. Examples of the rates payable for many of the most commonly used benefits are given on pages 285–6, but there are several useful guides which students wishing to make a more detailed study of this area could consult. See Child Poverty Action Group (1994); *Facts and Figures* 1994: *Social Security*; and the Welfare Benefits Chart 1994, available from Community Care. (Full details in References and Resources at the end of this chapter.)

The complexities of the social security system are highlighted by the fact that many people may be simply unaware of the overall structure of the benefits system and/or confused by the apparent complexities of the system, the administration and form-filling involved, and the mistakes, delays and waiting times which can occur. The National Audit Office has estimated that £716 million worth of errors in Income Support payments and accounts were made in 1992/93, with a net loss to the Exchequer of £329 million.

ACTIVITY

1 Use information from your local DSS office, Citizen's Advice Bureau or library to find out what financial help may be available to the particular group of clients you chose to study above (see Figure 5.4). Present this in poster form.

2 Anyone getting Family Credit or Income Support is automatically entitled to receive help with NHS costs. Others on a low income may also be entitled to this help. Find out which NHS costs may be covered.

3 Mary Smith lives alone with her four year-old daughter. She works 20 hours a week as a cleaner at the local hospital, for which she earns £100. She has no savings and her rent is £50 per week.
- To what benefits are she and her daughter entitled?
- Under what conditions would a cold weather payment be made to them?
- Mary's cooker stops working and she urgently wants to buy a new one. What help may she obtain from social security?

PRIVATE PROVISIONS

Some social care is delivered through private provision. For example, of the elders living in old people's homes, only about half are in local authority homes. The remainder are in private and voluntary homes. The number of private homes has increased by over 200% since 1979 (see Figure 5.5).

Local authorities may pay for children to be cared for in private community homes or, more widely, to be privately fostered. Private day nurseries and child-minding are further examples of private care for children.

Although privately run as profit-making schemes, these arrangements are regulated by Acts of Parliament and they have to be registered and inspected by the local authority. For example, private old people's homes are regulated by the Registered Homes Act 1984, which dictates that local authorities must carry out an annual inspection. The Foster Children Act 1980 dictates that all foster homes must register with the local authority and must be open to inspection.

ACTIVITY W

1 Find out what private provision for social care is available to your chosen client group:
- nationally;
- locally.

2 If possible, find out the cost to the client of using services provided through local private provision. Where appropriate (e.g. day nurseries, old people's homes), compare this cost with that of using state provision.

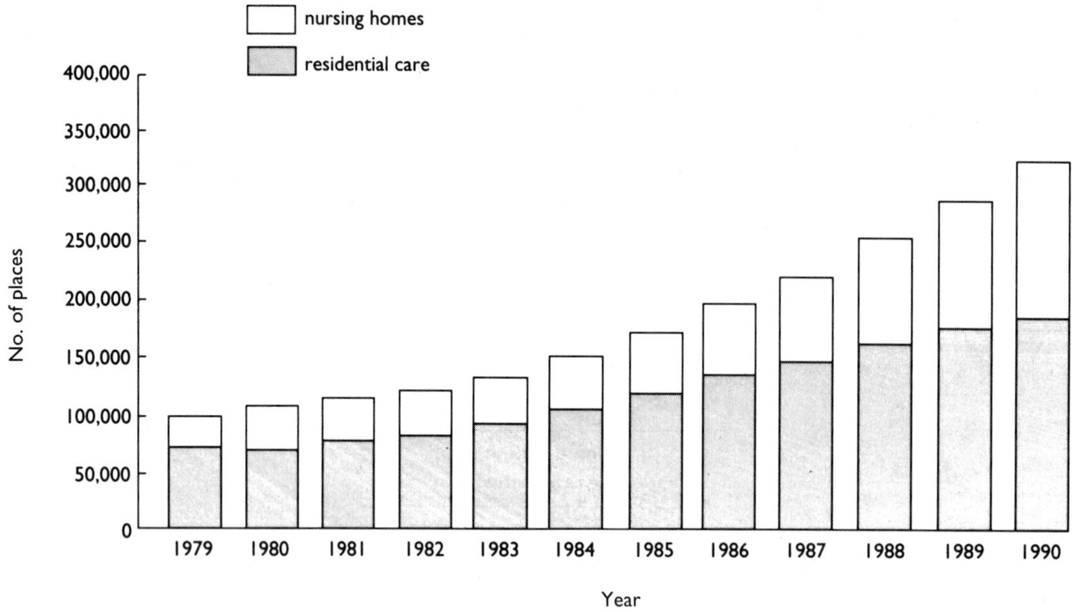

Figure 5.5 Private residential and nursing home places
Source: Audit Commission, *Community Care: Managing the Cascade of Change* (HMSO, 1992), after Laing's review of private health care 1990/1, reproduced by permission of the Controller of Her Majesty's Stationery Office.

3 What links with the local authority do these private establishments have?

4 What do you consider to be the advantages and disadvantages of the private provision of social care for your client group?

VOLUNTARY PROVISION

The provision of social care by voluntary bodies, charities and volunteers is considerable.

There are many formally organised voluntary bodies and CHARITIES involved in social care. Examples include The Samaritans, NSPCC, Relate, Shelter, MIND, Mencap, Dr Barnardo's, the WRVS and SCOPE.

Organisations may be pressure groups aiming to bring about changes in statutory care, or they may directly provide care to clients. Most organisations combine these two functions. With the introduction of the Community Care Act, Social Services Departments are now increasingly contracting out some of their services to local voluntary organisations, so that care can be provided on a domiciliary basis (in the home) instead of in a more expensive residential setting

ACTIVITY — W

1 What do you think are the advantages and disadvantages of voluntary organisations and volunteers providing social care, compared with statutory and private provision?

2 What voluntary provision is there for social care for your chosen client group:

- nationally?
- locally?

3 For the voluntary organisations involved, find out about:

- the services they provide;
- the roles of salaried and volunteer staff;
- how they are financed;
- the history of the organisations.

Table 5.1 Benefits available in 1994

(a) Family Credit
Beneficiaries 503,000 **Cost** £1,091 m

The amount of Family Credit that a working family can get depends on the family's income and savings, and on the number and ages of the children.

The maximum amount of Family Credit may be payable if net income is less than £71.70 per week. Families with much higher weekly incomes may be able to get smaller Family Credit payments. The maximum rate is made up of the following:

Adult credit (for 1 or 2 parents)	£44.30
and for each child aged	
under 11	£11.20
11–15	£18.55
16–17	£23.05
18	£32.20

(b) Housing Benefit

	Beneficiaries	Cost
Rent rebate (council tenants)	3,130,000	£5,004 m
Rent allowance (private tenants)	1,435,000	£3,817 m
Total		£8,821 m

The maximum amount of Housing Benefit payable is 100% of eligible rent. The rates used to calculate Housing Benefit are generally the same as the allowance and premiums that make up Income Support.

(c) Unemployment Benefit
Beneficiaries 701,000 **Cost** £1,742 m

Over pension age	£57.60
Extra benefit for dependent adult	£34.50
Under pension age	£45.45
Extra benefit for dependent adult	£28.05
under 40	£12.15
under 50	£7.60
under 60	£3.80
Extra benefit for dependent adult	£20.65
Extra benefit for dependent child	£11.00

(d) Sickness Benefit
Beneficiaries 159,000 **Cost** £385 m

Over pension age	£55.25
Under pension age	£43.45
Extra benefit for dependent adult (over pension age)	£33.10
Extra benefit for dependent adult (under pension age)	£26.90
Extra benefit for dependent child	£9.80–£11.00

(e) Income Support
Beneficiaries 5,670,000 **Cost** £15,773 m

Personal allowances, premiums, and payments to cover certain housing costs, together make up the benefit payment.

Personal allowances

Single
aged 16–17 (in certain

circumstances only)	£27.50 or £36.15
aged 18–24	£36.15
aged 25 or over	£45.70
Couple	
both aged under 18	
(depending on situation)	£54.55
one or both aged 18 or over	£71.70
Lone parent	
aged 16–17 (depending	
on circumstances)	£27.50 or £36.15
aged 18 or over	£45.70
Dependent children and young	
people aged	
under 11	£15.65
11–15	£23.00
16–17	£27.50
18	£36.15
Premiums	
Family	£10.05
Lone parent	£5.10
Pensioner	
single	£18.25
couple	£27.55
Enhanced pensioner	
single	£20.35
couple	£30.40
(f) Retirement Pension	
Beneficiaries 9,821,000	**Cost** £28.052 m
Basic Retirement Pension	
Man or woman (own contributions	
or late spouse's contributions)	£57.60
Man or woman (spouse's	
contributions)	£34.50
Extra benefit for dependent	
adult	£34.50
Extra benefit for	
dependent child	£9.80–£11.00
Non-contributory pensions	
full rate	£34.50
married woman's	£20.65
Over 80 addition	£0.25
Over 80 pension	
Beneficiaries 30,000	**Cost** £35 m
Rate	£34.50
(g) Severe Disablement Allowance	
Beneficiaries 322,000	**Cost** £686 m
Rate	£34.80

There are age-related additions based on when you became incapable of work.

4 Is there any contracting out of services for your client group to voluntary organisations by the local Social Services Department? Can you find any evidence for the success or failure of these schemes?

One important voluntary organisation which you have probably already used in the course of the research is the Citizens Advice Bureau (CAB). The CAB was set up in 1939 to provide the following:

- accurate information and skilled advice to individuals on the personal problems that arise in life generally;
- explanation of legislation;
- help to allow the citizen to benefit from and to use widely the services provided by the state;
- counsel to men and women in the many difficulties which beset them in an increasingly complex world.

There are approximately 1,200 Citizen's Advice Bureaux throughout the UK, staffed mainly by trained volunteers. Many bureaux offer on their premises legal advice from solicitors and financial advice sessions. Many CABs are under pressure, with an increasing number of people seeking help and advice, and so have requested statutory, and not voluntary, local authority funding.

A volunteer may offer a client advice, or may refer them on to other statutory or voluntary agencies.

INFORMAL PROVISION

The General Household Survey estimated that in 1990, 6.8 million people in Britain had some caring responsibilities for sick, disabled and/or frail elderly people. This represents an increase of almost 1 million people since 1985. Of these informal carers, 1.4 million adults are caring for 20 hours or more a week. The main carers of older people are families themselves, in particular women as mothers and daughters. Male carers are most likely to be caring for a spouse. Nearly one in five carers is 65 or over, but nearly one in three carers (29%) who care for the sick, elderly or disabled for more than 20 hours a week also has children under the age of 16 to care for. (International Year of the Family Factsheet 4, *Families and Caring*).

80-HOUR WEEK FOR CARERS OF DEMENTIA PATIENTS

Half the people caring for a relative or friend with dementia are having to do so for more than 80 hours a week and more than a quarter are spending at least £100 a month, according to a survey by the Alzheimer's Disease Society published yesterday.

An estimated 500,000 people in the United Kingdom suffer from Alzheimer's by which nerve cells in the brain become diseased and mental functions deteriorate.

By 2021, it is projected some 750,000 people will be suffering from the disease or another form of dementia.

The society, which has designated this week Alzheimer's awareness week, is calling for more support for the relatives and friends who have the burden of caring for the sufferers.

The April survey of 1,303 people who look after others with dementia found that 50 per cent of them – including 46 per cent of those over 80 – spend more than 80 hours a week in their caring role.

Twenty per cent of those surveyed had been forced to take early retirement to concentrate on caring, one in four losing full pension rights, and 41 per cent had met the costs by drawing on savings, taking out a loan, or selling property or other assets.

Twenty-seven per cent were paying more than £100 towards caring costs.

Of those over 80, 20 per cent were paying more than £300 a month.

Twenty-four per cent of the sample anticipated financial problems over the following year.

Only 36 per cent of carers expressed confidence that they would be able to carry on indefinitely and 21 per cent were sure they would be unable to do so. The survey also found lack of confidence in the medical profession's understanding of Alzheimer's.

Ninety-two per cent of carers thought that general practitioners were not sufficiently informed about the disease.

Thirty-two per cent of the carers said it had taken the sufferer's GP more than a year to diagnose the disease or another form of dementia.

The cause of Alzheimer's remains unknown although it was first observed in 1907 by Alois Alzheimer, a German neurologist.

Early symptoms of the disease are often attributed to the ageing process.

The society is calling for a full range of services for dementia sufferers and their carers, including access to a seven-days-a-week day centre open in the evenings.

In addition, the society wants social security benefit levels for people cared for at home to be brought into line with those for people in residential care. Where hospital wards have been closed, it says, the Government should take responsibility for providing alternative long-term care.

(The Guardian, 5 July 1993)

CASE STUDY: JENNY WALLACE

Jenny Wallace is 38, married with three children aged four, eight and ten. Her mother, Ruth, is a widow aged 74, who has lived alone in her own home since the death of her husband three years ago. Two months ago, Ruth had a severe stroke which left her with very restricted mobility and speech. Jenny has a part-time job (20 hours a week) as a college librarian and is currently studying for a Diploma in Management Studies with the Open University.

The hospital where Ruth has been for the past two months is ready to discharge her and Jenny now has to decide what form of care to arrange for her mother. Jenny is an only child and has always been fond of her mother, visiting her regularly before and after the stroke.

ACTIVITY

While this case study is not typical of most potential carers, it does illustrate some of the conflicts and strains faced by carers. Using the additional background information provided here, discuss what you think Jenny should do. What problems might she face in reaching a decision about care for her mother?

Background information

1 The only benefit specifically for carers is the Invalid Care Allowance (£34.50 a week in 1994). Jenny could claim this if she gave up her job and provided at least 35 hours of care a week. She would then not be allowed to earn more than around £30.00 a week from part-time work. Ruth would have to claim Attendance Allowance. This, at the higher rate paid for day and night care, would give Ruth £45.70 a week. Only about 17.5% of carers can claim Invalid Care Allowance because of these very specific rules for entitlement to it.

2 Only about 4% of the over-65 population are looked after in institutional care, however, there has been a sharp increase in the number of private residential homes since the late 1980s. The fees for private residential care can be as much as £500 per week. The Family Policy Studies Centre report *Disability and Dependency in Old Age* (McGlone, 1992) suggests that while the growth in the private sector may have increased choice in the kind of residential care on offer (public sector residential homes having often had a poor image and been subject to criticism), 'questions have also been asked about care in the private sector. Care for profit, low levels of inspection, no security of tenure, large fees for additional services, and low levels of staffing and training, have all been cited as areas of concern' (McGlone, 1992, p. 27).

3 The need for full-time care as in Ruth's situation typically (but of course not always) arises at the last stage of a four-step progression from impaired health to dependency in old age:

Stage 1: The person 'feels' older and certain mental and physical faculties become impaired (for example, there may be an onset of deafness).

Stage 2: The impairments become more acute but are manageable and the person can usually cope with living independently.

Stage 3: The management of the illnesses/impairments requires more but not total support from carers (family, community, friends).

Stage 4: This stage is characterised by an acute episode of illness, such as a stroke. The person loses independence and may be hospitalised. Total or near total support and care are required (Field, 1992, p. 19).

4 Under the NHS and Community Care Act, people with income or assets above £3,000 get reduced financial support for residential care home fees and those with income or assets above £8,000 get no help. If Jenny decided that Ruth's needs would be best served by residential care, she would probably have to sell Ruth's house to raise the money to pay for the fees.

5 If Jenny decided to care for Ruth at home, her loss of paid work would entail loss of family income and of a career for Jenny, at least in the short term. She is unlikely to receive much help or support from social services or voluntary agencies because this is usually targeted on the sick, elderly and disabled who are living alone. Breaks would be difficult to arrange, unless Jenny's family was willing and able to help out when needed.

INFORMAL PROVISION IN THE FUTURE

There is concern that families are becoming less willing to accept the major burden of care, and that older people too are less willing to depend on their children. How far, in the future, will family care for elderly, disabled and sick relatives continue to be available?

The following factors may decrease the pool of carers:

- Rising rates of divorce may make the care of elderly parents less straightforward. Will an ex-daughter-in-law care for her former husband's parents? The proportion of divorced elderly people is also likely to rise, reducing the potential supply of elderly husband and wife carers.
- There are far fewer unmarried daughters – the 'traditional' carers – in the population than there used to be.
- There are more married women in paid employment than formerly, although many work part time. This may mean women having to combine four roles: wife, mother, worker and carer.
- Some studies of social attitudes have found that the majority of people wanted community-based professional care – day care centres, day hospitals and sheltered housing – rather than informal care 'in the community'.

The following factors might maintain or even increase the pool of informal carers:

- The increasingly high cost of residential care.
- The government White Paper, *Caring for People: Community Care in the next Decade and Beyond*, which preceded the NHS and Community Care Act 1990, had as one of its principal objectives to enable people to remain as long as possible in their own homes, or some other domiciliary setting. It recognised the needs of carers; however, the Act itself makes no provision for any new forms of support for the carers of elderly and disabled people at home, and the availability of respite care is not always widespread or adequate.

Classification of health and social care services and facilities

Services and facilities can be classified in a number of different ways (Figure 5.6). For

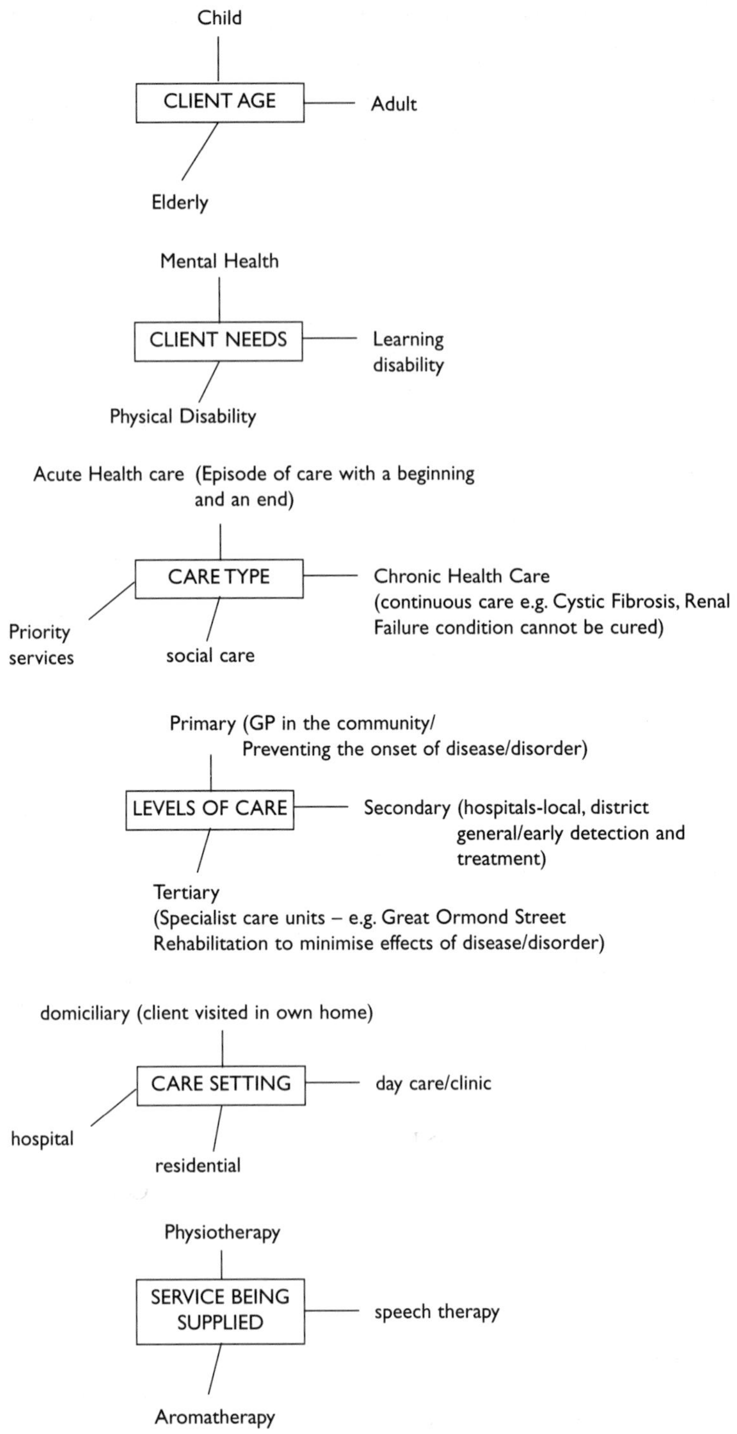

Figure 5.6 Possible ways of classifying health and social care services and facilities

example, in a hospital care may be divided into out-patient care, or in-patient care; wards may divide patients depending on their age group, for example, neonatal, children, adults and elderly; the hospital may be divided into units based on care type, for example, urology, maternity, gynaecology and obstetrics, neurology, accident and emergency, and intensive care. Departments may also be based on the service provided, for example, physiotherapy, radiography, pharmacy and surgery.

ACTIVITY

1 Check that you understand all the terms used in Figure 5.6. Can you think of any other examples of care services and facilities which may come under the headings given?

2 Look back at Figure 5.4 which shows the services and facilities generally available to different client groups through social services.
Divide them up under the following headings: client age; client needs; care setting; and service being supplied. For example, under client age you would list care of elders; care of adults; and care of children.

Because there are many different ways in which services may be classified, for example, by setting, client age, client needs, or service supplied, in reality there may be *inconsistencies in the ways in which health and social services are classified*, which may lead to patients falling between support services.

Resourcing of services

SOURCES OF FUNDING IN HEALTH AND SOCIAL CARE

There are four main sources of funding for health and social care. These are:

- central government;
- local government;
- registered charities;
- commercial sources.

Central government

The money available for public expenditure comes from:

- taxes;
- National Insurance contributions (paid by employees, the self-employed and employers – in fact a form of taxation);
- charges (direct payment by client e.g. rents, health service charges, etc.; see Table 5.2);
- government borrowing.

ACTIVITY W

1 Discuss within your group to what extent services should be resourced by the individual who needs the service, and to what extent services should be resourced by the nation through the taxation system.

2 Discuss what charges may be made by each of the five services listed in Table 5.2. What is provided free?

3 Where possible, find out the amount individuals may be asked to pay (for example, current prescription charges).

4 What exemptions are made?

5 If possible, interview a professional from each of the five areas to help you check your findings.

Table 5.2 National health and personal social services in England: charges to persons using the services (years ended 31 March)

	Charges (£m)							
Services	1981	1985	1986	1987	1988	1989	1990	1991*
All services	**524**	**808**	**930**	**925**	**1,020**	**1,072**	**1,441**	**1,606**
Hospital	54	78	86	91	97	107	399	471
Pharmaceutical	71	122	128	170	167	203	191	206
General dental	92	171	195	223	240	291	367	335
General ophthalmic	29	44	12	1	–	–	–	–
Personal social services	277	393	509	440	516	471	484	544

* 1991 figures are provisional.
Source: Health and Personal Social Services Statistics for England, 1992 (HMSO).

Figure 5.7 shows the sources of revenue and the main categories of expenditure. Figure 5.8 shows how finance flows from central government down to health and social care services.

Local government

Local authorities obtain their funds from the Council Tax (previously poll tax or Community Charge and, before that, Rates), and grants from central government. These grants are weighted, depending on the needs within the local authorities. Financial penalties are imposed on local authorities which overspend.

ACTIVITY

Discuss the arguments for and against local freedom in collecting taxes and managing services. Compile a list of each.

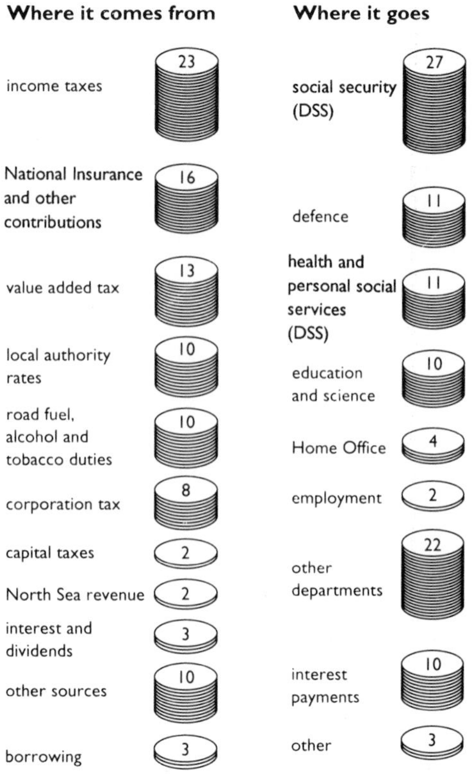

Figure 5.7 UK public income and expenditure, 1987/8, pence in every pound (to the nearest penny)
Source: G. F. Stanlake, *Introductory Economics* (Longman Group UK Ltd, 1990), using data from *Financial Statement and Budget Report 1987/8; Economic Progress Report Suplement, March–April 1987.*

Registered charities
HOW ARE CHARITIES FUNDED?

In the UK there are at present 175,000 registered charities, and this number is continually growing. Central government contributes a great deal to charities:

- Charitable status confers exemption from taxation, which amounts to about £3 billion of tax forgone per year.
- Various government departments may also give grants directly to charities; for example, the Department of the Environment funds many inner-city projects.

Local authorities, too, fund many charities. This may be through grants or, increasingly, with the introduction of the government's 'Care in the Community' programme, through payment for services provided.

It is often thought that charities obtain most money through donations, but in fact this accounts for less than 40% of charitable income. Donations may be gained:

- in the form of endowments;
- collected on flag-days;
- from employees at work who regularly donate part of their wage;
- from corporate sponsorship;
- from charity shops.

Recession hits charities hard and since the introduction of the National Lottery the amount of money donated to charities has fallen. It means less government money and donations at a time when demand for their services is increasing.

Some fund-raisers worry that as services provided by charities replace those previously provided by the state, people will be less willing to donate money.

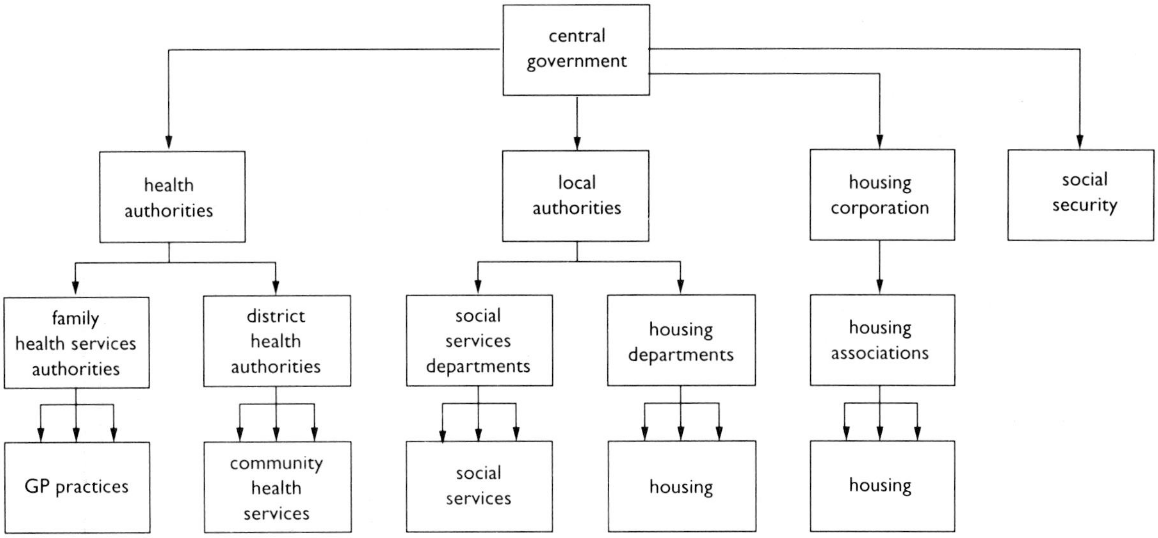

Figure 5.8 The flow of finance from central government
Source: Audit Commission, *Community Care: Managing the Cascade of Change* (HMSO, 1992) reproduced by permission of the Controller of Her Majesty's Stationery Office.

ACTIVITY

- Look at Figure 5.9.
- Discuss the distribution of charity donations. Why are some causes more 'popular' than others?

CHARITABLE FUNDING OF THE NHS

Charitable fund-raising is not limited to voluntary organisations. Before the NHS was funded in 1948, charity was at the forefront of health services. After this, up until 1980, charity in hospitals ceased to be of any significance.

In 1980 the Health Service Act empowered health authorities to fund-raise, and the amounts collected through this activity doubled every year during the late 1980s. Proceeds are now used to pay for basic patient care and hospital building, not just for small comforts for patients and staff and for research.

ACTIVITY W

1 What examples can you find of charitable funding of the NHS in your area?

2 What are the merits and drawbacks of the charitable funding of health care?

Commercial funding

Corporate sponsorship

An important aspect of charitable fund-raising is CORPORATE SPONSORSHIP. It is now common for local businesses to fund building programmes and pay for items of equipment in hospitals.

West Middlesex University Hospital marked its first day of NHS trust status by signing a deal for a new state-of-the-art endoscopy unit which will allow them to treat patients more efficiently.

Lister BestCare Limited are funding the building of the unit which can diagnose and treat conditions of the stomach and intestine without surgery,

(Richmond and Twickenham Guardian, April 1993)

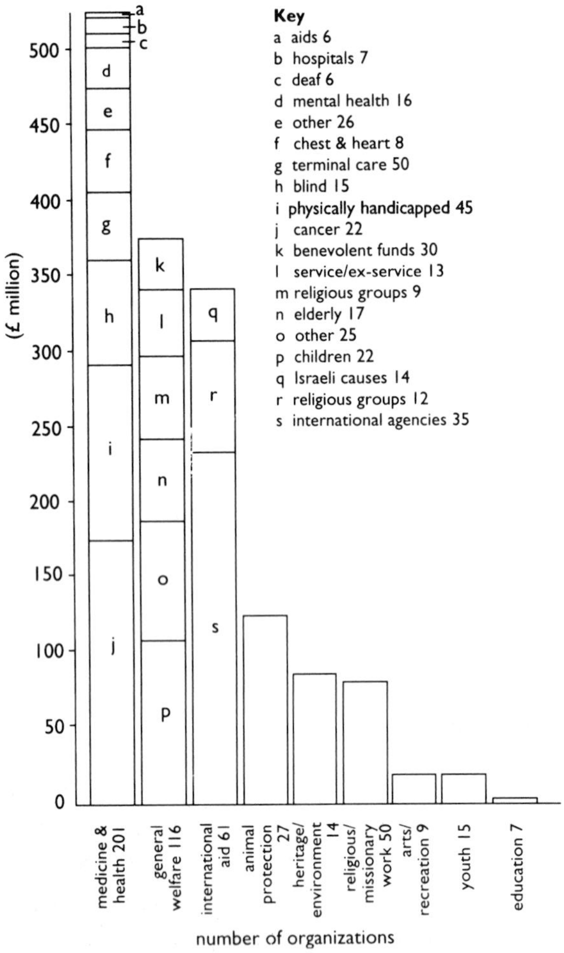

Figure 5.9 Voluntary income received by the largest 500 charities by sector
Source: *Charity Trends*. 16th edition, published by Charities Aid Foundation.

In another example, in an effort to boost take-up of child immunisation, St Helen's and Knowsley Health Authority on Merseyside struck up a deal with Iceland frozen foods to distribute £6,000 in grocery vouchers to families in the worst-performing neighbourhoods who completed all immunisation courses before their child's third birthday.

ACTIVITY **W**

1 Discuss the advantages to a business of donating funds.

2 Can you find examples of corporate sponsorship in your locality?

Selling goods and services

The selling of goods and services and private insurance schemes have been covered earlier in the chapter, in the sections on private provision.

There are increasing numbers of examples of the NHS raising funds through commercial transactions. For example, when staff at West Dorset Hospital in Dorchester found that 68% of new born babies were being taken home by car without any form of seat restraint, they introduced the sale of baby chairs and started to provide carriers for parents to take babies from the maternity department to the car.

The private sector also invests in profit-making schemes in hospitals; for example, there are privately managed shopping malls.

Recently the use of private finance has been widened. The limit above which NHS Trusts and health authorities need Treasury approval for contracts involving private finance has risen from £250,000 to £10 million. This has led to opposition from MPs accusing the Conservative government of trying to 'fudge' the difference between private and public health care.

THE GROWING DEMAND FOR HEALTH AND SOCIAL CARE

ACTIVITY

There are many factors which raise costs or create an increase in demand for health and social care. In a group, discuss what these factors may be and then compare your ideas with those given below.

Population changes

The population is constantly increasing (see Figure 5.10) (see Chapter 4 for latest population statistics). Obviously more people mean a higher demand for health and social care.

Perhaps even more important than the change in population size is the change in AGE STRUCTURE of the population. On average, one

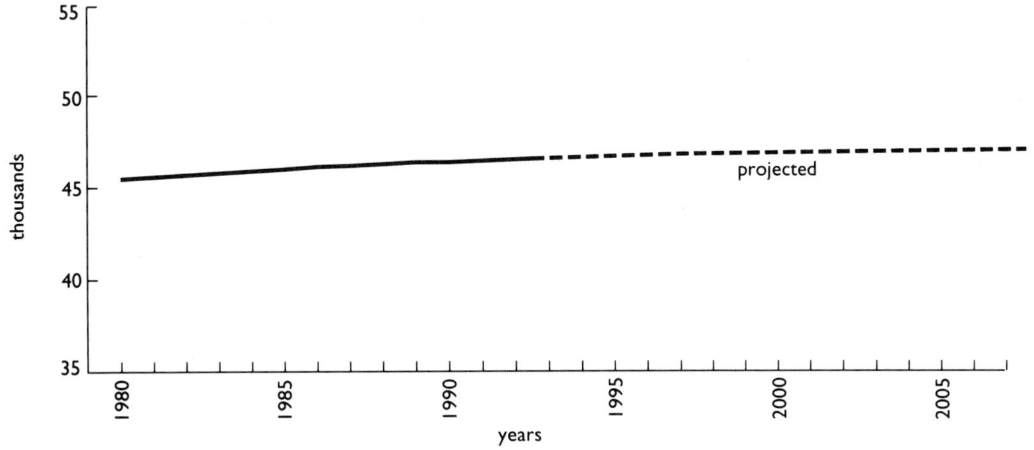

Figure 5.10 Population size in England
Source: Crown copyright. Reproduced with the permission of the Controller of Her Majesty's Stationery Office.

person aged 75 or over costs the health and personal social services seven times as much as one person of working age. By the year 2001 there will be 10.6 million pensioners, and by the year 2031, 14.6 million.

ACTIVITY

Explain why we have an 'ageing population'.

Advances in medical science

When the NHS started it was envisaged that the cost of health care would fall over the years as people became healthier. However, as medical technology advances, conditions which were previously incurable can now often be treated, and improvements in treatment are continuously being made. People expect these often expensive advances to be freely available. For example, improved anti-depressants have been developed which, if taken in an overdose as a suicide attempt, are far less likely than previous ones to be fatal. However, these new drugs are over 20 times more expensive than the old ones.

Increased expectations

Just as people expect increases in their standard of health care, so increases in the standards of housing and education are also expected.

ACTIVITY

Chat to elderly relations or friends about their living conditions and the health care and education they received when they were young. List the improvements there have been. Have there been any deteriorations in living standards?

Changed family patterns

Perhaps one of the most significant social changes in recent decades is the increase in the divorce rate. This has left a high number of families headed by a single parent, which has increased the demand on all the major social services (for example, housing, personal social services and social security benefits).

Coping with increased demand

In recent years the government has had to consider carefully the options open to it to cope with the increased demand for health and social care described above.

The amount of money collected (from charges, taxes and National Insurance contributions) could be increased, or the

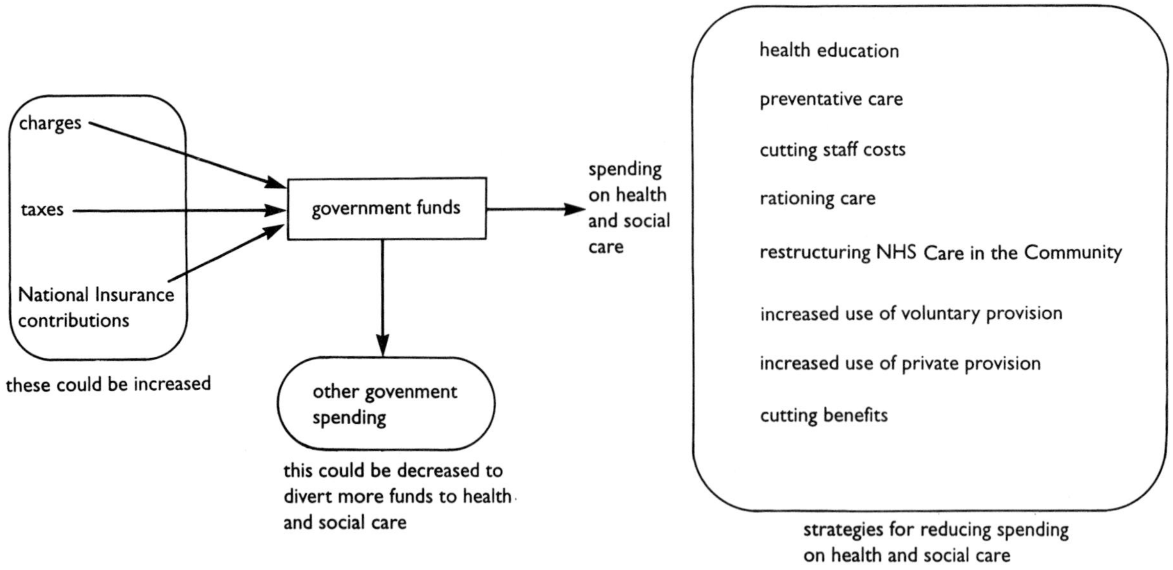

Figure 5.11 Possible strategies for coping with increased demand for statutory care

pattern of government spending could be changed (Figure 5.11).

INCREASING FUNDING

The funding available to the government is largely dependent upon the state of the economy. The higher the rate of employment, the more people are paying taxes and National Insurance contributions and the lower are social security claims.

ACTIVITY

1 Find out the current rates of the following sources of government funding and then discuss the relative advantages and disadvantages of increasing each of them:

- *Charges.* Consider in your discussion which charges could be increased or whether any new charges could be introduced. For example, it has been suggested that people convalescing in hospital would be asked to pay the equivalent of what they would spend at home.
- *Taxes.* What taxes are currently levied in the UK? Which could be increased (e.g. Income Tax, VAT, Council Charge)?
- *National Insurance contributions.*

  Conduct a survey to find out people's attitudes to paying each of the above.

2 Debate the advantages and disadvantages of the suggestions made in *The Observer* article reproduced here for increasing funding of the NHS through increased charges.

A MEANS-TEST FOR HEALTH CHARGES CAN SAVE THE NHS

The forecast by the architect of the modern welfare State, William Beveridge, that the cost of free health care would decline as the nation's health improved, has been shown to be, in Enoch Powell's phrase, 'a miscalculation of sublime proportions'. The cost of the NHS has grown 100 times since its inception in 1949. It is now about £40 billion a year, roughly £650 for every person in the country.

Rising life expectancy, advances in high-tech treatment and an ageing population mean health expenditure is certain to continue to increase ahead of inflation. By the end of the century, there will be twice as many people aged over 80 as now, and the cost of care for this group is roughly 10 times that for those in work.

So how is this bill for an ever-expanding health service going to be met? If demand for a service free at the point of supply is almost infinite, the sums can only be made to add up by queuing, rationing or simply removing some medical procedures, such as in-vitro fertilisation, from available treatment. And that is what is happening.

Conservative governments have increased spending on the NHS by 58 per cent in real terms since 1979, but the perception of a grossly underfunded service is widespread. Hospitals unable to perform urgently-needed operations, children having to wait months for routine procedures, wards left empty because of shortages of funds are everyday occurrences.

If the NHS is to prosper, it needs additional sources of revenue, and these can only come from charges. Before howls of fury rent the land, it is worth pointing out that we already have a crude charging system. Prescription charges have been increased by more than 2,000 per cent since 1979.

A far better system would be to charge for drugs according to income, using a computerised family income coding. The poor would pay nothing; the rich would pay nearly the full cost for most drugs.

Much of this would be very unpopular. But if the NHS continues to be grossly underfunded, the result is inevitable. A two-tier, separate system of private and public health care is well established. Spending on private health care is rising three times faster than spending on the NHS; more than one in six households is covered by private health insurance.

(The Observer, 28 March 1993)

CHANGING THE PATTERNS OF SPENDING

Prioritisation of government spending

The largest single category of public expenditure in the UK is spending on social services. Under this heading it is usual to include education, health and social security benefits, and these three items account for

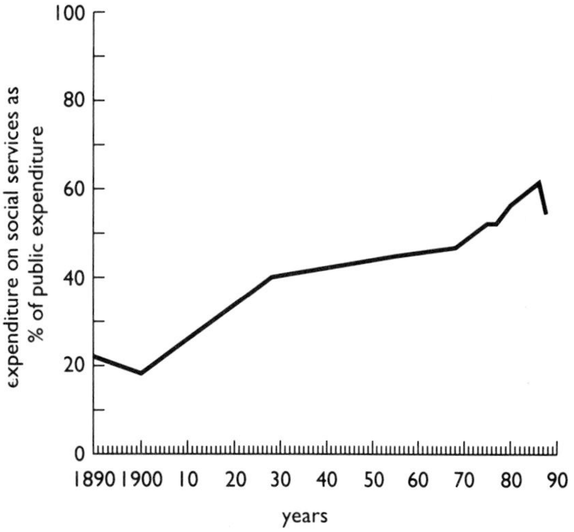

Figure 5.12 The proportion of public expenditure devoted to social services, 1890–1986
Source: Peacock and Wisemen, *The Growth of Public Expenditure*; *Annual Abstract of Statistics*; *Economic Trends* (CSO Publications)

about 50% of total public expenditure (Figure 5.7). This expenditure has increased over the years (Figure 5.12). The decision could be taken to meet increased demand by further increasing this percentage.

> **ACTIVITY**
>
> 1 What else accounts for government spending besides social services?
>
> 2 Discuss what expenditure could be decreased to allow extra funds to become available for social services. What opposition would the government meet?
>
> 3 How do policies which bring about cuts in the following areas influence health and social well-being?
>
> - transport;
> - housing;
> - education;
> - social welfare.

Within the social services sector the priority given to different aspects could be changed. For example, spending on health could be increased at the expense of spending on housing.

Within one social service priorities could be changed. For example, spending on welfare services for the elderly could be increased at the expense of spending on the handicapped.

Savings and efficiency

Health education

It has been suggested that increased spending on health education would result in a healthier population, and, therefore, a decrease in demand for health services.

> **ACTIVITY**
>
> Visit your local Health Promotion Unit (you can find the address in the telephone book). Find out:
>
> - what services it provided;
> - information on its funding;
> - how it measures its effectiveness.
>
> Does health promotion reach the more deprived sectors of a community who suffer the worst health?

Preventative care

In 1990, the government drew up new contracts for GPs and dentists which put the focus of intervention on *prevention* rather than cure. GPs are now expected to provide health checks for patients, and are rewarded for achieving certain targets of immunisation and screening.

> **ACTIVITY**
>
> 1 Visit your local GPs surgery to find out what health checks, screening and health promotion clinics are available.
>
> 2 Find out the levels of immunisation and screening required for the GP to obtain payments.
>
> 3 If possible, interview a GP about his or her opinion of the new contracts. For example, has the amount of paperwork increased?

Dentists are now paid an annual fee for each child on their list instead of being paid for each treatment. Incentives are given for quality rather than quantity; for example, if fillings fall out within a year, they have to be replaced free of charge.

Cutting staff costs

A high percentage of the expenditure on health and social care goes on staff costs. The NHS alone is one of Europe's biggest employers, and 75% of total NHS resources are spent on paying staff. This means that government can make savings by paying staff working in statutory health and social care less than they would earn outside.

> **ACTIVITY**
>
> 1 Find out how the wages of staff in statutory care compare with the wages of the equivalent staff in private care. Do they differ significantly?
>
> 2 How do the wages of staff in the 'caring sector' compare with the wages of staff in industry?

Some government advisers have recommended that the NHS could sack at least 200,000 people (one-fifth of the workforce) without any adverse effect. This would release an extra £4.6 billion a year for patient care.

Rationing care

While reading this section, it should have become apparent to you that in many cases, because of the availability of scarce resources, care may have to be rationed. NHS waiting lists are an example of the RATIONING OF CARE. Between 1987 and 1991 the government spent an extra £156 million to reduce waiting lists dramatically. The numbers of patients waiting more than one year dropped considerably; but the numbers of those waiting less than a year shot up.

Since the 1991 NHS reforms the income of hospitals depends far more on the number of patients treated. This has encouraged measures to move patients more quickly through the system. For example, day surgery is increasing, with a subsequent drop in waiting lists. It has been predicted that further increases in day surgery could reduce waiting lists in the UK as a whole by one-third.

Rationing may also be seen at work in the prescription of drugs. Some which the DoH regards as too expensive have now been placed on a 'restricted list', which means they cannot be prescribed on the NHS.

Restructuring the NHS

In the late 1980s an 'internal market' was created within the NHS by splitting the service into PURCHASERS and PROVIDERS. The aim was to make the NHS work more like private industry, where competition ideally keeps prices low and quality high. Purchasers buy treatment for patients, and providers provide the treatment. The main purchasers are the District Health Authorities, and the main providers are the hospitals and GPs.

As explained above, the District Health Authorities make annual contracts with hospitals, agreeing in advance the services the hospital will provide and the price to be paid for them.

The Family Health Services Authorities are the purchasers who make contracts with the providers of non-hospital care: GPs, dentists, pharmacists and opticians.

Fundholding GPs are purchasers as well as providers. They have their own budget to purchase drugs and hospital care for their patients.

The main criticism of the 'internal market' is that competition does not necessarily guarantee better quality. Providers might lower their standards in order to keep prices down. GPs may base their treatment decisions on cost rather than medical need. The following newspaper articles illustrate some of the problems which have been blamed on the market system.

NHS MARKET BLAMED FOR TREATMENT DELAYS

Patients facing delays in treatment at Papworth heart hospital in Cambridgeshire have been sent to St Bartholomew's in London, even though Bart's is unable to treat many of its own patients.

This has arisen as a result of the National Health Service market system.

Earlier this week, Mary Lambert, of Buckhurst Hill, Essex, told how her husband, Bert, died after being told by Bart's he could not have a coronary arteriogram, a form of X-ray, until April.

But Bart's has been treating patients unable to be seen by Papworth. Dr Ian Cooper, a consultant cardiologist at Papworth and at Bedford General, said he had been told to refer to Bart's 12 patients whom Papworth would not treat.

The district found it had spare cash 'on account' at Bart's. It agreed that the money could be used for coronary procedures and told Dr Cooper to refer 12 of his patients.

'The whole thing is completely stupid.' Dr Cooper said. 'We are told how the beauty of the market system is that the money follows the patient. In fact, you have got patients here being told to follow the money.'

The Department of Health has told hospitals and health districts that patients deemed urgent, like Mr Lambert, must not have treatments delayed until the new financial year.

A department spokesman said Mr Lambert's case was 'tragic' but that, at the time he was put on the Bart's waiting list, he had not been considered an emergency. 'Doctors, not administrators, are responsible for deciding which cases are emergencies.'

(The Guardian, 5 March 1993)

HOSPITAL IN CRISIS AS AXE FALLS ON ROUTINE OPS

The Lister Hospital, Stevenage, in the East and North Herts health authority, will be treating

3,000 fewer patients than last year. It will be axing 40 nursing jobs and closing 50 beds because of an estimated £20 million cash squeeze in the district health authority, due to the number of GP fundholders who take money out of health authority spending budgets.

The crisis at Stevenage underlines problems facing hundreds of hospitals as the start of the financial year looms. Many may be faced with a situation where they can only operate on urgent cases because there are no funds for routine waiting list surgery.

Lister managers have blamed the health authority for their lack of cash. The authority has said the Government's financial squeeze means there is no more money to treat non-urgent waiting list patients.

(The Observer, 13 March 1993)

Care in the community

Between 1979 and 1993 the cost to the state of residential care rose from £10 million to £2.5 billion. The main reason for this was that the Department of Social Security had to pay for the accommodation of anyone entitled to Income Support, which included the majority of those in residential care. For example, pensioners in private nursing homes had an automatic right to Income Support of up to £315 per week. With the increasing number of elderly people, it was apparent that these costs would continue to grow.

There were complaints that little help was available to people looking after relatives at home, and that the system therefore encouraged these carers to put their relatives into residential care.

The programme the government developed in an effort to solve these problems, CARE IN THE COMMUNITY, was introduced in April 1993 to cater for people with problems of ageing, mental illness, mental handicap, physical or sensory disabilities, or drugs and alcohol. The main change was that the money which had previously come from the DSS now goes to councils who work with local health authorities to decide who should be looked after in residential homes, who needs medical support, and who should be looked after at home, possibly with the assistance of professional carers. The councils also decide what should be paid for the various services required.

ACTIVITY

1 A 90-year-old man who has some mobility problems because of arthritis lives alone. What support is he likely to require from social services to allow him to continue living in his home?

2 Discuss the advantages and disadvantages (a) to the carer, and (b) to the dependent relative, of care in institutions compared with care in the community.

Although there are obvious advantages to giving people the opportunity to remain living in their own homes where possible, many criticisms have been made of the Care in the Community programme.

Inadequate funding. The chief complaint is that there is inadequate funding for the scheme. For example, for 1993/94, the local authorities in England received a transfer of £399 million from social security, plus £140 million to get things under way. It was claimed that this falls short of what is needed by £135 million.

Good home care is at least as expensive as residential care if the necessary support is provided. However, councils are required to spend 85% of their funds in the private sector, and most private provision is in residential care and nursing homes. This means that there will be little cash left for the promised new services to help people to stay in their own homes and provide temporary care to give relatives and other carers a break.

Another possible problem leading to lack of funds is the fact that in future years the community care budget may be raided to pay other council bills, as the money is only 'ring-fenced' for the first four years.

Although there is a cash shortage, councils could face legal action if they inform people about services and then fail to provide them because of insufficient funds. Therefore, in some circumstances, local authorities may record 'unmet choice', rather than conceding that it was an 'unmet need'. Research has also shown that on some occasions social services staff secretly ration the care and services available by failing to suggest services which are considered too expensive to provide.

Some clients are now contributing more to funding their care than they would have in the past. For example, the number of beds in long-stay geriatric wards in NHS hospitals (which are provided free to patients) are being cut, and the patients transferred to residential homes for which they are means-tested. It is likely that in the future there will be more emphasis on payment by the client from his or her savings of selling assets, or by payments by relatives. This may prove to be very expensive. On average a man spends the last three years of his life, and a woman spends the last five to six years, being looked after, either in nursing homes or in their own home with nursing or community care back-up. For this reason long-term care insurance plans are becoming increasingly popular.

ACTIVITY

- Find advertisements for long-term care insurance schemes. How do policies change with the age at which insurance is taken out, and what service does the insurance eventually cover?
- Read the newspaper article from *The Independent on Sunday* (22 January 1995). What three options are being considered by the government?

MINISTERS TO ACT ON HIGH CARE FEES

The growing problem of sons and daughters losing out on their inheritance because of the care fees they have to pay for elderly and infirm parents is to be addressed by the Government.

Ministers are considering plans for nationwide insurance schemes to protect people from massive bills if, in old age, they have to go into council care.

The current rules state that elderly people are obliged to pay in full if their assets exceed £8,000, although the value of their property will not be taken into account if a partner continues to live there. If not, councils can force a sale of the property to cover costs of care. On average, these are £199 a week in a residential home and £293 in a nursing home.

Among the models being considered is a form of compulsory insurance scheme, although this is viewed as anti-libertarian by some ministers.

More likely is tax relief for care insurance, putting it on a level playing field with pension investments. An alternative is to deduct all savings, including pensions, insurance and Personal Equity Plans from income tax.

(The Independent, 22 January 1995)

Changes in family structure and attitude. There is a worry that the number of family carers will not increase at the same rate as the number of dependants. An increasing divorce rate means that there may be fewer people caring for spouses and parents-in-law.

Many people have grown up with the belief that the state will care for elderly relatives. For example, in a recent survey two-fifths of the people questioned said that they felt 'no obligation to care for a parent'.

Abandonment. Already there are cases which are termed by the popular press as 'Granny-dumping', where stressed relatives, feeling unable to continue caring for elderly relatives at home, leave them at day centres or in hospital.

At present three-quarters of general hospitals say that this happens once a month; one-third say it happens once a week; and one-tenth say this happens every day. As more people are cared for in relatives' homes, these figures seem likely to increase.

NHS 'bed-blocking'. Hospitals may be unable to discharge patients who are otherwise ready to go because of delays in undertaking care assessments and arranging any further services they require.

Viability of 'low-priority' services. It is feared that hostels for homeless mentally ill people and residential drug and alcohol addiction clinics may be a low priority for local authorities and may, therefore, close.

ACTIVITY

Prepare a list of the advantages of the Care in the Community scheme and then debate whether, overall, these outweigh the disadvantages, or vice versa.

Increased use of voluntary provision

As you may have found through your research earlier in this chapter, an important aspect of the Care in the Community scheme is the increased role played by charities and voluntary organisations. They frequently replace and supplement some aspects of public social services.

Although local authorities will pay for services, many organisations are under financial pressure because of rising costs and cuts in local authority grants. There are complaints that by providing services for local authorities they have to operate under greater restrictions, ranging from staff qualifications to the colour of the carpets!

Increased use of private provision

Now that local authorities are playing a key role as 'commissioners' of services, they often 'contract out' to private organisations services which previously they would have supplied themselves. It is suggested that services may run more efficiently in private hands, but this opens up a debate on the question of EFFICIENCY.

If people can be persuaded to pay for their own private care this obviously saves money: examples include the use of private schools and hospitals. Commercial sponsorship will also save local authorities money.

Cutting social security

This is considered to be one of the most likely areas of cuts in both the long and the short terms, as it accounts for such a high percentage of government spending (Figure 5.13).

This may mean the extension of means-testing to target benefits where they are most needed. Younger people may become compelled to take out insurance against sickness and mortgage default, which will mean lower payments of state benefits.

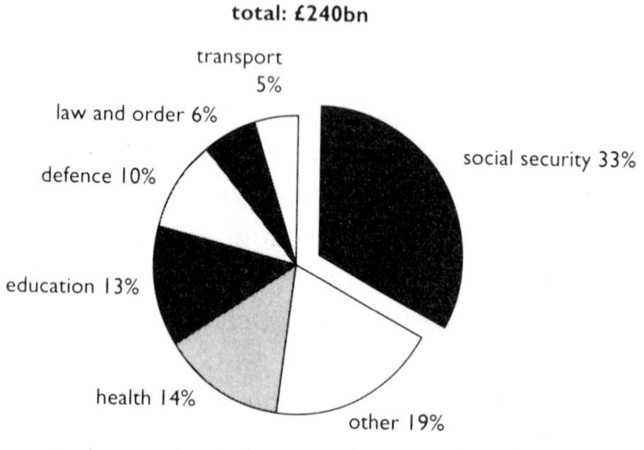

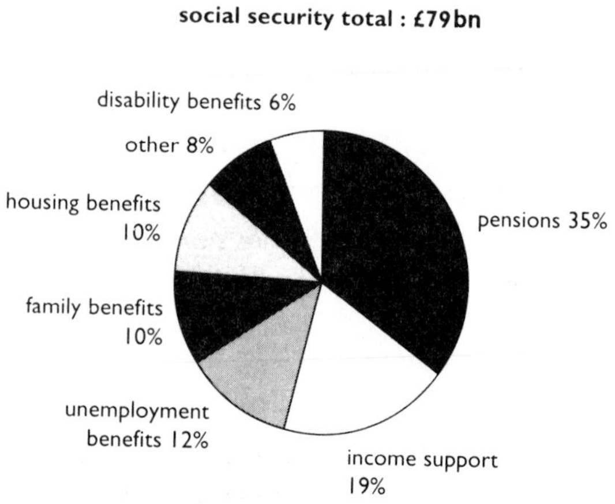

Figure 5.13 Where the money goes: public spending, 1992/93 (estimate, excluding debt interest and other accounting adjustments)
Source: *The Economist*, 13 February 1993.

Employers will also be required to take greater responsibility for Sick Pay and Maternity Benefit.

The retirement age for women is to be raised by five years so that there is a common retirement age of 65. This change will be phased in over ten to 15 years. Eventually the savings from this alone will be worth about £4 billion per year to the government.

Methods of access to health and social care provision

IMPLICATIONS OF RESOURCING AND CLASSIFICATION ON THE ACCESS AND SERVICES PROVIDED FOR CLIENTS

Figure 5.8 on page 293 shows how health and social care organisations are funded. Because different organisations may receive their funding from different sources, this means that some organisations may find it easier to receive funding than others. Obviously this will then have implications for the methods of access and services available to clients.

ACTIVITY

For example, an elderly disabled person could receive domiciliary care in the home under the Care in the Community scheme, or they could be cared for in a long-stay geriatric ward in a hospital.

- Ideally, what services would this person require from social services if they were to receive domiciliary care?
- If the services you listed above were available, which care setting, domiciliary or hospital ward, would you consider preferable?

Although domiciliary care may be considered preferable to living in a long-stay hospital ward, the resources available, or rather the lack of them, mean that in recent cases only the less favourable option may be available.

For example, in November 1994, the local authority on the Isle of Wight, which is responsible for funding local social services, and, therefore, domiciliary care and care in residential homes, said that it has run out of money and that people would have to stay in hospital.

Equally, health authorities have been criticised for increasingly dumping the costs of long-term care on to the local government-funded Care in the Community programme. For example, there have been cases of hospitals seeking a nursing home bed for unconscious patients on drips. In other words the NHS is moving towards providing acute medical care only and expecting local government, which is facing a cash cut in spending, to put patients needing longer-term care in private and independent nursing homes.

Ideally there should be genuine patient choice, based on information about the availability and quality of services. For example, it has been proved that the more specialised a surgeon or physician, the better the results will be for patients. However, not only is it difficult for patients to obtain accurate, up-to-date information, but under the new system of contracting it may not be possible for them to be treated by consultants of their own choice.

In practice, patients are restricted to being treated in hospitals where their District Health Authority has placed contracts, unless they have a fundholding GP.

If the patient wants to go to a specialist at another hospital, they have to get permission for what is called an 'extra-contractual referral', but money for these is extremely limited and there is no appeals procedure for appealing against refusals.

ACTIVITY

- Can you find other examples of lack of resources affecting the type of service offered to clients?

ACTIVITY

- Read the article below. In any experience you may have had in the workplace, or through any interviews you have had with clients (e.g. see Chapter 7), have you come across limits to the amount of service given to a person, or limits to whom the service is available?

WINTER OF NEGLECT LOOMS FOR ELDERLY

Almost 40 per cent of local authorities are cutting community-care provision to prevent big budget overspends. Gloucestershire council disclosed last week that it was providing care to the elderly only in emergencies. Days before, councillors on the Isle of Wight gave a warning that its community-care services were heading for collapse.

Elsewhere support services such as shopping, cleaning and cooking, and respite care to relieve round-the-clock pressure on relatives, are being axed.

According to the Association of Directors of Social Services, growing numbers of vulnerable elderly people have also become casualties of 'cost-shunting' between health authorities and local councils.

Hospital beds reserved for acute patients become 'blocked' as NHS managers and social services argue whether individual patients need social or medical care and about who should foot the bill. Nearly one-third of directors have reported that many elderly people have died within weeks of leaving hospital, suggesting they have been discharged too soon.

When community-care grants were fixed for the current year, Devon found itself £8.6 million short of what it had expected. Now it too is having to ration services to exclude 'lower priority categories' of elderly people. Demand for home help and respite care has been overwhelming. 'We have had 20,000 extra referrals across the board this year and we are looking after 100 more children,' said a spokesman. Next month the council may have to make more stringent cuts.

(The Sunday Observer, 20 November 1994)

ACTIVITY

- Recently a government 'brainstorming' seminar took place on how to contain the growing financial burden of looking after a population that is living longer. Organise a similar activity to produce a list of suggested options.
- To what extent do you consider that the focus of responsibility should be collective or individual?

Demographic characteristics affecting health and social care priorities

Throughout this book there are many examples of how population characteristics affect the provision of health and social care. Below is a summary of some of the population characteristics.

AGE PROFILE

ACTIVITY

- Refer back to pages 294–5 of this chapter where details are given for the projected number of pensioners in 2001 and 2031. Find out the predicted number of adults who will be paying taxes in these years, and work out the increase in the ratio of elderly people to taxpayers.
- List the examples given in this chapter on how the cost of providing the elderly with services may be kept to a minimum.
- Can you find evidence in your area of any planned increase in the future of provision for the elderly?

Table 5.3 Causes of death at all ages in England and Wales, 1991

Cause of death	Number	(%)
Diseases of the circulatory system (includes 150,090 deaths from heart disease)	261,834	(46.0)
Cancer	145,355	(25.7)
Diseases of the respiratory system	63,273	(11.1)
Diseases of the digestive system	18,508	(3.3)
Mental disorders	13,500	(2.4)
Diseases of the nervous system and sense organs	11,889	(2.1)
Endocrine, nutritional and metabolic diseases	10,538	(1.9)
Diseases of the genito-urinary system	6,464	(1.3)
Diseases of the musculoskeletal system	5,417	(1.0)
Diseases of the blood and blood-forming organs	2,446	(0.4)
Infectious and parasitic diseases	2,406	(0.4)
Diseases of the skin	930	–

Source: Davies and Davies (1993), *Community Health, Social Services and Preventative Medicine*, Baillière Tindall

INCIDENCE OF DISEASE

Potentially fatal diseases which occur frequently within a population will obviously be given a high health care priority. For example, heart disease, which is the greatest single cause of premature death, is targeted in the government's 'The Health of the Nation' document. The treatment and prevention of cancers, which cause 25% of all deaths, is also a high priority area (see Table 5.3 for a comparison of the incidence of fatal diseases).

INCIDENCE OF DISABILITY AND DYSFUNCTION

In 'The Health of the Nation', the government states its objective to 'enable people with physical disabilities to reach their optimum level of functioning', and so states its prevention to make rehabilitation a high priority area. The Office of Population, Censuses and Surveys (OPCS) has estimated that there are over six million people (14% of the total) in the adult population in Great Britain who have one or more significant disabilities. Figure 5.14 shows the incidence of types of disability.

GEOGRAPHICAL SPREAD

Areas of the country in which the population is most dense obviously attract more health and social care resources than more sparsely populated areas. For example, London has the highest concentration of hospitals, but even this is shrinking as the population of London declines.

ACTIVITY

Some diseases have a higher incidence in some geographical areas than others, and therefore receive a higher priority in those

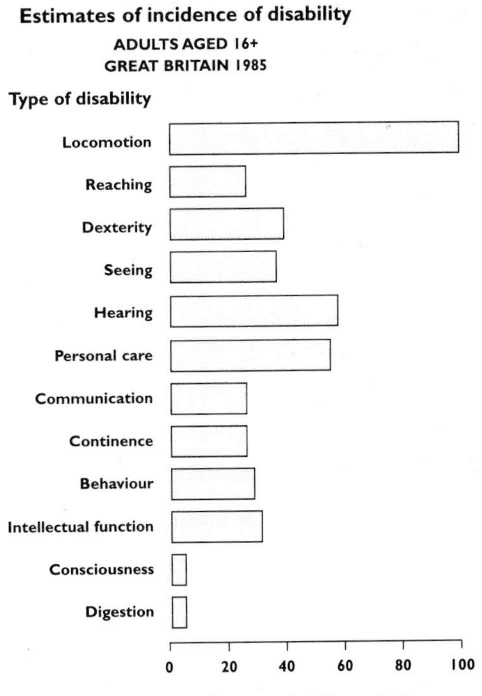

Figure 5.14 Estimates of incidence of disability
Source: OPCS Disability Survey. Taken from 'The Health of the Nation' – a consultative document for health in England, 1991.

Table 5.4 Standardised mortality ratios (SMRs) for coronary heart disease by Regional Health Authority (RHA) in England and Wales, 1989, and by Health Board in Scotland, 1980–85

England and Wales, RHA	SMR	Scotland, Health Board	SMR
Oxford	83	Lothian	92
South-east Thames	84	Borders	92
East Anglia	85	Grampian	93
North-west Thames	85	The Islands	94
North-east Thames	87	Tayside	96
Wessex	88	Highland	98
South Western	99	Forth Valley	98
West Midlands	106	Greater Glasgow	100
Wales	107	Fife	102
Trent	108	Dumfries and Galloway	105
Mersey	114	Ayr and Arran	108
Yorkshire	114	Argyll and Clyde	108
North Western	121	Lanarkshire	113
Northern	123		

Source: Davies and Davies (1993), *Community Health, Social Services and Preventative Medicine*, Baillière Tindall

areas. For example, heart disease has a significantly higher incidence in Scotland than anywhere else in the UK (see Table 5.4).

- Can you find examples of other diseases having a high incidence in some parts of the country compared with others?
- A higher incidence in the UK compared with other countries?

ACCESS TO HEALTH CARE

Self-referral

The first professional a person will generally visit if they have a health problem is a GENERAL PRACTITIONER (GP). A person should be registered with a GP to obtain regular health care. Every person has the right to be registered with a GP.

To register with a GP:

- Contact the FHSA, who will provide a list of GPs. (NB Children under 16 must be registered by their parents.)
- Take your medical card which shows your NHS number to the practice you choose and tell the receptionist you wish to register.
- If you are accepted, the FHSA will send you a new medical card and your medical records will be sent on to your new GP.
- If you are not accepted (e.g. if the GP's list is full), try at least two other GPs.
- If you are still not accepted, contact the FHSA who will allocate you a GP.

NB If you are staying in an area for less than three months you can be treated as a temporary resident by a local GP.

ACTIVITY

1 What factors would you take into consideration when choosing a GP?

2 Use a questionnaire to find out how other people have chosen their GP.

At any time a GP can remove a person from their list without giving a reason. The patient also has the right to leave a GP and register with another without asking permission or giving a reason. If the patient cannot find another, the FHSA is obliged to find one, who must accept the patient for a minimum of three months. Most general practices operate on an appointments system. Some practices have an 'open surgery' when patients can turn up and be seen on a first come, first served basis.

Most practices operate a combination of these two systems.

A GP only has to carry out a home visit if

'the condition of the patient so requires'. Out-of-hours home visits may be carried out by the GP, or he or she may make arrangements to provide alternative medical cover, for example, for other local doctors to work on a rota system.

Recall

To aid disease prevention, a person may occasionally be contacted by their dentist or GP and requested to make an appointment for a check-up or screening procedure.

The government provides various in-centre payments for GPs who reach given percentage targets for screening uptake. For example, between 1987 and 1990, £70 million was provided to set up and run the National Breast Screening Programme, in which all women aged 50–64 years old are invited for screening every three years. The target is for at least 70% of these eligible women to be screened. Women aged 20–64 are called for cervical cancer screening every five years, and 80% of these eligible women are actually screened. Of the women who do have a cervical smear, only about 5% are then recalled because of showing 'borderline abnormalities', or, in a few cases, the early warning signs of cancer. Trials are currently underway in Europe and the United States to establish whether screening men for prostate cancer would reduce its prevalence,

ACTIVITY

1 Visit your local GP's surgery or health centre to find out what you can about the type and scale of screening services available.

2 What are the benefits of screening for:

- the individual?
- the doctor?
- society as a whole

3 How would you evaluate the effectiveness of a screening programme?

Referral by a professional

A GP may refer a patient to a SPECIALIST. Generally, the professional to whom a GP will refer a patient will be a CONSULTANT. Unlike GPs, consultants are salaried employees of the NHS, although they may also have private patients. Consultants are specialists in particular:

- *diseases*, e.g. oncologist (cancer care);
- *age groups*, e.g. geriatrician (care of elders);
- *parts of the body*, e.g. urologist (bladder, prostate and kidney surgery).

In hospital the consultant normally heads a small team of doctors. In descending order of priority this team includes a senior registrar, a registrar, a senior house officer and a house officer.

It is the GP, and not the patient, who decides whether specialist attention is needed. If the patient disagrees with the GP about the need for an appointment with a consultant, he or she can request a second opinion (e.g. from another GP in the same practice).

If the GP thinks referral to a consultant is necessary, the following procedure is followed:

1 The GP writes a letter to a consultant to request an out-patient appointment. (Most GPs choose consultants in the hospitals with which their district health authority has a contract. GP fundholders have their own contracts with hospitals and may also pay for consultants to hold out-patient clinics at their health centres.)
2 The hospital writes directly to the patient with notification of the date and time of the out-patient appointment. (The waiting time for this appointment is generally about six weeks, or less if urgent.)
3 The patient attends an out-patient clinic where he or she will be seen by a consultant or registrar.
4 If the specialist finds it necessary to admit the patient for treatment (for example, an operation), he or she will be put on a waiting list. The Patient's Charter states that

patients have 'the right to be guaranteed admission for treatment by a specific date not later than two years from the day when your consultant places you on a waiting list'. Even two years may be considered an unacceptably long wait. Hospitals and health authorities are given targets and incentives by the Department of Health to keep their waiting lists within limits.

5 The consultant will send a letter to the GP to notify him or her of the proposed course of action.

6 After hospital treatment, the patient will receive care from his or her GP, and may also be given further appointments at the consultant's out-patient clinic.

ACTIVITY

W

1 Give as many examples as you can of specialists working in each of the three areas noted in the text (diseases, age groups, parts of the body).

2 In some countries, e.g. the United States and Germany, a patient can often go directly to a specialist without consulting the family doctor first. What do you think are the main advantages and disadvantages of the British system compared with the other?

3 Discuss the reasons for long waiting lists, and try to find out how hospitals are attempting to cut them.

There are two hospital departments for which the patient does not require professional referral:

- Accident and Emergency departments;
- Sexually Transmitted Diseases clinics;

In an emergency which is not life-threatening, the patient's GP should be the first point of contact. However, in a real emergency the 999 service should be called and an ambulance requested. The Patient's Charter states that an ambulance should arrive within 14 minutes in urban areas, and within 19 minutes in rural areas. Emergency ambulance crews are trained in emergency medical techniques, although the importance of basic first aid training for all members of the public cannot be over-emphasised.

In a large general hospital the ACCIDENT AND EMERGENCY DEPARTMENT ('casualty department') is open 24 hours a day. Usually the condition of the patient will be assessed initially by a nurse, who will either recommend immediate treatment or indicate the length of the waiting time before a doctor will see the patient for treatment.

A patient does not have to arrive at Accident and Emergency in an ambulance but treatment may not be given if it is thought the problem is not urgent and can be dealt with by their GP.

SEXUALLY TRANSMITTED DISEASES (STD) clinics are usually, but not always, attached to main hospitals. They give free, confidential advice and treatment to people of all ages with genito-urinary infections (for example, gonorrhoea and syphilis). They will also give HIV antibody tests. Telephone numbers of STD clinics are listed in the telephone book, and some clinics will see patients without them having to make appointments.

Before patients undergo invasive treatment (for example, surgery or radiotherapy), they are usually asked to sign a consent form. An example is given in Figure 5.15.

The standard NHS form includes the following:

- name of proposed treatment/operation;
- a statement that the nature and purpose of the treatment have been explained to the patient;
- a clause which gives consent for any other procedures which may be necessary if there is an urgent or unexpected complication.

In an emergency (i.e. if the patient is unconscious) permission will be sought from the patient's next of kin, if possible.

CONSENT FORM
For medical or dental investigation, treatment or operation

Health Authority .... Patient's Surname ....
Hospital .... Other Names ....
Unit Number .... Date of Birth ....
Sex: (*please tick*) Male ☐ Female ☐

DOCTORS OR DENTISTS (*This part to be completed by doctor or dentist. See notes*)

TYPE OF OPERATION INVESTIGATION OR TREATMENT

I confirm that I have explained the operation investigation or treatment, and such appropriate options as are available and the type of anaesthetic, if any (general/regional/sedation) proposed, to the patient in terms which in my judgement are suited to the understanding of the patient and/or to one of the parents or guardians of the patient

Signature .... Date ...../...../.......
Name of doctor or dentist ....

PATIENT/PARENT/GUARDIAN

1. Please read this form and the notes very carefully.
2. If there is anything that you don't understand about the explanation, or if you want more information, you should ask the doctor or dentist.
3. Please check that all the information on the form is correct. If it is, and you understand the explanation, then sign the form.

I am the patient/parent/guardian (*delete as necessary*)

I agree
- to what is proposed which has been explained to me by the doctor/dentist named on this form.
- to the use of the type of anaesthetic that I have been told about.
- to be examined, whilst under anaesthetic, by no more than two students.

I understand
- that the procedure may not be done by the doctor/dentist who has been treating me so far.
- that any procedure in addition to the investigation or treatment described on this form will only be carried out if it is necessary and in my best interests and can be justified for medical reasons.

I have told
- the doctor or dentist about any additional procedures I would *not* wish to be carried out straightaway without my having the opportunity to consider them first.

Signature ....
Name ....
Address ....
(*if not the patient*) ....
....

NOTES TO:

Doctors, Dentists
A patient has a legal right to grant or withold consent prior to examination or treatment. Patients should be given sufficient information, in a way they can understand, about the proposed treatment and the possible alternatives. Patients must be allowed to decide whether they will agree to the treatment and they may refuse or withdraw consent to treatment at any time. The patient's consent to treatment should be recorded on this form (further guidance is given in HC(90)22 (*A Guide to Consent for Examination or Treatment.*)

Patients

- The doctor or dentist is here to help you. He or she will explain the proposed treatment and what the alternatives are. You can ask any questions and seek further information. You can refuse the treatment.
- You may ask for a relative, or friend, or a nurse to be present.
- Training health professionals is essential to the continuation of the health service and improving the quality of care. Your treatment may provide an important opportunity for such training, where necessary under the careful supervision of a senior doctor or dentist. You may refuse any involvement in a formal training programme without this adversely affecting your care and treatment.

Figure 5.15 An example of a consent form

ACTIVITY

List the questions you would wish to be answered before you signed a consent form.

Consent is required from parents if their child is too young to have a full understanding of the treatment in question. If a doctor thinks consent is being withheld unreasonably, he or she can apply for a court order. However, a court order would be likely to go against parents' wishes only in life-and-death cases.

It is very rare for the wishes of an adult refusing to give consent for life-saving treatment to be overruled. For example, Jehovah's Witnesses, who believe that by accepting blood transfusions they will be denied eternal life, have had their wishes respected, even when this proves fatal. In the US courts an adult's refusal to accept a transfusion has been overridden only when the validity of the withholding consent was doubtful (for example, undue pressure had been put on the patient by relatives), or when the patient was a pregnant woman whose foetus was at risk, or whose child would be motherless. In the UK few cases have reached the courts, but instances of controversy from time to time make the news, as the following letter to *The Guardian* illustrates:

Doctor [name deleted] should not have the trauma of having to weigh the legal points about a Jehovah's Witness who does not wish for a blood transfusion, and may die as a result of not having it. Nor should there be expensive legal court cases on the point.

The medical establishment should ensure that all those who treat the sick and injured know that the patient's wish is paramount. There is no argument about it. If the Jehovah's Witness would prefer to die than accept someone else's blood, it is decided in the whole ethic of his of her life; there are countless thousands of people who would rather die than lose something they hold precious, whether it is their freedom or anything else.

I had thought it was perfectly understood that anyone is at liberty to refuse any form of medical treatment, when they are conscious and of sound mind. Not for nothing does one have to sign a disclaimer before an operation.

(The Guardian, 8 August 1992)

ACTIVITY

- Read the letter from *The Guardian* reproduced in the text about the refusal of a blood transfusion.
- Then consider the following four cases and discuss what recommendations you would have made in each of them.
- Finally, compare your conclusions with the court rulings given below.

The cases:

1 A 35-year-old Jehovah's Witness gave birth to twins. To save her life she required a blood transfusion. She refused this.

2 A 16-year-old anorexic refused to undergo treatment, even though she was aware that she would die without it.

3 T, who refused a blood transfusion, was 20. Her parents separated when she was three. Her mother was a fervent Jehovah's Witness, a faith which regards blood transfusions as sinful. T's father emphatically rejected the faith.

4 A 30-year-old woman who had two other children refused to have a Caesarian, although the surgeon was emphatic that the unborn child could not be delivered without the operation. The woman and her husband said the operation was against their principles as born-again Christians. Because it was an emergency, the case was brought and heard within an hour.

The court rulings:

1 The blood transfusion was not given and the woman died.

2 As the patient was under 18 her refusal was overruled.

3 It was judged that T was not in a fit state to make a decision and so her wishes were overruled; she received a transfusion. It was suggested that undue pressure from her mother had influenced her refusal.

4 The mother's wishes were overruled and the child was delivered by Caesarian. The baby died. This was the first case in the UK in which the rights of the unborn baby appear to have overruled those of the mother.

Compulsory admission to hospital

As has been shown, even if the patient's life is in danger, he or she can refuse to accept treatment and doctors and nurses treating patients against their will could face criminal prosecution. However, there are two circumstances in which compulsory admission to hospital occurs.

If MENTALLY ILL, patients may be detained under certain sections of the Mental Health Act. For this to occur, patients must have been SECTIONED for at least 28 days. Sectioning commits patients for treatment for their own safety or the protection of others. It requires the signature of two doctors, one of them a psychiatrist, as well as that of a psychiatric social worker or the patient's nearest relative. The patient's nursing care may include restraint or seclusion. Drug treatment can be given for up to three months, but after that a second doctor's opinion is required. Electroconvulsive therapy (ECT) also requires a second doctor's opinion. The patient's consent is required for invasive therapies, such as surgery or hormone implantation.

If patients are suspected of having a dangerous NOTIFIABLE DISEASE, for example, tuberculosis, they may be isolated from others at risk. This regulation would only be enforced if the public were at risk of infection, and although the patients would be isolated, they would still not be treated against their will.

Private self-referral

Even if a patient wants to be treated privately by a consultant, he or she must still be referred through a GP. Most complementary medical provision requires private self-referral even if this has been recommended by another professional, for example, making an appointment with an osteopath, chiropractor or faith healer.

ACTIVITY **W**

Refer back to the information obtained on voluntary organisations giving health care. How do clients gain access to the provision they offer? Is it by referral through professionals, or is it by private self-referral?

ACCESS TO SOCIAL CARE

Referral by a Professional

The following professionals and organisations may approach a social worker in their local Personal Social Services Department to request help for a client:

- health visitor;
- district nurse;
- GP;
- community psychiatric nurse;
- teacher;
- head of year;
- Education Welfare Department;
- magistrate;
- probation service;
- solicitor;
- Citizens Advice Bureau;
- police.

Referral by a member of the family or community

Non-professionals, such as neighbours or parents, may also ask for help, or the person requiring help may approach social services directly.

ACTIVITY

Examine the list of channels of referral to social services. Can you think of situations in which each might be used?

Once a person has been referred, or referred themselves, to the Social Services Department, an ASSESSMENT of the situation takes place to determine the most suitable course of action. Figure 5.16 shows a typical example of this assessment procedure.

ACTIVITY W

Refer back to the information obtained on voluntary organisations giving social care. How do users gain access to the provision they offer? Is it by referral through professionals, or is it by private self-referral?

ACCESS TO SOCIAL SECURITY PROVISION

There are many sources of information on social security payments. Any of the professionals and organisations listed above may advise a person to apply for benefits. Free leaflets are available from social security offices and advice centres, and the press and television sometimes carry advertisements giving details of particular benefits.

The applicants will complete the necessary forms, or this will be done for them if necessary. Their entitlement to benefit will then be assessed.

ACTIVITY

If a person thinks that a social security decision is wrong, he or she can appeal. Obtain the leaflet *How to Appeal* from your local social security office to find out about the appeals procedure.

WHY HEALTH AND SOCIAL CARE PROVISION DEVELOPS AND CHANGES

Policy developments

There have been important changes in the organisation, structure and 'delivery' of health and care services. What has influenced these changes? Some people observing and trying to describe developments since the nineteenth century have found it useful to try to summarise and classify different perspectives on social policy and welfare provision. They have looked at the ideas and values which lie behind a particular set of views and have tried to explain how these have affected the direction which social policy-making has taken. Usually these sets of ideas or perspectives involve attempts to explain social problems and devise appropriate solutions to them. In essence, these models of social policy provide different views on exactly where the burden and balance of responsibility for health and care provision should lie in any society.

Four models of social policy will be described:

- anti-collectivist/market models;
- non-socialist welfare collectivists/liberal collectivists/the mixed economy of welfare;
- the Fabian socialists;
- the political economy of welfare.

These outlines will be followed by feminist and anti-racist critiques of these models.

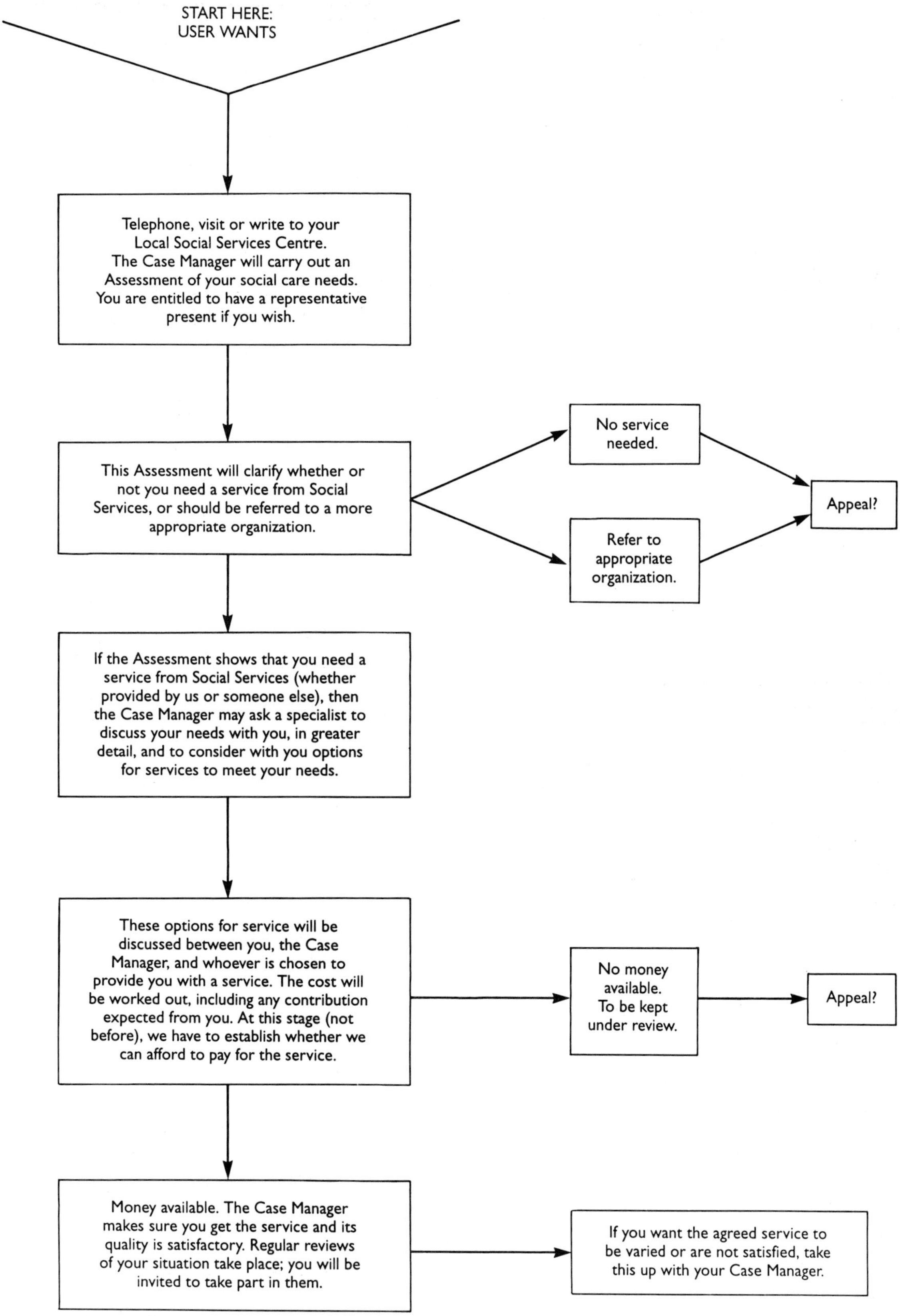
START HERE:
USER WANTS
Telephone, visit or write to your Local Social Services Centre. The Case Manager will carry out an Assessment of your social care needs. You are entitled to have a representative present if you wish.
This Assessment will clarify whether or not you need a service from Social Services, or should be referred to a more appropriate organization.
No service needed.
Refer to appropriate organization.
Appeal?
If the Assessment shows that you need a service from Social Services (whether provided by us or someone else), then the Case Manager may ask a specialist to discuss your needs with you, in greater detail, and to consider with you options for services to meet your needs.
These options for service will be discussed between you, the Case Manager, and whoever is chosen to provide you with a service. The cost will be worked out, including any contribution expected from you. At this stage (not before), we have to establish whether we can afford to pay for the service.
No money available. To be kept under review.
Appeal?
Money available. The Case Manager makes sure you get the service and its quality is satisfactory. Regular reviews of your situation take place; you will be invited to take part in them.
If you want the agreed service to be varied or are not satisfied, take this up with your Case Manager.

Figure 5.16 The assessment procedure carried out by social services
Source: Surrey County Council Social Services Department

ANTI-COLLECTIVIST/MARKET MODELS

Right-wing Conservative governments have believed that state intervention in society should be reduced. According to this approach, people should become more responsible for themselves and their families. They should 'stand on their own two feet'. The family and community should be the main source of care for children, the elderly and the infirm. State welfare limits individual freedom and choice, and leads to more demands on government than it can afford to pay for or administer. The real objective of state welfare is ultimately to make people do without it.

It is argued that people should not rely on the 'nanny state'. The way to reduce the cost of the welfare state is to promote SELECTIVIST health and welfare policies, where the benefits of the policies are available only to those assessed as in need of them. UNIVERSALIST policies, i.e. making services and benefits available to all, should be discouraged.

The term 'the New Right' has come to be used to describe the ideas of the Conservative governments led by Margaret Thatcher and John Major since 1979. New Right ideas involve the belief that:

- people lack choice if there is no readily available alternative to the state provision of services;
- state welfare services become wasteful and inefficient when they are faced with no competition or are not controlled by principles of cost-effectiveness;
- the more people get, the more they expect;
- state bureaucracies have created self-interested groups of professional workers and administrators who want the growth in the welfare state maintained because it is in their interests – it provides them with employment;
- the welfare state is morally disruptive; it saps people's will to find work and provide for themselves;
- the state is incapable of the efficient running of mass welfare schemes, e.g. insurance, pensions; private companies competing with each other in the marketplace could exercise these functions much more efficiently;
- the role of the state should be as a 'purchaser' of services for people rather than as a direct provider and financer of those services. State provision should be replaced by independent providers competing in 'internal' or 'quasi'-markets.

NON-SOCIALIST WELFARE COLLECTIVISTS/LIBERAL COLLECTIVISTS/THE MIXED ECONOMY OF WELFARE

These ideas originated with the Liberal Party in the early twentieth century and were taken up by figures such as Beveridge and Keynes and politicians of more recent years such as David Owen.

Liberal and Social Democratic (and more moderate Conservative) approaches have argued for a 'mixed economy of welfare' – a partnership between individuals, families, industry and the state in the provision of health and care services. Families and individuals cannot always function alone. They sometimes need professional support and help – financial, emotional and practical. There are times when state-employed professionals must 'step in' for the sake of those vulnerable to the 'downside' of capitalism, such as the unemployed and the poor, or to the 'bad' in people, e.g. children at risk of abuse.

There is a belief here that capitalism and free enterprise are the best ways to ensure people have freedom, but that welfare services are necessary to ensure political stability and the smooth maintenance of capitalism. Hence there is a belief in:

- the direct public provision of welfare benefits and services;
- the commitment to universal access to those services (but only at a minimal level);
- some 'targeting' of certain services to

particular individuals or groups, i.e. some selectivity;
- the role of the state in supporting the activities of voluntary agencies and self-help groups.

THE FABIAN SOCIALISTS

These ideas date from early Fabians such as the Webbs, and post-war writers such as Crosland and Titmuss.

The dominant values of these writers are equality, freedom and fellowship. They argue that capitalism is unethical, unjust and undemocratic, but that it can be transformed and changed. Government action can play a part in this process and the welfare state is one of the main ways in which this transformation can be achieved. There is thus a belief that:

- the Welfare State can be a springboard for change – a progressive force which can encourage the gradual development of citizenship rights;
- universal services should be provided by the State, with some positive discrimination for areas or groups defined as being in greater need;
- social change is generated by the State's action. If the State is seen to be just and altruistic, people will follow the 'good example' set.

More radical versions of this policy model suggest that:

- social policy is more important than economic policy and should certainly not just be a reaction to economic policy, dealing with the problems of capitalism as 'side-effects';
- social and economic policies need to be unified through a democratic, decentralised process of social planning according to need;
- any analysis of social problems must take into account the class structure of society;
- the assertion of socialist values can change capitalism.

THE POLITICAL ECONOMY OF WELFARE

This model applies Marxist economic and political theory to the development of the welfare state in the twentieth century. It suggests that the state should be highly committed to people's welfare and that people's values will change only when the economic organisation of society changes. Collectivist values will arise out of the struggle by the working class to achieve more power. Until this occurs, this perspective suggests that the Welfare State in capitalist societies is:

- on the one hand, used by the State to have more control over its workers;
- on the other hand, also partly the outcome of struggles by the working class to improve social and economic conditions for themselves.

FEMINIST CRITIQUE

Feminists suggest that welfare legislation has tended to reflect patriarchal attitudes in society. The 'caring' role of women within families (as mothers, as carers for the elderly and/or disabled) is assumed to be part of their 'normal' duties and responsibilities, and as such the State has tended to feel it should not subsidise women in these positions. There has been a reluctance by governments to replace the unpaid work of women within the family by health/welfare institutions and provision.

ANTI-RACIST CRITIQUE

This perspective identifies the Welfare State as part of the institutionalised racism in society – denying black peoples' access to benefits and provision, reproducing the racial division of labour within the Welfare State and using welfare agencies to police black people and immigrants. The State is seen as an agency of social control, coercing people into situations which may not necessarily mean they receive better health and care services.

Summary of Labour plans for health care (1992)

- More services outside the hospital by community health teams or GPs.
- Care of elderly or chronically ill patients must get a higher priority.
- Mental health services must get a fairer share of resources.
- Quality of treatment and services must be recognised as equally important as quantity.
- A permanent Cabinet committee on health promotion to be created.
- Tobacco advertising to be banned.
- Random breath-testing to be introduced.
- Nutritional guidelines for school meals to be restored.
- Free eye tests to be restored.
- GPs to be helped to make more time available for health promotion.

Conservative governments have been in power in Britain since 1979. The market model or approach to care has thus strongly directed a key idea in the organisation of health and social care services. This is the purchaser–provider 'split'.

In the business and industrial sectors of the economy there is a reasonably clear distinction between a purchaser and a provider. If I wish to purchase a pound of apples, I must go to a provider – a supermarket or greengrocer. If the apples are bruised, soft or too expensive, I will in future be more likely to buy them from another provider – a different shop. The shop which provides the best apples at the best price will, in theory, attract the most purchasers (customers). The Conservative government believes that such competition between providers improves the quality of the services or products they offer.

Can this approach be applied to health, welfare and other care services? The Conservative government believes that many of the existing social services can and must be split into different sectors of 'purchasers' and 'providers'. The split is not as simple as in the case outlined above, however. In most cases the purchasers will not be the public but professionals such as GPs and social workers, who will purchase services on their behalf – rather like allowing someone else to buy that pound of apples for you. The principle here will be that only the professional can really assess what the needs of the person are; it would not be appropriate for the potential patient or client to make their own decisions. It will be the professionals too, who have the money to pay; they control the purse. However, in some areas of social policy the government does intend to try to give the public more direct 'purchasing' power, as in its suggestions that students in further and higher education should be allocated education vouchers which they could spend on a range of courses.

THE ORGANISATION OF HEALTH AND SOCIAL CARE PLANNING AND PROVISION

The current structure of health and social care

The previous section discussed the influences of various social policy ideas on health and social care provision, and in particular the influence of current government policy. To summarise, the organisation of most health and social care provision now involves responding to the political pressure to become either:

- *a purchaser of services*. Some health and care organisations now have the resources and income to buy health and social care services for clients. These include Family Health Service Authorities and Local Purchasing Authorities;
- *a provider of services*. These health and care organisations are paid by the purchasers to provide services to clients. Examples here would include NHS Trusts and private

sector providers such as the owners of residential homes for the elderly.

- *a joint purchaser–provider*. For example, GP fundholders and Social Services Departments can purchase services on behalf of clients and provide them directly themselves.

Purchaser roles

The organisational changes of health and care services into purchaser and provider roles have meant that other changes are taking place within these organisations.

SINGLE AND MULTI-AGENCY PURCHASERS

Single agency purchasers are those, such as Social Services Departments, which control their own budget and use it to buy specific services for the clients they are responsible for. For example, places in residential care will be purchased on behalf of elderly clients by Social Services Departments. This would be an example of a service purchased for an individual.

Multi-agency purchasers refers to the growing trend for different purchaser organisations to jointly commission and pay for services. For example, health authorities and Social Services Departments may be joint purchasers of a child and adolescent mental health service. This service will be likely to be multi-disciplinary, i.e. there will be a range of professionals working together. In this example, psychotherapists, family therapists, counsellors, family assessment workers, psychologists and psychiatrists may all be involved in the provision of child and adolescent mental health services. These services are purchased by the joint commissioning agencies on behalf of the communities they serve.

PLANNING AND ASSESSMENT OF SERVICES

Now that purchasers have so much control over the budgets available to them, they are increasingly being expected to ensure that the best use is made of the money that they spend. Just as the person in charge of a family budget has to make careful calculations about who needs money spent on them in the family and whether the money subsequently spent represented good value, so purchasers are now expected to provide a 'service specification'. This means that they have to carefully assess:

- the past demand for their services;
- the current and projected future demands for their services;
- the nature and appropriateness of the services provided.

To do this they will consult:

- the results of research commissioned by them or other independent research;
- submissions from interested agencies, organisations and pressure groups;
- census information if relevant;
- estimates of cost and viability.

Changes in provider services

EMPLOYMENT STATUS

Providers generally feel the effects of the changes outlined above. Providers are beginning to need to demonstrate that they can effectively provide the services they sell. They are having to compete with other providers for the contracts of employment offered by the purchasers. In some areas of health and care provision this has led to organisations 'market-testing' parts of the services which they offer to assess whether these could be more effectively and cheaply provided by private companies. For example, fostering and adoption services which have traditionally been provided by local authority Social Services Departments are being market-tested in some boroughs as a prelude to their being sold off to the private sector and established as private agencies. Purchasing authorities would then buy fostering and adoption services from these agencies.

MANAGEMENT

Since the mid-1980s, in all social, health, education and care services there has been an encouragement and active creation of management posts and roles. These managers have essentially had the task of implementing the social legislation of the 1980s and 1990s in their organisations and institutions. In some services, personal social services in particular, those people promoted into lower or middle management posts have often previously been practitioners with limited or no previous 'management training'. Their new roles have left them with little direct work with the clients or 'clients' and have meant learning a new managerialist bureaucratic ethos.

On the other hand, at the higher management end of the organisation of health and care services, there has been a trend to appoint people to the most senior posts who have had no previous direct experience of that particular care service but may have had previous industrial and management experience. A survey for the Department of Health reported in *The Guardian* on 10th June 1994 showed that fewer than one in five top managers in the NHS has a background of medicine, nursing or any other clinical specialism.

These trends have caused some problems. Not all newly appointed lower and middle managers in social and care services agree with the social policy changes of the 1980s and 1990s; they find themselves attempting to implement policies with which they are not wholly comfortable and with which many of their staff also disagree. This has been one of the key themes in the BBC TV programme *Casualty*.

Secondly, the pay of some higher managers and executives, particularly in the NHS, has increased relatively faster than most other NHS employees. A report in 1993 by Income Data Services showed that, on average, the chief executives of Trust hospitals had received 9% pay rises over the previous year, with some getting 33%. The pay increases of most public sector workers were limited to 1.5% over the same period.

ADMIN IN THE 'NEW LOOK' NHS COSTS EXTRA £1.5BN

The National Health Service employs 36,000 more managers and clerks but 27,000 fewer nurses than it did before the Government started to introduce market-style changes, official figures disclose today.

Analysis of the figures by a Labour MP suggests that the service has spent, cumulatively, an extra £1.5 billion on bureaucracy over and above what would have been necessary to sustain the numbers of managers and administrative and clerical staff employed in 1989.

The figures are the most comprehensive and up to date available for the years straddling introduction of the NHS market in 1991. They have been obtained through parliamentary questions by Alan Milburn, Labour MP for Darlington.

His latest questions paint a picture for the entire United Kingdom, showing that the number of NHS managers rose from 6,091 in 1989/90 to 20,478 in 1992/93 – an increase of 236.2 per cent. In 1992/93 alone, the number rose 22.1 per cent.

Over the same period, administrative and clerical (A&C) staff rose from 144,582 to 166,363 – a 15.1 per cent increase. The rise in 1992/93 alone was 5.6 per cent. Taking together managers and A&C staff, the rise over the whole period was 36,168 or 24 per cent.

By contrast, the number of nursing and midwifery staff, expressed as whole-time equivalents, fell by 27,235 from 508,341 in 1989/90 to 481,106 in 1992/93 – a drop of 5.4 per cent, with a drop of 13,410 or 3.4 per cent in 1992/93 alone.

Ministers have responded to previous figures on staffing changes by arguing that some increase in management numbers was necessary to beef up the NHS in areas where it was weak, particularly finance. But they have said some of the rise, and some of the fall in nursing numbers, is explicable by reclassification of senior nurses as managers.

A Department of Health spokesman said yesterday this reclassification had started in 1989 and would still have been having an impact in 1992/93. Mr Milburn had also obtained figures for salary costs, consequent upon the staffing changes. Between 1989/90 and 1992/93, the bill for managers rose 205.9 per cent from £174.2 million to £532.9 million.

The bill for A&C staff rose 44.3 per cent from £1.3 billion to £1.8 billion. Taking both groups together, the service last year spent £925.9 million more on administration than in 1989/90.

The pay bill for nursing and midwifery staff rose only 23.2 per cent over the same period, from £6.2 billion to £7.6 billion.

The fact that the percentage increase in the managers' salary costs has been rather less than the percentage rise in their numbers indicates that recent appointments have been at lower grades. Nevertheless, Mr Milburn claimed there had been a 'managerial salary explosion' in the service.

Tom Sackville, Junior Health Minister, said the managerial salary bill represented only 3 per cent of total NHS pay costs, and more than 18,000 student nurses had been deleted from nursing numbers since 1990.

(The Guardian, 9 December 1993)

ACTIVITY

Using the article above, answer the following questions:

1 According to the official figures, how many NHS managers existed in 1989/90? How many existed in 1992/93? What percentage increase does this represent?

2 Over the same period, 1989/90–1992/93, by what percentage did the numbers of administration and clerical staff in the NHS rise?

3 Over the same period, 1989/90–1992/93; by what percentage did the number of nursing and midwifery staff fall?

4 How do Conservative Party ministers explain these figures?

5 To what extent do these figures support the suggestion that there is an increasing emphasis on management in the health profession?

6 Is an increasing emphasis on the role of managers in the health and care services a good thing or a bad thing?

ACTIVITY

Investigate the apparent growth in 'managerialism' in any institution with which you are familiar or can make contact. For example, in your school or college arrange to inverview anyone in a management position such as a headteacher, a manager of a curriculum section or a head of department. What changes have occurred to their jobs in the past few years? What has been their response to these changes? Do they think that students are getting a better service from the education system? What training in management have they had? Was it useful? Why?

SKILL MIX

To become more effective and efficient in the delivery of services many providers are now moving towards the multi-skilling of professionals – SKILL MIX. This means that teamwork is now encouraged so that skills can be used in a complementary way. For example, many GP practices are now group practices where the GPs can pool their resources and afford to buy in the additional services of other health professionals such as occupational therapists, nurses, health visitors, physiotherapists and alternative medicine practitioners (e.g. oesteopaths and homeopaths).

TRAINING AND DEVELOPMENT

The training and development of health and care professionals is now increasingly viewed as a provider service in its own right. Many training and development departments are now business units and have to respond carefully to the needs of the professionals they work with.

ADMINISTRATION AND COST-EFFECTIVENESS

As health and care organisations increasingly behave more like business organisations, there has been a desire to monitor more closely what staff do, how they do it and whether they are working cost-effectively.

The notion of cost-effectiveness is an economic term which is increasingly becoming a part of everyday speech. To make something cost effective simply means to ensure that the maximum financial profit or minimum financial loss is achieved by any organisation, industry or individual selling or providing a product or a service.

For example, it will not be cost-effective to take a job as, say, a nursery nurse, if the costs of accommodation, bills, travel, taxes and daily living exceed the annual wage. The 'costs' of doing the job have to be weighed against how effective the wage is as income.

The income or funding of health, education and social services is generally limited by a number of factors, and financial resourses are not infinite. For some people the way in which the idea of 'cost-effectiveness' has been applied in these areas is simply a euphemism for further 'cuts' in financial resources – the least-cost method of achieving a particular objective. However, 'cost-effectiveness' may be justified as a way of conserving scarce resources and avoiding unnecessary expenditure or waste.

Several issues and problems do, however, arise when trying to apply cost-effective measures to health, education and care contexts. Some of these will be considered below.

1 Short-term gains in cost-effectiveness have to be weighed up against the possible long-term consequences of the measures.

   For instance, a school managing its own overall budget may try to employ more 'beginning', newly qualified teachers in preference to older, more experienced teachers who would cost more in wages. Hence the school may in the short term save money from its overall wages bill. This saving would need to be measured against the following possible longer-term consequences:

   - The loss of effective teaching and leadership from more experienced staff could lead to a decline in examination results at the school. Fewer prospective students then apply to the school as its popularity falls.
   - As the 'roll' of the school falls, the school attracts a lower annual budget and may be forced to make teachers redundant.

2 Cost-effective measures in one part of a service may drive up costs in another, as the following extract suggests.

GPs URGED TO SAVE £425M ON DRUGS BILL

Family doctors give their patients too many drugs and the wrong types of drugs because they spend too little time seeing them, the Audit Commission says today in a report calling for more rational precribing.

Patient care could be improved and the National Health Service could save £425 million a year if all general practitioners prescribed as well as 50 medical practices studied by the commission, the report concludes.

The report will anger drugs companies. They point out that GPs write far fewer prescriptions

than their counterparts in most other European countries, as much as five times fewer than in France, and they maintain that good prescribing can save NHS money by keeping patients out of hospital.

The commission says it is not against prescribing more or costlier drugs and it acknowledges that the British record is good by international standards.

Drugs prescribed by GPs cost £3.6 billion in England and Wales in 1992/93, 10 per cent of the NHS budget. The bill is growing at an annual rate of 14 per cent and ministers are seeking ways to curb it.

The commission says the basic problem is that GPs spend too little time with their patients. Inadequate consideration may be given to a case, or alternative treatments, and a doctor under pressure may find it quicker to write a prescription to end a consultation.

Previous studies have shown that GPs who spend an average of 10 minutes or more with a patient prescribe fewer antibiotics, the report says. Doctors can make more time for patients by delegating to other members of the health team, keeping accurate and computerised records and seeing fewer drug company representatives.

The £425 million projected saving includes £275 million through less over-prescribing of drugs, such as antibiotics and laxatives, and £45 million through prescribing fewer drugs of limited clinical value, such as cough suppressants and nasal decongestants

It also includes £25 million through substituting cheaper drugs, such as Cimetidine, an ulcer healing brand 60 per cent cheaper than others; £50 million through prescribing 20 more generic alternatives to brands; and £30 million through more appropriate use of very expensive drugs.

One tranquilliser, buspirone, is said to cost 320 times more than an alternative, diazepam. Some practices do not prescribe it, but others do so in up to 56 per cent of cases on grounds of greater safety. The commission says there is only marginal evidence that it is safer.

On the other hand, the commission says, it would make good sense and save the NHS other costs if doctors spent £75 million more prescribing inhaled steroids to prevent asthma sufferers having attacks and possibly being admitted to hospital.

A summary of the report is being sent to every GP practice. Auditors will visit every family health services authority to check on procedures for monitoring prescribing.

The Royal Pharmaceutical Society welcomed the report, but the Association of the British Pharmaceutical Industry said the commission's recommendation would disadvantage patients, impose unnecessary restrictions on GPs and drive up health care costs.

(The Guardian, 8th March 1994)

ACTIVITY

Read the article above and use it to answer the following questions.

1 What does the Audit Commission mean by 'more rational' prescribing?

2 How does it suggest that more rational prescribing could cut costs in the NHS?

3 What arguments can you think of for and against the Audit Commission on this issue?

3 Cost-effectiveness measures sometimes indicate that a service could be improved by money being spent on it in different ways from the current arrangements. Money could be 'switched' from one area or aspect of a service to another without any overall increase in funding being needed.

For example, at present, family doctors have a contractual obligation with the Department of Health to provide 24-hour care, 365 days a year, to their patients. This means that they have to ensure that an emergency and night call-out service is provided. Some GPs argue that up to 60%

of emergency call-outs do not justify a home visit. They suggest that dealing with 'trivial' problems may hamper them in attending genuine emergencies. They may also be tired the next day when seeing patients in the surgery. They argue that it is therefore not 'cost-effective' to expect them to be on 24-hour call. Some doctors would like to see emergency night centres set up where patients could obtain out-of-hours care. Others have suggested that services could be better paid for if fines, removal from GP lists and loss of the right to visits at night and weekends were used to deter patients who demand home visits for 'trivial' reasons.

4 Finally, the issue of cost-effectiveness is at the heart of the debate over 'health care rationing', i.e. who makes the day-to-day decisions over the allocation of scarce resources and on what basis. The problem here is that it is not always clear to the public in what ways and for what reasons health and social services are offered to some people and not others. The public often assume that in health care at least, everything possible will be done to relieve suffering and save lives. But in practise decisions are taken about whether certain services are 'cost-effective'. For example, in 1994 hospital consultants in Manchester and Leicester have said that they will not offer non-urgent heart bypass operations to heavy smokers.

In some hospitals, attempts are being made to try to work out the cost-effectiveness of treatments offered in terms of 'quality-adjusted life-years' (QALYs) (see page 62). This assessment asks how many 'good-quality' years of life a patient is likely to gain, given the condition of the patient and the treatment received. Usually, older people are less likely than younger people to gain from these measures since they have fewer years to live.

INVOLVEMENT OF CLIENTS

Some people have suggested that in this brave new world of purchasers and providers, little has been done to involve clients in decisions about how money should be spent and on what services. That social workers, for example, should be 'purse-holders' deciding on behalf of others what care is required and where it should come from, may appear patronising and insulting to clients. The people most affected may wish to have a say in what kinds of Welfare State they want. There are already many disabled people and clients' movements which are demanding more say in health and social care provision. Some local authorities have attempted to consult the people to whom they provide services. For example, the Borough of Kensington and Chelsea in London has held consultation days for parents of children with disabilities where parents' views about how services should be provided and improved are sought.

A new Citizens' Commission on the future of the Welfare State will be established in 1995. This aims to open up discussion and provide an early opportunity for the people most affected to say what kind of Welfare State they want. It will be made up of Welfare State clients and will seek evidence and proposals from users across Britain. For more information contact:

Citizens' Commission
Tempo House
15 Falcon Road
London SW11 2PJ

The Conservative market-led changes of the past 15 or so years have tended to promote a somewhat different view of how clients might be more involved in the service they use. Here the concept of 'Consumer Choice' has been borrowed from industry.

In theory, this means that instead of health authorities, Social Services Departments and Education Departments providing services and then clients, patients and students being allocated those services according to what is available, the needs and/or choices of 'clients' should be identified and services tailored to their demands, requirements and concerns. It has been argued by Conservative governments that allowing care and health organisations to be organised more like businesses, competing in the market for customers, will encourage those organisations to respond more closely to 'what people want' because people will be able to pick and choose between the services offered.

In education, Conservative governments since 1979 have argued that there should be a greater choice and diversity in the type of secondary school which parents could choose for their children: grant-maintained, City Technology College, grammar, voluntary-aided, magnet, secondary–comprehensive, selective and non-selective, private.

ACTIVITY

To what extent is a variety of secondary schools available to all parents and their children in the borough or county where you live?

In April 1987 the government issued a White Paper, *Promoting Better Health*. It focused on:

- improving standards of General Practice;
- increasing the emphasis on health promotion;
- giving consumers more choice.

The government argued that the way to meet these objectives was to stimulate some degree of competition between GPs and to offer them some financial incentives to improve their work. As a result, the new GP contract was introduced in 1990. It allows GPs to hold their own budgets and, in theory at least, is intended to allow GPs and other health professionls to make more choices on behalf of their patients over what treatments or services can be bought for them.

Some patient consumer and advocacy groups have suggested that, if this is to be the case, patients need to be much better informed about the quality and success rates of different treatments at hospitals, health centres and clinics.

In June 1993 the Department of Health published for the first time 'league tables' of the numbers of cancelled operations and the times patients have to wait in accident and emergency departments before treatment. These statistics also include ambulance waiting times and the numbers of patients not admitted or seen within one month of having an operation cancelled at the last minute.

PATIENT GROUPS WANT LEAGUE TABLES OF HOSPITAL DEATH RATES PUBLISHED

League tables of hospital death rates should be made available to the public, and medical culture should be changed so that doctors do not feel threatened by well informed patients, researchers and patient groups said yesterday.

Far more information about medical advances needs to be given to patients, and they should be encouraged to ask questions about treatment options, the groups said.

Rabbi Julia Neuberger, chairman of Camden and Islington community health services, in London, said that despite the difficulties in comparing like with like, and taking account of the different mix of patients, there was still a case for publishing mortality league tables to give patients a better idea about good and bad hospitals.

Speaking at a conference in London organised by the King's Fund Centre, the health research organisation, Rabbi Neuberger said Britain should move towards a more American model of doctor–patient relationship, where it was assumed the patient would participate in questions about treatment.

'The assumption in America is that patients will be given detailed information about their treatment. They will ask questions, and if they don't like what they hear they will get more information. We need to find better ways to train patients in this country to ask questions.'

Other speakers at the meeting, on how to involve consumers in health research, said there should be a wider dissemination of research findings by consumer organisations, patient advocacy groups and the media.

Information leaflets and 'effectiveness bulletins', giving consensus views by doctors on the most effective treatments for various conditions, could be made available, and patients should be encouraged to ask why they were getting treatment which differed from this.

'Effectiveness bulletins can help patients participate in their own care. In two areas over recent years, AIDS and breast cancer, patients have become well informed enough to say they don't want certain treatments,' Rabbi Neuberger added.

(The Guardian, 10 November 1993)

ACTIVITY

1 Read the extract above. What problems might arise if the public tried to consult league tables of hospital mortality rates to judge the potential success of hospital treatments and surgical procedures?

2 There is currently a debate about whether GP fundholders are able to jump the queue for treatment on behalf of their patients in some hospitals because of their ability to 'shop around' for beds and because of the new funding arrangements for treatment. Investigate current media reports of 'fast-tracking', as this practice is known. Does more consumer choice for some patients mean less for others?

In the personal social services it is again difficult to see how 'consumer choice' could occur. In these services it is not really intended that 'clients' will be the direct purchasers or choosers of services. Rather, their needs will be assessed and a package of care decided upon in a care plan which works out current and future needs. Services to meet those needs would then be 'purchased' on behalf of the client by the social worker or 'care manager' in the Social Services Department.

It is the job of the social worker or care manager to identify who can provide the care required and then to see that this occurs. They will be aware that they cannot 'purchase' whatever they like and that they must remain within an overall budget. They will be encouraged to 'purchase' services from private and voluntary 'providers' wherever possible.

ACTIVITY

Interview social workers involved in care planning for the elderly, children or any other group of client. Do they feel that the choices or wishes of the clients are taken into account in the use of care plans?

ACTIVITY

Examine the list describing some of the plans for health care produced by the Labour Party prior to the 1992 election. Discuss the funding implications.

ASSESSMENT OPPORTUNITY ✔

1 Produce a project report which identifies five health and social services, and facilities available within your area. These should cover statutory, non-statutory and informal services.

- Describe how far there is statutory entitlement to these services.
- Classify the five services and facilities, describing variations between them and any difficulties you have experienced.
- Describe the major forms of resourcing for each of the services. How is this related to their classification?
- Describe how clients access these five services.

2 Produce a report which describes the following:

- How services and facilities have changed in the UK over the past 50 years.
- Three effects of recent government policy on the structure and funding of health and social services.
- The ways in which demographic characteristics affect priorities for health and social care. Give three examples.
- The role of the independent sector in influencing the provision of health and social care, giving specific examples.

3 Produce a report which covers the following:

- Describe the role of a local purchaser.
- Describe the changes required of a local provider in meeting the need of the purchaser.
- Give examples of different agencies involved in health and social care.

REFERENCES AND RESOURCES

Byrne, T. and Padfield, C. (1993), *Social Services*, Oxford: Butterworth-Heinemann. *Today's Health Services; A User's Guide* (1993), London: Channel Four Television Publications.

Tossel, D. and Webb, R. (1994), *Inside the Caring Services* (2nd edn). London: Edward Arnold.

In this rapidly changing area there are often relevant articles in the quality daily national newspapers and local press. Community care plans are available from your local authority.

USEFUL ADDRESSES

Council for Complementary and
Alternative Medicine
Suite 1
19A Cavendish Square
London W1M 9AD
Tel.: 0171 409 1440

Institute for Complementary Medicine
PO Box 194
London SE16 1QZ
Tel.: 0171 737 5165

NHS Trusts Unit
NHS Management Executive
Department of Health
Richmond House
79 Whitehall
London SW1A 2NS
Tel.: 0171 210 3000

6

HEALTH AND SOCIAL CARE PRACTICE

This chapter contains an introduction to the development and implementation of care plans, which are an increasingly important aspect of care provision. It should be read in conjunction with Chapter 2, which covers some of the skills necessary for producing a care plan. Students are given guidance on the investigation of care plans within the workplace. The opportunity is also provided for readers to find out about their chosen careers. The services concerned with the promotion and protection of health and social well-being are described, and the legislation and ethical issues involved in these areas are considered. Students are given guidance to carry out an investigation into how clients both experience and influence health and social care provision.

CARE PLANS

An important aspect of many professional carers' work is the development of care plans. This involves:

- assessing the client's needs;
- setting goals;
- listing the necessary action to meet the goals set;
- if necessary, justifying the actions set.

Care plans may be developed by:

- *one professional*, for example, a nurse or social worker;
- *multi-professionals* (team), for example, see Figure 6.5 which shows the team which may be responsible for developing a care plan for an elderly patient;
- *the client working alongside professionals* – empowering the client to take control of their care was covered in Chapter 2. An important part of this can be involving the client in the development of their care plan.

ACTIVITY

Consider the needs of the other client group shown in Figure 6.3. Draw a diagram similar to Figure 6.5 to show the roles of the key personnel who may be involved in developing and implementing care plans to meet these needs.

Once the care plan has been developed it is then implemented and regularly monitored and evaluated. Figure 6.1 shows an example of the stages in the development and implementation of a care plan by social workers involved in protecting children. Refer back to this for examples of the phases described throughout the chapter.

In Chapter 2, the assessment of clients and the development of care plans were considered using the case studies of Mrs Ivy Trent and Tracy Congdon. What follows in the first part of this chapter is a reiteration of the main stages in care plan development.

STAGE	Time-scale	Key activities	Areas for decision-making	Framework
STAGE 1 **Recognition...** *(referral or suspicion of abuse)*	24 hours	Discuss with referrer. Consult (where possible) with supervisor. Gather information from other key professionals. Involve other investigating agencies e.g. police, doctors, the Reporter (in Scotland). See child/other children/parents/carers/ alleged perpetrator as soon as possible if urgent. Evaluate initial data.	Is there cause for concern? Is action needed to protect the child? Protection in the family (or wider family) possible? Placement outside the family needed? Place of safety order? Access arrangements.	Legal. Children's Hearing system (in Scotland). Agency and inter-agency policies and procedures.
... and investigation *(initial assessment)*	Up to 1 week plus	Continue to gather information from child/other children/family members. Evaluate data. Consult with supervisor. Continue discussion and cooperation with other key professionals.	Emergency protection now, or still, needed? Maintain child in family with intervention? Call case conference? No further action needed? Care proceedings?	Legal. Children's Hearing system (in Scotland). Agency and inter-agency policies and procedures. Initial case conference arranged.
STAGE 2 **Assessment and Planning**	Up to 12 weeks maximum *(preferably less)*	Following case conference, decide if comprehensive assessment is needed. If so: gather information/ direct work with child/ family unit/wider family. Liaison with management and professional network. Evaluate data. Formulate action plan.	Care proceedings? Short-term separation continues? Access arrangements? Long-term separation indicated? Child stays in family with intervention? Long-term plan formulated?	Legal. Children's Hearing system (in Scotland). Agency and inter-agency policies and procedures. Review machinery: statutory (where appropriate) and inter-agency.
STAGE 3 **Implementation and Review**	6–12 months	Implementing action/ treatment plan. Reviewing progress. Direct work with child/parents/ family unit/wider family. Consult with supervisor and professional network.	If child is at home: No further action? Continued treatment? If child is in temporary, substitute care: Rehabilitation? Long-term separation and permanent substitute care?	Legal. Children's Hearing system (in Scotland). Agency policy and procedures. Review machinery: statutory (where appropriate) and inter-agency.
Leads to Rehabilitation	Can occur on any time-scale	Preparation for return: direct work with child and family. Protection plan/contract regarding treatment and monitoring after child's return, including child's health and development. Consult with supervisor and others in professional network.	What are the conditions of the return home? Is there a renewed need to intervene to protect?	Legal. Children's Hearing system (in Scotland). Agency policy and procedures. Review machinery: statutory (where appropriate) and inter-agency. Protection plan agreed with parents.
Leads to Separation *(permanent)*	Decision can be at any time but often after assessment or period of unsuccessful treatment	*Child* – bereavement and separation work, life story book, selection of and introduction to new family, continuing direct work. *Family* – bereavement, separation work, continued help and support where necessary.	Long-term family placement: adoption or long-term fostering placement? Alternative residential provision for child who cannot yet be placed in substitute family home? Access arrangements.	Legal. Children's Hearing system (in Scotland). Agency policy and procedures. Review machinery: statutory (where appropriate) and inter-agency.
Disengagement	At any time-scale	Consult and review progress with supervisor, management and others in professional network. Careful planning and preparation for disengagement with child and family.	Can parents care safely for child without further social work help? Are other support networks needed? Should any court order be revoked? Should (in Scotland) any supervision requirement be terminated?	Legal. Children's Hearing system (in Scotland). Agency policy and procedures. Review machinery: statutory (where appropriate) and inter-agency.

Figure 6.1 Stages in the development and implementation of a care plan

Source: Crown copyright. Reproduced with the permission of the Controller of Her Majesty's Stationery Office.

Phase 1: Initial assessment of needs

ACTIVITY

1 Refer back to Chapters 1, 2 and 4, where the following needs of clients were identified:

- social (Chapter 2);
- physical (Chapter 2);
- emotional (Chapter 2);
- communication (see 'Cognitive needs' (Chapter 2);
- identity (Chapter 4);
- cultural (Chapter 1);
- intellectual (Chapter 2).

Reread the section on Individual needs in Chapter 2 and check that you understand the meaning of each of these terms.

2 Refer back to the case histories of Ivy Trent and Tracy Congdon in Chapter 2. Remind yourself of their needs, dividing your list up into the seven categories shown above.

There are many METHODS OF ASSESSMENT of client needs (refer again to Chapter 2). Any or all of the following methods may be used by a professional assessing a client:

- Observation of:
  - physical condition;
  - behaviour;
  - behaviour;
  - personal circumstances.
- Questioning.
- Use of secondary sources, including:
  - relatives;
  - advocates;
  - support networks;
  - medical records.

When using any of these methods, the professional carer must bear in mind CLIENT RIGHTS with respect to assessment. The client has the right to:

- independence;
- identity maintenance;
- choice and control;
- confidentiality.

ACTIVITY

1 Refer back to Chapter 2.
- What methods were used to assess Ivy Trent's and Tracy Congdon's needs?
- Check that you understand the meaning of each of the client rights listed above.

2 Read through the two accounts of clients below. For both Rajpreet and Helen:
- suggest the methods of assessment that would be used to identify their needs;
- identify the needs that will have to be met;
- note any particular precautions for maintaining client rights that would have to be observed when using your suggested methods of assessment.

CASE HISTORY A

A young child, **Rajpreet** (five years), is admitted to a hospital paediatric ward via the accident and emergency department with asthma. She has been treated for asthma for six months but, on this occasion, the medication had not relieved her wheezing and difficulty in breathing. She is very distressed when her parents have to leave.

(If possible, watch the film made in the 1960s of children being admitted to hospital and separated from their parents: J. and J. Robertson, *Young Children in Brief Separation*. Ipswich: Concorde Films, 1969.)

CASE HISTORY B

A young mother, **Helen**, is referred to a voluntary agency because it is feared she may have a nervous breakdown as has happened in the past.

Helen's only income comes from Supplementary Benefit and she complains that her housing conditions are very bad. She is also worried because her 14-year-old son is getting into trouble with the police for shoplifting and she is unwilling to let her 13-year-old daughter out with her friends because the area is so 'rough'. A six-month-old baby completes the family.

You may wish to repeat the activity suggested above and the two following activities using the case histories of Ivy Trent and Tracy Congdon from Chapter 2.

Phase 2: Development of the care plan

Once the needs of the client have been assessed, and the needs which are not being met (i.e. the problems) identified, goals can then be set (i.e. the required outcome). The action required to meet these goals should then be identified and implemented.

Figure 6.2 shows an example of a table used by nurses to develop a care plan. Figure 6.3 shows an example of a table used by social workers involved in the protection of children to help with the development of a care plan.

ACTIVITY

Figure 6.4 shows a care plan for Rajpreet. Using the same format, develop a care plan for Helen.

- In the 'problem' column fill in all the needs you identified which were not being met.
- In the 'goal' column identify for each of the problems the desired outcome.
- In the 'action' column identify the action which must be taken by professionals to bring about the desired outcome.

Phase 3: Implementation and monitoring

You will notice in Figure 6.4 a column headed 'Review date'. Throughout the implementation of a care plan there should be both repeated assessment of the client's needs and constant MONITORING of progress so that the care plan can be adapted if necessary.

Monitoring can be defined as checking care and performance with criteria against agreed standards to produce a measurement of quality.

The Royal College of Nursing defines a STANDARD as 'a professionally agreed level of performance appropriate to the population addressed, which is observable, achievable, measurable and desirable'. In simple words, standards are statements of intent.

CRITERIA are the means of measuring whether a standard has been reached or not. For example:

- *Standard*: The cultural needs of all hospital patients will be met.
- Examples of *criteria*:
  - an appropriate menu is offered;
  - religious needs are considered;
  - cultural practices involved in childbirth, washing, family planning, etc., are considered.

Once standards and criteria have been set, a tick list or similar form can be designed and the care plan monitored.

A variety of sources of information can be used to enable the professional to monitor a care plan. For example:

- client interview;
- carer interview;
- client's records;
- observation of client, their care and environment;
- examination of support services.

ACTIVITY

1 Look back at the care plans you developed for Rajpreet and Helen. List

NURSING ASSESSMENT Usual routines, what s/he can and cannot do independently. (*delete as appropriate.) DATE: TAKEN BY: SIGN:	LABEL	Patient Perceived Problem	Nurse Perceived Problem	GOAL 1. Who 2. What is to be achieved 3. When	Nursing Action Review Date & Signature
1. MAINTAINING A SAFE ENVIRONMENT	*INFECTIOUS ALLERGIES IMMUNOSUPPRESSED				
2. COMMUNICATING	HEARING ______ AID USED YES/NO* SPEECH ______ SIGHT ______ GLASSES YES/NO* LANGUAGE ______ LENSES YES/NO* Present on Ward YES/NO*				
3. MENTAL ORIENTATION	*ANXIOUS/CHEERFUL/EUPHORIC/ORIENTED/DISTRESSED/CONFUSED/COOPERATIVE UNCOOPERATIVE/RESPONDS TO COMMANDS/RESPONDS TO PAIN STIMULI UNRESPONSIVE TO PAIN STIMULI				
4. BREATHING	COUGH PRODUCTIVE YES/NO* SMOKES: YES/NO* Number per day ______				
5. NUTRITIONAL NEEDS	DIET ______ APPETITE ______ MEALS per day ______ FOOD PREFERENCES ______ ORAL DRUGS: YES/NO* Present on Ward YES/NO*				
6. FLUID NEEDS	DRINK PREFERENCES ______ NORMAL DAILY FLUID INTAKE ______ mls. ALCOHOL DRUNK: YES/NO* Amount per week ______				
7. PERSONAL CLEANSING	ORAL HYGIENE ______ DENTURES TOP/BOTTOM* On Ward? YES/NO* *NO HELP REQUIRED/ASSIST/TOTAL HELP				
8. DRESSING	*NO HELP REQUIRED/ASSIST/TOTAL HELP				
9. BODY TEMPERATURE/ CIRCULATION	*NORMAL LIMITS/HYPOTHERMIA/PYREXIA				
10. MOBILISING	WALKING: IMMOBILE/NEEDS ONE PERSON/CAN MANAGE STAIRS/ INDEPENDENT. *USES AID: TYPE: ______				
11. LIFESTYLE/CULTURE					
12. SLEEPING/REST	HOURS PER NIGHT: ______ from: ______ to ______ SEDATION: YES/NO* WHAT HELPS ______				
13. ELIMINATING	*CONTINENT/CATHETER/STRESS INCONTINENCE/INCONTINENT BOWEL HABIT ______				
14. CONDITIONS OF SKIN	COMMENTS PRESSURE AREA WOUND LESIONS RASH				
15. SPECIAL PSYCHOLOGICAL NEEDS					

Figure 6.2 Table used by nurses to develop a care plan

Nursing Action
Sign and Date when completed

Nursing Action
Sign and Date when completed

Nursing Action
Sign and Date when completed

Nursing Action
Sign and Date when completed

PLANNING MODEL TABLE: ACTION BASED ON ASSESSMENT

IMPORTANT: The items listed on the table are examples only

Section	Main features: a) positive	Main features: b) negative	Changes needed	Factors helping change	Factors blocking change	Timescale	Resources needed	Action plan Goals to be achieved and action for achieving them
CAUSES FOR CONCERN		Neglect. Abuse: Repeated. Serious. Bizarre. Sadistic Sexual. Emotional Premedited etc. Poor standards of care.						
ATTITUDE OF PARENTS TO PROBLEMS	Shows remorse Concerned for child. Sought help quickly.	Denies or projects blame. Concerned for self. Little concern for child.						
ATTITUDE OF PARENTS TO INTERVENTION	Accepts need for change. Genuinely co-operates. Some insight.	Rejects need for help. Superficially co-operative.						
THE CHILD	Generally well cared for. Health and development satisfactory.	Neglected. Failing to thrive. Poor general health. Young and vulnerable child.						
FAMILY COMPOSITION	Information openly shared. Clear boundaries. Straightforward, stable structure.	Secretive. Difficult to obtain information. Confusing, blurred, ever-changing boundaries.						
INDIVIDUAL PROFILE OF PARENTS/CARERS	Good experiences in childhood. Come to terms with negative experiences in childhood. Able to make and sustain deep and warm relationships. Able to control behaviour and tolerate some frustration. Open and honest.	Poor experiences in childhood. Unresolved emotional issues in childhood. Coldness & superficiality. Authoritarian attitudes. Manipulative & plausible. Previous family violence. Alcohol to excess.						
COUPLE RELATIONSHIP *and...*	Stable sustained relationship. Complementary. Healthy mechanisms for resolving conflict. Evidence of trust, warmth, love. Sexual needs met.	Multiple partners. Unrealistic expectations of partner. Collusive. Violent. Mistrusting. Sexual frustrations.						
FAMILY INTERACTIONS	Child's needs put first. Realistic expectations of child. Loving, can have fun.	Parents needs first. Unrealistic expectations of child. Views child as naughty, powerful. Scapegoats child. Cold with child.						
NETWORKS	Supportive but separate. Good networks and lifelines.	Interfering. Enmeshed. Distant. Isolated. Unsupported.						
FINANCE	Manages financial affairs adequately. Acute problem – willing to seek help and accept advice.	Many debts. Impulsive with money. Chronic problems. Unwilling to follow advice.						
PHYSICAL CONDITIONS	Basic needs of child for shelter, warmth, food, sleep etc. adequately met.	Chronic problems. Basic needs of child unmet or vulnerable.						

Figure 6.3 Table used by social workers to develop a care plan

Source: Crown copyright. Reproduced with the permission of the Controller of Her Majesty's Stationery Office.

Name of client: Rajpreet Patel			Name of primary carer:	
Date	Problem	Goal	Action	Review date
	Difficulty breathing	Restore normal breathing	Observe condition Medication	
	Anxiety	Relieve anxiety	Reassure child Provide facilities for parents to stay with child	

N.B. Only the broad principles of care have been considered, not the actual physical care (for example, oxygen and ventolin).

Figure 6.4 Example of a care plan form

the sources of information you would use to monitor these care plans.

2 Why is it important to ensure that the client (or the client's representative) is consulted throughout the monitoring process?

Phase 4: Review and evaluation

Evaluation is a means of finding out whether the carer, or team of carers, have achieved what they set out to do when they developed the care plan. It is important that evaluation is OBJECTIVE and not SUBJECTIVE. For this reason, where possible, standards and criteria are needed to guide the evaluator.

In the light of the evaluation, shortcomings can be identified and, resources permitting, modification made to improve subsequent care plans. Any change in a client's needs should also be carefully evaluated, and if necessary a reassessment should be carried out.

Interventions

The interventions most commonly used by professionals in implementing a care plan can be divided into the following categories:

- *Enabling*. For example, enabling clients to develop new skills; enabling clients to regain their functioning; enabling clients to support others.
- *Caring*. For example, caring for clients who are unable to care for themselves, temporarily or permanently; caring for clients so that they die with dignity and minimum pain.

- *Treatment*. For example, surgery; medication; manipulation; specialist assessment services, such as radiography and physiological measurement.

ACTIVITY

It is likely that you have, or will have, the opportunity to observe in the workplace examples of interventions from at least one of the three categories above.

Write a brief account of these examples, remembering to observe client confidentiality.

Within your student group, discuss the examples you have written about, so that you can collect an account of interventions from each category (i.e. enabling, caring and treatment).

Health and social care personnel

As explained above, there is a wide variety of personnel who may be responsible for planning and implementing a care plan.

ACTIVITY

1 Have a 'brainstorming' session to produce a list of as many careers in health and social care as you can. Check your list against the following:

- care assistant;
- chiropodist;
- dentist;
- dietician;
- district nurse;
- homoeopath;
- housing officer;
- health visitor;
- hospital nurse;
- midwife;
- occupational therapist;
- osteopath;
- pharmacist;
- physiotherapist;
- probation officer;
- psychologist;
- social worker (field);
- social worker (residential);
- speech and language therapist;
- surgeon;
- teacher: special educational needs;
- warden: accommodation;
- youth and community worker.

2 Divide the occupations listed above into the following three groups, depending on the type of intervention they are usually involved in:

- enabling;
- caring;
- treatment.

3 For each of the careers, produce a profile including qualifications needed for entry, length of training, prospects, personal qualities and nature of the work. You may wish to divide the research between a group of you (e.g. choose a few careers each).
Suggested sources of information: college careers libraries, local careers offices and local libraries will have useful books, videos and computer programs. The list of addresses at the end of the chapter can be used to obtain further information.

4 Choose a career and devise a questionnaire about it. Use this to interview a professional about their work.

5 Use the information from this interview, and your careers profiles, to produce a 'careers resource pack'.

6 If facilities permit, make a short promotional video of 'caring careers'.

7 If you have the opportunity, set up a 'caring careers' stall at your college, using appropriate material.

8 Evaluate the effectiveness of the material you have produced.

ACTIVITY

Study Figure 6.5, which shows the roles of key personnel in caring for an elderly patient. Consider the needs of the other client groups shown in Figure 5.4 (page 281) and then draw diagrams to illustrate the roles of the key personnel involved in meeting these needs.

ACTIVITY W

If you can observe a patient or client being cared for by a multidisciplinary team, carry out the following tasks:

- List the occupations involved in delivering care.
- What are the major functions of each of these occupations in the care delivery?
- Who is the team leader? Why?
- Is communication good between team members?

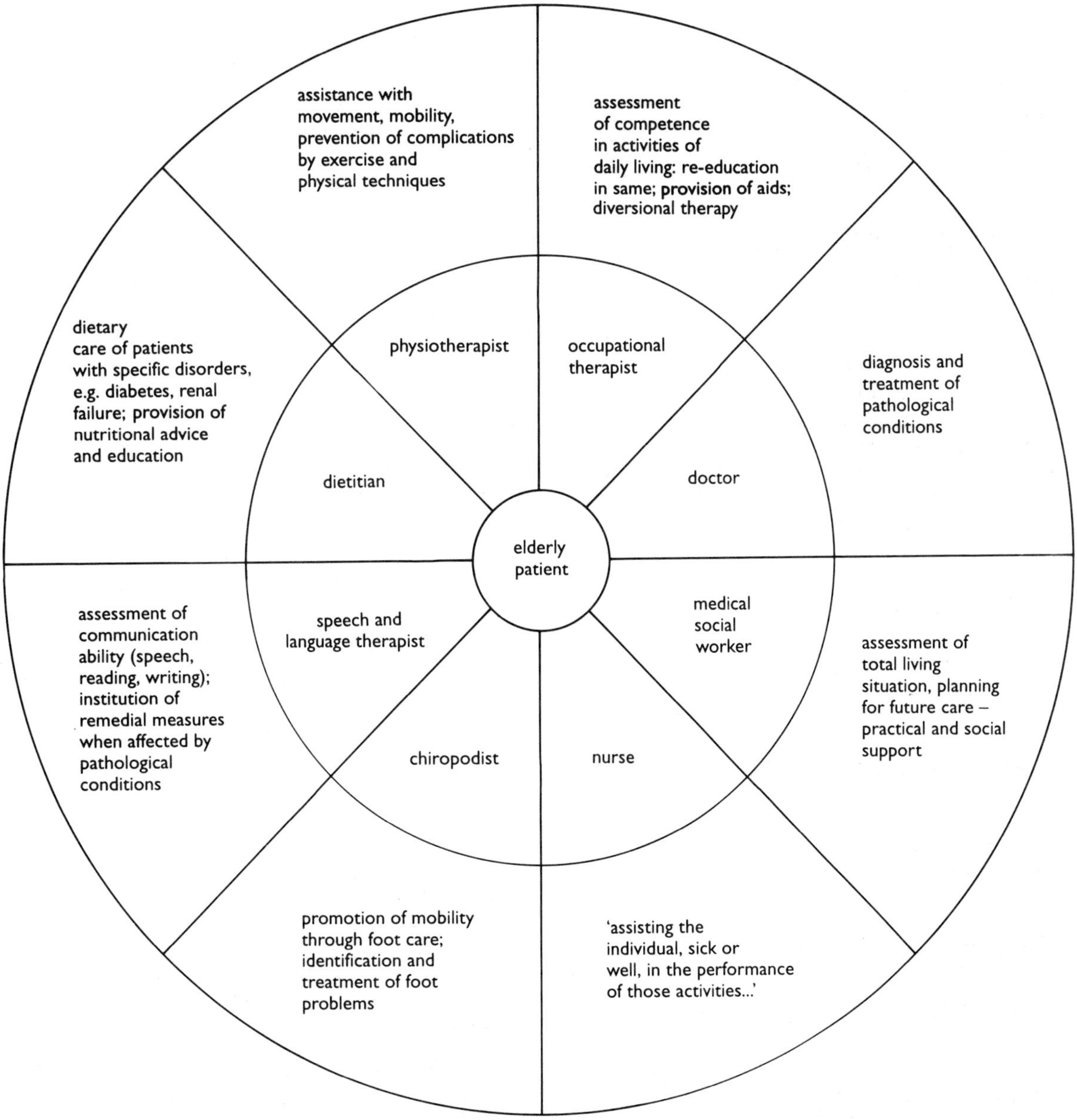

Figure 6.5 The multidisciplinary team caring for the elderly patient
Source: *The Essentials of Nursing: Health Needs of the Elderly* (Macmillan, 1987).

- How could communication be improved?

Trends and changes in practice

There have been many recent changes in health and social care practice. Some of the most significant changes include the following.

INCREASED SPECTRUM OF CARE

There are increasingly more types of care and treatment available to clients. Some of these new methods may be due to scientific advances, e.g., organ transplants. Other increases to the spectrum of care are because some professionals are taking a more HOLISTIC approach to care. Holistic care involves the treatment of the whole person. It takes into account the social, psychological and environmental influences, including nutrition, exercise and mental relaxation, that affect health.

COMPLEMENTARY MEDICINE is often linked to the holistic approach (see page 277, Chapter 5).

When modern medicine appeared unable to offer help in areas such as the chronic diseases, AIDS, and ME, many people turned to complementary therapies for help. There has been a gradual integration of complementary therapies and orthodox treatments within the NHS. For example, GPs can now refer patients to complementary therapists, or employ them in health centres and health promotion clinics. Complementary therapists are also working in hospital departments, such as oncology, AIDS units and maternity care.

A report by the National Association of Health Authorities and Trusts in 1993 showed that the NHS is spending about £1 million annually on complementary therapies.

GREATER USE OF SUPPORT STAFF

Many NHS Trusts are currently engaged in what is known as 'workforce re-profiling'. One aspect of this is the re-allocation of some jobs away from qualified to less or unqualified staff. Thus, for example, some tasks currently performed by nurses will be given to support workers; some radiographers' tasks will be transferred to radiography helpers; and some ambulance work will be given to health transport drivers.

ACTIVITY W

1 What do you consider the advantages and disadvantages to be of greater use of support staff?

2 If you have the opportunity, ask one or more professionals about the extent to which they rely on support workers. Has this reliance increased over recent years? What do they consider the advantages and disadvantages to be?

3 Make a list of health professions and their support workers. Try to make a comparison of their salaries, qualifications and responsibilities.

MULTI-SKILLING OF PROFESSIONALS AND EMPOWERMENT OF USERS TO TAKE CONTROL OF THEIR OWN CARE

Both these aspects of changes in health and care practice have been covered in Chapter 2. Read through Chapter 2 to check that you are aware of the ways in which greater user and care involvement is being encouraged.

ACTIVITY W

You may be able to observe directly the processes involved in developing, implementing, monitoring and evaluating a care plan. If this is not possible, interview a professional to obtain the information.

1 Describe the development of a care plan

for a client.

- Who was involved in the development of the care plan?
- How was the client involved in the development of the care plan?
- How are the client's needs assessed?
- What precautions are taken to protect the client's rights?
- What needs were identified?
- Is a standard assessment form used?
- Is a standard care plan form used?
- How has the development of a care plan changed over recent years?

2 Describe the interventions used in implementing the care plan.

- What types of intervention, enabling, caring and/or treatment were used in the implementation of the care plan?
- Give details of the examples of these that were used, explaining their purpose and how they were intended to meet the client's needs.
- How was the client encouraged to be involved in the interventions used?
- How have the interventions used changed over recent years?

3 Describe how the care plan is monitored and evaluated.

- Are standard forms used?
- What sources of information are used?
- For what purposes is the care plan monitored and evaluated?
- How has the monitoring and evaluation of a care plan changed over recent years?

NB Remember to observe confidentiality in writing up your notes.

If possible, carry out the above in both a health care *and* a social care setting. This will allow you to compare and contrast the methods used.

THE PROMOTION AND PROTECTION OF HEALTH AND SOCIAL WELL-BEING

Practitioners who promote health and social well-being

There are a range of practitioners who are involved in promoting the health and social well-being of the population. They work for a number of different agencies within the UK, and the main examples are as follows:

1. *Government departments:*
   - Department of Health;
   - Department of Education and Science;
   - Department of the Environment;
   - Central Office of Information.
2. *Health Education Council* (HEA). The HEA is a government-funded organisation which provides training, funds research and mounts national and regional campaigns on health issues. It is a QUANGO (quasi-autonomous non-governmental organisation).
3. *Health education or promotion teams.* Most district health authorities employ health promotion officers whose tasks vary widely between areas. Their main functions are:
   - to coordinate programmes of health education within the district;
   - to provide teaching materials, posters and leaflets;
   - to inform and work with the local mass media;
   - to implement strategies devised by the government for promoting the health of the population (see Chapter 7);
   - to provide support, advice and training for health professionals and other health educators.
4. *Community Health Councils* (CHC). The members of the CHC do not have a direct role in health promotion, but may play a part in influencing local health

promotion policies where there is a perceived need.

5 *Local Education Authority* (LEA). Each LEA is responsible for developing the promotion of health within schools and colleges through the work of teachers and lecturers.

6 *Voluntary organisations.*
National:

- RoSPA (Royal Society for the Prevention of Accidents);
- TACADE (Teachers' Advisory Centre for Alcohol and Drug Education);
- FPA (Family Planning Association).

National and local:

- NCT (National Childbirth Trust);
- MIND (National Association for Mental Health);
- CAB (Citizens Advice Bureaux).

There is also a vast range of smaller local and national voluntary organisations which aim to promote the health of selected groups within the population.

7 *Retail pharmacists.* The local chemist's shop is uniquely placed to offer health promotion advice because there is always a health professional as a resource for the general public. Recent advertisements on TV have urged the public to make better use of this resource.

8 *Manufacturers and retailers.* Many commercial organisations produce health information material to accompany the sale of their products (see Chapter 7)

9 *Environmental health officers* have a duty to provide information on air and water pollution, noise, home safety and food hygiene (see below).

10 *The Health and Safety Executive* has a duty to implement the Health and Safety at Work Act and provides training in first aid and safety at work programmes (see below).

11 *The Mass Media.* Television, radio, newspapers and magazines undertake health education, either in response to a specific problem or in the interest of the general public.

12 *Health professionals.* Doctors, dentists, nurses, health visitors, dietitians, chiropodists, therapists, etc., all have a role to play in the promotion of health; in particular, community nurses and school nurses view the promotion of a healthy lifestyle as the cornerstone of their practice.

13 *Trade unions* may, in response to specific problems, put pressure on the workplace to develop health promotion policies.

14 *Other specialists.* Drug outreach workers, police officers and many others working in service organisations have health promotion as part of their job description, e.g. police officers talk to groups in schools about road safety and 'stranger danger', and firemen give talks on fire prevention and emergency procedures.

15 *Occupational health services.* Many public and private organisations employ occupational health nurses who undertake regular surveillance and health education duties.

In addition to all these obvious agencies for health promotion, there is a huge network of **informal educators**, i.e. family and friends, who influence health behaviour and beliefs by example and by 'word-of-mouth' transfer of health information.

ACTIVITY

Look back at the activity you completed on health and social care personnel on page 334.

- Which of the professionals listed have the promotion of health and social well-being as one of their roles?

- Describe the nature of this role for each occupation. For example, which client groups will they be addressing? Which health and lifestyle factors may concern them?

Practitioners involved in creating healthy environments

'There are many practitioners involved in helping to create environments conducive to health and social well-being. Below are descriptions of the range of services for which they carry out their work. You are encouraged in the activities to contact individual practitioners to find out more directly about their work.'

NATURAL ENVIRONMENTS (E.G. WATER, AIR)

UK control

The central government is responsible for enforcing international directives and regulations, and setting national policies and legislation. The department within central government with the main responsibility for the national environment is the DEPARTMENT OF THE ENVIRONMENT. However, the policies of other departments, such as the Department of Transport, will also have an impact.

In 1990 an Act was passed which established a new pollution control system in England and Wales. It replaced many older laws and regulations to bring together pollution control under one central regime. It is called the Environmental Protection Act. This new approach has been designated integrated pollution control.

A new INSPECTORATE OF POLLUTION was set up. Certain industrial, commercial and other processes will be inspected and controlled from this central scheme. Releases of pollutants from most industrial processes to air, water and land come into its scope.

The Act allows the regulation of pollutants from a second tier of less polluting sources to be the responsibility of the *local authorities* for air and land pollution. Similarly, the NATIONAL RIVERS AUTHORITY (NRA) is able to regulate water pollution from more minor sources.

Water and air pollution are controlled by the UK government as follows:

1 *Water pollution.*
Control of water pollution is one of the main activities of the NRA and there are RIVER INSPECTORS whose job it is to ensure that the quality of water is maintained to a high standard. They take samples of water regularly, and these are analysed to see if there are any polluting substances present. They will also investigate the living organisms in the river to enable a judgement to be made about the cleanliness of the water.

2 *Air pollution.*
The Environmental Protection Act 1990 and the Clean Air Act 1993 are the most important laws in the control of air pollution. The Health and Safety at Work Act 1974 also grants powers to impose restrictions on emissions from industrial premises.

There are also regulations about the sulphur and lead contents of fuel used in motor vehicles, and the sulphur content of oil fuel used in engines and furnaces. Further regulations relate to the level of asbestos in the air of premises where people are working. Legislation also prohibits burning straw or stubble in fields after the crop has been harvested.

ACTIVITY

- Visit your local careers centre or library, and find out about the work of an environmental health officer.
- If possible, carry out an in-depth interview (see Chapter 8) with a local environmental health officer.
- Look in the front of *Yellow Pages* to find which areas of enquiry are referred to the Environmental Services Department of your local council.

Water supply and sewage services

To maintain clean rivers and to prevent the spread of disease it is necessary to ensure that there is:

- a source of clean water for domestic, industrial and agricultural purposes;
- an effective sewage disposal system.

ACTIVITY

- Discuss the following dilemma: Who should pay for cleaning up the consequences of past pollution? Should it be the government giving grants from taxpayers' money or should it be the industries that caused the problem?

Pressure groups

Although it is a role of central government, local authorities and industry to create or maintain a healthy natural environment, these organisations regularly receive criticism from pressure groups such as Friends of the Earth.

ACTIVITY

- Compile a list of voluntary organisations concerned with air and water pollution. (You will find the publication 'Who's Who in the Environment' useful for this. It also includes a list of organisations which will provide speakers.)

SOCIO-ECONOMIC CONDITIONS (e.g. HOUSING, SOCIAL WELFARE)

Housing

Housing is one of the basic needs for survival, and an important indicator of socio-economic conditions. There is a close relationship between health and housing, although because people who live in housing which is in poor repair, insanitary or over-crowded often suffer from other forms of social and economic disadvantage, it is difficult to separate the effects of bad housing on health from other factors related to poverty.

However, poor housing which is damp, over-crowded and insanitary can lead to increases in the incidence of communicable and other diseases related to poor hygiene and lack of cleanliness. It has been shown that children who live in small flats have higher rates of respiratory infection than those who live in houses. In housing that is in bad condition there may also be infestations with vermin and pests which spread disease. As well as physical disease, mental health, emotional disturbances and other stress-related problems also increase amongst inhabitants of poor housing.

There has been much recent legislation concerning housing. One of the most important relating to a healthy environment is the HOUSING ACT 1988. This Act reduced government controls over rent-fixing in the private sector of housing. It created HOUSING ACTION TRUSTS to take over and improve run-down council estates. It also identified HOUSING ASSOCIATIONS as the form of 'social housing' preferred by the government.

ACTIVITY

- Which department of central government is responsible for housing?
- Local authorities are responsible for the payment of housing benefit. Find out to whom this is available, and the different methods by which it may be paid to council tenants and private tenants.

At present, around 70% of all housing in the UK is owner-occupied, but recently there appears to have been a decline in demand. In 1991 there were 36,607 repossessions of houses by building societies and banks. Even though mortgage interest rates have now dropped, the fact that the concept of life-time employment is thought to be a thing of the past means that people are less willing to take out large loans to buy a house. The number of property transactions in England and Wales in 1994 was not much more than half that of the peak year, 1988, when 2.15 million were recorded.

ACTIVITY

- Find out how much the 'average' house in your area costs.
- Visit building societies and find out the typical monthly repayment on a mortgage for this sum.

Homelessness

The local authorities have the primary responsibility for dealing with homeless people. They are required to help homeless people in defined categories of 'priority need'. For example, families with young children, pregnant women, the elderly or ill. They do not have to provide local authority homes; they may make arrangements for the homeless to be housed by a Housing Association or help them find a private-sector tenancy. In 1992 local authorities in the UK secured permanent accommodation for 167,000 households.

ACTIVITY

Housing Associations account for 3% of all households. What Housing Associations provide accommodation in your locality? Find out what you can about their functions.

In practice, many homeless people either do not approach their local authority for accommodation, or are turned away by them. These people, who do not appear in official statistics on homelessness, may be helped by VOLUNTARY ORGANISATIONS, such as Shelter, or may end up living rough.

ACTIVITY

- What other voluntary organisations help the homeless? What services do they offer?
- The newspaper article from *The Daily Telegraph* (14 November 1994) shows that people leaving psychiatric hospitals often experience difficulty in finding accommodation. Find out if they are given any special help from voluntary organisations.

ONE IN FOUR HOMELESS HAS SCHIZOPHRENIA, SAYS STUDY

One in four homeless people suffers from schizophrenia – a prevalence up to 50 times greater than that for the general population, the Royal College of Physicians says today.

In a major report on poverty and ill health, the college bases its claim on studies of homeless in overnight hostels.

The report highlights poor co-ordination between the health authorities, social services and the housing authorities.

The upshot was that the mentally ill are not helped to find accommodation when they make contact with community nurses, leave hospital or seek a GP's help.

The Daily Telegraph, 14 November 1994

Building legislation

Building and housing legislation lays down standards to try to ensure good housing conditions. The structure of new buildings is controlled by very strict regulations and there are measures to rectify defects in older properties.

Plans of all proposed buildings must be submitted to the local authority for approval before building can begin. Plans may be rejected, for example, if a bathroom is not included with hot and cold water or if there is not adequate space for food storage. Much attention is given to adequate provision for drainage, and ensuring that proper arrangements exist for linking in to the sewerage system.

BUILDING INSPECTORS are employed by the local authority to work in the planning department. They inspect buildings at different stages of their construction and on completion.

It is an offence to contravene the provisions in the Building Regulations, and the local authority may require an owner to pull down or alter work which breaks the legislation. There is a right of appeal in a magistrates' court. There may be reference to the Secretary of State if there is a dispute.

Dealing with substandard housing

Under the Housing Act 1985 local authorities are empowered to issue repair notices to owners of dwelling houses which are defective or unfit for human habitation. The owner is required to carry out repairs so that the dwelling is of a reasonable standard. Dates are set for the completion of the work.

This Act also enables local authorities to improve whole areas of housing, by declaring housing action areas, general improvement areas and renewal areas. Central government funds can be made available. Slum clearance is also possible; local authorities can demolish buildings which are deemed to be unfit for human habitation or dangerous to health. Compulsory Purchase Orders are made. The courts have considerable powers of enforcement in this respect. Entry to premises for the purpose of valuation must be allowed, and any obstruction to the procedures leading to demolition is an offence.

ACTIVITY

Carry out a survey of the different types of housing in the area where you live. Contact your local Housing Department to help you. Are there any problem areas? The Environmental Health Department may be able to help you as well.

Social welfare

Social welfare provision is a term used to describe the services provided to help people. Many aspects of this provision are covered within this book under various headings, for example housing (see above); social conditions (see below); health care (Chapter 5); social care (Chapter 5); Social security provision (Chapter 5). Other issues sometimes considered under social welfare are education and unemployment. Obviously such a wide area requires the participation of a number of services from central and local government and private and voluntary organisations (see Tables 6.1 and 6.2).

There is much debate concerning 'universal versus selective welfare', i.e. should welfare services be provided universally, for all irrespective of income, or selectively on the criterion of need?

ACTIVITY

- Which social welfare provision is available on a universal basis and which is available on a selective basis?
- Which Social Security benefits are available on a universal basis and which are available on a selective basis?

SOCIAL CONDITIONS (e.g. CRIME, SOCIAL RELATIONSHIPS)

Crime

The central government department with responsibility for crime prevention is the HOME OFFICE. It is responsible for the following:

- *The Police Forces.* There are 50 regional Police Forces (e.g. The Metropolitan Police Force; The Avon and Somerset Constabulary). Each Police Force is subdivided into Districts of areas with police stations and offices. Some Forces have special departments such as Domestic Violence Units, Youth and Community Work, and Family Support.

Table 6.1 Services related to creating Healthy Environments

Examples of organisations with responsibility	Natural environment (e.g. water, air)	Socio-economic conditons (e.g. housing), (Social Welfare – see Table 6.2)	Public environments e.g. Leisure	Public environments Restaurants	Working environments	Social conditions e.g. Crime prevention	Social conditions Social relations
Central government departments	Department of the Environment Department of Transport	Department of the Environment	Department of National Heritage	Ministry of Agriculture, Fisheres and Food Department of Health	Department of Employment	The Home Office	Department of Health The Home Office
Local authority departments (county and borough councils)	Environment/ environmental health Transport planning	Building control/ housing/planning Environmental health Rent officer service	Leisure/amenities Libraries	Environmental health Consumer services	Environmental health (responsible for employees)	Influence of local authority on Police Force varies from area to area	Social services Environmental health (noise)
Public bodies/services	National Rivers Authority Inspectorate of Pollution Pesticides Safety Directorate Natural Environmental Research Council	Housing ActionTrusts The Housing Corporation Building Research Establishment Resettlement Agency	ADAS Sports Council Arts Council Regional Councils (sport and recreation) Regional Arts Boards	Health Education Council Health Promotion Units	Health and Safety Commission Advisory Committees Health and Safety Executive Occupational Health Service	Police Forces HM Prison Service Crown Prosecution Service The Probation Service Legal Aid Service	Commission for Racial Equality Family Court Welfare Service
Private/ commercial	Industries with the potential to pollute	Building societies Building industry	Health clubs Cinemas	Food outlets, e.g. restaurants, supermarkets, food suppliers	All employers and employees	Private security firms Education in prisons	Private counselling agencies
Voluntary/ charities/ trusts/ not-for-profit organisations	National Society for Clean Air Friends of the Earth National Pure Water Association	Housing Associations Shelter The Salvation Army CHAR (Campaign for the Homeless and Roofless)	Consumer groups, e.g. 'Which'		Trade union	Victims Helpline Victim Support Lifelife – help for victims of violence in the home The Howard League Neighbourhod Watch	Childine NSPCC National Association of Family Mediation and Conciliation Services Parent network Relate

ACTIVITY

Find out how the Police Force is organised in your area. Does it have any special departments?

- *The Prison Service.* There are approximately 130 prisons in England and Wales, including Remand Prisons, Young Offender Institutions and Open Prisons.

ACTIVITY

Check that you understand what is meant by each type of prison mentioned.

- *The Crown Prosecution Service.* This service runs regional offices.

ACTIVITY

What provision do you have within your area?

- *The Probation Service.* The service is organised into Regional and Area offices. The Probation Service may offer: Community Services; Family Day Centres; Employment Projects; Resettlement Units; Juvenile Liaison Teams; Probation and Bail Hostels; and Training Centres.

Table 6.2 Examples of social welfare services

	Health care	Social care	Social security	Education	Unemployment
Central government department	Department of Health	Department of Health	Department of Social Security	Department of Education	Department of Employment Department of Education (Training & Enterprise)
Local authority departments (county & borough councils)	N/A	Social services	Welfare Rights Units	Education	Education (Provides careers service)
Public bodies	NHS Management Executive Community Health Councils Health Department Executive Bodies Health Department Advisory Bodies	Social Services Inspectorate	Social Security Benefits Agency Child Support Agency Social Security Departments Executive Boards	Training and Enterprise Councils	Employment Service (has regional and area offices) Training, Enterprise and Education Directorate (in Northern Ireland, Training and Employment Agency)
Commercial/ private	Private hospitals, nursing homes and clinics	Private residential homes for the elderly, etc.	Private pensions/company pensions Unemployment insurance	Independent schools Private nurseries	Private employment agencies All businesses and industries
Voluntary/ charities/ not-for-profit	St Johns Ambulance Brigade MIND, SCOPE	Age Concern Community service volunteers	Citizens Advice Bureau The National Claimants Federation The Disablement Income Group Campaign against Child Support	The Dyslexia Centre The National Association for Special Educational Needs The National Campaign for Nursery Education	Low Pay Unit Job Concern Trade unions

ACTIVITY

Interview a probation officer about their work. How is the Probation Service organised within your area, and what services are offered?

- *Legal Aid Service*. This is administered locally.

ACTIVITY

Find out to whom Legal Aid is available.

- *The House of Lords (Law Lords), The Courts, The High Court.*

There are many voluntary organisations concerned with crime prevention and the support of victims of crimes.

ACTIVITY

Find out about the work of the following groups:

- The Howard League;
- The National Association for the Care and Resettlement of Offenders (NACRO);
- The National Association of Victim Support Services.

Although all these organisations and services described in this section are in place to reduce crime, it is thought by many that the most effective way to do this is to tackle the causes of crime.

ACTIVITY

Read the article below which appeared in *The Guardian*. Discuss the reasons why unemployment may lead to crime.

CRIME AND UNEMPLOYMENT LINK IS UNDENIABLE, SAYS STUDY FOCUSING ON THE ALIENATION OF YOUTH

Unemployment is one of the main reasons for a 120 per cent increase in crime in the last 14 years, according to a study published today.

Long-term and youth unemployment are major factors in a crime rate that now sees a total of 609 offences committed every hour, according to the report.

Professor John Benyon, director of the Centre for the Study of Public Order at Leicester University, who conducted the study, said that it was possible to reverse the trend, but to do so it was first of all necessary to understand the causes of crime.

Law and Order Review 1993: An audit of crime, policing and criminal justice issues, Centre of the Study of Public Order, University of Leicester, The Friars, 154 Upper New Walk, Leicester LE1 7QA. £8.50 inc p&p.

(The Guardian, 7 October 1994)

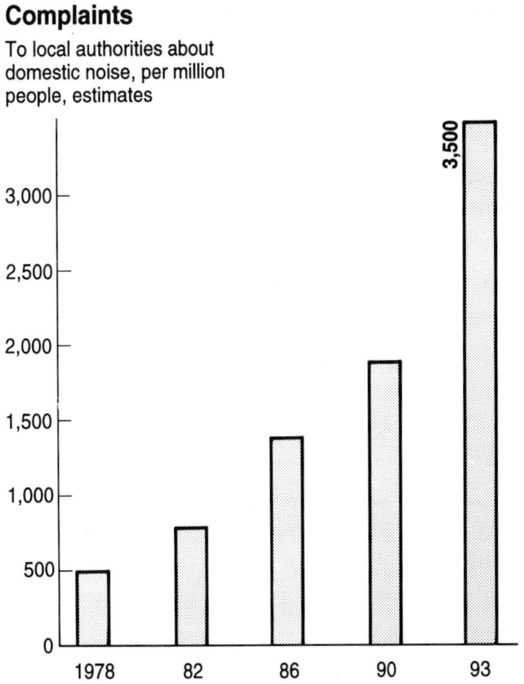

Figure 6.6 Complaints to local authorities about domestic noise, per million people (estimates)
Source: Chartered Institute of Environmental Health.

Quality of social relationships

Good social relationships are obviously an essential part of a healthy environment. These relationships may be with members of the family, employers and work colleagues, or neighbours.

There are many services concerned with FAMILY RELATIONSHIPS. The Social Services Department of each local authority will provide counselling services, for either individual members or a whole family (family therapy). This type of counselling is also available from private agencies and voluntary organisations, for example, Relate.

One of the main reasons for poor quality relationships between neighbours concerns disputes over noise. In recent years at least 17 deaths have resulted from these disputes, including suicides and murders. The government has promised a clamp down on neighbour noise. At present local authority environmental health officers can issue noise abatement notices and confiscate noisy hi-fi equipment or televisions. The maximum fine under the Environmental Protection Act for failing to obey an abatement notice is £5,000. However, although the number of complaints has increased significantly over the past years (Figure 6.6), only a very small percentage ever results in prosecution (e.g. 3% in 1993). For this reason, the pressure group 'The Right to Peace and Quiet Campaign' is pressing for persistent noise nuisance to be made a criminal offence.

Many disputes occur because of poor relationships between different racial groups. To counteract this, the Commission for Racial Equality was set up.

ACTIVITY

The provision of services related to creating and ensuring good quality social relationships varies from locality to locality. Give an account, for example, in the form of a poster, to show what services are available in your area.

(As a starting point you could look up the following in *Yellow Pages*: Counselling and Advice; Information Services; Social Services and Welfare Organisations; Youth and Community Groups.)

PUBLIC ENVIRONMENTS (e.g. LEISURE FACILITIES, RESTAURANTS)

Leisure

Leisure is essential for individuals to lead a healthy, balanced life. It encourages social contacts outside the workplace or home, and many leisure activities are concerned with fitness.

ACTIVITY

Carry out a survey of people's leisure activities (see Chapter 8 for research methods). What benefits to their health and well-being do these people feel they gain?

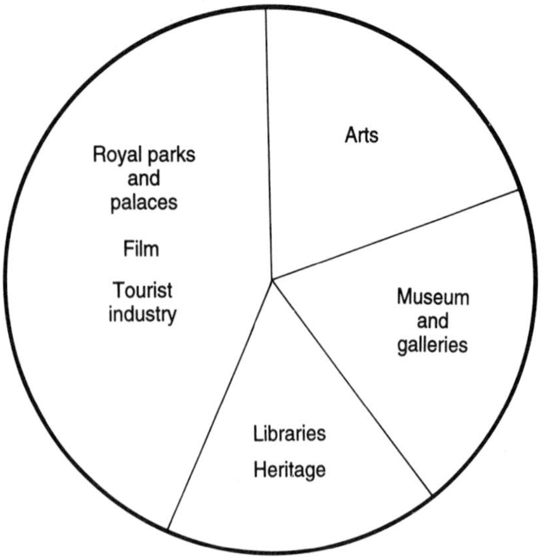

Figure 6.7 Breakdown of spending of the Department of National Heritage

The central government department with responsibility for leisure is the recently created DEPARTMENT OF NATIONAL HERITAGE, dubbed by some 'the Ministry of Fun'! The Department puts the emphasis of its role in improving the quality of life for British people, and its duties include overseeing the following:

- museums;
- libraries;
- sport;
- regulation of the newspaper press;
- preparation for the millennium;
- 'heritage'.

Figure 6.7 gives a breakdown of its spending.

There are various non-departmental public bodies concerned with leisure, for example the SPORTS COUNCIL which was set up to promote participation in sport and physical recreation, and the ARTS COUNCIL. These non-departmental bodies may also have a local presence which will work with local authorities. For example, there are REGIONAL COUNCILS FOR SPORT AND RECREATION and REGIONAL ARTS BOARDS.

Local authorities provide many leisure facilities, for example sport and leisure centres, libraries and gardens.

ACTIVITY

Look in the front of *Yellow Pages* to find which county and borough council departments are responsible for these different aspects of leisure.

Many leisure facilities are provided privately on a commercial basis, for example health clubs and cinemas. Large employers may also provide leisure facilities for their employees.

Some leisure facilities are run by voluntary organisations, which may rely on volunteers and fund-raising events to generate the necessary finance.

ACTIVITY

- Prepare a guide to the leisure facilities available in your locality. You may wish to focus on a particular type such as sports, family leisure, day-time leisure, night-time leisure or a diary of events. Include maps.
- Identify whether each facility is provided

by the state, privately or by a voluntary organisation.
- What facilities are available for the disabled?

Restaurants

Eating in restaurants is now a significant part of many people's leisure activities. There is legislation, and services to enforce this, to ensure that food outlets have adequate standards of hygiene to protect consumers from disease and ill health.

The legislative arrangements are the responsibility of central government, and are shared between two departments. These are the MINISTRY OF AGRICULTURE, FISHERIES AND FOOD, and the DEPARTMENT OF HEALTH.

While the food laws are generated centrally, their enforcement is devolved to local government.

The 1990 Food Safety Act empowers the local authority to appoint environmental health officers with special duties of food inspection. They have powers of entry and can enforce all aspects of the Act.

Public analysts can be appointed and microbiological laboratories can be set up. Arrangements can be made to collect and analyse samples.

Local authorities can seize and condemn suspected food, serve Improvement and Prohibition Orders and prosecute offenders.

Weights and Measures officers also play a role in ensuring that the Weights and Measures legislation is implemented.

ACTIVITY

1 Visit local restaurants, food shops and other food outlets and observe special precautions which are taken to avoid decay and contamination of food. You could specially investigate:

- a large supermarket;
- a fish shop;
- a bread and cake shop;
- an ice-cream stall;
- a hamburger stall;
- a self-service restaurant.

2 Food can be contaminated by a variety of toxic foreign materials and organisms. Find out about the following:

- chemical contamination;
- contamination by micro-organisms;
- infestations.

3 List five potential health hazards shown in Figure 6.8.

4 Local authority Departments of Environmental Health and Health Promotion Teams frequently publish packs to educate caterers. What 10 'Golden Rules' would you produce for people who work in restaurants?

5 Figure 6.9 is a poster produced by the Health Education Council. Do you think it is effective? Give reasons for your decision.

WORKING ENVIRONMENTS

In 1970 a committee was set up to investigate health and safety at work. It was found that the UK had the best legal and regulatory system in the world but it was not effective in preventing accidents at work. The law was very difficult to interpret and was often out of date. There were too many enforcement authorities and inspection was not systematic. Apathy was deemed to be the main cause of accidents at work. There are 100,000 major injuries caused by accidents at work every year, including 600 deaths.

The new Act which was introduced after this report was the Health and Safety at Work Act 1974. It was based on the following principles:

- All *employers* and *employees* should be aware of

Figure 6.8 Problems in the kitchen

health and safety matters. Personal responsibility is very important.
- There is one comprehensive framework which includes basic legislation, regulations covering specific hazards at work and codes of practice.
- There is one unified enforcement authority which carries out inspections, initiates legal proceedings, and gives help and advice.

THE HEALTH AND SAFETY COMMISSION was set up under the Act to administer the Health and Safety at Work Act. It also reviews health and safety legislation and submits proposals for new and revised regulations.

There are ADVISORY COMMITTEES which consider the following areas of employment:

1 Major hazards.
2 Toxic substances.
3 Dangerous substances.
4 Medical.
5 Nuclear safety.
6 Dangerous pathogens.
7 Industrial – paper, oil, agriculture, Health Services, printing, foundaries, construction, railways.

A major task is to formulate safety standards for every industry and to provide regulations and guidance.

THE HEALTH AND SAFETY EXECUTIVE is the major instrument of the Health and Safety Commission. It is responsible for the HEALTH AND SAFETY INSPECTORATE through which it enforces the health and safety law. It ensures that the regulations and guidance provisions are implemented. There are 21 regional offices of the Health and Safety Executive.

The health and safety inspectors have four main roles:

1 Inspection and enforcement of the law.
2 Help and advice to employers.

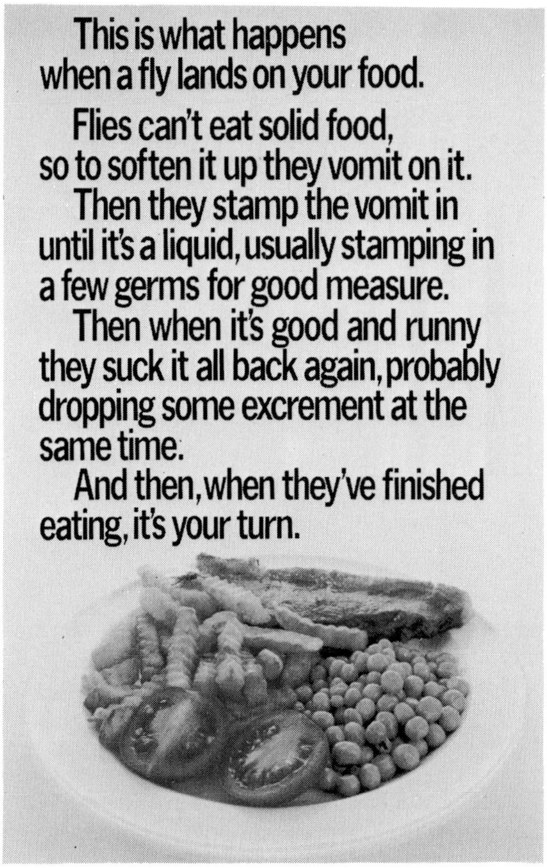
This is what happens
when a fly lands on your food.
Flies can't eat solid food,
so to soften it up they vomit on it.
Then they stamp the vomit in
until it's a liquid, usually stamping in
a few germs for good measure.
Then when it's good and runny
they suck it all back again, probably
dropping some excrement at the
same time.
And then, when they've finished
eating, it's your turn.

Figure 6.9 Health Education Authority poster

3 Serving improvement and prohibition notices.
4 Criminal proceedings as a last resort.

Criminal proceedings result in fines and compensation for victims of accidents if the employer is shown to be negligent. For severe breach the sentence can be imprisonment.

ACTIVITY

1 Write to the Health and Safety Executive for information on the Health and Safety at Work legislation.

2 **An investigation – health and safety at work in your college or school.** Imagine that you have been asked to produce a report for the Student Union called 'Potential Safety Hazards in the College/School'.

- In pairs, make a general survey of the health and safety facilities and considerations throughout the establishment. As you go around your school, department or college, make a note of safety equipment, for example fire escapes, facilities, displays and notices. Also make notes on possible dangerous equipment and furniture.
- Choose a specific area of the college/school or department and make a detailed survey of the health and safety problems and solutions in this area. Interview members of staff and students that use that area. Tape your interviews. Use photographs, diagrams, etc., to illustrate your report.
- In pairs, give a presentation to the class. Use visual aids to enhance your presentation.

Practitioners involved in protecting the public from risk

The Consultant in Communicable Disease Control, who works within each Department of Public Health, is in charge of all immunisation programmes, but it is the GPs who actually implement the programmes.

IMMUNISATION PROGRAMMES

The progress made in the control and prevention of infectious diseases has been the result of a number of factors, including improvements in water supply and sanitation, personal hygiene and nutritional status. However, the development of vaccines and immunisation programmes has been the most important factor in the prevention of many infectious diseases.

There is still a long way to go. Each year in developing countries almost four million children die and a similar number are

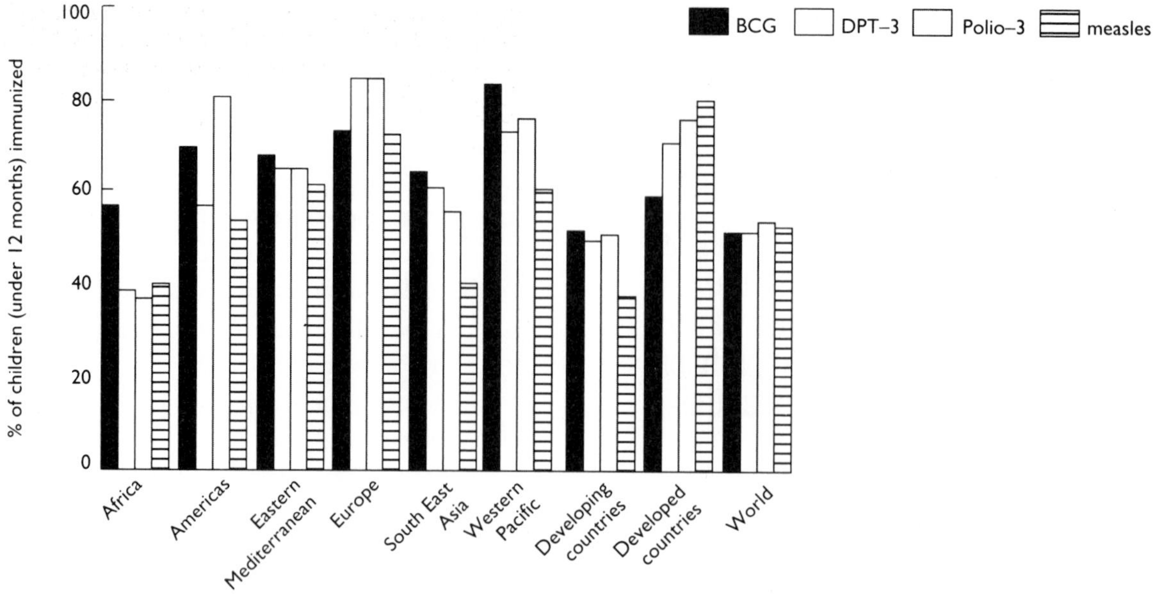

Figure 6.10 Immunisation coverage, by WHO region and level of development, in 1987 BCG = vaccine for tuberculosis
DPT-3 i = vaccine for diphtheria, pertussis and tetanus
Source: UNEP, 1989, *Environmental Data Report 1989* (Blackwell, 1989).

permanently disabled from six of the most common childhood diseases: pertussis (whooping cough), diphtheria, measles, poliomyelitis, tuberculosis and tetanus. Of these deaths nearly two million are from measles, 800,000 from neonatal tetanus, 600,000 from pertussis and 30,000 from tuberculosis. It is estimated that 250,000 cases of poliomyelitis occur annually (UNEP, 1990). There are effective vaccines against each of these diseases, but the immunisation levels, although improving, are still not adequate in many parts of the world (see Figure 6.10).

In England, as in most countries, immunisation coverage is continuing to rise (see Figure 6.11). The national target for childhood immunisation is 90% and this has been reached for all infections except pertussis (whooping cough). The targets will be increased to 95% by 1996.

As the immunisation uptake rate has increased, a corresponding fall in the relevant diseases has occurred. For example, in 1991 the lowest annual number of measles cases was reported since records began (see Figure 6.12). In October 1988 the MMR (mumps, measles and rubella) vaccine was introduced. Since then the number of cases of rubella has dropped, both for children and for pregnant women. There has been a corresponding drop in rubella-associated terminations of pregnancy and cases of congenital rubella.

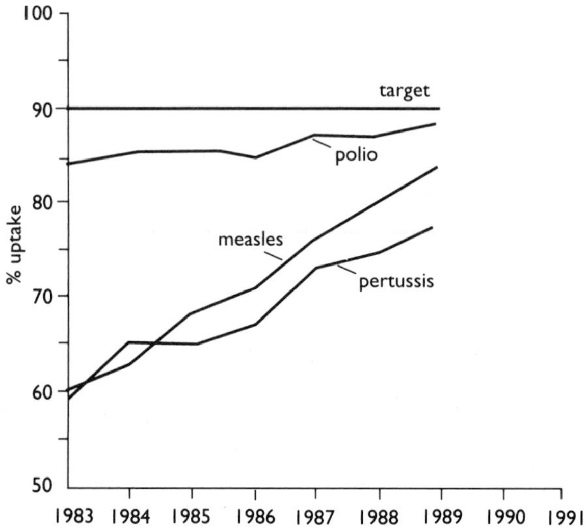

Figure 6.11 Immunisation uptake rate, England, 1983–91
Source: Crown copyright. Reproduced with the permission of the controller of Her Majesty's Stationery Office.

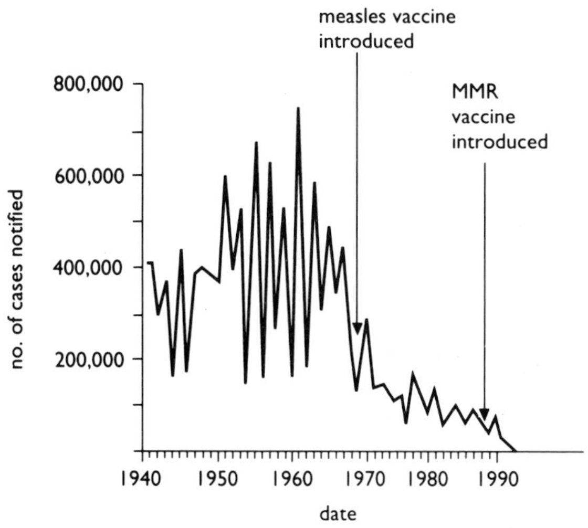

Figure 6.12 Notification of measles, 1940–91
Source: Crown copyright. Reproduced with the permission of the Controller of Her Majesty's Stationery Office.

The number of notifications of mumps has fallen to even lower levels than those for measles and rubella. It is likely that mumps will shortly disappear as a result of the very high uptake of MMR vaccine.

ACTIVITY

1 How does rubella harm the developing foetus?

2 Role-play the following situation. In advance gather together and prepare appropriate materials to help you (e.g. Figure 6.13).

You are a health visitor in an antenatal clinic. A mother with a three week-old baby comes to you for vaccination advice. Explain what the likely immunisation schedule will be for her child. She tells you that she has heard that vaccines contain viruses and so is worried that they may endanger her baby. Spend about ten minutes responding to this, using simple visual aids to help you with your explanation.

IMMUNISATION SCHEDULE

WHEN DUE	WHICH IMMUNISATIONS	TYPE
AT 2 MONTHS	Hib	ONE INJECTION
	DIPHTHERIA, WHOOPING COUGH, TETANUS – DTP	ONE INJECTION
	POLIO	BY MOUTH
AT 3 MONTHS	Hib	ONE INJECTION
	DIPHTHERIA, WHOOPING COUGH, TETANUS – DTP	ONE INJECTION
	POLIO	BY MOUTH
AT 4 MONTHS	Hib	ONE INJECTION
	DIPHTHERIA, WHOOPING COUGH, TETANUS – DTP	ONE INJECTION
	POLIO	BY MOUTH
AT 12–15 MONTHS	MEASLES, MUMPS, RUBELLA – MMR	ONE INJECTION
3–5 YEARS (around school entry)	DIPHTHERIA, TETANUS	BOOSTER INJECTION
	POLIO	BOOSTER BY MOUTH
GIRLS 10–14 YEARS	RUBELLA	ONE INJECTION
GIRLS/BOYS 13 YEARS	TUBERCULOSIS	ONE INJECTION (BCG)
SCHOOL LEAVERS	TETANUS, DIPHTHERIA	ONE INJECTION
15–19 YEARS	POLIO	BOOSTER BY MOUTH

Figure 6.13 Health Education Authority's Immunisation schedule
Source: Health Education Authority (1993).

3 Give an oral, visual or written presentation of an investigation into one named pathogen for which a vaccine is available. Your investigation should include the effect of the pathogen on the body, and the body's response. Investigate the effectiveness of the vaccine through the analysis of statistics, either globally or in one country.

SCREENING PROGRAMMES

(See 'Recall' on page 307 in Chapter 5 and information on New Immigrant Screening Programme in the next section.)

Within each Department of Public Health there is one person who has overall responsibility for screening programmes. This person advises and guides the GPs who receive payment for this from the District Health Authority. (Much of the actual screening is actually carried out by practice nurses.)

District Health Authorities may also set up BREAST SCREENING UNITS which go out into the community, for example into supermarket car parks.

Cervical screening may be carried out in Obstetrics and Gynaecology Units in hospitals, in Family Planning Units and by GPs.

CONTACT TRACING PROGRAMMES

The aim of health professionals involved in contact tracing is to find key people who have been in contact with patients suffering from certain diseases. Once traced, these people can then be tested for the disease; given prophylactic treatment (to prevent the disease occurring), and advice on how to limit the spread of the disease.

If a disease is classed as *notifiable*, once a case is suspected or diagnosed by the GP it has to be reported to the Department of Public Health (see the list of notifiable diseases below).

However, the only diseases which are presently included in Contact Tracing Programmes are usually tuberculosis and meningococcal meningitis. If a child is found to have the latter disease, any kissing contacts will be traced, and nasal swabs taken to test for the pathogen.

Recent studies show that 10% of tuberculosis cases are diagnosed by contact tracing and that the disease occurs in about 1% of contacts. People, particularly small children, sharing a house with someone who has tuberculosis are most at risk. Occasionally a contact at work or in a hospital ward is close enough to be equivalent to a household contact.

The incidence of tuberculosis is high among many immigrant groups in the UK. Because of this, screening of new immigrants from Asia, Africa, South and Central America, and other countries where tuberculosis is common is recommended.

The responsibility for screening and contact tracing rests in Scotland with the *Director of Public Health/Consultant in Public Health* (CDEM) and in England and Wales with the local *Consultant in Communicable Disease Control* (CCDC). But there must be close involvement with the local respiratory services. The Code of Practice 1994 produced by the Joint Tuberculosis Committee of the British Thoracic Society recommends that each Department of Public Health should have an agreed integrated policy which covers arrangements for contact tracing, new immigrant screening and contingency plans in the event of an outbreak. It also recommends that the minimum level of staffing is one full-time equivalent health visitor/nurse for every 50 notifications per annum, with full clerical support.

At Sexually Transmitted Disease (STD) Clinics patients will be given help in contact tracing if it is requested. For example, they are given printed leaflets which they are recommended to give to their sexual contacts and which advise the contacts of the need for treatment.

ACTIVITY

- What particular problems do you think may occur with STD contact tracing?

Notifiable diseases

The following are notifiable diseases:

- anthrax;
- cholera;
- cryptosoridiosis;

- diphtheria;
- dysentary (*Shingella*)
- food poisoning (*Salmonella*);
- hepatitis A, B, C, D;
- impetigo;
- jaundice;
- measles;
- meningitis;
- poliomyelitis;
- rabies;
- streptococcal infection associated with scarlet fever or rheumatic fever;
- tetanus;
- tuberculosis;
- typhoid, paratyphoid;
- whooping cough;
- yellow fever.

Legislation to restrict the liberty of individuals

As discussed earlier (Chapter 1), health and social care professionals are frequently engaged in applying legislation which restricts individual liberty, for the well-being either of the individual or of those with whom the individual may come into contact. The exercise of such powers often necessarily involves ethical questions, for example where it is not automatically clear that restricting an individual's liberty is a lesser 'evil' than the risk they may pose to others by remaining free. The health and social care worker owes a particular ethical duty to ensure that such powers are exercised fairly and justly.

MENTAL HEALTH ACT 1983

Under Section 2 of the Act, a person may be admitted to hospital for assessment of his or her mental disorder and held in hospital for up to 28 days. An Approved social worker, or nearest relative, completes an application supported by the recommendations of two doctors (one of whom will be a psychiatrist) who state that the detained person satisfies at least one of two criteria:

1 The person is suffering from a mental disorder that warrants detention in hospital for assessment and/or treatment.

2 The person ought to be detained in hospital in the interests of their health or safety or with a view to the protection of others.

Under Section 3 of the Act the same professionals can recommend detention of up to six months, which can be extended for a further six months and thereafter reviewed annually.

Clearly health and social care workers are here able to wield powers that otherwise would only be applied to those guilty of criminal offences. Great care must be exercised in such a fundamental restriction of civil liberties. A number of recent cases have led to concern that some sections of the population are much more likely to be 'sectioned' than others. In 1986 compulsory detention under the Mental Health Act was 25 times more likely for 16–25-year-old black people than for whites (*The Observer*, 1 January 1987), and women are similarly over-represented in Special (mental) hospitals as the following extract makes clear:

JUSTICE WEIGHTED AGAINST WOMEN

Women are diagnosed as psychiatric cases and sent to maximum-security hospitals at seven times the rate of men, an *Observer* investigation has found. And women are twice as likely as men to be sent for psychiatric treatment when they appear in criminal courts.

One result of this is that a woman may be held indefinitely in a maximum-security hospital originally designed for the 'criminally insane' while a man who committed a similar offence serves a prison sentence and returns home.

Until now, these 'forgotten women' have remained a hidden problem. But at a national conference on Tuesday, psychiatrists, social workers and lawyers will join former inmates to call for a big shake-up in the system. They want to see changes in the way women are sentenced by the courts and improvements in the way they are treated if detained in maximum-security hospitals.

Women as young as 16 and as old as 70 are locked up without limit of time in the harsh regimes of Broadmoor, Rampton and Ashworth, often because there are no other, more suitable, places for them. They are subjected to a stringent security system and cannot move out of the view of staff at any time.

According to an unpublished study which has been made available to *The Observer*, a woman already in jail is twice as likely as a man to be sent to Broadmoor, the high-security 'special hospital', without appearing again before the court. She can be sent there with the agreement of two doctors. This means that her relatively short prison term could turn into limitless detention.

ACTIVITY

1 One response to concern over the treatment of detainees was the establishment of the Mental Health Act Commission. Contact the Commission and find out what its responsibilities are.

2 People detained under the Mental Health Act can apply to have their case reviewed by a Mental Health Review Tribunal. Find out who sits on these tribunals and what evidence they consider in reaching a decision.

One response to recent incidents involving patients in the community has been a government proposal to introduce supervision registers (under the Mental Health (Supervised Discharge) bill) for patients discharged from hospital who may remain a danger to themselves or others (this means that their progress can be monitored by mental health professionals in the community). A more controversial proposal is for the compulsory treatment of patients in the community, i.e. forcing people to take medication (which, in the case of many psychotropic drugs, can have severe side-effects) when they have not been 'sectioned' and deemed in need of hospital treatment. Many people are opposed to such a measure because they believe that it would infringe patients' civil rights. A different argument claims that such measures would endanger patients who require constant monitoring and support whilst taking such medication.

ACTIVITY

Research the recent recommendations made by Lord Louis Blom-Cooper (January 1995) on the treatment of mentally ill people in the community. Write a short report considering arguments for and against the view that patients in the community should decide for themselves what medication they take.

CRIMINAL JUSTICE LEGISLATION

Criminal justice legislation (for example the Criminal Justice Acts of 1988 and 1991 and the Criminal Justice and Public Order Act of 1994) details criminal offences as identified by Parliament. Such legislation encompasses thousands of laws which, if broken, may result in the restriction of liberty, including imprisonment. It also frequently sets out sentencing guidelines for magistrates and the judiciary and outlines particular requirements concerning the treatment and sentencing of offenders. Health and social care workers will need to keep appraised of the legislation as it affects their particular field of practice and assessment of risk.

There are many situations in which the health and social care worker's assessment of risk to a client or their community is central to the criminal justice process, in determining both the treatment of an individual charged with an offence and the punishment if the individual is found guilty.

JUVENILE OFFENDERS

Successive legislation has demonstrated a rather contradictory attitude towards juvenile offenders. It has been recognised that young offenders have special needs if their first offence is not to become their introduction to a life-time of offending. The younger the offender the more vulnerable they are deemed to be and the more in need of social workers and probation officers to act as advocates for them. The Police and Criminal Evidence Act 1984 sets out strict guidelines on the treatment of young offenders and requires that an appropriate adult (possibly a social worker) is always present. However, it is also the case that Britain has one of the youngest ages of criminal responsibility in the world (ten in England and Wales and eight in Scotland) and the 1994 Criminal Justice Act provides for custodial sentences of up to 14 years for children who commit robbery, rape, assault or handle stolen goods.

BAIL

Bail refers to the temporary release from custody of either someone charged by the police and awaiting trial, or a prisoner. Security (money) is often paid to the police or court and forfeited if the suspect fails to appear. In the case of juvenile offenders bail will almost always be granted for a first offence unless he or she is deemed to be a risk to self or others or to be in danger. Frequently reports provided by health and social care workers will help to establish this.

Assessment by a social worker will also be taken into account by a court in determining the type of custody accommodation to be used. At present, juveniles may be sentenced to a variety of institutions, including remand support at home, a foster placement, a community home, a remand centre, secure accommodation or prison. The 1994 Criminal Justice Act proposes the establishment of a number of national secure units, run along prison lines, for young offenders aged 12–14. The United Nations has recently condemned these proposals as militating against the rights of the child as recognised in international agreements.

Ethical dilemmas for practitioners

The aim of health protection and promotion is to prevent illness, which must be a goal of all health care professionals. However, it is important to be aware that a number of health protection measures do raise ethical questions.

SCREENING

Screening does make an important contribution to public health, but some screening programmes raise difficult moral questions, particularly those tests now being developed to screen for genetic abnormalities. In many cases, for example cystic fibrosis and sickle-cell disease, there is no 'cure' and where carriers of a particular 'defective' gene are identified the only medical advice is to avoid having a family, or where prenatal testing is undertaken the preventative option is likely to be termination of the pregnancy.

This raises the question of individual liberty: should individuals be told that they must not have a family? If they ignore such advice will their child be refused the care that it will need because they 'chose' such an outcome?

Many people feel very uncomfortable at the thought that genetic screening may be used to attempt to create a 'perfect' population with pressure brought to bear on parents not to produce babies who will be less than 'perfect'. Others, however, find this a very unlikely scenario (not least because many disabilities are not genetic in origin), and many of those with children who have led painful and short lives would have wished to spare them.

A further dilemma is raised by the fact that screening is able to indicate that an individual is likely to develop an untreatable condition (e.g. Huntington's disease) at some time in the future.

ACTIVITY

What are the moral arguments for and against telling an apparently healthy 20 year-old that in ten years' time she is likely to have developed a terminal illness?

IMMUNISATION PROGRAMMES

The Department of Health's recent measles immunisation programme gave rise to a specific moral objection from the Catholic church when it was made public that aborted foetal tissue was used in the development of the vaccine. Abortion is not acceptable to many Catholics. However, immunisation programmes also raise wider moral questions. Whilst there are undoubtedly significant public health benefits to be gained from mass immunisation, side-effects for a small minority can be very severe. Some people argue that it is not morally acceptable to discount the potential disadvantages to the few solely on the grounds that a greater number are likely to benefit.

HEALTH EDUCATION CAMPAIGNS

Public health education campaigns aim to educate the public and to encourage them to change or adopt certain practices to improve or maintain their health. Such campaigns cover a wide range of issues from smoking and diet to sexual behaviour. They can be controversial because they are targeted at people who are not ill and because changes might be advocated in very personal areas of people's lives. They may also raise the question of individual freedom and liberty and the degree to which the medical profession can or should seek to force individuals to change their lifestyles.

Advice concerning sexual behaviour is a particular minefield. Sometimes the advice given may itself express a certain 'moral' viewpoint which is unacceptable to those it is targeted at, such as advice to young people to avoid all sexual contact outside of marriage.

Advice may be (unconsciously) motivated by a particular prejudice against certain kinds of sexual behaviour, and as such is unlikely to be successful in promoting public health.

Health workers need to always bear in mind that there is a significant difference between encouraging people to take responsibility for their own health and blaming them when they do not succeed.

ACTIVITY

How far can health workers legitimately go in seeking to persuade us to adopt a healthy lifestyle? Design your own health promotion campaign which falls within these limits.

ACTIVITY

Recently there have been a number of cases where doctors appear to have refused to treat patients because of their lifestyle, e.g. because they were smokers or severely overweight. Is the restriction of treatment in such cases ever justifiable on moral grounds?

ASSESSMENT OPPORTUNITY ✓

Produce a report which describes the range of practitioners who work in services which:

- promote health and social well-being;
- seek to create an environment conducive to health and social well-being;
- seek to protect individuals from risk.

Include in your report:

- a description of the legislation which may restrict the liberty of individuals for their or others health and social well-being;
- a discussion of the ethical dilemmas which practitioners may face when they are balancing the needs of different individuals and groups.

EVALUATE THE WAYS IN WHICH CLIENTS EXPERIENCE AND INFLUENCE HEALTH AND SOCIAL CARE PROVISION

This part of the chapter is designed to guide you in making your own investigation into clients' perceptions of health and social care. The investigations should be carried out after you have read Chapters 1–5, as well as the beginning of this chapter.

It would also be useful for you to read Chapter 8 on research methods.

ACTIVITY

Read the article entitled 'National Survey of Hospital Patients' by S. Bruster *et al.* in the British Medical Journal, 1994, vol. 309, pp. 1542–9.

- Summarise the problems highlighted by the survey.
- Note that asking a series of specific questions, e.g. 'Did a doctor explain your condition or treatment to you?', or 'Was the purpose of the tests explained to you by a doctor or other staff?', was much more successful than asking patients if they were satisfied with their care. Remember this when designing your questions.
- When you have completed your own investigation, compare your findings with those in this survey.

ASSESSMENT OPPORTUNITY ✓

Interview at *least* two clients with multiple needs of health and social care services to complete the following:

1 Describe the *client's perceptions* of health and social care services. (Give as many specific examples as possible, but don't forget to maintain confidentiality.)

To help you write your descriptions, ask the users about the following aspects of care:

- To what extent did they feel in control of the process?
- Did they feel respected as an individual?
- What did they think of the 'care' they received?
- Were they given enough information?
- Could they understand the information they were given?
- What did they think of the services and facilities on offer?

2 Describe the extent to which services user's perceive there to a *continuum of care*. Give as many specific examples as possible.

- Did they find the service they were offered 'seamless' or disjointed? For example was there:
  - continuity of provision?
  - a smooth transition from one care setting to another?
  - a smooth transition from one care worker to another?
  - a smooth flow of information from one care setting to another?
  - a smooth flow of information from one care worker to another?
  - a smooth flow of information to the client?
  - workers who could meet many of their needs?

3 Describe the *support* which clients were offered when receiving care.

- What examples of the following types of support were they offered?
  - physical (e.g. treatment, transport, etc.);
  - financial;

- emotional;
- knowledge and understanding.

4 Describe the ways in which the services users (and their carers) were able to *take control of the care* available or being received.

- What information was available? Was this adequate?
- What advice was given? Was this adequate?
- Was help given with development of skills?
- Was the client or carer given any responsibility for:
  - deciding how resources should be used?
  - deciding how care should be planned and delivered?
- Was any information given on, or contact made with, user/care networks and forums?
- Did users have any role in managing their own care?

5 Were there ways in which the health and social care services tried to *involve the clients to improve services*? For example:

- Were there recent improvements to buildings and furnishings to make users feel more relaxed and 'at home'?
- Was information available on what standards clients could expect (e.g. Charter of Service)?

- Were staff approachable, and did they have enough time available to listen to users' requests and suggestions?
- Did users know where they could find information, make complaints or give suggestions? For example, did they know about:
  - user forums?
  - Community Health Councils?
  - how to register a complaint?

6 In the light of your interviews with clients, and any visits to 'caring' establishments or interviews with professionals you can arrange:

- Write a summary of how health and social care services in your local area are attempting to improve their service.
- Make your own recommendations for how services could be improved on a day-to-day basis.

REFERENCES AND RESOURCES

Blom-Cooper, L. et al (1995), *The Falling Shadow*, London: Duckworth.

Bruster, S. *et al.* (1994), 'National Survey of Hospital Patients', *British Medical Journal*, vol. 309, pp. 1542–9.

Davey, B. and Popay, J. (1993), *Dilemmas in Health Care*. Buckinghamshire: Open University Press.

Department of Health (1988), *Protecting Children: A Guide for Social Workers Undertaking a Comprehensive Assessment*. London: HMSO.

Dynes, M. and Walter, D. (1995), *The Times Guide to the New British State: The Government Machine in the 1990s*. London: Times Books.

Joint Tuberculosis Committee of the British Thoracic Society (1994), 'Control and prevention of TB in the UK: Code of Practice 1994', *Thorax*, vol. 49, pp. 1193–1200.

Kemp, N. and Richardson, E. (1990), *Quality Assurance in Nursing Practice*. Oxford: Butterworth Heinemann.

MacKereth, P. and Harrison, T. (1995), 'Maintaining confidentiality when tracing contacts', *Nursing Times*, vol. 91, January 1995.

Mind/Liberty (1993), *Report 1 – People with Mental Health Problems and Learning Disability*. London: NCCL.

National Association of Health Authorities and Trusts (1993), 'Complementary Therapies in the NHS', Research Paper No. 10. London: NAHAT.

Social Services Inspectorate (1993), *Young People Detained and Remanded*. London: Department of Health.

Thames 'Help' Programme (1990), *The Health Directory*. London: Bedford Square Press.

Trevelyan, J. and Booth, B. (1994), *Complementary Medicine for Nurses, Midwives and Health Visitors*. London: Macmillan.

Who's Who in the Environment (regularly updated), The Environment Council, 80 York Way, London N1 9AG, Tel.: 0171-278-4736.

USEFUL ADDRESSES

Complementary and Alternative Medicines

British Complementary Medicine Association
St Charles Hospital
Exmoor Street
London W10 6DX

British Holistic Medicine Association
179 Gloucester Place
London NW1 6DX

Centre for Complementary Health Studies
University of Exeter
Streatham Court
Rennes Drive
Exeter EX4 4PU

Council for Complementary and Alternative Medicine
179 Gloucester Place
London NW1 6DX

Institute for Complementary Medicine
PO Box 194
London SE16 1QZ

Natural Medicines Society
Edith Lewis House
Ilkeston
Derbyshire DE7 8EJ

Research Council for Complementary Medicine
60 Great Ormond Street
London WC1N 3JF

Services related to creating healthy environments

Department of the Environment
Room A1.23
Romney House
43 Marsham Street
London SW1P 3PY
Tel.: 0171 276 8388

Department of the Environment for Northern Ireland
Clarence Court
10–18 Adelaide Street
Belfast BT2 8GB
Tel.: 01232 540540

EC Commission (London Information Office)
Jean Monnet House
8 Storey's Gate
London SW1P 3AT
Tel.: 0171 222 1992

Health and Safety Executive
St Hugh's House
Stanley Precinct
Bootle L20 3QY
Tel.: 0151 951 4000

Institute for European Environmental Policy
158 Buckingham Palace Road
London SW1W 9TR

The Institution of Environmental Health Officers
Chadwick Court
15 Hatfields
London SE1 8DJ
Tel.: 0171 928 6006

National Rivers Authority (NRA)
Rivers House
Waterside Drive
Aztec West
Almondsbury
Bristol BS12 4UD
Tel.: 01454 624400

The Royal Environmental Health Institute of Scotland
3 Manor Place
Edinburgh EH3 7DH
Tel.: 0131 225 6999

The Salvation Army
Territorial HQ
101 Queen Victoria Street
London EC4P 4EP
Tel.: 0171 236 5222

Shelter
88 Old Street
London EC1V 9HU
Tel.: 0171 253 0202

Sports Council
16 Upper Woburn Place
London WC1H 0QP
Tel.: 0171 388 1277

Sports Council for Northern Ireland
House of Sport
Upper Malone Road
Belfast BT9 5LA
Tel.: 01232 381222

USEFUL SOURCES OF CAREERS INFORMATION IN THE UK

Care assistant: see *Social worker*
Chiropodist:
Society of Chiropodists
53 Welbeck Street
London W1M 7HE
Tel.: 0171 486 3381

Institute of Chiropodists
91 Lord Street
Southport
Merseyside PR8 1SA
Tel.: 01704 546141

Dietitian:
The British Dietetic Association
7th Floor
Elizabeth House
22 Suffolk Street
Queensway
Birmingham B1 1LS
Tel.: 0121 643 5483

District nurse, health visitor, hospital nurse, midwife:
English National Board for Nursing
Midwifery and Health Visiting
ENB Careers Service
PO Box 356
Sheffield S8 0SJ

National Board for Nursing, Midwifery and Health Visiting for Scotland
22 Queen Street
Edinburgh EH2 1JX
Tel.: 0131 226 7371

Health Service Manager:
National Health Service Training Directorate
St Bartholomew's Court
18 Christmas Street
Bristol BS1 5BT
Tel.: 0117 9291 029

The Scottish Health Service Management Development Group
Scottish Health Service Centre
Crewe Road South
Edinburgh EG4 2LF
Tel.: 0131 332 2335

Homoeopath:
British Homoeopathic Association
27a Devonshire Street
London W1N 1RJ
Tel.: 0171 935 2163

The Society of Homoeopaths
2 Artizan Road
Northampton NN1 4HU
Tel.: 01604 21400

Housing officer:
Institute of Housing
Octavia House
Westwood Business Park
Westwood Way
Coventry
Warwickshire CV4 8JP
Tel.: 01203 694433

Institute of Housing in Scotland
6 Palmerston Place
Edinburgh EH12 5AA
Tel.: 0131 225 4544

Occupational therapist:
The College of Occupational Therapists/Occupational Therapy Training Clearing House/British Association of Occupational Therapy
6/8 Marshalsea Road
London SE1 1HL
Tel.: 0171 357 6480

Physiotherapist:
The Chartered Society of Physiotherapy
Central Applications Office for Diploma Courses in Physiotherapy
Room 422
Foulton House
Jessop Avenue
Cheltenham
Gloucestershire GL50 3SH

North London School of Physiotherapy for the Visually Handicapped
10 Highgate Hill
London N19 5ND
Tel.: 0171 288 5959

Probation officer:
Central Council for Educational and Training in
Social Work (CCETSW)
Derbyshire House
St Chads Street
London WC1H 8AD
Tel.: 0171 278 2455

Probation Service Division
Room 442
Home Office
50 Queen Anne's Gate
London SW1H 9AT
Tel.: 0171 273 2675

Psychologist:
British Psychological Society
St Andrews House
48 Princess Road East
Leicester LE1 7DR
Tel.: 0116 2549 568

Social worker (field/residential)/care assistant:
Central Council for Education and Training in Social Work (CCETSW)
Derbyshire House
St Chads Street
London WC1H 8AD
Tel.: 0171 278 2455

CCETSW Information Office
78–80 George Street
Edinburgh EH2 3BU
Tel.: 0131 220 0093

Speech and language therapist:
The College of Speech and Language Therapists (CSLT)
Harold Poster House
6 Lechmere Road
London NW2 5BU
Tel.: 0181 459 8521

Teacher: special educational needs:
Teaching as a Career (TASC)
Publicity Unit
Elizabeth House
39 York Road
London SE1 7PH
Tel.: 0171 925 6617/8

Scottish Office Education Department
Careers Service Branch
Room 5/32
New St Andrew's House
St James Centre
Edinburgh EH1 3SY
Tel.: 0131 224 4692/8

Volunteer organiser:
Volunteer Centre UK
29 Lower King's Road
Berkhamsted
Hertfordshire HP4 2AB
Tel.: 01442 873311

Volunteer Development Scotland
80 Murray Place
Stirling FK8 2BX
Tel.: 01786 79593

Youth and community worker:
National Youth Agency
17–23 Albion Street
Leicester LE1 6GD
Tel.: 0116 2471 200

Scottish Community Education Council
West Coates House
90 Haymarket Terrace
Edinburgh EH12 5LQ
Tel.: 0131 313 2488

7

EDUCATING FOR HEALTH AND SOCIAL WELL-BEING

Chapter 7 aims to raise health awareness by highlighting the areas in which people have genuine choices in following a healthier lifestyle: smoking, drug abuse in its widest sense, sexually transmitted diseases, HIV and AIDS, and personal safety and security. The reasons for, sources of and methods used in health campaigns are investigated and activities are structured to enable students to evaluate the effectiveness of a health education campaign.

INVESTIGATING A HEALTH EDUCATION CAMPAIGN

Aspects of health and social well-being on which health education campaigns focus

The World Health Organisation defines health as a 'state of complete physical, mental and social well-being and not merely the absence of disease or infirmity'

A person can be described as healthy provided that the three sides of the triangle – social, mental and physical – remain intact; if the natural equilibrium is damaged then a state of ill-health, often only temporary, results. This definition has been criticised as focusing too much on an IDEAL state. Health and social well-being can be categorised as follows:

- *physical health*. This is the easiest aspect of health to measure, and is concerned with the physical functioning of the body.
- *emotional health*. How we express emotions such as joy, grief, frustration and fear; this leads on to coping strategies for anxiety and stress.
- *mental health*. This relates to our ability to organise our thoughts in a coherent manner and is closely linked to emotional and social health.
- *social health*. How we relate to others and form relationships.
- *spiritual health*. This includes religious beliefs and practices, as well as personal codes of conduct and the quest for inner peace.
- *environmental health*. An individual's health also depends on the health of the society in which he or she lives, e.g. famine areas deny health to the inhabitants, and unemployed people cannot be healthy in a society which only values those who work.

In earlier times, disease or ill-health was seen as punishment from God or gods, or resulting from bad luck. Now, individuals take more of a personal responsibility for maintaining good health and rely on the public sector for the provision of sanitation and health care institutions and services.

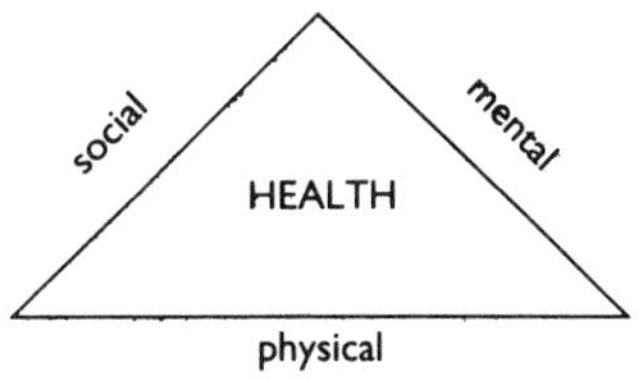

Figure 7.1 The three aspects of health

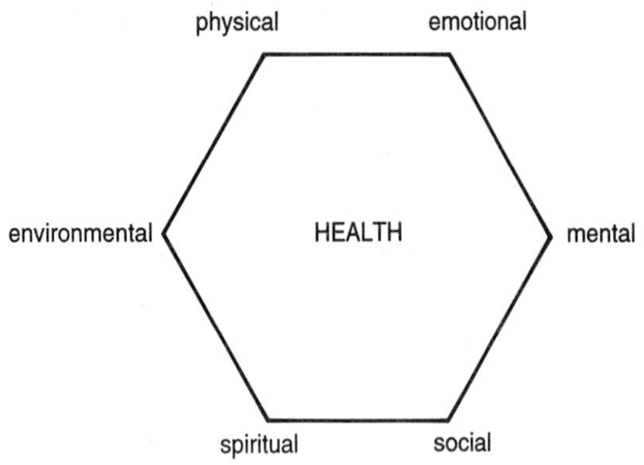

Figure 7.2 Six aspects of health

Health problems today

Medical advances, such as the development of new drugs, improved health services and high technology, have not managed to deal with a new generation of diseases – the CHRONIC DEGENERATIVE DISEASES:

- heart disease;
- cancers;
- stroke;
- arthritis.

All these represent the effects of wear and tear on the human body. In addition, new bacteria and viruses have emerged within the last 20 years:

- legionnaire's disease;
- campylobacter enteritis;
- helicobacter pylori gastritis (duodenal ulcer);
- human immunodeficiency virus (HIV and AIDS);
- bacterial spongiform encephalitis (BSE).

Aspects of health and social well-being

It is now recognised that people's lifestyles and behaviour are causative factors in most of the diseases mentioned above. Important factors are:

- diet;
- exercise and maintaining mobility;
- stress;
- recreation/leisure activities;
- smoking;
- alcohol and substance abuse;
- sexual behaviour;
- housing and sanitation.

What is health education?

Health education is a method of self-empowerment, i.e. it enables people to take more control over their own health and over the factors which affect their health. HEALTH PROMOTION is a term used to include all aspects of health education, but placing greater emphasis on changes in health policy and POSITIVE HEALTH as opposed to the rather negative prevention of ill-health.

The World Health Organisation (WHO) defines health promotion as:

'the process of enabling people to increase control over, and improve their health. To reach a stage of complete physical, mental and social well-being, an individual or group must be able to identify and to realise aspirations, to satisfy needs and to change or cope with the environment. Health is, therefore seen as a resource for everyday life, not the object of living. Health is a positive concept emphasising social and personal resources, as well as physical capacities. Therefore, health promotion is not just the responsibility of the health sector but goes beyond lifestyles to well-being'.

WHO (1985) Charter for Health Promotion.

PRIMARY, SECONDARY AND TERTIARY HEALTH EDUCATION

Health education may be described in the same way as the concept of primary, secondary and tertiary prevention in community medicine. Ewles and Simnett (1993) suggest three different levels of health education.

PRIMARY HEALTH EDUCATION

Primary health education is directed at healthy people. It is a prophylactic (or preventive) measure which aims to prevent ill-health from arising in the first instance.

Example: Children in school learn about:

- basic hygiene;
- nutrition;
- road safety;
- personal relationships.

SECONDARY HEALTH EDUCATION

Secondary health education is directed at people with a health problem or a reversible condition.

Examples:

- *Screening*. By routinely examining apparently healthy people, screening aims to detect either those who are likely to develop a particular disease or those in whom the disease is already present but not yet producing symptoms.
- *Reducing behaviours likely to damage health* – an overweight person can be encouraged to change their dietary habits or a smoker to quit smoking.

TERTIARY HEALTH EDUCATION

Tertiary health education is directed at those whose ill-health has not been, or could not be, prevented and who cannot be cured completely.

Examples:

- A child with brain damage can achieve his or her own potential through communication and structured play.
- A patient dying of cancer can do so with dignity if pain is kept under control.

Rehabilitation programmes are chiefly concerned with tertiary health education.

Reducing the likelihood of disease

The risks to health in society today differ greatly from those of the past. Diseases which were once major threats to life at all stages have been either eradicated or at least controlled:

- *Smallpox*: More than half the people of Europe would probably have had smallpox in their lifetime before Edward Jenner discovered the remedy, VACCINATION, in 1796.
- *Cholera*: The Public Health Acts in the 1870s halted the spread of cholera in the UK by improving water supplies and sewage disposal.
- *Tuberculosis*: In 1862, Robert Koch isolated the TB bacillus, leading to the development of a vaccine. (However, this disease is once again increasing in the 1990s, in both the developed and developing countries.
- *Diphtheria*: The anti-toxin was first used in 1890. Before then, death from diphtheria was common (see Figure 7.3).

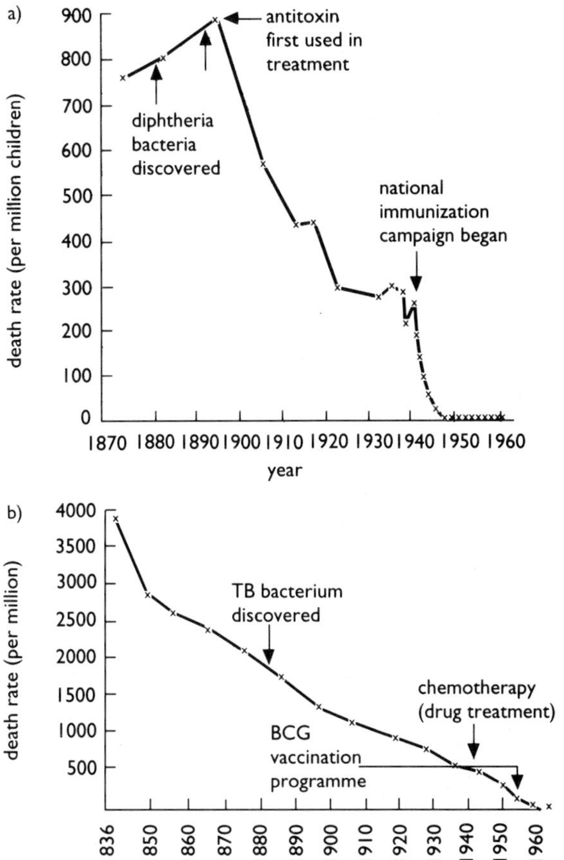

Figure 7.3 Decline in annual death rate from (a) diptheria and (b) tuberculosis, England and Wales

Source: L. Hartley, *History of Medicine* (Blackwell).

The problem of coronary heart disease

There are two main types of coronary heart disease: angina and heart attack (see also Chapter 3).

ANGINA PECTORIS is characterised by a crushing pain in the chest due to insufficient oxygen being carried to the heart muscles; it is often brought on by exercise or stress. The person will usually have special tablets (glyceryl trinitrate or Trinitrin) which dissolve under the tongue and bring rapid relief.

HEART ATTACKS are caused by either:

- *myocardial infarction*, when part of the heart muscle has died as a result of blood starvation;
- *coronary thrombosis*, when the blood supply to the heart muscles is stopped by a blood clot.

Both kinds of heart attack are usually caused by ATHEROSCLEROSIS, the build-up of fatty deposits, called ATHEROMA, in the blood vessels.

QUICK FACTS

- One *fatal* heart attack occurs in Britain every three minutes.
- Heart disease causes nearly one-third of all deaths in the UK in people *under* the age of 75.
- The United Kingdom has one of the highest levels of heart disease in the world.
- Smoking is a cause of one in every five fatal heart attacks.

REDUCING THE RISKS OF CORONARY HEART DISEASE

- Don't smoke.
- Take regular exercise – a brisk walk for 20 minutes each day will improve circulation.
- Drink alcohol sensibly – think of a pint of beer, or two glasses of wine, as the maximum for one day.
- Eat healthily.
- Try to avoid stress.

ACTIVITY **W**

Arrange a debate around a specific *lifestyle* issue, e.g. diet or smoking. Suggest topics:

- Should overweight people or smokers be refused a heart transplant by the NHS?
- Should smokers pay compensation directly to those damaged by passive smoking?
- Should health professionals prescribe courses to change health-damaging behaviour (e.g. an exercise programme at a leisure centre or a strictly-monitored diet)?

Cancer

There are over 200 different cancers, yet each starts in the same way – with a change in the normal make-up of a cell (see page 128). Experts have estimated that more than 80% of cancers may be avoidable by changing lifestyles or the environment.

QUICK FACTS

- 30% of all cancer deaths are caused by smoking.
- Every year smoking causes over 30,000 deaths from lung cancer.
- 3% of all cancers are related to excess alcohol consumption.
- Heavy drinkers are at risk of cirrhosis of the liver, which can lead to cancer in later life.
- About 35% of cancers are possibly related to diet.
- Diets containing a variety of fruits and vegetables seem to protect against certain cancers.
- Too much sun can lead to skin cancer.
- Skin cancer is the second most common cancer in the UK.
- Britain has the highest death rate from breast cancer in the world.
- 16,000 women die each year from breast cancer in the UK.
- About 2,000 women in the UK die each year from cervical cancer (cancer of the

cervix or neck of the womb).

- Testicular cancer is the commonest cancer in the UK in men aged 20–34, with 1,000 new cases reported each year.

THE RISKS OF RADIATION

Radiation is used therapeutically to treat various forms of cancer, but it can also cause cancer. Everyone is exposed to radiation which comes naturally from the earth and the sky; other sources of radiation need to be carefully monitored:

- X-ray examinations and treatment, including dental X-rays;
- houses found on certain types of ground in some counties in England, Scotland and Wales are more likely to have high levels of RADON, which is produced in granite and other rocks.

REDUCING THE RISKS OF CANCER

- Stop smoking, or better still don't start; after ten years your risk of lung cancer is about half that of a continuing smoker.
- Try to avoid places where you will be exposed to passive smoking.
- Know the limits of sensible drinking and keep within them.
- Eat more fruit and vegetables.
- Eat more starchy and fibre-rich foods.
- Eat less fatty foods.
- If you want to tan, do it gradually and protect against sunburn by using a sun lotion with the correct sun protection factor (SPF).
- Women aged between 50 and 64 should attend a breast screening centre every three years for mammography (X-rays) of both breasts; early detection gives a better chance of successful treatment.
- To reduce the risk of cervical cancer, use a BARRIER CONTRACEPTIVE (cap, condom, female condom or diaphragm) during intercourse; women aged 20–64 should attend a clinic for a free CERVICAL SMEAR TEST every 3 years.
- A good way of detecting testicular cancer in its early stages is for men to examine their own testicles.
- If you work with radiation, make sure that the safety regulations are fully observed.
- The radon level in your home can be

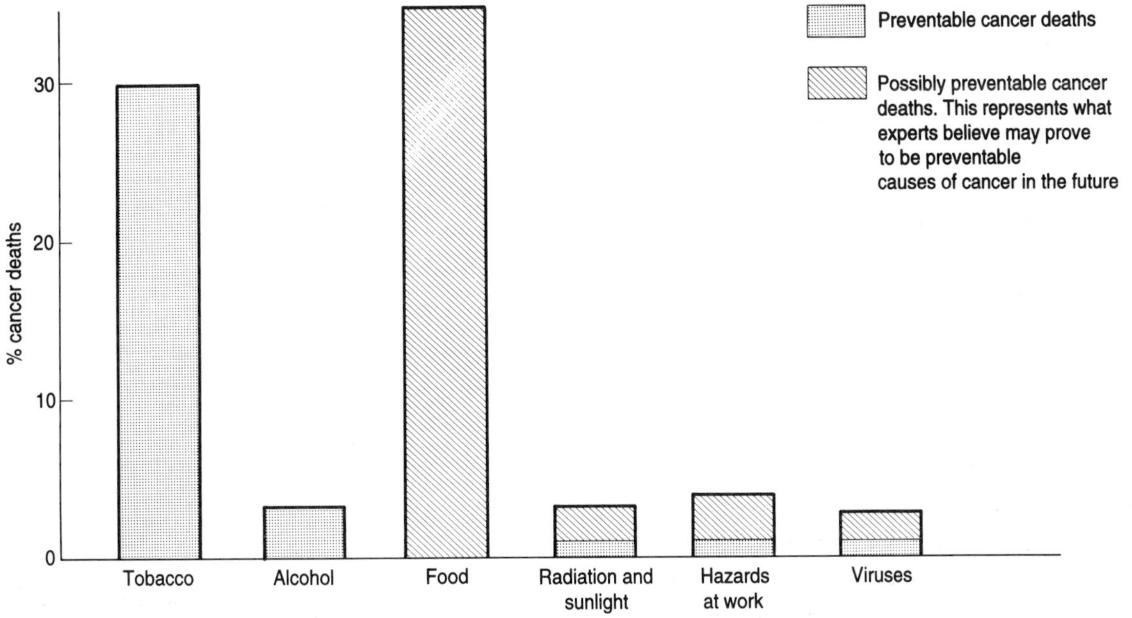

Figure 7.4 The main causes of preventable cancer deaths
Source: Table based on information in Doll, R. and Peto, R. (1981) *The Causes of Cancer*. Oxford University Press.

Table 7.1 Risk of cancer from drinking alcohol

MEN	WOMEN	Your risk of cancer from drinking
Less than 21 units a week spread throughout the week	Less than 14 units a week spread throughout the week	Low risk
22–49 units a week	15–34 units a week	Increased risk particularly if you are a smoker
50 or more units a week	35 or more units a week	Harmful – very high risk if you are a smoker

measured by writing to NRPB (see address panel).

EUROPE AGAINST CANCER is a campaign aimed at reducing the number of deaths from cancer by 15% by the year 2000. It has the support of all those active in the fight against cancer throughout the European Community – cancer specialists and general practitioners, the cancer charities, health education authorities, and other organisations concerned with the health of the public.

ACTIVITY W

Discuss in groups:

1 What social and cultural lifestyle changes might be responsible for the increased incidence of all forms of cancer?

2 Whose responsibility is it to educate and inform the public about risks to their health?

Tobacco and smoking

An estimated 110,000 people die in Great Britain each year directly from smoking-related illnesses. Meanwhile, tobacco companies spend an estimated £12 million each year sponsoring sports, such as motor racing, which would be hardest hit by a ban forbidding the display of brand logos.

The Nation's Health: A Strategy for the 1990s was an independent UK-wide report produced in 1988 by the King Edward's Hospital Fund for London. It examined current patterns of disease and of health-related behaviour and asked how they could be changed for the better. It concluded by proposing a health strategy for the 1990s and identified 17 priorities for public health action. One of these concerned the use of tobacco. The report sets out the general objectives:

- to create a physical and social environment where non-smoking is the norm;
- to support the creation of a generation of non-smokers;
- to maximise public awareness of the risks of smoking across all sectors of the community;
- to support the efforts of those who wish to stop smoking.

One of the targets set by the report – to be achieved by the year 2000 (or earlier) – is:

- to increase the proportion of children under 16 who are non-smokers to at least 95%;
- to reverse the trend towards increased smoking in girls.

According to the Law of Primacy, primary socialisation is both more powerful and more enduring than later socialising influences; research shows that a child is more likely to smoke if one or both parents smoke.

WHY DO PEOPLE START SMOKING?

Smoking usually begins in adolescence. There are various factors which might tempt a young person to smoke:

- If cigarettes are readily available at home,

there is a greater temptation to start smoking.

- Smoking is thought to be a social habit which gives confidence.
- A young person may start smoking as a gesture of defiance against authority.
- If role models, e.g. parents, teachers and friends, smoke, there is a desire to conform and copy their behaviour.

Studies have shown that a teenager who smokes just two or three cigarettes has a 70% chance of becoming addicted.

ACTIVITY

1 Set up a role-play scene in which one of you refuses to join friends in smoking, then is persuaded to give in. Notice what arguments are put forward and whether they appeal to the intelligence or to the emotions.

2 Set up the same scene. This time the non-smoker succeeds in persuading one other person to quit. Again, notice the language used.

3 Write to or visit your local Health Promotion Office. Ask for details on (a) helping addicted people to stop smoking and (b) teaching materials for use in junior schools.

4 Calculate the cost of smoking 20 cigarettes a day for one year.

HOW SMOKING AFFECTS YOUR BODY

Figures 7.5 and 7.6 show the physical effects of smoking. In addition to the diseases noted in Figure 7.7, many other diseases and health problems are caused or complicated by smoking, including:

- cancer of the mouth, lip, larynx, oesophagus, lung, pancreas, cervix, stomach, bladder and kidney (the direct evidence that cigarette smoking causes cancer of the lung is clear: fewer than 10% of lung cancers occur in non-smokers);
- emphysema;
- stroke (CVA or cerebro-vascular accident);
- leukaemia;
- chronic lung disease – bronchitis and COLD (chronic obstructive lung disease);
- fertility problems;

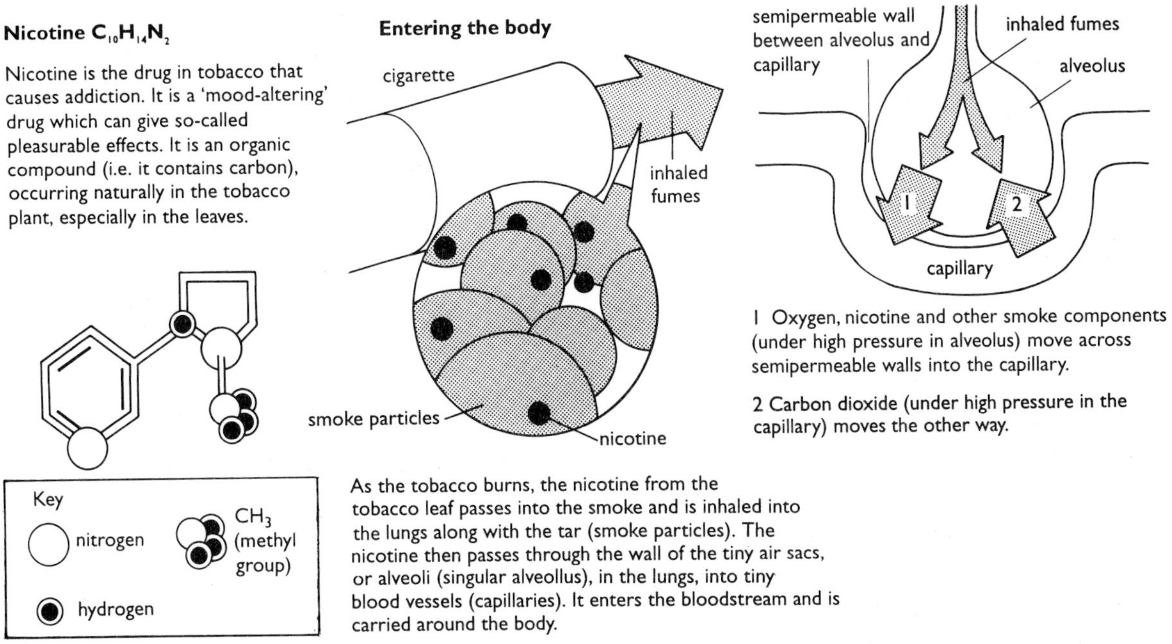
Nicotine $C_{10}H_{14}N_2$
Nicotine is the drug in tobacco that causes addiction. It is a 'mood-altering' drug which can give so-called pleasurable effects. It is an organic compound (i.e. it contains carbon), occurring naturally in the tobacco plant, especially in the leaves.
Key
nitrogen
hydrogen
CH_3 (methyl group)
Entering the body
cigarette
inhaled fumes
smoke particles
nicotine
As the tobacco burns, the nicotine from the tobacco leaf passes into the smoke and is inhaled into the lungs along with the tar (smoke particles). The nicotine then passes through the wall of the tiny air sacs, or alveoli (singular alveollus), in the lungs, into tiny blood vessels (capillaries). It enters the bloodstream and is carried around the body.
semipermeable wall between alveolus and capillary
inhaled fumes
alveolus
1
2
capillary
1 Oxygen, nicotine and other smoke components (under high pressure in alveolus) move across semipermeable walls into the capillary.
2 Carbon dioxide (under high pressure in the capillary) moves the other way.

Figure 7.5 How smoking affects the body (1)

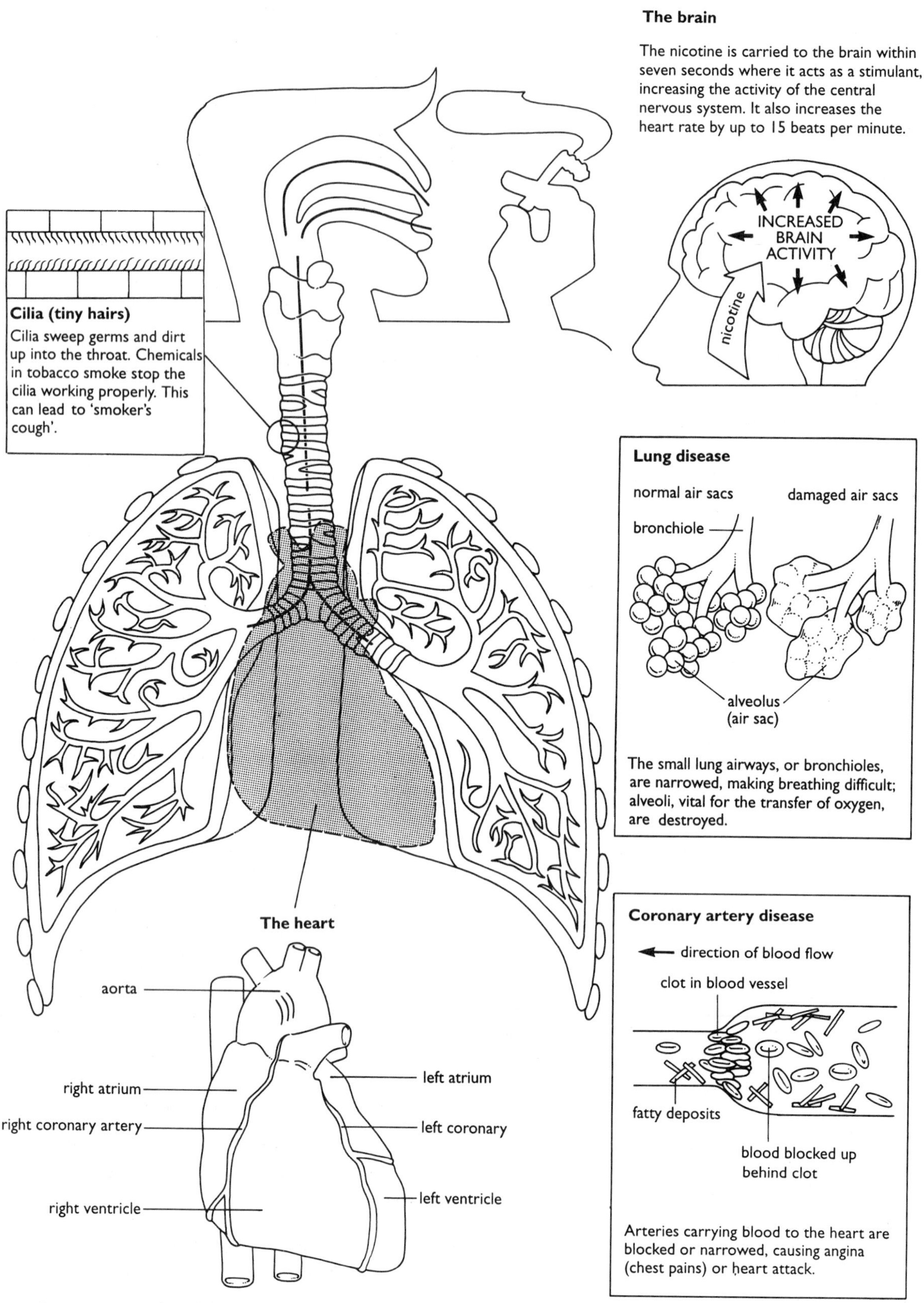

The brain
The nicotine is carried to the brain within seven seconds where it acts as a stimulant, increasing the activity of the central nervous system. It also increases the heart rate by up to 15 beats per minute.
INCREASED BRAIN ACTIVITY
nicotine
Cilia (tiny hairs)
Cilia sweep germs and dirt up into the throat. Chemicals in tobacco smoke stop the cilia working properly. This can lead to 'smoker's cough'.
Lung disease
normal air sacs
damaged air sacs
bronchiole
alveolus (air sac)
The small lung airways, or bronchioles, are narrowed, making breathing difficult; alveoli, vital for the transfer of oxygen, are destroyed.
The heart
aorta
right atrium
right coronary artery
right ventricle
left atrium
left coronary
left ventricle
Coronary artery disease
direction of blood flow
clot in blood vessel
fatty deposits
blood blocked up behind clot
Arteries carrying blood to the heart are blocked or narrowed, causing angina (chest pains) or heart attack.

Figure 7.6 How smoking affects the body (2)
Source: Imperial Cancer Research Fund.

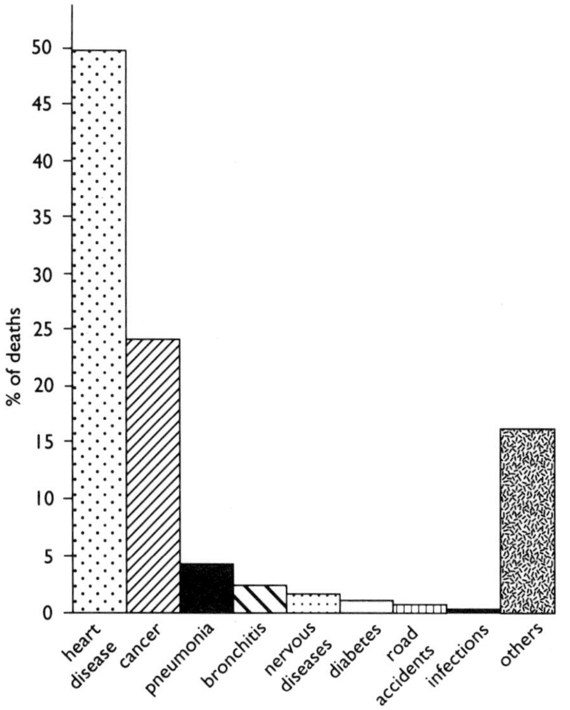

Figure 7.7 Causes of death in Britain in the 1980s
Source: L. Hartley, *History of Medicine* (Blackwell)

- early menopause;
- cataracts;
- male impotence;
- sickle-cell anaemia;
- stomach ulcers.

There are also diseases and health problems associated with PASSIVE SMOKING, i.e. inhaling the smoke from other people's cigarettes. MAINSTREAM SMOKE is that delivered directly to the smoker by inhalation and it tends to be filtered. The SIDESTREAM SMOKE emitted into the atmosphere from the burning end of a cigarette is unfiltered and contains a higher proportion of CARCINOGENS than mainstream smoke. Diseases caused are:

- lung cancer;
- bronchitis;
- heart disease;
- low birth weight;
- respiratory disease in children.

QUICK FACTS

- 33% of the adult population of the UK are smokers.
- Almost one in three of all school-leavers are regular smokers.
- Out of 1,000 smokers who die each year, one will be murdered, six will die on the roads and 250 will die from smoking-related disease.
- On average, babies whose mothers are smokers weigh 200 g less at birth than the babies of non-smokers.
- Out of every ten smokers, six say they would like to give up; they also say they need the support of a health professional.
- Giving up smoking reduces the risk of premature death; the risks return to those of a non-smoker within five to ten years.

ACTIVITY

Set up a 'No Smoking' campaign in college.

- Obtain posters from the local Health Promotion Unit or make some using the 'Quick Facts' section.
- Choose a prominent site to display posters and fact sheets.
- Obtain several PEAK FLOW METERS. Learn how to use them and to instruct others in their use. (NB follow the rules of hygiene.)
- Ask each volunteer if he/she smokes and offer them a chance to test their own peak flow.
- Record results from smokers and non-smokers on separate charts.
- At the end of the session, analyse the results and present them on a poster.

GIVING UP SMOKING

The Health Education Council gives the following advice to those who wish to give up smoking:

- Cut out the first cigarette of the day to start with, then the second, and so on.
- Start by cutting out the most 'enjoyable' cigarette of the day, like the one after a big meal.

- Give up with a friend.
- Tell everyone you are giving up smoking.

Think about the reasoning behind each piece of advice.

Drugs

A drug is any chemical substance which changes the function of one or more body organs or alters the process of a disease. Drugs may be:

- prescribed medicines;
- over-the-counter remedies;
- alcohol, tobacco and caffeine;
- illegal drugs.

DRUG ABUSE is the use of a drug for a purpose other than that for which it is usually prescribed.

DRUG DEPENDENCE is the compulsion to continue taking a drug, either to produce the desired effects that result from taking it, or to prevent the ill-effects that occur when it is withdrawn. There are two types of drug dependence:

- psychological;
- physical.

A person is psychologically dependent if he or she experiences craving or emotional distress when the drug is withdrawn. A person is physically dependent when the body has adapted to the presence of the drug and symptoms of withdrawal syndrome are caused when the drug is withdrawn.

DRUG TOLERANCE develops when the body becomes almost immune to the drug and requires larger doses to achieve the original effect.

There are four main groups of drugs which are commonly abused:

- stimulants ('uppers');
- depressants ('downers');
- psychedelics or hallucinogens;
- narcotics.

STIMULANTS

These drugs increase arousal and make the user feel temporarily more euphoric, alert and wide-awake. They are rarely prescribed for any 'medical' problem. Examples are:

- *Caffeine*, found in coffee, tea, chocolate and cola drinks. High daily dosage (such as six cups of coffee, i.e. 600 mg of caffeine) can induce agitation, tremor, insomnia and irregularities of the heart rhythm.
- *Cocaine*, derived from the leaves of *erythroxylum coca* trees. Cocaine was widely used in the nineteenth century (Sigmund Freud was an enthusiastic user and an advocate of its powers). In its purified form, it is usually taken intranasally ('snorted').
- *Crack*, a highly purified form of cocaine which is usually smoked or mixed with heroin and injected.
- *Nicotine*, a mild stimulant derived from the tobacco plant and usually smoked in cigars and cigarettes.

DEPRESSANTS

Drugs which depress the central nervous system produce a calming or relaxing effect. As the dose is increased, this feeling gives way to drowsiness and sleep. Tolerance develops to all the depressant drugs and they also cause physical and psychological dependence to a varying degree. Examples are:

- alcohol;
- sleeping tablets or hypnotics;
- tranquillizers;
- solvents (abused in glue-sniffing).

Alcohol

Alcohol (ethanol or ethyl alcohol) has been used and abused since prehistoric times and is probably the most commonly abused drug in the developed world. It is absorbed into the body through the stomach and intestines and distributed throughout the body by the bloodstream. In pregnant women, alcohol crosses the placental barrier to reach the developing baby.

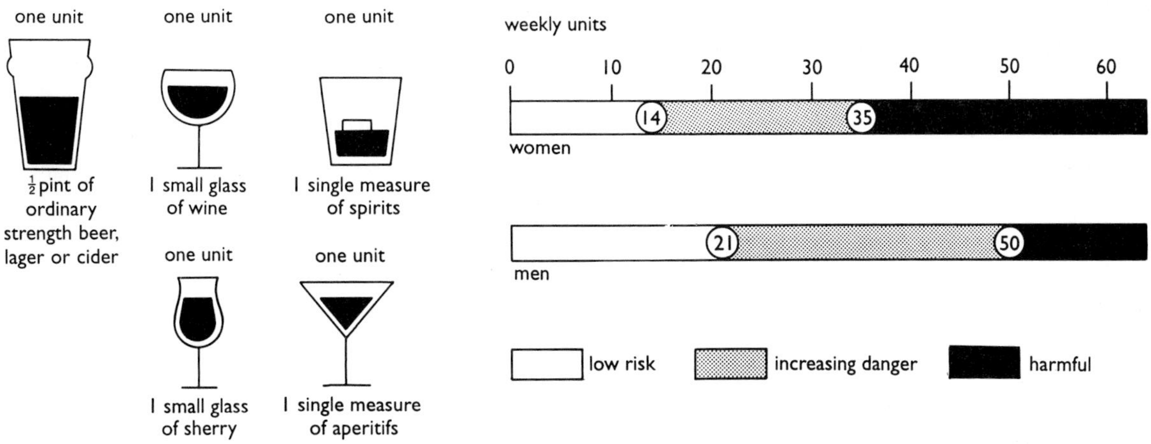

Figure 7.8 How much is too much?

Doctors recommend that sensible weekly limits on intake are up to 21 units of alcohol for men and up to 14 units for women. (See Figure 7.8 for what constitutes a unit.)

Alcohol problems occur at all educational and social levels and in every age group. There are several signals that a person is having difficulty controlling his or her alcohol intake:

- drinking for relief from pain and stress;
- pattern drinking (drinking every day or every week at a certain time, particularly in the morning);
- making alcohol the centre of life or of all pleasurable, relaxing activities.

Some quick facts on alcohol:

- After heart disease and cancer, alcohol is the third biggest health hazard today.
- Up to 30% of men admitted to hospitals are either 'problem drinkers' or physically dependent on alcohol.
- Drink is commonly believed to be an aphrodisiac, but, as Shakespeare wrote, it 'provokes the desire but takes away the performance'.
- There are many proven links between alcohol and violence. Alcohol is associated with 60–70% of homicides, 75% of stabbings and 70% of beatings.
- Recent research in the UK and America shows a connection between child abuse and problem drinking.
- Only 13% of single homeless people are heavy drinkers. Half of all single homeless people are light drinkers or abstain completely.
- A third of all deaths on the road are caused by drunken drivers.

In *The Nation's Health*, the authors have set out the following objectives in relation to alcohol use:

- to promote patterns of alcohol consumption that minimise its harm without jeopardising its benefits;
- to create an environment which minimises pressures to drink excessively and maximises choice of non-alcoholic alternatives;
- to improve understanding of the adverse medical, psychological and social effects of excessive drinking and to promote a better understanding of what constitutes 'safe' drinking patterns;
- to support the efforts of those with alcohol problems who wish to cut down on their drinking or remain abstinent.

The long-term effects of alcohol on the body are shown in Figure 7.9.

Table 7.2 How can alcohol affect physical and mental behaviour?

No. of drinks	Quantity of alcohol	Possible effects
1 pint of beer	30 mg	Likelihood of having an accident starts to increase
$1\frac{1}{2}$ pints of beer or 3 whiskies	50 mg	A feeling of warmth and cheer; impairment of judgement and inhibition
$2\frac{1}{2}$ pints of beer or 5 whiskies	80 mg	Loss of driving licence if discovered driving a vehicle
5 pints of beer or 10 whiskies	150 mg	Loss of self-control; exuberance; slurred speech; quarrelsomeness
6 pints of beer or 13 whiskies	200 mg	Stagger; double vision; memory loss
$\frac{1}{4}$ bottle of spirits	400 mg	Oblivion; sleeplessness; coma
1 bottle of spirits	500 mg 600 mg	Death possible Death certain

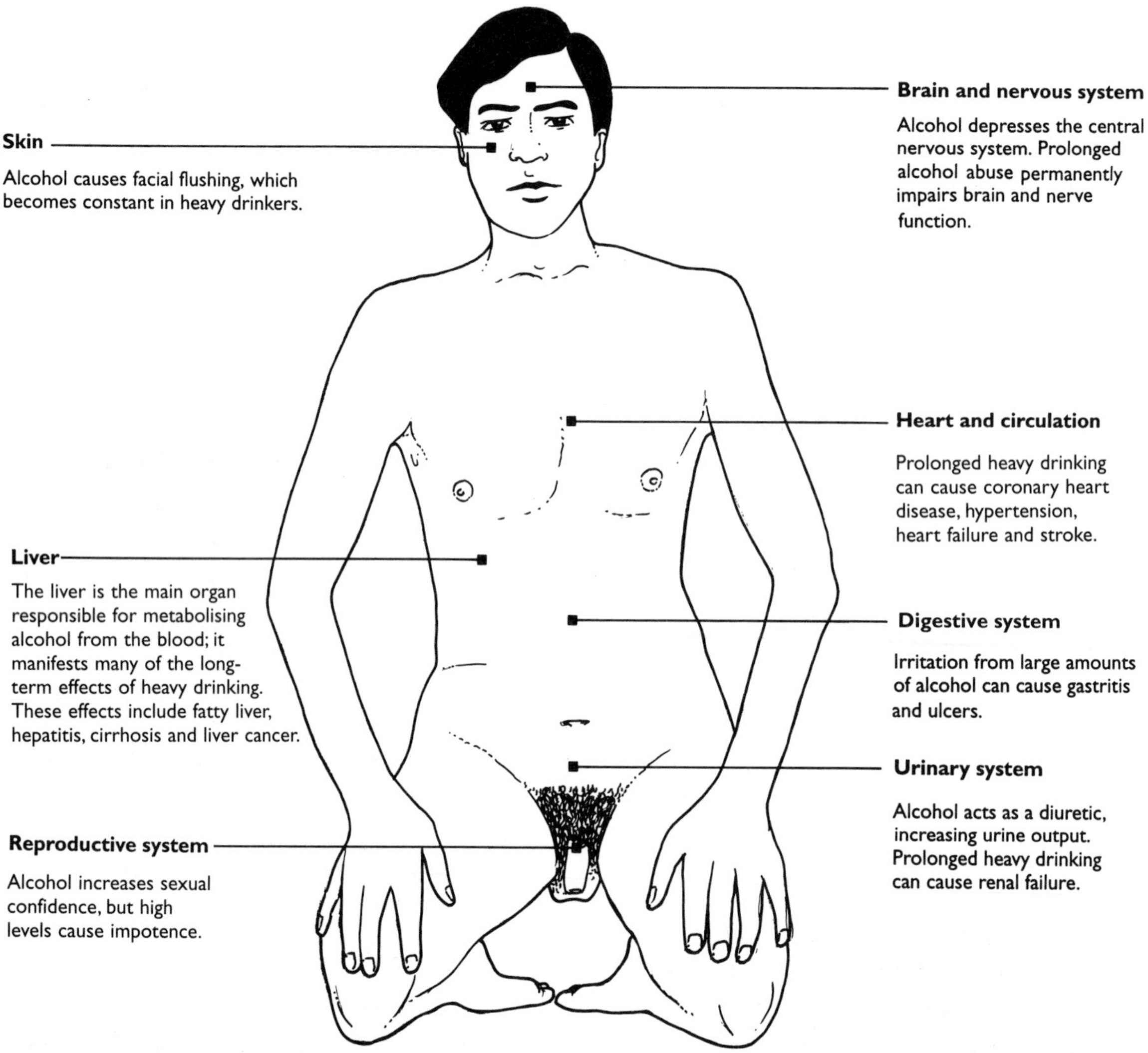
Brain and nervous system
Alcohol depresses the central nervous system. Prolonged alcohol abuse permanently impairs brain and nerve function.
Skin
Alcohol causes facial flushing, which becomes constant in heavy drinkers.
Heart and circulation
Prolonged heavy drinking can cause coronary heart disease, hypertension, heart failure and stroke.
Liver
The liver is the main organ responsible for metabolising alcohol from the blood; it manifests many of the long-term effects of heavy drinking. These effects include fatty liver, hepatitis, cirrhosis and liver cancer.
Digestive system
Irritation from large amounts of alcohol can cause gastritis and ulcers.
Urinary system
Alcohol acts as a diuretic, increasing urine output. Prolonged heavy drinking can cause renal failure.
Reproductive system
Alcohol increases sexual confidence, but high levels cause impotence.

Figure 7.9 The long-term physical effects of alcohol

ACTIVITY

1 Find out why women are more sensitive to comparable doses of alcohol than are men.

2 Find out what treatment or therapy is available for people with a drinking problem (alcoholism) in your area? What does the self-help group Alcoholics Anonymous offer?

ACTIVITY

1 Describe some of the ways in which people who drink excessive amounts of alcohol endanger (a) themselves and (b) other people.

2 Collect advertisements for drink from magazines, and also the posters and advertisements put out by bodies such as the Health Education Council which warn of the dangers of heavy drinking. Which posters are more effective? Design your own posters.

3 Research the condition known as foetal alcohol syndrome. How many babies are affected each year in the UK and what problems does it present?

Solvent abuse

Solvent abuse is the practice of inhaling the intoxicating fumes given off by certain volatile liquids. Glue-sniffing is the most common form of solvent abuse, but lighter fluid and paint thinner may also be used.

- The usual method of inhalation is from a plastic bag containing the solvent.
- It is usually a group activity and is common among boys from poor urban areas.
- Effects are similar to becoming drunk or getting 'high'.

Solvent abuse can cause:

- hallucinations;
- headache;
- vomiting;
- stupor;
- confusion and coma.

Occasionally, death occurs due to a direct toxic effect on the heart or by the inhalation of vomit. Signs and symptoms are:

- a flushed face;
- intoxicated behaviour;
- ulcers around the mouth;
- a smell of solvent;
- personality changes, e.g. edginess or moodiness.

Acute symptoms such as vomiting or coma must be treated following the basic principles of first aid:

- Maintain airway, breathing and circulation.
- Arrange urgent removal to hospital.
- Do NOT attempt to induce vomiting. It is often ineffective and may harm the casualty further.

PSYCHEDELICS OR HALLUCINOGENS

Drugs in this category produce disturbances of perception and a changed state of consciousness and awareness. The feelings experienced range from terror to ecstasy. Some, like LSD, are manufactured; others occur naturally as plants and fungi. As many as 25% of users of hallucinogens will experience a 'flashback' or return of the hallucinatory and delusional experience even months after the drug has been taken. The episode is usually brief, lasting only minutes, but it is often frightening and disturbing. Aldous Huxley wrote *The Doors of Perception* in 1954 whilst under the influence of the hallucinogen mescaline. Other examples of hallucinogens are:

- *LSD* (lysergic acid diethylamide). This is usually taken as tiny tablets. Its effects are unpredictable and depend very much on the individual. LSD is used socially in groups, with one person not 'using' to keep an eye on the others.

- *Cannabis* (or marijuana or hashish). This is produced from the plant Indian hemp. Visible effects of the drug include reddening of the eyes caused by dilation of the blood vessels. Effects on the mind and emotions vary. In general, perception is altered and ideas flow more quickly. This drug is not addictive and there is no evidence that it harms the body. Usually cannabis is smoked but it can also be made into cakes and eaten. There have been frequent calls for legalising the sale and use of cannabis, as has been done in The Netherlands.
- *Ecstasy* (MDMA). This substance was originally marketed as an appetite suppressant in 1914 and has been used in the 1970s by US psychotherapists to improve talking. It appeared in the UK in the 1980s and is mostly used in clubs. It is very expensive and comes in a variety of coloured tablets with exotic names such as Tangerine Dreams, California Sunshine, etc. Ecstasy is not addictive but has been known to cause death. Dancing for six hours at a stretch under its influence is not unusual. Excessive sweating leads to loss of fluid, hyperthermia and eventual collapse. The immediate effect is a rush – a feeling of warmth towards everyone. This may lead to unsafe sex with a stranger. There may also be a 'come down' the next day with feelings of depression and panic attacks.

NARCOTICS

Narcotics are ANALGESIC drugs (painkillers) used to treat moderate and severe pain. Abuse of narcotic drugs for their euphoric effects often causes tolerance and physical and psychological dependence. Examples are:

- heroin;
- morphine;
- pethidine;
- methadone;
- codeine;
- opium.

Heroin

Heroin is more potent than morphine and is derived from opium, which is harvested from the flower of the poppy, *Papaver somniferum* (see Figure 7.10). It is most active and effective

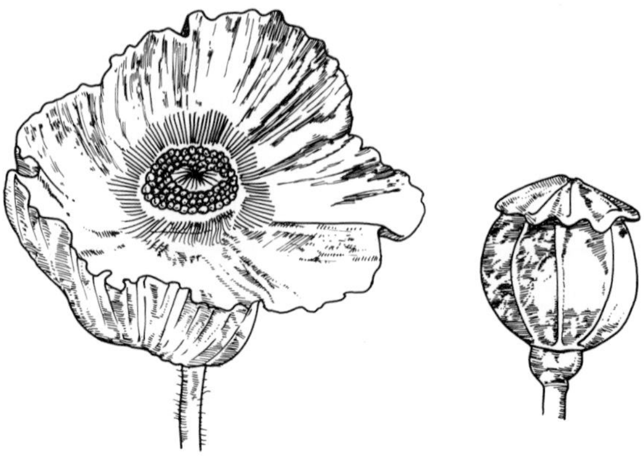

Figure 7.10 The poppy (*Papaver somniferum*) from which heroin is derived

when given by injection. Tolerance and physical dependence develop rapidly. Withdrawal symptoms are particularly unpleasant, and include:

- agitation;
- restless disturbed sleep;
- abdominal cramps;
- watering eyes and a running nose;
- dilated pupils;
- tremor.

These withdrawal symptoms last for a week or more.

Heroin addicts have a mortality rate 15 times higher than normal and, although death is not usually due to the direct effects of heroin use, it may result from:

- an overdose;
- mixing heroin with other substances;
- physical debility due to neglect;
- illness associated with unclean injection techniques, including venous thrombosis, septicaemia, hepatitis, HIV/AIDS.

Most users recognise the dangers of injection (mainlining) and yet prefer this method because of the 'rush' or intensity of the experience. Many users now choose to smoke heroin. The drug is placed in a strip of tinfoil and heated until it gives off smoke which is inhaled. The substance writhes above the foil while it is being heated, giving rise to the colourful phrase 'chasing the dragon'.

Methadone is a synthetic opiate which is much longer-acting than heroin, but still addictive. It is usually taken orally as a syrup and is often prescribed by clinics in maintenance therapy.

WHY DO PEOPLE TAKE DRUGS?

Obviously no one knows for certain why people abuse drugs, but Figure 7.11 shows some of the reasons which might be involved.

Figure 7.11 Why do people take drugs?
Source: BPI, Biology resource book.

Activity

1 Draw up a chart showing the 'pleasant' and 'unpleasant' effects of ecstasy, heroin, amphetamines and cocaine.

2 Choose one of the following drugs and research it:

- alcohol;
- tobacco;
- cocaine;
- heroin.

Include as much up-to-date information as you can; use your library's resources centre. The project should cover:

- What is the drug and what are its effects?
- Who uses the drug and why?
- How can health promoters change the patterns of drug abuse?

Substance abuse

The abuse of substances has been described in Chapter 3. THE NATION'S HEALTH report suggests the following measures to reduce cigarette consumption:

- regular increases on the real price of tobacco;
- a legislative ban on all forms of tobacco advertising or promotion;
- the creation of a non-smoking norm in public places;
- adequately funded public and professional education and information programmes;
- health warnings on all cigarette packs (and promotional material until a ban takes place).

Activity

1 How far do you think the measures listed above have been implemented?

2 Set up a role-play to determine reactions to the following scenarios:
- a 15-year-old girl is trying to persuade her father to give up smoking;
- a parent finds out that his/her 11-year-old child has been smoking.

Risks to personal safety

Many people believe that, as individuals, they have little control over risks to their health due to large-scale environmental problems such as acid rain or industrial pollution. While it is true that many environmental issues require global policies to be dealt with effectively, risks in one's immediate environment *can* be controlled.

SAFETY AT HOME

Although the most dangerous place for accidents is the road, the home is the setting for many *preventable* accidents (see Table 7.3).

Of all accidents resulting in death in the 0–4 year age group, the majority take place in the home.

Table 7.3 Causes of accidental death

Age (years)	Chief causes of accidental death (as % of total)	Commonest other causes (in order of frequency)
Under 1	Choking and suffocation (70%)	Falls; fire; road accidents
1–4	Road accidents (37%)	Fire; drowning; choking and suffocation
5–9	Road accidents (57%)	Drowning; fire; falls
10–14	Road accidents (53%)	Drowning; choking and suffocation; falls
15–24	Road accidents (76%)	Poisoning; falls; drowning
25–44	Road accidents (53%)	Poisoning; falls; choking and suffocation
45–64	Road accidents (44%)	Falls; poisoning; fire
Over 64	Falls (61%)	Road accidents; fire; poisoning

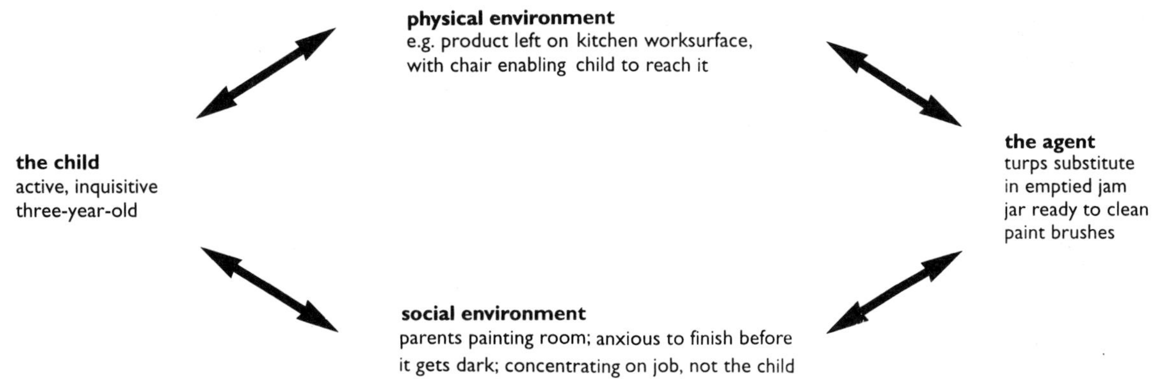

Figure 7.12 An accident waiting to happen

ACTIVITY

Arrange the following 'accidents waiting to happen' into the format outlined in Figure 7.12.

1 A six-year-old boy runs out into the road to retrieve his football which a friend kicked out of his hands.

2 A ten-month-old baby, sitting in her high chair, has been given a peeled banana to eat. Her mother is speaking on the telephone; the baby is silently choking.

Assuming that the worst happens, i.e. the six-year-old sustains a head injury, and the baby stops breathing because her airway is obstructed,

- state first aid measures you would take;
- how could the accident have been prevented?

Accidents in the home have a number of causes, varying with each age group involved. A young child's curiosity, an adult's carelessness or an old person's slower reactions may all be factors.

In addition to these mental and physical factors, accidents can be caused by:

- badly designed houses;
- faulty equipment;
- incorrect storage and use of dangerous substances.

ELECTRICAL INJURIES

Contact with high-voltage current, found in power lines and overhead high-tension (HT) cables, is usually immediately fatal.

The passage of electrical current through the body may cause breathing and even the heart to stop.

High-voltage current

- The power must be cut off and isolated before the casualty is approached.
- Call the emergency services immediately (dial 999).
- The casualty will be unconscious; check breathing and pulse; resuscitate if necessary.
- Treat burns and take steps to minimise shock.

Low-voltage current

Many injuries result from faulty switches, frayed flexes and defective domestic appliances. Water is a very good conductor of electricity. The risk of electrical injury is far greater if one has wet hands or is standing on a wet floor.

- Do not attempt first aid until contact with the electrical current has been broken. Pull the electric plug out. If this is impossible, stand on a dry, *insulating* object, e.g. rubber mat or thick pile of newspapers. Push the victim away using a broom or wooden chair.

- Check breathing and pulse; resuscitate if necessary.
- Cool any burns with plenty of cold water.
- Place in recovery position and wait for arrival of ambulance.

ACTIVITY

1 Suggest two methods of ensuring that an electrical accident does not occur in the home.

2 Find out the correct first aid treatment for burns and scalds.

DROWNING

Every year, about 350 people die in the UK from drowning. The victim is usually swimming or playing in water, although some deaths result from falling into water.

NB Infants can drown in a few centimetres of water.

Prevention

- Wear a lifejacket or buoyancy aid for all water sports, e.g. sailing and windsurfing.
- Never jump into deep water without ensuring there is a safe way out.
- Always obey the safety rules operated by lifeguards at pools and beaches.
- Do not drink alcohol before swimming or taking part in water sports.
- Never leave a child alone in the bath and always supervise water play.
- Children should never walk on an iced-over pond unless the ice has first been tested by an adult.

Symptoms and signs

General signs of asphyxia:

- difficulty in breathing;
- frothing around the mouth, lips and nostrils;
- confusion;
- possible unconsciousness;
- cyanosis (blueness of face, lips and fingernails).

Treatment

- Remove obstructions (e.g. seaweed) from casualty's mouth and check for breathing and pulse.
- Do not waste time trying to expel water from the casualty's lungs.
- Resuscitate if necessary.
- As soon as casualty begins breathing, place in recovery position.
- Keep casualty warm; if necessary, treat for hypothermia.

POISONING

A poison is a substance that, in relatively small amounts, disrupts the structure and/or function of cells, causing temporary or permanent damage.

Poisons enter the body by various routes. They may be:

- swallowed, e.g. contaminated foods, drugs or corrosives;
- inhaled, e.g. cases, solvents, vapours or fumes;
- absorbed through the skin, e.g. pesticides;
- injected under the skin, e.g. insect stings or snake bites.

Poisons may also originate within the body itself; for example, disorders such as liver failure may cause toxins to be produced.

Industrial poisons

Most cases of industrial poisoning involve poisonous fumes. Factories using potentially dangerous gases or chemicals may keep oxygen equipment, and must display notices indicating action to be taken in an emergency.

Poisonous plants

There are numerous different poisonous plants, including some common garden or house plants (see Table 7.4). Most cases of poisoning occur in young children who are attracted to brightly coloured berries and seeds and are liable to eat them.

Table 7.4 Plants that are poisonous if swallowed

Mushrooms	Seeds, bulbs and rhizomes	Berries
Death cap	Laburnum	Deadly nightshade
Spotted fly agaric	Lupin	Holly
Cortinarius speciosissimus	Daffodil	Laurel
	Iris	Mistletoe
	Foxglove	Yew
		Wild arum

ACTIVITY

1 A four-year-old child complains of 'tummy-ache' and you notice some red berries in her mouth. What action would you take? Use the first aid manual to help you.

2 Statistics show that there is a higher accident rate among boys than among girls. The discrepancy starts at the age of eight months and continues until the age of 14 years, when accident levels are again the same for the sexes. Suggest three reasons for this discrepancy.

3 Prepare a poster or leaflet warning parents of the dangers of poisons commonly available (remember tablets, medicines, bleaches, etc.).

4 

Where would you expect to see the labels above, and what do they tell us?

OCCUPATIONAL DISORDERS

Dust diseases

- *Pneumoconiosis*, or fibrosis of the lungs, is caused by the inhalation of organic and inorganic dusts. Those affected work in mining industries – coal and quartz mining and china clay factories – and in metal grinding and foundry work.
- *Asbestosis* is a similar hazard in the asbestos industry and is also a problem in the demolition industry (where buildings have involved the use of asbestos).

The most dangerous dusts are usually the ones so small that they cannot be seen with the naked eye. In general, the smaller a dust particle, the further it goes into the lungs and the more damage it causes. Less well-known sources of dust include wool, cotton, hay (fungal spores may cause farmer's lung), fibreglass, talcum powder and detergents.

Chemical poisoning

- *Cadmium fumes* (used in the welding and electroplating industries) may cause kidney damage.
- *Carbon tetrachloride* and *vinyl chloride* (used in the manufacture of chemicals and plastics) may cause liver disease.
- *Lead compounds* and *benzene* can damage the bone marrow, leading to anaemia.

Noise

Regular exposure to loud noise over a long time leads to increased deafness. Any noise above 90 decibels may cause damage (see Figure 7.13). Prolonged tinnitus (ringing or buzzing in the ears) occurring after a noise has ceased indicates that some damage has already occurred.

Regulations governing maximum noise levels apply to all places of work. Where exposure cannot be avoided (e.g. workers using pneumatic drills), ear protection should be worn.

Radiation hazards

- *Radiation from the sun*: people with outdoor occupations in sunny climates are at increased risk of skin disease, e.g. skin cancer.
- *Ionising radiation*: X-rays and radiation from nuclear waste may cause cancer (particularly leukaemia) if levels of

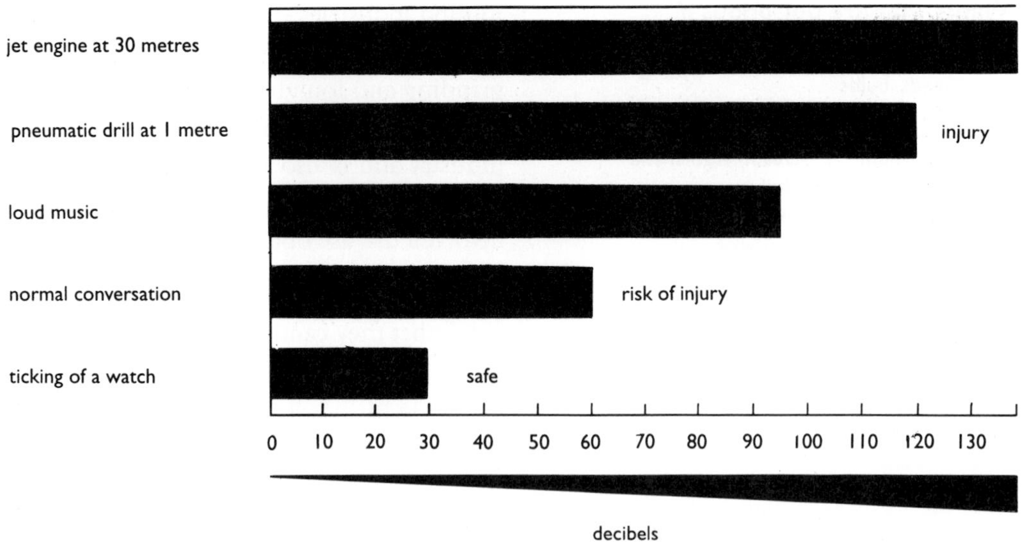

Figure 7.13 Comparative noise levels

exposure are not controlled. Controlled radiation, or radiotherapy, is however useful in the treatment of some cancers.

Repetitive strain injury (RSI)

This is a newly discovered hazard caused by repetitive movement of part of the body. The strain is felt in the joints and muscles, e.g. tennis elbow. Typists, assembly line workers and musicians may all experience pain and stiffness in the affected joints and muscles.

Symptoms usually disappear with rest.

> **ACTIVITY**
>
> 1 Find out about the Safety at Work Act.
>
> 2 When you are working in a health or social care setting, ask to see how accidents are reported and dealt with by staff.

SAFETY OF EQUIPMENT

All consumer products and appliances may be potentially dangerous. It is important to look for safety labels and to follow the manufacturer's instructions, particularly those with warnings.

Labels which show that equipment meets safety standards

Figure 7.14 Kitemark

The BSI Kitemark symbol means that the product has been made to the correct British Standard. It can be found on:

- domestic gas appliances;
- carry cots;
- prams;
- highchairs;
- pushchairs;
- oil heaters;
- pressure cookers.

Figure 7.15 BEAB Mark of Safety

The BEAB Mark of Safety symbol means that the goods meet government safety regulations for domestic electrical appliances (British Electrotechnical Approvals Board). It can be found on radiant fires, kettles, irons, toasters, hair dryers and refrigerators.

Figure 7.16 Flame resistant

The Fire resistant symbol means that the covers and filling of the goods meet fire resistance regulations. Fire safety labelling must, by law, be attached to all new and secondhand upholstered furniture sold in shops.

Figure 7.17 British Gas Seal of Service

The British Gas Seal of Service symbol means that the appliance has been tested and approved for safety. It is found on all domestic gas appliances.

ACTIVITY

1 Make a list of other safety labels and where they may be found.

2 List the gas hazards which can occur in the home and the appropriate emergency action you would take.

HOUSEHOLD SECURITY

Statistics from police records show an alarming increase in the number of burglaries and other crimes involving property, but it is important to remember that we live in an essentially peaceful society and that the approach of the millennium is an anxious time. There is even a phrase to describe it – 'fin-de-siecle anxiety'. Every society is symbolically anxious; the Victorians were anxious about sex – *we* focus our symbolic anxiety on crime and enjoy books and films about all its aspects.

Schemes such as NEIGHBOURHOOD WATCH operate in most areas, and all Police Forces have a CRIME PREVENTION OFFICER who specialises in this field; he or she will give advice to any individual on protecting a home and its contents.

ACTIVITY

You have lost your door key. Try to imagine that you have to break in to your own home and you will find out any weaknesses in the security system. Write down any obvious weak points and think of ways of making your home more secure.

ROAD SAFETY

From the age of one, the greatest risk to a child's life is an accident. Road traffic accidents (RTAs) account for one-half of all accidental deaths. In 1991 in Britain there were:

- 4,568 RTA deaths;
- 51,605 serious RTA injuries;
- 255,096 slight RTA injuries.

Educating children about safety on the roads should begin at a very early age, the best method being *by example*. There have been many campaigns over the years to reduce the number of accidents occurring on the roads – some targeting drink driving (particularly around Christmas holidays), some targeting the speeding driver, and others urging the use of seat belts.

Children need to learn about road safety in the same way as learning any new skill – repeating the message over and over again until the child really has learnt it. The Green Cross Code is a very good method of teaching road safety:

The Green Cross Code

1 Find a safe place to cross, then stop.
2 Stand on the pavement, near the kerb.
3 Look all around for traffic and listen.
4 If traffic is coming, let it pass. Look all round again.
5 When there is no traffic near, walk straight across the road.
6 Keep looking and listening for traffic while you cross. Repeat and use the code every time.

Every local authority employs a road safety officer and the Royal Society for the Prevention of Accidents (RoSPA) runs the Tufty Club for children aged three years and over.

ACTIVITY

As a group, discuss and list the risks to personal safety within the environment – these may include safety at work, hazardous substances, electrical accidents, etc.

Working in pairs, divide the list of risks between the pairs. Now complete the following task.

Task: To design a fact sheet on the risk to personal safety, to include the following information:

- the nature of the risk;
- possible causes;
- legal position and safety codes, with an evaluation of their success;
- ideas for minimising the risks.

Use illustrations to improve the overall effect.

HEALTH EDUCATION CAMPAIGNS

Identifying the objectives of health campaigns

Most health education campaigns are launched as a result of identifying a particular public health priority; **The Nation's Health – a Strategy for the 1990s** identified 17 areas for action:

- the reduction of tobacco consumption,
- the promotion of a healthy diet,
- the reduction of alcohol consumption,
- the promotion of physical activity,
- the promotion of road safety,
- the promotion of health at work,
- effective maternity services,
- child health surveillance,
- early cancer detection,
- high blood pressure detection and prevention,
- services for the elderly,
- the maintenance of social support,
- the promotion of dental health,
- the promotion of health in sexual activities,
- adequate income,
- safe housing.

These areas were then analysed in terms of feasibility in carrying out detailed plans for action, and grouped as follows:

Lifestyles for health prevention services

• Tobacco	• Maternity
• Diet	• Dental health
• Physical activity	• Immunisation
• Alcohol	• Early cancer detection
• Sexual behaviour	• High blood pressure detection
• Road Safety	

From the original 17 priority areas identified by the team working on **The Nation's Health**, six were excluded for the following reasons:

- the need for more evidence of the effectiveness of action, e.g. the government's advertising campaign to highlight the risks of illicit drug misuse (heroin) drew public attention away from more commonly abused drugs;
- the need for action beyond the scope of health promotion, e.g. whilst adequate income and housing were felt to be fundamental issues in promoting health for

all, they are more dependent on the development of socioeconomic policies.

ACTIVITY

Choose a health campaign which has focused on one of the six **Lifestyles for Health** above and try to identify the objectives of the campaign from its content. Consider the following points:

- What were the specific health targets?
- Were any special interest groups involved in the campaign?
- Did local community action play a part in the campaign?
- Were there any hidden messages, e.g. promoting a commercial interest?

You will need to refer to *Health of the Nation* and/or **Healthy Wales** to see if specific objectives were used.

Reasons for, sources of and methods used in health education campaigns

All health promotion programmes require careful planning; the planning process may be broken down into the following stages (see Figure 7.18):

STAGE 1

Identify the health issue, e.g. heart disease and/or the role of stress, exercise, nutrition; substance abuse – smoking, alcohol, solvents, etc.

STAGE 2

Identify the target group, e.g. middle-aged men are at particular risk from heart disease; you may wish to target young people who have just started or might be tempted to start smoking.

The age of the target group, i.e. whether they are children, adolescents or adults, will affect the way health promotion advice is presented to them. It is important to be aware of the different needs of the audience to

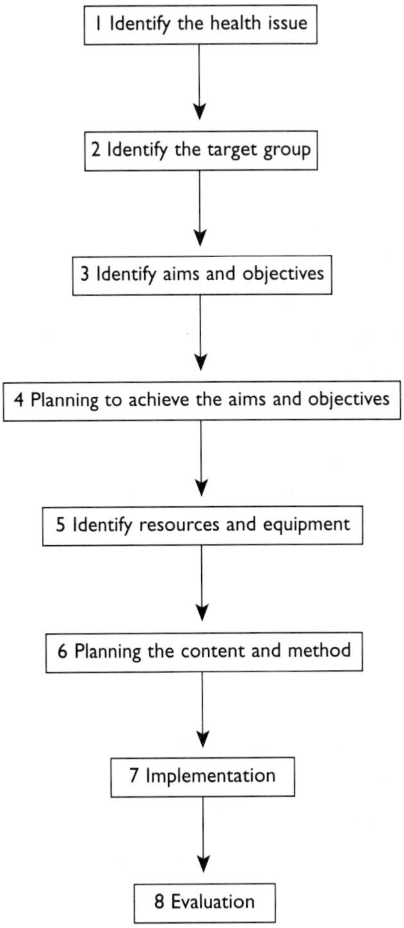

Figure 7.18 Flow chart showing the stages in planning a health education campaign

ensure that the information is presented at an appropriate level and using suitable resources.

STAGE 3

Identify the aims and objectives of the campaign. The AIMS (or goals) are broad statements of what you are trying to achieve from a single session or event, or from the whole campaign, e.g. to examine the issue of sexually transmitted diseases; to appreciate the role of exercise in preventing coronary heart disease; to explore the link between drinking and road accidents.

The OBJECTIVES are more specific aims; they help you to pinpoint the most realistic method of presenting health advice and information and to evaluate your success in achieving them, e.g. to provide parents with up-to-date information on immunisation, so that they can make an informed decision regarding their own children; to prepare a display on 'Safer Sex' – outlining the risks of contracting a sexually transmitted disease; to devise a questionnaire for adolescents to assess their knowledge about the effects of alcohol on behaviour.

STAGE 4

Planning to achieve the aims and objectives. Having identified your objectives, you now need to decide on the method of presentation; this will depend on such factors as cost, size of target group, ease of delivery, availability of material and/or equipment, and appropriateness for the target group.

Suitable methods may include:

- display, perhaps 'tying-in' with a national awareness day or week, e.g. AIDS awareness week or National No Smoking Day;
- video programme;
- leaflets;
- group workshop;
- formal lecture with slides or OHP transparencies.

STAGE 5

Identify resources and equipment. The choice of resources and equipment will depend on several factors:

- availability of resources, e.g. size of room, video rental, access to display boards and materials;
- cost of equipment;
- time available for promotion activity;
- knowing how to operate equipment, e.g. use of a video recorder;
- relevance to the target audience.

STAGE 6

Planning the content and method of the programme. This is where you work out *exactly* how to present the information, using the resources available. The OBJECTIVES and the target group will guide your choice of method, but it must be one with which you feel confident. The more effort put in at this stage, the greater the chance of success.

GUIDELINES FOR A PRESENTATION

- Produce a detailed timed plan.
- Allow time to introduce yourselves and the topic.
- Do a timed test run to ensure that you have enough material.
- Check the room for seating arrangements and equipment.
- Rehearse the delivery of the talk – try to use prompt cards which emphasise KEY POINTS even if you have written out the whole talk. Remember to maintain eye contact with your audience (see Chapter 2).
- Sum up the main points.
- Discussion time – let your audience know that there will be time for any questions or debate at the end. You may need to initiate this by asking a question yourself – have a few ideas ready or split the audience into smaller groups for the discussion of key points and arrange for the smaller groups to give feedback to the whole group.
- Empowering the audience – individuals need to make choices themselves; your task is to present them with clear, relevant and, above all, *accurate* information. If you don't know the answer to any questions, admit it and apologise!

STAGE 7

Implementation. Carry out the plan and remember to evaluate the programme as you go along.

STAGE 8

Evaluation. Evaluation is an important element in any health education campaign; it allows you to ASSESS and REVIEW all aspects of the programme. Always refer to the original aims and objectives and ask if these have been achieved. Before ending your presentation, ask the audience to complete an (anonymous) evaluation form so that you can review the outcome of the session (see Figure 7.19).

Questionnaire on presentation on

SMOKING AND HEALTH

We would be very grateful if you could spare a few minutes to complete this form. Any information received is confidential and will help us to improve our technique.

On a scale of 1–5 (1 = poor; 5 = good):

a) How would you rank the information on smoking and risks to health?

1 2 3 4 5

b) How useful was the information on ways to stop smoking?

1 2 3 4 5

c) How would you rank the OHP charts and diagrams as a learning tool?

1 2 3 4 5

d) How would you rank the display on 'Smoking: the facts'?

1 2 3 4 5

e) Did the session cover all you expected? Yes/No

Any other comments: ....

....

....

....

Thank you very much for your cooperation.

Figure 7.19 Sample evaluation form

RESOURCES USED IN HEALTH EDUCATION CAMPAIGNS

ACTIVITY

Look at Figure 7.20. For each of the following resources, brainstorm the advantages and disadvantages of each one, and arrange in the same format, including reference to target groups and any special considerations:

- leaflets;
- posters;
- role-play and games;
- OHP transparencies;
- handouts to accompany lecture;
- slides.

SOURCES OF HEALTH EDUCATION CAMPAIGNS

The Health Education Authority is a government-funded organisation set up in 1968 to promote health education in England, Wales and Northern Ireland. Its functions are to:

- mount national and regional campaigns;
- fund research;
- organise training and education events;
- provide information and resources for health educators (see Chapter 6);
- produce leaflets and posters.

In Scotland, a similar organisation is the Scottish Health Education Group.

Health For All is a global approach to health, originating from the World Health Organisation, which acknowledges the effect of the environment and lifestyle. The UK responded with the strategies:

- Health of the Nation;
- Healthy Wales.

The Nation's Health: A Strategy for the 1990s aims to identify measures likely to be effective in promoting the public health and outlines a national strategy for the next decade.

Government-run campaigns

In October 1994, the government launched a £20 million measles vaccination campaign; its aim was to vaccinate seven million schoolchildren, aged five to 16, against measles and rubella. The reason behind the campaign was a predicted measles epidemic which would result in many more deaths than the last epidemic in the early 1980s which saw 200,000 cases and 50 deaths.

Some campaigns continue for years and are jointly managed by the Department of Health and the Health Education Authority, e.g. Look after your HEART! which is a national programme which aims to prevent heart disease and encourage healthier lifestyles. Other campaigns have focused on smoking, diet and the risk of HIV and AIDS.

Local authorities also run campaigns which aim to give information about help available locally.

General Practitioners' waiting rooms usually have a selection of posters and leaflets on health issues, but research has shown that the public is not interested in being bombarded with educational messages while waiting to see the doctor; the survey results (published in 1994 in *Family Practice Journal*) showed that half the patients read a magazine, one-third had a chat, and most of the remainder did nothing. The conclusions were that GPs' premises should provide a calm ambience and not contribute to a guilty conscience.

Private companies

Manufacturers of 'healthy' products, such as wholemeal bread or high protein balanced foods for babies, often promote them by advertising *and* by using educational leaflets, which are offered free in health clinics, postnatal wards and supermarkets. Examples of these methods of health promotion are:

- booklets on 'Feeding your baby';
- child safety on the roads – by manufacturers of child car seats and harnesses;

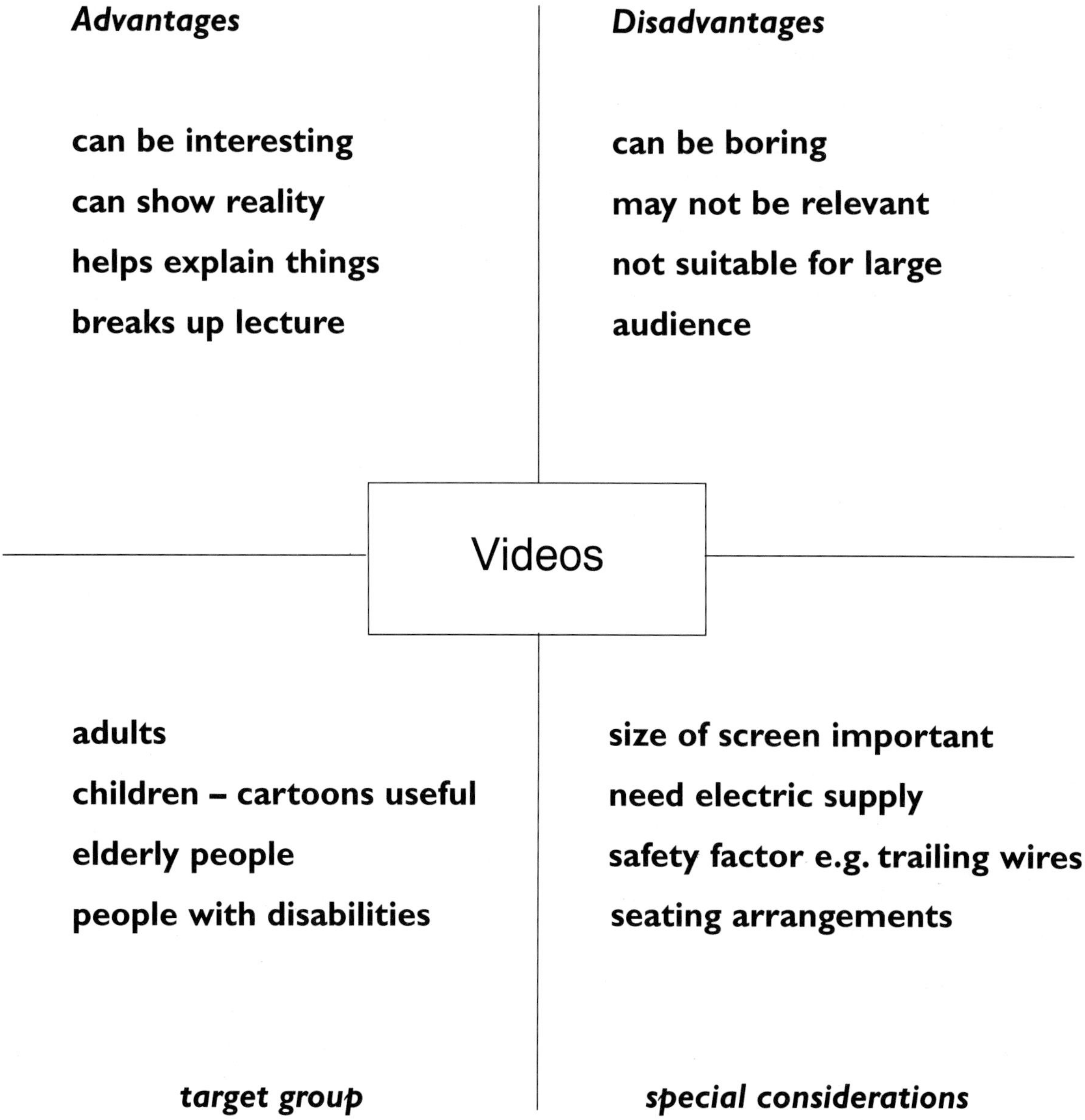

Figure 7.20 Video as a resource

- herbal remedies to encourage a stress-free life.

There are strict controls over the claims that manufacturers can make about the health-giving properties of their products.

Some products have traditionally been associated with promoting healthy lifestyles. Examples are:

- the advertising campaign for Guinness (Guinness is Good For You);
- Lucozade Promotes Rapid Recovery;
- Go to Work On An Egg.

ACTIVITY

1 Collect advertisements from magazines and newspapers for any product which claims to promote better health. Discuss their aims and objectives.

- Which groups are they targeting?
- Do they give any useful information on healthy living in addition to using their product?

2 Find out about the advertising standards

which apply to health product advertising.

3 Which television advertising campaigns for such products are memorable?

The voluntary sector

Voluntary organisations are in a strong position to enhance the health of the population by the following methods:

- through *self-help* – bringing people together to share common problems and to help them to gain more confidence and control over their own health;
- by *direct service provision* – e.g. British Red Cross has a network of shops for rental of equipment in the home (including walking frames, commodes and chairs);
- in *community health*, where voluntary organisations work with local people to identify and solve problems affecting their health, e.g. GASP – Group Against Smoking in Public, a Bristol-based group which campaigns for an increase in the provision of no-smoking areas in restaurants.
- health education and promotion, fund-raising and support for research, e.g. The Wellcome Trust is a medical research charity which provides funding for research in the biomedical sciences.

Charities which aim to promote health and inform the public of the risks to health from certain lifestyles also employ advertising methods to get their message across; they often work in conjunction with The Health Education Authority and/or private companies, e.g.:

- Child Accident Prevention Trust with financial support from Start-rite and Volvo produced a safety leaflet for parents, 'First Ride, Safe Ride', aimed at keeping a baby safe in the car.
- Age Concern, Help the Aged and Neighbourhood Energy Action joined the DSS to produce a booklet 'Keep Warm, Keep Well' which gives useful advice on all aspects of keeping warm, including where to apply for Community Care Grants.

REASONS FOR HEALTH CAMPAIGNS

Primary prevention

The Health of the Nation defined five key areas for health education and set targets in each area (see Figure 7.21):

- coronary heart disease and stroke;
- cancers;
- mental illness;
- HIV/AIDS and sexual health;
- accidents.

The report also emphasised the importance of considering the needs of specific groups of people within the population – children, women, elderly people, people in black and ethnic minority groups and certain socio-economic groups.

Work in and across the key areas has been developed by five TASK FORCES looking at nutrition, accidents, the workplace, physical activity and mental health:

- *The Nutrition Task Force* (NTF), working with food manufacturers, retailers, consumers, the Department of Health and the Ministry of Agriculture, Fisheries and Food (MAFF) developed 'Eat Well' – a national programme of action for promoting healthy eating.
- *The Accident Task Force* comprises eight government departments and three voluntary organisations: RoSPA, the Child Accident Prevention Trust and Age Concern. It is investigating the priorities for research into accidents and improving information on accidents.
- *The Workplace Task Force* is working towards more activity-based learning materials in the workplace and is encouraging the setting up of local groups comprising health promotion, occupational health and public health expertise, as well as representatives of trade unions, chambers

Coronary heart disease and stroke[1]

To reduce death rates for both CHD and stroke in people under 65 by at least 40% by the year 2000 *(Baseline 1990)*

To reduce the death rate for CHD in people aged 65–74 by at least 30% by the year 2000 *(Baseline 1990)*

To reduce the death rate for stroke in people aged 65–74 by at least 40% by the year 2000 *(Baseline 1990)*

Cancers[1]

To reduce the death rate for breast cancer in the population invited for screening by at least 25% by the year 2000 *(Baseline 1990)*

To reduce the incidence of invasive cervical cancer by at least 20% by the year 2000 *(Baseline 1986)*

To reduce the death rate for lung cancer under the age of 75 by at least 30% in men and by at least 15% in women by 2010 *(Baseline 1990)*

To halt the year-on-year increase in the incidence of skin cancer by 2005

Mental illness[1]

To improve significantly the health and social functioning of mentally ill people

To reduce the overall suicide rate by at least 15% by the year 2000 *(Baseline 1990)*

To reduce the suicide rate of severely mentally ill people by at least 33% by the year 2000 *(Baseline 1990)*

HIV/AIDS and sexual health

To reduce the incidence of gonorrhoea by at least 20% by 1995

(Baseline 1990), as an indicator of HIV/AIDS trends

To reduce by at least 50% the rate of conceptions amongst the under16s by the year 2000 *(Baseline 1989)*

Accidents[1]

To reduce the death rate for accidents among children aged under 15 by at least 33% by 2005 *(Baseline 1990)*

To reduce the death rate for accidents among young people aged 15–24 by at least 25% by 2005 *(Baseline 1990)*

To reduce the death rate for acccidents among people aged 65 and over by at least 33% by 2005 *(Baseline 1990)*

[1] The 1990 baseline for all mortality targets represents an average of the three years centred around 1990.

Figure 7.21 Health of the Nation main targets
Source: Department of Health (1992), *The Health of the Nation* (HMSO).

of commerce and the Employment Medical Advisory Service.

- *The Physical Activity Task Force* (PATF) is made up of government departments including health, education, environment, national heritage and transport, together with the HEA, the Association of District Councils, the Association of Metropolitan Authorities, the Sports Council and various professionals.
- *The Mental Health Task Force*, backed by a support group made up of 30–40 representatives from many mental health interests, identified where change is required to implement good practice – in the fields of leisure and occupation, supported accommodation and alternatives to hospital admission.

Each health authority in the United Kingdom is required to address the issues of health promotion by forming HEALTHY ALLIANCES for each of the key areas (see Chapter 6, page 337).

Preventative action

All immunisation programmes are an attempt to prevent disease and therefore to promote health – in both the individual and the general population. A recent initiative which followed on from research in New Zealand was to reduce the number of babies dying from Sudden Infant Death Syndrome (SIDS).

AND SO TO BED

The recent Cook Report into cot deaths was compulsive, yet almost unbearable to watch for new and prospective parents. Anything that sheds new light on this largely unexplained tragedy is welcome, but the combative, hard-hitting style of the TV programme has pushed many parental panic buttons without being able to offer a complete solution.

The debate started by the programme's conclusion that toxic chemicals in mattresses could be a cause of cot death is at least prompting further research and a re-evaluation of products by manufacturers. It is unlikely that all the answers are just around the corner but experts agree that certain practices appear to reduce the risk of cot death.

■ PLACE BABIES to sleep on their back or side

(with the underneath arm brought forward to prevent rolling on to the front).

■ DON'T SMOKE during pregnancy. A mother who smokes 20 or more cigarettes a day when pregnant increases her baby's risk of cot death by five times, according to the Foundation for the Study of Infant Deaths (FSID). Babies exposed to smoky atmospheres are also at greater risk.

■ DON'T LET babies overheat. A room temperature of 18°C is ideal. Remove bedding or clothing if the baby feels hot or sweaty. Don't give a hot water bottle or electric blanket. Make sure bedding and clothing does not prevent babies losing excess heat from their heads.

■ LOOK OUT for signs of illness needing medical attention. Emergency care is required if babies stop breathing, turn blue, have glazed eyes and are not focusing, cannot be woken or have a fit.

The cot death rate was cut by 50 per cent in one year after these measures were first promoted in 1991. But 10 babies still die every week and cot death is the leading cause of death in babies over one week old. The great majority are aged under six months.

Some studies have found that breastfeeding can protect against cot death, others that there is no proven link. Experts are divided on whether babies should sleep with their parents. Close contact with the mother appears to stabilise a baby's breathing, and makes the mother more aware of her child. But babies can overheat in a bed, and cot death risk is increased if the mother is a smoker.

Jane Silvester of FSID says: "We advise a separate cot, kept in the parent's bedroom. All babies need cuddling, but societies in which parents have traditionally slept with their babies don't tend to use very thick duvets and are likely to have harder mattresses."

Mattresses

Following the Cook Report, Boots has withdrawn all mattresses from its Children's World stores. Retailers who stock mattresses free of antimony, such as Mothercare, have been inundated with orders and have put customers on waiting lists. Manufacturers are stepping up production to fulfil orders as quickly as possible. FSID fears anxious parents are taking measures that may actually be dangerous for the baby, such as using pillows as mattresses.

■ THE MOST important advice is still to place babies on their backs – if The Cook Report's theory is correct, with their heads face down, babies breathe in toxic gases heavier than air.

■ MATTRESSES SHOULD be firm, clean, well-aired and dry (check secondhand ones very carefully). Don't make them up from soft materials which could cause suffocation.

■ ASK SHOPS or manufacturers about the content of mattresses.

■ IF YOU use a protective sheet, check that it doesn't contain toxic chemicals. It should be well-secured to avoid suffocation and shouldn't make the baby too hot.

Monitors

Various types of breathing monitors are available in the UK, but paediatricians do not recommend their use in the vast majority of cases and certainly not without medical supervision.

Monitors ring an alarm and flash a light when breathing movements stop for longer than 20 seconds. The three main types are: a sensor pad attached to the baby's stomach; a pressure pad or mattress on which the baby is placed; two electrodes attached to the baby's chest.

Monitors may be useful in some cases, where a baby has had an Apparent Life Threatening Event (ALTE), where the baby has stopped breathing, turned blue or white and may have gone floppy or choked.

Parents who have previously suffered a cot death may be advised to have a monitor for their next child. FSID's Care of the Next Infant scheme (CONI), run by district health authorities, offers an apnoea monitor.

While monitors offer some reassurance, there are disadvantages. They don't detect obstructive apnoea (where the windpipe is blocked but breathing or twitching movements continue). They are prone to false alarms. Some parents become dependent on the monitor, refusing to stop using it or failing to notice other signs of illness. There is no direct evidence that monitors reduce cot death.

Listeners

New parents are always nervous about their baby and most will buy a baby listener, even if their infant's noise is quite clearly detectable by ear.

Useful features include battery-operated mode, for moving from room to room or going outside; two channels, which avoids the confusion of hearing next door's baby when yours is sleeping peacefully nearby; a good volume control – you'll want it blasting at first, moving down as the baby gets older and you become more confident.

Some parents find it difficult to wean themselves off listeners until their child insists on some privacy; others cause trouble by forgetting it's switched on downstairs.

Tomy has a large range of listeners; Boots has own-brand equivalents for some.

(The Guardian, 29 November 1994)

METHODS OF PROMOTING HEALTH

Presenting the facts

The media have an important role to play in providing individuals with the information necessary to make decisions which affect their own health and that of their families. People are often confused by the wide variety of sometimes conflicting advice they receive on health matters. Most newspapers rely on interviews with professionals to inform their readers about health issues, but there can often be disagreement. For example:

- the link between BSE (bovine spongiform encephalopathy) and brain disease in humans;
- repetitive strain injury – is this an occupational hazard? – experts disagree;
- ME (myalgic encephalopathy) – often dismissed as 'yuppie flu'.

Analogy

The most common analogy used in health promotion is that of the body as an *engine*. If it is looked after properly, given the right fuel and exercise, then it should give years of trouble-free service. Unfortunately, this analogy does not take into account the inherited predispositions we all have to certain disorders.

Shock/scare stories

Every decade has its share of shock stories. There is usually a 'knee-jerk' reaction by the public, but the adoption of avoidance strategies is sustained only if the initial story is substantiated by informed debate and interest by health professionals. Examples are:

- the raw egg scare in the 1980s – when eggs were implicated in the spread of salmonellosis;
- the risk of listeria contamination of foods that had been cooked and then rapidly chilled;
- the role of toxins in cot mattresses as a contributory factor in cot deaths;
- the role of aluminium-coated saucepans as a cancer risk.

ACTIVITY

Read the article 'And so to bed' and evaluate it.

- Does the author describe the research methods used in the Cook report?
- Are the instructions for preventing cot death clear and detailed?
- If possible, arrange to view the relevant TV programme 'The Cook Report' and comment on the methods used to inform parents of all the risks.
- How would *you* mount a campaign to inform parents of the risks of cot death?

Role models

Supermodels are often accused of promoting an unrealistic role model for young girls to emulate. The 'emaciated waif' look can contribute to an adolescent's feelings of ambiguity and insecurity, and media images of thinness equating to health can increase the risk of anorexia nervosa (see page 229).

Sports personalities and their lifestyles are also very influential, particularly on young people; the recent case of a footballer being treated for drug addiction received much media publicity and increased health awareness.

Film stars and other people in the public eye advertise products and take part in health campaigns (see Figure 7.22).

TV and radio

Programmes such as 'Eastenders' and 'The Archers' draw the viewer or listener into their fictional world, but the messages can be very powerfully conveyed and lead to discussion of the wider issues:

- a character with HIV/AIDS will outline the measures for diagnosis and prevention;
- a character suffering from depression will seek help from the relevant agencies;
- an alcoholic may join a self-help group.

ACTIVITY

In small groups, discuss a serial on TV or radio. List all the health promotion messages you can remember within the story-lines:

- Do you think that TV or radio fiction is a good way of getting a message across?
- Does the inclusion of a telephone helpline number detract from or enhance the impact of a health problem?
- Does the programme mirror real life or is it viewed as escapism?

ASSESSMENT OPPORTUNITY ✔

Group Presentations – Health Campaign

These could be arranged as a *video* or as an *oral* presentation, depending on the resources available. Discuss with your tutor how and where you are going to make your presentation. Draw up an *individual* action plan, following the advice on page 386 to include:

- choice of health promotion area. Choose from:
  - smoking;
  - alcohol;
  - drug abuse;
  - safe sexual practices;
  - safety in the environment.
- detailed planning – delegate responsibility for different tasks to each group member. The presentation should:
- only contain correct information;
- outline your target group;
- include recommendations on the ways in which the audience can contribute to their own health;
- provide a 'question-and-answer' time at the end;
- ensure that all feedback made to the target audience is both constructive and non-judgemental.

After the presentation, write an individual *evaluation* of the exercise, commenting on:

- your own contribution;
- the audience response to your presentation;
- recommendations for the future (i.e. ways of improving the session).

EVALUATING THE EFFECTIVENESS OF HEALTH EDUCATION CAMPAIGNS

Health education campaigns – the forgotten issues

There have been many health education success stories over the last few decades:

- the recent campaign to increase awareness of the risk of Sudden Infant Death Syndrome (SIDS) – see pages 391–2;
- the Don't Drink and Drive campaigns each Christmas;
- the changes in food labelling which means

that the nutritional content of foods is now available and readily understood by the layman;
- the increased public awareness of the depletion of the *ozone layer* and the risk of skin cancer;
- immunisation campaigns have greatly reduced the incidence of infectious diseases.

Many other campaigns have had limited success, e.g. those which have focused on *secondary health promotion* such as persuading women to attend for breast cancer screening.

THE DIFFICULTIES OF EVALUATING THE SUCCESS OF HEALTH EDUCATION CAMPAIGNS

The success of *medical treatments* is comparatively easy to measure, e.g. the rapid recovery of servicemen with infections during the Second World War was certainly helped by the use of antibiotics, particularly penicillin. Most *health education campaigns* aim to increase public awareness and to affect lifestyle and behaviour; they are usually very difficult to evaluate. There are many reasons for this:

1. It is difficult to ensure strict comparability between targeted groups and a control group.
2. Any trial which aims to compare a targeted group with a control group must span a long period of time and cover a large population.
3. Primary prevention methods are usually matters of public policy, concerning healthy individuals who are not seeking care. How do we decide whether their continuing good health is directly influenced by a campaign?
4. The mass media plays a large part in raising public awareness of health issues, but messages received via television, radio and the press are often not acknowledged as being part of health education.

There are some issues which have not been the focus of recent health education campaigns:

- *Chlamydia* – the most common sexually transmitted disease in Britain today, yet most people have never heard of it;
- *dental decay* – one of the most costly avoidable health problems;
- *head lice* – the subject of infrequent campaigns;
- *back pain* – a common reason for absence from work;
- *stress and stress-related illnesses* – often work-related, these disorders can also result in many absences from work;
- *coronary heart disease* (CHD) – experts disagree on the exact causes of CHD, but it is the major killer of the over 75s in Britain.

ASSESSMENT OPPORTUNITY ✔

1. Select a recent health education campaign that is memorable to you. Evaluate the success of this campaign, with particular emphasis on the following:
   - A description of the aim of the campaign, e.g. a new government report may have emphasised an increase in alcohol-related road traffic accidents, which the campaign is seeking to address.
   - A description of the methods used, e.g. newspaper coverage, use of famous personalities, use of shock/scare tactics, and how these methods relate to the target population of the campaign.
2. Interview at least six individuals from the target group of the campaign, using a structured interview format.
3. Use the results of these interviews to draw conclusions and make recommendations about the effectiveness of the campaign.

REFERENCES AND RESOURCES

British Medical Association (1992), *Complete Family Health Encyclopedia*. London: Dorling Kindersley.

Ewles, L. and Simnett, I. (1993), *Promoting Health: A Practical Guide to Health Education*. Chichester: John Wiley and Sons Ltd.

First Aid Manual (1992), London: Dorling Kindersley.

Hartley, L. (1990), *History of Medicine*, Oxford: Blackwell Publishers.

Health Education Authority (1993), Cancer: How to Reduce your Risks.

Health of the Nation (1992), London: HMSO.

Inequalities in Health: The Black Report and the Health Divide (1992), London: Penguin Books.

Open University (1989), *Drug Use and Misuse: A Reader*. Chichester: John Wiley and Sons Ltd.

Smith, A. and Jackson, B. (eds) (1988), *The Nation's Health: A Strategy for the 1990s* (A report from an Independent Multidisciplinary Committee). London: King Edward's Hospital Fund for London.

Taylor, D. (1989), *Human Physical Health*. Cambridge: Cambridge University Press.

World Health Organisation (1985), *Health for All*, Geneva: WHO.

USEFUL ADDRESSES

British Heart Foundation
14 Fitzhardinge Street
London W1H 4DH
Tel.: 0171 935 0185

British Red Cross Society
9 Grosvenor Crescent
London SW1X 7EJ
Tel.: 0171 245 6315

Disability Alliance
1st Floor East
Universal House
88–94 Wentworth Street
London E1 7SA
Tel.: 0171 247 8763

Health Education Authority
Hamilton House
Mabledon Place
London WC1H 9JP
Tel.: 0171 631 0930

Help for Health Trust
Highcroft Cottage
Romsey Road
Winchester
Hants SO22 5DH
Tel.: 01962 849100

Mencap
123 Golden Lane
London EC1Y 0RT
Tel.: 0171 454 0454

MIND
22 Harley Street
London W1N 2ED
Tel.: 0171 637 0741

Radon Survey
National Radiological Protection Board
Chilton, Didcot
Oxfordshire OX11 0RQ

Royal Society for the Promotion of Health
RSH House
38A St George's Drive
London SW1V 4BH
Tel.: 0171 630 0121

St John Ambulance
1 Grosvenor Crescent
London SW1X 7EF
Tel.: 0171 235 5231

Directories of groups and organisations:

Directory for Disabled People, 6th ed. (1991), Woodhead-Faulkner.

Directory of Black and Ethnic Community Health Services in London (1990), London: MIND.

Disability Alliance (1993).

Disabled Rights Handbook (1993–94).

People Who Help, 3rd ed. (1992), Profile Publications.

The Voluntary Agencies Directory, 13th ed. (1993), NCVO Publications.

For free literature about HIV and AIDS, telephone 0800 555777.

8

RESEARCH PERSPECTIVES IN HEALTH AND SOCIAL CARE

This chapter provides a comprehensive guide to research methods used in health and social care. Guidance is given on how to plan, produce and present a research project, and the reader will find this chapter useful for reference when carrying out many of the pieces of research suggested throughout the rest of the book.

INVESTIGATING THE RESEARCH PROCESS

Health and social care embraces a variety of disciplines, drawing from the natural, behavioural and social sciences to cover health care issues. Although the subject matter of these different sciences may vary considerably, they all share a need to have defined investigative procedures, which are known as METHODS OF ENQUIRY. These methods may involve re-analysing records which already exist, such as statistics and historical documents, which are known as SECONDARY DATA. Alternatively, methods may be used employing participants to produce PRIMARY DATA, which are then analysed.

Purpose of research

There are a variety of reasons a research project may be carried out. The following list gives some examples of the purpose of a piece of research:

- to confirm policy;
- to question policy;
- to confirm practice;
- to disprove proportions;
- to extend knowledge and understanding;
- to improve practice.

ACTIVITY

1 Read the brief descriptions of the pieces of research described, and decide for which of the purposes listed above the work was carried out. (NB It is likely that a piece of research will be carried out for more than one reason.)

HEARTBREAKING TRUTH ABOUT WOMEN AND THE 'MAN'S DISEASE'

Last week the National Forum for Coronary Heart Prevention, an umbrella group of 35 medical and consumer groups, published a report which for the first time highlighted the coronary risks for women.

Imogen Sharp, director of the National Forum, said: "Despite the fact coronary heart disease is the leading single cause of death among women, it is typically seen as a male disease. As a result, women may not recognise coronary symptoms when they have them and GPs and other health professionals may not initially diagnose symptoms as heart disease.

"Women are less likely to receive investigations, medical and surgical treatments. They are referred later in their illness than men and take longer to recover."

It is women's own biology that is letting them down. Until they are about 50, women have an advantage over men because lower cholesterol levels and a higher proportion of the high density lipoproteins (blood fats) protect them against heart disease. Yet after this age, the low density lipoproteins that increase the risk of heart attack rise above those of men – and remain higher for the rest of a woman's life.

It is the female hormone oestrogen that is responsible for reducing cholesterol levels in women. In early research on post-menopausal women taking oestrogen-only hormone replacement therapy (HRT), a 50% reduction in deaths from coronary disease was reported.

(The Sunday Times, 25 November 1994)

EPIDURALS ARE NOT A PAIN IN THE BACK

Women who want an epidural anaesthetic during childbirth should not be afraid that it will trigger back pain later on, say doctors in the US. Back pain after childbirth is common, affecting between a quarter and a half of women, sometimes for as long as 18 months. However, researchers at Harvard University Medical School in Boston have found no link between this pain and epidurals.

The new finding contradicts several British studies which suggest that back pain after childbirth may be related to the administration of an epidural, in which a pain-relieving drug is injected near the spine during labour and delivery.

(New Scientist, 12 November 1994)

'NO CANCER LINK TO BREAST IMPLANTS'

A study of women who had silicone breast implants failed to find any extra cancer or connective tissue disease risk, a plastic surgeon said yesterday.

The results of research into their safety, announced by Antony Watson, consultant plastic surgeon at St John's Hospital near Livingston, West Lothian, come as thousands of UK women who have suffered problems after surgery prepare to apply for compensation through the US courts.

Mr Watson told a London news conference that a study carried out in Edinburgh between 1982 and 1991 compared 319 women with silicone gel breast implants, most of whom had undergone breast reconstruction after mastectomy, with those of carefully matched women without them.

None was found to have an increased risk of developing cancer or connective tissue diseases compared with the control group without implants.

(The Independent, 2 December 1994)

DRUG BRINGS RELIEF TO BIG SPENDERS

Compulsive shopping is probably closest in nature to a series of psychiatric complaints known as impulse control disorders, which include uncontrollable urges to light fires, steal or pull out one's hair. But it also resembles obsessive compulsive disorder (OCD), a strange complaint that causes sufferers endlessly to repeat pointless tasks like washing their hands, or to hoard obsessively.

The similarity to OCD led Black to test the drug fluvoxamine on compulsive shoppers. Fluvoxamine is already being used to treat people with depression in Britain, and is awaiting approval by the Food and Drug Administration for treatment of OCD in the US. In Black's study, patients take the drug for eight weeks, and the effect on their shopping urges is monitored. Then the patients are taken off the drug and watched for another month.

In the seven patients examined so far, the results are clear and dramatic, says Black: the urge to shop and the time spent shopping decrease markedly. When the patient stops taking the drug, however, the symptoms slowly return.

(New Scientist, 12 November 1994)

CARE FEARS OF TERMINALLY ILL

The fear of becoming a burden to others rather than the fear of pain is the main reason people request euthanasia, according to a new study.

The researchers looked in detail at the categories of suffering which drove people to ask for euthanasia, and found this was only weakly linked to pain, although those in severe pain were twice as likely to ask for this as those in no pain, 5 per cent against 2.6 per cent.

The main reason for requesting euthanasia was either real or perceived dependency. Of those suffering from high dependency, 5.9 per cent of the deceased had said they wanted euthanasia, as had 5.3 per cent of those with mental problems and 5.2 per cent of those with severe breathing difficulties.

Religious faith, or lack of it, appeared to make no difference to the numbers who had asked for euthanasia.

Dr Seal and Dr Addington-Hall, publishing the studies in the journal Social Science and Medicine, say: "If good care is to obviate the desire to die sooner, the hospice movement needs to address the problem of dependency as well as to provide symptom control in which hospice practitioners have developed impressive experience."

(The Guardian, 19 October 1994)

NHS CONSULTANTS FALL PREY TO STRESS

Nearly half National Health Service consultants, general practitioners and senior hospital managers suffer stress and depression, according to a report in the British Medical Journal today.

Some have even thought of suicide, Richard Caplan, a psychiatrist at Lincoln County Hospital, found in a survey. He sent questionnaires to 81 consultants, 322 general practitioners and 121 senior hospital managers which showed 47 per cent were suffering from stress and depression.

These 'disturbing' levels were much higher than in the professional and managerial class as a whole. He said that senior doctors and managers suffered far more from stress than expected. "This stress may have far reaching effects on the National Health Service and patient care."

'I have no explanation. The research that has been done in the past on medical specialities, looking at stress, has always assumed certain causes, and has asked questions which in a sense predisposed a person to answer about a particular type of stress.

'I wanted to avoid that, because I didn't want to get bogged down in cause. I just wanted to know whether it was there or not.'

(The Guardian, 11 November 1994)

2 When you read descriptions of other pieces of research, for example in newspapers, try to decide on its purpose using the list above.

METHODS OF ENQUIRY USING PRIMARY SOURCES

Experimentation (scientific, psychological)

Experimentation is the method of enquiry most widely used by natural scientists. It is also frequently used by behavioural scientists. The process in which experimentation is used can be broken down into stages (Figure 8.1).

The first stage involves the researcher making an OBSERVATION. For example, you may notice that, even if the water from a certain tap is always at the same temperature, if your hands are cold, it may feel hot, and yet if your hands are warm, it may feel only lukewarm.

From the researcher's observation, a HYPOTHESIS or an educated guess can be made to explain the observation. Using the example given, the researcher might guess 'skin receptors detect *changes* in temperature rather

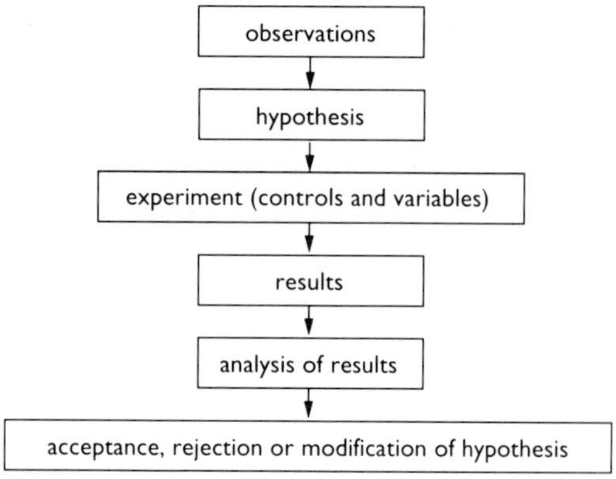

Figure 8.1 Stages involved in the process of experimentation

than *actual* temperature'. This is the hypothesis which the experiment will test.

In a CONTROLLED EXPERIMENT only one condition at a time should be changed. The conditions which can change are known as VARIABLES. Those remaining constant are FIXED VARIABLES, and that being changed by the experimenter is the MANIPULATED VARIABLE (or INDEPENDENT VARIABLE). The DEPENDENT VARIABLE is the factor which is then measured.

ACTIVITY

1 Think of observations that you have made in your everyday surroundings. Can you suggest hypotheses to explain these observations?

2 Design a simple experiment to test the hypothesis: 'Skin receptors detect *changes* in temperature rather than *actual* temperature'.

ACTIVITY

1 In the experiment you were asked to design in the previous activity, apparatus could be set up as shown.

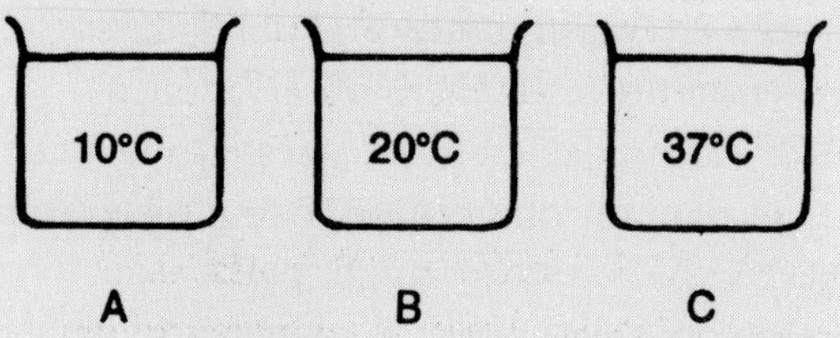

The subjects could then put one hand in A and the other in C for one minute, then place both hands in B, and then record their observations.

2 Which of the following are fixed variables and which is the manipulated variable?

- volume of water;
- temperature of water;
- time hand is placed in initial temperature.

3 Carry out the experiment shown above for testing the hypothesis 'Skin receptors detect change in temperature rather than actual temperature'. For accuracy, test at least three people, preferably more. From your results do you accept or reject the hypothesis?

The observations made in an experiment may be QUALITATIVE or QUANTITATIVE.

- A qualitative observation describes without measurement.
- A quantitative observation involves measuring an amount or quantity (such as length, volume, mass or time).

The observation made in the experiment above is qualitative, as the subject would just be recording whether the water felt hot, cold, tepid, etc. This is a DESCRIPTION and not a MEASUREMENT.

ACTIVITY

The observations below were recorded by a nurse working in the casualty department in a hospital. Which of her observations are quantitative and which are qualitative?

At 23.00 h a young man was brought in. He was semi-conscious and incoherent, but from his driving licence he was found to be 23 years old. His temperature was 36°C, but his skin was sweaty. His lips had a bluish tinge. His pulse rate was 120 per min., and his blood pressure 90/50 mm/Hg. His breath smelt quite strongly of pear drops.

Refer to a first aid book, and you should be able to make a diagnosis.

PSYCHOLOGICAL EXPERIMENTS

Psychological experiments are based on the scientific method and proceed along similar stages of observation, hypothesis, experiment (control and variables), results, analysis of results, acceptance, rejection or modification of hypothesis. However, because humans are involved, special modifications have to be made to the scientific method.

HYPOTHESIS

Whenever psychologists carry out a study, as with Scientists, they must start with a hypothesis, i.e. an intelligent guess as to what they are likely to discover – an idea or theory which makes certain predictions.

One-tailed and two-tailed hypotheses

A *one-tailed* hypothesis predicts the direction in which the results are expected to go. A two-tailed hypothesis does not state a direction but states that one factor affects another, or that there will be a difference between two sets of scores without stating the direction of that difference.

ACTIVITY

Decide whether the following hypotheses are one- or two-tailed.

1 Alcohol affects reaction time.

2 The likelihood of two people being friends depends on how similar their attitudes are.

3 What someone expects to see influences what they actually perceive.

4 Individuals are more likely to conform when in groups of five than when in pairs.

5 Anxiety affects the level of adrenalin in the blood.

INDEPENDENT AND DEPENDENT VARIABLES

In psychological experiments (as in experiments in other fields), attempts are made to keep all aspects of the situation constant (fixed variables) except for the one being investigated.

ACTIVITY

For the following hypotheses state:

- whether the hypothesis is one- or two-tailed;
- the independent or manipulated variable;
- the dependent variable.

1 Lack of sleep affects learning in ten-year-old boys.

2 A baby under nine months of age will not search for a hidden object.

3 Social class affects IQ scores.

4 Aggressive children are emotionally insecure.

5 It is easier to remember items which are ‘chunked’ together than it is to remember individual, unconnected items.

CONFOUNDING VARIABLES

These are all the other variables which might

affect the results and therefore prevent you from unequivocally attributing the changes you find in the dependent variable to your manipulation of the independent variable. It is very difficult and time-consuming to identify and eliminate all confounding variables in an experiment, especially in the fields of social and developmental psychology, but every attempt must be made to do so or the experiment will not be effective.

ACTIVITY

- What confounding variables might affect the results of an experiment based on hypotheses 1–5 above?
- Why would the elimination of confounding variables be easier in hypothesis 5?

VARIABLES OF PRESENTATION

The following procedures are used to eliminate variables of presentation:

- *Standardised procedures* – every step of the experiment is described beforehand, so that all subjects receive identical experiences.
- *Standardised instructions* – these ensure that all the subjects are given exactly the same information, with no variation in style, content and delivery. Therefore, if you choose to read your instructions to your subject, you must make sure that you do so in the same manner, and with the same inflections, throughout. Instructions should be friendly and clear, explaining the task required, but it is usually necessary, in psychology experiments, to conceal the real purpose of the experiment. Writing them is a skill.

ACTIVITY

Write standardised procedures and standardised instructions for an experiment to test hypothesis 5 above.

SUBJECT AND EXPERIMENTER EXPECTATION

Further confounding variables arise from the fact that a psychology experiment is a social situation in which neither the subjects nor the experimenters are inanimate objects; rather they are active, thinking human beings.

Subject expectations, also known as demand characteristics

Typically, subjects who take part in a psychological experiment are motivated to find out the purpose of the experiment, and then possibly to respond in support of what they think is the hypothesis being tested. Cues which convey to the subject the purpose of the experiment include: the non-verbal behaviour of the experimenter, the type of person the experimenter is, the setting of the experiment, and what the subject may already have heard about the experiment.

Experimenter expectations

The experimenter unconsciously conveys to subjects how they should behave – the cues may be extremely subtle, but they still have an influence. For example, in one of his studies Rosenthal (1966) found that male researchers were far more likely to smile at female subjects that at male subjects, a factor which would undoubtedly affect the results of studies looking at sex differences in any kind of behaviour – verbal ability, memory, non-verbal communication, etc.

METHODS OF REDUCING BIAS CAUSED BY SUBJECT AND EXPERIMENTER EXPECTATIONS

The single-blind condition

In this condition the subjects do not know under which condition they are being tested. An example of this is in drugs testing, when no subject knows whether they are taking the drug or a placebo, i.e. whether they are a member of the experimental or the control group.

The double-blind condition

Here the condition each subject is in is not known to the experimenter. In the example above, the experimenter would not know whether he or she is administering the drug or the placebo.

LABORATORY EXPERIMENTS

Advantages

- Experiments are the only means by which cause and effect can be established.
- Variables may be controlled precisely.

Disadvantages

- Behaviour in the laboratory, in which the situation is controlled so precisely, is necessarily limited.
- People are likely to behave differently from normal in the artificial conditions of the laboratory, even if the true nature of the study is concealed from them (the single-blind condition); their behaviour will be unnatural especially if they feel nervous. This is perhaps of less importance in a memory experiment that it is in an experiment on, for example, body language.

THE FIELD EXPERIMENT

Sometimes it is possible to carry out experiments in a more natural setting, i.e. in the field. A well-known example of this is Hoflings study (1966) showing the power of social roles in eliciting obedient behaviour.

Identical boxes of capsules were placed in 22 wards of both public and private psychiatric hospitals. The capsules were, in fact, placebos (consisting of glucose). But the containers were labelled '5 mg capsules of Astrofen'; the labels also indicated that the normal dose is 5 mg with a maximum daily dose of 10 mg.

While the nurse was on duty, a 'doctor' (a confederate of the experimenter: 'Dr Smith from the Psychiatric Department') instructed the nurse, by telephone, to give 20 mg of Astrogen to his patient, a Mr Jones, as he was in a desperate hurry and the patient needed the capsules. He said that he would come in to see Mr Jones in 10 minutes' time and that he would sign the authorisation document for the drug when he got there.

To comply with this request, the nurse would be breaking three basic procedural rules:

1 The dose was above the maximum daily dose of 10 mg.
2 Drugs should only be given after written authority has been obtained.
3 The nurse must be absolutely sure that 'Dr Smith' is a genuine doctor.

A real doctor was posted nearby, unseen by the nurse, and observed what the nurse did following the telephone call – did the nurse comply, did he/she refuse, or did he/she try to contact another doctor?

Whatever the nurse's course of action, the observer-doctor then revealed what was really going on.

21 out of 22 nurses complied unhesitatingly. Eleven later said they had not noticed the dosage discrepancy.

EXPERIMENTAL DESIGN

A common method of designing an experiment in psychology is to divide the subjects into two groups, the experimental group and the control group, and then change the independent variable for the experimental group and not for the control group. The experimental and the control groups must be matched on all important characteristics, e.g. age, sex, experience, etc.

Independent measures design

If two groups in an experiment consist of different individuals then this is an independent measures design. For example, if the hypothesis to be tested predicts that girls and boys show different levels of aggression, then two separate groups are obviously required, boys and girls.

Repeated measures design

Sometimes it is possible to use the same individuals and to test them on two or more occasions, so that each subject experiences each condition of the independent variable. This is called a repeated measures design and is often more accurate than the independent measures design. The example above could be conducted using the repeated measures design.

However, this design introduces other confounding variables which must be carefully controlled:

- practice effects;
- fatigue/boredom effects.

Using hypothesis 5 from the activity on page 401, in remembering items which are chunked and those which are not: if the chunked items are always placed in the second trial the fact that they are memorised more easily might simply be due to the fact that the subject is now more familiar with the requirements of the experiment – practice effects. If the unconnected items are always placed in the second trial then the fact that the subject is slower at learning them may be due to fatigue/boredom effects. To control the effects of practice and fatigue/boredom, half the subjects should be presented with the chunked items first, and half with the unconnected items first. This procedure is called counterbalancing.

Matched pairs design

If a repeated measures design cannot be used, it is sometimes possible to match every subject in one group with a very similar person in the other group. The ideal subjects for matched pairs design would be pairs of identical twins.

Characteristics of a good experiment

A good experiment should include the following:

1. It should be possible to generalise from the study.
2. The study should be replicable, i.e. it should be possible to copy exactly what the first experimenter did, and obtain the same results.
3. The measures used in the study must be valid, i.e. they must measure what they set out to measure.

BANDURA'S STUDIES

A classic psychology experiment, conducted in the laboratory, is Bandura's series of studies investigating imitation in children.

Bandura *et al.* (1963) carried out a series of experiments investigating imitation in children. They took 96 children aged between three and six years old, and divided them into four groups (24 children in each group). The groups were then shown different scenes.

Based on a bobo doll. *Psychology an Introduction*, by N. Hayes and S. Orrell, Longman.

- *Group 1* watched an adult behaving aggressively towards a large rubber 'bobo' doll. The adult punched the doll, shouted at it and hit it with a hammer.
- *Group 2* watched the same adult behaving in exactly the same way, but instead of seeing it in real life, they saw it on film.
- *Group 3* saw the same sequence of actions towards the doll, but they were shown it as a cartoon set in a fantasy land.
- *Group 4* saw no violent behaviour at all – the control group.

After watching the scenes, the children were

shown into a room to play with toys, among which was a bobo doll similar to the one they had seen. The experimenters then deliberately frustrated the children by taking the toys away from them just as they were enjoying their play. The children were then observed through a one-way mirror as they carried on playing. Hidden observers rated each child's behaviour, and counted the number of aggressive actions they performed during a 20 minute period. The following results were found:

Average number of aggressive acts

Group 1	real-life model	83
Group 2	filmed model	92
Group 3	cartoon model	99
Group 4	no model	54

From these results it may be seen that the children who had watched an aggressive model performed far more aggressive actions than the control group, who had not. Bandura also found that the children who had observed the real-life model copied more of the specific aggressive actions of the model, while those who had seen the film or the cartoon showed more general aggressive behaviour.

ACTIVITY

Write a two-tailed hypothesis for the above study.

- Which design was used for the experiment, independent measures or repeated measures?
- Which variables would have to be considered when subjects were selected and would have to be eliminated to avoid a meaningless set of results?
- What steps were taken to eliminate other confounding variables in this experiment?
- What method of sampling should be used for this study?
- Do you think children of this age would be likely to act artificially in the setting described?
- What sort of action, in this age group, do you think the observers would count as aggressive?
- How would the observers achieve inter-rater reliability, i.e. making sure that they were each observing, measuring and counting the same things?
- Is this investigation open to criticism on ethical grounds?

Bandura also found that the children did not imitate all models equally: they were much more likely to imitate models which they saw as similar to themselves, such as those of the same age and sex, with whom they could identify.

WRITING UP A PSYCHOLOGICAL REPORT

A psychological report is written in a style similar to a report on a scientific experiment, but it must include details of the special modifications described in this section.

WRITING UP AN EXPERIMENT

An important part of research is communicating your findings to others. The following guidelines will help you produce a comprehensive written report of your experiment.

- Use an informative *title*, e.g. 'Experiment to investigate the detection of temperature by skin receptors'.
- Write a short summary of the investigation, briefly outlining the aims, methods and main conclusions. This is known as the *abstract*.
- State your *hypothesis*.
- Explain your experimental *method*.
  Some do's and don'ts for writing your experimental method
  - DO write in sufficient detail for someone unfamiliar with the method to repeat the experiment exactly.
  - DO write in short, simple sentences.

  - DON'T use long words if short words will do.
  - DO write in the past tense, for example: 'The test tubes were placed in a water bath.'
  - DON'T write as a list of instructions – NOT, for example: 'Place the test tubes in a water bath.'
  - DON'T use personal pronouns – NOT, for example: 'I placed the test tubes in a water bath' or 'We placed the test tubes in a water bath.'
- Record your *results*. This might be in the form of, for example, a table, graph, bar chart, pie chart, drawing or written description (see section on 'Data handling').
- In your *discussion* do the following:
  (a) Draw your *conclusions*, i.e. explain whether your results mean that you are accepting, rejecting or modifying your hypothesis.
  (b) Write a critical *evaluation* of your results. Addressing the following questions may help you to do this.
    - Are your results *valid*, i.e. has the method measured what it set out to measure?
    - Are your results *reliable*, i.e. would the method used give consistent results?
    - Did you have any unexpected results? If so, can you explain them?
    - Were there any sources of inaccuracy?
    - How could you improve your method?
    - How could you extend your research?
- List your *references*. Any information you have given from other sources, or direct quotes, should be followed by the name of the author and the year of publication. For example: 'It is considered that by 1991 the Health Service had spent around 2 billion pounds in computer developments and is currently spending 50 million pounds a year buying in computer and information technology consultancy to develop and rectify computer systems' (Proctor, 1992).

  At the end of your report you should list the authors alphabetically, and include the following details so that the reference may be found by the reader.

  For books, give:
  - author's surname, followed by initials;
  - date of publication;
  - title;
  - place of publication;
  - publisher.

  For example: Procter, P. (1992), *Nurses, Computers and Information Technology*, London, Chapman and Hall.

  For journal articles, give:
  - author's surname, followed by initials;
  - date of publication;
  - title of article;
  - name of journal;
  - volume number;
  - issue number;
  - page range.

  For example: Weedon, P. and Curry, M. (1992), 'Diabetes: Switching to Insulin', *Nursing Times*, vol. 88, no. 49, 34–36.
- Any information which is relevant to the research but which is perhaps too bulky to fit into the main report can be put in an *appendix*. Examples of appendices include raw data, secondary data, statistical workings, useful addresses and telephone numbers.

ACTIVITY

1 Look in journals to find lists of references. Can you find variations in the ways in which these are given?

2 How does a bibliography differ from a list of references?

Correlation

A CORRELATION STUDY is a method of enquiry widely used by natural and behavioural scientists.

In the experimental method of enquiry described earlier, generally the scientist manipulates one variable, and observes the response of a second variable.

However, it is often not possible to do this, and so observations must be made of two variables, neither of them manipulated.

To see if there is a relationship between the two variables, the results should be plotted on a SCATTERGRAM. For example, in an investigation to find whether there is a relationship between shoe size and height in females, the following data were obtained from eight women:

Height (c)	*Shoe size*
158	4
162	3
161	5
162	5
162	6
164	7
168	6
166	7

To plot these data on a scattergram, create a graph with one variable measured on the vertical (*y*) axis and the other on the horizontal (*x*) axis; then enter a point on the graph for each pair of data.

In a correlation study you can put each variable on either axis as neither is manipulated; in a controlled experiment it is conventional to put the manipulated variable on the *x* axis.

If there is a relationship (correlation) between two variables, the points will lie along an imaginary line. The more scattered they are, the less likely that there is a correlation between the two variables.

ACTIVITY

1 Plot the height/shoe size data given in the text on a scattergram.

2 From the scattergram, say whether you think there is a correlation between height and shoe size or not.

3 Study Figure 8.2. In which graph, (a) or (b), is a correlation more likely to exist?

If there is a correlation, to show the line around which the points are scattered the LINE OF BEST FIT can be drawn. Although statistical methods can be used to find out where this straight line lies, it is often satisfactory to judge this by eye. (A transparent ruler helps, as this enables the points on both sides of the line to be seen at once.)

If the line of best fit slopes upwards from left to right, as shown in Figure 8.3(a), we say that there is a POSITIVE CORRELATION. If it slopes downwards from left to right, as shown in Figure 8.3(b), we say that there is a NEGATIVE CORRELATION.

ACTIVITY

1 Using the information given on positive and negative correlations, select the

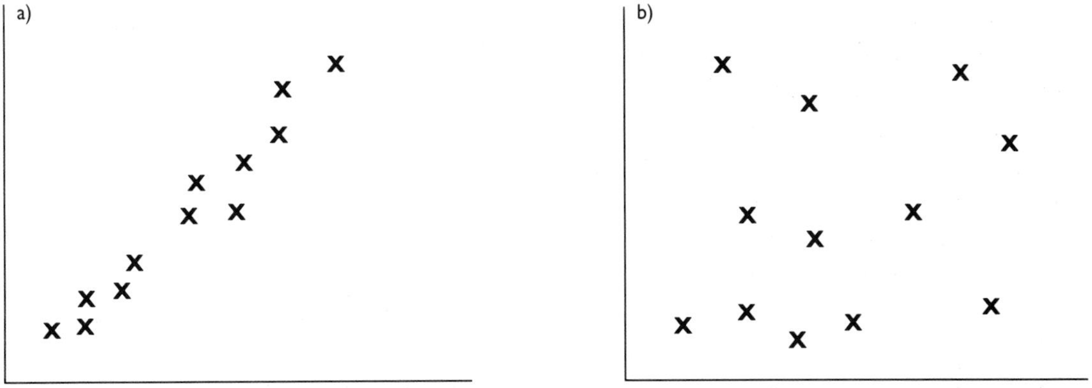

Figure 8.2 Which graph shows the closest correlation, (a) or (b)?

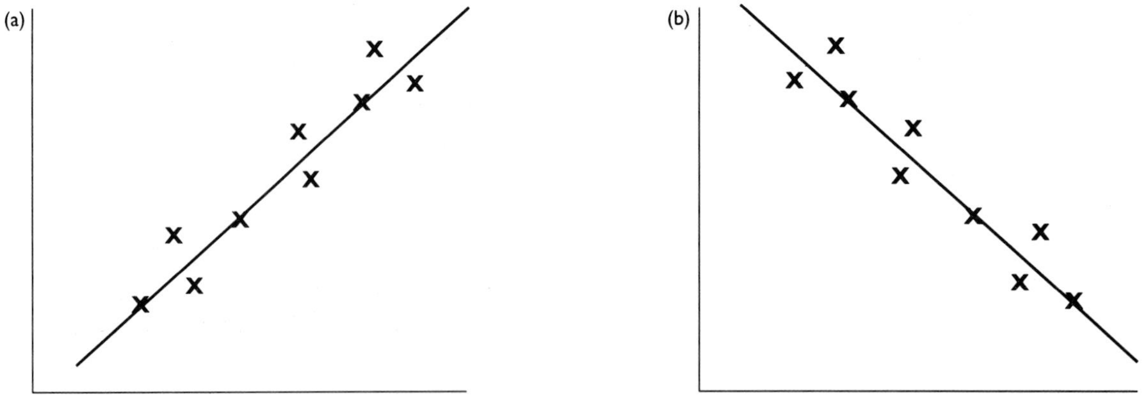

Figure 8.3 (a) Positive correlation; (b) negative correlation

correct alternative in each of the following statements:

- When there is a positive correlation, as measurements of one variable increase, the measurements of the other variable tend to *decrease/increase/stay the same*.
- When there is a negative correlation, as measurements of one variable increase, the measurements of the other variable tend to *decrease/increase/stay the same*.
- When there is no relationship between the measurements of two variables, the variables show a *positive/negative/zero correlation*.

2 Did your first scattergram (of height and shoe size) show a positive or negative correlation?

3 Which of the following pairs of variables do you think would show a positive correlation, which do you think would show a negative correlation and which would show no correlation?

- the cost of 100 g of a food and the energy content (kJ) of the food (you may find this an interesting topic to research).
- the length of gestation and the birthweight of a baby.
- the number of cigarettes smoked per week by pregnant women and the length of gestation.
- the age of a person and skin elasticity.
- the breathing rate and pulse rate in a number of people performing a standard exercise (research this yourself using at least ten volunteers).

4 Try to think of one further example of your own of positive correlation, one example of negative correlation and one example of zero correlation.

A word of warning: Even if a correlation can be shown between two variables, it does not necessarily mean that one *causes* the change in the other. There may be another variable (or variables) involved which causes the correlation. This is illustrated by the following example:

Over the past 40 years there has been a steady trend to hospitalise all mothers in labour. In Britain, 99 per cent of mothers now deliver in hospital. This shift away from home has coincided with a steady drop in the perinatal mortality rate (meaning the percentage of babies who are stillborn or who die shortly after birth). But just because two things happen simultaneously doesn't mean that one causes the other. Reduced perinatal mortality reflects all sorts of things, such as improved maternal health, smaller family size and better nutrition.

Exactly where people give birth may be irrelevant. Currently, a third of all Dutch mothers deliver at home, and the perinatal mortality in Holland is roughly the same as ours.

(The Observer Sunday Magazine, 25 October 1992)

And a more trivial example:

Between 1981 and 1988, consumption of white bread in the UK fell by 29 per cent.

Between 1981 and 1988, convictions for bigamy in the UK fell by 29 per cent.

Eating white bread causes marital complications.

(The Observer Sunday Magazine, 6 November 1992)

ACTIVITY

Suggestion for an investigation using a correlation study

It is widely accepted that smoking has a negative effect on health, although demonstrating this is not always easy.

How does smoking actually affect the physical condition of people? Is there a relationship between the number of cigarettes smoked and indicators of physical fitness?

A correlation study could be used to investigate this issue, and your task is to design and execute a study to determine whether there is a relationship between cigarette smoking and one or more health indicators of your choice. (For example, the number of step-ups done in one minute; pulse rate after a short period of vigorous exercise; time for this pulse rate to return to the resting rate.) Write:

- your hypothesis;
- methods (including precautions taken to fix as many variables as possible);
- results (plot a scattergram with line of best fit if appropriate);
- conclusions (is a correlation likely? If there is, is it negative or positive?);
- discussion (i.e. consider the limitations of your methods and suggest improvements).

Quantitative methods in social science research: surveys and field research

Is it appropriate for social scientists, in their study of human behaviour, to use the experimental and quantitative methods of research employed by natural scientists such as physicists and chemists? Can social scientists be *objective* (free of any subjective elements, desires, biases and preferences) when they choose areas of research and carry out and interpret the results of their studies? Is it possible for social scientists to explain and predict, with levels of certainty equivalent to those claimed by natural scientists investigating non-human or biological phenomena, reasons for human behaviour?

This debate can be studied in more depth by reference to most A Level or undergraduate textbooks in sociology or psychology. What we can highlight here are the *possibilities* and *problems* associated with the use of quantitative methods by social scientists. These can be briefly outlined as follows.

POSSIBILITIES

- Through the use of social surveys, researchers can gain information from a large number of people. From this information, generalisations about the population as a whole can be made.
- Questions can be pre-set and, because everyone can be asked the same questions, answers can be compared. If respondents fill in their own answers, there is no problem of interviewer bias.
- The form of a survey can vary widely, ranging from, at one extreme, a long list of closed, short-answer or multiple-choice questions to, at the other, a fairly brief list of structured but 'open-ended' questions

forming an 'interview schedule'.

- A pilot survey can be carried out to test the appropriateness, validity and wording of the questions asked.
- Surveys can be administered relatively cheaply and easily. With the aid of computers, the results can be collated swiftly and accurately.
- Large-scale surveys, such as the ten-yearly Census, can generate massive amounts of vital information for use by government departments, social scientists and others.

PROBLEMS

- Choosing a representative sample is not always straightforward. If samples are biased in a particular direction, the results of the survey may be open to criticism.
- The wording of questions in surveys can be extremely difficult to get right. Ambiguous questions can lead to confusion on the part of the respondent and to non-comparable answers.
- The answers to open-ended questions are often difficult to classify and interpret. Closed questions do not always allow the respondent to answer in the way he or she would want. All questions can be interpreted differently by people. They may not be answered honestly or with much care or thought.
- Information from surveys can 'date' very quickly. Large-scale analysis of a mass of complex data may not, in the end, prove much use if events have outstripped the findings of the survey.
- A legally enforceable survey, such as the Census, may ensure a high response rate. Other researchers may be less successful in finding people willing to complete their surveys.

In practice, many social scientists use a wide range of variety of methods of research, both quantitative and qualitative. Some social scientists find this distinction between types of research in itself limiting. Quantitative research in the natural and social sciences often has a higher status and prestige than qualitative research, despite the fact that many researchers find that different methods of research can complement each other by compensating for the inadequacies in any single methodology. Others suggest that the use of observation or interviews in field research can also involve the rigorous and careful collection and analysis of data. In the study of health and illness, social scientists often work closely with natural scientists, sharing and combining methods and approaches.

Quantitative methods in social science research therefore usually involve several of the following elements.

- *Sampling*, i.e. the careful consideration of the representativeness of the group of people/documents/situations chosen for study.
- *Counting*, i.e. precise enumeration of a particular phenomenon recorded by answers to survey questions, observed in field research or a laboratory: for example, how often and why a person takes vigorous physical exercise per day.
- *A comparative method*, i.e. the comparison and/or contrast of two or more similar or different variables occurring in the sample in question: for example, how often *men* and *women* (the variable being sex) take physical exercise per day and the different reasons they may have for doing so.
- The generation and testing of *hypotheses* and/or *generalisations* about the group of people being studied, i.e. suggesting and checking theories to accounting for existing or to predict future social phenomena. For example, a survey might indicate that if people take little vigorous physical exercise, they are more likely to be overweight, unhealthy and enjoy life less.

HALF OF ADULTS IN ENGLAND 'LIKELY TO FAIL FITNESS TEST'

Eighty per cent of people believe themselves to

be fit, about half of them wrongly, according to a survey published yesterday.

In addition, Dr Jacky Chambers, director of Public Health at the Health Education Authority, said that half of the male population was now overweight, compared with four out of ten in 1982, and four out of ten women were overweight compared with three out of ten, 10 years ago.

'If we continue at this rate the majority of the adult population will be overweight by the year 2000,' she said.

Nearly 4,500 adults took part in the survey which involved questions about lifestyle, diet, and physical activity and their attitude to it. Then researchers measured their fitness.

The report defines levels of fitness into five grades; from exercising vigorously on more than 12 occasions in the previous four weeks to deliberately not taking any exercise.

It defines vigorous activity as brisk hill-walking, playing squash and running; or tennis, football and cycling provided the participant got a bit sweaty and out of breath.

Moderate activity would be heavy housework or heavy gardening, swimming, tennis, football or cycling if not out of breath; or a long walk at a fast pace. Light activity would include long walks at a slow pace, DIY, fishing or darts and social dancing and 'exercises', if not out of breath.

ACTIVITY LEVEL SCALE

Level	Activity of 20 minutes in previous 4 weeks
Level 5	12+ occasions of vigorous activity
Level 4	12+ occasions of moderate/vigorous activity
Level 3	12+ occasions of moderate activity
Level 2	5–11 occasions of moderate/vigorous activity
Level 1	1–4 occasions of moderate/vigorous activity
Level 0	None

TARGETS

Age	Target levels
16–34	Activity level 5
35–54	Activity level 4
55–74	Activity level 3

(The Independent, 16 June 1992)

MOST ADULTS TOO UNFIT FOR A HEALTHY LIFE

Seven out of 10 men and eight out of 10 women in England do not take enough exercise to keep themselves healthy, according to the largest ever survey into activity levels.

The survey, published yesterday by the Health Education Authority and the Sports Council, interviewed 4,316 adults over the age of 16 about daily activity including sports and recreation pastimes, with two-thirds of the group being given laboratory assessments of fitness levels.

Among 16–24 year olds, 70 per cent of men and 91 per cent of women were below activity levels necessary for a fit and healthy life.

Professor Peter Fenton, head of physiology at Nottingham University, who acted as scientific adviser to the survey, said although the levels of unfitness came as no surprise, they had to be scientifically quantified, if policies were to be formulated to improve activity levels.

The survey divided activity levels into five categories, with level five being people who exercised vigorously at least 12 times for 20 minutes or more in the previous four weeks, and level zero those who took no exercise.

	Men (%)	Women (%)
Level 5	14	4
Level 4	12	12
Level 3	23	27
Level 2	18	25
Level 1	16	18
Level 0	17	16

(The Guardian, 16 June 1992)

ACTIVITY

Look at the two newspaper reports of a survey carried out by the Health Education Authority and the Sports Council on fitness levels among the adult British population. Then answer the following questions.

1 What was the size of the sample chosen for the study?

2 Would you describe this as a large-scale or small-scale sample. Why?

3 Which methods of research did the study choose to use in attempting to measure fitness levels?

4 What variables among the overall sample were the researchers comparing?

5 What elements of this study could be described as:
(a) mainly of interest to biologists?
(b) mainly of interest to sociologists and psychologists?

6 A hypothesis (in this case a future prediction) is suggested by the Director of Public Health for the HEA as a result of this survey. What is it?

7 Briefly summarise the results of this survey. Given the information you have about the survey in the extracts above, how reliable and valid do you think this survey is?

Sampling

Once a particular research problem has been identified, the question of WHOM TO STUDY arises. Defining the population to be studied usually involves deciding upon a SAMPLE. There are various methods for choosing the type of sample most appropriate to the research in question.

The SAMPLING FRAME is a list from which the sample is chosen. Some examples are:

- The Small User Post Office Address File (PAF), which gives addresses and postcodes of all domestic residences in the UK.
- The Electoral Register, which lists names and addresses of all registered voters in the UK.
- A list of all schools, colleges and institutes of higher education in a particular area.
- A list of all students enrolled in an institution.

ACTIVITY

As you have seen, sampling frames can be large scale or small scale. What other sampling frames might researchers into health and social care issues use?

TYPES OF SAMPLING

Random sampling

A random sample ensures that every member of the sampling frame has an equal chance of selection. This can be undertaken by:

- selecting every, for example, fifth name on a list;
- putting each name on the list on a slip of paper and drawing the required number from a closed box, as in a raffle;
- using tables of random numbers. By numbering the members of the sampling frame, the tables then indicate to the researcher which numbers to select for interview. There are computer facilities for this procedure if very large samples are used.

In general, the larger the sample, the more likely it is that 'randomness' is achieved. However, this method can be expensive and must be strictly adhered to if it is chosen. If the random numbering has indicated that the resident of number 10 Tree Walk is to be interviewed, but he/she is then found to be unavailable or will not cooperate, residents in numbers 8 or 12 will not 'do' instead. The respondent is 'lost' from the survey.

If applied carefully to large samples, this method is the most likely to ensure that the sample is representative of all sections of the wider population.

Stratified random sampling

This method is used when researchers want to 'match' the subgroups in their overall sample with the size of particular subgroups in the population studied.

For example, a researcher wishes to study the attitudes towards trade unions among the whole staff of a particular hospital. Having consulted the sampling frame, which in this case might be a list of all hospital employees, the researcher calculates that 60% of the hospital staff are women and that 40% are men.

When choosing her sample of hospital staff to interview, she therefore randomly selects from this staffing list a sample made up of 60% women and 40% men. She has thus matched the proportions in her sample with the proportions existing in the staff as a whole.

ACTIVITY

The main problem with stratified random sampling is how to ensure that the sampling frame used can be divided into the categories or subgroups the researcher requires. It might be easy, for example, to work out the sex of employees from a list such as the one mentioned in the case above; but what difficulties might a researcher face in dividing up a list of hospital employees by:

- ethnic origin?
- social class?
- age?
- type of job?

Quota sampling

In this type of sampling, a 'sampling frame' is often unnecessary. Quota samples are often used when the researcher wants a certain number of people in a number of defined categories. Filling a quota sample therefore involves deciding upon what numbers of respondents to include in any category and then interviewing those respondents until the quota is 'full'.

For example, an interviewer may have been given instructions to interview 20 people aged over 65 and 20 people aged 45–64 on their attitudes towards diet, health and lifestyle. Standing outside a local supermarket, the interviewer gradually fills up the 'quotas' in each age category.

However, the final sample may be unrepresentative of these age groups in the population as a whole. Two ways in which this could come about are:

- a special offer at the supermarket for cut-price cigarettes that day may have attracted relatively more smokers than usual into the quota sample.
- the people who actually agree to stop and answer the questions may have a particular interest in the topic being researched.

How might this lack of genuine randomness affect the study?

Non-representative or convenience sampling

There are occasions when the researcher cannot or does not wish to ensure representativeness in the sample. It is not always easy to gain access to the people you wish to study and contacts might have to be built up tentatively and as the opportunity arises. An initial contact with one interviewee might lead him or her to suggest other suitable people to interview and the sample may be built up in that way ('snowballing'). Often a sample may be made up of subjects who are simply available in a convenient way to the researcher. This is often the case when 'sensitive' subjects are being researched. The following extract from Mary Eaton's book *Women after Prison* illustrates this process:

> At this stage I was fortunate in receiving encouragement and help from Women in Prison, particularly from the director. She contacted a number of women on my behalf and asked if they would be willing to be interviewed. All agreed – I do not know whether this was a result of the director's skill in choosing possible subjects or her persuasive powers when explaining the

project. I then telephoned each woman and arranged to meet her. In most cases the interviews took place in the woman's home, usually within the following two days. Five women were interviewed at their place of work in a voluntary sector organization. Three women were interviewed at the offices of WIP. One woman was interviewed at my office in Central London. One interview was conducted in a pub but later followed up at the offices of WIP.

When I first described the project to the director of WIP I said that I was interested in the prison experiences and post-prison experiences of all women and I asked that none should be excluded on the grounds of the untypicality of her crime or her circumstances. There was a deliberate decision at this stage to include four women imprisoned for action at Greenham Common. Three of these women (Barbara, Judith and Martha) felt that their experiences were too unlike those of other prisoners to be useful. However, there was in these differences the source of useful comment on the more usual experiences of other women prisoners. Throughout their sentences, members of the Greenham Common peace camp received letters and flowers from those outside. This lessened their sense of separation from the wider world. Indeed, these women were not excluded by their community and were continually reminded, through the letters and flowers, of their inclusion, by their actions, in the aims and objectives of camp members. However, even though prison was a rational choice, made to further the cause, and even with the extraordinary level of support that these women received, it was not enough to counteract the impact of prison on their sense of self. With less support and longer sentences other women are likely to be even more susceptible to the influences of the prison regime.

(Eaton, 1993)

In practical terms this is likely to be the method of sampling most used in student research. This is perfectly acceptable as long as the risk of bias is duly noted.

Question wording

This is a surprisingly difficult part of constructing a questionnaire or interview schedule. If a large-scale piece of research is being carried out and the reliability of the data generated is therefore an important feature of the research, it is vital that the wording of questions is clear, unambiguous and likely to mean the same to researcher and respondent. This is also true of smaller-scale, face-to-face, less structured interviewing; but in this case there is at least the possibility of explaining, elaborating upon and probing further into the initial questions asked.

SOME TECHNIQUES IN QUESTION WORDING

Closed questions

The simplest method of asking questions is to give the respondent the choice of a fixed and limited number of pre-set possible answers. Closed questions can vary from a simple:

Have you ever been in hospital for an operation?

YES ☐ NO ☐

to a more complex series of options, such as:

What were your immediate feelings when waking up after your hospital operation? Please tick any which apply.

Drowsiness	☐
Nausea	☐
Disorientation	☐
Dizziness	☐
Panic	☐
Thirst	☐
Pain	☐
Discomfort	☐
Need to urinate	☐
Other (please state)	☐

The obvious advantage of closed questions is that the responses can be easily and quickly collated and analysed, perhaps using a computer. The disadvantage is that the respondent's range of possible replies is structured in advance and may therefore be unrepresentative of his or her 'true' feelings, or may fail to convey any complexity or ambiguity within them.

ACTIVITY

1 Suggest areas of research where closed questions might be useful and effective.

2 Design a short questionnaire using only closed questions.

Rating scales/semantic differential technique

Social scientists (in particular social psychologists) may use these question-wording techniques as part of a larger questionnaire or interview schedule, or as a complete piece of research in itself.

Rating scales are used to ascertain the respondent's attitudes across an established range of positions set by the researcher. They are useful for making comparisons across large samples of respondents relatively quickly and cheaply. They can take a variety of forms and combinations of forms.

Numerical rating scales explore ways in which people can use numerical measures to assess feelings. For example:

If 1 = low satisfaction and 10 = high satisfaction, on a scale of 1–10, how would you rate:

(a) the hospital care you received prior to your operation?
1 2 3 4 5 6 7 8 9 10
(please ring)
(b) the hospital care you received after your operation?
1 2 3 4 5 6 7 8 9 10
(please ring)

Written/verbal rating scales explore ways in which people can use words to assess and describe situations. For example:

How would you rate the hospital care you received prior to your operation?

(a) excellent ☐
(b) good ☐
(c) adequate ☐
(d) poor ☐
(e) very poor ☐

The SEMANTIC DIFFERENTIAL TECHNIQUE is a specialised method which:

allows a researcher to explore the similarities and the differences between perceptions of situations, people and things. It is an underlying assumption of the technique, that certain words have similar meanings for different individuals.

The technique offers subjects a series of bipolar dimensions along which they rate themselves, other people or activities. For example, a subject may be asked to consider his/her ability to care. This is done by placing a tick on a scale like the one below. Ratings along the scale can be compared.

(Burnard and Morrison, 1990)

CHARTS or other GRAPHICAL methods may be used to provide respondents with a means of rating attitudes, ideas, feelings, etc. For example, the respondent may be asked to use the chart shown in Figure 8.4 to rate the general state of his/her health at different life periods.

Open questions

These are simply open-ended questions to which respondents are invited to reply in any way they wish. For example:

Do you regard yourself as a healthy person? Why or why not?

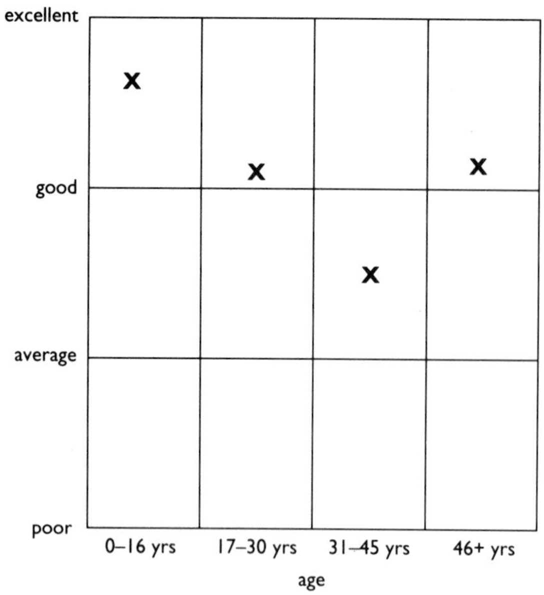

Figure 8.4 Chart for rating health
Source: Burnard and Morrison (1990), *Nursing Research in Action* (Macmillan).

The answers to open questions can provide more detailed and interesting answers but can prove difficult to analyse.

ACTIVITY

Write an open-ended question on any subject which interests you and ask everyone in your class or your family to write an answer. How can the answers you receive be analysed and summarised?

Leading questions

Questions which, through the use of emotive language or suggestiveness, 'lead' to a certain type of response should be avoided. An example might be: 'Do you think that dentists are completely wrong to refuse absolutely to take new adult NHS patients?'

Administering questionnaires in survey research

All research costs money and researchers have to consider the most effective way of using the money available to them. Spending much time and effort constructing a survey which then achieves a LOW RESPONSE RATE is disappointing for all concerned.

A range of factors can affect the likelihood of achieving a high or low response rate to a piece of research. A study carried out by Kay Wellings *et al.* (1994), *Sexual Behaviour in Britain: The National Survey of Sexual Attitudes and Lifestyles*, is used here to illustrate the range of factors involved in choosing a method of delivery for a piece of research.

This study, sponsored by the Wellcome Trust, was interested in two broad questions:

- What patterns of sexual behaviour exist in the population of the UK, and how might these contribute to the spread of HIV/AIDS?
- What patterns of sexual behaviour exist in the population of the UK, and how might these contribute to an understanding of the ways to prevent the spread of HIV/AIDS?

The researchers wished to choose a method of delivery for their research which would:

- achieve a very large overall random sample and therefore ensure representativeness and the sampling of sufficiently high proportions of minority, uncommon sexual behaviours;
- overcome the problems in administering a survey on very sensitive, personal issues associated with sexual practices, experience and behaviours.

POSTAL QUESTIONNAIRES were therefore rejected. Although sending questionnaires through the post and requesting that respondents post them back when completed is a relatively cheap and straightforward method, other studies using postal questionnaires have found that the response rate is often as low as 30%. In the sensitive subject area of this survey, the response rate was likely to be even lower – or might only reflect a 'self-selected sample' of those who had a particular interest in the subject matter of the survey.

TELEPHONE INTERVIEWS were also rejected. Again, these are convenient and relatively easy

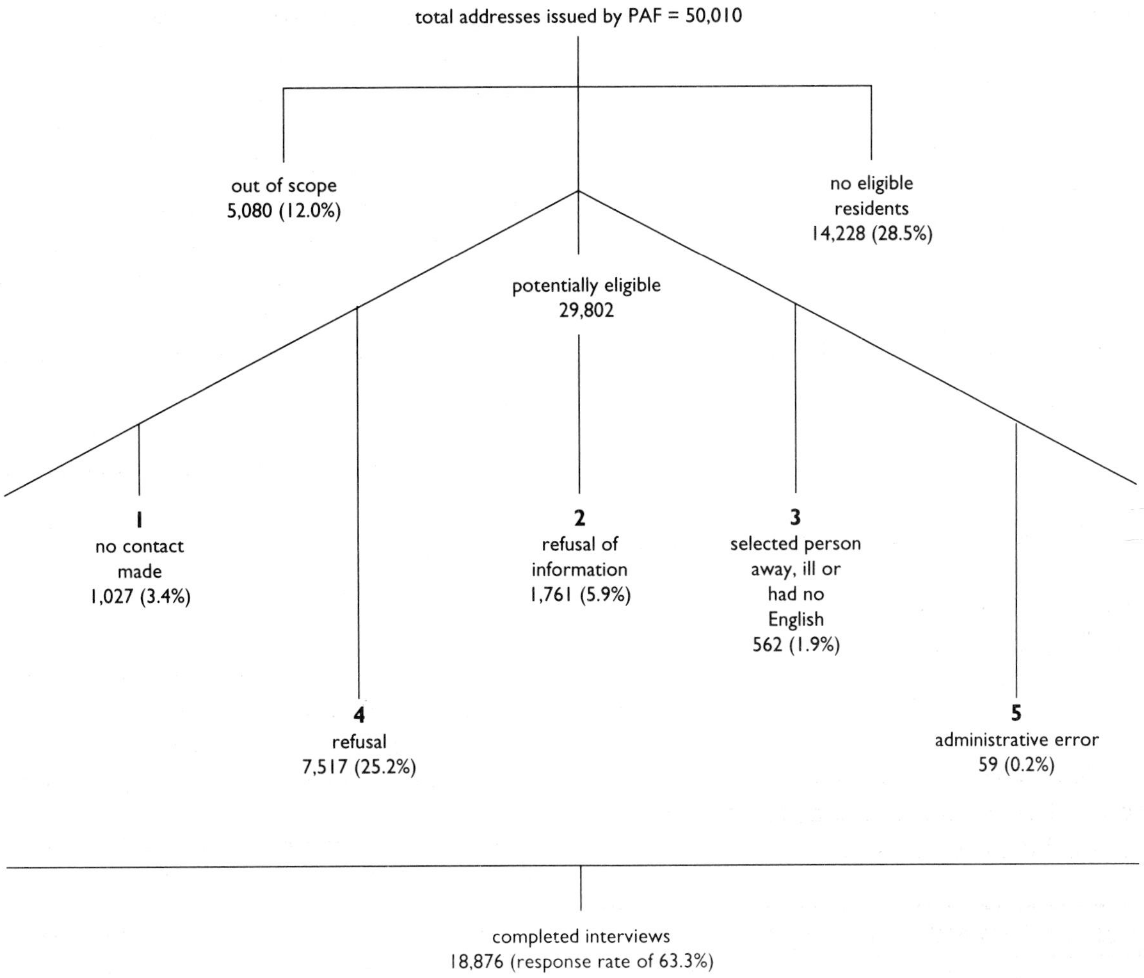

Figure 8.5 500 interviewers attempted to interview a total of 50,000 people aged between 16 and 59 in their homes

to carry out, but in this sensitive area the interviewer could not be sure who might be in the same room as any interviewee and what inhibiting effect this might have on interviewees' responses.

Finally it was decided to employ and train a team of 500 interviewers who would VISIT and attempt to interview people aged between 16 and 59 in their homes. Fifty thousand names and addresses were selected from the PAF (see the section on 'Sampling'), covering 100 electoral wards representative of metropolitan, urban and rural areas in the UK.

Figure 8.5 shows the response rate to this survey.

ACTIVITY

1 Make a list of reasons why researchers may not achieve a 100% response rate to their research.

2 What methods could researchers employ to minimise the risks of a low response rate?

Interviews

For many people the word 'interview' conjures up two types of image. On the one hand there is the stressful, very formal and often highly structured situation of a job interview or, for children, an interview with a headteacher. On the other hand there is the seemingly relaxed, spontaneous, jokey and conversational interviewing of the famous or not so famous by television or radio presenters such as Terry Wogan or Chris Tarrant. Some people may also have experienced MARKET RESEARCH, where they have been interviewed by someone employed by a company or agency and asked for their opinion on and consumption patterns of a specific product or service.

TYPES OF INTERVIEW

Social scientists use a similar range of types of interview with individuals or groups of people. There are some situations where highly structured interviews using pre-set lists of questions and a fairly formal relationship between interviewer and interviewee may be more appropriate and may suit the research aims of the study. For example, if the researcher wishes to interview a fairly large number of people reasonably quickly to compare their experiences, attitudes, beliefs or intentions, it may be more practical, financially and methodologically, to conduct a structured interview. The researcher may use a pre-designed QUESTIONNAIRE (a list of questions for self-completion by the respondent) or an INTERVIEW SCHEDULE (a list of questions to be asked by the interviewer, face to face or on the telephone).

AMBIGUITY

The structured interview is most successfully used where there is likely to be the least ambiguity over the wording and possible interpretations of the questions.

Problems arise when interviewees experience difficulty in understanding the intended meaning of a question. Interviewers may then have to prompt or explain questions and in so doing may unintentionally 'steer' the respondent towards a particular response to a question.

ACTIVITY

Study the following interview schedule.

Which of the following questions might raise problems of interpretation?

1 Are you a
(a) vegetarian
(b) non-vegetarian?
(Please tick)

Questions for vegetarians

2 How long have you followed this healthy lifestyle?

3 Are you a vegetarian:
(a) for health reasons?
(b) for political reasons?
(c) for social reasons?
(d) for religious reasons?
(e) other (please state)?
Please tick the one above that applies to you.

4 How do you think most other people react to you being a vegetarian?
(a) very positively;
(b) regard you as 'deviant' or 'strange'.

Questions for non-vegetarians

5 How many times have you eaten meat today?

6 How do you feel about people who kill animals?

Try rewriting this short interview schedule on vegetarianism and non-vegetarianism, making the questions as unambiguous and as clear as possible.

Some social scientists believe that if an interviewer does intentionally or unintentionally prompt or steer respondents towards certain answers, the research data are then invalidated because one can never be really certain that the interviewee's 'true' feelings, beliefs, attitudes and intentions have been established. There is the suspicion that the research data have become 'tainted' by the values, perspectives and approach of the interviewer and are thus no longer objective.

INTERVIEWING TECHNIQUE

Other social scientists suggest that this issue is less important than using an interview technique which is designed to elicit the most detailed and insightful information about the lives of the people being studied. Unstructured, informal, open-ended interviewing encourages the interviewer:

- to be flexible;
- to respond to what the interviewee is saying;
- to probe a little deeper than surface attitudes and beliefs;
- to establish a relationship of mutual trust and confidence;
- to encourage the interviewee to relax and talk freely and thus allow the conversation to develop naturally.

In their study of mixed-race relationships, *The Colour of Love*, Yasmin Alibhai-Brown and Anne Montague say that the aim of the interviews they conducted with people (and their children) in mixed-race relationships was to gain insights by:

> asking people with immediate personal experience to talk about the subject – people who, through their relationships with partners, parents and children, have insights that no neat journalistic analysis or ponderous research tome can hope to capture ... The conversations were unstructured in a formal sense and self-determined by our interviewees. Their views were taken on board, they had access to us and we did not impose any pre-packaged notions on the people we spoke to.
>
> *(Alibhai-Brown and Montague, 1992)*

As with the more formal, structured interview, the open interview requires considerable care in preparing the ground to be covered in the interview and the range of possible questions/approaches to be taken, and the establishment of trust and a relaxed context in which to carry out the interviews.

Sometimes the interviewer may feel the need to interview the same person or group of people several times over a certain period, to allow time for ideas to develop or to note changes in attitudes and experiences during a particular period in the person's life.

The interviewer also has to make decisions about what might be the most appropriate techniques to 'get people talking'. Should the researcher:

- be non-directive?
- refrain from offering personal opinions?
- avoid approval or disapproval of what is said?
- be disingenuous and pretend to know less than he or she does?
- be aggressive and provocative?
- be sceptical?
- be totally honest about the aims of his or her questioning?

Alibhai-Brown and Montague (1992) made it clear that their approach to interviewing was NON-DIRECTIVE. Other sociologists have found problems in establishing a relationship with interviewees if the issue under discussion frequently turns into argument rather than discussion. Signifying an understanding of what the interviewee is saying, rather than agreement or disagreement, may ease the progress of the interview, even if in practice this may give the impression that the interviewer agrees with what is being said when he or she does not. This technique may be useful where there are relatively minor areas of disagreement. Where potentially explosive areas of conflict might arise between the interviewer's own social, political, religious and moral perspectives and those of the interviewee, it makes more sense to avoid this method of research altogether or to deliberately choose issues more likely to coincide with the researcher's own interests. Many social scientists have noted that women find it easier to interview women, and men to interview men. As Ann Oakley, a feminist sociologist, has said: 'The point is that academic research projects bear an intimate relationship to the researcher's life; however 'scientific' a sociologist pretends to be, personal dramas provoke ideas that generate books and research projects.' (Oakley, 1981)

'PUBLIC' AND 'PRIVATE' ACCOUNTS

Some of the very complex and less immediately obvious problems with interviews are discussed by Jocelyn Cornwall in her book *Hard-Earned Lives*, an enquiry into people's experiences of health and illness and health services which focuses upon the lives of 24 people who live in East London (Cornwall, 1984).

Cornwall used interviews which were constructed around a schedule of topics. She included some standard questions which were put to everyone and also questions developed specifically for each individual each time he or she was interviewed. All interviews were recorded on tape and took place in people's homes. She interviewed the same people repeatedly and took her cue from them, 'to let them direct the course of the interview and to follow their interest in the topics proposed to them'.

The problem with interviews which Cornwall highlights is that differences in social class, gender, race and educational background between interviewer and interviewee, as well as the artificial situation of the interview itself, can result in the interviewees giving what Cornwall describes as 'public accounts' rather than 'private accounts' of situations they experience or ideas and beliefs they hold. By this Cornwall means that people tend to give the answers they feel would be acceptable to other people, not what they really think themselves. When Cornwall asked people to 'tell stories' about their experiences rather than answer questions, she found that interviewees could more readily control what they said and were less self-conscious and more likely to give both 'public' and 'private' accounts of experience. This helped Cornwall to explore the difference between the two and to link her findings to the major theme of her book: the relationship between medicine and the medical profession on the one hand and society – 'ordinary people' – on the other.

Despite these and other problems with interviewing, there is no doubt that many interviewees, given the opportunity to reflect upon, explore and analyse their beliefs and ideas in a relatively systematic way, find the experience extremely positive. Alibhai-Brown and Montague (1992) claim that:

> The people we talked to gave us endless amounts of time and coffee and allowed us intimate access to their lives, even when it was incredibly painful or when, as well-known figures, they could so easily have held back. Some people found the conversations cathartic after years of burying feelings about the issue. Others talked to each other as we talked to them, often for the first time, about their worries and realisations. Some claim to have found renewed joy and vigour by being forced to excavate the past and remember what they gave up in order to be with one another. Theirs were exceptional insights.

ACTIVITY

In practice, social scientists adapt the interview method (open or more formal) to the particular situation to be researched. Discuss which types of interview might work best in the following research projects:

1. A study of nurses' experiences of sexual and/or racial discrimination in the NHS.

2. A study of refugees in Britain to establish their health needs and the use they make of the health services.

3. A study of returning overseas travellers to investigate the range of health-related

problems they experienced while abroad.

4 A study to compare the experiences of fundholding GPs with those who are not fundholders. (In 1991, 1,720 GPs in 306 practices became fundholders.)

5 A study looking at the causes of Sudden Infant Death Syndrome (SIDS). In England and Wales about two infant deaths per 1,000 live births are attributed to SIDS.

Case studies

Case studies are most commonly used when the researcher wishes to focus, in depth, upon individual people, small groups, an organisation, a community, a nation or an event. The aim of the case study is usually to throw light on wider issues by studying carefully the case in question. Factors which exist in one case may need to be taken into account when explaining others. The researcher recognises that the case chosen may not be typical (and would therefore have to exercise caution in making generalisations), but may use the case study to do the following:

- Study the lives of particular individuals – particularly if they have made a significant political, historical or social impact upon the world. For example, studying the life of Marie Stopes would reveal social attitudes towards contraception, sex and abortion in the late nineteenth and early twentieth centuries.
- Develop a better professional understanding of a client, group of clients or institution (the method here being more akin to a case history).
- Provide a base or 'trial run' for larger-scale research by generating hypotheses and indicating at least some of the facts and situations which will need to be taken into account.
- Give a basis for comparison between two or more similar cases (NHS Trust and non-Trust hospitals) or between two or more apparently different cases (NHS and private-sector hospitals).
- Look at the lessons which could be learned from an apparently 'deviant' or 'atypical' case. The film *The Silence of the Lambs* illustrated the way in which psychologists, criminologists and psychiatrists are currently interested in studying the individual cases of serial killers and psychopaths in the hope that this will lead to an understanding of the pathologies of other killers and make detection and arrest easier.
- 'Balance' or 'give colour to' a large-scale quantitative study by selecting cases which graphically illustrate some of the issues in question. For example, a researcher studying the extent to which an 'alternative' therapy, such as homoeopathy or acupuncture, is used in Britain may illustrate any statistical data generated by the study with a number of detailed, descriptive cases of the users of such therapies. This technique is often used in the 'investigative reporting' of TV documentaries such as *Panorama*, *Public Eye*, etc., and in print journalism.

The key problem with case studies is the question of the VALIDITY of wider generalisations based on the often rich and detailed insights generated by this method. Therefore case studies are often best used in conjunction with other methods of research.

ACTIVITY

1 Consider the GP surgery you use. If you were asked to carry out a case study of the way this surgery was run, how might you approach this task? What factors do you think might make it typical or atypical of other GP surgeries in your area?

2 What useful insights might a case study of this kind give you?

3 How might the ideas generated from this case study be used in a larger-scale piece of research?

Observation

Of all the research methods mentioned in this chapter, observation is possibly the most difficult to carry out skilfully. This may seem strange, because we spend our lives observing, using a variety of senses, albeit with very different and constantly changing levels of attention and perception. For example, what different kinds of observation might be involved in the following situations?

- a mother or father looking at their newly-born child;
- a teacher watching and listening to children in his or her class discuss a project in a lesson;
- staring out of the window of a bus;
- noticing your friend has had a haircut;
- meeting your girlfriend's or boyfriend's parents for the first time.

To each of these situations we bring feelings, emotions, memories of past experiences and knowledge. We make judgements on the basis of our observations and these ideas go on to structure the way we continue to 'see' situations or people. For much of the time we do not question or doubt our observations – although we can be discomfited if someone 'sees' a situation differently from us, as this reminds us that our perceptions are not necessarily the only ones possible.

For those working in the caring professions, whether they are carrying out 'research' or not, careful observation becomes a vital skill, one which is practised and improved. Social workers may need to make careful and sensitive observations about people's circumstances and behaviour, for example in assessing whether a child should remain in the care of his or her parents. Residential workers and foster-parents may have to look out for signs of distress or unhappiness. Nurses will become skilled in detecting physical and psychological changes in the patients in their care. The professional practice of observation is similar to the social science use of observation as a research tool, in that both are conscious and deliberate 'ways of looking': there are specific reasons for the observation.

REASONS FOR OBSERVATION

Perhaps the researcher wishes deliberately to take part in a social situation or join a social group which has previously been unfamiliar to him or her. The aim of the study is to understand and attempt to explain to others how the people the researcher is studying 'see' the world from their PERSPECTIVE. Sociologists have studied the behaviour and attitudes of groups of people 'from the inside' either by joining them COVERTLY (i.e. by deception and pretending to be 'one of them' and/or by joining them but not revealing the nature of the research which is being carried out) or OVERTLY (by openly joining groups and getting to know the people involved extremely well). Here social scientists aim to remind us about what we in our everyday lives can easily forget, ignore or misunderstand – what it might be like to 'be' other people in social situations very different from our own. Observational studies of the mentally ill, of criminals and deviants, of gangs and of religious sects have frequently been carried out for this reason.

Alternatively, a researcher may wish to observe others systematically, over specific periods of time, to 'test' whether a usual, taken-for-granted or commonsense perception of a situation is actually accurate. Most people do not have time for such systematic observation, but social scientists are interested in the ways patterns of interaction and behaviour develop and come to define and structure particular situations. Some social scientists, for example, are interested in the differences between what people say happens, or what they think will happen, in certain situations and the actual events which occur – including apparently unintended consequences.

In this context, there have been studies of classroom behaviour – looking for patterns in the interactions observed and asking questions which seem to arise from these observations, e.g.

- Do boys receive more attention than girls from teachers?
- In what ways does the behaviour of boys and girls in classes differ?
- What consequences do these patterns appear to have for the lives of the individuals involved?

There are also occasions when researchers wish to record and analyse their observations of particular situations or behaviours in an extremely structured way. Here social experiments (in 'the field' or in a laboratory) may be set up in a way very similar to experiments used by natural scientists (see the section on 'Experiments' earlier in this chapter). Some examples of experiments of this kind are discussed throughout this book.

DIFFICULTIES IN OBSERVATION

There are two key difficulties in using observation as a method of research, each of which you can test out for yourself by trying out the Activity in this section:

- Does the presence of the observer (covert or overt) alter the behaviour of those observed in any way? Does this make a difference to the situation he or she is observing? Does it matter?
- Is it possible to observe situations objectively, without any preconceptions or prejudices which might alter the way you 'see' things?

ACTIVITY

1 When next using a bus or a train, spend a few minutes actively observing the people around you. Do not read or look out of the window but instead closely observe the passengers. You could (mentally) count them; try to put them into categories; decide what they might have been doing and where they might be going; observe who is talking to whom, and so on.

Did your active observation of the passengers make any difference to them? Can you think of situations where observation may make a difference?

2 Observe any situation with which you are very familiar – a family meal, for example. First write a paragraph describing this situation. Then write a paragraph trying to describe this situation as if you and the person reading your description had never seen or experienced that situation before.

Do your accounts differ? If so, why might this have happened?

METHODS OF ENQUIRY USING SECONDARY SOURCES

Secondary sources of data are very useful in identifying patterns and trends over time. They can be used in two contrasting ways:

- They can be examined and then a hypothesis can be formulated.
- They can be used to test an existing hypothesis.

Official statistics

Advantages:

- Statistics are readily available on a wide range of issues (see suggestions of sources on page 424).
- Research based on secondary data is cheaper than that involving the collection of primary data.

Table 8.1 Population age and sex structure 1991, and changes by age, England, 1981–91

Age (in years)	Resident population at mid-1991 (thousands) Persons	Males	Females	Percentage changes (persons) 1981–91	1988–89	1989–90	1990–91
Under 1	663	339	324	10.8	−0.8	0.9	2.3
1–4	2,575	1,318	1,257	15.2	2.5	1.1	1.3
5–15	6,465	3,318	3,147	−13.2	−0.6	0.6	0.9
16–29	10,206	5,191	5,016	3.5	−0.5	−1.1	−1.6
30–44	10,153	5,084	5,069	10.7	0.7	1.0	1.2
45–64/59*	9,122	5,138	3,984	0.2	0.8	0.8	0.9
65/60–74**	5,436	1,897	3,539	−3.7	−0.5	−0.4	0.1
75–84	2,618	968	1,650	16.4	1.4	0.6	−0.2
85+	770	199	571	50.6	5.0	3.9	4.1
All ages	48,008	23,451	24,557	2.5	0.3	0.3	0.4

*45–64 years for males and 45–59 years for females.
**65–74 years for males and 60–74 years for females.
Notes: i. Figures may not add precisely to totals due to rounding.
ii. These estimates are based on the 1981 Census with allowance for subsequent changes. Revised estimates will be prepared, first for mid-1991 and eventually for earlier years, when 1991 Census results become available.
Source: OPCS.

Disadvantages:

- Not all statistics are reliable. They may include biases and inaccuracies.
- The researcher must find out how concepts have been defined and measured. This might have changed over time.

Tables 8.1 and 8.2 give examples of information published by the Office of Population Censuses and Surveys (OPCS).

ACTIVITY

1 Study Table 8.1. Then answer the following questions:
- Which age group has shown the most rapid increase in number?
- Suggest possible reasons for this increase (i.e. formulate hypotheses to account for the increase).
- If you were to test these hypotheses, what statistics would you require access to?
- Do these statistics support the hypothesis 'Women are more likely to live longer than men'.

2 Formulate *two* hypotheses supported by observations made from Table 8.2.
- Can you think of possible explanations for these trends?
- On what basis are people allotted to a social class?

Table 8.2 Mean age of women at first live birth within marriage, according to social class of husband, England, 1981, 1990 and 1991

Social class of husband	Mean age of women at first birth within marriage 1981	1990	1991
All social classes	25.4	27.2	27.5
I and II	27.6	28.7	29.0
III Non-manual	26.1	27.4	27.7
III Manual	24.5	26.4	26.7
IV and V	23.4	25.3	25.8

Note: Figures for social class are based on a 10% sample.
Source: OPCS.

USEFUL SOURCES OF OFFICIAL STATISTICS

Official reports and other government

documents are available from HMSO (for address see list at end of chapter).

The Department of Health produces:

- *The Health Service in England* (annual report).
- *On the State of the Public Health* (the annual report of the Chief Medical Officer of the Department of Health).
- Health and Personal Social Services Statistics for England.

The Office of Population Censuses and Surveys (OPCS) publishes annual medical and population tables published in separate, topic-oriented volumes on: family statistics, deaths, morbidity, population estimates and projections, births, cancer, communicable diseases, congenital malformations, demographic review, general household survey, hospital in-patient enquiry, labour force, longitudinal study, marriage and divorce, abortion statistics, migration, local authority vital statistics and electoral statistics.

Content analysis

Content analysis is most commonly used when studying the output of forms of the mass media (television, radio, newspaper, magazines, books, film, music on disc/tape/LP, etc.), although the content of other documents may also be worthy of systematic study. Photographs, letters, official documents, reports and pictures/drawings can all be used to look at the ways in which *issues*, *groups of people* (such as those with mental disorders, drug users or AIDS sufferers) or *images* are most commonly represented. Different forms of content can be compared and the question of BIAS can then be raised. Because reporting in television and newspapers has been shown to be biased, it is more useful to use this method to show *how an item is reported*, rather than as a *source of information*.

CARRYING OUT A CONTENT ANALYSIS

The first step is to identify an area of concern to investigate and then to establish the purpose of the investigation: for example, the way in which tabloid and broadsheet newspapers report cases of AIDS sufferers could be compared. A clearer 'picture' of the range of images most commonly shown makes it possible to go on to discuss the potential impact of these images on audiences and the public.

ACTIVITY

Think of other issues related to health and social care which could be explored through content analysis. How many can you list? Why do you think this form of investigation is suitable for them?

The next task is to devise a SCHEME OF ANALYSIS. Depending upon the issue and form of content chosen to study, this would usually involve:

- a QUANTITATIVE ASSESSMENT of the content examined (i.e. counting the number of times a theme or issue appears and recording the form in which it does so);
- the subsequent construction of THEORIES to interpret and explain the findings.

AN EXAMPLE OF CONTENT ANALYSIS

Hypothetical task: '*Examine the influence of the mass media upon the socialisation of young children, choosing a theme related to a health and social care context.*'

One possibility here would be to carry out a content analysis of children's TV programmes and/or advertising, choosing to focus upon one or more of the following issues which have prompted general public concern over the past decade or so:

- How do children interpret and react to violence on television? What implications does exposure to screen violence have for children's health and development?
- Are children absorbing sexist and/or racist images from children's television?
- In what ways might children's television programmes and advertising be influencing

their families' consumption of toys and games (e.g. video games)?
- Are standards of literacy and numeracy 'declining' because children are watching too much of the 'wrong' sort of television programmes (e.g. animation and cartoons, which may encourage more passive viewing, rather than programmes like *Blue Peter*, which encourage more active involvement)?

While content analysis in itself cannot provide a complete answer to any of these questions, it can be used to establish possible trends, effects and influences. Depending, therefore, upon the emphasis chosen for the investigation, the content analysis itself might involve one or more of the following elements over a specified period of time (a week, a month, longer . . .):

- An analysis of the hours devoted to children's programming on each television channel, including an assessment of the time devoted to each different type of programme (drama, animation, 'factual' programmes, etc.).
- An analysis of the timing of these children's programmes and/or advertising.
- An analysis of the age ranges catered for by the programmes.
- An analysis of comparisons between the content of specific programmes/adverts for their approach to issues of gender, race, disability, etc.

After carrying out such an analysis, some INTERPRETATION of the results needs to be carried out. This could lead to a theory or hypothesis explaining the phenomena/trends observed which may, in turn, be tested choosing different methods of research.

The crucial limitation of content analysis is that, in itself, it tells us nothing about how audiences might be interpreting or reacting to the media content or form of content chosen as the subject of study. It is a very useful method of research, however, for generating theories and hypotheses and is most productively employed in association with other methods of research.

Below is a report of the content analysis carried out by the Broadcasting Standards Council, published in *The Guardian*:

CHILDREN'S TV 'LEANS MORE ON CARTOONS'

The factual content of children's television has declined in favour of cartoons and entertainment formats, the Broadcasting Standards Council said yesterday.

It warned of a further creeping erosion, caused by the squeeze on funds, more severe competition for ratings and the reduced power of regulators to defend quality.

A council report reveals that ITV has cut spending on children's programmes by 40 per cent over the past five years – from £50 million to £30 million – and the BBC has cut its children's budget by 5 per cent a year over the past two years.

By 1991, more than half of BBC1's and ITV's children's hours were devoted to animation and other predominantly entertaining formats, up from between a quarter and a third in 1981.

One of the report's researchers, said that drama like the BBC's Chronicles of Narnia were high quality and sold well, but there was a danger that contemporary drama, without an overseas market, was at risk.

(The Guardian, 10 December 1992)

ACTIVITY

Study the extract from *The Guardian* on children's television.

1 What broad conclusions did this analysis reach regarding the content of children's television programming in 1991?

2 If you were asked to check whether these findings of the BSC still applied, using a fortnight's television programming for children over the next month, how would you go about this task?

3 Given the conclusions reached in the BSC study, can you suggest any possible hypotheses about how current children's programming might be affecting the children who watch? What other research methods could you employ to test your hypothesis?

Documents

A document is, broadly speaking, any written or graphic material which can generate data for research. The use of books, statistics and the media as secondary sources and for the purposes of content analysis has been discussed earlier in this chapter; here we will be concentrating upon the almost endless variety of other documents which can prove useful to researchers. These include:

- official and unofficial reports;
- minutes of meetings;
- memos and other records of the business and administration of organisations;
- publicity and promotional material;
- leaflets;
- diaries;

. . . and many others.

ACTIVITY

1 You have been asked to compare the way truancy is approached and dealt with in two secondary schools in your area.

What documents might you wish to study and analyse? Give reasons for your choices.

2 A student health visitor is carrying out research into how effectively new parents use the 'Personal Child Health Record' books issued in several health authorities to enable parents to record developments in their children's health – dates of vaccinations, visits to the GP, major illnesses, treatments, medicines prescribed, etc. (see Figure 8.6).

Assuming that the student has sought and gained permission from a sample of parents to look at their use of these 'Child Health' books, how might he or she go about analysing the information within them? What trends or patterns in their use might he or she look for? To what use might the information collected be put?

There are often problems associated with the use of documents. Medical records, which could prove an invaluable source of research material in the study of health and illness, are of course confidential while the person to whom they relate is still alive. The secrecy and non-availability in whole or in part of some documents is therefore a potential obstacle to research.

Researchers also need to check whether the documents they use are:

- complete and reliable;
- written with sincerity or written with the intention to mislead;
- representative.

WRITING UP A RESEARCH REPORT

Whatever your method of research, an essential element is communicating your findings to others.

For the basic guidelines on writing a research report, refer back to the section on 'Writing up an experiment' earlier in the chapter. These principles apply whether you are describing a simple experiment or a complex survey project – although for more involved pieces of research you will probably want to add an *introduction* after the abstract before you go on to describe your research method. This introduction should state your

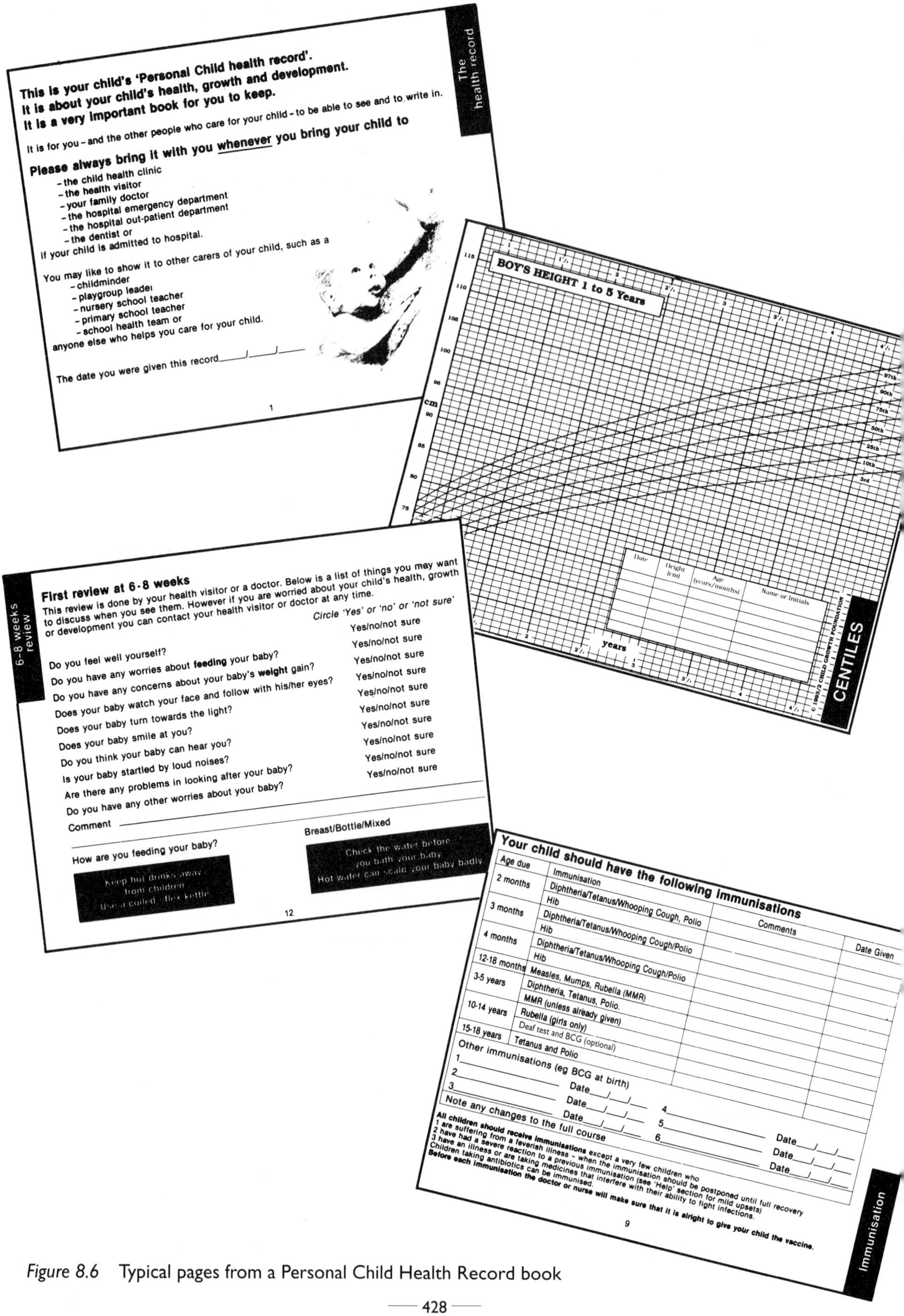

The health record

This is your child's 'Personal Child health record'.
It is about your child's health, growth and development.
It is a very important book for you to keep.

It is for you – and the other people who care for your child – to be able to see and to write in.

Please always bring it with you <u>whenever</u> you bring your child to
- the child health clinic
- the health visitor
- your family doctor
- the hospital emergency department
- the hospital out-patient department
- the dentist or

if your child is admitted to hospital.

You may like to show it to other carers of your child, such as a
- childminder
- playgroup leader
- nursery school teacher
- primary school teacher
- school health team or

anyone else who helps you care for your child.

The date you were given this record____/____/____

1

6-8 weeks review

First review at 6-8 weeks

This review is done by your health visitor or a doctor. Below is a list of things you may want to discuss when you see them. However if you are worried about your child's health, growth or development you can contact your health visitor or doctor at any time.

Circle 'Yes' or 'no' or 'not sure'

Do you feel well yourself?	Yes/no/not sure
Do you have any worries about **feeding** your baby?	Yes/no/not sure
Do you have any concerns about your baby's **weight** gain?	Yes/no/not sure
Does your baby watch your face and follow with his/her eyes?	Yes/no/not sure
Does your baby turn towards the light?	Yes/no/not sure
Does your baby smile at you?	Yes/no/not sure
Do you think your baby can hear you?	Yes/no/not sure
Is your baby startled by loud noises?	Yes/no/not sure
Are there any problems in looking after your baby?	Yes/no/not sure
Do you have any other worries about your baby?	Yes/no/not sure

Comment ________________

How are you feeding your baby? Breast/Bottle/Mixed

Keep hot drinks away from children
Use a coiled flex kettle

Check the water before you bath your baby
Hot water can scald your baby badly

12

Your child should have the following immunisations

Age due	Immunisation	Comments	Date Given
2 months	Diphtheria/Tetanus/Whooping Cough, Polio		
	Hib		
3 months	Diphtheria/Tetanus/Whooping Cough/Polio		
	Hib		
4 months	Diphtheria/Tetanus/Whooping Cough/Polio		
	Hib		
12-18 months	Measles, Mumps, Rubella (MMR)		
3-5 years	Diphtheria, Tetanus, Polio.		
	MMR (unless already given)		
10-14 years	Rubella (girls only)		
	Deaf test and BCG (optional)		
15-18 years	Tetanus and Polio		

Other immunisations (eg BCG at birth)

1________ Date___/___/___ 4________ Date___/___/___
2________ Date___/___/___ 5________ Date___/___/___
3________ Date___/___/___ 6________ Date___/___/___

Note any changes to the full course

All children should receive immunisations except a very few children who
1 are suffering from a feverish illness – when the immunisation should be postponed until full recovery
2 have had a severe reaction to a previous immunisation (see 'Help' section for mild upsets)
3 have an illness or are taking medicines that interfere with their ability to fight infections.
Children taking antibiotics can be immunised.
Before each immunisation the doctor or nurse will make sure that it is alright to give your child the vaccine.

9

Immunisation

Figure 8.6 Typical pages from a Personal Child Health Record book hypothesis and outline succinctly any relevant background information, for example, previous research that has been conducted on the same topic.

DATA HANDLING

Arithmetical techniques

You will need to understand the following:

- addition;
- subtraction;
- multiplication;
- division;
- fractions;
- decimals;
- percentages;
- ratios;
- means;
- range;
- plotting coordinates.

It is not within the scope of this book to cover these techniques; if you need further help with them, refer to *Calculations for Health and Social Care* by Gordon Gee (1994), or other appropriate mathematics books.

Data presentation

Unless results are very clear-cut, it can be difficult to draw conclusions from raw data. However, if data are presented in the correct way, patterns, trends and relationships can become obvious.

TABLES

Generally, the first way in which you will organise your data is in the form of a table. Essential points about tables are as follows:

- Each table should have a title.
- Don't include too much information on one table.
- Label columns and rows clearly (include any units of measurement used).
- Construct your table *before* you start recording any results.
- Do not leave blanks. Show a zero value as 0, and a missing observation as –.

ACTIVITY

Refer back to the experiment described at the beginning of this chapter for investigating temperature detection by the skin. Design a table which would be suitable for recording the results from ten subjects.

LINE GRAPHS

Two variables can be plotted on a line graph, which will show any relationship existing between them.

Points to remember when plotting a graph are as follows:

- The values for the *manipulated variable* (i.e. the variable controlled by the experimenter) go on the horizontal or *x* axis. The values for the *dependent variable* (i.e. the 'unknown quantity') go on the vertical or *y* axis.
- Each axis should be labelled, including the unit of measurement.
- A scale should be used which is simple and produces a graph large enough to be clear. (The axes do not have to begin at 0.)
- The coordinates should be marked by an × or ⊙, not just a dot, as a dot is not visible when a line passes over the point.
- Points may be joined by a series of straight lines (i.e. from point to point), a smooth curve, or a 'line of best fit' (see the section on 'Correlation').
- The graph should have a full title, such as 'Graph showing the relationship between . . .'
- Two or more lines can be plotted on the same axes, but you must label each line clearly. For example, use an × to mark each point on one line, and join them with a solid line, and use a ⊙ for each point on another line, joining the points with a broken or dashed line (- - - - - -). Show these symbols clearly in a key.

ACTIVITY

Practise constructing a line graph by plotting the data in the following table.

Prevalence of cigarette smoking in adults (aged 16 years and over) in England and Wales, 1974–90

	Men %	Women %
1974	51	41
1976	46	38
1978	45	37
1980	42	37
1982	38	33
1984	36	32
1986	35	31
1988	33	30
1990	31	29

Source: OPCS.

- Consider whether to join the points with a series of straight lines, to draw a curved 'line of best fit' or to draw a straight 'line of best fit'. Use the most appropriate method. Which do you consider the least appropriate method?
- During this time period (i.e. 1974–90), is the rate of decrease in smoking faster in men or women? (NB The steeper the graph, the faster the rate of decrease.)
- INTERPOLATION is the estimating of other values by reading off coordinates at any point along the line. What percentage of women would you estimate were smokers in 1983?
- EXTRAPOLATION involves extending the line outside the range of the graph to estimate further values. Use this method to estimate the percentage of male smokers in 1992.
- Compare your answers to the last two questions with others; it must be emphasised that these interpolated and extrapolated values are only estimates, so it is likely you will not agree on identical figures.

Table 8.3 The initial capacity of 50 male subjects

Vital capacity (dm^3)	Tally chart	Frequency
2.80–2.99		2
3.00–3.19		5
3.20–3.39		10
3.40–3.59		16
3.60–3.79		11
3.80–3.99		4
4.00–4.19		2

HISTOGRAMS

In a FREQUENCY TABLE the data are grouped in some way, and the number in each group (frequency) is recorded. For an example, see Table 8.3, recording an experiment in which the VITAL CAPACITY (i.e. the maximum amount of air exchanged during forced breathing) was recorded for 50 males. These data can be plotted in the form of a HISTOGRAM, where the areas of the bars represent frequency. If a curve is joined to link the mid-points of the top of each rectangle in Figure 8.7, a 'bell-

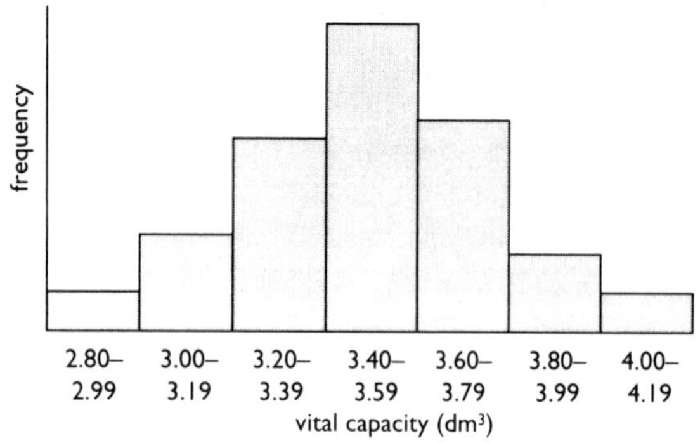

Figure 8.7 Histogram displaying data shown in Table 8.3

shaped' curve is seen. This is known as a NORMAL DISTRIBUTION CURVE, which will generally be found whenever the frequency distribution of a physical parameter such as height or weight is displayed.

ACTIVITY

1 Measure the length of the index finger of 20 people. Record your results in a tally chart, and draw a histogram to show frequency distribution.

2 The most common value, or range of values, is known as the MODE. The MEDIAN is obtained by arranging the values in order and taking the 'middle' value. What are the mode and median values of your data?

BAR CHARTS

Bar charts are essentially the same as histograms, but are used when one variable is not numerical, and the height rather than the area of each 'bar' represents the frequency. As the groups are quite distinct (i.e. not on a scale of measurements as with histograms), the bars have gaps between them. For examples, see Figure 8.8.

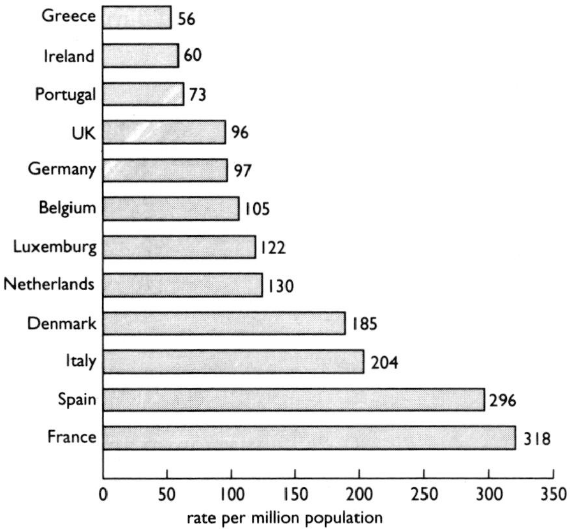

Figure 8.8 Reported AIDS cases in Europe: cumulative rates to December 1991
Source: Crown copyright. Reproduced with the permission of Her Majesty's Stationery Office.

A variation of the bar chart is the PICTOGRAM, where the length of each bar is represented by an appropriate pictorial image. For an example see Figure 8.9.

ACTIVITY

Look for examples of pictograms illustrating health-related statistics in newspapers and magazines.

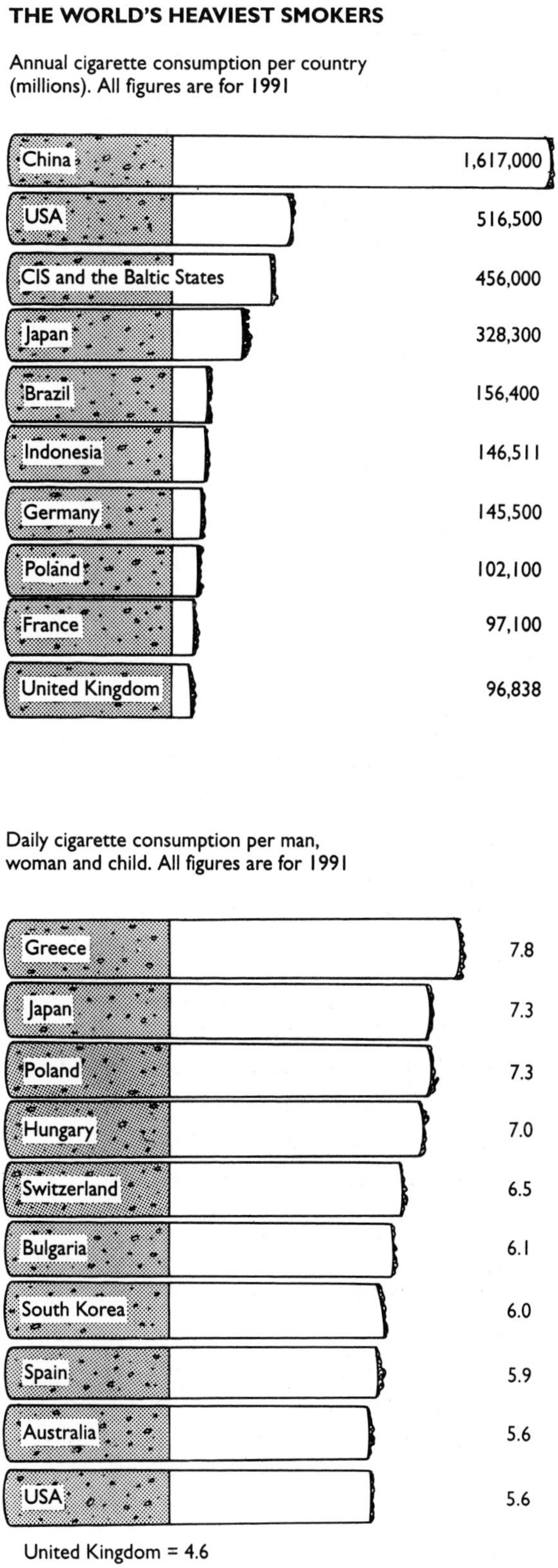

Figure 8.9 Pictogram showing cigarette consumption per country, 1991
Source: *Sunday Observer* magazine, 8 November 1991.

PIE CHARTS

Pie charts can be used as an alternative to bar charts to display data. For examples see Figure 8.10.

ACTIVITY

1 Study Figure 8.10 and then answer the following questions.

- In developed countries, which cancers are most common in:
  (a) males?
  (b) females?
- In developing countries, which cancers are most common in:
  (a) males?
  (b) females?
- Overall, the *number* of cases of cancer were divided almost equally between developed and developing countries. Can the pie charts show this information?

2 The following table shows the numbers of staff in four hospital occupations in the UK in 1990

	Total	Females	Males
Medical (e.g. consultants, registrars, house officers)	48,018	12,951	35,067
Dental	2,051	524	1,527
Nursing	385,878	341,629	44,250
Midwifery	22,606	22,539	67

Source: Health and Personal Social Service Statistics for England, 1992 (HMSO).

From the table:

- Find the total number of people employed in the four occupational areas.
- Draw a pie chart to show the proportions of staff employed in each of the four occupational areas.

Calculate the angle of each sector by using the equation:

Number of people in an occupation × 360 = total number employed.

- Now draw two separate pie charts, to show the relative proportions of males and females.
- There are far more females (377,643) compared with males (80,911) employed in these four occupational areas. Do your pie charts show this difference in total number?

TEXT

Very often data will not be displayed in a figure (e.g. table, graph or pie chart), but will be included in the text. For example: 'Currently 65% of children and 58% of adults are registered with a dentist. Most adults, except those on Supplementary Benefit, pay 80% of the cost of dental treatment.'

ACTIVITY

Find care-related newspaper articles which include data in the text. Convert these data into a diagrammatic form (e.g. table, graph or pie chart). Which is the most effective form of communication? What are the advantages and disadvantages of presenting data in text?

Conveying messages with statistics

How data are presented can affect the messages conveyed. There are various ways in which statistics can be presented in a form which, although not incorrect, is misleading.

USE OF A 'FALSE ORIGIN'

Take the following data:
Total NHS expenditure (£ millions):

1991/92	1992/93
23,260	24,430

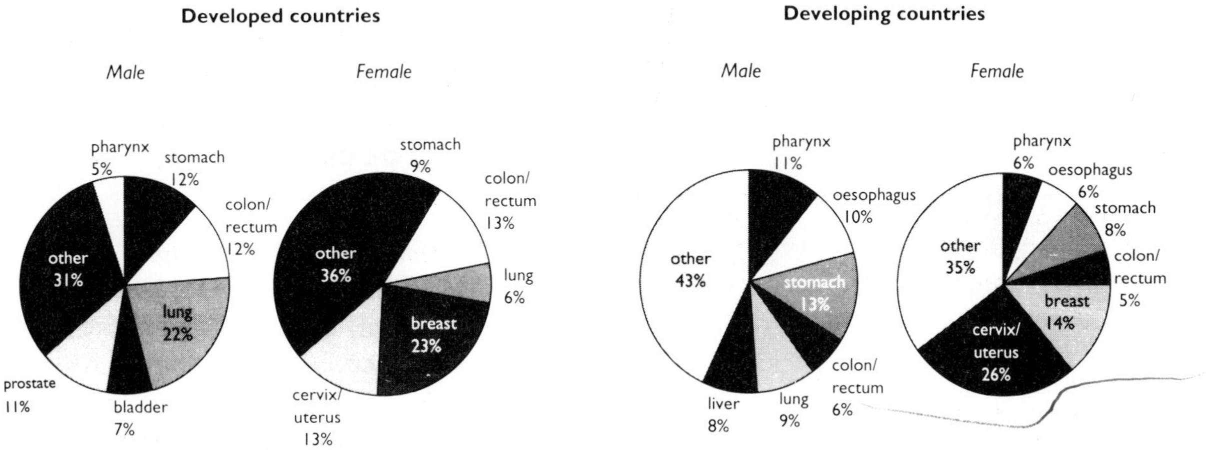

Figure 8.10 Pie charts showing distribution of cancer incidence by type and level of development for males and females, 1980
Source: UNEP. *Environment Data Report 1989* (Blackwell, 1989).

The most obvious way of expressing these data is shown in Figure 8.11(a). However, if a politician wanted to make the point that there had been a large increase in spending, most of the vertical scale could be deleted, as shown in Figure 8.11(b).

To the casual reader the clear conclusion would seem to be that there was a huge increase in expenditure from one year to the next.

BARS OF DIFFERENT WIDTHS

Although it is the *height* of a bar on a bar chart which gives information, different widths may be used to mislead the reader.

For example, the manufacturer of a low-fat yogurt, Brand A, may produce the advertisement shown in Figure 8.12 in a slimming magazine. Without careful inspection of the bar chart, Brand A would appear to the casual reader to have less fat than the other brands shown.

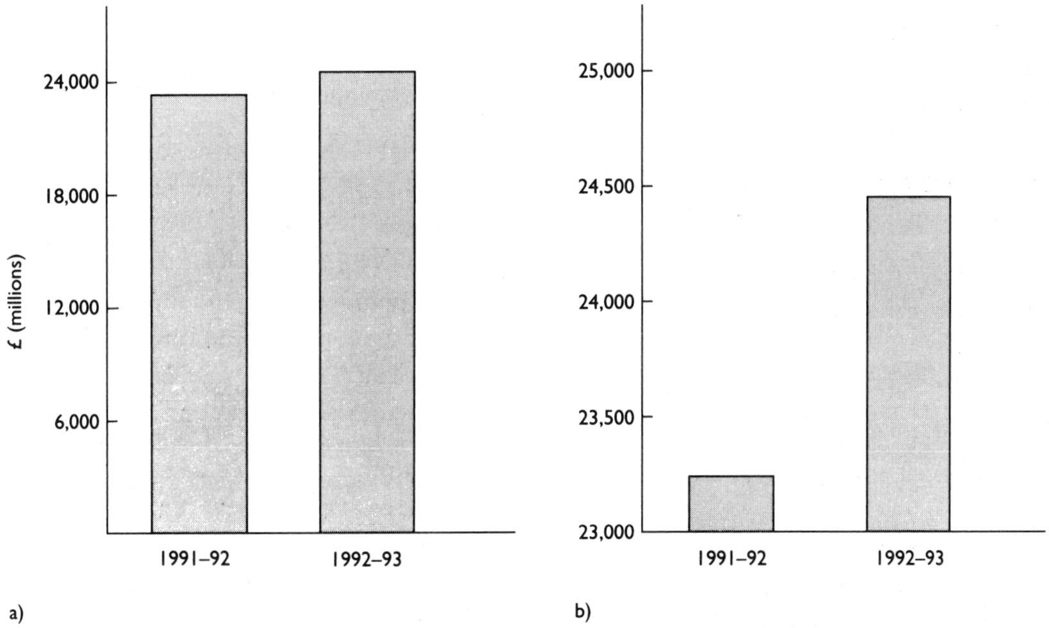

Figure 8.11 Changing the vertical scale changes the impression given by the same data

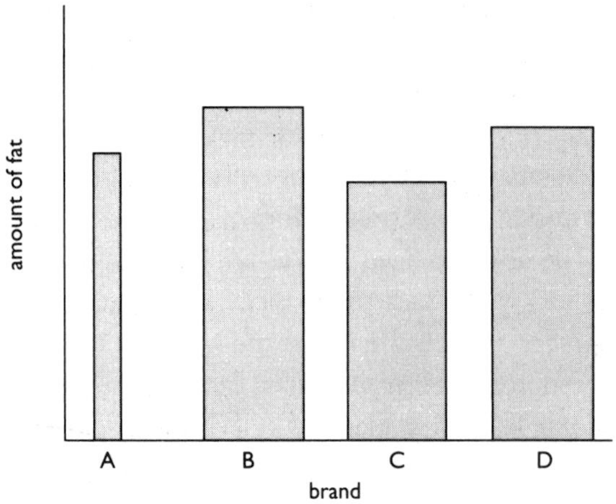

Figure 8.12 Changing the widths of bars changes the impression given by the same data

SELECTION OF FIGURES

Data to illustrate a point are often chosen very selectively. Although the data used are themselves accurate, this can give a misleading impression.

For example, a £2 million government campaign, introduced in December 1991, to reduce cot deaths by putting babies to sleep on their backs, was judged to be a huge success. The death rate dropped by 50%, and the Health Department held a press conference to call attention to its success. What it failed to point out was that the rate of cot deaths was already falling before the campaign was introduced (see Figure 8.13).

Although the campaign advice is obviously very sound, it was felt by many researchers that further lessons could be learned by endeavouring to explain the drop in cot death rate prior to the campaign.

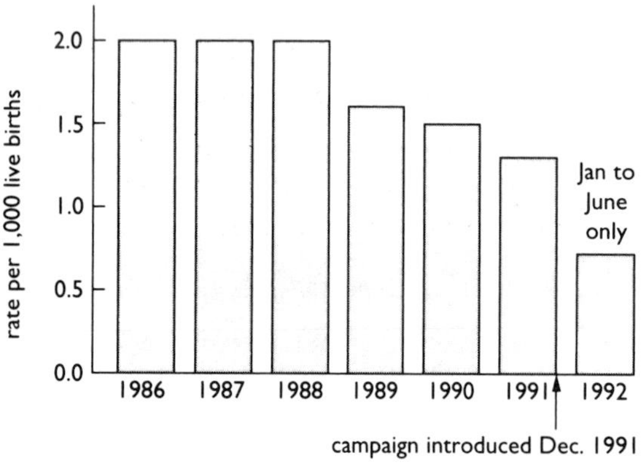

Figure 8.13 Sudden Infant Death Syndrome ('cot death'), England and Wales, 1986–92
Source: *The Observer*, 30 May 1993.

Data processing and computers

Computers are often used to help collect, store and analyse data. However, it must be remembered that there is legislation which restricts the storage and access of data on computer.

The DATA PROTECTION ACT, which was passed by Parliament in 1985, has eight main principles. These are:

- personal data (i.e. information about a living individual) must be obtained fairly and the data user must register the source of such data;
- personal data must be held for specified purposes only;
- personal data must not be held for any other purpose;
- personal data must be both relevant and adequate to the specific purpose;
- personal data must be accurate and updated as necessary;
- personal data must not be held for any longer than is necessary;
- personal data must be made available to the data subject on request and provision made for the correction of data;
- personal data must be kept securely.

In May 1987 the ACCESS TO PERSONAL FILES ACT was introduced. This complements the Data Protection Act, and gives people the right to see their own records kept on computer. This may include, for example, records kept by social services, banks and doctors.

ACTIVITY

Read the section on 'Data processing and computers'.

What are the possible advantages and disadvantages of giving people access to their files?

ACTIVITY W

Talk to professionals working in health and social care about the Data Protection and Access to Personal Files Acts, to find out how this legislation affects their work.

ETHICAL ISSUES IN RESEARCH

Neither natural nor social scientists can avoid considering ethical issues when carrying out their research.

In MEDICAL SCIENCE ethical issues often arise as a result of the widespread use of CLINICAL TRIALS for new drugs or treatments. To test the effectiveness and safety of such new drugs and treatments, patients or volunteers participating in trials may not know whether they are part of a CONTROL GROUP receiving the PLACEBO or standard conventional treatment, or whether they are part of the TREATMENT GROUP receiving the new drug or treatment. Occasionally, and very controversially, clinical trials are conducted without the consent or knowledge of the participants.

Using people as 'human guinea pigs' does raise questions about the risks to those people exposed to new drugs and treatments, and these risks have to be set against the potential benefits for a particular group of people in the population as a whole.

WOMEN AT RISK FROM BREAST CANCER PIN HOPES ON HORMONE DRUG STUDY

The Royal Marsden Hospital, in London, announced that it had just recruited its 2,000th volunteer into a study it has been running since 1986 into possible protective effects of tamoxifen against breast cancer.

The drug has been used as back-up therapy for women with breast cancer since 1971, but the Marsden study is the first in the world to try to investigate whether tamoxifen can prevent the disease in the first place.

It is planned to recruit another 500 women to the study. All receive six-monthly check-ups, with breast X-rays each year. The screening costs about £500 a year each, with the drug costing about £7 a month and the placebo £2.

If there is a marked protective effect it should be possible to detect it sometime between 1996 and 1998, Dr Powles, the study co-ordinator, said.

Dr Powles said so far 11 cancers had been spotted, all at an early stage. It was not possible to say yet if these had occurred in the tamoxifen or the placebo women, but the number was smaller than might have been expected in a high risk group.

Some 20 to 25 cancers might have been expected in such a group, but it was too early to say if the drug was successful.

The women all have a family history of breast cancer, with a close relative affected. Most are aged between 35 and 70.

Plans for a national tamoxifen trial involving 15,000 women are being delayed while the Department of Health makes a decision about possible side effects. The Committee on Safety of Medicines has approved the national study, but the Medical Research Council has raised questions because some rats given the drug developed liver cancer.

Yesterday Dr Powles said no liver cancer had been seen in his group, or in the 6 million women around the world given the drug as part of breast cancer therapy. Side effects were either non-existent or mild.

Dr Powles said 15 per cent of women experienced hot flushes, and 10 per cent had some irregularity of periods. There was no evidence it caused an early menopause, and no medical reason why it could not be taken by women receiving hormone replacement therapy.

(The Guardian, 22 April 1993)

Activity

Study *The Guardian* article on the clinical trials for tamoxifen.

1 What is the purpose of this clinical trial?

2 How is the clinical trial being carried out?

3 What special characteristics apply to the group of women who are involved in this trial?

4 What possible risks in taking tamoxifen have been suggested?

5 Ask other people whether they would be prepared to be involved in a clinical trial such as this? What kinds of response did you find?

6 Do you think that it can ever be justifiable to involve someone in a clinical trial without their consent or knowledge?

Interestingly, it might be argued that using people in clinical trials receives less publicity, and appears to arouse less concern, than the use of ANIMALS IN EXPERIMENTS.

The Animals (Scientific Procedures) Act 1986 requires that before a doctor or scientist can conduct research involving animals, he or she must have special licences. These are granted by the Home Secretary.

Such licences are granted only if:

- the potential results of the research are important enough to justify the use of animals;
- the research cannot be performed using non-animal methods;
- the minimum number of animals will be used;
- dogs, cats and primates are only used when absolutely necessary;
- any discomfort or suffering is kept to a minimum by the appropriate use of anaesthetics or painkillers;
- the researchers conducting the experiments have the necessary skill and experience with laboratory animals;
- the research laboratory has the necessary facilities to look after the animals properly.

The law says that animals must be examined every day and a vet must be on call at all times. Any animal judged to be in severe pain or distress which cannot be relieved must be painlessly destroyed. To enforce the Act the Home Office employs a team of inspectors who are all qualified vets or medical doctors. These people ensure that all animal-based research is carried out strictly according to these controls.

Activity

1 Animals have long been used in health research. Examples which have attracted considerable publicity include the use of beagles in smoking studies, and the research using mice which are genetically engineered to die from cancer.

What other examples of animal experimentation in health research can you find?

2 What are the alternatives to animal experimentation?

3 'Animal experimentation is justified by the medical benefits it brings to human beings'.

Organise a debate to discuss this motion. Information can be obtained from the organisations listed at the end of this chapter.

In SOCIAL SCIENCE ethical (and sometimes legal) dilemmas arise precisely because social research intrudes into the lives of those studied. For some, completing a questionnaire or participating in an interview may be an interesting, perhaps even a rewarding or enlightening, experience. For others, especially those involved in research into 'sensitive' issues or subject to a prolonged period of observation or case study, the experience may be less positive. People may feel that their privacy is being invaded. Feelings or thoughts suppressed for a long time may be uncomfortably re-awoken and prove disturbing. Some people may feel very anxious about the uses to which the research data will be put. People may feel that they want a wider involvement in the whole research project than merely answering a questionnaire or agreeing to be interviewed. They may wish to comment upon or contribute to the planning, interpretation and evaluation of the research, as well as to raise questions about the validity and reliability of the methods of research used. Covert participant observation raises serious questions about whether researchers should always be honest and open with the people and organisations they are studying.

There are occasions when social scientists (and other professionals, such as journalists) have used covert participant observation to uncover injustices or to investigate what would otherwise be closed and secret areas of social life. However, there are considerable practical risks to the researcher using this method, and many social scientists suggest that more open forms of observation study can engender a trust and acceptance of the researcher which allows him or her to gain an intimate and privileged insight into the lives of the people being researched. This said, there may be unexpected and unanticipated barriers to effective and productive communication between researcher and researched. We have already mentioned (p. 419) how female researchers may feel more comfortable interviewing women rather than men in certain circumstances. There are other cultural experiences and expectations which may influence both the value and outlook of researchers, and the responses of 'the researched'.

Gender, ethnicity, class, age, sexuality, language and accent are just some of the CULTURAL FACTORS which can, consciously or unconsciously, shape the direction of research, the question asked, the responses given, and the results achieved.

Whether or not it is possible or even desirable to try to 'screen out' all these factors and approach research from a completely objective and 'value-free' position is an interesting question for discussion and debate.

In general, as a STUDENT RESEARCHER, if you have the opportunity to carry out research of your own, consider the following points.

- Try to obtain and consult any statement of ethical practice issued by academic associations in the particular field of research you are considering; for example, the British Sociological Association issues its own 'Statement of Ethical Practice'.
- Think carefully about any ethical issues which may be raised by the research you wish to carry out. Yours may be a relatively small-scape piece of research compared with professionally commissioned research. You may be working under considerable pressure to meet deadlines. Nevertheless, how will you approach the people you want to involve in your research? If you want your respondent or interviewees to take your questions seriously, you need to motivate, encourage, respect and thank them.
- Always obtain consent from the people you involve in your research. If observing or interviewing children, ensure you obtain consent to do so from the adults responsible for them.
- Ensure that the participants in your research are aware of the true nature of your research.
- Be sensitive to the privacy and feelings of the participants in your research. Even if you involve people you think you know well in your research, you may be taken by surprise at an unexpected reaction to a

particular question asked.

- Reassure your participants that they will be afforded anonymity and confidentiality and that they will not be identified by name. Ensure that this is the case when writing, recording and presenting your research. Consider using pseudonyms when referring to organisations and institutions studied in a project.
- For your own personal safety, never agree to interview anyone whom you do not know if you are at all unsure about the circumstances and location of the interview.

THE PROCESS OF RESEARCH – AN EVALUATIVE EXERCISE

The following article is a summary of the research into MULTIPLE SCLEROSIS carried out by Colin Young, a senior social worker at the Neurology Unit of the University Hospital of Wales, Cardiff (reprinted with permission of *Community Care Magazine*).

Read this article carefully, and then answer the questions which follow.

TRUTH AND MYTHS

Multiple sclerosis is both unpredictable and this country's most common potentially disabling disease. Symptoms range from a slight limp to paraplegia and severe intellectual impairment. It is all the more traumatic because it strikes at an average age of 30, when people are in the middle of responsibilities such as a career, or raising a family.

How then do those with MS and those who care for them cope, and how do health and social services meet their needs? My seven-year research study[1] involved 379 people; 220 of whom returned questionnaires. I also interviewed 25 people with MS, and 18 carers in depth about their quality of life.

The research offered an opportunity to study the whole population, not just those known to social services. Social workers often have a distorted view of the world, tending to see only those people with major physical or emotional problems. This research gave me a more balanced view by making direct contact with those who were managing without outside assistance.

Some commonly encountered myths about MS and its consequences have been challenged by the research. For example, 35 of those who returned questionnaires reported that they did not use any walking aid at all. This offered the reassurance that MS can be a relatively mild illness for many.

I explored the person's perception of what the illness demanded of them, and what resources the person had to deal with these demands. Two types of coping have been identified by Lazarus and Folkman[2], the first being about problem-solving, and the second about emotional responses to aspects of situations that cannot be 'solved'. A balanced assessment needs to include both elements.

This led to some interesting results. For example, one person who was a wheelchair user described his approach to life 'as if the wheelchair was not there', and felt it did not intrude. Among these more disabled people, it appeared that all those interviewed were realistic about their physical abilities, and had a complex system of coping strategies, rooted in a clear understanding of the disease.

For example, one man said: 'I have a strong belief in a cure being around the corner, and it keeps me going – it's mental physiotherapy for me.' For him, this was not an unrealistic belief, but an active way of coping.

In some cases, it was clear that coping was about responding to problems caused by particular symptoms, rather than coping with an amorphous label of 'MS'. Continence problems appeared the most difficult symptom to cope with – 40 per cent complained of them. One person said: 'I suffered from acute urine retention, and have had a number of operations.

[1] D C Young, *Aspects of Coping with MS*, unpublished PhD thesis, Cardiff University, 1993

[2] R S Lazarus and S Folkman, *Stress, Appraisal and Coping*, Springer Publishing, 1984

These left me wet all the time. I was encouraged to have an artificial sphincter in the bladder. This was unsuccessful. I am one of the few "albatrosses" around the surgeon's neck.'

Another person said: 'I can cope with the wheelchair, but not the bowel pain. If I watch TV, I cannot forget it. If it was not for this, I would be quite happy.' Counselling should perhaps focus more on helping the person with MS to manage specific symptoms such as these.

The much-reported high occurrence of marital breakdown among those with MS was not evident – 70 per cent were married. However, the interviews with carers, 16 of whom were spouses, indicated that many felt under great stress but had no plans to leave.

There was a strong commitment to caring, but little sense of fulfilment in doing so. One woman said: 'I have to care for him all the time. There's no lovey-dovey any more. I have never felt so alone.'

Social workers often do not fully appreciate the stress suffered by carers, nor the difficulties caused by restrictions on family and social life. Only seven out of 12 carers in the largest group interviewed reported positive experiences as a result of caring, such as: 'The illness has brought us closer together. We feel as if we're still on honeymoon.'

Carers, especially, appreciated regular contact with the medical research team with whom I worked and were disappointed when it was disbanded. They felt that interest and commitment were shown, despite the frequent lack of a clear medical solution. The research also offered a way to talk constructively to doctors about how to help people tackle such an illness.

Such research is needed if community care is going to develop into more than just looking after the immediate personal needs of those with a disability or chronic illness. Emotional responses to disability are of central importance, constituting an essential part of a realistic assessment for community care. For instance, the research fed into social care plans for South Glamorgan.

For most people, MS is not a static disability, but a chronic illness with fluctuating and often concealed symptoms.

Carers often pay a high price in terms of their own health. Only by going deeper into the experience of MS can we assist those with the illness, and carers, to cope.

(Community Care, 3–9 November, 1994)

ACTIVITY

1. What is multiple sclerosis?
2. What did Colin Young want to find out about this disease?
3. What quantitative and qualitative research methods did Colin Young use? Why do you think he chose this mixture of methods?
4. What response to the questionnaires did Young's study achieve? How might you explain this?
5. Summarise briefly the main results and conclusions of this research.
6. Why does Colin Young feel that research like this is needed? What uses could be made of the research?
7. What possible effects on those being researched might this study have had?
8. 'Multiple sclerosis research should ideally be carried out by those with the disease themselves'. How far do you agree or disagree with this statement?
9. In what ways could the conclusions and results of research such as this be communicated to wider audiences?

PRACTISING RESEARCH SKILLS

Choosing a research topic

You will be expected to undertake your own piece of research into health and social well-being and/or related services and facilities. This will be a fairly extensive piece of work, covering approximately two term's work.

Figure 8.14 shows how scientists, psychologists and sociologists may be involved in health and social care, and how their areas of research may overlap. As a starting point to choosing your topic of research, you may like to consider which area you would find most interesting. Table 8.4 gives suggestions for possible research projects. Of course, your choice of research topic cannot only be based on your interests. You must also take into account many other factors. You must think carefully about the difficulties you would encounter with your chosen area, and whether and how you could get around these difficulties. Some examples of some of the difficulties are listed below.

Ethical issues

Consider carefully the ethical issues involved. For example:

- It is highly unlikely that you would find it possible to collect primary data on a sensitive issue such as cot deaths, because of the potential effects of research on participants.
- It is unlikely that you could guarantee the necessary confidentiality to persuade participants to be entirely honest on subjects such as their personal experience of contraception or drug taking.
- The Animals (Scientific Procedures) Act 1986 forbids any unlicensed person to

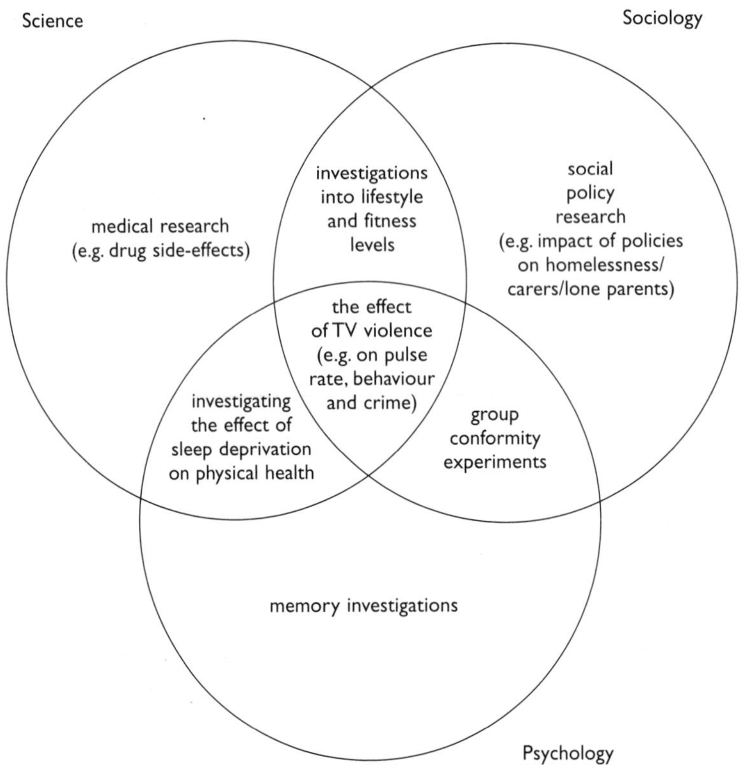

Figure 8.14 Examples of topics of scientific, psychological and sociological research into health and social well-being

apply procedures to a vertebrate that 'may have the effect of causing that animal pain, suffering, distress, or lasting harm'.

Cost

It is unlikely that you will want to spend a large amount of money on carrying out your project, so do a 'costing' exercise at the start. Don't forget to include items such as photocopying, postage and travel costs.

Appropriate Sample

You must be realistic when deciding upon your sample. For example, if it is difficult for you to have access to a significant number of very old or very young people, and you are studying in a sixth-form or further education college, you would be sensible to carry out research in which an age range of 16–18 year-olds is appropriate. Be realistic about the size of your sample as well. Whilst it is an advantage to have as large a sample as possible, think carefully about the amount of time available to you. If you are planning to interview others, think carefully about the amount of time available to *them*!

Equipment available

If you are interested in carrying out a scientific or psychological experiment, find out to what equipment you have access. For example, don't base your research project on the use of a reaction time or a sphygmomanometer (for measuring blood pressure), and then find out that these are not available.

ASSESSMENT OPPORTUNITY ✔

Before you start choosing a research project, in a group have a brainstorming session to list any other difficulties you may have with the choice of topic.

Planning and undertaking your research

Once you have decided on your topic of research:

1 Clearly describe the rationale for the research.

- What is the research trying to find out?
- Who might have an interest in the results?
- What links are there to previous research?

2 Identify the sources of data to be used.

- Will you use primary or secondary sources?

3 Decide on an appropriate research method.

- Which of the following will you use:
  - experiments (e.g. scientific, psychological)?
  - questionnaire (e.g. self-report, administered)?
  - interviews (e.g. structured, semi-structured, behaviour relevant)?
  - observation?
  - do you need to carry out a pilot study?
  - will you use quantitative or qualitative methods for analysing the data?

4 Identify the ethical issues raised, and propose ways of handling or resolving them.

- What are the potential benefits of research?
- What will be the potential effect on participants?
- How will you maintain confidentiality?
- How will you allow participants the right to choose involvement?
- What opportunity will you give for participants to comment on outcomes?

5 Obtain and record your data.
6 Analyse your data.
7 Draw conclusions from the data available.

Table 8.4 Suggested topics and areas for a research project

Scientific

- The effect of a factor (e.g. caffeine, exercise, smoking, etc.) on heart rate and/or breathing rate/blood pressure/reaction time.
- The effect of a factor (e.g. disinfectant, toothpaste, temperature, etc.) on microbial growth.
- Investigations into an aspect of diet.
- An investigation into an aspect of food storage (e.g. milk and the effect of temperature; the amount of vitamin C in fruit juice, etc.).
- Investigation into an aspect of exercise (e.g. on muscle development).

Sociological

Investigations into aspects of:

- provision for working parents, including childcare facilities;
- public perception of AIDS/HIV;
- the role of alternative/complementary medicine;
- the role of a professional (e.g. a midwife);
- provision of care (e.g. for elders).

Psychological

- Hand and foot reaction times.
- Effect of sleep deprivation/time of day, etc., on reaction time.
- Investigation into an aspect of memory (e.g. related to age, etc.).
- Measuring the apparent extent of optical illusions.

NB These are suggestions which may help you to get started. There are many other suggestions made throughout the book, and you will have your own ideas based on your interests and the resources available.

Producing and presenting your research report

Your final written report should be between 5,000 and 6,000 words in length, and must contain the following:

- A description of the research process (include who the report will be of interest to; methods of obtaining data; the nature of the research population; sampling methods; a copy of any questionnaire used – this can go in an appendix).
- A description of the data obtained and the method(s) by which the data were analysed (use diagrams and charts where necessary).
- Valid conclusions.
- A description of any ethical issues raised, and how these were handled.
- An assessment of the limitations of the research.
- Recommendations for further research and development.

Give an oral presentation of your report to a small audience of at least five other people. You should expect to answer questions on your research and findings. Figure 8.15 shows the points on which you may be assessed.

REFERENCES AND RESOURCES

Alibhai-Brown, Y. and Montague, A. (1992), *The Colour of Love*. London: Virago.

British Sociological Association, 'Statement of Ethical Practice'. Durham: BSA. Burnard, P. and Morrison, P. (1990), *Nursing Research in Action: Developing Basic Skills*. London: Macmillan.

Cornwall, J. (1984), *Hard-Earned Lives*, Social Science Paperbacks.

Eaton, M. (1993), *Women after Prison*. Milton Keynes: Open University Press.

Gee, G. (1994), *Calculations for Health and Social Care*. London: Hodder and Stoughton.

Harris, P. (1989), Designing and Reporting Experiments. Milton Keynes: Open University Press.

NAME	
UNIT	
ASSIGNMENT	

PERFORMANCE	PASS	MERIT	DISTINCTION
INTRODUCTION			
DELIVERY			
VISUAL AIDS			
CLARITY			
INTEREST			
SUMMARY			
PLANNING			
TEAMWORK			

GENERAL COMMENTS

GRADE AWARDED:

Figure 8.15 Schema for assessing oral presentation

Heyes, S., Hardy, M., Humphreys, P. and Rootes, P. (1986), *Starting Statistics in Psychology and Education*. London: Weidenfeld and Nicolson.

Kalsi, N. and Constantinides, P. (1989), *Working towards Racial Equality in Health Care: The Haringey Experience*. London: King's Fund Centre for Health.

Methodology and Statistics Package for A and AS Level Psychology. Psychology Resources, 230 Desborough Avenue, High Wycombe, Buckinghamshire.

Oakley, A. (1981), *From Here to Maternity*. London: Penguin.

Reid, N. G. and Boore, J. R. P. (1987), *Research Methods and Statistics in Health Care*. London: Edward Arnold.

Sapsford, R. and Abbott, P. (1992), *Research methods for Nursing and the Caring Professions*. Oxford: OUP.

Wellings, K. et al. (1994), *Sexual Behaviour in Britain: The National Survey of Sexual Attitudes and Lifestyles*. London: Penguin.

USEFUL ADDRESSES

Animals in Medicines Research Information Centre
12 Whitehall
London SW1A 2DY

Biomedical Research Education Trust
58 Great Marlborough Street
London W1V 1DD

British Union for the Abolition of Vivisection
16a Crane Grove
Islington
London N7 8LB

Disabled Against Animal Research and Exploitation
PO Box 8
Daventry
Northamptonshire NN11 4RQ

Fund for the Replacement of Animals in Medical Experiments
Eastgate House
34 Stoney Lane
Nottingham NG1 1NB

HMSO
49 High Holborn
London WC1V 6HB
Tel.: 0171 873 0011

Humane Research Trust
Brook House
29 Bramhall Lane South
Bramhall
Southport
Cheshire SK7 2DN

Nurses' Anti-Vivisectionist Movement
2 Hillcrest Cottage
Hillcrest
Uppertown
Bonsall
Derbyshire DE4 2AW

Research Defence Society
58 Great Marlborough Street
London W1V 1DD

Research for Health Charities Group
PO Box 1417
Shepton Mallet
Somerset BA4 4YZ

RSPCA
Causeway
Horsham
West Sussex RH12 1HG

Seriously Ill for Medical Research
PO Box 504
Houghton Regis
Dunstable

Social Work Research Association
c/o David Allan
3 Corbett Street
Droitwich
Worcestershire WR9 7BQ

Appendix A

EXPERIENCE IN THE WORKPLACE

An important part of a vocational health and social care course is one or more work placements.

FUNCTIONS OF A WORK PLACEMENT

1 It allows a student to find out first-hand about various careers. Many students find their true vocation on a work experience placement. (Equally, some students find that their chosen career is not, after all, for them!)
2 The work placement is a 'learning experience'. Not all learning has to take place in the classroom.
3 The work placement allows students to put into practice the theory learnt in the classroom – for example, assessment of client needs (Chapter 6).
4 Students can develop skills in the workplace, for example, communication.
5 Students may have the opportunity to carry out research in the workplace.
6 Positive comments on a student's performance on a work placement are viewed favourably in references or Records of Achievement. In an interview the student will have an advantage if he or she can talk knowledgeably about practical work experience.

ACTIVITY

Study the list of functions of a work placement. Can you think of any others?

SUGGESTIONS FOR HEALTH AND SOCIAL CARE PLACEMENTS

Your choice of placement(s) will obviously be limited to those within an acceptable travelling distance, your previous experience and your future aspirations. The following list should help you consider some of the options:

- hospitals (private, NHS Trust/non-Trust);
- community health clinics;
- Probation Service;
- Education Welfare Department;
- social services;
- public health authorities;
- Citizens Advice Bureaux;
- other voluntary agencies;
- nurseries/playgroups;
- schools (including special schools, day or residential);
- probation hostels;
- day care centres for physically or mentally handicapped people;
- residential homes for physically or mentally handicapped people;
- day care centres for elders;
- residential homes for elders.

To find these establishments locally check libraries, *Yellow Pages* and the CAB.

PLANNING YOUR PLACEMENT

An important aspect to be planned is the LENGTH OF TIME you spend at your placement.

This may be beyond your control, but if you have the choice it requires careful consideration.

Some colleges send their students out on a BLOCK of work experience (for example, four continuous weeks per year); others send them out for SINGLE DAYS (for example, a day a week throughout the course).

ACTIVITY

1 What do you consider to be the advantages and disadvantages of the two work experience schemes, block and single day?

2 On a full-time, two-year health and social care course, what would you consider to be an adequate length of time to spend in the workplace?

If a student is to have more than one block of work experience, he or she may find it useful to progress on to a different establishment where clients have greater needs.

PERMISSION TO VISIT an establishment can be requested by letter or telephone. Be willing to give a concise description of your course, your intended career, and what you hope to achieve from the placement.

Confirm in writing when you will be visiting and, if possible, arrange a PRELIMINARY VISIT. Obviously you will find out all you can about the placement before this first visit, but actually going there will allow you to meet staff and to find out:

- how to get there;
- the hours you will be working;
- likely tasks you will be involved in;
- what style of dress will be suitable;
- practical arrangements, for example, where to have lunch.

You should take a copy of the TASKS you are required to do during your placement, and explain the assessment procedure.

Check with your school or college that the necessary INSURANCE has been arranged.

WORK EXPERIENCE TASKS

Tasks to be carried out prior to the placement

To gain the maximum benefit from the work placement it is important to be well prepared. The following tasks are suggestions to help you with this preparation.

1 Following your preliminary visit, discuss your feelings and reactions with other students. The following areas should be covered:

- your initial impressions;
- the atmosphere;
- the clients;
- the staff involved in the care of the patients/clients;
- your expectations of your future placements in terms of self-development, job satisfaction and problem areas.

2 Copy the 'skills checklist' in Figure A.1 and use it to make a self-appraisal before you go to visit your workplace. Grade yourself on each skill: 4 for very good; 3 for good; 2 for acceptable; and 1 for poor.

From the complete skills checklist you will see that you have positive attributes to offer the workplace. If there are any areas you've identified that you feel might cause some problems at the workplace, DISCUSS these on a one-to-one basis with your tutor to enable you to plan strategies on how to deal with them before you go to the workplace.

Make a list of the practical skills you have already acquired on your course so far, or on previous courses you have followed. Be proud of your accomplishments so far, and use this recognition as a basis for starting a PRACTICAL SKILLS PROFILE which can be added on to throughout the whole course, including subsequent work placements. This will give you valuable information to put into your curriculum vitae or future applications for further training or jobs.

Skill	Score 1	2	3	4
Motivation				
Effort				
Self-confidence				
Enthusiasm				
Ability to follow instructions				
Ability to assess when to ask for help				
Listening skills				
Co-operation				
Relationships with colleagues				
Accuracy in practical work				
Punctuality				
Attendance				
Time management				
Ability to take criticism				
Ability to present written reports				
Ability to handle calculations				

Figure A.1 Checklist for scoring relevant skills

Write a statement of your PERSONAL CAREER AIMS identifying the career you might want to follow and the progression route which you think you will follow to this career. You can get advice from the local careers service and your teachers or lecturers.

How do you think the workplace that you are going to could help you acquire the practical and personal skills that you will need in the career you want to follow?

3 Before you go into the workplace it is important that you are aware of CONFIDENTIALITY issues (see Chapter 2).

Tasks to be carried out in the workplace

Throughout this book many suggestions have been made for activities which either can or should be carried out in the workplace. In addition, the following written tasks may be performed to help you benefit from your work experience.

1 Keep a DIARY or LOG BOOK on your work experience.

- Note activities undertaken each day and the time spent on them.
- Record your feelings and reactions to your experiences.

2 Describe:

- the SERVICE(S) provided by your work experience establishment;
- the needs of the CLIENTS using these services;
- the work of the PROFESSIONALS with whom you come into contact.

What do you think are the main qualities/skills they each require?

3 Conduct one or more of the following CASE STUDIES. NB This task should be carried out only after a preliminary discussion with placement staff as to what aspects of the task are considered to be both permissible and possible. Confidentiality and respect for the individual and family should be maintained.

(a) Conduct a case study on one employee/pupil/client, to include:
- reasons for selection;
- personal details of the individual, such as age, sex, family situation, special interests and abilities, etc.;
- an analysis of the role of the individual in the establishment and the demands made on him/her by the establishment.

(b) Make brief notes on different attitudes patients/clients have to themselves and their care, focusing on two case studies.

(c) Make notes on cases you observe where professionals influence the way in which patients/clients view their own identity.

(d) Examine and record one example of group interactions and dynamics.

4 Investigate and comment on the following aspects of HEALTH AND SAFETY in your workplace:

- fire prevention and drill;
- safety policy, officers, first aiders;
- actual/potential hazards to staff and clients;
- provision of rest/reaction areas for clients.

5 Evaluate the role of COMPUTERS in the workplace: how they are used, the tasks they perform and the software employed. Consider other tasks being performed that could be computerised and assess how valuable the computer is as a work aid.

6 Throughout your work experience period make a note of any issues arising that you wish to discuss, or any questions that arise and are unanswered. You can then raise these issues later with your visiting tutor or other students.

Tasks to be carried out following the placement

1 Produce an ASSESSMENT OF YOUR OWN STRENGTHS AND WEAKNESSES during your placement. Refer back to your 'skills checklist' completed prior to the time spent in the workplace.

- Has your self-appraisal changed?
- Have your career aims changed?
- Have you gained skills which will be necessary for your chosen career?

Update your CV and, if possible, plan strategies for overcoming any remaining areas of weakness.

2 Give an ORAL PRESENTATION of your work experience to other students. Your presentation should include:
an outline of the organisation(s) and type of work;

- your own role and tasks;
- the challenges and problems you faced;
- an assessment of what has been learned and the personal development that has taken place.

There should also be an opportunity for a more informal debriefing session to allow the discussion of any points raised in Task 6 which was completed during the placement.

3 Write a LETTER OF THANKS to the employer(s) at your placement.

4 EVALUATE the usefulness of your placement.

- What aspects were most satisfactory?
- What aspects were least satisfactory?
- Do you have any suggestions for improvements?
- Would you recommend the placement to another student?

This feedback should be used to help students with their organisation of future work placements.

ASSESSMENT

It will be useful for you to receive as much feedback as possible on your performance in the workplace. The possible sources of assessment will be:

- yourself;
- your placement supervisor and colleagues;
- your visiting tutor;
- your written work.

It is advisable to give your supervisor in the workplace a standard form to enable him or her to comment on your performance. Figure A.2 shows an example of this.

Your supervisor should also be encouraged to give feedback on the organisational aspects of the work experience. These comments should then be considered when planning future placements.

ROLE OF THE VISITING TUTOR

Although assessment by your visiting tutor was mentioned above, the main role he or she will have is to support you and if necessary help solve any problems you may encounter. He or she may also give feedback on the

Student's name ....

Name of establishment ....

Employer's Comments

Please comment on the following:

1. Student's attitude with reference to attendance, punctuality, etc.

2. Student's interest and enthusiasm.

3. Ability to work and cooperate with others.

4. Suitability of the student for this type of work.

5. Any other comments.

Signed .... Date ....

Position ....

Figure A.2 Example of employer's comment form

suitability of the workplace for student placements. Make sure you know how to contact the visiting tutor if the need arises.

and finally . . .

Many workers in caring professions are under a great deal of pressure, perhaps because of understaffing, or perhaps because of the nature of the job. It may be an added pressure for them to work with a student. If you observe the following points it will help your working relationship to flourish:

- Find out as much as you can about the placement before you arrive.
- Be punctual.
- Inform your supervisor and college tutor of any unavoidable absences.
- Be prepared for shift-work hours.
- Be cooperative.
- Treat clients and staff with respect.
- Observe confidentiality.
- Show an interest by asking questions at convenient times.

Remember, the impression you give may affect the employer's willingness to offer students placements in the future, and, you never know, you may eventually return for an interview for a full-time post!

Appendix B

THE SCOTTISH DIMENSION

DIFFERENCES IN HEALTH AND SOCIAL CARE IN SCOTLAND

Although most of this book is as relevant to Scotland as to any other part of the United Kingdom, there are some differences in institutions which mean that health and social care workers in Scotland often work with a different frame of reference. These differences, guaranteed through the Act of Union of 1707, are perpetuated to this day. This Act permitted Scotland its own legal, educational and religious systems. Differences in the legal system are particularly relevant to workers in social care, with Scottish law being as intractably different in this field as in many others. Health legislation does, however, remain broadly similar to that of England and Wales, with provision through the National Health Service.

One of the most important pieces of legislation which health and social carers should familiarise themselves with is the Social Work (Scotland) Act 1968. This Act created a generic service in Scotland through the formation of Social Work Departments. Thus Scotland does not have Social Services Departments, neither does it have a separate Probation Service. The 1968 Act also legislated for the creation of a system of children's hearings, recommended by the Kilbrandon committee in 1964, to deal with children in need of compulsory measures of care, for whatever reason. This includes groups which would previously have come before the courts and reflects the underlying philosophy of a need for education, training and family responsibility. In this way most juvenile offenders do not come before the courts at all but are dealt with by a children's panel at a children's hearing.

ACTIVITY

1 Find out what services are provided by your local Social Work Department if you work in Scotland.

2 Look at the parts of the 1968 Act which apply particularly to your work.

The Children Act 1989, which has received so much publicity and which made fundamental changes to child care law in England and Wales, hardly applies to Scotland except in relation to reviewing day care provision for the under eights, and the registration of child minders and those providing day care services for the same group. Scotland has its own new Children Bill which is likely to pass into law in 1995. Among the provisions of this new legislation there is likely to be an exclusion of the alleged Abuser Order and a duty to assist care leavers up to their 19th birthday, with discretion to help up to the age of 21.

ACTIVITY

Find out what other changes are likely to be brought about by the new Children Act for Scotland.

Unlike many other pieces of legislation, some Acts do apply to Scotland as well as to other parts of the UK. The National Health Service and Community Care Act 1990 makes similar

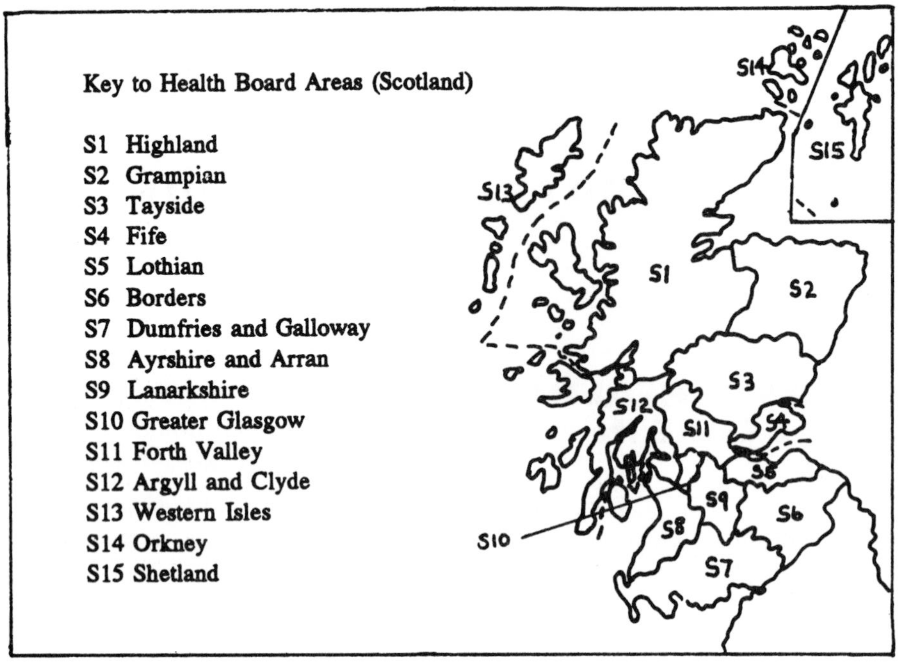

Figure B.1 Scottish health board areas

provisions for Scotland as for England and Wales, although there are separate sections for Scotland since this Act amends some sections of Scottish legislation. The Equal Pay Act 1970, the Sex Discrimination Act 1975 and the Race Relations Act 1976 all apply equally in Scotland, England and Wales. Scotland does, however, have its own Mental Health Acts (see especially the Mental Health (Scotland) Act 1984) and Education Acts. It also has its own courts system and legal personnel.

With these brief examples in mind, the reader working in Scotland should research those particular pieces of legislation which apply to their work. Familiarity with relevant law enables workers not only to guide clients through the legal maze, but also to understand where their work fits into the legal framework.

Key texts

Carstairs, V. and Morris, R. (1991), *Deprivation and Health in Scotland*. Aberdeen: Aberdeen University Press.

English, J. (ed.) (1992), *The Social Services in Scotland*. 3rd edition. Edinburgh: Scottish Academic Press.

Fabb, J. and Guthrie, T.G. (1992), *Social Work and the Law in Scotland*. Edinburgh: Butterworths.

Linklater, M. and Denniston, R. (eds) (1992), *Anatomy of Scotland*. Edinburgh: Chambers.

INDEX